# Readings in Public Finance

## Second Edition

Samuel Baker
The College of William and Mary

Catherine Elliott
New College of The
University of South Florida

**THOMSON**

™

**CUSTOM PUBLISHING**

Editor: Louis Schwartz
Production Manager: Staci Powers
Production Coordinator: Mary Snelling
Marketing Coordinator: Sara L. Hinckley

Printed in the United States of America

**Thomson Learning Custom Publishing**
**5191 Natorp Blvd.**
**Mason, Ohio 45040**
**USA**

For information about our products, contact us:
**1-800-355-9983**
http://www.custom.thomsonlearning.com

**International Headquarters**
Thomson Learning
International Division
290 Harbor Drive, 2$^{nd}$ Floor
Stamford, CT 06902-7477
USA

**UK/Europe/Middle East/South Africa**
Thomson Learning
Berkshire House
168-173 High Holborn
London WCIV 7AA

**Asia**
Thomson Learning
60 Albert Street, #15-01
Albert Complex
Singapore 189969

**Canada**
Nelson Thomson Learning
1120 Birchmount Road
Toronto, Ontario MIK 5G4
Canada
United Kingdom

Visit us at www.e-riginality.com and learn more about this book and other titles published by Thomson Learning Custom Publishing

ISBN 0-538-86524-5

The Adaptable Courseware Program consists of products and additions to existing Custom Publishing products that are produced from camera-ready copy. Peer review, class testing, and accuracy are primarily the responsibility of the author(s).

# P R E F A C E

...........................................................................................

We see at least two objectives in using *Readings in Public Finance* to supplement public finance textbooks: to present policy issues, allowing students an opportunity to apply the theory discussed in class, and to show students how material is developed in the literature by having them read some of the classics and contemporary contributions. To fulfill these goals, we have attempted to bring together thought-provoking policy pieces, good examples of economic argument, well-done surveys, and classic works. Supplementary readings are indispensable in achieving a broad, thorough understanding of the issues as well as the relevance of economic methodology to current government expenditure and financing policies.

This volume is the outgrowth of our experience in teaching public finance. Because of the large literature in public finance economics, we were forced to choose from among many outstanding contributions in order to limit the readings to a manageable number. Fortunately, we were able to reprint a large number of selections that provide a broad range of topics. Individual instructors and students can choose those readings most suitable to their interests. *Readings in Public Finance* could also be used in courses on public policy as well as public finance. In addition, the anthology could serve as a main text itself, particularly in a survey course with the instructor providing appropriate foundational material.

A number of fine textbooks have been written on public finance, providing an expanded scope that accommodates both core material and recent developments in the field. Thus, we have not tied the readings in this book to any one text. But in developing this second edition, we have had a new goal to direct us in compiling the current collection of readings: to make certain that each selection corresponds to at least one chapter in each of the major textbooks, and that no text chapter is without a supplementary reading. The Cross Reference Chart that follows the Table of Contents illustrates how this volume complements the major undergraduate texts in this field. This chart can be used straightforwardly to link chapter and reading assignments.

Each prospective reading had to meet the two additional general criteria of "readability" and "supplemental." Readability was met if the selection was suitable for the undergraduate student who had taken only principles of economics, and if the selection could be understood without a high level of mathematical sophistication. Supplemental, not surprisingly, was met if the reading not only did not duplicate material presented in the major textbooks, but also represented an addition in some way—e.g., a classic providing linkage to foundational research in public finance, a discussion of issues by a distinguished economist renowned for work in the field, or an interesting application expounding upon text material (and one which might help students answer the question: "just how relevant is this?").

Each reading is prefaced by a short introduction to the issues and brief summary, and a list of questions to guide the students through the selection. Together, the prefaces and questions motivate the readings by eliciting the primary themes. The introductions help to connect the work to textbook discussions in the same subject area, place the article within a relevant context in the field of public finance, and provide some additional background. The questions, as guides to the reading, cover the majority of the key points in each reading. Thus, the answer to each question can be found in the readings themselves. When appropriate, these questions also link the article to the conceptual framework of the subject matter as presented in the textbooks or in the public finance literature.

While this volume attempts to provide an overall balance of views, some of the individual readings do not take a middle-of-the-road stance. Readers have the chance to judge for themselves the shades of gray—the areas of controversy. To aid in this pursuit, the final component of this volume is the bibliographic section Suggested Further Readings. These references range in subject matter, providing additional readings for the topics of the selections in this book as well as more generally for the subject areas focused on in the textbook chapters. The references also range from articles written for noneconomists to those written for professional economics journals. *Readings in Public Finance* thus should serve as a useful supplement to public finance textbooks, helping students to build and weigh arguments, to identify strengths and weaknesses of opposing viewpoints, and ultimately to draw their own conclusions.

Samuel H. Baker
Catherine S. Elliott

# ACKNOWLEDGMENTS

*Readings in Public Finance* has benefited from the suggestions of colleagues at numerous universities and colleges, and from the reactions of the students who class-tested the readings, selection introductions, and questions. Such advice and feedback proved crucial. We invite more of it, for we harbor hopes that future editions will continue to track new developments and policy issues, thus further serving this lively field.

We are indebted to a number of specific individuals for their help and advice: Don Hayward, Donald Campbell, Robert Tollison, Richard Coe, Richard McGrath, Alfredo Pereira, Sebastian Canon, and Harvey Stewart. Members of the staff at South-Western College Publishing who deserve mention include: Jack Calhoun, John Alessi, Andrea Shaw, Scott Person, and Peggy Buskey. We are also grateful to the publishers and authors who kindly allowed us to reprint these articles. Finally, we remain appreciative of the efforts of everyone who helped us develop the first edition.

S.H.B.
C.S.E.

# C O N T E N T S

**Preface** ii

**Acknowledgments** v

**Cross Reference Chart** xi

**General Introduction**
Volume Overview and General Introduction to the Study of Public Finance  1
  *Samuel H. Baker and Catherine S. Elliott*

**Roles of Government - Topic of Interest:**
***Restructuring Who Does What***
  1. Distinguished Lecture on Economics in Government: Strengthening the
     Economy by Rethinking the Role of Federal and State Governments  11
     *Alice M. Rivlin*

**Public Finance Analysis - Classic**
  2. Positive Economics, Welfare Economics, and Political Economy  23
     *James M. Buchanan*

**Externalities - Classic**
  3. The Problem of Social Cost  37
     *Ronald H. Coase*

**Externalities - Topic of Interest:**
***Environmental Economics and the Market***
  4. The Design and Implementation of Environmental Policy  53
     *Maureen L. Cropper and Wallace E. Oates*

**Externalities - Topic of Interest:**
***Efficient Consumption of Alcohol and Cigarettes***
  5. Alcohol and Cigarette Taxes  79
     *Michael Grossman, Jody L. Sindelar, John Mullahy, and Richard Anderson*

**Public Goods - Classic**
  6. The Logic  93
     *Mancur Olson, Jr.*

**Public Goods - Classic**

7.  The Tragedy of the Commons     107
    *Garrett Hardin*

**Optimal Government Intervention - Topic of Interest:**
**Public versus Private Provision**

8.  Economic Perspectives on Privatization     121
    *John Vickers and George Yarrow*

**Optimal Government Intervention - Topic of Interest:**
**Infrastructure**

9.  Infrastructure Spending: Where Do We Go from Here?     145
    *Charles R. Hulten and Robert M. Schwab*

**Public Choice - Topic of Interest:**
**The Public-Choice Paradigm**

10. Public Finance and Public Choice     163
    *James M. Buchanan*

**Public Choice - Topic of Interest:**
**A Real-World Voting Cycle**

11. A Paradox of Voting: Cyclical Majorities and the Case of Muscle Shoals     181
    *John L. Neufeld, William J. Hausman, and Ronald B. Rapoport*

**Public Choice - Topic of Interest:**
**Rent Seeking and Lobbying**

12. Rent Seeking: A Survey     197
    *Robert D. Tollison*

**Cost-Benefit Analysis - Topic of Interest:**
**HIV Testing for Employment?**

13. Benefits and Costs of HIV Testing     207
    *David E. Bloom and Sherry Glied*

**Distribution of Income - Topic of Interest:**
**Changing Definitions of Income at the Census Bureau**

14. Measuring the Effects of Benefits and Taxes on Income and Poverty     225
    *Charles T. Nelson and John F. Coder*

**Poverty Programs - Topic of Interest:**
**Investment in Children**

15. Children's Prospects and Children's Policy     239
    *Robert Haveman and Barbara Wolfe*

**Public Education - Topic of Interest:**
**College Loans**

16. Income-Contingent College Loans     263
    *Alan B. Krueger and William G. Bowen*

## Social Insurance - Topic of Interest:
### Social Security Reform
17. Putting Social Security to Work: How to Restore the Balance Between
    Generations   273
    *Barry Bosworth*

## Health Care - Topic of Interest:
### Lessons Learned
18. The Economics of Health and Health Care: What Have We Learned?
    What Have I Learned?   281
    *Martin Feldstein*

## Taxation - Classic
19. The Bridge between Tax and Expenditure in the Fiscal Decision Process   289
    *James M. Buchanan*

## Taxation - Topic of Interest:
### Excess Burden of "Green" Taxes
20. Green Taxes: Can We Protect the Environment and Improve the
    Tax System at the Same Time?   299
    *Wallace E. Oates*

## Taxation - Topic of Interest:
### Lifetime versus Annual Incidence
21. Lifetime versus Annual Perspectives on Tax Incidence   311
    *Don Fullerton and Diane Lim Rogers*

## Taxation - Topic of Interest:
### Comprehensive Income Tax
22. The Future of the Income Tax   325
    *Joseph A. Pechman*

## Personal Income Tax - Topic of Interest:
### Tax Reform and Behavioral Changes
23. Behavioral Responses to Tax Rates: Evidence from the Tax Reform
    Act of 1986   353
    *Martin Feldstein*

## Personal Income Tax - Topic of Interest:
### Compliance Costs and Simplicity
24. Did the Tax Reform Act of 1986 Simplify Tax Matters?   361
    *Joel Slemrod*

## Corporation Income Tax - Topic of Interest:
### Eliminating Double Taxation
25. Corporate Tax Integration: A View from the Treasury Department   375
    *R. Glenn Hubbard*

**Other Taxes - Topic of Interest:**
*Flat Tax versus "USA" Tax*

26. The Tax Restructuring Phenomenon: Analytical Principles and
    Political Equation                                               395
    *Ernest S. Christian*

**Other Taxes - Topic of Interest:**
*Value-Added Tax*

27. Value-Added Taxation: A Tax Whose Time Has Come?              411
    *Gilbert E. Metcalf*

**Other Taxes - Topic of Interest:**
*Taxing the Rich*

28. Reassessing the Role for Wealth Transfer Taxes               433
    *Henry J. Aaron and Alicia H. Munnell*

**Other Taxes - Topic of Interest:**
*State Lotteries*

29. On the Economics of State Lotteries—Updated                 457
    *Charles T. Clotfelter and Philip J. Cook*

**Government Deficits and Debt - Topic of Interest:**
*Generational Accounts*

30. Generational Accounting: A Meaningful Way to Evaluate Fiscal Policy   473
    *Alan J. Auerbach, Jagadeesh Gokhale, and Laurence J. Kotlikoff*

**Fiscal Federalism - Classic**

31. An Economic Approach to Federalism                          491
    *Wallace E. Oates*

**Fiscal Federalism - Classic**

32. A Pure Theory of Local Expenditures                         503
    *Charles M. Tiebout*

**Suggested Further Readings**                                  513

# CROSS REFERENCE CHART

| | Browning & Browning | Hyman | Marlow | Rosen |
|---|---|---|---|---|
| **GENERAL INTRODUCTION** | | | | |
| Preface | 1 | 1 | 1, 2 | 1, 2 |
| Volume Overview | 1 | 1 | 1, 2 | 1, 2 |
| General Introduction to the Study of Public Finance | 1 | 2 | 3 | 3, 4 |
| *Samuel H. Baker and Catherine S. Elliott* | | | | |
| **ROLES OF GOVERNMENT - TOPIC OF INTEREST:** | | | | |
| ***RESTRUCTURING WHO DOES WHAT*** | | | | |
| 1. Distinguished Lecture on Economics in Government: Strengthening the Economy by Rethinking the Role of Federal and State Governments | 1 | 1 | 1, 2 | 1, 2 |
| *Alice M. Rivlin* | (16) | (18) | (22) | (21) |
| **PUBLIC FINANCE ANALYSIS - CLASSIC** | | | | |
| 2. Positive Economics, Welfare Economics, and Political Economy | 1, 3 | 2, 5 | 3, 6, 7 | 3, 4, 7 |
| *James M. Buchanan* | (8) | (7) | (11) | (8) |
| **EXTERNALITIES - CLASSIC** | | | | |
| 3. The Problem of Social Cost | 2 | 3 | 4 | 6 |
| *Ronald H. Coase* | | | | |
| **EXTERNALITIES - TOPIC OF INTEREST:** | | | | |
| ***ENVIRONMENTAL ECONOMICS AND THE MARKET*** | | | | |
| 4. The Design and Implementation of Environmental Policy | 2 | 3 | 4 | 6 |
| *Maureen L. Cropper and Wallace E. Oates* | | | | |
| **EXTERNALITIES - TOPIC OF INTEREST:** | | | | |
| ***EFFICIENT CONSUMPTION OF ALCOHOL*** | | | | |
| ***AND CIGARETTES*** | | | | |
| 5. Alcohol and Cigarette Taxes | 2 | 3 | 4 | 6 |
| *Michael Grossman, Jody L. Sindelar,* | (10) | (11) | (16) | (13) |
| *John Mullahy, and Richard Anderson* | | | | |

The numbers listed in each column correspond to chapter numbers in the four textbooks; citations are at the end of the chart.

| | Browning & Browning | Hyman | Marlow | Rosen |
|---|---|---|---|---|
| **PUBLIC GOODS - CLASSIC**<br>6. The Logic<br>*Mancur Olson, Jr.* | 2, 3 | 4, 5 | 5, 6 | 5, 7 |
| **PUBLIC GOODS - CLASSIC**<br>7. The Tragedy of the Commons<br>*Garrett Hardin* | 2 | 4, 3 | 5, 4 | 5, 6 |
| **OPTIMAL GOVERNMENT INTERVENTION -**<br>**TOPIC OF INTEREST:** *PUBLIC VERSUS*<br>*PRIVATE PROVISION*<br>8. Economic Perspectives on Privatization<br>*John Vickers and George Yarrow* | 2, 3<br>(4) | 4, 5, 10 | 5, 7, 6 | 5, 7 |
| **OPTIMAL GOVERNMENT INTERVENTION -**<br>**TOPIC OF INTEREST:** *INFRASTRUCTURE*<br>9. Infrastructure Spending: Where Do We Go<br>From Here?<br>*Charles R. Hulten and Robert M. Schwab* | 4, 2<br>(3) | 6, 4, 10<br>(7) | 9, 5, 14 | 5, 12 |
| **PUBLIC CHOICE - TOPIC OF INTEREST:**<br>*THE PUBLIC-CHOICE PARADIGM*<br>10. Public Finance and Public Choice<br>*James M. Buchanan* | 3<br>(2) | 5<br>(4) | 6, 7<br>(5, 10) | 7<br>(5) |
| **PUBLIC CHOICE - TOPIC OF INTEREST:**<br>*A REAL-WORLD VOTING CYCLE*<br>11. A Paradox of Voting: Cyclical Majorities and the<br>Case of Muscle Shoals<br>*John L. Neufeld, William J. Hausman, and*<br>*Ronald B. Rapoport* | 3 | 5 | 7 | 7 |
| **PUBLIC CHOICE - TOPIC OF INTEREST:**<br>*RENT SEEKING AND LOBBYING*<br>12. Rent Seeking: A Survey<br>*Robert D. Tollison* | 3 | 5 | 7, 8, 9<br>(3) | 7 |
| **COST-BENEFIT ANALYSIS - TOPIC OF INTEREST:**<br>*HIV TESTING FOR EMPLOYMENT?*<br>13. Benefits and Costs of HIV Testing<br>*David E. Bloom and Sherry Glied* | 4 | 6 | 14 | 12 |
| **DISTRIBUTION OF INCOME - TOPIC OF INTEREST:**<br>*CHANGING DEFINITIONS OF INCOME AT*<br>*THE CENSUS BUREAU*<br>14. Measuring the Effects of Benefits and Taxes on<br>Income and Poverty<br>*Charles T. Nelson and John F. Coder* | 8<br>(11) | 7<br>(13) | 11<br>(18) | 8<br>(16) |
| **POVERTY PROGRAMS - TOPIC OF INTEREST:**<br>*INVESTMENT IN CHILDREN*<br>15. Children's Prospects and Children's Policy<br>*Robert Haveman and Barbara Wolfe* | 8, 9<br>(5) | 7 | 11 | 9 |

| | Browning & Browning | Hyman | Marlow | Rosen |
|---|---|---|---|---|
| **PUBLIC EDUCATION - TOPIC OF INTEREST: COLLEGE LOANS** | | | | |
| 16. Income-Contingent College Loans<br>*Alan B. Krueger and William G. Bowen* | 5<br>(8) | 3<br>(7) | 9, 10<br>(11) | 6<br>(8) |
| **SOCIAL INSURANCE - TOPIC OF INTEREST: SOCIAL SECURITY REFORM** | | | | |
| 17. Putting Social Security to Work: How to Restore the Balance Between Generations<br>*Barry Bosworth* | 7, 13 | 8<br>(13) | 12<br>(16) | 10<br>(13) |
| **HEALTH CARE - TOPIC OF INTEREST: LESSONS LEARNED** | | | | |
| 18. The Economics of Health and Health Care: What Have We Learned? What Have I Learned?<br>*Martin Feldstein* | 6 | 9 | 13 | 11 |
| **TAXATION - CLASSIC** | | | | |
| 19. The Bridge between Tax and Expenditure in the Fiscal Decision Process<br>*James M. Buchanan* | 10 | 10<br>(12) | 15, 9, 10<br>(17) | 13, 7<br>(19) |
| **TAXATION - TOPIC OF INTEREST: EXCESS BURDEN OF "GREEN" TAXES** | | | | |
| 20. Green Taxes: Can We Protect the Environment and Improve the Tax System at the Same Time?<br>*Wallace E. Oates* | 10, 2 | 11, 3 | 15, 16, 4 | 14, 15, 6 |
| **TAXATION - TOPIC OF INTEREST: LIFETIME VERSUS ANNUAL INCIDENCE** | | | | |
| 21. Lifetime versus Annual Perspectives on Tax Incidence<br>*Don Fullerton and Diane Lim Rogers* | 10 | 11 | 16 | 13 |
| **TAXATION - TOPIC OF INTEREST: COMPREHENSIVE INCOME TAX** | | | | |
| 22. The Future of the Income Tax<br>*Joseph A. Pechman* | 11, 15 | 13, 14, 16 | 18, 21 | 15, 16, 20 |
| **PERSONAL INCOME TAX - TOPIC OF INTEREST: TAX REFORM AND BEHAVIORAL CHANGES** | | | | |
| 23. Behavioral Responses to Tax Rates: Evidence from the Tax Reform Act of 1986<br>*Martin Feldstein* | 11, 15 | 13, 14 | 19 | 17 |
| **PERSONAL INCOME TAX - TOPIC OF INTEREST: COMPLIANCE COSTS AND SIMPLICITY** | | | | |
| 24. Did the Tax Reform Act of 1986 Simplify Tax Matters?<br>*Joel Slemrod* | 11 | 14, 10 | 16, 18 | 15, 16 |
| **CORPORATION INCOME TAX - TOPIC OF INTEREST: ELIMINATING DOUBLE TAXATION** | | | | |
| 25. Corporate Tax Integration: A View from the Treasury Department<br>*R. Glenn Hubbard* | 12 | 15 | 20 | 18 |

| | Browning & Browning | Hyman | Marlow | Rosen |
|---|---|---|---|---|
| **OTHER TAXES - TOPIC OF INTEREST:** *FLAT TAX VERSUS "USA" TAX* | | | | |
| 26. The Tax Restructuring Phenomenon: Analytical Principles and Political Equation<br>*Ernest S. Christian* | 11, 15 (12) | 13, 14 (15) | 15, 18 (20) | 15, 16 (18) |
| **OTHER TAXES - TOPIC OF INTEREST:** *VALUE-ADDED TAX* | | | | |
| 27. Value-Added Taxation: A Tax Whose Time Has Come?<br>*Gilbert E. Metcalf* | 13, 15 | 16 | 21 | 20 |
| **OTHER TAXES - TOPIC OF INTEREST:** *TAXING THE RICH* | | | | |
| 28. Reassessing the Role for Wealth Transfer Taxes<br>*Henry J. Aaron and Alicia H. Munnell* | 13 | 17 (11) | 21 | 20 |
| **OTHER TAXES - TOPIC OF INTEREST:** *STATE LOTTERIES* | | | | |
| 29. On the Economics of State Lotteries—Updated<br>*Charles T. Clotfelter and Philip J. Cook* | 16 (13) | 10, 18 (17) | 22 (21) | 21 |
| **GOVERNMENT DEFICITS AND DEBT - TOPIC OF INTEREST:** *GENERATIONAL ACCOUNTS* | | | | |
| 30. Generational Accounting: A Meaningful Way to Evaluate Fiscal Policy<br>*Alan J. Auerbach, Jagadeesh Gokhale, and Laurence J. Kotlikoff* | 14 | 12 | 17, 9 | 19 |
| **FISCAL FEDERALISM - CLASSIC** | | | | |
| 31. An Economic Approach to Federalism<br>*Wallace E. Oates* | 16 | 18 | 22 | 21 |
| **FISCAL FEDERALISM - CLASSIC** | | | | |
| 32. A Pure Theory of Local Expenditures<br>*Charles M. Tiebout* | 16 | 18 | 22 | 21 |

Browning, Edgar K. & Jacquelene M. Browning. *Public Finance and the Price System* (4th edition). New York: Macmillan Publishing, 1994.

Hyman, David N. *Public Finance: A Contemporary Application of Theory to Policy* (5th edition). Fort Worth: Dryden Press, 1996.

Marlow, Michael L. *Public Finance: Theory and Practice*. Fort Worth: Dryden Press, 1995.

Rosen, Harvey S. *Public Finance* (4th edition). Chicago: Irwin, 1995.

Samuel H. Baker
Catherine S. Elliott

# Volume Overview and General Introduction to the Study of Public Finance

Public finance (also called public economics and public sector economics) examines both how democratic governments make finance and expenditure choices, and how these decisions influence the economy and thus the welfare of its members. Even though economies like that of the United States are primarily market based, substantial resources are allocated by government. Often questions arise about what economic activities a government should undertake and how a government should allocate resources. Indeed, these questions are linked. Both involve an evaluation of the alternative methods for a government to do something as well as an evaluation of the possibility of the market being involved in addition to—or instead of—the government.

Public finance has substantially broadened its content over the last four decades. Along with standard material on taxation, progress in the theory of collective decision making and advances in expenditure analysis have immensely improved economists' understanding of the public sector. The expansion in the field is most evident when one compares the table of contents of Richard Musgrave's classic text (*The Theory of Public Finance*, 1959) with those of texts published in the last few years. Both Musgrave and more recent books contain chapters on taxation, deficit financing, and budget determination through voting. But newer texts also include chapters on externalities, cost-benefit analysis, health care, Social Security, and various expenditure programs designed to provide assistance to the poor.

## VOLUME OVERVIEW

The readings in this book correspond to the major areas of study and research in public finance and public policy economics. The first selection by Alice Rivlin addresses the basic question of the appropriate roles for governments. In the second selection, James Buchanan's classic article sets the stage for the discussion of modes of analysis for public finance in general and for economists particularly interested in policymaking.

The next five selections focus on two principal rationales for public sector activity—externalities and public goods. Economists use the term *externality* to refer to any consequences of private market exchanges that "spillover" onto third parties. A family restoring (destroying) the exterior of its home bestows positive (negative) externalities on neighbors, whose properties appreciate (depreciate) in value as a result. The readings on externalities include the classic by Ronald Coase, and two others examining policy implementation issues. Maureen Cropper and Wallace Oates highlight issues in the design of economic policy instruments for controlling pollution, and Michael Grossman and colleagues explore the arguments for using excise taxes to influence alcohol and cigarette consumption.

A second principal rationale for government activity is a failure of private markets to provide efficient levels of public goods. For example, given a large number of citizens, an individual's private decision not to purchase national defense or mosquito control will not significantly affect the amount available to everyone else. This creates an incentive for each person to "free ride," attempting to benefit from others' purchases without paying. If collectively-shared goods such as national defense or mosquito control are desired, compulsory payment in the form of taxation becomes necessary when the incentives to free ride are strong. The readings on public goods include two classic articles: Mancur Olson's investigation into "the logic of collective action," and Garrett Hardin's treatment of "the tragedy of the commons."

Underlying the economic analysis of public sector activity is the basic question of optimal government intervention. In the first of two selections, John Vickers and George Yarrow deal with issues of privatization of goods and services provided by the public sector. No longer are concerns over market failure paramount; complex policy choices now depend on assessments of the social costs of government failure. In the second selection, Charles Hulten and Robert Schwab direct attention to a more specific policy matter—public spending on highway infrastructure. Government infrastructure spending has been viewed by some as a crucial link to economic growth.

The following three selections on public choice reflect the efforts of economists, as well as political scientists, to understand the political process. This topic intrigues economists, often because of the influence of politics on the implementation of economic policy recommendations. For instance, efficient policy proposals are frequently not adopted. Also, policies that are adopted frequently do not perform as predicted. Considered by many to have pioneered the study of public choice, James Buchanan introduces the public-choice paradigm which provides the framework for research in this influential branch of public finance. In the second reading, John Neufeld, William Hausman, and Ronald Rapoport report on their exciting discovery of a real-world voting cycle. Robert Tollison then introduces rent seeking—an activity in which private parties attempt to manipulate government policies to profitable advantage.

The next group of readings apply economic analysis to particular expenditure programs affecting the choices of individuals, the allocation of resources, and the distribution of income. These papers raise a number of critical issues concerning the desirability of various public policies. David Bloom and Sherry Glied ask whether HIV testing should be a condition of employment. Charles Nelson and John Coder, both of the U.S. Census Bureau, consider how income should be defined and used to measure distribution, poverty levels, and tax burdens. Robert Haveman and Barbara Wolfe pose the question: How do social programs impact children's welfare? Alan Krueger and William Bowen focus on an innovative funding option for student college loans. Whether social security can be reformed to ensure financial solvency is the subject of Barry Bosworth's article. Martin Feldstein examines what lessons have been learned about health care, and how the United States might better meet the challenge to make the system operate more effectively.

The two selections by James Buchanan and Wallace Oates reflect the volume's change in emphasis from the expenditure to the revenue side of government activities. However, instead of focusing solely on methods of raising revenue, James Buchanan addresses the inherent linkages between spending and taxing—discussing how inefficiency is likely to be the result of separating spending policy decisions from taxing decisions. Wallace Oates cautions against relying too heavily on what might be wishful thinking of those who believe the revenues from "green taxes" can replace or reduce other types of taxation.

Revenue issues are the traditional core of the public finance field: how government pays for its activities through taxation and borrowing. But new questions and developments continue to make this branch of public finance exciting and controversial. Don Fullerton and Diane Rogers introduce a novel approach to measuring tax incidence, asking what the burden of taxation is over an entire lifetime as opposed to just during a single year. With tax reform part of the past, present, and certainly the future, Joseph Pechman's impassioned argument for maintaining the federal income tax remains particularly timely—and his plea for greater progressivity continues to evoke debate.

But in order to evaluate new proposals for tax reform, a clear understanding of the impacts of what Martin Feldstein calls "the most important natural experiments since the start of the income tax" is crucial. Thus, two selections focus directly on evaluations of the U.S. Tax Reform Act of 1986. First, Martin Feldstein looks at the effects on individual incentives, and specifically, the evidence concerning changes in labor supply, taxable income, and realized capital gains. Joel Slemrod next investigates whether or not the Tax Reform Act of 1986 made good on one of its celebrated promises—to simplify taxes. Was the plan to streamline the federal tax system waylaid by policy tradeoffs and political expediencies?

Not surprisingly, proposals for tax reform are abundant, varying from specific modifications to thorough overhauls of the existing tax system to completely new methods of taxation. Glenn Hubbard, of the U.S. Treasury Department, focuses on a specific modification to the corporation tax. Corporate tax integration is proposed to eliminate the double taxation of dividend income. Ernest Christian discusses plans for a thorough overhaul of the federal income tax by instituting a "flat tax." Several versions of the flat tax exist, including the Unlimited Saving Allowance (USA) tax which was introduced in a U.S. Senate bill in 1995. In the next selection, Gilbert Metcalf asks whether it might be time to institute a value-added tax in the United States—to replace all or part of the federal income tax. Many proponents of value-added or consumption taxation believe the benefits of a complete substitution would far outweigh the transition costs involved in changing to a new system of taxation.

Each of the topics of the next three selections have also generated considerable debate. Henry Aaron and Alicia Munnell argue in favor of tightening the collection of estate and inheritance taxes. Should wealth transfer taxes be used to dilute the concentration of wealth in the United States, and by doing so, disperse any wealth-related power? Charles Clotfelter and Philip Cook take a unique perspective on state lotteries, a relatively new and very popular source of state revenue. While the revenue-collection properties of lotteries are examined, the primary focus is on lotteries as consumption goods—and on questions of why people play lottery games and what are the socioeconomic characteristics of those who play. Alan Auerbach, Jagadeesh Gokhale, and Laurence Kotlikoff provide a systematic method of addressing the problem of the burden of the national debt on today's and future generations. Generational accounting offers a way to determine a particular generation's "public account"—a new approach to measuring the intergenerational incidence of budget deficits.

The final two selections in this volume examine some of the interactions arising in a federal system of government. Because the United States was originally formed as a federation of thirteen colonies, the national government became known as the federal government. Under the federal government are state and local governments, forming descending layers of the system of American federalism. The first selection is the classic analysis of a federal system by Wallace Oates. Why might a federal system be preferable to having one level of government provide all public sector output? What comparative advantages might the federal and state levels have in performing the various functions of government? Charles Tiebout, in another classic paper, focuses on the advantages of numerous local governments. He introduces the well-known concept of "voting with your feet"—if unsatisfied with the policies of one local government, voters have the option of moving to another jurisdiction.

## GENERAL INTRODUCTION TO THE STUDY OF PUBLIC FINANCE

Economic analysis is an invaluable tool in the formulation, evaluation, and understanding of public policy. Public finance economists base most of their analyses on concepts of economic efficiency and distributional welfare. The following discussion introduces these concepts, illustrating the main points with a numerical example. While every textbook includes explanations of economic efficiency and equity considerations, every reader of this volume may not be using a text. Additionally, the illustration may serve to supplement the discussions found in accompanying textbooks.

## Economic Efficiency versus Economic Inefficiency

The criterion of economic efficiency is easy to grasp, and seemingly, easy to apply. Once it is explained, almost everyone intuitively feels that it is a worthwhile and beneficial goal for a society to pursue. Simply put, arrangements are said to be economically efficient if the only possible way to make any one person in the economy better off is to make someone else worse off. Economic efficiency is also referred to as Pareto optimality. Contrast this state of affairs with an economy that is operating inefficiently. Someone could be better off *without anyone else having to suffer*: a "free lunch." What could be a more reasonable goal than to institute all policy changes that would benefit society in this way? It seems that both politicians and their constituents would find themselves in the unusual position of agreement on this question.

Economic efficiency and inefficiency are linked to the *Pareto-improvement criterion* for judging when government can and cannot act strictly in the public interest. When a public policy makes any individual worse off, it is not in the interest of every member of the public, and therefore does not meet the Pareto-improvement criterion. On the other hand, if no one is harmed by the policy, the Pareto criterion is met, and the change is said to reflect a Pareto improvement. By definition, it is impossible to institute a Pareto improvement if the economy is operating efficiently. It follows, then, that if the Pareto-improvement criterion has been met by a policy change, the original state of affairs must have been economically inefficient.

Actual examples of inefficiencies that can be readily corrected without hurting anyone are not easy to find, usually because common sense already has led to an efficient arrangement. Consider the gains that result from traffic regulation on streets. Assume that initially roads are completely unregulated, with vehicles moving in opposite directions on either side of the road. Drivers operate slowly to make certain they have enough time to dodge vehicles coming from the other direction, particularly when they are going around sharp turns and over hills. On flat, open roads, on the other hand, drivers can travel faster by using turn signals, for example, to indicate a desire to pass approaching vehicles on one side or the other.

Despite drivers' reducing their speed at blind spots in the road, and signaling on the flat stretches, head-on collisions occur often—injuring travelers and damaging vehicles. Therefore, a traffic regulation that requires all vehicles to travel on the right side (or left side) of the road represents a Pareto improvement to an economically-efficient arrangement: such coordination should make all drivers better off, without making any driver worse off.

However, any two randomly chosen voters are likely to disagree over who should receive the benefits and who should bear the costs of two different, but equally efficient, allocations of resources. In the example above, a policy that requires individuals to drive on the right side of the road, coupled with a regulation that steering wheels be placed on the left, is equally as efficient as left-side driving and right-side steering. But present-day drivers might disagree strongly on which policy is more desirable, depending upon the type of car they currently own or prefer to drive, and who is made responsible for the cost of changing policies.

Once an economy is operating efficiently, hard choices must be made if any additional changes are desired, such as in the distribution of income. It becomes no longer possible to improve the welfare of one group without imposing a cost on another group, i.e., there are no more free lunches. Although economists would certainly vote in favor of any policy that benefits society at no one else's expense, their personal beliefs and preferences would have to come into play for them to choose between different, yet equally efficient, public policies.

## Employing the Economic Efficiency Criterion: A Numerical Illustration

Economists often use a method of judging economic efficiency that is analogous to a private business achieving the greatest possible profits. If all benefits and costs of a public policy can be quantified, then economic efficiency is equivalent to maximizing total social benefits (benefits to all members of a community) net of total social costs (costs to all members of a community). This difference is termed *net social benefits*, and is sometimes referred to as society's surplus—the extra benefits, above cost, enjoyed by the members of an economy at any given time.

Consider a small municipality that has the task of determining how to allocate $1.2 million for residential fire protection services. The overall budget, also an important policy issue, has already been resolved. Thus, for simplicity, the economic efficiency criterion will be employed only to evaluate alternative allocations of the $1.2 million earmarked for this project. Fire protection services consist of fire engines and the accompanying labor, building, land, and water. These services may be provided either on the town's affluent south end, or on its poorer north end, or on both ends by splitting the services in some way.

In Table 1, the annual total social cost (TSC) to the community of operating and financing a fire station on either end of town is assumed to be the same, rising as the number of fire engines ($Q$) increases. Residents have a certain maximum willingness to pay for any given level of $Q$, determined by, among other things, the amount an increase in $Q$ lowers both the insurance rates and psychic costs associated with the threat of fire. The combined maximum willingness to pay of all south-enders is given by $TB_S$, and of all north-enders, by $TB_N$. Note that residents of one end of town benefit when a fire engine is placed at the other end of town, but not as much as when a fire engine is at their end of town.

**Table 1** Benefits and Costs of Alternative Fire Stations ($1,000s)

| Both | | South-End Station | | | | North-End Station | | | |
|---|---|---|---|---|---|---|---|---|---|
| Q | TSC | TB$_S$ | TB$_N$ | TSB | NSB | TB$_S$ | TB$_N$ | TSB | NSB |
| 1 | 400 | 450 | 170 | 620 | 220 | 116 | 340 | 456 | 56 |
| 2 | 500 | 550 | 200 | 750 | 250 | 140 | 420 | 560 | 60** |
| 3 | 600 | 645 | 225 | 870 | 270 | 160 | 496 | 656 | 56 |
| 4 | 700 | 735 | 245 | 980 | 280* | 176 | 568 | 744 | 44 |
| 5 | 800 | 818 | 257 | 1075 | 275 | 186 | 634 | 820 | 20 |

The total social benefit (TSB) schedules in Table 1 give the combined benefits to south- and north-end residents for different levels of Q at the two fire station locations. The difference between TSB and TSC is then the net social benefits, or social surplus, enjoyed by the entire community for any given level of fire protection. While schedules of marginal benefits and marginal costs could easily be constructed as well, the use of total values will facilitate the discussion of Pareto improvements and alternative decision criteria in the next section.

The economically-efficient choice maximizes net social benefits (NSB)—the excess of TSB over TSC. Given the figures in Table 1, economic efficiency will be accomplished by providing unequal levels of fire protection on both ends of town. Because the two NSB columns represent all net social benefits from each station for each level of Q, the efficient solution is found by (1) determining where the sum of south-end NSB plus north-end NSB is maximized, and at the same time, (2) making certain that the budget constraint is satisfied. Given the budget allotment of $1.2 million, net social benefits are maximized when $700,000 is spent on four engines in the south end, and $500,000 is spent on two engines in the north end. The two maximum levels of NSB are designated with single and double asterisks in Table 1 ($280,000 and $60,000). Thus, a total expenditure of $1,200,000 provides maximum net social benefits of $340,000.

## Alternative Decision Criteria: Equity and Distributional Concerns

Economic analysis helps to identify efficient policies as well as the distributional consequences of these policies, but it cannot judge the overall desirability of the resulting distribution of benefits among members of a community. Whether or not an efficient policy is fair or equitable is a separate issue which must be decided through a political process that includes voters, elected officials, and relevant government agencies. Equity is more difficult to analyze than efficiency, because equity means different things to different people.

While an attractive goal on both equity and efficiency grounds, the Pareto-improvement criterion is also an incomplete guide to policymaking. Even if public policy achieves an economically-efficient allocation, one cannot conclude that the Pareto-improvement criterion has been met at each step along the way—a controversy surrounding the use of the efficiency criterion. Further, inefficient policies may be judged more equitable than economically-efficient policies. (Or, as the traffic example demonstrates, more than one efficient policy may exist.) In these cases, the Pareto-improvement criterion cannot be used to choose between the policies, and society must apply a different decision criterion. These issues will be illustrated below by referring again to the numerical example in Table 1.

A policy choice made on the basis of a criterion of fairness or equity could require the same number of fire engines at both ends of the city. Given the budget allotment of $1.2 million and the cost data in Table 1, the community could afford three fire engines per station. Net social benefits would then equal $326,000, representing a loss in social surplus of $14,000 when compared to the economically-efficient solution. Because net social benefits are less than those resulting from the solution of four fire engines in the south and two in the north, this arrangement is economically inefficient.

Nevertheless, the members of this community still may decide to place three fire engines at each station. If this solution is adopted, it would have to be justified on different grounds than those of economic efficiency. Proponents of this policy could argue that the gain in equity more than makes up for the loss of $14,000 in net social benefits. This argument could be further strengthened, for example, if policymakers were persuaded that a dollar's worth of benefits to the residents of the poorer north end was of greater value than a dollar's worth of benefits to the residents of the affluent south end.

These alternative solutions serve to demonstrate the difference between the efficiency criterion and the Pareto-improvement criterion. If each side of town originally had three fire engines, and a change were made simply by edict to the unequal, but economically-efficient allocation, then the resulting policy change would not meet the Pareto-improvement criterion. Although net social benefits would be greater, the efficient solution would not be instituted without causing harm to some residents. Using the values from Table 1 again, the north-end residents benefit an additional $20,000 when the fourth fire engine is placed in the south, but they lose $76,000 in total benefits because only two engines remain in the north station. In contrast, the south-enders are more than willing to give up the $20,000 they lose when the number of engines in the north end decreases from three to two—they gain $90,000 in benefits from the additional fire services in the south end. The south-enders gain net benefits of $70,000; the north-enders lose net benefits of $56,000. Therefore, the $14,000 gain in net social benefits derived from changing from the economically-inefficient solution to the economically-efficient solution violates the Pareto-improvement criterion.

If the south-enders compensated the north-enders in some way for the loss of $56,000, the policy would meet the Pareto-improvement criterion. In practice, however, actual compensation may be difficult to arrange. To avoid this problem, some economists advocate use of a "potential" Pareto-improvement criterion. Under this decision rule, policies in which compensation is possible are acceptable, but actual compensation is not required. The solution of four fire engines in the south and two in the north would fulfill the criterion of a potential Pareto improvement—and additionally, would maximize net social benefits. Thus, application of the potential Pareto-improvement criterion is equivalent to maximizing net social benefits because sufficient social surplus is generated for gainers potentially to compensate losers.

## Economic Analysis

Economic analysis makes a genuine contribution by generating information on the benefits and costs associated with particular policy proposals, and on the distribution of such gains and losses among citizens. Almost every economic policy decision affects society's distribution of resources. Judicious use of the efficiency and Pareto criteria can clarify when value judgments have a critical role to play in policymaking. Such information is indispensable to the democratic process used to make real policy choices.

# S E L E C T I O N  1

Alice M. Rivlin

# Distinguished Lecture on Economics In Government: Strengthening the Economy by Rethinking the Role of Federal and State Governments

Public finance, simply put, studies government spending and taxation decisions. But which government? Because we have a federal form of government in the United States, national, state and local governments all have the power to create new expenditure programs or cut old programs, levy new taxes or reform old taxes. Thus, very basic to public finance is the question: Who should do what? This issue has become increasingly important. In recent federal budgetary deliberations, intense debate has focused on efforts to redefine the responsibilities of the federal and state governments—i.e., the current structure of American federalism.

In this selection, Alice Rivlin attempts to extend and refine the answer to the question "who should do what" to better meet the challenges of today's world. More specifically, Rivlin argues that our economic performance in the last decades is an indicator of the flaws of the present system of American federalism, and that a reconfiguration of federal-state governmental responsibilities is needed to strengthen the United States economy. Rivlin proposes three fundamental structural reforms: (1) consolidate programs at the federal level for which national uniformity is desirable (such as most social insurance programs—in particular, Medicaid); (2) reinvigorate the role of states by returning to their jurisdiction non-national

Rivlin, Alice M. "Distinguished Lecture on Economics in Government: Strengthening the Economy by Rethinking the Role of Federal and State Governments." *Journal of Economic Perspectives 5* (Spring 1991): 3–14. This selection is an abridged version of the original article.

**Alice M. Rivlin** is Vice-Chair, Board of Governors of the Federal Reserve System.

public investment programs (such as education and infrastructure); and (3) institute state-level common taxes aimed to strengthen each state's revenue base (such as a shared value-added tax).

### Questions to Guide the Reading

1. Why does Rivlin believe the federal government should increase national saving? How could a federal budget surplus contribute to national saving?
2. Rivlin asserts that "disharmony at the federal level has been extremely costly." What are the nature of these costs? What basic factor is causing this disharmony?
3. Distinguish between the views of the "sorters out" and the "marble cake folks" on the optimal structure of American federalism. Which view does Rivlin believe to be the most appropriate? Why?
4. What types of spending programs seem to belong in the federal budget? Why? What types of spending programs should be the responsibility of the state governments? Why?
5. As Rivlin points out, if these structural changes are to be considered seriously, a fundamental question must be addressed: "where will the states get the money?" How does Rivlin answer this question?
6. What state-level tax problems would this new system attempt to correct? How might this system help guarantee the participation of both rich and poor states?

---

This lecture brings together two subjects that are not often discussed together: national economic policy and the structure of American federalism. My thesis is that the policies needed to improve the health of the U.S. economy over the next decade or two require a new look at the division of responsibilities between the federal government and the states. In particular, I will argue that the states should have much clearer responsibility for most kinds of public investment, especially for improving the skills of the labor force and upgrading public infrastructure. The federal government should concentrate on a different set of missions, including interaction with the rest of the world, strengthening social insurance, and contributing to national saving by running a surplus in the unified federal budget.

This line of reasoning suggests devolution to the states of federal spending programs for education, housing, training and most other types of investment—a move that would clarify which level of government is accountable for performance in these areas and make a federal surplus easier to achieve. The added responsibilities would require the states to find more effective ways of financing their activities. I will argue for a new approach to state taxation called "uniform shared taxes." The idea is that the states, with the support of the federal government, should move toward greater uniformity in business and consumption taxation by enacting one or more common taxes and sharing the proceeds on a formula basis.

These are drastic and rather unlikely sounding suggestions. They grow out of a perception, which I believe is widely shared, that neither the economy nor the federal government has been operating satisfactorily for some years. There is a strong need for the country to be thinking about structural reforms that might improve the performance of both.

## THE POOR PERFORMANCE OF THE ECONOMY

\* \* \*

Americans should aspire to have an economy that produces significant and sustainable growth in the standard of living in which all groups share. But since the early 1970s, the U.S. economy has not measured up to any part of that standard. Real wages have been falling (Executive Office of the President, *Economic Report of the President* 1990, 344). Average family income has remained constant (*ERP* 328), despite the increase in women's employment (U.S. Department of Commerce 1990, 45–48). Moreover, the prosperity of the 1980s, such as it was, had many unsustainable elements. These included environmental damage; accumulation of wastes; profligate use of oil, forests, land, water, and other natural resources; and failure to maintain and improve the nation's infrastructure. The most dramatically unsustainable element was living on borrowed money. The 1980s ended with an overleveraged economy and heavy national dependence on foreign capital to finance investment. Moreover, the only part of the population which was doing better was at the top of the economic heap. The top fifth, especially the top tenth, increased its share of total income while the bottom fifth lost both relatively and absolutely (Committee on Ways and Means 1990). The poor got poorer and certain groups— blacks, Hispanics, the less educated, and young families, especially those with only one parent—dropped behind the rest of the population.

Hence, polls showing that Americans are worried about the economic future are hardly surprising. There is much to worry about.

This dismal diagnosis is widely recognized, as are the main elements of a corrective policy agenda. The nation needs to save and invest more. It needs a higher level of public and private investment, with special emphasis on improving the skills of the workforce, staying on the forefront of research and development, and improving the nation's infrastructure. The agenda should emphasize "twofers"— that is, policies that move toward two objectives at once. Increasing the skills of poor and minority young people is an obvious "twofer," since it would contribute to raising productivity as well as improving the chances of those young people sharing in the resulting increase in standard of living.

This policy agenda is by now conventional wisdom, with broad support from economists, business and labor leaders, and politicians at all levels of government. Not being discussed, however, are dilemmas this agenda poses for the division of responsibility between the federal government and the states. Which level of government is going to generate the saving? Which will take the lead in public investment?

The federal government is the most promising locus of responsibility for increasing national saving. A higher level of national saving could be achieved by moving the federal budget (the old-style unified budget, which includes social security) into surplus. A strong case can be made for running such surplus on the average, at least for the next several decades when the social security system will be accumulating reserves in anticipation of the retirement of the baby boom generation. The social security surpluses could be used to buy federal debt held by the public. The government would then be adding to the nation's savings pool, not using it up; indirectly, the social security surplus would be flowing into private investment.

Budget surpluses would put downward pressure on interest rates and make investment more attractive, both to the private sector and to state and local governments. Lower debt and lower interest rates would also reduce government debt service costs, thus ensuring that a greater fraction of the federal taxpayers' dollar actually ended up funding federal services, rather than paying interest on past debt.

\* \* \*

Unless major increases in federal taxes become acceptable, which hardly seems likely, the federal surplus scenario will require a continued squeeze on federal spending. Hence, although achieving federal surplus has much to recommend it, it prohibits a significantly increased federal role in improving education and training, revitalizing public infrastructure, or indeed, major federal initiatives of any kind. Some of those who favor increasing expenditures for public investment at the federal level reject the federal surplus scenario on the grounds that a federal contribution to public investment is more likely to produce social benefits than would channeling resources into the private sector by running a surplus. The choice, however, is not solely between the federal government and the private sector. A third possibility is to look to the state level of government for much of the public investment the economy needs.

## DISARRAY IN THE FEDERAL GOVERNMENT

Before pursuing that argument, let us turn to another source of public dissatisfaction, the process by which the federal government arrives at policy decisions. The framers of the Constitution purposely designed the federal government with divided powers and potential for deadlock. Pluralism, hostility between Congress and the administration (and within both), messiness and delay in decision making are more the rule than the exception in the history of federal affairs.

In the last few years, however, disharmony at the federal level has been extremely costly. The decade-long wrangle between the president and the Congress over the budget deficit and the inability of government to face the savings and loan crisis early on have weakened both the economy and the credibility of the U.S. government. To be sure, Washington's style is worse than its substance. After the bickering, name-calling, finger-pointing and posturing, reasonably sensible decisions often get made. The Social Security Reform of 1983, the Tax Reform Act of 1986, the Clean Air Act of 1990, all were considerable legislative achievements. . . .

Nevertheless, the process of getting to "yes" on these and other pieces of legislation has been ugly and time-consuming. At a moment when Americans are encouraging eastern Europeans to make the wrenching decisions required to restructure their economic systems, it is embarrassing that the far richer United States exhibits so little ability to face the less painful decisions of reducing the federal budget deficit, containing environmental damage, and improving public services.

Many reasons have been offered for the current stalemate in domestic policy at the federal level, from the decline of party discipline to the rise of selfishness, but one plausible explanation has been largely overlooked; namely, what used to be a fairly broad public consensus on the role of the federal government has fallen apart. If this is true, then decision making at the federal level is likely to remain embarrassingly ugly until a new consensus forms on what the federal government ought to do.

## FEDERAL AND STATE RESPONSIBILITIES

From the depths of the Depression of the 1930s to the late 1970s, the division of governmental responsibilities between the federal government and the states was hotly debated. Typically, the question was whether the federal government should take on some new role hitherto regarded as a state function, a question usually resolved in the affirmative, although frequently after years of vociferous argument. In this period, the federal government set up the social security system, took responsibility for managing the macroeconomy, assured easy access to affordable credit for homeowners, insured bank deposits, built the interstate highways, set up the welfare system, financed health care for the elderly, trained the unemployed and created jobs, lent money to students, funded education for poor children, and took on many other new tasks. Some of the new functions were carried out directly, most by grants to states and localities for specific purposes.

In some cases, the argument for federal action was that the function was truly national and could not be performed by the states. In others, the call for federal involvement reflected frustration with state neglect or inadequacy in areas, like education, in which no one disputed the states should have primary responsibility.

By the late 1970s, the pendulum had swung the other way. The Reagan administration called for major cuts in federal domestic spending. Efforts to reduce the huge federal budget deficits in the 1980s fell heavily on discretionary spending for domestic programs. Revenue sharing was eliminated and federal grants to states and localities (other than payments to individuals, such as welfare and Medicaid) dropped sharply.

The retrenchment, however, generated little debate over appropriate federal and state roles. The argument was about the level of federal spending: less vs. more. Few programs were eliminated, most were simply squeezed down or not allowed to grow. At the same time, states were required to spend increasing funds on Medicaid (jointly funded by states and the federal government) and on complying with federal mandates. The states were not able to increase their autonomy in exchange for less federal support. Overlap of authority between Washington and state capitals remained high.

The history of the 1980s contains some clues about public views of the appropriate federal role. Clearly, the events of the 1980s represent a strong national vote of confidence in social security, including Medicare. The public not only made clear that it does not want social security and Medicare benefits cut, it indicated a willingness to pay for them, even to build up surpluses out of which to pay future benefits. To the surprise of some political pundits, Senator Daniel Patrick Moynihan's proposal to cut the social security surplus by reducing the payroll tax received little public support. Apparently, the public is not enthusiastic about tinkering with social security, even if the result would be lower taxes.

The persistence of a large structural deficit in the general fund (the budget excluding social security) suggests that the public may not be firmly enough committed to the activities covered by the general fund to pay their full cost even when the economy is functioning tolerably well. Indeed, some doubts are not surprising. Nearly 30 percent of general fund spending is devoted to debt service costs (including interest paid to social security). Paying interest is hardly likely to generate broad taxpayer enthusiasm (GAO, 1990, A116). About a third goes for defense. While defending the country is clearly an important federal government function, agreement on how much to spend for it has eroded with the decline of the Soviet threat and the widespread perception that Pentagon procurement practices are wasteful. Remaining general fund spending is divided among a long list of programs. Some have clear identities and widespread public support, like the Coast Guard, the National Park Service, the Veterans Administration. Others, one suspects, are rather fuzzy in the minds of most citizens. In the case of long-standing federal grants to states and localities for the support of services also funded by lower levels of government—for example, vocational education, Medicaid, social services—the connection between federal taxes paid and services received may seem to the taxpayer quite remote and unclear. A sharper distinction between the responsibilities of the federal government and those of states might help generate the support needed to move the general fund toward balance.

## A CLEANER DISTINCTION

Those who think and write about the division of responsibilities between states and the central government in the American federal system fall into two general categories. One group, the "sorters out," believe that distinctions between state and federal functions ought to be as clean as possible. If the overlap in functions is minimized, accountability is enhanced. Voters have a clearer idea what their tax dollars are buying and whom to blame if policy is not to their liking. Sorters out believe that it is possible to identify programs for which the national government is best suited and others in which state or local choices are more appropriate.

The other camp, which I call the "marble cake folks" (after Morton Grodzins' image of state and federal functions intimately intertwined like the flavors of a marble cake), believes it is impractical to make sharp distinctions between state and federal functions (Grodzins, 1960, 265). Marble cake folks would use the powers of the federal government to nudge, bribe, or require states to do whatever a majority of the Congress finds in the national interest.

For much of this century, the marble cake view was clearly in the ascendancy. Especially in the 1960s and 1970s, the federal government funded and regulated a wide variety of activities previously deemed to be the province of state and local governments. The driving force was an increased national concern with social problems, combined with a perception that state and local governments were unable or unwilling to take the action deemed appropriate at the national level.

However, there are at least three reasons for thinking that a swing back to sorting out might be appropriate to the realities of the 1990s. First, states are much stronger, more capable governments than they used to be, a point to which I will return below. Second, technology has shrunk the globe and intertwined the United States far more closely than ever before with the world economy and political system. One consequence of internationalization has been a quantum leap in the complexity of federal policymakers' jobs and a huge increase in the time and energy that both the President and the Congress are forced to spend on international affairs, both political and economic. Domestic policy issues and management of domestic programs are getting less attention at the federal level and may be suffering as a result. Third, at least a partial explanation of negative public attitudes toward government, especially at the federal level, and reluctance to pay the cost of public services may be a perception that the federal government is engaged in some activities for which it is not suited and which might be carried out more effectively by the states.

If a new effort is to be made to sort out state and federal responsibilities, three types of spending programs clearly belong in the federal budget. First, defense and international affairs are inherently national responsibilities. The end of the cold war may make defense less costly, but can only make defense policy more complex and difficult to manage. Moreover, the growing importance of international trade, the increasing vulnerability of the U.S. economy to shocks from the outside, the interlinking of the American banking and financial system with that of the rest of the world, the growing necessity for world cooperation to reduce threats to the environment and the likelihood of frequent waves of international refugees and migrants—all these mean that federal policymakers in both the executive and legislative branches are going to be increasingly occupied with international matters in the future.

Second, the federal government must play a role in solving problems that spill over state lines, like acid rain and river pollution. Individual states do not have incentives to undertake programs that will heavily benefit other states. Nor can they be counted on to invest as much as the nation needs in programs, such as scientific and technological research, whose benefits are both uncertain and impossible to contain within state borders.

Third, spending programs in which national uniformity is important to effective functioning belong on the federal docket. Air traffic control is one of these. So is social insurance. No one would want fifty different social security systems, each with its own rules for payment and eligibility.

These three criteria do not lead to a definitive list of federal responsibilities. Views differ, for example, on whether national uniformity would be desirable in all income maintenance programs. Should there be a national standard for welfare benefits to raise benefit levels in the poorest states and reduce any tendency of beneficiaries to migrate in search of higher payments? Would it be desirable to have a uniform national health insurance system? Should aid to students be handled at the national level?

However these questions are answered, there are unquestionably a set of government activities for which national uniformity is *not* desirable and attempts to attain it could only lead to rigidity and loss of effectiveness. Service delivery programs are "non-national." Education and job training, child care and social services, law enforcement and public health, housing and economic development, roads and most other infrastructure—all require flexibility, experimentation, and adaptation to local conditions. They work best when citizen involvement and participation is high; when visible, identifiable, accountable public officials are in charge. In a country as large and diverse as this one, it is hard to imagine a uniform national system for education or social services or road building being anything but an overbureaucratized disaster. Indeed, hardly anyone has ever proposed such an absurd idea.

Is there a cogent rationale for federal funding for services that almost everyone would agree should *not* be "run from Washington"? Are the possible advantages of federal involvement in non-national programs sufficient to outweigh the disadvantages of dividing responsibility, weakening accountability, and confusing citizens about who is in charge of what? (That the confusion is major was amply illustrated by the 1988 presidential campaign in which candidate Bush promised to be the "education president" and implied he would be tough on criminals, although, in fact, the federal government has little influence over either education or criminal justice and the candidate was not proposing that it should.)

Two lines of argument have been important in federal assumption of partial responsibilities for these "non-national" programs. One is the allegation that the states are incompetent and unresponsive to national goals, such as delivering service to the poor. The other is that states have inadequate and unequal resources. The first is a lot less true than it used to be. The second could be remedied by the new approach to state revenue proposed below.

## NEW STRENGTHS IN STATE GOVERNMENTS

In the 1960s, when many of the "non-national" programs of the federal government were initiated, the states were subject to much justified criticism. State legislatures were frequently unrepresentative. They were dominated by rural constituencies and vested interests. They were frequently not responsive to the problems of the poor, minorities, and urban areas. Being a legislator was often a part-time job. Legislatures met infrequently and had little staff or professional expertise available to them. Many state governors had weak staffs. State bureaucracies, especially in the smaller states, were less professional and had less training than the federal civil service. Many state governments were overtly or tacitly racist.

Some proponents of active government intervention to improve the lot of the poor and alleviate urban problems had little reason to trust the states. They turned to the federal government. They lobbied for narrow categorical grants to the states with strict rules about how the federal money was to be spent. They worked for direct federal aid to cities, not channeled through state capitals.

The states of the 1990s, however, are radically different from those of the 1960s. The credit goes partly to the Supreme Court, whose rule of "one person, one vote" made legislatures far more representative of state populations as a whole. Legislatures increasingly hold longer sessions and are acquiring more and better staff help. Part of the credit goes to civil rights enforcement at the federal level, which has made the state governments more responsive to minorities. Part of the credit also goes to state reform movements which have strengthened governors' offices and raised the quality of state government staffs. Some of the credit also goes to the Reagan revolution. With less federal help available, states had to meet rising needs on their own. Bright young people seeking careers in government gravitated to state capitals where the action was, rather than to Washington where domestic programs were being reduced. In recent years, innovation and experimentation in education, social welfare, and other programs has been mostly at the state, not the federal, level (Bowman and Kearney, 1986).

In the same period, the federal government has lost some of its former luster. Inept handling of programs at the Department of Housing and Urban Development, scandals in Pentagon procurement and the ever-escalating savings and loan crisis indicates weakness in federal administrative capacity, especially where the government has to deal with a large number of diverse situations in different parts of the country. Quite apart from the federal deficit, the states now look like a better bet than the federal government for carrying out the high quality public investments the economy needs in the 1990s.

## COMMON SHARED TAXES

If the federal government were to devolve its "non-national" programs to the states, and the nation were to rely on the states for most of the public investment it needs, an obvious question must be answered: Where will the states get the money? States in recent years have modernized their revenue systems, but they still face two major difficulties in raising funds to provide public services. First, they compete with each other. Each is reluctant to raise tax rates out of line with its neighbors for fear that sales, businesses, and people will migrate across the border. Second, states have unequal resources. The poorest states have trouble maintaining adequate service levels even with substantial tax effort.

The first problem is getting more serious, as the economy becomes less local and regional and more national and international. Workers and businesses are more mobile than they used to be. Service production is increasing relative to goods production, and some services (in legal, computing, accounting, advertising, and so on) can be performed easily at substantial distances from the client. Mail order sales largely escape retail sales taxation, except in states where the mail order house has substantial operations.

The second problem, inequality among the states, remains large. The common shared tax approach could be a partial solution to both problems.

The basic idea is that the states, with or without the help of the federal government, share the proceeds of a common tax on a formula basis. The tax is imposed at the same rate on a uniform base. It could be an existing tax, such as a sales tax, or a new tax, such as a value-added tax. It could be a broad-based tax, such as a general retail sales tax, or a narrower one, such as a tax on mail order sales or professional services. The group of states agreeing to share the tax could include all fifty or could be a smaller regional grouping, like the New England states.

In principle, states could adopt a common shared tax by interstate compact. The compact approach would require the acquiescence but not the participation of the federal government. Alternatively, and more realistically, the federal government could enact the tax and collect it on behalf of the states. For example, the federal government could enact a 5 percent value-added tax, which would raise about $100 billion a year, and distribute it directly to the states. It would not be necessary to run this money through the federal budget, since the tax would not be a federal tax. It would be a state tax collected on behalf of the states by the federal government. The idea is reminiscent of revenue sharing, but is really quite different because no federal revenue would be shared. Since a separate tax earmarked for the states would be enacted, there would be less danger of the revenue disappearing in a federal budget crisis, as revenue sharing funds disappeared in the 1980s.

However the funds were collected, agreement would have to be reached on how to divide them. Ideally, the formula should be simple and should redistribute resources to some extent toward the poorer states. Dividing the revenue on a population basis would be both simple and redistributive. If the tax were a sales tax, for example, the poorer states with lower sales per capita would get back somewhat more than their citizens paid.

Why would richer states participate in such a scheme? The answer is that both rich and poor states would gain if total revenues were significantly increased by the fact that the new tax would bring in revenue from activities that now escape taxation because they move (or threaten to move) across state lines. All states would benefit from a tax on mail order sales, for example, since a large fraction of these sales are not now taxed.

## A NEW VISION OF AMERICAN FEDERALISM

The directions sketched here would change the American federal system substantially. The federal government would be clearly in charge of international affairs, both economic and political. Federal responsibilities would include strengthening the social insurance system, perhaps by adding basic health insurance. They might include a stronger role for the federal government in means-tested payments, like a national welfare minimum. Other clearly national functions, those whose costs or effects spill over state borders, would be retained by the federal government. The central government would continue to regulate financial institutions and support of scientific research. It would also run a significant surplus in the unified budget.

Federal funding for "non-national" services would cease. Federal programs devoted to the states would include: education (except college student aid and grants for research), health services (as opposed to health financing), housing, community and economic development, employment and training, social services, airports, and roads. One might argue for continued federal funding of interstate highways, although now that most of the money goes for maintenance and improving access to the system, the need for such federal jurisdiction is declining.

With these shifts, the states would be clearly and unequivocally in charge of human services, improving the skills of the labor force and upgrading most public infrastructure. Economic development, sometimes known as "industrial policy," would be the hallmark of activist governors and state legislative leaders.

As common shared taxes became part of the states' revenue structure, business and sales taxation would tend to become more uniform across the country. Economic competition among the states would increasingly take the form of efforts to attract business on the basis of excellent public services, rather than tax reductions. Companies would be urged to come to a particular state because of the high quality of the education or child care system or the fine state of roads, bridges, and airports, rather than to get a tax break.

This new approach to the roles of state and local government might contribute significantly to higher levels of saving and both public and private investment in the years ahead. If it did, it would improve the chances of achieving an economy with sustainable growth in the standard of living in which all groups share.

## NOTE

This article is a slightly condensed version of the Distinguished Lecture on Economics in Government, presented to a joint session of the Society of Government Economists and the American Economic Association in Washington on December 29, 1990.

## REFERENCES

Bowman, Ann O'M., and Richard C. Kearney. *The Resurgence of the States.* Englewood Cliffs. New Jersey: Prentice Hall (1986).

Committee on Ways and Means, United States House of Representatives. *The Green Book.* Washington, D.C.: United States Government Printing Office (1990), 1069–1147.

Executive Office of the President, Council on Economic Advisers. *The Economic Report of the President.* Washington, D. C.: United States Government Printing Office (1990), 328–329, 336–339, 344.

Executive Office of the President, Office of Management and Budget. *Budget of the U.S. Government Fiscal Year 1991,* section 2. Washington, D.C.: United States Government Printing Office (1990), 116–122.

Grodzins, Morton. "The Federal System," in U.S. President's Commission on National Goals, *Goals for Americans.* Englewood Cliffs, New Jersey: Prentice Hall (1960), 265.

Schultze, Charles L. "The Federal Budget and the Nation's Economic Health," in Aaron, Henry J., ed., *Setting National Priorities.* Washington, D.C.: The Brookings Institution (1990), 19–63.

U.S. Department of Commerce, Bureau of the Census. *Current Population Reports,* Series P-60, No. 168. Washington, D.C.: United States Government Printing Office (1990), 45–48.

U.S. General Accounting Office. *The Budget Deficit: Outlook, Implications and Choices.* Washington, D.C.: GAO (1990), 54.

# S E L E C T I O N   2

James M. Buchanan

# Positive Economics, Welfare Economics, and Political Economy

In this classic article, Nobel laureate James Buchanan addresses the question: Can political economists practice positive economics? Essentially, Buchanan considers a political economist to be any economist who is interested in making policy recommendations in the social or political arena. Positive economic analysis is both descriptive and predictive, modeled after the scientific method of examining "what is" and hypothesizing "what will be" under different circumstances. The application of positive economics is thus hoped to stand in stark contrast to normative analysis, wherein nonscientific assessments or value judgments are given an explicit role in deciding "what ought to be."

Buchanan argues that political economists can practice positivist methods, but only if they accept the polling place as their testing ground. Policy recommendations are to be considered hypotheses about societal welfare improvements. Because economists are not omniscient with respect to individual preferences, voting must be relied upon to reflect the public choice. And only unanimous consent will prove a Pareto improvement. In this way, the political economist can still employ the positivist method—testing policy proposals in a polling booth just as a scientist tests propositions in a laboratory. Both the political economist and the scientist rely upon the "choices" of their subjects to validate their hypotheses. However, while acknowledging that many will be sorely tempted to throw off the "scientific cloak" and invoke personal value judgments to recommend a course of action, Buchanan urges the political economist to declare the normative nature of these judgments openly so that they may be seen as clearly distinct from the positivist policy proposals.

Buchanan, James M. "Positive Economics, Welfare Economics, and Political Economy." *Journal of Law and Economics 2* (October 1959): 124–138. Reprinted by permission of the author and The University of Chicago. This selection is an abridged version of the original article.

**James M. Buchanan** is Harris University Distinguished Professor of Economics and General Director of The Center for Study of Public Choice at George Mason University. He received a Nobel Prize in Economics in 1986.

### Questions to Guide the Reading

1. What is the difference between Pareto efficiency (also known as Pareto optimality) and the Pareto rule (also known as the Pareto-improvement criterion)? How is the Pareto rule asserted to avoid the requirement that interpersonal comparisons of utility be made?

2. According to Buchanan, why is the "presumption of ignorance" more valid than welfare theory's implicit requirement of omniscience?

3. Compare the concepts of Pareto efficiency and "presumed efficiency." How does the use of presumed efficiency make the task of the political economist consistent with the positivist or scientific method?

4. What does Buchanan mean when he states that full compensation is "the only device available to the political economist"? Why is this a controversial position?

5. What is a social welfare function? Why does Buchanan believe a free society has little use for the decision-making approach of the social welfare function?

6. Buchanan states that he has assumed "the social group is composed of reasonable men." What are possible implications of the existence of unreasonable individuals?

7. How does majority rule limit "severely the efforts of the political economist"? What additional responsibilities does this place upon political economists in a democratic society?

8. How would the policy advice of Buchanan's three types of economists—the positive economist, the "positive" political economist, and the economist who discards the "scientific cloak"—differ in the case of a specific public policy issue such as removal of tariffs on sugar cane or textiles?

---

Economic theory, as we know it, was developed largely by utilitarians. Admitting the measurability and interpersonal comparability of utility and accepting the maximization of utility as an ethically desirable social goal, neoclassical economists were able to combine an instinctively human zeal for social reform with subjectively satisfactory scientific integrity. The positivist revolution has sharply disturbed this scholarly equilibrium. If utility is neither cardinally measurable nor comparable among persons, the economist who seeks to remain "pure" must proceed with caution in discussing social policy. The "positive" economist becomes an inventor of testable hypotheses, and his professional place in policy formation becomes wholly indirect.

Milton Friedman has provided the clearest statement of the positivist position,[1] and he has called for a distinct separation between the scientific and the nonscientific behavior of individuals calling themselves economists. But economics, as a discipline, will probably continue to attract precisely those scholars who desire to assist in policy formation and to do so professionally. The social role of the economist remains that of securing more intelligent legislation, and the incremental additions to the state of knowledge which "positive" economics may make seems to shut off too large an area of discussion from his professional competence. Does there exist a role for the political economist as such? This essay will examine this question and suggest an approach.[2]

## I. THE NEW WELFARE ECONOMICS

The "new" welfare economics was born in response to the challenge posed by the positivist revolution. The intellectual source of this subdiscipline is Pareto, whose earlier attempts to introduce scientific objectivity into the social studies led him to enunciate the now-famous definition of "optimality" or "efficiency." This definition states that any situation is "optimal" if all possible moves from it result in some individual being made worse off. The definition may be transformed into a rule which states that any social change is desirable which results in (1) everyone being better off or (2) someone being better off and no one being worse off than before the change. This Pareto rule is itself an ethical proposition, a value statement, but it is one which requires a minimum of premises and one which should command wide assent. The rule specifically eliminates the requirement that interpersonal comparisons of utility be made. As stated, however, a fundamental ambiguity remains in the rule. Some objective content must be given to the terms "better off" and "worse off." This is accomplished by equating "better off" with "in that position voluntarily chosen." Individual preferences are taken to indicate changes in individual well-being, and a man is said to be better off when he voluntarily changes his position from A to B when he could have remained in A.

The theoretical work completed during the last twenty years has consisted, first of all, in a refinement and development of the Paretian conditions for "optimality." Much attention has been given to a careful and precise definition of the necessary and sufficient attributes of a social situation to ensure its qualification as a Paretian P-point, that is, a point on the "optimality surface." The application of this theoretical apparatus has taken two lines of development. The first, which is sometimes more specifically called the "new welfare economics," is an attempt to devise tests which will allow changes in social situations to be evaluated. This work, which has been associated with Kaldor, Hicks, and Scitovsky, includes the discussion of the "compensation principle" and the distinction between actual and potential increases in "welfare." The second line of development has been, in one sense, a critique of the Kaldor-Hicks approach. The ethical purity of the compensation tests proposed has been questioned, and additional ethical norms have been deliberately reintroduced through the device of a "social welfare function," which, conceptually, orders all possible states of society. With this, the problem of genuine choice among alternatives disappears, and the single "best" state of the world may be selected. This function may take any form, but its users have normally conceived the Paretian conditions to be relevant in defining a preliminary subset of social configurations. This approach, which is associated with Bergson, Samuelson, and Graaff, now appears to have more widespread support than the alternative one. Its supporters, notably Samuelson, argue that the Kaldor-Hicks efforts were "misguided" and erroneous[3] and that only the "social welfare function" construction offers real promise of further development. In the latter, allegedly, "the foundation is laid for the 'economics of the good society.' "[4]

## II. OMNISCIENCE AND EFFICIENCY

Welfare economists, new and old, have generally assumed omniscience in the observer, although the assumption is rarely made explicit, and even more rarely are its implications examined.[5] The observing economist is considered able to "read" individual preference functions. Thus, even though an "increase in welfare" for an individual is defined as "movement to a preferred position," the economist can unambiguously distinguish an increase in welfare independent of individual behavior because he can accurately predict what the individual would, in fact, "choose" if confronted with the alternatives under consideration.

The omniscience assumption seems wholly unacceptable. Utility is measurable, ordinally or cardinally, only to the individual decision-maker. It is a *subjectively* quantifiable magnitude. While the economist may be able to make certain presumptions about "utility" on the basis of observed facts about behavior, he must remain fundamentally ignorant concerning the actual ranking of alternatives until and unless that ranking is revealed by the overt action of the individual in choosing.

If a presumption of ignorance replaces that of omniscience, the way in which "efficiency" as a norm enters into the economist's schemata must be drastically modified. No "social" value scale can be constructed from individual preference patterns, since the latter are revealed only through behavior. Hence "efficiency" cannot be defined independently; it cannot be instrumentally employed as a criterion for social action. Discussions of "ideal output" and "maximization of real income" become meaningless when it is recognized that the economizing process includes as data *given ends* as conceived by individuals. Ends are not *given* for the social group in any sense appropriate to the solution of problems in political economy, and the normally accepted definition of the economizing problem is seriously incomplete in not having made this clear.

"Efficiency" in the sense of maximizing a payoff or outcome from the use of limited resources is meaningless without some common denominator, some value scale, against which various possible results can be measured. To the individual decision-maker the concept of an "efficiency criterion" is a useful one, but to the independent observer the pitfalls of omniscience must be carefully avoided. The observer may introduce an efficiency criterion only through *his own estimate of his subjects' value scales*. Hence the maximization criterion which the economist may employ is wholly in terms of his own estimate of the value scales of individuals other than himself. *Presumptive efficiency* is, therefore, the appropriate conception for political economy.

The relationship of the *presumptive efficiency* criterion to the Paretian construction remains to be clarified. Given the assumption of ignorance, Paretian "efficiency" cannot be employed in aiding a group in choosing from among a set of possible social policy changes. A specific change may be judged to be Pareto-optimal or "efficient" only after it has, in fact, been proposed and the individual preferences for or against the change revealed. Nevertheless, in discussing proposals before individual preferences are revealed, the economist may utilize a *presumed efficiency* notion which retains the Paretian features. In diagnosing a specific proposal, the economist makes a judgment as to its "efficiency" on the basis of *his own* estimates of individual preferences. The Paretian elements are retained in the sense that the observer makes no attempt to do other than to "translate" what he considers to be individual preferences. He accepts these preferences, or tastes, as *he thinks they exist*. He does not evaluate social alternatives on the basis of individual preferences as he thinks they should be.

This characteristic behavior of the political economist is, or should be, ethically neutral; the indicated results are influenced by his own value scale only insofar as this reflects his membership in the larger group. Conceptually, the economist may present a social policy change as "presumed Pareto-optimal," the results of which are wholly indifferent to him as an individual member of society. The propositions which the economist is able to develop through the procedure outlined are operational in the modern sense of this term. The presentation of a policy shift is a hypothesis concerning the structure of individual values and is subject to conceptual contradiction. The failure of recent methodological discussion to recognize this operational aspect of political economy appears to be based on an attempt to place the practitioner in a false position in the decision-making complex. The political economist is often conceived as being able to *recommend* policy A over policy B. If, as we have argued above, no objective social criterion exists, the economist qua scientist is unable to recommend. Therefore, any policy discussion on his part appears to take on normative implications. But there does exist a positive role for the economist in the formation of policy. His task is that of diagnosing social situations and presenting to the choosing individuals a set of possible changes. He does not recommend policy A over policy B. He presents policy A as a hypothesis subject to testing. The hypothesis is that policy A will, in fact, prove to be Pareto-optimal. The conceptual test is *consensus* among members of the choosing group, not objective improvement in some measurable social aggregate.

Political economy is thus "positivistic" in a different sense from the more narrowly conceived positive economics. Both allow the expert to make certain predictions about the real world—predictions which are operationally meaningful. Propositions of positive economics find their empirical support or refutation in observable economic quantities or in observable market behavior of individuals. Propositions in political economy find empirical support or refutation in the observable behavior of individuals *in their capacities as collective decision makers*—in other words, in politics.

Propositions advanced by political economists must always be considered as tentative hypotheses offered as solutions to social problems. The subjective bases for these propositions should emphasize the necessity for their being considered as alternatives which may or may not be accepted. But this is not to suggest that one proposition is equally good with all others. Just as is the case with positive economics, the skill of the observer and his capacity in drawing upon the experience which has been accumulated will determine the relative success of his predictions.

There are no fully appropriate analogies to this task of the political economist, but the role of the medical diagnostician perhaps comes closest. The patient is observed to be ill; a remedy is prescribed. This remedy is a hypothesis advanced by the diagnostician. If the illness persists, an alternative remedy is suggested and the first hypothesis discarded. The process continues until the patient is restored to health or the existence of no solution is accepted. While this analogy is helpful, it can also be misleading. In political economy the observer isolates an "illness" or rather what he believes to be an "illness" through his knowledge of the system. He presents a possible change. But this change is a "cure" only if *consensus* is attained in its support. The measure of "wellness" for the political economist is not improvement in an independently observable characteristic but rather agreement. If no agreement can be attained, the presumed "illness" persists, and the political economist must search for still other possible solutions. The political behavior of individuals, not market performance or results, provides the criteria for testing hypotheses of political economy.

## III. COMPENSATION AND EXTERNALITY

The "welfare economics" suggested here is simpler than that which assumes omniscience on the part of the observer. Much of the discussion in the subdiscipline has been devoted to two problems, both of which will be substantially eliminated in the approach suggested. First, the appropriateness or inappropriateness of compensation has been a central topic along with the discussion of the legitimacy or illegitimacy of certain tests. But, quite clearly, if the political economist is presumed to be ignorant of individual preference fields, his predictions (as embodied in suggested social policy changes) can only be supported or refuted if full compensation is, in fact, paid.[6] The potential compensation argument disappears, and the whole controversy over the appropriate tests becomes meaningless at this level of argument.

Many scholars have objected to the requirement that compensation be paid on the grounds that such requirement creates a serious bias toward the initial or status quo distribution of "welfare" among individuals of the group. This criticism seems misdirected and inapplicable if the purposes of compensation are conceived to be those outlined. Full compensation is essential, not in order to maintain any initial distribution on ethical grounds, but in order to decide which one from among the many possible social policy changes does, in fact, satisfy the genuine Pareto rule. Compensation is the only device available to the political economist for this purpose.

If the observing economist is assumed omniscient, the actual payment of compensation may seem unnecessary, and the requirement for payment may appear to introduce the bias mentioned. No additional information about individuals' preference fields is needed, and none can be revealed by behavior. A proposed change is no longer a hypothesis to be tested, and the relatively neutral ethics imposed by the Pareto rule may prove too restrictive. And, if the observer does not move in the direction of the Bergson-Samuelson welfare function, he may attempt to devise tests for potential compensation. In this way the whole debate about the Kaldor-Hicks-Scitovsky criteria for improvement has arisen. This approach constitutes a distortion of the Pareto rule. If ethical evaluations on the part of the observer are to be introduced, there is no place for the Pareto rule. This rule is designed for use in situations where individual values must count, not because they possess some inherent ethical superiority (which is quite a different point), but because individual action provides the only guide toward acceptable collective action.

The full-compensation requirement need not imply—indeed, it will not normally imply—the maintenance of the status quo in the distribution of either income or welfare. Presumably, if a given social change is approved by all parties, each must be better off in absolute terms. Therefore, at the simplest level of discussion, there is more "welfare" to go around than before the change. To be sure, the relative distribution of "welfare" may be modified significantly by a fully compensated change. This is true because the order of presentation will determine the final point chosen from among a whole subset of acceptable points. The political economist cannot, however, say anything concerning the relative merits of the separate points in this subset. This amounts to saying that the political economist's task is completed when he has shown the parties concerned that there exists mutual gains "from trade." He has no function in suggesting specific contract terms within the bargaining range itself.

An additional simple, but often overlooked, point on compensation needs to be made. The requirement of full compensation as here interpreted need not imply that the measured incomes of individuals or groups may not be reduced by acceptable social policy changes. "Welfare" is defined as that which is expressed by individual preference as revealed in behavior. And individual behavior may be fully consistent with a reduction in measured personal income or wealth. For example, a policy which combines progressive income taxation and public expenditure on the social services may command unanimous support even though the process involves a reduction in the measured real incomes of the rich. The existence of voluntary charity indicates that individuals are, in fact, willing to reduce their own incomes in order to increase those of others. And the peculiar nature of collective choice makes support for collective or governmental action perhaps even more likely. Many individuals may find themselves saying: "I should be willing to support this proposal provided that other equally situated individuals do likewise." Thus collective action may command relatively widespread support, whereas no purely voluntary action might be taken in its absence.[7]

A second major problem which has concerned theorists in welfare economics has been the possible existence of external effects in individual consumption and production decisions, sometimes called "spillover" or "neighborhood" effects. But this annoying complication also disappears in the approach to welfare economics suggested here. If, in fact, external effects are present, these will be fully reflected in the individual choices made for or against the collective action which may be proposed. External effects which are unaccounted for in the presumptive efficiency criterion of the economist and the proposal based upon this criterion will negate the prediction of consensus represented in the alternative suggested. The presence of such effects on a large scale will, of course, make the task of the political economist more difficult. His predictions must embody estimates of a wider range of individual preferences than would otherwise be the case. The compensations included in the suggested policy changes must be more carefully drawn and must be extended to include more individuals who might otherwise be neglected.[8]

Both the compensation and the externality problems may be illustrated by reference to the classical example of the smoking chimney. The economist observes what he considers to be smoke damage and discontent among families living adjacent to the smoke-creating plant. Using a presumptive efficiency criterion, he suggests a possible course of action which the group may take. This action must include, on the one hand, the payment of some tax by the previously damaged individuals who stand to gain by the change. On the other hand, the action must include some subsidization of the owners of the firm to compensate them for the capital loss which is to be imposed by the rule of law which states that henceforward the full "social" costs of the operation must be shouldered. Some such tax-compensation–smoke-abatement scheme will command unanimous consent from the group which includes both individuals living within the damaged area and the owners of the firm. The problem for the political economist is that of searching out and locating from among the whole set of possible combinations one which will prove acceptable to all parties. If the smoke nuisance is a real one, at least one such alternative must exist. If no agreement of this sort is possible, the economist can only conclude that the presumptive efficiency criterion was wrongly conceived and the hypothesis based upon it falsified.[9]

* * *

## V. THE SOCIAL WELFARE FUNCTION

The approach to political economy suggested in this essay may be compared with the Bergson-Samuelson approach which deliberately introduces ethical evaluations in the form of the "social welfare function." Both approaches aim at establishing a role for the economist qua scientist beyond positive economics narrowly defined. The differences between the two approaches lie in the treatment of individual values.

The "social welfare function" is an explicit expression of a value criterion. It incorporates fully the required information concerning the relative importance of conflicting aims, including the relative importance of separate individuals within the social group. The function orders all possible social situations and allows an external observer to select one as "best." Presumably, this "best" point will lie on a "welfare frontier" which contains a sub-infinity of possible points. But the precise meaning of this "welfare frontier" is not entirely clear. If social situations are to be ordered *externally*, the "individual welfare scales" embodied must be those akin to those which enter into the presumptive efficiency criterion discussed above. Individual preferences, insofar as they enter the construction (and they need not do so) must be those which *appear to the observer* rather than those revealed by the behavior of the individuals themselves. In other words, even if the value judgments expressed in the function say that individual preferences are to count, these preferences must be those presumed by the observer rather than those revealed in behavior.

Several questions may be raised. Unless the relevant choices are to be made by some entity other than individuals themselves, why is there any need to construct a "social" value scale? There would seem to be no reason for making interpersonal comparisons of "welfare" based on hypothetical individual preferences except for the purpose of assisting in the attainment of *given ends* for the group or some subgroup. This central feature of the approach seems, therefore, to be contrary to one of the presuppositions of the free society. The function may be useful as a device in assisting the decision-making of a despot, benevolent or otherwise, and organic state, or a single-minded ruling group. But, once this limitation is recognized, individual preferences, even as presumed by the observer, need not enter into the construction at all except insofar as it becomes necessary to consider predicted individual reaction to coercively imposed changes. The Pareto conception of "optimality" loses most of its significance.

The approach adopted here is based upon the idea that no "social" values exist apart from individual values. Therefore, the political economist, instead of choosing arbitrarily some limited set of ethical norms for incorporation into a "social welfare function," searches instead for "social compromises" on particular issues. His proposals are hypotheses about individual values, hypotheses which are subjected to testing in the collective choice processes. Actual values are revealed only through the political action of individuals, and consensus among individual members of the choosing group becomes the only possible affirmation of the "social" value. The order which is present among "social" decisions, if indeed there is one, is revealed in the decision process itself, not external to it. Whereas the "social welfare function" approach searches for a criterion independent of the choice process itself, presumably with a view toward influencing the choice, the alternative approach evaluates results only in terms of the choice process itself.

## VI. CONSENSUS AMONG REASONABLE MEN

In developing the argument of this essay, I have assumed that the social group is composed of reasonable men, capable of recognizing what they want, of acting on this recognition, and of being convinced of their own advantage after reasonable discussion. Governmental action, at the important margins of decision, is assumed to arise when such individuals agree that certain tasks should be collectively performed. To this extent, my argument rests on some implicit acceptance of a contract theory of the state. Since it is carried out only after general agreement, collective action is essentially voluntary action. State or governmental coercion enters only insofar as individuals, through collectively imposed rules, prevent themselves from acting as they would act in the absence of such rules.

I am aware of the limitations of this conception of society, and I can appreciate the force of the objection that may be raised on these grounds. Societies in the real world are not made up exclusively of reasonable men, and this fact introduces disturbing complications in any attempt to discuss the formation of social policy.

In outlining the structure of a possible nonevaluative political economy, I am suggesting that we proceed on an *as if* assumption. Despite our knowledge that some men are wholly unreasonable, we assume this away just as we have done in the organization of our whole democratic decision-making processes. Insofar as "antisocial" or unreasonable individuals are members of the group, consensus, even where genuine "mutual gains" might be present, may be impossible. Here the absolute unanimity rule must be broken; the political economist must try, as best he can, to judge the extent of unanimity required to verify (not refute) his hypothesis. Some less definitive rule of relative unanimity must be substituted for full agreement, as Wicksell recognized and suggested.

This necessary modification does not materially reduce the strength of the argument presented. But it does place an additional responsibility upon the political economist. He is forced to discriminate between reasonable and unreasonable men in his search for consensus. This choice need not reflect the introduction of personal evaluation. Relatively objective standards may be adduced to aid in the discrimination process. Reflection from everyday experience with groups which use unanimity as the customary, but not essential, means of reaching decisions should reveal that the genuinely unreasonable individual can be readily identified. This reduction of the unanimity requirement to some relative unanimity does not suggest that "unreasonable" as a characteristic behavior pattern can be determined on the basis of one issue alone. And it should be emphasized that in no way whatsoever does continuing disagreement with majority opinion suggest unreasonableness.

## VII. MAJORITY RULE, CONSENSUS, AND DISCUSSION

The hypotheses which the political economist presents are tested by the measure of agreement reached, qualified only by the relative unanimity requirement introduced in the preceding section. But there remain two major practical difficulties to be confronted at this testing stage. These make the empirical testing difficult and, in some cases, impossible. First, collective decisions in democratically organized societies may be, and normally are, made on the basis of some variant of majority rule rather than consensus or unanimity, even if the latter is qualified to rule out limited "antisocial" dissent.

The economist, employing his presumptive efficiency criterion, presents for consideration a policy change which embodies the hypothesis that the adoption of this change will constitute "improvement" in the "welfare" of the group in accordance with the Pareto rule. This proposal is then voted upon, either by all individuals in a referendum or by their representatives in a legislative body. If a majority rejects the proposal, the economist's hypothesis is clearly refuted, and alternatives must be sought. The hypothesis is equally refuted if a minority dissents, but the proposal may be carried on the basis of majority decision. This adoption tends to preclude the presentation of alternative hypotheses more acceptable to the minority. Majority rule, considered as a final means of making decisions, has the effect of closing off discussion and of thereby limiting severely the efforts of the political economist.

This result of majority rule places before the political economist a great temptation and also places upon him significant responsibility. Knowing that collective decisions are made by majority rule, he will be tempted to present social alternatives which may command majority support rather than consensus. Adequate compensations for damaged minorities may be omitted in the proposals suggested with a view toward making the majority more receptive. Deliberate attempts in this direction would violate the neutral position outlined for the political economist here, but, given the inherently subjective basis for the presumptive efficiency criterion at best, the proposals presented may tend to reflect majority-oriented biases quite unintentionally. The danger that this bias will occur places upon the practitioner the responsibility of insuring that suggested proposals do, in fact, include compensations to damaged minorities estimated to be adequate and, contrariwise, do not include overcompensations to damaged majorities.

The probability that decisions will be made without consensus being attained adds responsibility to the economist's task. Much greater care must be taken with the construction and application of the presumptive efficiency criterion. Again the analogy with the medical diagnostician may be helpful. Majority rule tends to place the political economist in the position of the diagnostician who may propose a fatal dosage if his diagnosis should prove incorrect. Hence he must be more careful than otherwise in proposing alternative remedies.

The practical difficulties introduced by majority rule may not be great if there exists consensus that all collective decisions reached in this way are temporary or provisional and are subject to reversal and modification. If majority rule is understood to be, not a means of making final decisions, but rather as one of making provisional choices while discussion continues, the possibility remains that alternative hypotheses can be presented subsequent to a favorable majority vote. No barrier to discussion need be introduced by majority rule conceived in this way.

But if majority rule is conceived as merely a step in the discussion process leading toward final agreement, a second major problem of practical importance arises. The whole process of discussion which characterizes the democratic idea implies that, insofar as their behavior in making collective decisions is concerned, individuals do not have explicitly defined ends of an instrumental sort. If they do, discussion is bound to be fruitless, and an initial disagreement will persist. The purpose of political discussion is precisely that of changing "tastes" among social alternatives. The political economist, therefore, in constructing and applying his presumptive efficiency criterion, must try to incorporate the predicted preferences of individuals, not as they exist at a given moment, but as they will be modified after responsible discussion. In other words, he must try to predict "what reasonable individuals will reasonably want" after discussion, not what they "do want in a given moment" before discussion or what they "ought to want" if they agreed in all respects with the observer.

This recognition that individuals do not have *given ends* which can, at any moment, be taken as data by the observer appears to blur the sharp dividing line between "positive" political economy as here outlined and "normative" political economy which allows the observer to introduce his own ethical evaluations. This makes it more important that the attempt be made to test propositions in terms of expressed individual values instead of first attempting to estimate such values as a basis for decision.

## VIII. CONCLUSION

Positive science is concerned with the discovery of "what is"; normative science, with "what ought to be." Positive economics, narrowly conceived, overly restricts the "what is" category. Political economy has a non-normative role in discovering "what is the structure of individual values." The political economist, in accomplishing this task, can remain as free of personal value judgment as the positive economist. To be sure, the objectivity of the political economist is more difficult to preserve, and his behavior in departing from it more difficult for observers to detect. His hypotheses must take the form of policy propositions, and these may tend to appear as recommendations rather than hypotheses. And, since such hypotheses must be based on some presumptive efficiency criterion, an element of subjectivity is necessarily introduced. But the presence of subjective evaluation of the outside world (which includes the preference fields of other individuals) does not imply the infusion of an individual value judgment concerning the "goodness" of the proposal presented.

In a sense, the political economist is concerned with discovering "what people want." The content of his efforts may be reduced to very simple terms. This may be summed up in the familiar statement: *There exist mutual gains from trade.* His task is that of locating possible flaws in the existing social structure and in presenting possible "improvements." His specific hypothesis is that *mutual* gains do, in fact, exist as a result of possible changes (trades). This hypothesis is tested by the behavior of private people in response to the suggested alternatives. Since "social" values do not exist apart from individual values in a free society, consensus or unanimity (mutuality of gain) is the only test which can ensure that a change is beneficial.

In his diagnosis and prescription, the economist must call upon all the skills and resources which he possesses. These include the traditional "efficiency" tools, but, in utilizing these, he must beware of slipping into the easy assumption of omniscience. The individual preference patterns which he incorporates into his models must be conceived as presumed or predicted, and the changes which are based on these must always be considered tentative hypotheses to be subjected to testing in the polling places. The economist can never say that one social situation is more "efficient" than another. This judgment is beyond his range of competence. He presents a hypothesis that one situation is "presumed Pareto-Efficient," and he allows the unanimity test (appropriately modified) to decide whether his prediction is correct or incorrect. From this it follows that all his proposals must embody estimated full compensations.

The role of the political economist as outlined here may be quite limited. The applicability of political economy is inversely related to the rate at which majoritarian conceptions of the democratic process replace the classical liberal conceptions. Even in a world seemingly dominated by majoritarian views, however, the approach outlined here can be useful in establishing some norms for scientific objectivity. Beyond the area of "positive" political economy, there may be room for the individual to serve in a normative capacity as an especially well-informed citizen. Here his own ethical evaluations may be explicitly introduced, and he may choose to utilize certain welfare function constructions in this task. But this behavior must be sharply distinguished from his professional role, either as positive economist or as political economist.

Perhaps this essay may best be summarized by the consideration of a single example: the removal of a long-established tariff. The positive economist can predict that imports of the commodity will increase, that domestic prices of the commodity will fall, that exports will increase, that resources will be shifted from the domestic to the export industries, etc. The "positive" political economist, building on the fundamental theorems of positive economics, attempts to devise a proposal or proposals which will remove or reduce the tariff and be approved by an overwhelming majority of the whole social group. He advances a proposal which embodies a tariff reduction, along with estimated full compensation to the damaged industries financed out of a tax imposed on benefited groups. This proposal is advanced as a hypothesis. If the proposal is accepted by the whole group, the hypothesis is not refuted. If it is rejected, or approved by only a majority, the political economist should search for alternative schemes. In all this, as an observer, he is ethically neutral. His own evaluations of the alternatives considered do not, and should not, influence his behavior in any way other than that necessarily arising out of his membership in the group.

If complexities of the collective decision-making process arise to prevent a genuine testing of the hypothesis, the economist may, if he desires, discard his "scientific" cloak. He may introduce his own ethical evaluations and state openly and frankly that he thinks tariff reductions would be "good" for the whole group.

It seems useful that these three types of behavior of individuals calling themselves economists be separated and classified, even if practical politics reduce the second type to relative insignificance.

## NOTES

1. Friedman, M., *Essays in Positive Economics* (1953), 3–43.
2. The approach which will be suggested here involves an extension of some of Wicksell's ideas on fiscal theory to modern welfare economics. For a recently published translation of Wicksell's fiscal theory, see "A New Principle of Just Taxation," in *Classics in the Theory of Public Finance* (Musgrave and Peacock, ed., 1958), 72.
3. Samuelson, "Comment", *A Survey of Contemporary Economics 2* (Haley, ed., 1952): 37.
4. Samuelson, "Social Indifference Curves," *Quarterly Journal of Economics 70* (1956): 1, 22.
5. J. de V. Graaff in his book, *Theoretical Welfare Economics* (1957, 13), makes the assumption explicitly, but after one short paragraph proceeds with his argument.
6. There are two distinct meanings of the word "compensation." In ordinary discussion, compensation is conceived as an objectively measurable quantity; this conception has no relevance for welfare economics. Compensation must be defined in terms of the individual choice process, and it becomes measurable only through an observation of choices made. Full or adequate compensation is defined as that set of payments required to secure the agreement of all parties to the proposed change.
7. This point has been stressed by W. J. Baumol in *Welfare Economics and the Theory of the State* (1952).
8. The discussion of this paragraph assumes that the membership in the group making the collective choice is at least as large as the "neighborhood" defined by the presence of external effects.
9. Objections will be raised to the procedure suggested here because its acceptance seems to leave the door open to exploitation of some parties to the contract by other unscrupulous parties. The owners of the smoke-creating firm may refuse to agree to any scheme except the one which grants them compensation equal to the full benefits of the proposed change. This possibility, or its converse, exists. But, in refusing to agree to any proffered compensation equal to or above the estimated value of the capital losses undergone, the owners must recognize that such opportunities might not recur.

   As a second point, if the distributional results of a change are significantly important, this fact alone may reduce the extent of the bargaining range. Even though the objectively measured "income" of the previously damaged group were demonstrably increased by the adoption of the tax-compensation–smoke-abatement plan, this group might not agree if the owners secured the predominant share of the total benefits. They might veto the plan on distributional grounds, thereby preventing unanimity.

# S E L E C T I O N 3

Ronald H. Coase

# The Problem of Social Cost

Economists use the term *externality* to refer to an effect that takes place outside the mutual voluntary exchange of the market system. For example, a firm polluting a river with a chemical that kills fish imposes a negative externality on fishermen whose incomes are reduced. But is government intervention the only way to secure an optimal allocation of resources when externalities exist? Nobel laureate Ronald Coase has demonstrated that the answer is "not necessarily."

What has become known as the Coase theorem is his proposition that resource misallocation will not occur if all relevant property rights are clearly assigned and if the involved parties can negotiate at no cost to their mutual benefit. Such costless negotiation assumes that the parties incur no "transactions costs" (i.e., costs of becoming informed, of bargaining, and of enforcing agreements). Under this condition, negotiation leads to an arrangement either with the polluting party compensating the "victim" or the potential victim paying the potential polluter to reduce the harmful acts. This result is in stark contrast to schemes requiring social intervention as typified by taxation under what Coase refers to as the "Pigouvian tradition"—essentially, the levying of a corrective tax on a polluter equal to the divergence between private and social costs (resulting from the externality).

**Questions to Guide the Reading**
1. What are some implications of Coase's assertion that the responsibility for damages resulting from externalities is reciprocal in nature?
2. In the arithmetic example involving wandering cattle, why is it useful (in demonstrating the Coase theorem) to consider the "crop loss

..................................................................................................................
Coase, Ronald. "The Problem of Social Cost." *Journal of Law and Economics 3* (October 1960): 1–44. Reprinted by permission of the author and The University of Chicago. This selection is an abridged version of the original article.

**Ronald Coase** is Clifton R. Musser Professor of Economics, Emeritus, at the University of Chicago. He received a Nobel Prize in Economics in 1991.

per additional steer" as a marginal "bribe" schedule offered by the wheat farmer to the cattle rancher?

3. Coase assumes "for purposes of simplicity that the farmer owns the land." Why does the efficient solution *not* depend upon who is actually assigned the property rights?

4. Under what conditions would the parties involved in an externality be unable to prevent resource misallocation by bargaining to their mutual advantage?

5. What is the importance of transactions costs in determining the correct policy to deal with an externality?

6. According to Coase, what are some possible problems with the Pigouvian tradition of a tax-based solution to negative externalities?

## I. THE PROBLEM TO BE EXAMINED

This paper is concerned with those actions of business firms which have harmful effects on others. The standard example is that of a factory the smoke from which has harmful effects on those occupying neighbouring properties. The economic analysis of such a situation has usually proceeded in terms of a divergence between the private and social product of the factory, in which economists have largely followed the treatment of Pigou in *The Economics of Welfare*. The conclusion to which this kind of analysis seems to have led most economists is that it would be desirable to make the owner of the factory liable for the damage caused to those injured by the smoke, or alternatively, to place a tax on the factory owner varying with the amount of smoke produced and equivalent in money terms to the damage it would cause, or finally, to exclude the factory from residential districts (and presumably from other areas in which the emission of smoke would have harmful effects on others). It is my contention that the suggested courses of action are inappropriate, in that they lead to results which are not necessarily, or even usually, desirable.

## II. THE RECIPROCAL NATURE OF THE PROBLEM

The traditional approach has tended to obscure the nature of the choice that has to be made. The question is commonly thought of as one in which A inflicts harm on B and what has to be decided is: how should we restrain A? But this is wrong. We are dealing with a problem of a reciprocal nature. To avoid the harm to B would inflict harm on A. The real question that has to be decided is: should A be allowed to harm B or should B be allowed to harm A? The problem is to avoid the more serious harm. I instanced in my previous article[1] the case of a confectioner the noise and vibrations from whose machinery disturbed a doctor in his work. To avoid harming the doctor would inflict harm on the confectioner. The problem posed by this case was essentially whether it was worthwhile, as a result of restricting the methods of production which would be used by the confectioner, to secure more doctoring at the cost of a reduced supply of confectionery products. Another example is afforded by the problem of straying cattle which destroy crops on neighbouring land. If it is inevitable that some cattle will stray, an increase in the supply of meat can only be obtained at the expense of a decrease in the supply of crops. The nature of the choice is clear: meat or crops. What answer should be given is, of course, not clear unless we know the value of what is obtained as well as the value of what is sacrificed to obtain it. To give another example, Professor George J. Stigler instances the contamination of a stream.[2] If we assume that the harmful effect of the pollution is that it kills the fish, the question to be decided is: is the value of the fish lost greater or less than the value of the product which the contamination of the stream makes possible? It goes almost without saying that this problem has to be looked at in total *and* at the margin.

## III. THE PRICING SYSTEM WITH LIABILITY FOR DAMAGE

I propose to start my analysis by examining a case in which most economists would presumably agree that the problem would be solved in a completely satisfactory manner: when the damaging business has to pay for all damages caused *and* the pricing system works smoothly (strictly this means that the operation of a pricing system is without cost).

A good example of the problem under discussion is afforded by the case of straying cattle which destroy crops growing on neighbouring land. Let us suppose that a farmer and cattle-raiser are operating on neighbouring properties. Let us further suppose that, without any fencing between the properties, an increase in the size of the cattle-raiser's herd increases the total damage to the farmer's crops. What happens to the marginal damage as the size of the herd increases is another matter. This depends on whether the cattle tend to follow one another or to roam side by side, on whether they tend to be more or less restless as the size of the herd increases and on other similar factors. For my immediate purpose, it is immaterial what assumption is made about marginal damage as the size of the herd increases.

To simplify the argument, I propose to use an arithmetical example. I shall assume that the annual cost of fencing the farmer's property is $9 and that the price of the crop is $1 per ton. Also, I assume that the relation between the number of cattle in the herd and the annual crop loss is as follows:

| Number in Herd (steers) | Annual Crop Loss (tons) | Crop Loss per Additional Steer (tons) |
|---|---|---|
| 1 | 1 | 1 |
| 2 | 3 | 2 |
| 3 | 6 | 3 |
| 4 | 10 | 4 |

Given that the cattle-raiser is liable for the damage caused, the additional annual cost imposed on the cattle-raiser if he increased his herd from, say, 2 to 3 steers is $3 and in deciding on the size of the herd, he will take this into account along with his other costs. That is, he will not increase the size of the herd unless the value of the additional meat produced (assuming that the cattle-raiser slaughters the cattle) is greater than the additional costs that this will entail, including the value of the additional crops destroyed. Of course, if, by the employment of dogs, herdsmen, aeroplanes, mobile radio and other means, the amount of damage can be reduced, these means will be adopted when their cost is less than the value of the crop which they prevent being lost. Given that the annual cost of fencing is $9, the cattle-raiser who wished to have a herd with 4 steers or more would pay for fencing to be erected and maintained, assuming that other means of attaining the same end would not do so more cheaply. When the fence is erected, the marginal cost due to the liability for damage becomes zero, except to the extent that an increase in the size of the herd necessitates a stronger and therefore more expensive fence because more steers are liable to lean against it at the same time. But, of course, it may be cheaper for the cattle-raiser not to fence and to pay for the damaged crops, as in my arithmetical example, with 3 or fewer steers.

It might be thought that the fact that the cattle-raiser would pay for all crops damaged would lead the farmer to increase his planting if a cattle-raiser came to occupy the neighbouring property. But this is not so. If the crop was previously sold in conditions of perfect competition, marginal cost was equal to price for the amount of planting undertaken and any expansion would have reduced the profits of the farmer. In the new situation, the existence of crop damage would mean that the farmer would sell less on the open market but his receipts for a given production would remain the same, since the cattle-raiser would pay the market price for any crop damaged. Of course, if cattle-raising commonly involved the destruction of crops, the coming into existence of a cattle-raising industry might raise the price of the crops involved and farmers would then extend their planting. But I wish to confine my attention to the individual farmer.

I have said that the occupation of a neighbouring property by a cattle-raiser would not cause the amount of production, or perhaps more exactly the amount of planting, by the farmer to increase. In fact, if the cattle-raising has any effect, it will be to decrease the amount of planting. The reason for this is that, for any given tract of land, if the value of the crop damages is so great that the receipts from the sale of the undamaged crop are less than the total costs of cultivating the tract of land, it will be profitable for the farmer and the cattle-raiser to make a bargain whereby the tract of land is left uncultivated. This can be made clear by means of an arithmetical example. Assume initially that the value of the crop obtained from cultivating a given tract of land is $12 and that the cost incurred in cultivating this tract of land is $10, the net gain from cultivating the land being $2. I assume for the purposes of simplicity that the farmer owns the land. Now assume that the cattle-raiser starts operations on the neighbouring property and that the value of the crops damaged is $1. In this case $11 is obtained by the farmer from the sale on the market and $1 is obtained from the cattle-raiser for damage suffered and the net gain remains $2. Now suppose that the cattle-raiser finds it profitable to increase the size of his herd, even though the amount of damage rises to $3; which means that the value of the additional meat production is greater than the additional costs, including the additional $2 payment for damage. But the total payment for damage is now $3. The net gain to the farmer from cultivating the land is still $2. The cattle raiser would be better off if the farmer would agree not to cultivate his land for any payment less than $3. The farmer would be agreeable to not cultivating the land for any payment greater than $2. There is clearly room for a mutually satisfactory bargain which would lead to the abandonment of cultivation.[3] But the same argument applies not only to the whole tract cultivated by the farmer but also to any subdivision of it. Suppose, for example, that the cattle have a well-defined route, say, to a brook or to a shady area. In these circumstances, the amount of damage to the crop along the route may well be great and if so, it could be that the farmer and the cattle-raiser would find it profitable to make a bargain whereby the farmer would agree not to cultivate this strip of land.

But this raises a further possibility. Suppose that there is such a well-defined route. Suppose further that the value of the crop that would be obtained by cultivating this strip of land is $10 but that the cost of cultivation is $11. In the absence of the cattle-raiser, the land would not be cultivated. However, given the presence of the cattle-raiser, it could well be that if the strip were cultivated, the whole crop would be destroyed by the cattle. In which case, the cattle-raiser would be forced to pay $10 to the farmer. It is true that the farmer would lose $1. But the cattle-raiser would lose $10. Clearly this is a situation which is not likely to last indefinitely since neither party would want this to happen. The aim of the farmer would be to induce the cattle-raiser to make a payment in return for an agreement to leave this land uncultivated. The farmer would not be able to obtain a payment greater than the cost of fencing off this piece of land nor so high as to lead the cattle-raiser to abandon the use of the neighbouring property. What payment would in fact be made would depend on the shrewdness of the farmer and the cattle-raiser as bargainers. But as the payment would not be so high as to cause the cattle-raiser to abandon this location and as it would not vary with the size of the herd, such an agreement would not affect the allocation of resources but would merely alter the distribution of income and wealth as between the cattle-raiser and the farmer.

I think it is clear that if the cattle-raiser is liable for damage caused and the pricing system works smoothly, the reduction in the value of production elsewhere will be taken into account in computing the additional cost involved in increasing the size of the herd. This cost will be weighed against the value of the additional meat production and, given perfect competition in the cattle industry, the allocation of resources in cattle-raising will be optimal. What needs to be emphasized is that the fall in the value of production elsewhere which would be taken into account in the costs of the cattle-raiser may well be less than the damage which the cattle would cause to the crops in the ordinary course of events. This is because it is possible, as a result of market transactions, to discontinue cultivation of the land. This is desirable in all cases in which the damage that the cattle would cause, and for which the cattle-raiser would be willing to pay, exceeds the amount which the farmer would pay for the use of the land. In conditions of perfect competition, the amount which the farmer would pay for use of the land is equal to the difference between the value of the total production when the factors are employed on this land and the value of the additional product yielded in their next best use (which would be what the farmer would have to pay for the factors). If damage exceeds the amount the farmer would pay for use of the land, the value of the additional product of the factors employed elsewhere would exceed the value of the total product in this use after damage is taken into account. It follows that it would be desirable to abandon cultivation of the land and to release the factors employed for production elsewhere. A procedure which merely provided for payment for damage to the crop caused by the cattle but which did not allow for the possibility of cultivation being discontinued would result in too small an employment of factors of production in cattle-raising and too large an employment of factors in cultivation of the crop. But given the possibility of market transactions, a situation in which damage to crops exceeded the rent of the land would not endure. Whether the cattle-raiser pays the farmer to leave the land uncultivated or himself rents the land by paying the land-owner an amount slightly greater than the farmer would pay (if the farmer was himself renting the land), the final result would be the same and would maximize the value of production. Even when the farmer is induced to plant crops which it would not be profitable to cultivate for sale on the market, this will be a purely short-term phenomenon and may be expected to lead to an agreement under which the planting will cease. The cattle-raiser will remain in that location and the marginal cost of meat production will be the same as before, thus having no long-run effect on the allocation of resources.

## IV. THE PRICING SYSTEM WITH NO LIABILITY FOR DAMAGE

I now turn to the case in which, although the pricing system is assumed to work smoothly (that is, costlessly), the damaging business is not liable for any of the damage which it causes. This business does not have to make a payment to those damaged by its actions. I propose to show that the allocation of resources will be the same in this case as it was when the damaging business was liable for damage caused. As I showed in the previous case that the allocation of resources was optimal, it will not be necessary to repeat this part of the argument.

I return to the case of the farmer and the cattle-raiser. The farmer would suffer increased damage to his crop as the size of the herd increased. Suppose that the size of the cattle-raiser's herd is 3 steers (and that this is the size of the herd that would be maintained if crop damage were not taken into account). Then the farmer would be willing to pay up to $3 if the cattle-raiser would reduce his herd to two steers, up to $5 if the herd were reduced to 1 steer and would pay up to $6 if the cattle-raising was abandoned. The cattle-raiser would therefore receive $3 from the farmer if he kept 2 steers instead of 3. This $3 foregone is therefore part of the cost incurred in keeping the third steer. Whether the $3 is a payment which the cattle-raiser has to make if he adds the third steer to his herd (which it would be if the cattle-raiser was liable to the farmer for damage caused to the crop) or whether it is a sum of money which he would have received if he did not keep a third steer (which it would be if the cattle-raiser was not liable to the farmer for damage caused to the crop) does not affect the final result. In both cases $3 is part of the cost of adding the third steer, to be included along with the other costs. If the increase in the value of production in cattle-raising through increasing the size of the herd from 2 to 3 is greater than the additional costs that have to be incurred (including the $3 damage to crops), the size of the herd will be increased. Otherwise, it will not. The size of the herd will be the same whether the cattle-raiser is liable for damage caused to the crop or not.

It may be argued that the assumed starting point—a herd of 3 steers—was arbitrary. And this is true. But the farmer would not wish to pay to avoid crop damage which the cattle-raiser would not be able to cause. For example, the maximum annual payment which the farmer could be induced to pay could not exceed $9, the annual cost of fencing. And the farmer would only be willing to pay this sum if it did not reduce his earnings to a level that would cause him to abandon cultivation of this particular tract of land. Furthermore, the farmer would only be willing to pay this amount if he believed that, in the absence of any payment by him, the size of the herd maintained by the cattle-raiser would be 4 or more steers. Let us assume that this is the case. Then the farmer would be willing to pay up to $3 if the cattle-raiser would reduce his herd to 3 steers, up to $6 if the herd were reduced to 2 steers, up to $8 if one steer only were kept and up to $9 if cattle-raising were abandoned. It will be noticed that the change in the starting point has not altered the amount which would accrue to the cattle-raiser if he reduced the size of his herd by any given amount. It is still true that the cattle-raiser could receive an additional $3 from the farmer if he agreed to reduce his herd from 3 steers to 2 and that the $3 represents the value of the crop that would be destroyed by adding the third steer to the herd. Although a different belief on the part of the farmer (whether justified or not) about the size of the herd that the cattle-raiser would maintain in the absence of payments from him may affect the total payment he can be induced to pay, it is not true that this different belief would have any effect on the size of the herd that the cattle-raiser will actually keep. This will be the same as it would be if the cattle-raiser had to pay for damage caused by his cattle, since a receipt foregone of a given amount is the equivalent of a payment of the same amount.

It might be thought that it would pay the cattle-raiser to increase his herd above the size that he would wish to maintain once a bargain had been made, in order to induce the farmer to make a larger total payment. And this may be true. It is similar in nature to the action of the farmer (when the cattle-raiser was liable for damage) in cultivating the land on which, as a result of an agreement with the cattle-raiser, planting would subsequently be abandoned (including land which would not be cultivated at all in the absence of cattle-raising). But such manoeuvres are preliminaries to an agreement and do not affect the long-run equilibrium position, which is the same whether or not the cattle-raiser is held responsible for the crop damage brought about by his cattle.

It is necessary to know whether the damaging business is liable or not for damage caused since without the establishment of this initial delimitation of rights there can be no market transactions to transfer and recombine them. But the ultimate result (which maximizes the value of production) is independent of the legal position if the pricing system is assumed to work without cost.

\* \* \*

## VI. THE COST OF MARKET TRANSACTIONS TAKEN INTO ACCOUNT

The argument has proceeded up to this point on the assumption (explicit in Sections III and IV . . .) that there were no costs involved in carrying out market transactions. This is, of course, a very unrealistic assumption. In order to carry out a market transaction it is necessary to discover who it is that one wishes to deal with, to inform people that one wishes to deal and on what terms, to conduct negotiations leading up to a bargain, to draw up the contract, to undertake the inspection needed to make sure that the terms of the contract are being observed, and so on. These operations are often extremely costly, sufficiently costly at any rate to prevent many transactions that would be carried out in a world in which the pricing system worked without cost.

In earlier sections, when dealing with the problem of the rearrangement of legal rights through the market, it was argued that such a rearrangement would be made through the market whenever this would lead to an increase in the value of production. But this assumed costless market transactions. Once the costs of carrying out market transactions are taken into account it is clear that such a rearrangement of rights will only be undertaken when the increase in the value of production consequent upon the rearrangement is greater than the costs which would be involved in bringing it about. When it is less, the granting of an injunction (or the knowledge that it would be granted) or the liability to pay damages may result in an activity being discontinued ( or may prevent its being started) which would be undertaken if market transactions were costless. In these conditions the initial delimitation of legal rights does have an effect on the efficiency with which the economic system operates. One arrangement of rights may bring about a greater value of production than any other. But unless this is the arrangement of rights established by the legal system, the costs of reaching the same result by altering and combining rights through the market may be so great that this optimal arrangement of rights, and the greater value of production which it would bring, may never be achieved. ... In this section, I will take the initial delimitation of rights and the costs of carrying out market transactions as given.

It is clear that an alternative form of economic organisation which could achieve the same result at less cost than would be incurred by using the market would enable the value to production to be raised. As I explained many years ago, the firm represents such an alternative to organising production through market transactions.[4] Within the firm individual bargains between the various cooperating factors of production are eliminated and for a market transaction is substituted an administrative decision. The rearrangement of production then takes place without the need for bargains between the owners of the factors of production. A landowner who has control of a large tract of land may devote his land to various uses taking into account the effect that the interrelations of the various activities will have on the net return of the land, thus rendering unnecessary bargains between those undertaking the various activities. Owners of a large building or of several adjoining properties in a given area may act in much the same way. In effect, using our earlier terminology, the firm would acquire the legal rights of all the parties and the rearrangement of activities would not follow on a rearrangement of rights by contract, but as a result of an administrative decision as to how the rights should be used.

It does not, of course, follow that the administrative costs of organising a transaction through a firm are inevitably less than the costs of the market transactions which are superseded. But where contracts are peculiarly difficult to draw up and an attempt to describe what the parties have agreed to do or not to do (e.g., the amount and kind of smell or noise that they may make or will not make) would necessitate a lengthy and highly involved document, and, where, as is probable, a long-term contract would be desirable,[5] it would be hardly surprising if the emergence of a firm or the extension of the activities of an existing firm were not the solution adopted on many occasions to deal with the problem of harmful effects. This solution would be adopted whenever the administrative costs of the firm were less than the costs of the market transactions that it supersedes and the gains which would result from the rearrangement of activities greater than the firm's costs of organising them. I do not need to examine in great detail the character of this solution since I have explained what is involved in my earlier article.

But the firm is not the only possible answer to this problem. The administrative costs of organising transactions within the firm may also be high, and particularly so when many diverse activities are brought within the control of a single organisation. In the standard case of a smoke nuisance, which may affect a vast number of people engaged in a wide variety of activities, the administrative costs might well be so high as to make any attempt to deal with the problem within the confines of a single firm impossible. An alternative solution is direct government regulation. Instead of instituting a legal system of rights which can be modified by transactions on the market, the government may impose regulations which state what people must or must not do and which have to be obeyed. Thus, the government (by statute or perhaps more likely through an administrative agency) may, to deal with the problem of smoke nuisance, decree that certain methods of production should or should not be used (e.g., that smoke preventing devices should be installed or that coal or oil should not be burned) or may confine certain types of business to certain districts (zoning regulations).

The government is, in a sense, a superfirm (but of a very special kind) since it is able to influence the use of factors of production by administrative decision. But the ordinary firm is subject to checks in its operations because of the competition of other firms, which might administer the same activities at lower cost and also because there is always the alternative of market transactions as against organisation within the firm if the administrative costs become too great. The government is able, if it wishes, to avoid the market altogether, which a firm can never do. The firm has to make market agreements with the owners of the factors of production that it uses. Just as the government can conscript or seize property, so it can decree that factors of production should only be used in such-and-such a way. Such authoritarian methods save a lot of trouble (for those doing the organising). Furthermore, the government has at its disposal the police and the other law enforcement agencies to make sure that its regulations are carried out.

It is clear that the government has powers which might enable it to get some things done at a lower cost than could a private organisation (or at any rate one without special governmental powers). But the governmental administrative machine is not itself costless. It can, in fact, on occasion be extremely costly. Furthermore, there is no reason to suppose that the restrictive and zoning regulations, made by a fallible administration subject to political pressures and operating without any competitive check, will necessarily always be those which increase the efficiency with which the economic system operates. Furthermore, such general regulations which must apply to a wide variety of cases will be enforced in some cases in which they are clearly inappropriate. From these considerations it follows that direct governmental regulation will not necessarily give better results than leaving the problem to be solved by the market or the firm. But equally there is no reason why, on occasion, such governmental administrative regulation should not led to an improvement in economic efficiency. This would seem particularly likely when, as is normally the case with the smoke nuisance, a large number of people are involved and in which therefore the costs of handling the problem through the market or the firm may be high.

There is, of course, a further alternative which is to do nothing about the problem at all. And given that the costs involved in solving the problem by regulations issued by the governmental administrative machine will often be heavy (particularly if the costs are interpreted to include all the consequences which follow from the government engaging in this kind of activity), it will no doubt be commonly the case that the gain which would come from regulating the actions which give rise to the harmful effects will be less than the costs involved in government regulation.

The discussion of the problem of harmful effects in this section (when the costs of market transactions are taken into account) is extremely inadequate. But at least it has made clear that the problem is one of choosing the appropriate social arrangement for dealing with the harmful effects. All solutions have costs and there is no reason to suppose that government regulation is called for simply because the problem is not well handled by the market or the firm. Satisfactory views on policy can only come from a patient study of how, in practice, the market, firms, and governments handle the problem of harmful effects. Economists need to study the work of the broker in bringing parties together, the effectiveness of restrictive covenants, the problems of the large-scale real estate development company, the operation of government zoning and other regulating activities. It is my belief that economists, and policy-makers generally, have tended to overestimate the advantages which come from governmental regulation. But this belief, even if justified, does not do more than suggest that government regulation should be curtailed. It does not tell us where the boundary line should be drawn. This, it seems to me, has to come from a detailed investigation of the actual results of handling the problem in different ways. But it would be unfortunate if this investigation were undertaken with the aid of a faulty economic analysis. The aim of this article is to indicate what the economic approach to the problem should be.

* * *

## IX. THE PIGOUVIAN TRADITION

It is strange that a doctrine as faulty as that developed by Pigou should have been so influential, although part of its success has probably been due to the lack of clarity in the exposition. Not being clear, it was never clearly wrong. Curiously enough, this obscurity in the source has not prevented the emergence of a fairly well-defined oral tradition. What economists think they learn from Pigou, and what they tell their students, which I term the Pigouvian tradition, is reasonably clear. I propose to show the inadequacy of this Pigouvian tradition by demonstrating that both the analysis and the policy conclusions which it supports are incorrect.

I do not propose to justify my views as to the prevailing opinion by copious references to the literature. I do this partly because the treatment in the literature is usually so fragmentary, often involving little more than a reference to Pigou plus some explanatory comment, that detailed examination would be inappropriate. But the main reason for this lack of reference is that the doctrine, although based on Pigou, must have been largely the product of an oral tradition. Certainly economists with whom I have discussed these problems have shown a unanimity of opinion which is quite remarkable considering the meagre treatment accorded this subject in the literature. No doubt there are some economists who do not share the usual view but they must represent a small minority of the profession.

The approach to the problems under discussion is through an examination of the value of physical production. The private product is the value of the additional product resulting from a particular activity of a business. The social product equals the private product minus the fall in the value of production elsewhere for which no compensation is paid by the business. Thus, if ten units of a factor (and no other factors) are used by a business to make a certain product with a value of $105; and the owner of this factor is not compensated for their use, which he is unable to prevent; and these ten units of the factor would yield products in their best alternative use worth $100; then, the social product is $105 minus $100 or $5. If the business now pays for one unit of the factor and its price equals the value of its marginal product, then the social product rises to $15. If two units are paid for, the social product rises to $25 and so on until it reaches $105 when all units of the factor are paid for. It is not difficult to see why economists have so readily accepted this rather odd procedure. The analysis focuses on the individual business decision and since the use of certain resources is not allowed for in costs, receipts are reduced by the same amount. But, of course, this means that the value of the social product has no social significance whatsoever. It seems to me preferable to use the opportunity cost concept and to approach these problems by comparing the value of the product yielded by factors in alternative uses or by alternative arrangements. The main advantage of a pricing system is that it leads to the employment of factors in places where the value of the product yielded is greatest and does so at less cost than alternative systems (I leave aside that a pricing system also eases the problem of the redistribution of income). But if through some God-given natural harmony factors flowed to the places where the value of the product yielded was greatest without any use of the pricing system and consequently there was no compensation, I would find it a source of surprise rather than a cause for dismay.

The definition of the social product is queer but this does not mean that the conclusions for policy drawn from the analysis are necessarily wrong. However, there are bound to be dangers in an approach which diverts attention from the basic issues and there can be little doubt that it has been responsible for some of the errors in current doctrine. The belief that it is desirable that the business which causes harmful effects should be forced to compensate those who suffer damage . . . is undoubtedly the result of not comparing the total product obtainable with alternative social arrangements.

The same fault is to be found in proposals for solving the problem of harmful effects by the use of taxes or bounties. Pigou lays considerable stress on this solution although he is, as usual, lacking in detail and qualified in his support.[6] Modern economists tend to think exclusively in terms of taxes and in a very precise way. The tax should be equal to the damage done and should therefore vary with the amount of the harmful effect. As it is not proposed that the proceeds of the tax should be paid to those suffering the damage, this solution is not the same as that which would force a business to pay compensation to those damaged by its actions, although economists generally do not seem to have noticed this and tend to treat the two solutions as being identical.

Assume that a factory which emits smoke is set up in a district previously free from smoke pollution, causing damage valued at $100 per annum. Assume that the taxation solution is adopted and that the factory-owner is taxed $100 per annum as long as the factory emits the smoke. Assume further that a smoke-preventing device costing $90 per annum to run is available. In these circumstances, the smoke-preventing device would be installed. Damage of $100 would have been avoided at an expenditure of $90 and the factory-owner would be better off by $10 per annum. Yet the position achieved may not be optimal. Suppose that those who suffer the damage could avoid it by moving to other locations or by taking various precautions which would cost them, or be equivalent to a loss in income of, $40 per annum. Then there would be a gain in the value of production of $50 if the factory continued to emit its smoke and those now in the district moved elsewhere or made other adjustments to avoid the damage. If the factory owner is to be made to pay a tax equal to the damage caused, it would clearly be desirable to institute a double tax system and to make residents to the district pay an amount equal to the additional cost incurred by the factory owner (or the consumers of his products) in order to avoid the damage. In these conditions, people would not stay in the district or would take other measures to prevent the damage from occurring, when the costs of doing so were less than the costs that would be incurred by the producer to reduce the damage (the producer's object, of course, being not so much to reduce the damage as to reduce the tax payments). A tax system which was confined to a tax on the producer for damage caused would tend to lead to unduly high costs being incurred for the prevention of damage. Of course this could be avoided if it were possible to base the tax, not on the damage caused, but on the fall in the value of production (in its widest sense) resulting from the emission of smoke. But to do so would require a detailed knowledge of individual preferences and I am unable to imagine how the data needed for such a taxation system could be assembled. Indeed, the proposal to solve the smoke-pollution and similar problems by the use of taxes bristles with difficulties: the problem of calculation, the difference between average and marginal damage, the interrelations between the damage suffered on different properties, etc. But it is unnecessary to examine these problems here. It is enough for my purpose to show that, even if the tax is exactly adjusted to equal the damage that would be done to neighbouring properties as a result of the emission of each additional puff of smoke, the tax would not necessarily bring about optimal conditions. An increase in the number of people living or of business operating in the vicinity of the smoke-emitting factory will increase the amount of harm produced by a given emission of smoke. The tax that would be imposed would therefore increase with an increase in the number of those in the vicinity. This will tend to lead to a decrease in the value of production of the factors employed by the factory, either because a reduction in production due to the tax will result in factors being used elsewhere in ways which are less valuable, or because factors will be diverted to produce means for reducing the amount of smoke emitted. But people deciding to establish themselves in the vicinity of the factory will not take into account this fall in the value of production which results from their presence. The failure to take into account costs imposed on others is comparable to the action of a factory-owner in not taking into account the harm resulting from his emission of smoke. Without the tax, there may be too much smoke and too few people in the vicinity of the factory; but with the tax there may be too little smoke and too many people in the vicinity of the factory. There is no reason to suppose that one of these results is necessarily preferable.

I need not devote much space to discussing the similar error involved in the suggestion that smoke producing factories should, by means of zoning regulations, be removed from the districts in which the smoke causes harmful effects. When the change in the location of the factory results in a reduction in production, this obviously needs to be taken into account and weighed against the harm which would result from the factory remaining in that location. The aim of such regulation should not be to eliminate smoke pollution but rather to secure the optimum amount of smoke pollution, this being the amount which will maximize the value of production.

## X. A CHANGE OF APPROACH

It is my belief that the failure of economists to reach correct conclusions about the treatment of harmful effects cannot be ascribed simply to a few slips in analysis. It stems from basic defects in the current approach to problems of welfare economics. What is needed is a change of approach.

Analysis in terms of divergencies between private and social products concentrates attention on particular deficiencies in the system and tends to nourish the belief that any measure which will remove the deficiency is necessarily desirable. It diverts attention from those other changes in the system which are inevitably associated with the corrective measure, changes which may well produce more harm than the original deficiency. In the preceding sections of this article, we have seen many examples of this. But it is not necessary to approach the problem in this way. Economists who study problems of the firm habitually use an opportunity cost approach and compare the receipts obtained from a given combination of factors with alternative business arrangements. It would seem desirable to use a similar approach when dealing with questions of economic policy and to compare the total product yielded by alternative social arrangements. In this article, the analysis has been confined, as is usual in this part of economics, to comparisons of the value of production, as measured by the market. But it is, of course, desirable that the choice between different social arrangements for the solution of economic problems should be carried out in broader terms than this and that the total effect of these arrangements in all spheres of life should be taken into account. As Frank H. Knight has so often emphasized, problems of welfare economics must ultimately dissolve into a study of aesthetics and morals.

A second feature of the usual treatment of the problems discussed in this article is that the analysis proceeds in terms of a comparison between a state of laissez-faire and some kind of ideal world. This approach inevitably leads to a looseness of thought since the nature of the alternatives being compared is never clear. In a state of laissez-faire, is there a monetary, a legal, or a political system and if so, what are they? In an ideal world, would there be a monetary, a legal, or a political system and if so, what would they be? The answers to all these questions are shrouded in mystery and every man is free to draw whatever conclusions he likes. Actually very little analysis is required to show that an ideal world is better than a state of laissez-faire, unless the definitions of a state of laissez-faire and an ideal world happened to be the same. But the whole discussion is largely irrelevant for questions of economic policy since whatever we may have in mind as our ideal world, it is clear that we have not yet discovered how to get to it from where we are. A better approach would seem to be to start our analysis with a situation approximating that which actually exists, to examine the effects of a proposed policy change, and to attempt to decide whether the new situation would be, in total, better or worse than the original one. In this way, conclusions for policy would have some relevance to the actual situation.

A final reason for the failure to develop a theory adequate to handle the problem of harmful effects stems from a faulty concept of a factor of production. This is usually thought of as a physical entity which the businessman acquires and uses (an acre of land, a ton of fertiliser) instead of as a right to perform certain (physical) actions. We may speak of a person owning land and using it as a factor of production but what the land-owner in fact possesses is the right to carry out a circumscribed list of actions. The rights of a land-owner are not unlimited. It is not even always possible for him to remove the land to another place, for instance, by quarrying it. And although it may be possible for him to exclude some people from using "his" land, this may not be true of others. For example, some people may have the right to cross the land. Furthermore, it may or may not be possible to erect certain types of buildings or to grow certain crops or to use particular drainage systems on the land. This does not come about simply because of government regulation. It would be equally true under the common law. In fact it would be true under any system of law. A system in which the rights of individuals were unlimited would be one in which there were no rights to acquire.

If factors of production are thought of as rights, it becomes easier to understand that the right to do something which has a harmful effect (such as the creation of smoke, noise, smells, etc.) is also a factor of production. Just as we may use a piece of land in such a way as to prevent someone else from crossing it, or parking his car, or building his house upon it, so we may use it in such a way as to deny him a view or quiet or unpolluted air. The cost of exercising a right (of using a factor of production) is always the loss which is suffered elsewhere in consequence of the exercise of that right—the inability to cross land, to park a car, to build a house, to enjoy a view, to have peace and quiet, or to breathe clean air.

It would clearly be desirable if the only actions performed were those in which what was gained was worth more than what was lost. But in choosing between social arrangements within the context of which individual decisions are made, we have to bear in mind that a change in the existing system which will lead to an improvement in some decisions may well lead to a worsening of others. Furthermore we have to take into account the costs involved in operating the various social arrangements (whether it be the working of a market or of a government department), as well as the costs involved in moving to a new system. In devising and choosing between social arrangements we should have regard for the total effect. This, above all, is the change in approach which I am advocating.

## NOTES

This article, although concerned with a technical problem of economic analysis, arose out of the study of the Political Economy of Broadcasting which I am now conducting. The argument of the present article was implicit in a previous article dealing with the problem of allocating radio and television frequencies ("The Federal Communications Commission," *Journal of Law and Economics 2* [1959]) but comments which I have received seemed to suggest that it would be desirable to deal with the question in a more explicit way and without reference to the original problem for the solution of which the analysis was developed.

1. Coase, R. "The Federal Communications Commission," *Journal of Law and Economics 2* (1959): 26–27.
2. Stigler, G. J. *The Theory of Price*, New York: Macmillan Co. (1952): 105.
3. The argument in the text has proceeded on the assumption that the alternative to cultivation of the crop is abandonment of cultivation altogether. But this need not be so. There may be crops which are less liable to damage by cattle but which would not be as profitable as the crop grown in the absence of damage. Thus, if the cultivation of a new crop would yield a return to the farmer of $1 instead of $2, and the size of the herd which would cause $3 damage with the old crop would cause $1 damage with the new crop, it would be profitable to the cattle-raiser to pay any sum less than $2 to induce the farmer to change his crop (since this would reduce damage liability from $3 to $1) and it would be profitable for the farmer to do so if the amount received was more than $1 (reduction in his return caused by switching crops). In fact, there would be room for a mutually satisfactory bargain in all cases in which change of crop would reduce the amount of damage by more than it reduces the value of the crop (excluding damage)—in all cases, that is, in which a change in the crop cultivated would lead to an increase in the value of production.
4. See Coase, "The Nature of the Firm," *Economica 4*, New Series, (1937): 386. Reprinted in *Readings in Price Theory*, Homewood, Illinois: Richard D. Irwin (1952): 331.
5. For reasons explained in my earlier article, see *Readings in Price Theory*, n. 14 at 337.
6. Pigou, *The Economics of Welfare*, London: Macmillan (1920): 192–194, 381, and *Public Finance*, London: Macmillan Co. (3d ed. 1947), 94–100.

## S E L E C T I O N  4

Maureen L. Cropper and Wallace E. Oates

# The Design and Implementation of Environmental Policy

In properly functioning markets, private parties must pay for the resources they use, and an additional unit of a resource is used only if benefits exceed costs. However, there may be no payment required for using the environment—for pouring pollutants into water resources, for allowing fumes to escape into the atmosphere, and so on. In such cases, the environment is a free good, littered with wastes even when private benefits are smaller than the external costs or externalities. Governments have the power to prohibit or regulate environmental abuses by decree. However, economic policy instruments for controlling pollution can help place the environment within the operation of an efficient market system. In particular, marketable pollution permits are transferable permits to emit a specified amount of a waste product into the air or water during a given time period. Regulatory authorities determine the maximum desirable amount of a particular pollutant in the environment, and then issue the appropriate quantity of pollution "rights" to firms. Unlike penalty taxes, pollution permits give regulators strict control over the amount of emissions.

In this selection, Maureen Cropper and Wallace Oates examine the policy potential of marketable pollution permits and effluent fees (penalty taxes), as well as legal liability for pollution damages. They focus on the U.S. and European experiences with economic incentives for pollution control. In the United States, marketable permits have increasingly become the policy instrument of choice—particularly for air pollution. As early as 1977, the Environmental Protection Agency

Cropper, Maureen L., and Wallace E. Oates. "Environmental Economics: A Survey." *Journal of Economic Literature 30* (June 1992): 675–740. This selection is an abridged version of the original article.

Both **Maureen L. Cropper** and **Wallace E. Oates** are Professors of Economics at the University of Maryland and Fellows at Resources for the Future.

adopted an emission banking procedure under which a polluter could receive (and sell) credit for reducing emissions by amounts exceeding required levels. More recently, the nation's largest commodity market, the Chicago Board of Trade, voted in 1991 to create a trading market for rights to emit sulfur dioxide.* Cropper and Oates also examine a number of other regulatory issues: centralization versus decentralization of regulatory power, enforcement measures, and the international effects of domestic environmental policies.

### Questions to Guide the Reading

1. What is the source of the large potential cost-savings of economic incentives?
2. Why may marketable pollution permits be preferable to effluent fees as a mechanism for providing incentives for pollution control? When would fees be preferable to permits?
3. In light of the U.S. experience with marketable permits, why are the authors optimistic about the prospects for the functioning of the market for sulfur allowances?
4. What are the strengths and limitations of legal liability as a policy instrument for environmental protection?
5. When would regionally-decentralized environmental decisions (environmental federalism) be efficient?
6. In spite of modest enforcement efforts and small fines, why might substantial compliance with environmental regulation exist?
7. Contrary to early fears, why hasn't "industrial flight" been a major problem?

---

When the environmental revolution arrived in the late 1960s, the economics profession was ready and waiting. Economists had what they saw as a coherent and compelling view of the nature of pollution with a straightforward set of policy implications. The problem of externalities and the associated market failure had long been a part of microeconomic theory and was embedded in a number of standard texts. Economists saw pollution as the consequence of an absence of prices for certain scarce environmental resources (such as clean air and water), and they prescribed the introduction of surrogate prices in the form of unit taxes or "effluent fees" to provide the needed signals to economize on the use of these resources. While much of the analysis was of a fairly general character, there was at least some careful

---

**\*Editors' note:** For current information on prices and trades in the market for rights to emit sulfur dioxide, see the U.S. Environmental Protection Agency's World-Wide Web page on acid rain: http://www.epa.gov/docs/acidrain/ardhome.html

research underway exploring the application of economic solutions to certain pressing environmental problems (e.g., Allen Kneese and Blair Bower 1968).

The economist's view had—to the dismay of the profession—little impact on the initial surge of legislation for the control of pollution. In fact, the cornerstones of federal environmental policy in the United States, the Amendments to the Clean Air Act in 1970 and to the Clean Water Act in 1972, *explicitly* prohibited the weighing of benefits against costs in the setting of environmental standards. The former directed the Environmental Protection Agency to set maximum limitations on pollutant concentrations in the atmosphere "to protect the public health"; the latter set as an objective the "elimination of the discharge of *all* [our emphasis] pollutants into the navigable waters by 1985."[1]

The evolution of environmental policy, both in the U.S. and elsewhere, has inevitably brought economic issues to the fore; environmental regulation has necessarily involved costs—and the question of how far and how fast to push for pollution control in light of these costs has entered into the public debate. Under Executive Order 12291 issued in 1981, many proposed environmental measures have been subjected to a benefit-cost test. In addition, some more recent pieces of environmental legislation, notably the Toxic Substances Control Act (TSCA) and the Federal Insecticide, Fungicide, and Rodenticide Act (FIFRA), call for weighing benefits against costs in the setting of standards. At the same time, economic incentives for the containment of waste discharges have crept into selected regulatory measures. In the United States, for example, the 1977 Amendments to the Clean Air Act introduced a provision for "emission offsets" that has evolved into the Emissions Trading Program under which sources are allowed to trade "rights" to emit air pollutants. And outside the United States, there have been some interesting uses of effluent fees for pollution control.

This is a most exciting time—and perhaps a critical juncture—in the evolution of economic incentives for environmental protection. The Bush Administration proposed, and the Congress has introduced, a measure for the trading of sulfur emissions for the control of acid rain under the new 1990 Amendments to the Clean Air Act. More broadly, an innovative report from within the U.S. Congress sponsored by Senators Timothy Wirth and John Heinz, *Project 88: Harnessing Market Forces to Protect Our Environment* (Robert Stavins 1988), explores a lengthy list of potential applications of economic incentives for environmental management. Likewise, there is widespread, ongoing discussion in Europe of the role of economic measures for pollution control. Most recently in January of 1991, the Council of the Organization for Economic Cooperation and Development (OECD) has gone on record urging member countries to "make a greater and more consistent use of economic instruments" for environmental management. Of particular note is the emerging international concern with global environmental issues, especially with planetary warming; the enormous challenge and awesome costs of policies to address this issue have focused interest on proposals for "Green Taxes" and systems of tradable permits to contain global emissions of greenhouse gases. In short, this seems to be a time when there is a real opportunity for environmental economists to make some valuable contributions in the policy arena—if, as we shall argue, they are willing to move from "purist" solutions to a realistic consideration of the design and implementation of policy measures.

* * *

## A. INTRODUCTION: FROM THEORY TO POLICY

Consider environmental policy as a two-step process: first, standards or targets for environmental quality are set, and, second, a regulatory system is designed and put in place to achieve these standards. This is often the way environmental decision making proceeds. Under the Clean Air Act, for example, the first task of the EPA was to set standards in the form of maximum permissible concentrations of the major air pollutants. The next step was to design a regulatory plan to attain these standards for air quality.

In such a setting, systems of economic incentives can come into play in the second stage as effective regulatory instruments for the achievement of the predetermined environmental standards. Baumol and Oates (1971) have described such a system employing effluent fees as the "charges and standards" approach. But marketable permit systems can also function in this setting—a so-called "permit and standards" approach (Baumol and Oates 1988, ch. 12).[2]

The chief appeal of economic incentives as the regulatory device for achieving environmental standards is the large potential cost-savings that they promise. There is now an extensive body of empirical studies that estimate the cost of achieving standards for environmental quality under existing command-and-control (CAC) regulatory programs (e.g., Scott Atkinson and Donald Lewis 1974; Seskin et al. 1983; Alan Krupnick 1983; Adele Palmer et al. 1980; Albert McGartland 1984). These are typically programs under which the environmental authority prescribes (often in great detail) the treatment procedures that are to be adopted by each source. The studies compare costs under CAC programs with those under a more cost effective system of economic incentives. The results have been quite striking: they indicate that control costs under existing programs have often been several times the least-cost levels. (See Thomas Tietenberg 1985, ch. 3, for a useful survey of these cost studies.)

The source of these large cost savings is the capacity of economic instruments to take advantage of the large differentials in abatement costs across polluters. The information problems confronting regulators under the more traditional CAC approaches are enormous—and they lead regulators to make only very rough and crude distinctions among sources (e.g., new versus old firms). In a setting of perfect information, such problems would, of course, disappear. But in the real world of imperfect information, economic instruments have the important advantage of economizing on the need for the environmental agency to acquire information on the abatement costs of individual sources. This is just another example of the more general principles concerning the capacity of markets to deal efficiently with information problems.[3]

The estimated cost savings in the studies cited above result from a more cost effective allocation of abatement efforts within the context of existing control technologies. From a more dynamic perspective, economic incentives promise additional gains in terms of encouraging the development of more effective and less costly abatement techniques. As John Wenders (1975) points out in this context, a system that puts a value on any discharges remaining after control (such as a system of fees or marketable permits) will provide a greater incentive to R&D efforts in control technology than will a regulation that specifies some given level of discharges (see also Wesley Magat 1978, and Scott Milliman and Raymond Prince 1989).

## B. THE CHOICE OF POLICY INSTRUMENTS[4]

Some interesting issues arise in the choice between systems of effluent fees and marketable emission permits in the policy arena (John H. Dales 1968; Donald Dewees 1983; David Harrison 1983). There is, of course, a basic sense in which they are equivalent: the environmental authority can, in principle, set price (i.e., the level of the effluent charge) and then adjust it until emissions are reduced sufficiently to achieve the prescribed environmental standard, or, alternatively, issue the requisite number of permits directly and allow the bidding of polluters to determine the market-clearing price.

However, this basic equivalence obscures some crucial differences between the two approaches in a policy setting; they are by no means equivalent policy instruments from the perspective of a regulatory agency. A major advantage of the marketable permit approach is that it gives the environmental authority direct control over the quantity of emissions. Under the fee approach, the regulator must set a fee, and if, for example, the fee turns out to be too low, pollution will exceed permissible levels. The agency will find itself in the uncomfortable position of having to adjust and readjust the fee to ensure that the environmental standard is attained. Direct control over quantity is to be preferred since the standard itself is prescribed in quantity terms.

This consideration is particularly important over time in a world of growth and inflation. A nominal fee that is adequate to hold emissions to the requisite levels at one moment in time will fail to do so later in the presence of economic growth and a rising price level. The regulatory agency will have to enact periodic (and unpopular) increases in effluent fees. In contrast, a system of marketable permits automatically accommodates itself to growth and inflation. Since there can be no change to the aggregate quantity of emissions without some explicit action on the part of the agency, increased demand will simply translate itself into a higher market-clearing price for permits with no effects on levels of waste discharges.

Polluters (that is, *existing* polluters), as well as regulators, are likely to prefer the permit approach because it can involve lower levels of compliance costs. If the permits are auctioned off, then of course polluters must pay directly for the right to emit wastes as they would under a fee system. But rather than allocating the permits by auction, the environmental authority can initiate the system with a one-time distribution of permits to existing sources—free of charge. Some form of "grandfathering" can be used to allocate permits based on historical performance. Existing firms thus receive a marketable asset, which they can then use either to validate their own emissions or sell to another polluter.[5] And finally, the permit approach has some advantages in terms of familiarity. Regulators have long-standing experience with permits, and it is a much less radical change to make permits effectively transferable than to introduce a wholly new system of regulation based on effluent fees. Marketable permits thus have some quite appealing features to a regulatory agency—features that no doubt explain to some degree the revealed preference for this approach (in the U.S. at least) over that of fees.

Effluent charges have their own appeal. They are sources of public revenue, and, in these days of large budget deficits, they promise a new revenue source to hard-pressed legislators. From an economic perspective, there is much to be said for the substitution of fees or other sources of revenues that carry sizable excess burdens (Lee and Misiolek 1986). In a study of effluent charges on emissions of particulates and sulfur oxides from stationary sources into the atmosphere, David Terkla (1984) estimates, based on assumed levels of tax rates, that revenues in 1982 dollars would range from $1.8 to $8.7 billion and would, in addition, provide substantial efficiency gains ($630 million to $3.05 billion) if substituted for revenues from either the federal individual income tax or corporation income tax.

Moreover, the charges approach does not depend for its effectiveness on the development of a smoothly functioning market in permits. Significant search costs, strategic behavior, and market imperfections can impede the workings of a permit market (Hahn 1984; Tietenberg 1985, ch. 6). In contrast, under a system of fees, no transfers of permits are needed—each polluter simply responds directly to the incentive provided by the existing fee. There may well be circumstances under which it is easier to realize a cost-effective pattern of abatement efforts through a visible set of fees than through the workings of a somewhat distorted permit market. And finally, there is an equity argument in favor of fees (instead of a free distribution of permits to sources). The Organization for Economic Cooperation and Development (OECD), for example, has adopted the "Polluter Pays Principle" on the grounds that those who use society's scarce environmental resources should compensate the public for their use.

There exists a large literature on the design of fee systems and permit markets to attain predetermined levels of environmental quality. This work addresses the difficult issues that arise in the design and functioning of systems of economic incentives—issues that receive little or only perfunctory attention in the purely theoretical literature but are of real concern in the operation of actual policy measures. For example, there is the tricky matter of spatial differentiation. For most pollutants, the effect of discharges on environmental quality typically has important spatial dimensions; the specific location of the source dictates the effects that its emissions will have on environmental quality at the various monitoring points. While, in principle, this simply calls for differentiating the effluent fee according to location, in practice this is not so easy. The regulatory agency often does not have the authority or inclination to levy differing tax rates on sources according to their location. Various compromises including the construction of zones with uniform fees have been investigated (Tietenberg 1978; Seskin et al. 1983; Kolstad 1987).

Similarly, problems arise under systems of transferable permits where (as is often the case) the effects of the emissions of the partners to a trade are not the same. (The seminal theoretical paper is W. David Montgomery 1972.) Several alternatives have been proposed including zoned systems that allow trades only among polluters within the specified zones, ambient permit systems under which the terms of trade are determined by the relative effects of emissions at binding monitors, and the pollution-offset system under which trades are subject to the constraint of no violations of the prevailing standard at any point in the area (Atkinson and Tietenberg 1982; Atkinson and Lewis 1974; Hahn and Noll 1982; Krupnick et al. 1983; McGartland and Oates 1985; McGartland 1988; Tietenberg 1980, 1985; Walter Spofford 1984; Baumol and Oates 1988, ch. 12). For certain pollutants, these studies make clear that a substantial portion of the cost-savings from economic-incentive approaches will be lost if spatial differentiation is not, at least to some degree, built into the program (Robert Mendelsohn 1986).

The actual design of systems of economic incentives inevitably involves some basic compromises to accommodate the range of complications to the regulatory problem (Albert Nichols 1984). It is instructive to see how some of these issues have been dealt with in practice.

## C. EXPERIENCE WITH ECONOMIC INCENTIVES FOR ENVIRONMENTAL MANAGEMENT[6]

In the United States proposals for effluent fees have met with little success; however, there has been some limited experience with programs of marketable permits for the regulation of air and water quality. In Europe, the experience (at least until quite recently) has been the reverse: some modest use of effluent charges but no experience with transferable permits. We shall provide in this section a brief summary of these measures along with some remarks on their achievements and failures.

Largely for the reasons mentioned in the preceding section, policymakers in the U.S. have found marketable permits preferable to fees as a mechanism for providing economic incentives for pollution control.[7] The major program of this genre is the EPA's Emission Trading Program for the regulation of air quality. But there are also three other programs worthy of note: the Wisconsin system of Transferable Discharge Permits (TDP) for the management of water quality, the lead trading program (known formally as "interrefinery averaging"), and a recent program for the trading of rights for phosphorus discharges into the Dillon Reservoir in Colorado.[8]

By far the most important of these programs in terms of scope and impact, Emissions Trading has undergone a fairly complicated evolution into a program that has several major components. Under the widely publicized "Bubble" provision, a plant with many sources of emissions of a particular air pollutant is subjected to an overall emissions limitation. Within this limit, the managers of the plant have the flexibility to select a set of controls consistent with the aggregate limit, rather than conforming to specified treatment procedures for each source of discharges within the plant. Under the "Netting" provision, firms can avoid stringent limitations on new source of discharges by reducing emissions from other sources of the pollutant within the facility. Hahn and Hester (1989b) report that to date there have been over 100 approved Bubble transactions in the U.S. and a much larger number of Netting "trades" (somewhere between 5,000 and 12,000). The estimated cost savings from these trades have been quite substantial; although the estimates exhibit a very wide range, the cost savings probably amount to several billion dollars.

There are provisions under Emissions Trading for external trades across firms—mainly under the Offset provision which allows new sources in nonattainment areas to "offset" their new emissions with reductions in discharges by existing sources. Offsets can be obtained through either internal (within plant) or external trades. Hahn and Hester (1989b) indicate that there have been about 2,000 trades under the Offset policy; only about 10 percent of them have been external trades—the great bulk of offsets have been obtained within the plant or facility.

Emissions Trading, as a whole, receives mixed marks. It has significantly increased the flexibility with which sources can meet their discharge limitations—and this has been important for it has allowed substantial cost savings. The great majority of the trades, however, have been internal ones. A real and active market in emissions rights involving different firms has not developed under the program (in spite of the efforts of an active firm functioning as a broker in this market). This seems to be largely the result of an extensive and complicated set of procedures for external trades that have introduced substantial levels of transactions costs into the market and have created uncertainties concerning the nature of the property rights that are being acquired. In addition, the program has been grafted onto an elaborate set of command-and-control style regulations which effectively prohibit certain kinds of trades. Many potentially profitable trades simply have not come to pass.[9]

Likewise, the experience under the Wisconsin TDP system has involved little external trading. The program establishes a framework under which the rights to BOD discharges can be traded among sources. Since the program's inception in 1981 on the Fox River, there has been only one trade: a paper mill which shifted its treatment activities to a municipal wastewater treatment plant transferred its rights to the municipal facility. The potential number of trades is limited since there are only about twenty major sources (paper mills and municipal waste treatment plants) along the banks of the river. But even so, preliminary studies (O'Neil 1983; O'Neil et al. 1983) indicated several potentially quite profitable trades involving large cost savings. A set of quite severe restrictions appears to have discouraged these transfers of permits. Trades must be justified on the basis of "need"—and this does not include reduced costs! Moreover, the traded rights are granted only for the term of the seller's discharge permit (a maximum period of five years) with no assurance that the rights will be renewed. The Wisconsin experience seems to be one in which the conditions needed for the emergence of a viable market in discharge permits have not been established.

In contrast, EPA's "interrefinery averaging" program for the trading of lead rights resulted in a very active market over the relatively short life of the program. Begun in 1982, the program allowed refiners to trade the severely limited rights to lead additives to gasoline. The program expired in 1986, although refiners were permitted to make a use of rights that were "banked" through 1987. Trading became brisk under the program: over the first half of 1987, for example, around 50 percent of all lead added to gasoline was obtained through trades of lead rights, with substantial cost savings reported from these trades. Although reliable estimates of cost-savings for the lead-trading program are not available, Hahn and Hester (1989b) surmise that these savings have run into the hundreds of millions of dollars. As they point out, the success of the program stemmed largely from the absence of a large body of restrictions on trades: refiners were essentially free to trade lead rights and needed only to submit a quarterly report to EPA on their gasoline production and lead usage. There were, moreover, already well established markets in refinery products (including a wide variety of fuel additives) so that refinery managers had plenty of experience in these kinds of transactions.[10]

Finally, there is an emerging program in Colorado for the trading of rights to phosphorous discharges into the Dillon Reservoir. This program is noteworthy in that among those that we have discussed, it is the only one to be designed and introduced by a local government. The plan embodies few encumbrances to trading; the one major restriction is a 2:1 trading ratio for point/nonpoint trading, introduced as a "margin of safety" because of uncertainties concerning the effectiveness of nonpoint source controls. The program is still in its early stages; although no trades have been approved, some have been requested.

The U.S. experience with marketable permits is thus a limited one with quite mixed results. In the one case where the market was allowed to function free of heavy restrictions, vigorous trading resulted with apparently large cost savings. In contrast, under Emissions Trading and the Wisconsin TDP systems, stringent restrictions on the markets for trading emissions rights appear to have effectively increased transaction costs and introduced uncertainties, seriously impeding the ability of these markets to realize the potentially large cost savings from trading. Even so, the cost savings from Emissions Trading (primarily from the Netting and Bubble provisions) have run into several billion dollars. Finally, it is interesting that these programs seem not to have had any significant and adverse environmental effects; Hahn and Hester (1989a) suggest that their impact on environmental quality has been roughly "neutral."

In light of this experience, the prospects, we think, appear favorable for the functioning of the new market in sulfur allowances that is being created under the 1990 Amendments to the Clean Air Act. The measure, designed to address the acid rain problem by cutting back annual sulfur emissions by 10 million tons, will permit affected power plants to meet their emissions reduction quotas by whatever means they wish, including the purchase of "excess" emissions reductions from other sources. The market area for this program is the nation as a whole so that there should be a large number of potential participants in the market. At this juncture, plans for the structure and functioning of the market do not appear to contain major limitations that would impede trading in the sulfur allowances. There remains, however, the possibility that state governors or public utility commissions will introduce some restrictions. There is the further concern that regulated firms may not behave in a strictly cost-minimizing fashion, thereby compromising some of the cost-effectiveness properties of the trading scheme. But as we suggested earlier, this may not prove to be a serious distortion.

The use of effluent fees is more prevalent in Europe where they have been employed extensively in systems of water quality management and to a limited extent for noise abatement (Ralph Johnson and Gardner Brown, Jr. 1976; Bower et al. 1981; Brown and Hans Bressers 1986; Brown and Johnson 1984; Tietenberg 1990). There are few attempts to use them for the control of air pollution. France, Germany, and the Netherlands, for example, have imposed effluent fees on emissions of various water pollutants for over two decades. It should be stressed that these fee systems are not pure systems of economic incentives of the sort discussed in economics texts. Their primary intent has not been the regulation of discharges, but rather the raising of funds to finance projects for water quality management. As such, the fees have typically been low and have tended to apply to "average" or "expected" discharges rather than to provide a clear cost signal at the margin. Moreover, the charges are overlaid on an extensive command-and-control system of regulations that mute somewhat further their effects as economic incentives.

The Netherlands has one of the oldest and most effectively managed systems of charges—and also the one with relatively high levels of fees. There is some evidence suggesting that these fees have, in fact, had a measurable effect in reducing emissions. Some multiple regression work by Hans Bressers (1983) in the Netherlands and surveys of industrial polluters and water board officials by Brown and Bressers (1986) indicate that firms have responded to the charges with significant cutbacks in discharges of waterborne pollutants.

In sum, although there is some experience with systems of fees for pollution control, mainly of water pollution, these systems have not, for the most part, been designed in the spirit of economic incentives for the regulation of water quality. This role has been more that of a revenue device to finance programs for water quality management.

These systems, it is worth noting, have addressed almost exclusively so-called "point-source" polluters. Nonpoint source pollution (including agricultural and urban runoff into waterways) has proved much more difficult to encompass within systems of charges or permits. Winston Harrington, Krupnick, and Henry Peskin (1985) provide a useful overview of the potential role for economic incentives in the management of nonpoint sources. This becomes largely a matter of seeking out potentially effective second-best measures (e.g., fees on fertilizer use), since it is difficult to measure and monitor "discharges" of pollutants from these sources. Kathleen Segerson (1988) has advanced an ingenious proposal whereby such sources would be subject to a tax (or subsidy payment) based, not on their emissions, but on the observed level of environmental quality; although sources might find themselves with tax payments resulting from circumstances outside their control (e.g., adverse weather conditions), Segerson shows that such a scheme can induce efficient abatement and entry/exit behavior on the part of nonpoint sources.

## D. LEGAL LIABILITY AS AN ECONOMIC INSTRUMENT FOR ENVIRONMENTAL PROTECTION

An entirely different approach to regulating sources is to rely on legal liability for damages to the environment. Although we often do not include this approach under the heading of economic instruments, it is clear that a system of "strict liability," under which a source is financially responsible for damages, embodies important economic incentives.[11] The imposition of such liability effectively places an "expected price" on polluting activities. The ongoing suits, for example, following upon the massive Exxon-Valdez oil spill suggest that such penalties will surely exert pressures on potential polluters to engage in preventive measures.

Under this approach, the environmental authority, in a setting of uncertainty, need not set the values of any price or quantity instruments; it simply relies on the liability rule to discipline polluters. Two issues are of interest here. The first is the capacity, in principle, for strict liability to mimic the effects of a Pigouvian tax. And the second is the likely effectiveness, in practice, of strict liability as a substitute for other forms of economic incentives. There is a substantial literature in the economics of the law that addresses these general issues and a growing number of studies that explore this matter in the context of environmental management (see, for example, Steven Shavell 1984a, 1984b; Segerson 1990).

It is clear that strict liability can, in principle, provide the source of potential damages with the same incentive as a Pigouvian tax. If a polluter knows that he will be held financially accountable for any damages his activities create, then he will have the proper incentive to seek methods to avoid these damages. Strict liability serves to internalize the external costs—just as does an appropriate tax. Strict liability is unlike a tax, however, in that it provides compensation to victims. The Pigouvian tax possesses an important asymmetry in a market sense; it is a charge to the polluter—but not a payment to the victim. And, as noted earlier, such payments to victims can result in inefficient levels of defensive activities. Strict liability thus does not get perfect marks on efficiency grounds, even in principle, for although it internalizes the social costs of the polluter, it can be a source of distortions in victims' behavior.

The more important concern, in practice, is the effectiveness of legal liability in disciplining polluter behavior. Even if the basic rule is an efficient one in terms of placing liability on the source of the environmental damage, the actual "price" paid by the source may be much less than actual damages because of imperfections in the legal system: failures to impose liability on responsible parties resulting from uncertainty over causation, statutes of limitation, or high costs of prosecution.[12] There is the further possibility of bankruptcy as a means of avoiding large payments for damages. The evidence on these matters is mixed (see Segerson 1990), but it seems to suggest that legal liability has functioned only very imperfectly.

An interesting area of application in the environmental arena involves various pieces of legislation that provide strict liability for damages from accidental spills of oil or leakage of hazardous wastes. The Comprehensive Environmental Responses, Compensation, and Liability Act (CERCLA) of 1980 and its later amendments (popularly known as "Superfund") are noteworthy for their broad potential applicability (Grigalunas and Opaluch 1988). Such measures may well provide a useful framework for internalizing the external cost of spills (Opaluch and Grigalunas 1984). In particular, the liability approach appears to have its greatest appeal in cases like those under Superfund where damages are infrequent events and for which monitoring the level of care a firm takes under conventional regulatory procedures would be difficult.[13]

## E. ENVIRONMENTAL FEDERALISM

In addition to the choice of policy instrument, there is the important issue of the locus of regulatory authority. In the case of fees, for example, should a central environmental authority establish a uniform fee applicable to polluters in all parts of the nation or should decentralized agencies set fee levels appropriate to their own jurisdictions? U.S. environmental policy exhibits considerable ambivalence on this matter. Under the Clean Air Act in 1970, the U.S. Congress instructed the Environmental Protection Agency to set uniform national standards for air quality—maximum permissible concentrations of key air pollutants applicable to all areas in the country. But two years later under the Clean Water Act, the Congress decided to let the individual states determine their own standards (subject to EPA approval) for water quality. The basic question is "Which approach, centralized decision making or environmental federalism, is the more promising?"

Basic economic principles seem to suggest, on first glance, a straightforward answer to this question. Since the benefits and costs of reduced levels of most forms of pollution are likely to vary (and vary substantially) across different jurisdictions, the optimal level of effluent fees (or quantities of marketable permits) will also vary (Sam Peltzman and T. Nicolaus Tideman 1972). The first-best outcome must therefore be one in which fees or quantities of permits are set in accord with local circumstances, suggesting that an optimal regulatory system for pollution control will be a form of environmental federalism.

Some environmental economists have raised an objection to this general presumption. John Cumberland (1981), among others, has expressed the concern that in their eagerness to attract new business and jobs, state or local officials will tend to set excessively lax environmental standards—fees that are too low or quantities of permits that are too high. The fear is that competition among decentralized jurisdictions for jobs and income will lead to excessive environmental degradation. This, incidentally, is a line of argument that has appeared elsewhere in the literature on fiscal federalism under the title of "tax competition." The difficulty in assessing this objection to decentralized policy making is that there exists little systematic evidence on the issue; most of the evidence is anecdotal in character, and, until quite recently, there has been little theoretical work addressing the phenomenon of interjurisdictional competition.[14]

In a pair of recent papers, Oates and Schwab (1988a, 1988b) have set forth a model of such competition in which "local" jurisdictions compete for the mobile national stock of capital using both tax and environmental policy instruments. Since the production functions are neoclassical in character, an increase in a jurisdiction's capital stock raises the level of wages through an associated increase in the capital-labor ratio. In the model, local officials simultaneously employ two policy tools to attract capital: a tax rate on capital itself which can be lowered or even set negative (a subsidy) to raise the return to capital in the jurisdiction, and a level of allowable pollutant emissions (or, alternatively, an effluent fee). By increasing the level of permissible waste discharges either directly or by lowering the fee on emissions, the local authority increases the marginal product of capital and thereby encourages a further inflow of capital. The model thus involves two straightforward tradeoffs: one between wage income and tax revenues, and the other between wage income and local environmental quality. The analysis reveals that in a setting of homogeneous worker-residents making choices by simple majority rule, jurisdictions select the socially optimal levels of these two policy instruments. The tax rate on capital is set equal to zero, and the level of environmental quality is chosen so that the willingness to pay for a cleaner environment is equal to marginal abatement cost. The analysis thus supports the case for environmental federalism: decentralized policy making is efficient in the model.[15]

In one sense, this is hardly a surprising result. Since local residents care about the level of environmental quality, we should not expect that they would wish to push levels of pollution into the range where the willingness to pay to avoid environmental damage exceeds the loss in wage income from a cleaner environment. At the same time, this result is not immune to various "imperfections." If, for example, local governments are constrained constitutionally to use taxes on capital to finance various local public goods, then it is easy to show that not only will the tax rate on capital be positive, but officials will select socially excessive levels of pollution. Likewise, if Niskanen bureaucrats run the local public sector, they will choose excessively lax environmental standards as a mechanism to attract capital so as to expand the local tax base and public revenues. Finally, there can easily be conflicts among local groups of residents with differing interests (e.g., workers vs. nonworkers) that can lead to distorted outcomes (although these distortions may involve too little or too much pollution).

The basic model does at least suggest that there are some fundamental forces promoting efficient decentralized environmental decisions. If the regions selected for environmental decision making are sufficiently large to internalize the polluting effects of waste discharges, the case for environmental federalism has some force. Exploration of this issue is admittedly in its infancy—in particular, there is a pressing need for some systematic empirical study of the effects of "local" competition on environmental choices.[16]

## F. ENFORCEMENT ISSUES

The great bulk of the literature on the economics of environmental regulation simply assumes that polluters comply with existing directives: they either keep their discharges within the prescribed limitation or, under a fee scheme, report accurately their levels of emissions and pay the required fees. Sources, in short, are assumed *both* to act in good faith and to have full control over their levels of discharges so that violations of prescribed behavior do not occur.

Taking its lead from the seminal paper by Gary Becker (1968) on the economics of crime and punishment, a recent literature has addressed enforcement issues as they apply to environmental regulations.[17] As this literature points out, violations of environmental regulation can have two sources: a polluter can willfully exceed his discharge limitation (or underreport his emissions under a fee system) to reduce compliance costs *or* a stochastic dimension to discharges may exist so that the polluter has only imperfect control over his levels of emissions. In such a setting, the regulatory problem becomes a more complicated one. Not only must the regulatory agency set the usual policy parameters (emissions limitations or fees), but it must also decide upon an enforcement policy which involves both monitoring procedures and levels of fines for violations.

The early literature explored these enforcement issues in a wholly static framework. The seminal papers, for example, by Paul Downing and William Watson (1974) and by Jon Harford (1978), established a number of interesting results. Downing and Watson show that the incorporation of enforcement costs into the analysis of environmental policy suggests that optimal levels of pollution control will be less than when these costs are ignored. Harford obtains the especially interesting result that under a system of effluent fees, the level of *actual* discharges is independent both of the level of the fine for underreporting and of the probability of punishment (so long as the slope of the expected penalty function with respect to the size of the violation is increasing and the probability of punishment is greater than zero). The polluter sets the level of actual wastes such that marginal abatement cost equals the effluent fee—the efficient level! But he then, in general, underreports his discharges with the extent of underreporting varying inversely with the level of the fines and the probability of punishment.

Arun Malik (1990) has extended this line of analysis to the functioning of systems of marketable permits. He establishes a result analogous to Harford's: under certain circumstances, noncompliant polluters will emit precisely the same level of wastes for a given permit price as that discharged by an otherwise identical compliant firm. The conditions, however, for this equivalence are fairly stringent ones. More generally, Malik shows that noncompliant behavior will have effects on the market-clearing price in the permit market—effects that will compromise to some extent the efficiency properties of the marketable permit system.

One implication of this body of work is the expectation of widespread noncompliance on the part of polluters. But as Harrington (1988) points out, this seems not to be the case. The evidence we have from various spot checks by EPA and GAO suggests that most industrial polluters seem to be in compliance most of the time.[18] Substantial compliance seems to exist in spite of modest enforcement efforts: relatively few "notices of violation" have been issued and far fewer polluters have actually been fined for their violations. Moreover, where such fines have been levied, they have typically been quite small. And yet in spite of such modest enforcement efforts, "cheating" is not ubiquitous—violations are certainly not infrequent, but they are far from universal.

This finding simply doesn't square at all well with the results from the static models of polluter behavior.[19] An alternative line of modeling (drawing on the tax-evasion literature) seems to provide a better description of polluter behavior; it also has some potentially instructive normative implications. This approach puts the problem in a dynamic game-theoretic framework. Both polluters and regulators react to the activities of one another in the previous period. In a provocative paper, Harrington (1988) models the enforcement process as a Markov decision problem. Polluters that are detected in violation in one period are moved to a separate group in the next period in which they are subject to more frequent inspection and higher fines. Polluting firms thus have an incentive to comply in order to avoid being moved into the second group (from which they can return to the original group only after a period during which no violations are detected). In such a framework, firms may be in compliance even though they would be subject to no fine for a violation. Following up on Russell's analysis (Russel et al. 1986, 199–216), Harrington finds that the addition of yet a third group, an absorbing state from which the polluter can never emerge, can result in a "spectacular reduction in the minimum resources required to achieve a given level of compliance" (p. 47). In sum, the dynamic game-theoretic approach can produce compliance in cases in which the expected penalty is insufficient to prevent violations in a purely static model. Moreover, it suggests some potentially valuable guidelines for the design of cost-effective enforcement procedures. Enforcement is an area where economic analysis may make some quite useful contributions.

# G. THE EFFECTS OF DOMESTIC ENVIRONMENTAL POLICY ON PATTERNS OF INTERNATIONAL TRADE

The introduction of policy measures to protect the environment has potential implications not only for the domestic economy but also for international trade. Proposed environmental regulations are, in fact, often opposed vigorously on the grounds that they will impair the "international competitiveness" of domestic industries. The increased costs associated with pollution control measures will, so the argument goes, result in a loss of export markets and increased imports of products of polluting industries.

These potential effects have been the subject of some study. It is clear, for example, that the adoption of costly control measures in certain countries will, in principle, alter the international structure of relative costs with potential effects on patterns of specialization and world trade. These trade effects have been explored in some detail, making use of standard models of international trade (Kazumi Asako 1979; Baumol and Oates 1988, ch. 16; Anthony Koo 1974; Martin McGuire 1982; John Merrifield 1988; Rüdiger Pethig 1976; Pethig et al. 1980; Horst Siebert 1974; James Tobey 1989; Ingo Walter 1975). In particular, there has been a concern that the less developed countries, with their emphasis on economic development rather than environmental protection, will tend over time to develop a comparative advantage in pollution-intensive industries. In consequence, they will become the "havens" for the world's dirty industries; this concern has become known as the "pollution-haven hypothesis" (Walter and Judith Ugelow 1979; Walter 1982).

Some early studies made use of existing macroeconometric models to assess the likely magnitudes of these effects. These studies used estimates of the costs of pollution control programs on an industry basis to get some sense of the effects of these programs on trade and payments flows. Generally, they found small, but measurable, effects (d'Arge and Kneese 1971; Walter 1974).

We are now in a position to examine historically what has, in fact, happened. To what extent have environmental measures influenced the pattern of world trade? Have the LDC's become the havens of the world's dirty industries? Two recent studies, quite different in character, have addressed this issue directly. H. Jeffrey Leonard (1988), in what is largely a case study of trade and foreign-investment flows for several key industries and countries, finds little evidence that pollution-control measures have exerted a systematic effect on international trade and investment. After examining some aggregate figures, the policy stances in several industrialized and developed countries, and the operations of multinational corporations, Leonard concludes that "the differentials in the costs of complying with environmental regulations and in the levels of environmental concern in industrialized and industrializing countries have not been strong enough to offset larger political and economic forces in shaping aggregate international comparative advantage" (p. 231).

Tobey (1989, 1990) has looked at the same issue in a large econometric study of international trade patterns in "pollution-intensive" goods. After controlling for effects of relative factor abundance and other trade determinants, Tobey cannot find any effects of various measures of the stringency of domestic environmental policies. Tobey estimates two sets of equations that explain, respectively, patterns of trade in pollution-intensive goods and changes in trade patterns from 1970 to 1984. In neither set of equations do the variables measuring the stringency of domestic environmental policy have the predicted effect on trade patterns.

Why have domestic environmental measures not induced "industrial flight;" and the development of "pollution havens?" The primary reason seems to be that the costs of pollution control have not, in fact, loomed very large even in heavily polluting industries. Existing estimates suggest that control costs have run on the order of only 1 to 2½ percent of total costs in most pollution-intensive industries; H. David Robison (1985, p. 704), for example, reports that total abatement costs per dollar of output in 1977 were well under 3 percent in all industries with the sole exception of electric utilities where they were 5.4 percent. Such small increments to costs are likely to be swamped in their impact on international trade by the much larger effects of changing differentials in labor costs, swings in exchange rates, etc. Moreover, nearly all the industrialized countries have introduced environmental measures—and at roughly the same time—so that such measures have not been the source of significant cost differentials among major competitors. There seems not to have been a discernible movement in investment in these industries to the developing countries because major political and economic uncertainties have apparently loomed much larger in location decisions than have the modest savings from less stringent environmental controls.

In short, domestic environmental policies, at least to this point in time, do not appear to have had significant effects on patterns of international trade. From an environmental perspective, this is a comforting finding, for it means that there is little force to the argument that we need to relax environmental policies to preserve international competitiveness.

## H. COMMAND-AND-CONTROL VS. ECONOMIC INCENTIVES: SOME CONCLUDING OBSERVATIONS

Much of the literature in environmental economics, both theoretical and empirical, contrasts in quite sharp and uncompromising terms the properties of systems of economic incentives with the inferior outcomes under existing systems of command-and-control regulations. In certain respects, this literature has been a bit misleading and, perhaps, unfair. The term command-and-control encompasses a very broad and diverse set of regulatory techniques—some admittedly quite crude and excessively costly. But others are far more sophisticated and cost sensitive. In fact, the dividing line between so-called CAC and incentive-based policies is not always so clear. A program under which the regulator specifies the exact treatment procedures to be followed by polluters obviously falls within the CAC class. But what about a policy that establishes a fixed emissions limitation for a particular source (with no trading possible) but allows the polluter to select the form of compliance? Such flexibility certainly allows the operation of economic incentives in terms of the search for the least-cost method of control.

The point here is that it can be quite misleading to lump together in a cavalier fashion "CAC" methods of regulatory control and to contrast them as a class with the least-cost outcomes typically associated with systems of economic incentives. In fact, the compromises and "imperfections" inherent in the design and implementation of incentive-based systems virtually guarantee that they also will be unable to realize the formal least-cost result.

Empirical studies contrasting the cost effectiveness of the two general approaches have typically examined the cost under each system of attaining a specified *standard* of environmental quality—which typically means ensuring that at no point in an area do pollutant concentrations exceed the maximum level permissible under the particular standard. As Atkinson and Tietenberg (1982) and others have noted, CAC systems typically result in substantial "over-control" relative to incentive-based systems. Since it effectively assigns a zero shadow price to any environmental improvements over and above the standard, the least-cost algorithm attempts to make use of any "excess" environmental capacity to increase emissions and thereby reduce control costs. The less cost-sensitive CAC approaches generally overly restrict emissions (relative to the least-cost solution) and thereby produce pollutant concentrations at nonbinding points that are less than those under the least-cost outcome. In sum, at most points in the area, environmental quality (although subject to the same overall standard) will be higher under a CAC system than under the least-cost solution. So long as there is some value to improved environmental quality beyond the standard, a proper comparison of benefits and costs should give the CAC system credit for this increment to environmental quality. One recent study (Oates, Paul Portney, and McGartland 1989) which does just this for a major air pollutant finds that a relatively sophisticated CAC approach produces results that compare reasonably well to the prospective outcome under a fully cost effective system of economic incentives.

Our intent is not to suggest that the economist's emphasis on systems of economic incentives has been misplaced, but rather to argue that policy structure and analysis is a good deal more complicated than the usual textbooks would suggest (Nichols 1984). The applicability of systems of economic incentives is to some extent limited by monitoring capabilities and spatial complications. In fact, in any meaningful sense the "optimal" structure of regulatory programs for the control of air and water pollution is going to involve a combination of policy instruments—some making use of economic incentives and others not. Careful economic analysis has, we believe, an important role to play in understanding the workings of these systems. But it can make its best contribution, not through a dogmatic commitment to economic incentives, but rather by the careful analysis of the whole range of policy instruments available, insuring that those CAC measures that are adopted are effective devices for controlling pollution at relatively modest cost (Kolstad 1986).

At the same time, it is our sense that incentive-based systems have much to contribute to environmental protection—and that they have been much neglected in part because of the (understandable) predisposition of regulators to more traditional policy instruments.[20] There are strong reasons for believing, with supporting evidence, that this neglect has seriously impaired our efforts both to realize our objectives for improved environmental quality and to do so at the lowest cost. A general realization of this point seems to be emerging with a consequent renewed interest in many countries in the possibility of integrating incentive-based policies into environmental regulations.

* * *

## NOTES

We are grateful for many valuable comments on earlier drafts of this paper to a host of economists: Nancy Bockstael, Gardner Brown, Richard Carson, John Cumberland, Diane DeWitt, Anthony Fisher, A. Myrick Freeman, Tom Grigalunas, Winston Harrington, Robert Hahn, Charles Howe, Dale Jorgenson, Charles Kolstad, Ray Kopp, Allen Kneese, Alan Krupnick, Randolph Lyon, Ted McConnell, Albert McGartland, Robert Mitchell, Arun Malik, Roger Noll, Raymond Palmquist, John Pezzey, Paul Portney, V. Kerry Smith, Tom Tietenberg, and James Tobey. Finally, we want to thank Jonathan Dunn, Joy Hall, Dan Mussatti, and Rene Worley for their assistance in the preparation of the manuscript.

1. Although standards were to be set solely on the basis of health criteria, the 1970 Amendments to the Clean Air Act did include economic feasibility among its guidelines for setting source-specific standards. Roger Noll has suggested that the later 1977 Amendments were, in fact, more "anti-economic" than any that went before. See McCubbins et al. (1989) for a careful analysis of this legislation.

2. This is admittedly a highly simplified view of the policy process. There is surely some interplay in debate and negotiations between the determination of standards and the choice of policy instruments. More broadly, there is an emerging literature on the political economy of environmental policy that seeks to provide a better understanding of the process of instrument choice—see, for example, McCubbins et al. (1989), and Robert Hahn (1990).

3. There is also an interesting literature on incentive-compatible mechanisms to obtain abatement cost information from polluters—see, for example, Evan Kwerel (1977).

4. For a useful, comprehensive survey of the strengths and weaknesses of alternative policy instruments for pollution control, see Peter Bohm and Clifford Russell (1985).

5. In an interesting simulation study, Randolph Lyon (1982) finds that the cost of permits to sources under the auction system can be quite high; for one of the auction simulations, he finds that aggregate payments for permits will exceed treatment costs. Lyon's results thus suggest potentially large gains to polluting firms from a free distribution of permits instead of their sale through an auction. These gains, of course, are limited to current sources. Polluting firms that arrive on the scene at a later date will have to purchase permits from existing dischargers.

6. The OECD (1989) has recently provided a useful "catalog" and accompanying discussion of the use of economic incentives for environmental protection in the OECD countries.

7. One case in which there has been some use of fees in the U.S. is the levying of charges on industrial emissions into municipal waste treatment facilities. In some instances these charges have been based not only on the quantity but also on the

strength or quality of the effluent. The charges are often related to "average" levels of discharges and have had as their primary objective the raising of funds to help finance the treatment plants. Their role as an economic incentive to regulate levels of emissions has apparently been minor (see James Boland 1986; Baumol and Oates 1979, 258–63). There are also a variety of taxes on the disposal of hazardous wastes, including land disposal taxes in several states.

8. Tietenberg's book (1985) is an excellent, comprehensive treatment of the Emissions Trading Program. Robert Hahn and Gordon Hester have provided a series of recent and very valuable descriptions and assessments of all four of these programs of marketable permits. See Hahn and Hester (1989a,1989b), and Hahn (1989). For analyses of the Wisconsin TDP system, see William O'Neil (1983), and O'Neil et al. (1983).

9. In an interesting analysis of the experience with Emissions Trading, Roger Raufer and Stephen Feldman (1987) argue that some of the obstacles to trading could be circumvented by allowing the leasing of rights.

10. We should also note that various irregularities and illegal procedures were discovered in this market—perhaps because of lax oversight.

11. The major alternative to strict liability is a negligence rule under which a polluter is liable only if he has failed to comply with a "due standard of care" in the activity that caused the damages. Under strict liability, the party causing the damages is liable irrespective of the care exercised in the polluting activity.

12. As one reviewer noted, in these times of heightened environmental sensitivity, liability determinations could easily exceed actual damages in some instances. However, this seems not to have happened in the recent Exxon-Valdez case. The case was settled out of court with Exxon agreeing to pay some $900 million over a period of several years. Some observers believe that this falls well short of the true damages from the Exxon-Valdez oil spill in Alaska.

13. A more complicated and problematic issue relates to the permission of the courts to sue under Superfund for damages from toxic substances using "the joint and several liability doctrine." Under this provision, *each* defendant is potentially liable for an amount up to the *entire* damage, irrespective of his individual contribution. For an analysis of this doctrine in the Superfund setting, see Tietenberg (1989).

14. Two recent studies, one by Virginia McConnell and Schwab (1990), and the other by Timothy Bartik (1988c), find little evidence of strong effects of existing environmental regulations on the location decisions of firms within the U.S. This, of course, does not preclude the possibility that state and local officials, in fear of such effects, will scale down standards for environmental quality.

15. Using an alternative analytical framework in which local jurisdictions "bid" against one another for polluting firms in terms of entry fees, William Fischel (1975) likewise finds that local competition produces an efficient outcome.

16. For some other recent theoretical studies of interjurisdictional fiscal competition, see Jack Mintz and Henry Tulkens (1986), John Wilson (1986), David Wildasin (1989), and George Zodrow and Peter Mieszkowski (1986).

17. Russell, Harrington, and William Vaughan (1986, ch. 4) provide a useful survey of the enforcement literature in environmental economics up to 1985. Harrington (1988) presents a concise, excellent overview both of the more recent literature and of the "stylized facts" of actual compliance and enforcement behavior. See also Russell (1990).

18. Interestingly, noncompliance seems to be more widespread among municipal waste treatment plants than among industrial sources! (Russell 1990, 256). Some of the

most formidable enforcement problems involve federal agencies. The GAO (1988), for example, has found the Department of Energy's nuclear weapons facilities to be a source of major concern; the costs of dealing with environmental contamination associated with these facilities are estimated at more than $100 billion.

19. Perhaps public opprobrium is a stronger disciplinary force than economists are typically inclined to believe!

20. See Steven Kelman (1981) for a fascinating—if somewhat dismaying—study of the politics and ideology of economic incentives for environmental protection.

## REFERENCES

Asako, Kazumi. "Environmental Pollution in an Open Economy." *Economic Record 55:*151 (December 1979): 359–367.

Atkinson, Scott E., and Donald H. Lewis. "A Cost-Effectiveness Analysis of Alternative Air Quality Control Strategies." *Journal of Environmental Economics and Management 1:*3 (November 1974): 237–250.

Atkinson, Scott E., and T. H. Tietenberg. "The Empirical Properties of Two Classes of Designs for Transferable Discharge Permit Markets." *Journal of Environmental Economics and Management 9:*2 (June 1982): 101–121.

Bartik, Timothy J. "The Effects of Environmental Regulation on Business Location in the United States." *Growth Change 19:*3 (Summer 1988c): 22–44.

Baumol, William J., and Wallace E. Oates. "The Use of Standards and Prices for Protection of the Environment." *Swedish Journal of Economics 73:*1 (March 1971): 42–54.

———. *Economics, Environmental Policy, and Quality of Life.* New York: Prentice-Hall (1979).

———. *The Theory of Environmental Policy,* Second Edition. Cambridge, England: Cambridge University Press (1988).

Becker, Gary S. "Crime and Punishment: An Economic Approach," *Journal of Political Economy 76:*2 (March/April 1968): 169–217.

Bohm, Peter, and Clifford F. Russell. "Comparative Analysis of Alternative Policy Instruments," in *Handbook of Natural Resource and Energy Economics.* Volume 1. Eds.: Allen V. Kneese and James L. Sweeney. Amsterdam: North-Holland (1985): 395–460.

Boland, James. "Economic Instruments for Environmental Protection in the United States," ENV/ECO/86.14. Paris, France: Organization for Economic Cooperation and Development (September 11, 1986).

Bower, Blair et al. *Incentives in Water Quality Management: France and the Ruhr Area.* Washington, D.C.: Resources for the Future (1981).

Bressers, Hans. "The Effectiveness of Dutch Water Quality Policy." *Mimeo.* The Netherlands: Twente University of Technology, 1983.

Brown, Gardner, Jr., and Hans Bressers. "Evidence Supporting Effluent Charges." *Mimeo.* The Netherlands: Twente University of Technology (September 1986).

Brown, Gardner, Jr., and Ralph W. Johnson. "Pollution Control by Effluent Charges: It Works in the Federal Republic of Germany, Why Not in the U.S." *Natural Resource Journal 24*:4 (October 1984): 929–966.

Cumberland, John H. "Efficiency and Equity in Interregional Environmental Management," *Review of Regional Studies 10*:2 (Fall 1981): 1–9.

Dales, John Harkness. *Pollution, Property, and Prices.* Toronto, Ontario: University of Toronto Press (1968).

D'Arge, Ralph C., and Allen V. Kneese. "International Trade, Domestic Income, and Environmental Controls: Some Empirical Estimates," in *Managing the Environment: International Economic Cooperation for Pollution Control.* Eds.: Allen V. Kneese, Sidney E. Rolfe, and Joseph W. Harned. New York: Praeger (1971): 289–315.

Dewees, Donald N. "Instrument Choice in Environmental Policy." *Economic Inquiry 21*:1 (January 1983): 53–71.

Downing, Paul B., and William D. Watson, Jr. "The Economics of Enforcing Air Pollution Controls," *Journal of Environmental Economics and Management 1*:3 (November 1974): 219–236.

Fischel, William A. "Fiscal and Environmental Considerations in the Location of Firms in Suburban Communities," in *Fiscal Zoning and Land Use Controls.* Eds.: Edwin S. Mills and Wallace E. Oates. Lexington, Massachusetts: Heath (1975): 119–173.

Grigalunas, Thomas A., and James J. Opaluch. "Assessing Liability for Damages Under CERCLA: A New Approach for Providing Incentives for Pollution Avoidance?" *Natural Resource Journal 28*:3 (Summer 1988): 509–533.

Hahn, Robert W. "Market Power and Transferable Property Rights," *Quarterly Journal of Economics 99*:4 (November 1984): 753–765.

———. "Economic Prescriptions for Environmental Problems: How the Patient Followed the Doctor's Orders," *Journal of Economic Perspectives 3*:2 (Spring 1989): 95–114.

———. "The Political Economy of Environmental Regulation: Towards a Unifying Framework," *Public Choice 65*:1 (April 1990): 21–47.

Hahn, Robert W., and Gordon L. Hester. "Marketable Permits: Lessons for Theory and Practice," *Ecology Law Quarterly 16*:2 (1989a): 361–406.

———. "Where Did All the Markets Go? An Analysis of EPA's Emissions Trading Program," *Yale Journal of Regulation 6*:1 (Winter 1989b): 109–153.

Hahn, Robert W., and Roger G. Noll. "Designing a Market for Tradable Emission Permits," in *Reform of Environmental Regulation.* Ed.: Wesley Magat. Cambridge, Massachusetts: Ballinger (1982): 119–146.

Harford, Jon D. "Firm Behavior Under Imperfectly Enforceable Pollution Standards and Taxes," *Journal of Environmental Economics and Management 5*:1 (March 1978): 26–43.

Harrington, Winston. "Enforcement Leverage When Penalties Are Restricted." *Journal of Public Economics 37*:1 (October 1988): 29–53.

Harrington, Winston; Alan J. Krupnick, and Henry M. Peskin. "Policies for Nonpoint-Source Water Pollution Control." *Journal of Soil and Water Conservation 40* (January–February 1985): 27–32.

Harrison, David H. "The Regulation of Aircraft Noise," in *Incentives for Environmental Protection*. Ed.: Thomas C. Schelling. Cambridge, Massachusetts: MIT Press (1983): 41–143.

Johnson, Ralph W., and Gardner M. Brown, Jr. *Cleaning up Europe's Waters*. New York: Praeger (1976).

Kelman, Steven J. *What Price Incentives? Economists and the Environment*. Boston, Massachusetts: Auburn House (1981).

Kneese, Allen V., and Blair T. Bower. *Managing Water Quality: Economics, Technology, Institutions*. Baltimore, Maryland: Johns Hopkins University Press for Resources for the Future (1968).

Kolstad, Charles D. "Empirical Properties of Economic Incentives and Command-and-Control Regulations for Air Pollution Control." *Land Economics 62*:3 (August 1986): 205–268.

———. "Uniformity versus Differentiation in Regulating Externalities." *Journal of Environmental Economics and Management 14*:4 (December 1987): 386–399

Koo, Anthony Y. C. "Environmental Repercussions and Trade Theory." *Review of Economics and Statistics 56*:2 (May 1974): 235–244.

Krupnick, Alan J. "Costs of Alternative Policies for the Control of NO₂ in the Baltimore Region." Unpub. working paper. Washington, D.C.: Resources for the Future (1983).

Krupnick, Alan J.; Wallace E. Oates, and Eric Van De Verg. "On Marketable Air-Pollution Permits: The Case for a System of Pollution Offsets." *Journal of Environmental Economics and Management 10*:3 (September 1983): 233–247.

Kwerel, Evan R. "To Tell the Truth: Imperfect Information and Optimal Pollution Control." *Review of Economic Studies 44*:3 (October 1977): 595–601.

Lee, Dwight R. and Walter S. Misiolek. "Substituting Pollution Taxation for General Taxation: Some Implications for Efficiency in Pollution Taxation." *Journal of Environmental Economics and Management 13*:4 (December 1986): 338–347.

Leonard, H. Jeffrey. *Pollution and the Struggle for the World Product*. Cambridge, England Cambridge University Press (1988).

Lyon, Randolph M. "Auctions and Alternative Procedures for Allocating Pollution Rights," *Land Economics 58*:1 (February 1982): 16–32.

Magat, Wesley A. "Pollution Control and Technological Advance: A Dynamic Model of the Firm." *Journal of Environmental Economics and Management 5*:1 (March 1978): 1–25.

Malik, Arun. "Markets for Pollution Control When Firms Are Noncompliant." *Journal of Environmental Economics and Management 18*:2, Part 1 (March 1990): 97–106.

McConnell, Virginia D., and Robert M. Schwab. "The Impact of Environmental Regulation in Industry Location Decisions: The Motor Vehicle Industry." *Land Economics 66* (February 1990): 67–81.

McCubbins, Matthew D., Roger G. Noll, and Barry R Weingast. "Structure and Process, Politics and Policy: Administrative Arrangements and the Political Control of Agencies." *Virginia Law Review 75*:2 (March 1989): 431–482.

McGartland, Albert M. *Marketable Permit Systems for Air Pollution Control: An Empirical Study*. Ph.D. Dissertation, University of Maryland, College Park, Maryland (1984).

———. "A Comparison of Two Marketable Discharge Permits Systems," *Journal of Environmental Economics and Management 15:1 (*March 1988): 35–44.

McGartland, Albert M., and Wallace E. Oates. "Marketable Permits for the Prevention of Environmental Deterioration." *Journal of Environmental Economics and Management 12*:3 (September 1985): 207–228.

McGuire, Martin. "Regulation, Factor Rewards, and International Trade." *Journal of Public Economics17:3 (*April 1982): 335–354.

Merrifield, John D. "The Impact of Selected Abatement Strategies on Transnational Pollution, the Terms of Trade, and Factor Rewards: A General Equilibrium Approach." *Journal of Environmental Economics and Management 15*:3 (September 1988): 259–284.

Milliman, Scott R., and Raymond Prince. "Firm Incentives to Promote Technological Change in Pollution Control." *Journal of Environmental Economics and Management 17*:3 (November 1989): 247–265.

Mintz, Jack M., and Henry Tulkens. "Commodity Tax Competition Between Member States of a Federation: Equilibrium and Efficiency." *Journal of Public Economic 29*:2 (March 1986): 133–172.

Montgomery, W. David. "Markets in Licenses and Efficient Pollution Control Programs." *Journal of Economic Theory 5*:3 (December 1972): 395–418.

Nichols, Albert L. *Targeting Economic Incentives for Environmental Protection*. Cambridge, Massachusetts: MIT Press (1984).

Oates, Wallace E.; Paul R. Portney, and Albert M. McGartland. "The *Net* Benefits of Incentive-based Regulation: A Case Study of Environmental Standard Setting." *American Economic Review 79*:5 (December 1989): 1233–1242.

Oates, Wallace E., and Robert M. Schwab. "Economic Competition Among Jurisdictions: Efficiency Enhancing or Distortion Inducing?" *Journal of Public Economics 35*:3 (April 1988a): 333–354.

———. "The Theory of Regulatory Federalism: The Case of Environmental Management." Working Paper No. 88-26, Dept. of Economics. University of Maryland (1988b).

O'Neil, William B. "The Regulation of Water Pollution Permit Trading Under Conditions of Varying Streamflow and Temperature," in *Buying a Better Environment: Cost-Effective Regulation Through Permit Trading*. Eds. Erhard F. Joeres and Martin H. David. Madison, Wisconsin: University of Wisconsin Press (1983): 219–231.

O'Neil, William, et al. "Transferable Discharge Permits and Economic Efficiency: The Fox River." *Journal of Environmental Economics and Management 10*:94 (December 1983): 346–355.

Opaluch, James J., and Thomas A. Grigalunas. "Controlling Stochastic Pollution Events through Liability Rules: Some Evidence from OCS Leasing." *Rand Journal of Economics* 15:1 (Spring 1984): 142–151.

Organization for Economic Cooperation and Development. *The Application of Economic Instruments for Environmental Protection*. Paris: OECD (1989).

Palmer, Adele R., et al. "Economic Implications of Regulating Chlorofluorocarbon Emissions from Nonaerosol Applications." Report R-2524-EPA. Santa Monica, California: Rand Corporation (1980).

Peltzman, Sam, and T. Nicolaus Tideman. "Local versus National Pollution Control: Note," *American Economic Review* 62:5 (December 1972): 959–963.

Pethig, Rüdiger. "Pollution, Welfare, and Environmental Policy in the Theory of Comparative Advantage." *Journal of Environmental Economics and Management* 2:3 (February 1976): 160–169.

Pethig, Rüdiger, et al. *Trade and Environment: A Theoretical Inquiry.* Amsterdam: Elsevier (1980).

Raufer, Roger K., and Stephen L. Feldman. *Acid Rain and Emissions Trading*. Totowa, New Jersey: Rowman & Littlefield (1987).

Robison, H. David. "Who Pays for Industrial Pollution Abatement?" *Review of Economics and Statistics* 67:4 (November 1985): 702–706.

Russell, Clifford S. "Monitoring and Enforcement," in *Public Policies for Environmental Protection*. Ed.: Paul Portney. Washington, D.C.: Resources for the Future (1990): 243–274.

Russell, Clifford S.; Winston Harrington, and William J. Vaughan. *Enforcing Pollution Control Laws*. Washington D.C.: Resources for the Future (1986).

Segerson, Kathleen. "Uncertainty and Incentives for Nonpoint Pollution Control." *Journal of Environmental Economics and Management 15:1* (March 1988): 87–98.

———. "Institutional 'Markets': The Role of Liability in Allocating Environmental Resources," in *Proceedings of AERE Workshop on Natural Resource Market Mechanisms*. Association of Environmental and Resource Economists (June 1990).

Seskin, Eugene P., Robert J. Anderson, Jr., and Robert O. Reid. "An Empirical Analysis of Economic Strategies for Controlling Air Pollution." *Journal of Environmental Economics and Management 10:2* (June 1983): 112–124.

Shavell, Steven. "A Model of the Optimal Use of Liability and Safety Regulations." *Rand Journal of Economics 15:2* (Summer 1984a): 271–280.

———. "Liability for Harm versus Regulation of Safety." *Journal of Legal Studies 13:2* (1984b): 357–374.

Siebert, Horst. "Environmental Protection and International Specialization." *Weltwirtsch. Arch. 110:3* (1974): 494–508.

Spofford, Walter O., Jr. "Efficiency Properties of Alternative Control Policies for Meeting Ambient Air Quality Standards: An Empirical Application to the Lower Delaware Valley." Discussion Paper D-118. Washington, D.C.: Resources for the Future (February 1984).

Stavins, Robert N., ed. *Project 88—Harnessing Market Forces to Protect Our Environment: Initiatives for the New President.* A Public Policy Study Sponsored by Senator Timothy E. Wirth, Colorado, and Senator John Heinz, Pennsylvania. Washington, D.C. (December 1988).

Terkla, David. "The Efficiency Value of Effluent Tax Revenues." *Journal of Environmental Economics and Management 11:2* (June 1984): 107–123.

Tietenberg, Thomas H. "Spatially Differentiated Air Pollutant Emission Charges: An Economic and Legal Analysis." *Land Economics 54:93* (August 1978): 265–277.

————. "Transferable Discharge Permits and the Control of Stationary Source Air Pollution: A Survey and Synthesis." *Land Economics 56:4* (November 1980): 391–416.

————. *Emissions Trading: An Exercise in Reforming Pollution Policy.* Washington, D.C.: Resources for the Future (1985).

————. "Indivisible Toxic Torts: The Economics of Joint and Several Liability." *Land Economics 65* (November 1989): 305–319.

————. "Economic Instruments for Environmental Regulation." *Oxford Review of Economic Policy 6* (March 1990).

Tobey, James A. "The Impact of Domestic Environmental Policies on International Trade." Ph.D. dissertation, Department of Economics, University of Maryland, College Park (1989).

————. "The Effects of Domestic Environmental Policies on Patterns of World Trade: An Empirical Test." *Kyklos (*1990) Fasc. 2.

Walter, Ingo. "Pollution and Protection: U.S. Environmental Controls as Competitive Distortions." *Welwirtsch. Arch. 110:1* (1974): 104–113.

————. "Trade, Environment and Comparative Advantage." in *International Economics of Pollution.* Ed.: Ingo Walter. New York: Wiley (1975): 77–93.

————. "Environmentally Induced Industrial Relocation in Developing Countries." in *Environment and Trade.* Eds.: Seymour J. Rubin and Thomas R. Graham. Totowa, New Jersey: Allanheld, Osmun and Co., (1982): 67–101.

Walter, Ingo, and Judith Ugelow. "Environmental Policies in Developing Countries." *Ambio 8:2,3,* (1979): 102–109.

Wenders, John T. "Methods of Pollution Control and the Rate of Change in Pollution Abatement Technology." *Water Resources Research 11:3* (1975): 393–396.

Wildasin, David E. "Interjurisdictional Capital Mobility: Fiscal Externality and a Corrective Subsidy." *Journal of Urban Economics 25:2* (March 1989): 193–212.

Wilson, John D. "A Theory of Interregional Tax Competition." *Journal of Urban Economics 19:3* (May 1986): 296–315.

Zodrow, George R., and Peter Mieszkowski. "Pigou, Tiebout, Property Taxation and the Under-Provision of Local Public Goods." *Journal of Urban Economics 19:3* (May 1986): 356–370.

# S E L E C T I O N    5

Michael Grossman, Jody L. Sindelar,
John Mullahy, and Richard Anderson

# Alcohol and Cigarette Taxes

Much public policy attention has been focused on proposals to increase federal excise taxes on alcohol and tobacco. Optimal tax policy in this area depends critically upon one's particular perspectives and objectives. For example, public health officials and economists tend to differ greatly in their rationales for taxing alcohol and cigarettes. From a medical perspective, these "sin taxes" are a way to "help people help themselves" eliminate bad habits. Economists, on the other hand, use two distinctly different types of arguments: First, based on externality theory, excise taxes should be levied on the commodities in order to correct for external costs. This is the same justification used for levying a penalty tax on polluting firms. Second, the best way to collect a certain amount of tax revenue is to levy the highest excise taxes on commodities with the lowest price elasticities. Many believe alcohol and cigarette price-elasticities qualify these goods for this type of taxation.

Michael Grossman, Jody Sindelar, John Mullahy, and Richard Anderson discuss how taxes on alcohol and tobacco affect consumption, and investigate how higher taxes may help to internalize negative externalities. Implications for raising tax revenues are also examined. Estimates of price elasticities of demand vary greatly, and thus play a crucial role in determining the effects of taxing these products. For instance, if demand is inelastic, then the increase in price from a higher tax rate

Grossman, Michael; Jody L. Sindelar; John Mullahy; and Richard Anderson. "Alcohol and Cigarette Taxes." *Journal of Economic Perspectives* 7 (Fall 1993): 211–222. This selection is an abridged version of the original article.

**Michael Grossman** is Distinguished Professor of Economics at City University of New York Graduate School, and Research Associate and Program Director of Health Economics at the National Bureau of Economic Research. **Jody Sindelar** is Associate Professor at the Yale University School of Public Health and Research Associate at National Bureau of Economic Research. **John Mullahy** is Associate Professor of Economics at Trinity College and Research Associate at National Bureau of Economic Research. **Richard Anderson** is Assistant Professor of Economics at Jersey City State College.

could yield significant amounts of new tax revenues—by one estimate, $18 billion a year from additional cigarette taxation. But the greatest declines in consumption would occur if demand is price elastic—the lives of over 1,000 people aged 18 to 20 might have been saved each year if the 1951 beer tax had been indexed to the rate of inflation.

### Questions to Guide the Reading

1. If adjusted for inflation since 1951, what would be the federal excise tax rates on cigarettes, beer and wine, and distilled spirits?
2. Aside from taxation, what deterrents to smoking and drinking have been attempted?
3. Why are cigarette smoking and alcohol consumption not linked in the same way to adverse health effects? How might this complicate tax policy, especially with respect to teenagers and young adults?
4. The "rational addiction" framework predicts that even consumers of addictive commodities will change their consumption when the prices change—in essence, contradicting the view that the price elasticity of demand for addictive substances is zero. How do the empirical studies cited by the authors support this prediction? What are the implications of these studies for increases in federal excise taxes on cigarettes and on alcohol?
5. In what ways do smokers and alcohol abusers bear less than the full costs of their habits? What types of costs are considered external by some economists, but internal by others?
6. What estimates of appropriate tax rates for cigarettes and alcohol are presented by the authors? Upon what economic perspective are these estimates based?

## INTRODUCTION

Increased excise taxes on cigarettes and alcohol were suggested as a means to finance (at least partially) the Clinton administration's proposed program of health care reform. From a public health perspective, these tax hikes are appealing because cigarette smoking and alcohol abuse have detrimental health effects. Politically, sin tax increases are increasingly acceptable, especially (in light of the sharply declining number of smokers) for cigarettes. From an economic efficiency perspective, these tax hikes may be justified because smokers and alcohol abusers impose costs on others which exceed current tax levels. From a revenue raising perspective, higher tax rates would be justified if the demand functions for alcohol and cigarettes were relatively inelastic.

The federal excise tax rates on cigarettes and alcohol have been stable in nominal terms for long periods of time. The federal excise tax rate on cigarettes was fixed at 8 cents per pack between November 1, 1951, and the end of 1982. It rose to 16 cents per pack effective January 1, 1983, as part of the Tax Equity and Fiscal Responsibility Act of 1982. The tax was increased further to 20 cents per pack effective January 1, 1991, and to 24 cents per pack effective January 1, 1992, as part of the Omnibus Budget Reconciliation Act of 1990. But if the tax had simply been adjusted for inflation since 1951, it would be 42 cents per pack today.

January 1,1991, marked the first increases in the federal excise tax rates on beer and wine since November 1, 1951. In addition, the tax rate on distilled spirits—increased by about 19 percent effective October 1, 1985, as part of the Deficit Reduction Act of 1984—was raised for only the second time since 1951. As part of the Omnibus Reconciliation Act of 1990, the tax on beer doubled from 16 cents per six-pack to 32 cents, the tax on wine jumped from just over 3 cents per 750 milliliter bottle to about 21 cents, and the tax on a 750 milliliter bottle of 80 proof distilled spirits rose from $1.98 to $2.14. But the distilled spirits tax rate would have to be 75 percent higher and the beer tax rate would have to be 162 percent higher to maintain their real values as of 1951.[1]

Since the first Surgeon General's Report on Smoking and Health in 1964, federal and state governments have carried out policies designed to increase public knowledge about the harmful effects of smoking, along with restrictions on advertising by cigarette manufacturers, and assuring no-smoking areas in public places and in the workplace. A similar campaign to reduce alcohol-involved motor vehicle deaths dates to the mid-1970s, a program which has included higher minimum legal ages for the purchase and consumption of alcoholic beverages, and stricter penalties for drunk driving. The relative stability of tax rates on cigarettes and alcohol is somewhat inconsistent with these campaigns (Grossman 1989; Grossman et al. forthcoming). In fact, the real prices of alcohol and cigarettes (their prices after accounting for the effects of inflation) have declined significantly for long periods during which the campaigns have been in effect, as shown in Figure 1.[2] In what follows, we will address some key issues involved in raising these taxes.

## REVENUE POTENTIAL OF CIGARETTE AND ALCOHOL TAX HIKES

Two alternative proposals to increase the federal excise tax on cigarettes were discussed extensively when President Clinton formed his Task Force on National Health Care Reform in January 1993: an increase from 24 cents a pack to 48 cents a pack and an increase to $2.24 a pack. The Congressional Budget Office (1993) estimates that the former policy would increase tax revenue from the $5 billion figure yielded by the 24-cent tax in 1992 to $8 billion in the first year of the tax hike. This projection is based on a demand function for cigarettes with a constant price elasticity equal to –0.40 (personal conversation with Frank Sammartino of CBO).

**Figure 1**   Real Alcohol and Cigarette Prices, 1975–1992

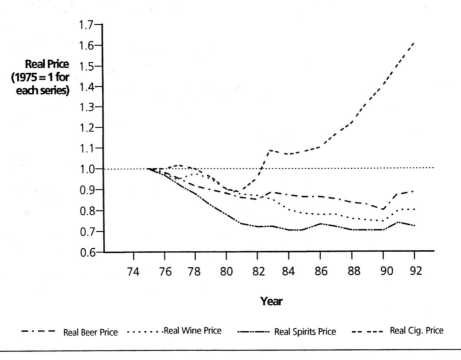

Source: Distilled spirits prices from 1975 through 1977 are based on the whiskey price index. Alcoholic beverage prices and the Consumer Price Index for all items are from Bureau of Labor Statistics, U.S. Department of Labor, *Monthly Labor Review,* various issues, and *Consumer Price Index–Detailed Report,* various issues. Cigarette prices are from the Tobacco Institute, *The Tax Burden on Tobacco,* Volume 27, Washington, D.C., 1992. All four prices include federal and state excise taxes.

Based on unstated assumptions, the Congressional Joint Committee on Taxation estimates that a $2 a pack tax hike would yield $18 billion a year in additional revenue (unpublished memorandum). Using a lower and constant price elasticity of approximately –0.50, Harris (1993) offers computations that indicate a revenue increase of $28 billion. Based on the cigarette demand functions obtained by Becker, Grossman, and Murphy (1993) and by Chaloupka (1991), Grossman (1993) predicts that a tax rate of $1.26 a pack would maximize federal revenue from the excise tax at $16 billion. Higher tax rates, such as the $2.24 suggested by Harris, would yield less additional revenue than the $11 billion generated by a tax hike of $1.02 from 24 cents to $1.26. Grossman's computations are based on a linear demand function, rather than one with a constant elasticity, so that the higher taxes at some point lead to such substantial decreases in demand that total tax revenue falls.[3]

The pure alcohol in one ounce of distilled spirits is currently taxed at about 21 cents, which is substantially higher than the 10 cents per ounce for beer or 8 cents per ounce for wine. Before the 1990 legislation was enacted, the Bush administration proposed taxing the pure alcohol in any alcoholic beverage at 25 cents per ounce. This policy would raise the tax on a 750 milliliter bottle of distilled spirits from $2.14 to $2.54, the tax on a six-pack of beer from 32 cents to 81 cents, and the tax on a 750 milliliter bottle of table wine from 21 cents to 70 cents. Clinton administration officials have revived the proposal, although the president has not supported it.

The Congressional Budget Office (1993) estimates that such a tax increase would increase federal revenue from alcohol excise taxes from the $8 billion figure yielded by the current taxes to $12 billion in the first year. Higher beer tax revenue accounts for 73 percent of this $4 billion increase, with higher wine and spirits revenue accounting for 19 percent and 8 percent, respectively. These projections assume constant price elasticities of demand for beer, wine, and spirits equal to –0.30, –0.70, and –0.80, respectively. They also assume no cross substitution among beverages (personal conversation with Frank Samartino of CBO).

## EFFECTS ON CONSUMPTION AND RELATED OUTCOMES

Much of the research on how prices of alcohol and tobacco affect consumption capitalizes on the substantial variation in their prices across states, primarily because of the very different state tax rates on these goods. It controls in a variety of ways for factors such as pro- and antismoking or drinking sentiment that may jointly determine tax rates and consumption. Before turning to a discussion of this research, we must address some conceptual issues.

First, cigarette smoking and alcohol use are not linked to adverse health consequences in the same way. There is overwhelming evidence that smoking has detrimental health effects. One can usefully focus on whether and how much individuals smoke since these measures are highly correlated with the smoking-related costs of interest. With alcohol, the situation is more complex. Unlike cigarettes, many persons regularly consume small quantities of alcohol. Most individuals who consume alcohol do not harm themselves or others; indeed, some evidence suggests that moderate alcohol consumption lowers the risk of coronary heart disease in men (Rimm et al. 1991). Instead, the adverse effects of alcohol spring from overuse (cirrhosis of the liver) or misuse (drunk driving crashes). For these reasons, we emphasize outcomes other than per capita alcohol consumption by all segments of the population.

Second, since current consumption is positively related to past consumption for addictive goods, the response to higher taxes grows over time. For example, a hike in the price of cigarettes in 1993 would reduce consumption in 1993, which would cause consumption in 1994 and all future years to fall.[4] Under certain circumstances, the long-run price elasticity rises as the degree of addiction rises (Becker, Grossman, and Murphy 1991; Becker 1992).

Third, it is important to focus on teenagers and young adults, because cigarette smoking and alcohol abuse are addictive behaviors that generally begin early in life. Thus, policies to prevent their onset might be the most effective means to reduce them in all segments of the population (Mullahy and Sindelar 1990b; forthcoming). The focus on the younger age group is particularly urgent for alcohol, because motor vehicle accident mortality is the leading cause of death of persons under the age of 35, and alcohol is involved in over half these fatal accidents (National Highway Traffic Safety Administration 1986). Youths are more sensitive to changes in money prices of addictive goods, whereas adults respond more to changes in the perceived or actual harmful consequences that take place in the future. This is because future costs tend to be less important to younger consumers since they have lower time discount factors, and because youths have more stringent budget constraints. Interactions between peer pressure and addiction also predict greater price sensitivity by youths. Bandwagon or peer effects are much more important in the case of youth smoking or alcohol consumption than in the case of adult smoking or alcohol consumption. To the extent that higher taxes help prevent a bandwagon effect, such taxes will have larger effects on youth.

Cigarette demand functions estimated in the context of the rational addiction model (Becker and Murphy 1988) yield long-run price elasticities for per capita consumption (at the mean values of consumption and price) that range from –0.45 to –0.75. The corresponding range of short-run price elasticities is –0.20 to –0.45 (Chaloupka 1991; Becker, Grossman, and Murphy 1993; Keeler et al. 1993). Clearly, an increase in the federal excise tax rate on cigarettes is a potent policy to curtail smoking

Higher cigarette prices may result in diverse changes in smoking behavior. Some smokers maintain their rates of smoking by substituting discount brands—which now account for almost one-third of the cigarette market—for the more expensive name brands. Smokers who reduce the number of cigarettes consumed may compensate by switching to higher tar and nicotine brands, by inhaling more deeply, or by reducing idle burn time. But more than half of the effect of a higher price on cigarette consumption is due to a reduction in the number of smokers (Lewit, Coate, and Grossman 1981; Lewit and Coate 1982; Wasserman et al. 1991), so the factor of more intense smoking can be given fairly minor weight in evaluating the impact of excise tax changes.

The demand elasticity studies also indicate that the elasticities for youth participating in smoking are larger than adult smoking participation elasticities. The relevant figures are –1.20 for youths aged 12–17, –0.74 for 20–25 year olds, –0.44 for 26–35 years olds, and –0.15 for persons above the age of 35 (Lewit, Coate, and Grossman 1981; Lewit and Coate 1982).[5] Because of its effect in discouraging teenage smoking participation, a tax increase that is maintained in real terms over a period of several decades could decrease aggregate smoking substantially.

With regard to youth alcohol consumption, the incidence of frequent consumption and the incidence of heavy consumption appear inversely related to the price of alcohol (Grossman, Coate, and Arluck 1987; Coate and Grossman 1988; Kenkel 1993; Grossman et al., forthcoming.)[6] Kenkel (1993) reports that the price elasticity of demand for the heavy drinking outcome is –0.92 for persons 18 years of age and older, while it is –2.24 for youth between the ages of 18 and 21. This suggests that young drinkers, like young smokers, are quite sensitive to price. Kenkel also reports a strong positive association between the number of days with five or more drinks of alcohol in the past year and the reported number of occasions of drunk driving in the past year.

Alcohol abuse can cause deaths in motor vehicles and from liver cirrhosis and other diseases. If the federal excise tax on beer had been indexed to the rate of inflation since 1951, the lives of about 1,022 youths aged 18 to 20 who died in motor vehicle accidents would have been saved in a typical year in the 1975–81 period (Saffer and Grossman 1987). Chaloupka, Saffer, and Grossman (1993) report that the beer tax policy would have had an even larger effect in the 1980s, saving about 1,660 lives per year in the 1982–88 period. The same policy would have prevented over 5,000 people of all ages from being killed annually in fatal motor vehicle crashes.

Cook and Tauchen (1982) report that a $1 increase in the state excise tax rate on a gallon of distilled spirits lowers the age-adjusted cirrhosis mortality rate by approximately the same percentage as it lowers per capita consumption of distilled spirits. In the context of the rational addiction model, Chaloupka et al. (1993) find that the long-run price elasticity of demand for distilled spirits is –1.00, substantially larger than the short-run elasticity of –0.79. The estimates indicate either that heavy drinkers greatly reduce their consumption when alcohol becomes more expensive or that the number of heavy drinkers is sensitive to the price of alcohol.

Along with these deaths, alcohol abuse has a number of other harmful side effects. Chaloupda and Saffer (1992) and Cook and Moore (1992b) find that increases in alcoholic beverage excise tax rates would lead to significant reductions in crime rates. For example, Chaloupka and Saffer predict that a doubling of the federal beer tax would reduce total crimes by approximately 1.3 percent, murders by 3 percent, rapes by 3 percent, robberies by 4.7 percent, and burglaries and thefts by 1.3 percent each. Ohsfeldt, Morrisey, and Henderlite (1991) estimate that a 12 percent increase in the beer tax in 1989 would have resulted in about 130,000 fewer industrial injury cases among full-time workers. Furthermore, the tax increase would have lowered work-loss days resulting from industrial injuries by 1.5 million in 1989. Cook and Moore (1992a) document that school completion rates are positively related to state beer tax rates.

Some concern has been expressed that raising the price of alcohol may lead to the substitution of illegal drugs. For example, Chaloupka and Laixuthai (1992) and DiNardo and Lemieux (1992) find that marijuana and alcohol are substitutes. But the lower motor vehicle mortality rates in states with relatively high beer excise tax rates suggest that, while marijuana may have some impact on the ability to drive an automobile, any substitution does not offset the gains from reducing alcohol consumption.

## INDIRECT COSTS, EXTERNAL COSTS, AND OPTIMAL SIN TAXES

The optimal rate of taxation for cigarettes and alcohol is hotly debated. Public health officials often favor imposing taxes to help people help themselves to adopt healthier behaviors. Economists tend to argue that if individuals are informed about their choices and yet still choose to consume cigarettes and alcohol, consumer sovereignty should reign, and taxes should be imposed only to correct for externalities. Still others argue for maximizing tax revenue, or collecting revenue in a manner that minimizes welfare losses due to price distortions.

In their penetrating and comprehensive study of the external costs of smoking and drinking, Manning et al. (1989, 1991) point out that the principal common external cost of these behaviors, and the most important external cost of smoking, is the fact that premiums paid by smokers and alcohol abusers for health and life insurance do not fully reflect their excess use of medical care services and their higher probability of premature death.[7] While many external costs will be captured by thinking about the consequences in the insurance market, others will not. Consider, for example, a sober passenger who knowingly agrees to ride in a motor vehicle operated by an intoxicated driver: If the driver causes a crash in which the passenger is killed, is this premature death an external cost of alcohol abuse, or was the risk taken voluntarily (and thus internalized) by the passenger?

Other controversial issues arise for both smoking and drinking. Is the harm done to their fetuses by pregnant women who smoke and drink excessively an external cost? What about the detrimental health effects suffered by nonsmokers from secondhand smoke, estimated to include annually roughly 3,000 lung cancer deaths as well as a host of other respiratory illnesses (U.S. EPA 1992)? Manning et al. (1989, 1991) treat most of the costs associated with such outcomes as internal costs. Hay (1991) criticizes this treatment, possibly because the decisions at issue are made with less than full information. The extent to which information is imperfect is yet to be resolved. Individuals are likely to be aware of some costs, like passive smoking and fetal alcohol syndrome, yet may overestimate others. For instance, Viscusi (1992) cites survey results that both smokers and nonsmokers overestimate the probability of death and illness from tobacco, and that teenagers attach a higher risk to smoking than the rest of the population.

Even if smoking, drinking, and imperfect information engender costs that are ignored by consumers, government intervention in general—and taxation in particular—are not necessarily the best remedies. For example, parents may be better able to internalize the costs ignored by their children than the government. Further, more vigorous enforcement of laws restricting the use of tobacco in public places (Viscusi, 1992) or of drunk driving laws may be preferable to higher tax rates, although the costs of enforcement may favor the tax policy. These issues will continue to be debated.

With these warnings in mind, we present some estimates of the social costs and implied optimal tax rates on cigarettes and alcohol. These tax rates are from the perspective of taxing to correct for externalities. Manning et al. (1989, 1991) estimate that a tax of 19 cents on a pack of cigarettes would have equaled the per pack external cost of smoking (in 1991). This figure excludes the costs of low birthweight and passive smoking, which might be measured by the cost of premature death and the cost of neonatal intensive care. If these costs are treated as externalities, the optimal tax becomes 65 cents, and this upper-bound figure exceeded the average federal and state tax of 44 cents on a pack of cigarettes in 1991. Based on these estimates, a tax hike in excess of 24 cents could not be justified on externality grounds. However, Manning et al. exclude the long-term intellectual and physical developmental consequences of low birthweight. Hay (1991) estimates that the inclusion of these costs raises the optimal tax to more than $4.80 a pack. Clearly, the range of choice here is considerable, particularly since programs to modify the behavior of pregnant women who smoke are alternatives to a broad-based cigarette tax.

The story with respect to alcohol is somewhat different. Based on external cost estimates on a study by Harwood et al. (1984), Pogue and Sgontz (1989) and Saffer and Chaloupka (1992) estimate the optimal tax on alcohol in 1991 at $73 and $79 per gallon of pure alcohol, respectively. Based on similar cost estimates by Manning et al. (1989, 1991), Blumberg (1992) obtains an optimal tax of $73 per gallon. Although these studies examine differing estimates of the costs of alcohol abuse, all conclude that the optimal tax is significantly greater than the average federal and state tax of $35 per gallon of pure alcohol. The studies also take account of the welfare losses suffered by consumers who do not abuse alcohol when the tax rate rises.[8]

Revenue yield and the fact that sin taxes tend to be regressive must also be considered in setting optimal tax rates. If the aim of tax hikes is to correct for externalities, small changes in individual income tax rates could easily compensate for the effect of increased excise taxes on the distribution of income (Manning et al., 1989). But if revenue yield also is important, offsetting tax cuts are not a viable option. Moreover, the fairness standard described by Cook and Moore (forthcoming) calls for smokers and drinkers to pay for the full costs of their behavior regardless of whether taxes are levied to raise revenue or to correct for externalities.

The conventional view is that alcohol and cigarettes are attractive targets from Ramsey's (1927) standard of efficient taxation. As shown by Ramsey, under certain conditions the way to raise a fixed amount of revenue while minimizing welfare losses due to price distortions is to tax inelastically demanded goods more heavily. While fairly inelastic in the short run, the estimated price elasticities of cigarette smoking and heavy alcohol consumption cited earlier (which were based on theories of rational addiction) imply that in the long run these behaviors may be no less sensitive to price than other goods. An alternate efficiency argument is that goods that are complements to leisure should be taxed at higher rates to offset the disincentive effects of income taxation of labor supply (Corlett and Hague, 1953); indeed, Cook and Moore (forthcoming) argue that the negative effects of excessive alcohol consumption on earnings and investment in human capital documented by Mullahy and Sindelar (1989, 1990a, 1993) suggest that alcohol is a complement for leisure. In any case, there is no particular relationship between the optimal tax rate to correct for externalities and the tax rate required to yield a given amount of revenue while minimizing welfare losses due to price distortions.

The bulk of the evidence presented here does support higher taxes on cigarettes and alcohol. It should be remembered, however, that an "optimal" tax rate for these commodities cannot be defined without reference to one's particular perspective and objectives—enhancing public health, maximizing tax revenues, or properly pricing external effects—and that political value judgments are involved throughout (for example, should regressive taxes be used to raise revenue?). In addition, with both cigarette and alcohol taxes, a primary unresolved issue relates to what harmful consequences should be classified as external. For alcohol in particular, an important open question is how to enact taxes focused on the abusers of alcohol, while avoiding undue costs for the majority of drinkers who do not abuse alcohol.

# NOTES

We are indebted to Alan B. Krueger, Carl Shapiro, and Timothy Taylor for helpful comments. This paper has not undergone the review accorded official NBER publications; in particular, it has not been submitted for approval by the Board of Directors.

1. The average U.S. federal and state tax on a pack of cigarettes in 1992 was lower than any other developed country except Spain (Coalition on Smoking OR Health 1993). The U.S. taxes beer and wine at rates significantly below the average rates imposed by developed countries, while it taxes spirits at about the average rate (Sparrow et al. 1989). Analyses of the sources of these differences and their impacts on the consumption must take account of the political setting in which these rates are determined and cultural attitudes towards smoking and drinking (Laugesen and Meads 1991; Saffer 1991).

2. The real price of cigarettes fell by 15 percent between 1975 and 1980 (and by 20 percent between 1965 and 1980) before rising by 62 percent between 1980 and 1990. One factor in this trend is that the legislation which raised the federal excise tax from 8 cents to 16 cents in 1983 contained a clause which provided for the resumption of the old 8 cent rate at the end of fiscal 1985. After a half-dozen temporary extensions, Congress made the 16 cent rate permanent in 1986. Harris (1987) argues that part of the trend can be explained by viewing the tax increase as a coordinating device for oligopolistic price increases. Becker, Grossman, and Murphy (1993) attribute it to monopolistic pricing behavior by the producers of an addictive good faced with expected future declines in the demand for smoking.

3. One may question the use of a linear demand function for global, optimal tax calculations. But it is equally questionable to forecast the impacts of large tax hikes by using a demand function with a constant elasticity that is smaller than one, particularly since the long-run price response or elasticity exceeds the short-run elasticity in the case of addictive goods such as cigarettes (see the next section). Grossman's computation takes account of this difference and pertains to the long-run revenue yield. In the short-run the revenue yield would be larger. Strictly speaking, a present value measure is required to summarize the revenue yield. Since the precise adjustment period is not known and since annual estimates are presented by other forecasters, Grossman does not make present value computations.

4. Indeed, studies based on the "rational addiction" framework (Becker and Murphy 1988) have considered the demand function for an addictive good as negatively related to its price in that period, but positively related to past and future consumption. Chaloupka (1991), Becker, Grossman, and Murphy (1993), and Chaloupka, Grossman, Becker, and Murphy (1993) use estimates of this type of demand function to compute long-run and short-run price elasticities of demand for cigarettes and excessive alcohol consumption.

5. Wasserman et al. (1991) contradict the conclusion that youth smoking is more responsive to price than adult smoking. Their study should be interpreted with caution for rea-

sons indicated by Grossman (1991). Ferrence et al. (1991) report that recent Canadian tax hikes on cigarettes have caused substantial declines in teenage smoking participation rates in that country. As more studies dealing with the price sensitivity of teenage smoking are undertaken, the conclusions reached above may have to be modified. Since smoking participation rates rise with age, larger smoking participation elasticities do not necessarily translate into larger declines in smoking participation rates when prices rise. According to the elasticities cited in the text, a 10 percent increase in price would lower smoking participation rates of 12–17 year olds, 20–25 year olds, 26–35 year olds, and persons over the age of 35 by 2 percentage points, 3 percentage points, 2 percentage points, and less than 1 percentage point, respectively. Based on this measure, persons under the age of 36 are more responsive to price than older persons.

6. Grossman et al. (forthcoming) estimated the consequences for youth if the federal excise of tax rate on beer—the alcoholic beverage of choice among youth—had been indexed to the rate of inflation since 1951. This policy would have reduced the number of high school seniors who drank frequently (more than 30 times) in the past year (21 percent of all seniors) by 45 percent, the number who drank frequently (more than 9 times) in the past month (16 percent of all seniors) by 43 percent, and the number with at least one heavy drinking episode (consumption of five or more drinks) in the past two weeks (40 percent of all seniors) by 18 percent. These declines are greater than those associated with an alternative policy simulation: a uniform legal drinking age of 21 in all states of the United States in 1982.

7. This external cost is net of smokers' and alcohol abusers' implicit pension transfers to other persons.

8. To maintain the optimal alcohol tax in real terms after 1991, it would have to be indexed to the rate of inflation. The same objective could be accomplished by converting to an ad valorem alcoholic beverage excise tax system under which the tax rate is expressed as a fixed percentage of the manufacturer's price. The Congressional Budget Office (1993) points out that the latter option might induce manufacturers to lower sales prices to company-controlled wholesalers to avoid part of the tax. Similar comments apply to optimal cigarette taxes.

## REFERENCES

Becker, Gary S. "Habits, Addictions, and Traditions." *Kyklos 45* (1992): 327–346.

Becker, Gary S., and Kevin M. Murphy. "A Theory of Rational Addiction." *Journal of Political Economy 96:4* (August 1988): 675–700.

Becker, Gary S., Michael Grossman, and Kevin M. Murphy. "Rational Addiction and the Effect of Price on Consumption." *American Economic Review 81:2* (May 1991):237–241.

———. "An Empirical Analysis of Cigarette Addiction." Cambridge: National Bureau of Economic Research Working Paper No. 3322. Revised March 1993 (first version April 1990).

Blumberg, Linda J. "Second Best Alcohol Taxation: Balancing Appropriate Incentives with Deadweight Loss." Ph.D. dissertation, University of Michigan, 1992.

Chaloupka, Frank J. "Rational Addictive Behavior and Cigarette Smoking." *Journal of Political Economy 99:4* (August 1991): 722–742.

Chaloupka, Frank J., Michael Grossman, Gary S. Becker, and Kevin M. Murphy. "Alcohol Addiction: An Econometric Analysis." Presented at the annual meeting of the American Economic Association, Anaheim, California, January 1993.

Chaloupka, Frank J., and Adit Laixuthai. "Do Youths Substitute Alcohol and Marijuana? Some Econometric Evidence." Presented at the annual meeting of the Southern Economic Association, Washington, D.C., November 1992.

Chaloupka, Frank J., and Henry Saffer. "Alcohol, Illegal Drugs, Public Policy, and Crime." Presented at the annual meeting of the Western Economic Association, San Francisco, California, July 1992.

Chaloupka Frank J., Henry Saffer, and Michael Grossman. "Alcohol-Control Policies and Motor-Vehicle Fatalities." *Journal of Legal Studies 22:1* (January 1993): 161–186.

Coalition on Smoking OR Health. "Saving Lives and Raising Revenue: The Case for Major Increases in State and Federal Tobacco Taxes." Washington, D.C., January 1993.

Coate, Douglas, and Michael Grossman. "Effects of Alcoholic Beverage Prices and Legal Drinking Ages on Youth Alcohol Use." *Journal of Law and Economics 31:1* (April 1988): 145–171.

Congressional Budget Office, U.S. Congress. *Reducing the Deficit: Spending and Revenue Options.* Washington, D.C.: U.S. Government Printing Office (1993).

Cook, Philip J., and Michael J. Moore. "Drinking and Schooling." Presented at the Third Annual Health Economics Workshop at Johns Hopkins University, Baltimore, Maryland, May 1992a.

———. "Economic Perspectives on Reducing Alcohol-Related Violence." Presented at the National Institute on Alcohol Abuse and Alcoholism Working Group on Alcohol-Related Violence, Washington, D.C., May 1992b.

———. "Taxation of Alcoholic Beverages." In Gregory Bloss and Michael Hilton, eds., *Economic and Socioeconomic Issues in the Prevention of Alcohol-Related Problems.* Rochville: National Institute on Alcohol Abuse and Alcoholism (forthcoming).

Cook, Philip J., and George Tauchen. "The Effect of Liquor Taxes on Heavy Drinking." *Bell Journal of Economics 13:2* (Autumn 1982): 379–390.

Corlett, W. J., and D. C. Hague. "Complementarity and the Excess Burden of Taxation." *Review of Economic Studies 21:54* (1953): 21–30.

DiNardo, John, and Thomas Lemieux. "Alcohol, Marijuana, and American Youth: The Unintended Effects of Government Regulation." Cambridge: National Bureau of Economic Research Working Paper No. 4212, November 1992.

Ferrence, Roberta G., et al. "Effects of Pricing on Cigarette Use among Teenagers and Adults in Canada, 1980–1989." Working paper, Addiction Research Foundation, Toronto, February 1991.

Grossman, Michael. "Health Benefits of Increases in Alcohol and Cigarette Taxes." *British Journal of Addiction 84:10* (October 1989): 1193–1204.

———. "Editorial: The Demand for Cigarettes." *Journal of Health Economics 10*:1 (May 1991): 101–103.

———. "For Best Revenue, Tax Cigarettes $1.26." *New York Times* (June 18, 1993): A26.

Grossman, Michael, Frank J. Chaloupka, Henry Saffer, and Adit Laixuthai. "Effects of Alcohol Price Policy on Youth: A Summary of Economic Research." *Journal of Research on Adolescence* (forthcoming).

Grossman, Michael, Douglas Coate, and Gregory M. Arluck. "Price Sensitivity of Alcoholic Beverages in the United States." In Holder, Harold D., eds., *Control Issues in Alcohol Abuse Prevention: Strategies for States and Communities.* Greenwich: JAI Press, Inc. (1987): 169–198.

Harris, Jeffrey E. "The 1983 Increase in the Federal Cigarette Excise Tax." In Summers, Lawrence H., ed., *Tax Policy and the Economy,* Volume 1. Cambridge: MIT Press (1987): 87–111.

Harris Jeffrey E., "Two Bucks Will Finance Health for 10 Million." *New York Times* (June 4, 1993): A27.

Harwood, Henrick J., Diane M. Napolitano, Patricia L. Kristiansen, and James J. Collins, eds. *Economic Costs to Society of Alcohol and Drug Abuse and Mental Illness: 1980.* Research Triangle Park, North Carolina: Research Triangle Institute (1984).

Hay, Joel W. "The Harm They Do to Others: A Primer on the External Costs of Drug Abuse." In Krauss, Melvyn B., and Edward P. Lazear, eds., *Searching for Alternatives: Drug-Control Policy in the United States.* Stanford: Hoover Institution Press (1991): 200–225.

Keeler, Theodore E., Teh-wei Hu, Paul G. Barnett, and Willard G. Manning. "Taxation, Regulation, and Addiction: A Demand Function for Cigarettes Based on Time-Series Evidence." *Journal of Health Economics 12*:1 (April 1993): 1–18.

Kenkel, Donald S. "Drinking, Driving, and Deterrence: The Social Costs of Alternative Policies." *Journal of Law and Economics 36*:2 (October 1993),

Laugesen, Murray, and Chris Meads. "Tobacco Advertising Restrictions, Price, Income, and Tobacco Consumption in OECD Countries, 1960–1986." *British Journal of Addiction 86* (1991): 1343–1354.

Lewit, Eugene M., and Douglas Coate. "The Potential for Using Excise Taxes to Reduce Smoking." *Journal of Health Economics 1*:2 (August 1982): 121–145.

Lewit, Eugene M., Douglas Coate, and Michael Grossman. "The Effects of Government Regulation on Teenage Smoking," *Journal of Law and Economics 24*:3 (December 1981): 545–569.

Manning, Willard G., et al. "The Taxes of Sin: Do Smokers and Drinkers Pay Their Way?" *Journal of the American Medical Association 261*:11 (March 1989): 1604–1609.

Manning, Willard G., et al., eds. *The Costs of Poor Health Habits.* Cambridge: Harvard University Press (1991).

Mullahy, John, and Jody L. Sindelar. "Life Cycle Effects of Alcoholism on Education, Earnings, and Occupation." *Inquiry 26* (Summer 1989): 272–282.

Mullahy, John, and Jody L. Sindelar. "Gender Differences in the Labor Market Effects of Alcoholism." *American Economic Review 81*:2 (May 1990a): 161–165.

Mullahy, John, and Jody L. Sindelar. "An Ounce of Prevention: Productive Remedies for Alcoholism." *Journal of Policy Analysis and Management 9*:2 (Spring 1990b): 249–253.

Mullahy, John, and Jody L. Sindelar. "Alcoholism, Work and Income." *Journal of Labor Economics 11*:3 (July 1993): 494–520.

Mullahy, John, and Jody L. Sindelar. "Direct and Indirect Effects of Alcoholism on Human Capital." *Milbank Quarterly* (forthcoming).

National Highway Traffic Safety Administration, U.S. Department of Transportation. *Fatal Accident Reporting System,* 1984, DOT HS 806 919 (February 1986).

Ohsfeldt, Robert L., Michael A. Morrisey, and Stephen Henderlite. "Alcohol Taxes and Industrial Injury," working paper, University of Alabama at Birmingham School of Public Health, November 1991.

Pogue, Thomas F., and Larry G. Sgontz. "Taxing to Control Social Costs: The Case of Alcohol." *American Economic Review 79*:1 (March 1989): 235–243.

Ramsey, Frank P. "A Contribution to the Theory of Taxation." *Economic Journal 37*:1 (March 1927): 47–61.

Rimm, Eric B., et al. "Prospective Study of Alcohol Consumption and Risk of Coronary Disease in Men." *The Lancet 338* (August 24, 1991): 464–468.

Saffer, Henry. "Alcohol Advertising Bans and Alcohol Abuse: An International Perspective." *Journal of Health Economics 10*:1 (May 1991): 65–79.

Saffer, Henry, and Frank J. Chaloupka. "Alcohol Tax Equalization and Social Cost," working paper. Cambridge: National Bureau of Research (July 1992).

Saffer, Henry, and Michael Grossman. "Beer Taxes, the Legal Drinking Age, and Youth Motor Vehicle Fatalities." *Journal of Legal Studies 16*:2 (June 1987): 351–374.

Sparrow, Margo, Ron Brazeau, Howard Collins, R. A. Morrison. *International Survey: Alcoholic Beverage Taxation and Control Policies,* seventh edition. Ontario: Brewers Association of Canada (1989).

U.S. Environmental Protection Agency. *Respiratory Health Effects of Passive Smoking: Lung Cancers and Other Disorders.* Publication EPA/600/6-90/ 006F (December 1992).

Vicusi, W. Kip. *Smoking: Making the Risky Decision.* New York: Oxford University Press, 1992.

Wasserman, Jeffrey, Willard G. Manning, Joseph P. Newhouse, and John D. Winkler. "The Effects of Excise Taxes and Regulations on Cigarette Smoking." *Journal of Health Economics 10*:1 (May 1991): 43–64.

# S E L E C T I O N 6

Mancur Olson, Jr.

# The Logic

This reading summarizes and extends the arguments in Mancur Olson's classic work *The Logic of Collective Action*. The larger the number of individuals with a common interest, the larger the probability that nothing will be done by those same individuals to further that interest. The student of public finance will recognize this as the free rider problem—or as Olson puts it, the "let George do it" philosophy.

Private groups, organized around collective interests, cannot rely upon the same means as governments—compulsory taxation—to solve the problem of free riders. Yet such special interest groups exist, and often act as lobbies or pressure groups at the federal, state, or local levels of government. The attainment of favorable government policies can be considered a public good, as the ramifications are nonrival—shared by all relevant constituents. Olson describes the conditions under which collective action by private organizations can be successful (while at the same time illustrating when collective action will not be likely). Of particular interest are the methods used by these organizations to address the problem of free riding. The most effective incentives embody some type of private good consumption, thereby employing the rivalness characteristic to limit the free riders normally associated with public good provision.

### Questions to Guide the Reading
1. What is the nature of the benefit-cost calculation that leads members of large groups to choose (rationally) not to act in the interest of the group?

Olson, Mancur Jr. "The Logic," in *The Rise and Decline of Nations: Economic Growth, Stagflation, and Social Rigidities*, New Haven: Yale University Press (1982), 17–35. Reprinted with permission of Yale University Press. This selection is an abridged version of the original article.

**Mancur Olson, Jr.** is Distinguished University Professor of Economics, and Chairman, Center of Institutional Reform and Informal Sector (IRIS) at the University of Maryland.

2. Today's special interest groups are numerous and varied—from the Teamsters to the American Heart Association to the Sierra Club. How might private organizations such as these substitute selective incentives (negative or positive) for compulsory taxation used by governments?

3. Under what circumstances are *social* selective incentives available to a group? When might social selective incentives be ineffective?

4. How does the concept of "rational ignorance" explain the effectiveness of lobbying, acts of terrorism, and the existence of government policies which are seemingly inconsistent with the egalitarian goals of a democracy?

5. Collective action is argued to be more likely to occur in small groups than in large ones. But what might prevent or disrupt collective action even in small groups?

It has often been taken for granted that if everyone in a group of individuals or firms had some interest in common, then there would be a tendency for the group to seek to further this interest. Thus many students of politics in the United States for a long time supposed that citizens with a common political interest would organize and lobby to serve that interest. Each individual in the population would be in one or more groups and the vector of pressures of these competing groups explained the outcomes of the political process. Similarly, it was often supposed that if workers, farmers, or consumers faced monopolies harmful to their interests, they would eventually attain countervailing power through organizations such as labor unions or farm organizations that obtained market power and protective government action. On a large scale, huge social classes are often expected to act in the interests of their members; the unalloyed form of this belief is, of course, the Marxian contention that in capitalist societies the bourgeois class runs the government to serve its own interests, and that once the exploitation of the proletariat goes far enough and "false consciousness" has disappeared, the working class will in its own interest revolt and establish a dictatorship of the proletariat. In general, if the individuals in some category or class had a sufficient degree of self-interest and if they all agreed on some common interest, then the group would to some extent also act in a self-interested or group-interested manner.

If we ponder the logic of the familiar assumption described in the preceding paragraph, we can see that it is fundamentally and indisputably faulty. Consider those consumers who agree that they pay higher prices for a product because of some objectionable monopoly of tariff, or those workers who agree that their skill deserves a higher wage. Let us now ask what would be the expedient course of action for an individual consumer who would like to see a boycott to combat a monopoly or a lobby to repeal the tariff, or for an individual worker who would like a strike threat or a minimum wage law that could bring higher wages. If the consumer or worker contributes a few days and a few dollar to organize a boycott or a union or to lobby for favorable legislation, he or she will have sacrificed time and money. What will this sacrifice obtain? The individual will at best succeed in advancing the cause of a small (often imperceptible) degree. In any case he will get only a minute share of the gain from his action. The very fact that the objective or interest is common to or shared by the group entails that the gain from any sacrifice an individual makes to serve this common purpose is shared with everyone in the group. The successful boycott or strike or lobbying action will bring the better price or wage for everyone in the relevant category, so the individual in any large group with a common interest will reap only a minute share of the gains from whatever sacrifices the individual makes to achieve this common interest. Since any gain goes to everyone in the group, those who contribute nothing to the effort will get just as much as those who made a contribution. It pays to "let George do it," but George has little or no incentive to do anything in the group interest either, so (in the absence of factors that are completely left out of the conceptions mentioned in the first paragraph) there will be little, if any, group action. The paradox, then, is that (in the absence of special arrangements or circumstances to which we shall turn later) large groups, at least if they are composed of rational individuals, will *not* act in their group interest.

This paradox is elaborated and set out in a way that lets the reader check every step of the logic in a book I wrote entitled *The Logic of Collective Action.* That book also shows that the evidence in the United States, the only country in which all powerful interest groups were considered, systematically supported the argument, and that the scattered evidence that I was aware of from other countries was also consistent with it. Since the present book is an outgrowth of *The Logic of Collective Action* and in large part even an application of the argument in it, the most serious critics or students of the present book should have read that one. For the many readers who naturally would not want to invest the time needed to do so without knowing what might be gained, and for those with a more casual interest, the first part of this chapter will explain a few features of the argument in *The Logic* that are needed to understand the rest of the present volume. Other parts of the chapter, however, should not involve any repetition.

**II**

One finding in *The Logic* is that the services of associations like labor unions, professional associations, farm organizations, cartels, lobbies (and even collusive groups without formal organization) resemble the basic services of the state in one utterly fundamental respect. The services of such associations, like the elemental services or "public goods" provided by governments, if provided to anyone, go to everyone in some category or group. Just as the law and order, defense, or pollution abatement brought about by government accrue to everyone in some country or geographical area, so the tariff obtained by a farm organization's lobbying effort raises the price to all producers of the relevant commodity. Similarly, as I argued earlier, the higher wage won by a union applies to all employees in the pertinent category. More generally, every lobby obtaining a general change in legislation or regulation thereby obtains a public or collective good for everyone who benefits from that change, and every combination—that is, every "cartel"—using market or industrial action to get a higher price or wage must, when it restricts the quantity supplied, raise the price for every seller, thereby creating a collective good for all sellers.

If governments, on the one hand, and combinations exploiting their political or market power, on the other, produce public or collective goods that inevitably go to everyone in some group or category, then both are subject to the paradoxical logic set out above: that is, the individuals and firms they serve have in general no incentive voluntarily to contribute to their support. It follows that if there is only voluntary and rational individual behavior,[1] then for the most part neither governments nor lobbies and cartels will exist, unless individuals support them for some reason *other* than the collective goods they provide. Of course, governments exist virtually everywhere and often there are lobbies and cartelistic organizations as well. If the argument so far is right, it follows that something *other* than the collective goods that governments and other organizations provide accounts for their existence.

In the case of governments, the answer was explained before *The Logic of Collective Action* was written; governments are obviously supported by compulsory taxation. Sometimes there is little objection to this compulsion, presumably because many people intuitively understand that public goods cannot be sold in the marketplace or financed by any voluntary mechanism; as I have already argued, each individual would get only a minute share of any governmental services he she paid for and would get whatever level of services was provided by others in any event.

In the case of organizations that provide collective goods to their client groups through political or market action, the answer has not been obvious, but it is no less clear-cut. Organizations of this kind, at least when they represent large groups, are again not supported because of the collective goods they provide, but rather because they have been fortunate enough to find what I have called *selective incentives*. A selective incentive is one that applies selectively to the individuals depending on whether they do or do not contribute to the provision of the collective good.

A selective incentive can be either negative or positive; it can, for example, be a loss or punishment imposed only on those who do *not* help provide the collective good. Tax payments are, of course, obtained with the help of negative selective incentives, since those who are found not to have paid their taxes must then suffer both taxes and penalties. The best-known type of organized interest group in modern democratic societies, the labor union, is also usually supported, in part, through negative selective incentives. Most of the dues in strong unions are obtained through union shop, closed shop, or agency shop arrangements which make dues paying more or less compulsory and automatic. There are often also informal arrangements with the same effect; David McDonald, former president of the United Steel Workers of America, describes one of these arrangements used in the early history of that union. It was, he writes, a technique

> which we called ... visual education, which was a high-sounding label for a practice much more accurately described as dues picketing. It worked very simply. A group of dues-paying members, selected by the district director (usually more for their size than their tact) would stand at the plant gate with pick handles or baseball bats in hand and confront each worker as he arrived for his shift.

As McDonald's "dues picketing" analogy suggests, picketing during strikes is another negative selective incentive that unions sometimes need; although picketing in industries with established and stable unions is usually peaceful, this is because the union's capacity to close down an enterprise against which it has called a strike is clear to all; the early phase of unionization often involves a great deal of violence on the part of both unions and antiunion employers and scabs.

Some opponents of labor unions argue that, since many of the members of labor unions join only through the processes McDonald described or through legally enforced union-shop arrangements, most of the relevant workers do not want to be unionized. The Taft-Hartley Act provided that impartial governmentally administered elections should be held to determine whether workers did in fact want to belong to unions. As the collective-good logic set out here suggests, the same workers who had to be coerced to pay union dues voted for the unions with compulsory dues (and normally by overwhelming margins), so that this feature of the Taft-Hartley Act was soon abandoned as pointless. The workers who as individuals tried to avoid paying union dues at the same time that they voted to force themselves all to pay dues are no different from taxpayers who vote, in effect, for high levels of taxation, yet try to arrange their private affairs in ways that avoid taxes. Because of the same logic, many professional associations also get members through covert or overt coercion (for example, lawyers in those states with a "closed bar"). So do lobbies and cartels of several other types; some of the contributions by corporate officials, for instance, to politicians useful to the corporation are also the result of subtle forms of coercion.

Positive selective incentives, although easily overlooked, are also commonplace, as diverse examples in *The Logic* demonstrate. American farm organizations offer prototypical examples. Many of the members of the stronger American farm organizations are members because their dues payments are automatically deducted from the "patronage dividends" of farm cooperatives or are included in the insurance premiums paid to mutual insurance companies associated with the farm organizations. Any number of organizations with urban clients also provide similar positive selective incentives in the form of insurance policies, publications, group air fares, and other private goods made available only to members. The grievance procedures of labor unions usually also offer selective incentives, since the grievances of active members often get most of the attention. The symbiosis between the political power of a lobbying organization and the business institutions associated with it often yields tax or other advantages for the business institution, and the publicity and other information flowing out of the political arm of a movement often generates patterns of preference or trust that make the business activities of the movement more remunerative. The surpluses obtained in such ways in turn provide positive selective incentives that recruit participants for the lobbying efforts.

## III

Small groups, or occasionally large "federal" groups that are made up of many small groups of socially interactive members, have an additional source of both negative and positive selective incentives. Clearly most people value the companionship and respect of those with whom they interact. In modern societies solitary confinement is, apart from the rare death penalty, the harshest legal punishment. The censure or even ostracism of those who fail to bear a share of the burdens of collective action can sometimes be an important selective incentive. An extreme example of this occurs when British unionists refuse to speak to uncooperative colleagues, that is, "send them to Coventry." Similarly, those in a socially interactive group seeking a collective good can give special respect or honor to those who distinguish themselves by their sacrifices in the interest of the group and thereby offer them a positive selective incentive. Since most people apparently prefer relatively like-minded or agreeable and respectable company, and often prefer to associate with those whom they especially admire, they may find it costless to shun those who shirk the collective action and to favor those who oversubscribe.

Social selective incentives can be powerful and inexpensive, but they are available only in certain situations. As I have already indicated, they have little applicability to large groups, except in those cases in which the large groups can be federations of small groups that are capable of social interaction. It also is not possible to organize most large groups in need of a collective good into small, socially interactive subgroups, since most individuals do not have the time needed to maintain a huge number of friends and acquaintances.

The availability of social selective incentives is also limited by the social heterogeneity of some of the groups or categories that would benefit from a collective good. Everyday observation reveals that most socially interactive groups are fairly homogeneous and that many people resist extensive social interaction with those they deem to have lower status or greatly different tastes. Even Bohemian or other nonconformist groups often are made up of individuals who are similar to one another, however much they differ from the rest of society. Since some of the categories of individuals who would benefit from a collective good are socially heterogeneous, the social interaction needed for selective incentives sometimes cannot be arranged even when the number of individuals involved is small.

Another problem in organizing and maintaining socially heterogeneous groups is that they are less likely to agree on the exact nature of whatever collective good is at issue or on how much of it is worth buying. All the arguments showing the difficulty of collective action mentioned so far in this chapter hold even when there is perfect consensus about the collective good that is desired, the amount that is wanted, and the best way to obtain the good. But if anything, such as social heterogeneity, reduces consensus, collective action can become still less likely. And if there is nonetheless collective action, it incurs the extra cost (especially for the leaders of whatever organization or collusion is at issue) of accommodating and compromising the different views. The situation is slightly different in the very small groups to which we shall turn shortly. In such groups differences of opinion can sometimes provide a bit of an incentive to join an organization seeking a collective good, since joining might give the individual a significant influence over the organization's policy and the nature of any collective good it would obtain. But this consideration is not relevant to any group that is large enough so that a single individual cannot expect to affect the outcome.

Consensus is especially difficult where collective goods are concerned because the defining characteristic of collective goods—that they go to everyone in some group or category if they are provided at all—also entails that everyone in the relevant group gets more or less of the collective good together, and that they all have to accept whatever level and type of public good is provided. A country can have only one foreign and defense policy, however diverse the preferences and incomes of its citizenry, and (except in the rarely attainable case of a "Lindahl equilibrium") there will not be agreement within a country on how much should be spent to carry out the foreign and defense policy. . . . Heterogeneous clients with diverse demands for collective goods can pose an even greater problem for private associations, which not only must deal with the disagreements but also must find selective incentives strong enough to hold dissatisfied clients.

In short, the political entrepreneurs who attempt to organize collective action will accordingly be more likely to succeed if they strive to organize relatively homogeneous groups. The political managers whose task it is to maintain organized or collusive action similarly will be motivated to use indoctrination and selective recruitment to increase the homogeneity of their client groups. This is true in part because social selective incentives are more likely to be available to the more nearly homogeneous groups, and in part because homogeneity will help achieve consensus.

# IV

Information and calculation about a collective good is often itself a collective good. Consider a typical member of a large organization who is deciding how much time to devote to studying the policies or leadership of the organization. The more time the member devotes to this matter, the greater the likelihood that his or her voting and advocacy will favor effective policies and leadership for the organization. This typical member will, however, get only a small share of the gain from the more effective policies and the leadership: in the aggregate, the other members will get almost all the gains, so that the individual member does not have an incentive to devote nearly as much time to fact-finding and thinking about the organization as would be in the group interest. Each of the members of the group would be better off if they all could be coerced into spending more time finding out how to vote to make the organization best further their interests. This is dramatically evident in the case of the typical voter in a national election in a large country. The gain to such a voter from studying issues and candidates until it is clear what vote is truly in his or her interest is given by the difference in the value to the individual of the "right" election outcome as compared with the "wrong" outcome, *multiplied by the probability a change in the individual's vote will alter the outcome of the election.* Since the probability that a typical voter will change the outcome of the election is vanishingly small, the typical citizen is usually "rationally ignorant" about public affairs. Often, information about public affairs is so interesting or entertaining that it pays to acquire it for these reasons alone—this appears to be the single most important source of exceptions to the generalization that *typical* citizens are rationally ignorant about public affairs.

Individuals in a few special vocations can receive considerable rewards in private goods if they acquire exceptional knowledge of public goods. Politicians, lobbyists, journalists, and social scientists, for example, may earn more money, power, or prestige from knowledge of this or that public business. Occasionally, exceptional knowledge of public policy can generate exceptional profits in stock exchanges or other markets. Withal, the typical citizen will find that his or her income and life chances will not be improved by zealous study of public affairs, or even of any single collective good.

The limited knowledge of public affairs is in turn necessary to explain the effectiveness of lobbying. If all citizens had obtained and digested all pertinent information, they could not then be swayed by advertising or other persuasion. With perfectly informed citizens, elected officials would not be subject to the blandishments of lobbyists, since the constituents would then know if their interests were betrayed and defeat the unfaithful representative at the next election. Just as lobbies provide collective goods to special-interest groups, so their effectiveness is explained by the imperfect knowledge of citizens, and this in turn is due mainly to the fact that information and calculation about collective goods is also a collective good.

This fact—that the benefits of individual enlightenment about public goods are usually dispersed throughout a group or nation, rather than concentrated upon the individual who bears the costs of becoming enlightened—explains many other phenomena as well. It explains, for example, the "man bites dog" criterion of what is newsworthy. If the television newscasts were watched or newspaper were read solely to obtain the most important information about public affairs, aberrant events of little public importance would be ignored and typical patterns of quantitative significance would be emphasized; when the news is, by contrast, for most people largely an alternative to other forms of diversion or entertainment, intriguing oddities and human-interest items are in demand. Similarly, events that unfold in a suspenseful way or sex scandals among public figures are fully covered by the media, whereas the complexities of economic policy or quantitative analyses of public problems receive only minimal attention. Public officials, often able to thrive without giving the citizens good value for their tax monies, may fall over an exceptional mistake striking enough to be newsworthy. Extravagant statements, picturesque protests, and unruly demonstrations that offend much of the public they are designed to influence are also explicable in this way: they make diverting news and thus call attention to interests and arguments that might otherwise be ignored. Even some isolated acts of terrorism that are described as "senseless" can, from this perspective, be explained as effective means of obtaining the riveted attention of a public that otherwise would remain rationally ignorant.

This argument also helps us to understand certain apparent inconsistencies in the behavior of modern democracies. The arrangement of the income-tax brackets in all the major developed democracies is distinctly progressive, whereas the loopholes are more often tilted toward a minority of more prosperous taxpayers. Since both are the result of the same democratic institutions, why do they not have the same incidence? As I see it, the progression of the income tax is a matter of such salience and political controversy that much of the electorate knows about it, so populist and majoritarian considerations dictate a considerable degree of progression. The details of tax laws are far less widely known, and they often reflect the interests of small numbers of organized and usually more prosperous taxpayers. Several of the developed democracies similarly have adopted programs such as Medicare and Medicaid that are obviously inspired by the concerns about the cost of medical care to those with low or middle incomes, yet implemented or administered these programs in ways that resulted in large increases in income for prosperous physicians and other providers of medical care. Again, these diverse consequences seem to be explained by the fact that conspicuous and controversial choices of overall policies become known to the majorities who consume health care, whereas the many smaller choices needed to implement these programs are influenced primarily by a minority of organized providers of health care.

The fact that the typical individual does not have an incentive to spend much time studying many of his choices concerning collective goods also helps to explain some otherwise inexplicable individual contributions toward the provision of collective goods. The logic of collective action that has been described in this chapter is not immediately apparent to those who have never studied it; if it were, there would be nothing paradoxical in the argument with which this chapter opened, and students to whom the argument is explained would not react with initial skepticism. No doubt the practical implications of this logic for the individual's own choices were often discerned before the logic was ever set out in print, but this does not mean that they were always understood even at the intuitive and practical level. In particular, when the costs of individual contributions to collective action are very small, the individual has little incentive to investigate whether or not to make a contribution or even to exercise intuition. If the individual knows the costs of a contribution to collective action in the interest of a group of which he is a part are trivially small, he may rationally not take the trouble to consider whether the gains are smaller still. This is particularly the case since the size of these gains and the policies that would maximize them are matters about which it is usually not rational for him to investigate.

This consideration of the costs and benefits of calculation about public goods leads to the testable prediction that voluntary contributions toward the provision of collective goods for large groups without selective incentives will often occur when the costs of the individual contributions are negligible, but that they will *not* often occur when the costs of the individual contributions are considerable. In other words, when the costs of individual action to help to obtain a desired collective good are small enough, the result is indeterminate and sometimes goes one way and sometimes the other, but when the costs get larger this indeterminacy disappears. We should accordingly find that more than a few people are willing to take the moment of time needed to sign petitions for causes they support, or to express their opinions in the course of discussion, or to vote for the candidate or party they prefer. Similarly, if the argument here is correct, we should not find many instances where individuals voluntarily contribute substantial sums of resources year after year for the purpose of obtaining some collective good for some large group of which they are a part. Before parting with a large amount of money or time, and particularly before doing so repeatedly, the rational individual will reflect on what this considerable sacrifice will accomplish. If the individual is a typical individual in a large group that would benefit from a collective good, his contribution will not make a perceptible difference in the amount that is provided. The theory here predicts that such contributions become less likely the larger the contribution at issue.

## V

Even when contributions are costly enough to elicit rational calculation, there is still one set of circumstances in which collective action can occur without selective incentives. This set of circumstances becomes evident the moment we think of situations in which there are only a few individuals or firms that would benefit from collective action. Suppose there are two firms of equal size in an industry and no other firms can enter the industry. It still will be the case that a higher price for the industry's product will benefit both firms and that legislation favorable to the industry will help both firms. The higher price and the favorable legislation are then collective goods to this "oligopolistic" industry, even though there are only two in the group that benefit from the collective goods. Obviously, each of the oligopolists is in a situation in which if it restricts output to raise the industry price, or lobbies for favorable legislation for the industry, it will tend to get half of the benefit. And the cost-benefit ratio of action in the common interest easily could be so favorable that, even though a firm bears the whole cost of its action and gets only half the benefit of this action, it could still profit from acting in the common interest. Thus if the group that would benefit from collective action is sufficiently small and the cost-benefit ratio of collective action for the group sufficiently favorable, there may well be calculated action in the collective interest even without selective incentives.

When there are only a few members in the group, there is also the possibility that they will bargain with one another and agree on collective action—then the action of each can have a perceptible effect on the interests and the expedient courses of action of others, so that each has an incentive to act strategically, that is, in ways that take into account the effect of the individual's choices on the choices of others. This interdependence of individual firms or persons in the group can give them an incentive to bargain with one another for their mutual advantage. Indeed, if bargaining costs were negligible, they would have an incentive to continue bargaining with one another until group gains were maximized, that is, until what we shall term a *group-optimal outcome* (or what economists sometimes call a "Pareto-optimal" outcome for the group) is achieved. One way the two firms mentioned in the previous paragraph could obtain such an outcome is by agreeing that each will bear half the costs of any collective action; each firm would then bear half the costs of its action in the common interest and receive half the benefits. It therefore would have an incentive to continue action in the collective interest until the aggregate gains of collective action were maximized. In any bargaining, however, each party has an incentive to seek the largest possible share of the group gain for itself, and usually also an incentive to threaten to block or undermine the collective action—that is, to be a "holdout"—if it does not get its preferred share of the group gains. Thus the bargaining may very well not succeed in achieving a group-optimal outcome and may also fail to achieve agreement on any collective action at all. The upshot of all this, as I explain elsewhere, is that "small" groups can often engage in collective action without selective incentives. In certain small groups ("privileged groups") there is actually a presumption that some of the collective good will be provided. Nonetheless, even in the best of circumstances collective action is problematic and the outcomes in particular cases are indeterminate.

Although some aspects of the matter are complex and indeterminate, the essence of the relationship between the size of the group that would benefit from collective action and the extent of collective action is beautifully simple—yet somehow not widely understood. Consider again our two firms and suppose that they have *not* worked out any agreement to maximize their aggregate gains or to coordinate their actions in any way. Each firm will still get half the gains of any action it takes in the interest of the group, and thus it may have a substantial incentive to act in the group interest even when it is acting unilaterally. There is, of course, also a *group external economy*, or gain to the group for which the firm acting unilaterally is not compensated, of 50 percent, so unilateral behavior does not achieve a group-optimal outcome. Now suppose there were a third firm of the same size—the group external economy would then be two thirds, and the individual firm would get only a third of the gain from any independent action it took in the group interest. Of course, if there were a hundred such firms, the group external economy would be 99 percent, and the individual firm would get only 1 percent of the gain from any action in the group interest. Obviously, when we get to large groups measured in millions or even thousands, the incentive for group-oriented behavior in the absence of selective incentives becomes insignificant and even imperceptible.

Untypical as my example of equal-sized firms may be, it makes the general point intuitively obvious: other things being equal, *the larger the number of individuals or firms that would benefit from a collective good, the smaller the share of the gains from action in the group interest that will accrue to the individual or firm that undertakes the action. Thus, in the absence of selective incentives, the incentive for group action diminishes as group size increases, so that large groups are less able to act in their common interest than small ones.* If an additional individual or firm that would value the collective good enters the scene, then the share of the gains from group-oriented action that anyone already in the group might take must diminish. This holds true whatever the relative sizes or valuations of the collective good in the group.

* * *

The number of people who must bargain if a group-optimal amount of a collective good is to be obtained, and thus the costs of bargaining, must rise with the size of the group. This consideration reinforces the point just made. Indeed, both everyday observation and the logic of the matter suggest that for genuinely large groups, bargaining among all members to obtain agreement on the provision of a collective good is out of the question. The consideration mentioned earlier in this chapter, that social selective incentives are available only to small groups and (tenuously) to those larger groups that are federations of small groups, also suggests that small groups are more likely to organize than large ones.

The significance of the logic that has just been set out can best be seen by comparing groups that would have the same net gain from collective action, if they could engage in it, but that vary in size. Suppose there are a million individuals who would gain a thousand dollars each, or a billion in the aggregate, if they were to organize effectively and engaged in collective action that had a total cost of a hundred million. If the logic set out above is right, they could not organize or engage in effective collective action without selective incentives. Now suppose that, although the total gain of a billion dollars from collective action and the aggregate cost of a hundred million remain the same, the group is composed instead of five big corporations or five organized municipalities, each of which would gain two hundred million. Collective action is not an absolute certainty even in this case, since each of the five could conceivably expect others to put up the hundred million and hope to gain the collective good worth two hundred million at no cost at all. Yet collective action, perhaps after some delays due to bargaining, seems very likely indeed. In this case any one of the five would gain a hundred million from providing the collective good even if it had to pay the whole cost itself; and the costs of bargaining among five would not be great, so they would sooner or later probably work out an agreement providing for the collective action. The numbers in this example are arbitrary, but roughly similar situations occur often in reality, and the contrast between "small" and "large" groups could be illustrated with an infinite number of diverse examples.

The significance of this argument shows up in a second way if one compares the operations of lobbies or cartels within jurisdictions of vastly different scale, such as a modest municipality on the one hand and a big country on the other. Within the town, the mayor or city council may be influenced by, say, a score of petitioners or a lobbying budget of a thousand dollars. A particular line of business may be in the hands of only a few firms, and if the town is distant enough from other markets only these few would need to agree to create a cartel. In a big country, the resources needed to influence the national government are likely to be much more substantial, and unless the firms are (as they sometimes are) gigantic, many of them would have to cooperate to create an effective cartel. Now suppose that the million individuals in our large group in the previous paragraph were spread out over a hundred thousand towns or jurisdictions, so that each jurisdiction had ten of them, along with the same proportion of citizens in other categories as before. Suppose also that the cost-benefit ratios remained the same, so that there was still a billion dollars to gain across all jurisdictions or ten thousand in each, and that it would still cost a hundred million dollars across all jurisdictions or a thousand in each. It no longer seems out of the question that in many jurisdictions the groups of ten, or subsets of them, would put up the thousand-dollar total needed to get the thousand for each individual. Thus we see that, if all else were equal, small jurisdictions would have more collective action per capita than large ones.

Differences in intensities of preference generate a third type of illustration of the logic at issue. A small number of zealots anxious for a particular collective good are more likely to act collectively to obtain that good than a large number with the same aggregate willingness to pay. Suppose there are twenty-five individuals, each of whom finds a given collective good worth a thousand dollars in one case, whereas in another there are five thousand, each of whom finds the collective good worth five dollars. Obviously, the argument indicates that there would be a greater likelihood of collective action in the former case than in the latter, even though the aggregate demand for the collective good is the same in both. The great historical significance of small groups of fanatics no doubt owes something to this consideration.

# VI

The argument in this chapter predicts that those groups that have access to selective incentives will be more likely to act collectively to obtain collective goods than those that do not, and that smaller groups will have a greater likelihood of engaging in collective action than larger ones. The empirical portions of *The Logic* show that this prediction has been correct for the United States. More study will be needed before we can be utterly certain that the argument also holds for other countries, but the more prominent features of the organizational landscape of other countries certainly do fit the theory. In no major country are large groups without access to selective incentives generally organized—the masses of consumers are not in consumers' organizations, the millions of taxpayers are not in taxpayers' organizations, the vast number of those with relatively low incomes are not in organizations for the poor, and the sometimes substantial numbers of underemployed have no organized voice. These groups are so dispersed that it is not feasible for any nongovernmental organization to coerce them; in this they differ dramatically from those, like workers in large factories or mines, who are susceptible to coercion through picketing. Neither does there appear to be any source of the positive selective incentives that might give individuals in these categories an incentive to cooperate with the many others with whom they share common interests. By contrast, almost everywhere the social prestige of the learned professions and the limited numbers of practitioners of each profession in each community has helped them to organize. The professions have also been helped to organize by the distinctive susceptibility of the public to the assertion that a professional organization, with the backing of government, ought to be able to determine who is "qualified" to practice the profession, and thereby to control a decisive selective incentive. The small groups of (often large) firms in industry after industry, in country after country, are similarly often organized in trade associations or organizations or collusions of one kind or another. So, frequently, are the small groups of (usually smaller) businesses in particular towns or communities.

\* \* \*

## NOTE

1. *Rational* need not imply *self-interested.*

# S E L E C T I O N   7

Garrett Hardin

# The Tragedy of the Commons

Common property includes such resources as air, water, and fish. Externality theory is traditionally applied when common resources can easily be converted into private property, as in the classic examples of open fisheries and pastures. However, when property rights cannot readily be assigned, as in the case of the destruction of world-wide natural resources, public goods theory is applied. In particular, the problem of large-group collective action, as described by Mancur Olson in the previous reading, is used to understand ozone depletion, deforestation, and acid rain.

In this selection, Garrett Hardin, a biologist, provides a classic statement of the problem of the depletion of common property resources and applies his analysis to overpopulation in particular. Common-property or common-pool resources are characterized by the unrestricted access of potential users. The "tragedy" of common-property ownership then occurs when users are capable of decreasing the potential benefits others can derive from the common asset, and thus impose an external cost. With respect to the Hardin's primary concern—population growth—each newborn has both unrestricted access to the world and the capacity to consume food (energy) to the exclusion of others. Thus, common property resources are also similar to "congestible" or "impure" public goods—goods which are initially distinguished by non-rivalness until crowding effectively diminishes shared benefits.

### Questions to Guide the Reading
1. How does pursuit of one's "own best interest" contribute to the tragedy of the commons?
2. How can you explain that in the American West during the 1800s buffalo were hunted practically to extinction, yet the cattle population increased as more cattle were consumed?

**Garrett Hardin** is Professor Emeritus, Department of Biology, Environmental Studies, and Human Ecology at the University of California at Santa Barbara, and Member of the Board for Federation of American Immigration Reform (FAIR).

3. What public policy steps can be taken to avoid the tragedy of the commons?
4. Do you agree with Hardin that the "freedom to breed is intolerable"? Explain.
5. According to Hardin, how might social arrangements of "mutual coercion mutually agreed upon" prevent the tragedy of the commons? How effective do you believe mutual coercion can be in generating effective collective action or preventing free riding?

---

*The population problem has no technical solution; it requires a fundamental extension in morality.*

At the end of a thoughtful article on the future of nuclear war, Wiesner and York[1] concluded that: "Both sides in the arms race are ... confronted by the dilemma of steadily increasing military power and steadily decreasing national security. *It is our considered professional judgment that this dilemma has no technical solution.* If the great powers continue to look for solutions in the area of science and technology only, the result will be to worsen the situation."

I would like to focus your attention not on the subject of the article (national security in a nuclear world) but on the kind of conclusion they reached, namely that there is no technical solution to the problem. An implicit and almost universal assumption of discussions published in professional and semipopular scientific journals is that the problem under discussion has a technical solution. A technical solution may be defined as one that requires a change only in the techniques of the natural sciences, demanding little or nothing in the way of change in human values or ideas of morality.

In our day (though not in earlier times) technical solutions are always welcome. Because of previous failures in prophecy, it takes courage to assert that a desired technical solution is not possible. Wiesner and York exhibited this courage; publishing in a science journal, they insisted that the solution to the problem was not to be found in the natural sciences. They cautiously qualified their statement with the phrase, "It is our considered professional judgment. . . . " Whether they were right or not is not the concern of the present article. Rather, the concern here is with the important concept of a class of human problems which can be called "no technical solution problems," and, more specifically, with the identification and discussion of one of these.

It is easy to show that the class is not a null class. Recall the game of tick-tack-toe. Consider the problem, "How can I win the game of tick-tack-toe?" It is well known that I cannot, if I assume (in keeping with the conventions of game theory) that my opponent understands the game perfectly. Put another way, there is no "technical solution" to the problem. I can win only by giving a radical meaning to the word "win." I can hit my opponent over the head; or I can drug him; or I can falsify the records. Every way in which I "win" involves, in some sense, an abandonment of the game, as we intuitively understand it. (I can also, of course, openly abandon the game—refuse to play it. This is what most adults do.)

The class of "No technical solution problems" has members. My thesis is that the "population problem," as conventionally conceived, is a member of this class. How it is conventionally conceived needs some comment. It is fair to say that most people who anguish over the population problem are trying to find a way to avoid the evils of overpopulation without relinquishing any of the privileges they now enjoy. They think that farming the seas or developing new strains of wheat will solve the problem—technologically. I try to show here that the solution they seek cannot be found. The population problem cannot be solved in a technical way, any more than can the problem of winning the game of tick-tack-toe.

Population, as Malthus said, naturally tends to grow "geometrically," or, as we would now say, exponentially. In a finite world this means that the per capita share of the world's goods must steadily decrease. Is ours a finite world?

A fair defense can be put forward for the view that the world is infinite; or that we do not know that it is not. But, in terms of the practical problems that we must face in the next few generations with the foreseeable technology, it is clear that we will greatly increase human misery if we do not, during the immediate future, assume that the world available to the terrestrial human population is finite. "Space" is no escape.[2]

A finite world can support only a finite population; therefore, population growth must eventually equal zero. (The case of perpetual wide fluctuations above and below zero is a trivial variant that need not be discussed.) When this condition is met, what will be the situation of mankind? Specifically, can Bentham's goal of "the greatest good for the greatest number" be realized?

*No*—for two reasons, each sufficient by itself. The first is a theoretical one. It is not mathematically possible to maximize for two (or more) variables at the same time. This was clearly stated by von Neumann and Morgenstern,[3] but the principle is implicit in the theory of partial differential equations, dating back at least to D'Alembert (1717–1783).

The second reason springs directly from biological facts. To live, any organism must have a source of energy (for example, food). This energy is utilized for two purposes: mere maintenance and work. For man, maintenance of life requires about 1,600 kilo-calories a day ("maintenance calories"). Anything that he does over and above merely staying alive will be defined as work, and is supported by "work calories" which he takes in. Work calories are used not only for what we call work in common speech; they are also required for all forms of enjoyment, from swimming and automobile racing to playing music and writing poetry. If our goal is to maximize population it is obvious what we must do: We must make the work calories per person approach as close to zero as possible. No gourmet meals, no vacations, no sports, no music, no literature, no art. . . . I think that everyone will grant, without argument or proof, that maximizing population does not maximize goods. Bentham's goal is impossible.

In reaching this conclusion I have made the usual assumption that it is the acquisition of energy that is the problem. The appearance of atomic energy has led some to question this assumption. However, given an infinite source of energy, population growth still produces an inescapable problem. The problem of the acquisition of energy is replaced by the problem of its dissipation, as J. H. Fremlin has so wittily shown.[4] The arithmetic signs in the analysis are, as it were, reversed; but Bentham's goal is still unobtainable.

The optimum population is, then, less than the maximum. The difficulty of defining the optimum is enormous; so far as I know, no one has seriously tackled this problem. Reaching an acceptable and stable solution will surely require more than one generation of hard analytical work—and much persuasion.

We want the maximum good per person; but what is good? To one person it is wilderness, to another it is ski lodges for thousands. To one it is estuaries to nourish ducks for hunters to shoot; to another it is factory land. Comparing one good with another is, we usually say, impossible because goods are incommensurable. Incommensurables cannot be compared.

Theoretically this may be true; but in real life incommensurables *are* commensurable. Only a criterion of judgment and a system of weighting are needed. In nature the criterion is survival. Is it better for a species to be small and hideable, or large and powerful? Natural selection commensurates the incommensurables. The compromise achieved depends on a natural weighting of the values of the variables.

Men must imitate this process. There is no doubt that in fact he already does, but unconsciously. It is when the hidden decisions are made explicit that the arguments begin. The problem for the years ahead is to work out an acceptable theory of weighting. Synergistic effects, nonlinear variation, and difficulties in discounting the future make the intellectual problem difficult, but not (in principle) insoluble.

Has any cultural group solved this practical problem at the present time, even on an intuitive level? One simple fact proves that none has: there is no prosperous population in the world today that has, and has had for some time, a growth rate of zero. Any people that has intuitively identified its optimum point will soon reach it, after which its growth rate becomes and remains zero.

Of course, a positive growth rate might be taken as evidence that a population is below its optimum. However, by any reasonable standards, the most rapidly growing populations on earth today are (in general) the most miserable. This association (which need not be invariable) casts doubt on the optimistic assumption that the positive growth rate of a population is evidence that it has yet to reach its optimum.

We can make little progress in working toward optimum population size until we explicitly exorcise the spirit of Adam Smith in the field of practical demography. In economic affairs, *The Wealth of Nations* (1776) popularized the "invisible hand," the idea that an individual who "intends only his own gain," is, as it were, "led by an invisible hand to promote . . . the public interest."[5] Adam Smith did not assert that this was invariably true, and perhaps neither did any of his followers. But he contributed to a dominant tendency of thought that has ever since interfered with positive action based on rational analysis, namely, the tendency to assume that decisions reached individually will, in fact, be the best decisions for an entire society. If this assumption is correct it justifies the continuance of our present policy of laissez-faire in reproduction. If it is correct we can assume that men will control their individual fecundity so as to produce the optimum population. If the assumption is not correct, we need to reexamine our individual freedoms to see which ones are defensible.

## TRAGEDY OF FREEDOM IN A COMMONS

The rebuttal to the invisible hand in population control is to be found in a scenario first sketched in a little-known pamphlet[6] in 1833 by a mathematical amateur named William Forster Lloyd (1794–1852). We may well call it "the tragedy of the commons," using the word "tragedy" as the philosopher Whitehead used it:[7] "The essence of dramatic tragedy is not unhappiness. It resides in the solemnity of the remorseless working of things." He then goes on to say, "This inevitableness of destiny can only be illustrated in terms of human life by incidents which in fact involve unhappiness. For it is only by them that the futility of escape can be made evident in the drama."

The tragedy of the commons develops in this way. Picture a pasture open to all. It is to be expected that each herdsman will try to keep as many cattle as possible on the commons. Such an arrangement may work reasonably satisfactorily for centuries because tribal wars, poaching, and disease keep the numbers of both man and beast well below the carrying capacity of the land. Finally, however, comes the day of reckoning, that is, the day when the long-desired goal of social stability becomes a reality. At this point, the inherent logic of the commons remorselessly generates tragedy.

As a rational being, each herdsman seeks to maximize his gain. Explicitly or implicitly, more or less consciously, he asks, "What is the utility *to me* of adding one more animal to my herd?" This utility has one negative and one positive component.

(1) The positive component is a function of the increment of one animal. Since the herdsman receives all the proceeds from the sale of the additional amimal, the positive utility is nearly +1.

(2) The negative component is a function of the additional overgrazing created by one more animal. Since, however, the effects of overgrazing are shared by all the herdsmen, the negative utility for any particular decision-making herdsman is only a fraction of –1.

Adding together the component partial utilities, the rational herdsman concludes that the only sensible course for him to pursue is to add another animal to his herd. And another; and another. . . . But this is the conclusion reached by each and every rational herdsman sharing a commons. Therein is the tragedy. Each man is locked into a system that compels him to increase his herd without limit—in a world that is limited. Ruin is the destination toward which all men rush, each pursuing his own best interest in a society that believes in the freedom of the commons. Freedom in a commons brings ruin to all.

Some would say that this is a platitude. Would that it were! In a sense, it was learned thousands of years ago, but natural selection favors the forces of psychological denial.[8] The individual benefits as an individual from his ability to deny the truth even though society as a whole, of which he is a part, suffers. Education can counteract the natural tendency to do the wrong thing, but the inexorable succession of generations requires that the basis for this knowledge be constantly refreshed.

A simple incident that occurred a few years ago in Leominster, Massachusetts, shows how perishable the knowledge is. During the Christmas shopping season the parking meters downtown were covered with plastic bags that bore tags reading: "Do not open until after Christmas. Free parking courtesy of the mayor and city council." In other words, facing the prospect of an increased demand for already scarce space, the city fathers reinstituted the system of the commons. (Cynically, we suspect that they gained more votes than they lost by this retrogressive act.)

In an approximate way, the logic of the commons has been understood for a long time, perhaps since the discovery of agriculture or the invention of private property in real estate. But it is understood mostly only in special cases which are not sufficiently generalized. Even at this late date, cattlemen leasing national land on the western ranges demonstrate no more than an ambivalent understanding, in constantly pressuring federal authorities to increase the head count to the point where overgrazing produces erosion and weed-dominance. Likewise, the oceans of the world continue to suffer from the survival of the philosophy of the commons. Maritime nations still respond automatically to the shibboleth of the "freedom of the seas." Professing to believe in the "inexhaustible resources of the oceans," they bring species after species of fish and whales closer to extinction.[9]

The National Parks present another instance of the working out of the tragedy of the commons. At present, they are open to all, without limit. The parks themselves are limited in extent—there is only one Yosemite Valley—whereas population seems to grow without limit. The values that visitors seek in the parks are steadily eroded. Plainly, we must soon cease to treat the parks as commons or they will be of no value to anyone.

What shall we do? We have several options. We might sell them off as private property. We might keep them as public property, but allocate the right to enter them. The allocation might be on the basis of wealth, by the use of an auction system. It might be on the basis of merit, as defined by some agreed-upon standards. It might be by lottery. Or it might be on a first-come, first-served basis, administered to long queues. These, I think, are all the reasonable possibilities. They are all objectionable. But we must choose—or acquiesce in the destruction of the commons that we call our National Parks.

## POLLUTION

In a reverse way, the tragedy of the commons reappears in problems of pollution. Here it is not a question of taking something out of the commons, but of putting something in—sewage, or chemical, radioactive, and heat wastes into water; noxious and dangerous fumes into the air; and distracting and unpleasant advertising signs into the line of sight. The calculations of utility are much the same as before. The rational man finds that his share of the cost of the wastes he discharges into the commons is less than the cost of purifying his wastes before releasing them. Since this is true for everyone, we are locked into a system of "fouling our own nest," so long as we behave only as independent, rational, free-enterprisers.

The tragedy of the commons as a food basket is averted by private property, or something formally like it. But the air and waters surrounding us can not readily be fenced, and so the tragedy of the commons as a cesspool must be prevented by different means, by coercive laws or taxing devices that make it cheaper for the polluter to treat his pollutants than to discharge them untreated. We have not progressed as far with the solution of this problem as we have with the first. Indeed, our particular concept of private property, which deters us from exhausting the positive resources of the earth, favors pollution. The owner of a factory on the bank of a stream—whose property extends to the middle of the stream—often has difficulty seeing why it is not his natural right to muddy the waters flowing past his door. The law, always behind the times, requires elaborate stitching and fitting to adapt it to this newly perceived aspect of the commons.

The pollution problem is a consequence of population. It did not much matter how a lonely American frontiersman disposed of his waste. "Flowing water purifies itself every 10 miles," my grandfather used to say, and the myth was near enough to the truth when he was a boy, for there were not too many people. But as population became denser, the natural chemical and biological recycling processes became overloaded, calling for a redefinition of property rights.

## HOW TO LEGISLATE TEMPERANCE?

Analysis of the pollution problem as a function of population density uncovers a not generally recognized principle of morality, namely: *the morality of an act is a function of the state of the system at the time it is performed.*[10] Using the commons as a cesspool does not harm the general public under frontier conditions, because there is no public; the same behavior in a metropolis is unbearable. A hundred and fifty years ago a plainsman could kill an American bison, cut out only the tongue for his dinner, and discard the rest of the animal. He was not in any important sense being wasteful. Today, with only a few thousand bison left, we would be appalled at such behavior.

In passing, it is worth noting that the morality of an act cannot be determined from a photograph. One does not know whether a man killing an elephant or setting fire to the grassland is harming others until one knows the total system in which his act appears. "One picture is worth a thousand words," said an ancient Chinese; but it may take 10,000 words to validate it. It is as tempting to ecologists as it is to reformers in general to try to persuade others by way of the photographic shortcut. But the essence of an argument cannot be photographed: it must be presented rationally—in words.

That morality is system-sensitive escaped the attention of most codifiers of ethics in the past. "Thou shalt not . . ." is the form of traditional ethical directives which make no allowance for particular circumstances. The laws of our society follow the pattern of ancient ethics, and therefore are poorly suited to governing a complex, crowded, changeable world. Our epicyclic solution is to augment statutory law with administrative law. Since it is practically impossible to spell out all the conditions under which it is safe to burn trash in the back yard or to run an automobile without smog-control, by law we delegate the details to bureaus. The result is administrative law, which is rightly feared for an ancient reason—*Quis custodiet ipsos custodes?*—"Who shall watch the watchers themselves?" John Adams said that we must have "a government of laws and not men." Bureau administrators, trying to evaluate the morality of acts in the total system, are singularly liable to corruption, producing a government by men, not laws.

Prohibition is easy to legislate (though not necessarily to enforce); but how do we legislate temperance? Experience indicates that it can be accomplished best through the mediation of administrative law. We limit possibilities unnecessarily if we suppose that the sentiment of *Quis custodiet* denies us the use of administrative law. We should rather retain the phrase as a perpetual reminder of fearful dangers we cannot avoid. The great challenge facing us now is to invent the corrective feedbacks that are needed to keep custodians honest. We must find ways to legitimate the needed authority of both the custodians and the corrective feedbacks.

## FREEDOM TO BREED IS INTOLERABLE

The tragedy of the commons is involved in population problems in another way. In a world governed solely by the principle of "dog eat dog"—if indeed there ever was such a world—how many children a family had would not be a matter of public concern. Parents who bred too exuberantly would leave fewer descendants, not more, because they would be unable to care adequately for their children. David Lack and others have found that such a negative feedback demonstrably controls the fecundity of birds.[11] But men are not birds, and have not acted like them for millenniums, at least.

*If* each human family were dependent only on its own resources; *if* the children of improvident parents starved to death; *if*, thus, overbreeding brought its own "punishment" to the germ line—*then* there would be no public interest in controlling the breeding of families. But our society is deeply committed to the welfare state,[12] and hence is confronted with another aspect of the tragedy of the commons.

In a welfare state, how shall we deal with the family, the religion, the race, or the class (or indeed any distinguishable and cohesive group) that adopts over-breeding as a policy to secure its own aggrandizement?[13] To couple the concept of freedom to breed with the belief that everyone born has an equal right to the commons is to lock the world into a tragic course of action.

Unfortunately this is just the course of action that is being pursued by the United Nations. In late 1967, some thirty nations agreed to the following:[14]

> The Universal Declaration of Human Rights describes the family as the natural and fundamental unit of society. It follows that any choice and decision with regard to the size of the family must irrevocably rest with the family itself, and cannot be made by anyone else.

It is painful to have to deny categorically the validity of this right; denying it, one feels as uncomfortable as a resident of Salem, Massachusetts, who denied the reality of witches in the seventeenth century. At the present time, in liberal quarters, something like a taboo acts to inhibit criticism of the United Nations. There is a feeling that the United Nations is "our last and best hope," that we shouldn't find fault with it; we shouldn't play into the hands of the archconservatives. However, let us not forget what Robert Louis Stevenson said: "The truth that is suppressed by friends is the readiest weapon of the enemy." If we love the truth we must openly deny the validity of the Universal Declaration of Human Rights, even though it is promoted by the United Nations. We should also join with Kingsley Davis[15] in attempting to get Planned Parenthood – World Population to see the error of its ways in embracing the same tragic ideal.

## CONSCIENCE IS SELF-ELIMINATING

It is a mistake to think that we can control the breeding of mankind in the long run by an appeal to conscience. Charles Galton Darwin made this point when he spoke on the centennial of the publication of his grandfather's great book. The argument is straightforward and Darwinian.

People vary. Confronted with appeals to limit breeding, some people will undoubtedly respond to the plea more than others. Those who have more children will produce a larger fraction to the next generation than those with more susceptible consciences. The difference will be accentuated, generation by generation.

In C. G. Darwin's words: "It may well be that it would take hundreds of generations for the progenitive instinct to develop in this way, but if it should do so, nature would have taken her revenge, and the variety *Homo contracipiens* would become extinct and would be replaced by the variety *Homo progenitivus*."[16]

The argument assumes that conscience or the desire for children (no matter which) is hereditary—but hereditary only in the most general formal sense. The result will be the same whether the attitude is transmitted through germ cells, or exo-somatically, to use A. J. Lotka's term. (If one denied the latter possibility as well as the former, then what's the point of education?) The argument has here been stated in the context of the population problem, but it applies equally well to any instance in which society appeals to an individual exploiting a commons to restrain himself for the general good—by means of his conscience. To make such an appeal is to set up a selective system that works toward the elimination of conscience from the race.

## PATHOGENIC EFFECTS OF CONSCIENCE

The long-term disadvantage of an appeal to conscience should be enough to condemn it; but has serious short-term disadvantages as well. If we ask a man who is exploiting a commons to desist "in the name of conscience," what are we saying to him? What does he hear?—not only at the moment but also in the wee small hours of the night when, half asleep, he remembers not merely the words we used but also the nonverbal communication cues we gave him unawares? Sooner or later, consciously or subconsciously, he senses that he has received two communications, and that they are contradictory: (1) (intended communication) "If you don't do as we ask, we will openly condemn you for not acting like a responsible citizen"; (2) (the unintended communication) "If you *do* behave as we ask, we will secretly condemn you for a simpleton who can be shamed into standing aside while the rest of us exploit the commons."

Everyman then is caught in what Bateson has called a "double bind." Bateson and his co-workers have made a plausible case for viewing the double bind as an important causative factor in the genesis of schizophrenia.[17] The double bind may not always be so damaging, but it always endangers the mental health of anyone to whom it is applied. "A bad conscience," said Nietzsche, "is a kind of illness."

To conjure up a conscience in others is tempting to anyone who wishes to extend his control beyond the legal limits. Leaders at the highest level succumb to this temptation. Has any President during the past generation failed to call on labor unions to moderate voluntarily their demands for higher wages, or to steel companies to honor voluntary guidelines on prices? I can recall none. The rhetoric used on such occasions is designed to produce feelings of guilt in noncooperators.

For centuries it was assumed without proof that guilt was a valuable, perhaps even an indispensable, ingredient of the civilized life. Now, in this post-Freudian world, we doubt it.

Paul Goodman speaks from the modern point of view when he says: "No good has ever come from feeling guilty, neither intelligence, policy, nor compassion. The guilty do not pay attention to the object but only to themselves, and not even to their own interests, which might make sense, but to their anxieties."[18]

One does not have to be a professional psychiatrist to see the consequences of anxiety. We in the Western world are just emerging from a dreadful two-centuries-long Dark Ages of Eros that was sustained partly by prohibition laws, but perhaps more effectively by the anxiety-generating mechanisms of education. Alex Comfort has told the story well in *The Anxiety Makers*;[19] it is not a pretty one.

Since proof is difficult, we may even concede that the results of anxiety may sometimes, from certain points of view, be desirable. The larger question we should ask is whether, as a matter of policy, we should ever encourage the use of a technique the tendency (if not the intention) of which is psychologically pathogenic. We hear much talk these days of responsible parenthood; the coupled words are incorporated into the titles of some organizations devoted to birth control. Some people have proposed massive propaganda campaigns to instill responsibility into the nation's (or the world's) breeders. But what is the meaning of the word responsibility in this context? Is it not merely a synonym for the word conscience? When we use the word responsibility in the absence of substantial sanctions are we not trying to browbeat a free man in a commons into acting against his own interest? Responsibility is a verbal counterfeit for a substantial *quid pro quo*. It is an attempt to get something for nothing.

If the word responsibility is to be used at all, I suggest that it be in the sense Charles Frankel uses it.[20] "Responsibility," says this philosopher, "is the product of definite social arrangements." Notice that Frankel calls for social arrangements—not propaganda.

## MUTUAL COERCION MUTUALLY AGREED UPON

The social arrangements that produce responsibility are arrangements that create coercion, of some sort. Consider bank-robbing. The man who takes the money from a bank acts as if the bank were a commons. How do we prevent such action? Certainly not by trying to control his behavior solely by a verbal appeal to his sense of responsibility. Rather than rely on propaganda we follow Frankel's lead and insist that a bank is not a commons; we seek the definite social arrangements that will keep it from becoming a commons. That we thereby infringe on the freedom of would-be robbers we neither deny not regret.

The morality of bank-robbing is particularly easy to understand because we accept a complete prohibition of this activity. We are willing to say "Thou shalt not rob banks," without providing for exceptions. But temperance also can be created by coercion. Taxing is a good coercive device. To keep downtown shoppers temperate in their use of parking space we introduce parking meters for short periods, and traffic fines for longer ones. We need not actually forbid a citizen to park as long as he wants to; we need merely make it increasingly expensive for him to do so. Not prohibition, but carefully biased options are what we offer him. A Madison Avenue man might call this persuasion; I prefer the greater candor of the word coercion.

Coercion is a dirty word to most liberals now, but it need not forever be so. As with the four-letter words, its dirtiness can be cleansed away by exposure to the light, by saying it over and over without apology or embarrassment. To many, the word coercion implies arbitrary decisions of distant and irresponsible bureaucrats; but this is not a necessary part of its meaning. The only kind of coercion I recommend is mutual coercion, mutually agreed upon by the majority of the people affected.

To say that we mutually agree to coercion is not to say that we are required to enjoy it, or even to pretend we enjoy it. Who enjoys taxes? We all grumble about them. But we accept compulsory taxes because we recognize that voluntary taxes would favor the conscienceless. We institute and (grumblingly) support taxes and other coercive devices to escape the horror of the commons.

An alternative to the commons need not be perfectly just to be preferable. With real estate and other material goods, the alternative we have chosen is the institution of private property coupled with legal inheritance. Is this system perfectly just? As a genetically trained biologist I deny that it is. It seems to me that, if there are to be differences in individual inheritance, legal possession should be perfectly correlated with biological inheritance—that those who are biologically more fit to be the custodians of property and power should legally inherit more. But genetic recombination continually makes a mockery of the doctrine of "like father, like son" implicit in our laws of legal inheritance. An idiot can inherit millions, and a trust fund can keep his estate intact. We must admit that our legal system of private property plus inheritance is unjust—but we put up with it because we are not convinced, at the moment, that anyone has invented a better system. The alternative of the commons is too horrifying to contemplate. Injustice is preferable to total ruin.

It is one of the peculiarities of the warfare between reform and the status quo that it is thoughtlessly governed by a double standard. Whenever a reform measure is proposed it is often defeated when its opponents triumphantly discover a flaw in it. As Kingsley Davis has pointed out,[21] worshippers of the status quo sometimes imply that no reform is possible without unanimous agreement, an implication contrary to historical fact. As nearly as I can make out, automatic rejection of proposed reforms is based on one of two unconscious assumptions: (1) that the status quo is perfect; or (2) that the choice we face is between reform and no action; if the proposed reform is imperfect, we presumably should take no action at all, while we wait for a perfect proposal.

But we can never do nothing. That which we have done for thousands of years is also action. It also produces evils. Once we are aware that the status quo is action, we can then compare its discoverable advantages and disadvantages with the predicted advantages and disadvantages of the proposed reform, discounting as best we can for our lack of experience. On the basis of such a comparison, we can make a rational decision which will not involve the unworkable assumption that only perfect systems are tolerable.

## RECOGNITION OF NECESSITY

Perhaps the simplest summary of this analysis of man's population problems is this: the commons, if justifiable at all, is justifiable only under conditions of low-population density. As the human population has increased, the commons has had to be abandoned in one aspect after another.

First we abandoned the commons in food gathering, enclosing farm land and restricting pastures and hunting and fishing areas. These restrictions are still not complete throughout the world.

Somewhat later we saw that the commons as a place of waste disposal would also have to be abandoned. Restrictions on the disposal of domestic sewage are widely accepted in the Western world; we are still struggling to close the commons to pollution by automobiles, factories, insecticide sprayers, fertilizing operations, and atomic energy installations.

\* \* \*

Every new enclosure of the commons involves the infringement of somebody's personal liberty. Infringements made in the distant past are accepted because no contemporary complains of a loss. It is the newly proposed infringements that we vigorously oppose; cries of "rights" and "freedom" fill the air. But what does "freedom" mean? When men mutually agreed to pass laws against robbing, mankind became more free, not less so. Individuals locked into the logic of the commons are free only to bring on universal ruin; once they see the necessity of mutual coercion, they become free to pursue other goals. I believe it was Hegel who said, "Freedom is the recognition of necessity."

The most important aspect of necessity that we must now recognize, is the necessity of abandoning the commons in breeding. No technical solution can rescue us from the misery of overpopulation. Freedom to breed will bring ruin to all. At the moment, to avoid hard decisions many of us are tempted to propagandize for conscience and responsible parenthood. The temptation must be resisted, because an appeal to independently acting consciences selects for the disappearance of all conscience in the long run, and an increase in anxiety in the short.

The only way we can preserve and nurture other and more precious freedoms is by relinquishing the freedom to breed, and that very soon. "Freedom is the recognition of necessity"—and it is the role of education to reveal to all the necessity of abandoning the freedom to breed. Only so, can we put an end to this aspect of the tragedy of the commons.

# NOTES

This article is based on a presidential address presented before the meeting of the Pacific Division of the American Association for the Advancement of Science at Utah State University, Logan, 25 June 1968.

1. J. B. Wiesner and H. F. York. *Scientific American 211*:4 (1964): 27.
2. G. Hardin. *Journal of Heredity* 50, 68(1959); S. Von Hoernor, *Science 137* (1962): 18.
3. J. Von Neumann and O. Morgenstern. *Theory of Games and Economic Behavior.* Princeton, New Jersey: Princeton University Press (1947): 11.
4. J. H. Fremlin. *New Scientist 415* (1964): 285.
5. A. Smith. *The Wealth of Nations.* New York: Modern Library (1937): 423.

6. W. F. Lloyd. *Two Lectures on the Checks of Population*, Oxford, England: Oxford University Press (1833), reprinted (in part) in *Population, Evolution, and Birth Control*, G. Hardin, ed. San Francisco: Freeman (1964): 37.
7. A. N. Whitehead. *Science and the Modern World*, New York: Mentor, (1948): 17.
8. G. Hardin, ed. *Population, Evolution, and Birth Control*, San Francisco: Freeman (1964): 56.
9. S. McVay. *Scientific American 216* (1966): 13.
10. J. Fletcher. *Situation Ethics*, Philadelphia: Westminster (1966).
11. D. Lack. *The Natural Regulations of Animal Numbers*, Oxford: Clarendon Press (1954).
12. H. Girvetz. *From Wealth to Welfare*, Stanford, California: Stanford University Press (1950).
13. G. Hardin. *Perspectives in Biology and Medicine 6* (1963): 366.
14. U. Thant. *International Planned Parenthood Federation Medical Bulletin 168* (February 1968): 3.
15. K. Davis. *Science 158* (1967).
16. S. Tax, ed. *Evolution after Darwin*, vol. 2. Chicago: University Of Chicago Press (1960): 469.
17. G Bateson, D. D. Jackson, J. Haley, and J. Weakland. *Behavioral Science 1*:251 (1956).
18. P. Goodman. *New York Review of Books 10* (May 23, 1968): 22.
19. A. Comfort. *The Anxiety Makers*, London: Nelson (1967).
20. C. Frankel. *The Case for Modern Man*, New York: Harper (1955): 203.
21. J. D. Roslansky. *Genetics and the Future of Man*. New York: Appleton-Century-Crofts (1966): 177.

## S E L E C T I O N    8

John Vickers and George Yarrow

# Economic Perspectives on Privatization

The question of public versus private provision of goods and services
has many dimensions: welfare costs of market failure versus government failure, comparative efficiency of public versus private production of specific goods or services, and purely ideological and political
concerns over the appropriate role of government in a market economy. As concern over federal debt has grown, even the revenue-raising potential of selling government assets and enterprises has entered
the discussion. However, there seems to be no single answer for any
of these debates. Nevertheless, it is clear that privatization is an
important and current public policy issue—not only for recently-
formed market economies in Eastern Europe and the former Soviet
Union, but also for mature industrialized nations such as the United
States and Great Britain.

In this selection, John Vickers and George Yarrow explore policies of
ownership reform. The discussion is organized around three types of
privatizations: (1) privatization of state-run enterprises with already-
active private sector competitors (e.g., railroads); (2) privatization of
state-run enterprises with no private sector competitors (e.g., telecommunications); and (3) contracting out to private firms services previously provided by the public sector (e.g., garbage collection). The authors
examine how privatization and continuing government intervention
can alter an enterprise's objectives as well as the ability to measure
managerial performance. The role of product market competition in
creating incentives for the efficient operation of privatized firms is

Vickers, John, and George Yarrow. "Economic Perspectives on Privatization." *Journal of Economic Perspectives* 5 (Spring 1991): 111–132.

**John Vickers** is Drummond Professor of Political Economy at Oxford University and a Fellow of All Souls College. **George Yarrow** is Oxford University Lecturer in the Economics of the Firm, and Fellow and Tutor in Economics at Hertford College, Oxford, United Kingdom.

investigated. The authors also detail the actual experiences of privatization programs in Britain, Chile, and Poland.*

**Questions to Guide the Reading**
1. According to the "simple benchmark model" of Shapiro and Willig,[†] how might the objectives of public and private decision makers differ? When might private ownership be clearly advantageous? When might public ownership have the advantage?
2. In what ways might government intervention continue after privatization?
3. How does the monitoring of managers in the public sector contrast with that in the private sector?
4. In the United States, the most relevant form of privatization is contracting out. How does the role of competition in contracting out compare with the other two forms of privatization? What are some of the potential pitfalls of contracting out?
5. In general, what is the empirical evidence on the comparative performance of the three types of privatization?
6. What are some of the distributional issues involved in privatization? In privatizing a state-owned enterprise, what might be the advantages of distributing shares to citizens directly and free of charge?
7. What lessons can be drawn from the experiences in Britain, Chile, and Poland?

---

Despite being one of the most fundamental issues in political economy, the question of the appropriate boundary between public and private enterprise received relatively little attention in mainstream economic analysis until quite recently. In the 1980s, however, programs of ownership reform were started in many developed and developing countries. Dramatic though some of these policies have been, they are likely to be overshadowed in the 1990s by even greater privatization in the reforming socialist economies.

The opening sections of this paper are organized around three broad and interrelated questions. How does ownership matter for the efficiency of enterprise

---

\* *Editors' note:* If desired because of length or other considerations, the reader may omit these country-specific discussions without loss of continuity, and skip directly to the final section "Concluding Remarks."

† *Editors' note:* Students familiar with models of bureaucracy should recognize that the Shapiro and Willig bureaucrat is based, at least in part, on the influential model developed by William Niskanen (see Suggested Further Readings, Niskanen 1971). Niskanen argued that bureaucrats were essentially monopoly suppliers of public services, and that their primary objective was to maximize power by maximizing the size of their budgets.

performance? What is the role for privatization in financing public debts and deficits? What are the distributional and political implications of privatization? Such questions obviously cannot be given general answers: what holds for a developed, market-based economy in western Europe may not hold for a developing country with a thin domestic capital market or severe debt problems, still less for an economy emerging from decades of state control. Nevertheless, we hope to show that a relatively small set of economic principles can be applied to various cases of privatization.

One way to characterize the privatization programs of different countries is in terms of the relative importance given to three types of privatization: (1) privatization of competitive firms—or, more generally, transfer to the private sector of state-owned enterprises operating in competitive product markets free from substantial market failures; (2) privatization of monopolies—transfer to the private sector of state-owned enterprises with substantial market power, like network utilities in telecommunications or electricity; and (3) contracting out of publicly financed services, previously performed by public sector organizations, to the private sector. These three types will serve as benchmarks throughout the discussion.

An important difference between types 1 and 2 is that governments frequently retain some rights of control, in the form of regulation, where monopoly power and other market failures are present. Indeed, where government involvement in the affairs of a private enterprise is substantial, the differences between public and private can become a matter of degree. Within type 2 it is important to distinguish between natural monopolies (like electricity transmission), where technological conditions imply monopoly, and "artificial" monopolies, where competition from domestic or foreign firms could exist but is thwarted by anticompetitive industrial and commercial policies. Type 3, the contracting out case, does not involve the sale of physical assets, but it is a kind of privatization: the asset sold is a service contract or franchise agreement. Rights over any financial surplus arising from the activities concerned are transferred to the private contractor, and rights to residual earnings are central to what is meant by ownership.

France is an example of a country where privatization (in 1986–1988) concerned firms in more or less competitive industries, like banking and insurance. In Britain, while numerous privatizations of all types have occurred, utility privatizations (telecommunications, gas, electricity, and water) have been of greater significance than elsewhere. In the United States, where the scope of state-owned enterprises has been relatively limited, privatization has been mostly concerned with contracting out; for example, garbage collection or hospital cleaning. In the formerly socialist economies of central and eastern Europe, a large proportion of privatizations will concern (potentially) competitive industries. Three illustrative country case studies of privatization—Britain, Chile, and Poland—will be examined in later sections of this paper.

The possible methods of privatization will not be discussed in any detail here. Assets can be sold, or distributed at zero price, for example via voucher schemes. If the decision is taken to sell, there are questions of whom to sell to (individual, shareholders, managers, other employees, banks, mutual funds, corporations, domestic residents, foreigners); how to sell (private negotiation, stock market offer for sale, tender, auction); what form of private participation to adopt (majority/minority stake, joint venture); what initial debt-equity ratio to set; and so on (World Bank 1988). Other policy instruments—like competition and regulatory policies, the ability of the government to raise money without selling assets, and the existing system of redistribution—will influence both what method is chosen, and whether privatization is appropriate. The general point is that privatization policies should be evaluated not only with regard to given objectives but also in the light of alternative ways of attaining those objectives.

## HOW DOES PRIVATIZATION AFFECT THE EFFICIENCY OF AN ENTERPRISE?

The relationship between ownership, incentives, and efficiency are numerous and complex, and our analysis will proceed in steps. We shall consider how privatization can change the objectives of the firm's ultimate owners, the possibilities for government intervention, and ways of monitoring managerial performance. We also discuss relationships between ownership and competition in determining incentives for efficiency. Finally, the empirical evidence on ownership and efficiency is mentioned. The evidence suggests that private ownership has efficiency advantages in competitive conditions, but does not show either public or private ownership to be generally superior when market power is present. Policy towards competition and regulation appears to be very important in the latter case. Indeed, the need to consider the effects of ownership, competition, and regulation jointly will be central to the analysis that follows.

### Owners' Objectives

Let us begin with a simple benchmark model. Following Shapiro and Willig (1990), suppose that under public ownership the firm is run by a minister or government bureaucrat who maximizes an objective function that is a weighted average of social welfare and his or her personal agenda. The personal agenda could consist of a variety of elements: redistribution to favoured interest groups, high wage and employment levels in particular enterprises or sectors, patronage, and so on.[1] Under private ownership, by contrast, suppose that firm is run for the maximization of profit. Profit is a component of social welfare, but there might also be external effects on welfare from the activities of the firm. These include effects on consumer suprlus if the firm has market power, effects due to input market distortions, distributional effects, and so on.[2]

In each case, social welfare and the objectives of the decision makers diverge. In competitive market conditions (and in the absence of other market failures), externality effects are small, so private profit and social welfare objectives are closely aligned, and private ownership is likely to have the advantage, especially if the public bureaucrat has considerable scope to pursue his or her personal agenda. On the other hand, public ownership may have the advantage if externalities are larger and the pursuit of personal agendas is more constrained, for example by a well-functioning political system.

## Government Intervention

This simple approach assumes (among other things) that privatization entails the transfer of all decision-making authority to private hands. But is it credible or desirable for there to be no government intervention in the decisions taken by the firm?

Sappington and Stiglitz (1987) argue that privatization affects the transaction costs of government intervention in enterprise decision-making. For example, subsidies to loss-making activities are fairly common under public ownership. Privatization does not imply a binding commitment by government not to subsidize losses—as witnessed by Chrysler in the United States and British Leyland in the UK—but subsidization is clearly easier under public ownership. Similarly, cross-subsidies that serve political and distributional goals are often a feature of public enterprise pricing. Taxes and subsidies could induce a privatized firm to maintain such a pattern of pricing, but with less ease and less covertly than under public ownership. Of course, competition is even more likely to undermine cross-subsidies in pricing, irrespective of whether there is public or private ownership.

Where monopoly power (or other externalities) are important—that is, in type 2 privatization—intervention by government is likely to be desirable on welfare grounds, and regulation is called for. When a firm is both privatized and regulated, much depends upon the nature of the game between the firm and the government. For example, if the firm chooses sunk investment expenditures to reduce costs, it runs the risk that the government might opportunistically decide to enforce low prices, without allowing the firm to recover its costs. This kind of problem is familiar from the work of Oliver Williamson (1975). It can give rise to problems of underinvestment.[3]

It follows that the welfare effects of privatizing monopolies depend significantly upon how well regulatory problems are overcome. Regulation might even reinstate the problems of public officials acting in their own interest that privatization was intended to sidestep.[4]

## Monitoring Managers

A criticism often made of public ownership is that incentives to monitor managerial behavior are poor, leaving managers considerable discretion to pursue their personal agendas. However, managers of state-owned enterprises are typically responsible to political decision makers, and while the discretion of politicians to impose their own private agendas can be explained by the limitations of political institutions as monitoring systems, it is not obvious that this will also lead to managerial discretion. Political fortunes might not normally be very sensitive to overall state-owned enterprise performance, and politicians may lack strong incentives to monitor enterprise management. However, some decisions (like plant closures) tend to be very sensitive politically, and the performance of state-owned enterprises may become a priority item on political agendas at certain times, like when the enterprises are losing money and state budgets are being tightened. In such situations, managerial discretion in public enterprises may be more limited.

Privatization alters the means of monitoring managerial behavior. In particular, capital market pressures may be brought to bear.[5] The transferability of private ownership rights reveals information via prices, like share prices. If the stock market is efficient, these prices capitalize the consequences of current action for future profits. The resulting information can be used in contracts between shareholders and managers—remuneration packages may include stock options, for example—and it might have further incentive effects via the managerial labor market (Fama 1980; Holmstrom 1982b). However, if the efficient markets hypothesis is not true (the evidence on this is mixed—see the symposium on bubbles in the Spring 1990 issue of the *Journal of Economic Perspectives*), then the information conveyed by share prices has less value for monitoring purposes.

Moreover, most important cases of privatization (of types 1 and 2) have concerned large corporations with numerous shareholders. With dispersed shareholding, which was actively promoted in privatizations that aimed to widen share ownership (like the utility industries in Britain), obvious free-rider problems remain for shareholder monitoring. It is here that the threats of takeover and bankruptcy become important. The effectiveness of the discipline on managers arising from the threat of takeover remains a subject of controversy (for example, see the symposium in the Winter 1988 issue of the *Journal of Economic Perspectives*), and the dispute has clear implications for privatization.

The threat of bankruptcy, which is also a kind of monitoring device, is another difference between public and private ownership. It can significantly affect bargaining over matters like wages and employment.[6] But the differences should not be exaggerated. Hard budget constraints have been successfully applied to state-owned enterprises, at least at times. Regulators of privatized utility companies in Britain are effectively required to ensure that they do not go bankrupt. And government has many ways to loosen the budget constraints for private firms, including subsidies, loan guarantees, trade protection, and ultimately nationalization.

## The Role of Competition

Competition, which is conceptually distinct from ownership, can greatly improve monitoring possibilities, and hence incentives for productive efficiency. In particular, competition facilitates performance comparisons, which can generally improve tradeoffs between incentives and risk when several agents (managers) facing correlated uncertainties are being monitored (Hart 1983; Holmstrom 1982a; Nalebuff and Stiglitz 1983). Thus, product market competition is important for performance not only for familiar reasons of allocative efficiency but also because it enhances productive efficiency. As Adam Smith (1776/1976, page 163) put it two centuries ago: "Monopoly, besides, is a great enemy to good management, which can never be universally established but in consequence of that free and universal competition which forces every body to have recourse to it for the sake of self-defence."

But head-to-head product market competition, or even the threat of it, does not always exist. If competition has been suppressed by the state through legal barriers to entry, trade protection and the like, as in much of central and eastern Europe, then deregulation and liberalization of markets may suffice for a reasonably rapid transition to competitive markets. Then privatization can be of type 1 (competitive) rather than type 2 (monopolistic). On the other hand, experience in Britain (described below) shows that the legalization of entry does not always lead to effective competition by itself. Regulation for competition may then be a desirable complement to privatization.

The bundling of privatization with the promotion of competition is precisely what contracting out (type 3 privatization) involves. The shift is from monopolistic public supply to private supply (unless the public enterprise wins the contract) with competition. However, contracting out has some potential pitfalls (Williamson 1976). First, competition for contracts may be ineffective from the outset, perhaps because of collusion, or subsequently as advantages of incumbency accumulate. Second, depending on the observability and transferability of investment, underinvestment can cause problems of dynamic efficiency. Third, for all but the simplest of goods and services, there is generally a continuing role for government authority in contract administration—monitoring, enforcing, bargaining over unspecified contingencies, and so on—and these activities may be only a short step from regulation or having the public agency oversee the work directly. In the end, what matters is how the combination of ownership and regulation under private ownership compares with ownership and (implicit or explicit) regulation in the public sector.

## Evidence on Ownership and Efficiency

What follows is simply a summary of some of the main conclusions from empirical studies of the comparative performance of public and private enterprise. (For detail, see Vickers and Yarrow 1988, chapter 2; Boardman and Vining 1989.) First, some of the difficulties facing empirical analysis must be noted. They include problems of measuring key variables (like allocative efficiency), the relative scarcity of cases where like-with-like comparisons can be made between public and private firms, the limited time that has elapsed since many major privatizations, and difficulties in distinguishing between the effects on efficiency of changes in ownership, competition, and regulatory policies.

In competitive environments (relevant for type 1 privatization) some like-with-like comparisons of performance have been made. An example is the study of Canadian railroads by Caves and Christensen (1980). Once competition was introduced, there was no evidence of inferior performance by publicly-owned Canadian National relative to Canadian Pacific, its private rival. The authors concluded that public ownership was not inherently less efficient than private ownership in this case, and that competition rather than ownership per se was the key to efficiency. However, in competitive conditions, the two types of ownership are likely to be of similar efficiency if state-owned enterprises are not unfairly supported. Boardman and Vining (1989), in their international cross-section analysis of competitive industries, find that state-owned enterprises are less profitable and less efficient than private firms. Overall, the evidence suggests that in competitive industries private ownership is generally (though not universally) preferable on efficiency grounds, and that competition may be a more important influence than ownership.

Studies of contracting out (type 3 privatization), which implies an immediate increase in competition, reach similar conclusions. Donahue (1989) concludes from his study of U.S. privatization that most of the benefits of contracting out have come from the greater scope for rivalry than from private provision per se. However, it may be difficult to introduce rivalry without some private ownership, and, in this context, some privatization may be necessary but not sufficient for substantial performance improvements.

Turning to cases of industries with natural monopoly elements (relevant for type 2 privatization), like water and electric utilities, the results of the empirical studies are very mixed: some give the advantage to public ownership, others to private ownership, and yet others can find no significant difference between the two. Substantial performance differences among utilities do, nevertheless, exist, both within and between countries. The major factor that appears to be at work is regulatory policy. This point is supported by before-and-after comparisons of enterprise performance when there is a major shift of regulatory regime. Foe example, there have been significant changes in the productivity performance of some protected nationalized industries in Britain since the regulatory reforms of the late 1970s and early 1980s, which emphasized tighter financial constraints (Molyneux and Thompson, 1987). British Steel is a very good example.

Perhaps the most important point to emerge from the evidence is the importance of competitive conditions and regulatory policies, as well as ownership, for incentives and efficiency.

## RAISING REVENUE

Privatization is likely to influence the profit streams of firms, for all the reason just discussed. Moreover, it gives governments the opportunity to capitalize those profit streams and raise immediate revenue (or promote distributional ends by underpricing assets as described in the next section). Like the sale of government bonds, privatization converts future cash streams into present cash sums.

Where privatization increases profits in ways not feasible under public ownership (for example, because of greater efficiency), revenue-raising advantages can enhance the already existing case for privatization (Jones, Tandon, and Vogelsang 1988).[7] If privatization does not increase profits, can it nevertheless have advantages on revenue-raising grounds? To examine this question, let us assume that privatization has no effect on the firm's earning prospects.

In terms of transaction costs, selling bonds would appear to be a less costly way of raising revenue than privatization (selling equities). Many countries, especially in the developed world, have liquid bond markets, so that bonds can be priced quite accurately (or simply auctioned), whereas with equities there can be a tendency to underpricing (as explained further in the next section). Direct costs of sale—prospectuses, advertising, underwriting, and so on—are also higher with equity sales.

Governments constrained in their ability to sell bonds, like some Latin American countries facing debt crises, might nevertheless favor equity sales. The private discount rate applied to bonds might be higher than that applied to equities if the perceived risk of default on bonds is higher than the equity risk; that is, if the government commitment not to expropriate equity holders is more credible than the commitment not to expropriate bondholders. Expropriation of bondholders can occur by inflation (unless the bonds are indexed), by the withholding of interest payments, or by non-repayment of the principal. Expropriation of equity returns can occur by outright nationalization (without proper compensation), or less directly, by tightening price or environmental regulation once privately financed investments have been sunk. The credibility of government commitment not to "default on equity" is likely to vary by industry, as sunk costs and the extent of regulation vary, and by country, as legal and political institutions and international relations differ. It may also depend on the way that privatization is carried out, such as whether the assets are sold to domestic residents or foreigners, or whether large or small investors are encouraged to buy.

Finally, another reason government may feel constrained in selling bonds is that many have promised not to do so. For example, the British government in the early 1980s was committed to limits on public sector borrowings to make its anti-inflationary stance more credible. These constraints had led to what were considered undesirable limitations on the investment programs of state-owned enterprises such as British Telecom. Privatization moved the borrowings of these state-owned enterprises out of the public sector accounts, and thereby freed them from the government-imposed constraints. Since the real macroeconomics effects of the firms' borrowings are much the same irrespective of whether they are deemed "public" or "private," this seems rather curious. Maybe signalling considerations can explain how privatization could save anti-inflationary face in these circumstances?

The revenue-raising argument for privatization depends on the circumstances of a particular country and the credit rating of its bonds. For a developed economy with a stable financial and political system, the risk of default on bonds is likely to be low, and it is hard to make the case for privatization purely on revenue grounds. But for a less developed country prone to bouts of rapid inflation, bond sales may be constrained in such a way that there is a pure revenue motive for the privatization of firms in sectors where the "default" risk on equity is not too great. Because this risk is related to the availability of regulatory instruments, these tend to be the more competitive (and hence less regulated) sectors, where the efficiency case for privatization is already the strongest.

## POLITICAL AND DISTRIBUTIONAL ISSUES

Privatization presents significant opportunities for redistribution of income and wealth. Just as aspects of regulation can be analyzed in terms of their implicit tax and subsidy aspects (Posner 1971), so too can some aspects of privatization programs.

In discussing distributional issues, it is useful to identify the major groups which might be affected by privatization. Apart from political decision makers themselves, these include consumers, employees (including managers), new shareholders, taxpayers, suppliers of inputs other than labor, and suppliers of "privatization services" like financial institutions responsible for handling the sales, recipients of advertising revenues, consultants, and lawyers.

Consumers will be affected by changes in both the level and structure of prices of newly privatized enterprises. Here, as elsewhere, policies towards competition and regulation are also very important. For example, the creation of a privatized monopoly subject to weakened price controls could be a method of raising revenue less overtly than by an equivalent increase in commodity taxation. Peltzman (1989) has put forward the hypothesis that state intervention in the utility industries has tended to suppress spatial (often urban versus rural) price differentials associated with economies of density, usually by creating monopoly rents which are partly used (implicitly or explicitly) to cross-subsidize high-cost consumers. If the policy preference survives privatization, then the promotion of competition may be sacrificed to the distributional objective, since competition will undermine the cross-subsidization unless explicit taxes and subsidies are used.

Many privatization programs, as in Britain, have included schemes to allow enterprise employees to acquire shares in their organization on particularly favorable terms. The rationale for these policies may be based upon the perceived efficiency-enhancing incentive effects of employee share ownership, but these are questionable in large firms. There may also be a desire to compensate employees for potential loss of rents accrued under public ownership, or to influence the longer-term probability of renationalization.

However, this last point is questionable. Pressure from workers for public ownership is likely to be strongest when their firm is in financial difficulties. But share values will tend to be low in that case, and, even if employee shareholding exists on a substantial scale, protecting returns to labor may be the overriding priority. Moreover, employee share ownership gives workers extra incentives to oppose policies promoting effective competition and regulation. Thus, what was initially a compensation for loss of privileges may, at a later date, provide stronger incentives for the restoration of those privileges.

The most immediate and dramatic distributional effects of privatization are those resulting from the pricing of privatized assets. Discounts on the market clearing price are a transfer of wealth to the new owners from the wider public, and from taxpayers in particular. Generous pricing may be politically attractive both because it reduces the risk of the shares being unsold (which could be embarrassing), and because the beneficiaries tend to be more aware of their gains than the losers feel the losses. It is costly in (national) welfare terms, however, if there is a premium on public funds, if part of the windfall goes abroad, of if the gainers tend to be wealthier than the losers and, other things equal, there is a preference for more egalitarian wealth distribution.

Pricing at substantial discounts to market values is often associated with policies to promote wide share ownership, together with measures like share allocation rules that favor small investors, and inducements for them to hold on to their shares rather than sell out at a quick profit (for example, loyalty bonuses and discounts on purchases of goods or services from the privatized enterprises). Such methods have been used in the sales of utility industries in Britain, for example.

In the limit, shares can simply be distributed free of charge, either directly or in the form of vouchers that are redeemable for shares in former state-owned enterprises. For example, in 1979 the government of British Columbia in Canada gave each resident five shares in its Resources Investment Corporation. Government revenues are foregone in this process, which is costly to the economy depending upon the social costs of public funds, but it satisfies fairness criteria, may reduce transactions costs, and avoids the transfer abroad of windfall gains that may be a feature of alternative methods of privatization. Free distribution of shares, or something close to it, might be the only practicable means of rapid domestic privatization (as opposed to sales to foreigners) in economies where individual savings are meagre. On the other hand, in some circumstances, selling shares might be a way of absorbing "monetary overhang" resulting from forced saving due to past rationing in nonmarket economies.

Finally, another motive for wider share ownership is to make it more difficult for a future government to reverse privatization. The numerous new shareholders acquire some financial interest in the continuation of policies (and governments) beneficial to the profitability of the firms that they own, and in the avoidance of policies (and governments) liable to cause them capital losses, such as renationalization on poor terms.

## PRIVATIZATION IN PRACTICE IN THREE COUNTRIES

### Britain

Privatization in Britain has involved various policies. Large amounts of public sector housing stock were sold in the early 1980s. There has been considerable contracting out of services at local government level and in organizations such as the National Health Service. However, the discussion here will focus on the transfer of state-owned enterprises to private ownership, which is the aspect of the policy that has attracted the most international attention. Vickers and Yarrow (1988) provide a detailed account of this program.

In 1979, at the beginning of the privatization program, state-owned enterprises accounted for about 10.5 percent of Britain's gross domestic product. The greater part of public enterprise output came from state monopolies in telecommunications, gas, electricity, water, rail transport, and postal services. However, major state-owned enterprises also existed in competitive or potentially competitive industries such as steel, coal, oil, and vehicles.

Studies of the performance of the state-owned enterprise sector during the 1960s and 1970s found numerous specific examples of inefficient resource allocation, but overall productivity growth was broadly in line with that in the British private sector (Molyneux and Thompson 1987). The state-owned enterprise sector did, however, have substantial persistent financial deficits in the preprivatization period. This deficit amounted to over 20 percent of the state-owned enterprises' contribution to GDP in 1979, which was down from a high of over 35 percent in 1975. This reduction reflected changes in public policy that placed much greater stress on financial objectives for public enterprises, and the emphasis on financial objectives was increased further by the Conservative government that came to power in 1979.

Privatization of state-owned enterprises was barely mentioned in the Conservative party manifesto of that year, but the great majority of state-owned enterprise assets have now been privatized, leaving coal, rail, and postal services as the only major industries still in the public sector. This transfer of enterprises to the private sector can usefully be divided into three phases, corresponding to the periods between national election years.

*Phase 1, 1979–83.* Asset sales in the first phase were concentrated on enterprises other than the major monopolies that lay at the heart of the public sector. These included Associated British Ports (port operations), British Aerospace (aircraft and defense contracting), Britoil (North Sea oil exploration and production), Cable and Wireless (telecommunications operations), National Freight (road haulage), and sales of stock in British Petroleum (already part privately owned). Although some of these firms possessed pockets of market power, to a first approximation they can be regarded as examples of the first of our three benchmark cases of privatization. Total privatization proceeds were no higher than £500 million per annum during this period.

Both efficiency and revenue objectives were involved in these privatizations. For example, National Freight was a deeply discounted management/worker buyout, which had incentive effects, but raised little revenue for the Treasury. On the other hand, the sale of shares in British Petroleum, which could not be expected to make much difference to incentives, raised substantial amounts. Similarly, the sale by tender of shares in Britoil in 1982 can be viewed as a forward sale of oil motivated chiefly by revenue considerations. At the time British macroeconomic policy was committed to limiting the public sector deficit, which was under pressure because of recession.

During this period, the government was also active in competition and regulatory policy. Stricter budget constraints were placed on state-owned enterprises and were sometimes accompanied by new management, most notably in the steel industry. Legislation was introduced with the aim of increasing competitive pressures on state-owned enterprises in the telecommunications, gas, electricity, and road transport industries. In telecommunications, for example, a second public network operator, Mercury (owned by Cable and Wireless), was licensed in 1982 to compete with British Telecom. Although the impact of some of these measures turned out to be disappointing (because entry-deterring strategies of incumbent firms went largely unchecked) the legislation does indicate that increasing efficiency was an important policy goal at the time.

*Phase 2, 1983–87.* Sales of enterprises operating in reasonably competitive industries continued, including Enterprise Oil (oil exploration and production), Jaguar (motor cars), the Trustee Savings Bank, British Airways, and Rolls-Royce (airplane engines). The distinguishing feature of this second period, however, was the first sale of a utility/network industry, in the form of the flotation of £3,900 million less costs, followed by the sale of British Gas in December 1986 (£5,600 million). These two privatizations mark a shift in emphasis in the program toward the second benchmark type of privatization.

When the government announced its intention to privatize British Telecom in 1982, it emphasized allowing British Telecom access to capital markets, so that investment in new technology could be undertaken without increasing public sector borrowings (which were constrained by the macroeconomic commitments referred to above). In addition, because privatization proceeds are treated in British public sector accounts as negative public expenditure, selling BT would help the short-term deficit, whatever its effect on the net worth of the public sector in the long run. As explained in the discussion of revenue-raising above, selling bonds and selling equities are rather similar in economic terms, but their very different accounting treatments enhanced the attractiveness of privatization.

Another important innovation of the BT sale was the extent to which the share issue was targeted at small investors by advertising, generous pricing, share allocation rules, and loyalty bonuses to encourage individuals to hold on to their shares. For the first time, successful applicants for shares were numbered in millions, and the offer price was such that first day capital gains amounted to 33 percent on the full price and 86 percent on a partly-paid basis. A similar pattern was followed during the second phase of privatization, including British Airways, Rolls-Royce, British Gas, and the Trustee Savings Bank, and with the subsequent water and electricity sales. While new equity issues by private companies typically go to a premium on the opening of trading, the average premium with these privatization issues was considerably higher. Moreover, there was a shift in methods of sale. In the earlier period, sale by tender offer and privatization of companies in stages were common. These methods facilitate accurate pricing; for example, it is easier to price shares in a company if some of its shares are already traded on the stock market. But later, especially after 1985, tendering was rarely used, and sales tended to be all in one go. This suggests that the weight attached by the government to political and distributional objectives, for example wider share ownership, had substantially increased.

The privatization of BT, the monopoly supplier of telecommunications services, raised the question of whether or not to restructure the industry before transfer to the private sector (the restructuring of AT&T in the United States was in progress at the time) and how to regulate the industry. The restructuring option was rejected: although it might have facilitated the development of competition it would have delayed privatization, perhaps considerably, and hence would have delayed the political benefits from the asset transfer. The incumbent management, whose cooperation was important in the privatization process, was also strongly opposed to restructuring. Similar remarks also apply in the case of gas.

New regulatory bodies, the Office of Telecommunications (Oftel) and the Office of Gas Supply (Ofgas), were established in connection with these privatizations. Their job is to apply price controls to the regulated firms and, within limits, to promote competition. Some of the powers initially given to these bodies were rather limited—the aim was to have "regulation with a light touch"—but they have been increasingly active in influencing market conduct. For example, in its 1988 review, Oftel successfully tightened the original pricing constraint on BT from a rule specifying that real prices must, on average, fall by 3 percent per year to one requiring a 4.5 percent per annum reduction. And a review in 1988 of British Gas's conduct in the industrial market led to a tightening of regulation.

*Phase 3, 1987–91.* Although these years included major asset sales such as British Steel and the British Airports Authority, the third phase of the program was dominated by the sales of the water (1989) and electricity (1990–91) industries. These later utility sales were similar to the earlier telecommunications and gas privatizations in that new bodies were established to regulate the industries and the sales were heavily targeted at small investors. Unlike telecommunications and gas, however, in both cases there was substantial restructuring of the state-owned enterprises before privatization. The purpose of restructuring the water industry was to separate environmental regulation, which used to be a duty of the public enterprises, from the business of water supply, rather than any notion that competition might be increased as a result. Indeed, the government explicitly recognized that the prospects for competition in the supply of basic services were poor, and instead emphasized the potential for the development of "competition by comparison" that existed by virtue of the fact that there are a number of regionally-based water utilities.

Pressures for improved water quality (for example, to meet European regulatory standards) meant that the industry was planning for a large-scale investment program. Privatization raised fears of possible underinvestment by privately-owned water utilities. Initial price controls therefore took the form of formulae which promised the regional utilities future prices which, year by year, would rise substantially faster than the general rate of inflation, provided that key investment objectives in each region,were met. In effect, "regulatory contracts" were struck with the utilities allowing the latter to obtain finance for investment from consumers.

In contrast, industrial restructuring in electricity has been motivated by an attempt to increase competition. The monopoly generation and transmission enterprise in England and Wales, the Central Electricity Generating Board, has been split into four parts: two non-nuclear generating companies, one nuclear generating company, and a national transmission grid company, owned jointly by the regional distribution companies. The whole industry was originally to be privatized, but the nuclear power stations were later withdrawn from the sale and will remain in state ownership. While a number of significant limitations on competition remain associated with this structure and with the associated regulatory regime, by international standards the measures taken with electricity supply are the most radical of the whole privatization program. In particular, generation and transmission have been de-integrated, and a quasi-spot market for wholesale power supplies has been set up. In addition, generating companies can compete with electricity distributors to supply power to larger customers, and they have successfully done so. Given its experimental nature, however, it remains to be seen how effectively the system will work in the longer term. One unanswered question is whether the essentially duopolistic structure of electricity generation will be compatible with developing effective competition in the bulk power market (Vickers and Yarrow 1991).

The British privatization program has raised tens of billions of pounds for the Treasury, has created millions of new shareholders, and has significantly reduced state involvement in enterprise decision making in a number of industries. However, its impact on economic efficiency is rather less clear (Bishop and Kay 1988; Yarrow 1989). Inferences are necessarily limited by the short elapsed time since some of the more important privatizations, but, thus far, radical shifts in conduct and performance appear to have occurred in only a few cases, all of which are characterized by a reasonable degree of product market competition (like Associated British Ports, National Freight, Cable and Wireless). To complicate the interpretation of these cases, the most dramatic changes have occurred in state-owned enterprises like (preprivatization) British Steel and British Coal, where productivity gains have been massive by any standards. In steel and coal there was less scope to meet tighter financial constraints by price rises than in more monopolized industries, and the government successfully confronted the coal miners' union. Perhaps the only sound conclusion at this stage, therefore, is that the British evidence is consistent with the view that competitive conditions and regulatory environments (in the broad sense) are key determinants of performance.

## Chile

The history of state-owned enterprises in Chile dates back well into the nineteenth century, with the development of industries such as railroads, ports, postal services, and finance. The public sector was expanded during the 1940s and 1950s, a period when the state-owned investment bank CORFO created large enterprises in sectors like steel, petroleum, and electricity. Difficulties in securing imports of industrial goods, investment finance and technology in wartime conditions were motivating factors in this expansion, and the result was a state-owned enterprise sector that accounted for approximately 15 percent of GDP by the late 1960s (Luders 1990).

During 1970–73, the Allende government sought to turn Chile into a fully socialist economy. This involved a dramatic increase in the size of the state-owned enterprise sector to around 40 percent of GDP (a significant fraction of which was accounted for by the nationalization of the copper industry) and a range of other measures that included land nationalization, the establishment of state monopoly in international trade, the extensions of state control over enterprises and markets outside the state sector itself.

When the military government ousted Allende, privatization was part of a general policy designed to reverse the measures introduced by the Allende government. It was accompanied by measures of deregulation and liberalization, including liberalization of international trade. The privatization program in Chile, which was to become very far-reaching, has had four main stages (World Bank 1988, vol. 2).

*Phase 1, 1974–75.* The first phase of privatization consisted largely in the simple return to their original owners of enterprises that had been nationalized in the immediately preceding period, and these transfers did not involve payments either to or from the government.

*Phase 2, 1975–83.* More than 100 enterprises were privatized in the second phase, including firms in which the Allende government had taken an ownership stake or which it had created. Over this period, the principal objective of privatization was to raise revenues for the state. In the peak year of 1975, for example, privatization raised revenues equal to approximately 3.3 percent of GDP. Though large in relation to programs in other countries (in Britain that ratio was a little over 1 percent in the late 1980s), this was but a small fraction of the fiscal deficit, which had soared to a level equal to 25 percent of Chile's GDP in 1973. Privatization proceeds fell to approximately 1.5 percent of GDP in 1976, and then to less than 1 percent per annum.

The priority attached to raising revenue had a strong influence on how assets were sold during the second phase of privatization. The main sales method was public auction followed by negotiation with the most qualified bidder. The buyers included corporations, notably banks, but not individual investors. Many of the sales involved partial payment, with the balance financed by loans from the state. The granting of loans lowered the net revenue on any given asset sale, but the procedure was intended greatly to increase the number of state-owned enterprises that could be sold quickly. One consequence of the approach was a commercial structure characterized by highly leveraged financial and industrial conglomerates and by concentrations of ownership. This structure failed to withstand the financial crisis of the 1982–83 period, when widespread bankruptcies, including bank failures, led to many of the newly privatized enterprises again being placed under state control.

*Phase 3, 1985–86.* The third phase was motivated by desires to reverse the renationalizations that had taken place during the 1982–83 financial crisis, and to promote "popular capitalism" by wider share ownership, including employee share ownership, by appropriate share pricing and allocation rules. A major goal was to foster a more broadly-based ownership structure less vulnerable to collapse and more resistant to further renationalization, and thereby to enhance the durability of privatization.

*Phase 4, 1986–.* Though its objectives have been a continuation of those in the immediately preceding period, most of the enterprises targeted for privatization in this fourth stage have been the state-owned enterprises whose establishment predated the Allende government, including state monopolies such as the main electricity utility. In these cases, the issues and tradeoffs are, in broad terms, similar to those already discussed in relation to Britain.

The fate of many of the enterprises sold during the second phase of Chile's privatization policy illustrates the problems that can arise when different parts of public policy are not properly aligned. In attempting to privatize quickly, the government sold assets in a way that jeopardized the survival of the new enterprises, at a time when increases in market pressures were being promoted by liberalization and trade policies. While an efficiency case may sometimes exist for selling state-owned enterprises with highly leveraged capital structures, a general policy of this type, implemented in conditions of economic turbulence, would appear to have been misguided. Liberalization in advance of privatization might have been a safer policy sequence (World Bank 1988, vol. 2). But although the second phase of privatization in Chile can generally be deemed a failure, the policy of promoting competition and regulatory reform may have had more durable effects (Luders 1990).

Perhaps the most important lesson to draw from the Chilean experience is that privatization per se is not always an effective way to establish credible commitments to new incentive structures, and that the method of privatization may well be of crucial importance in this regard.

## Poland

Privatization policies in Poland are part of a much wider package of policies aimed at fostering the development of a market economy, as they are in the rest of central and eastern Europe (Kawalec 1989; Lipton and Sachs 1990a). There are some similarities here with post-Allende Chile, although the scale of problem is greater in Poland, given both the extent and duration of state control over economic activity. Thus, in the late 1980s, state ownership dominated both the industrial and service sectors of the economy, which together accounted for over 85 percent of GDP. In the industrial sector, for example, private production accounted for less than 6 percent of measured output (although it was growing quite rapidly, and there was also considerable black market activity). Only in agriculture was private ownership prevalent.

The first priority of the incoming Solidarity government in 1989 was macroeconomic stabilization in the face of hyperinflation. Price reforms allowed enterprises to set their own prices (although state control was retained in politically sensitive areas like energy), but the aim was largely to achieve a more realistic level of prices in relation to wages. Given the nature and structure of socialized enterprises and markets, there was little expectation that the resulting price structure would provide accurate signals for the next round of resource allocation decisions.

A more distinctive feature of the Polish situation has been uncertainty about initial property rights (Lipton and Sachs 1990b). Economic reforms in the 1980s had sought to decentralize planning functions, increase enterprise autonomy, and expand the influence of workers on enterprise decisions. Partly as a result, it was possible to find the state treasury, the relevant local government body, and employees (including management) each claiming ownership rights in a particular enterprise. Lack of clarity concerning property rights is particularly damaging because it can lead to sereve incentive failure. For example, managers and employees might begin to expropriate potentially productive capital. Moreover, uncertainty can lead rival claimants to devote their energies and resources to influencing the allocation of property rights, rather than to more socially productive activities. Hence, it was important for Polish government to give a high priority to securing an acceptable property rights settlement, implying that at least some distributional issues had to be tackled before privatization could even begin. Unfortunately, conflict over the distributional consequences (including the distribution of control as well as wealth) of alternative privatization schemes acted as a brake on the development of the enabling legislation for privatization during the course of 1990.

Another distinctive feature of the situation in formerly communist economies like Poland is the lack of capitalist financial markets and institutions (like a stock market, pension funds, private banks, mutual funds, and so on). Their creation must accompany the process of privatization. Various techniques of privatization have been proposed, including distribution of shares to individuals, employees, and financial intermediaries (Lipton and Sachs 1990b).

The desirable pace of privatization has been another subject of heated debate. There are tensions between objectives—for example, between state revenue objectives and the desire to privatize rapidly—so as not to delay the benefits of privatization and not to risk the whole process being mired down. (The difficulty of combining vigorous pursuit of revenue objectives with rapid privatization is illustrated by the outcome of phase 2 of Chile's program). Given the squeeze on household liquidity and wealth that resulted from the 1989/90 stabilization program, sale of assets to domestic nationals at anything but the lowest of prices would require a relatively slow pace of privatization. Alternatively, assets could be sold on a large scale to overseas investors, but this would risk a political backlash.

It should be noted that this argument applies to the privatization of state-owned enterprises, and not to contracting out forms of privatization. Given the extent of state involvement in service activities in the Polish economy, there is considerable scope for efficiency gains via contracting out of service provision by, for example, local government bodies. As argued earlier, the achievement of financial benefits through contracting goes hand-in-hand with the promotion of efficiency via competition for the relevant contract. Pressures on public sector budgets could, therefore, act as a factor making for the speeding up, rather than the slowing down, of this type of privatization.

An important argument against rapid privatization is that it might leave inadequate time for the creation of durable incentive structures for efficiency. For example, without market liberalization, many of the state-owned enterprises would simply be transformed into private monopolies, as happened with some of the larger privatizations in Britain. In Poland, however, the greater proportion of the state-owned enterprise sector is made up of enterprises that could quickly be subjected to increased competition by the liberalization of international trade and the withdrawal of industrial subsidies, policies that the Solidarity government has chosen to adopt independently of privatization.

A related argument for delay is that, even if the Chilean pitfall of creating highly leveraged enterprises were avoided, the withdrawal of industrial subsidies and the opening up of markets to international competition might proceed too quickly to allow efficient response. Hence, enterprises that might be economically viable in the longer term could find it hard to survive in the short term. On this view, the better sequence is to promote competition first, to establish more realistic price signals that can be used by the state to restructure enterprises, and, finally, only when these stages are completed, to privatize (a sequence followed, with great success, by the British government in the case of British Steel).

This is rather like the infant industry argument. It relies upon state ownership, rather than tariffs, to provide the necessary degree of protection, and can therefore be assumed to rest upon a favorable view of the operation of state-owned enterprises and a relatively unfavorable view of the efficiency with which capital markets function. The difficulty with it is a familiar one: the protection may never be removed.

Analysis of the tradeoffs between distributional, revenue, and efficiency objectives in the Polish case, therefore, brings us back to the basic issues discussed earlier. If market failures are large relative to government failures in the new political situation, then state-owned enterprises might perform better relative to privately-owned enterprises in the period of transition than when market failures are smaller and political agendas are less constrained. If reality in Poland lies closer to the former situation, the analysis would point toward a policy sequence of partial liberalization (liberalization cannot be said to be complete when enterprise-specific subsidies are retained), enterprise restructuring within the public sector and, only then, privatization. On the other hand, a situation close to the second possibility would point towards full liberalization and rapid privatization, leaving restructuring and other major resource allocation decisions to be taken by owners or managers within the new structure of property rights.

Perhaps the most difficult aspect of the problems confronting Poland, however, is that reality does not lie close to either of the above two hypothesized situations. Rather, what will be observed through the 1990s will be the simultaneous existence of substantial externalities in several major markets (largely the result of the socialist inheritance) and of the implementation of discretionary political agendas (associated, for example, with interest group capture of parts of the state apparatus). In the Polish case, the tradeoffs facing privatization policy appear particularly difficult.

## CONCLUDING REMARKS

Any form of ownership is inevitably imperfect. Market failures can lead to divergence between profit and welfare objectives in private firms. Government failure leads to divergence between political/bureaucratic and welfare objectives in state-owned enterprises. Monitoring failure leads to divergence between the objectives of enterprise managers and their principals, whether the principals are private owners or political superiors. The effects of ownership changes on welfare will depend upon the relative magnitudes of these imperfections. As a first approximation, privatization can be viewed as a means of reducing the impact of government failure, albeit at the risk of increasing market failures, and of changing monitoring arrangements.

Of course, it would be simplistic to view privatization as a universally effective remedy for agency problems in the public sector. First, where market failures are significant (and sometimes where they are not), government intervention frequently continues after privatization, so that significant opportunities for the direct implementation of political and bureaucratic agendas will often remain. Second, while privatization may increase the obstacles to government intervention, commitments not to intervene at all may lack credibility or be undesirable, especially in industries with monopoly power or other market failures. This can result in inefficient underinvestment. And the possibility of partial "default on equity" via renationalization, tighter regulation, high profits taxation, and so on, is important for the issue of whether the government should raise revenue by selling bonds or equities. Third, privatization is itself a government activity, and one with potentially large distributional and political consequences. The process of asset transfer will tend to open new opportunities for the pursuit of private agendas by political decision makers. As with other areas of public policy, privatization cannot be expected to be exempt from the impact of government failure.

The effects of privatization in any particular context will, therefore, be highly dependent upon the wider market, regulatory, and institutional environments in which it is implemented. The challenge to economic analysis of privatization is to develop a more complete understanding of the implications for business conduct and performance of these complex interactions among ownership, market structure, regulatory, and political variables.

## NOTES

We are grateful to the UK Economic and Social Research Council and Office of Fair Trading for research support, and to Carl Shapiro, Joe Stiglitz, and Timothy Taylor for very helpful comments on an earlier version of the paper, and to Mark Armstrong for research assistance. The views expressed are entirely our own, and we are responsible for any errors.

1. More formally, let us assume that under public ownership the firm is run by a minister or government bureaucrat whose objective $V$ is a weighted average of social welfare and his/her personal agenda $P$: $V = W(x) + \mu P(x)$, where $x$ is a vector of decision variables. The parameter $\mu$ here reflects the weight given to the private agenda relative to social welfare.

2. Denoting welfare by $W$, profit by $\pi$, and the externalities, notably including consumer benefits, by $E(x)$, we have $W = \pi + E$, or equivalently: $\pi (x) = W(x) - E(x)$.

3. This underinvestment problem, which arises if the regulator cannot fully commit not to behave opportunistically, is to be contrasted with the well-known overinvestment problem under rate-of-return regulation explored by Averch and Johnson (1962). Greenwald (1984) argues that rate-of-return regulation can be viewed as a means of commitment that addresses the underinvestment concern. Gilbert and Newbery (1988) describe how this problem may be less severe in a multi-period framework, since opportunistic behavior by a regulator today can have negative consequences for future regulatory objectives. Grossman and Hart (1986) provide related analysis about the importance of the institutional setting.

4. That is not, of course, to say that public ownership and regulated private ownership have identical consequences. One possible difference lies in the information available to the government decision maker (Shapiro and Willig 1990).

5. In economies where capital markets are undeveloped, privatization may be used as an element of policy to promote their development.

6. It is important to distinguish between the distributional and efficiency effects of soft budget constraints. High wages, for example, show up in firm deficits, but do not necessarily imply (technological) inefficiency.

7. Note that this argument depends on the gains in profits being unobtainable under public ownership. For example, it would certainly be fallacious to favor on revenue grounds the privatization of a monopoly because it would lead to greater exercise of monopoly power and hence profits, which would be capitalized in privatization proceeds, if monopolistic pricing could also be implemented in the public sector.

## REFERENCES

Alchian, Armen, and Harold Demsetz. "Production, Information Costs and Economic Organization." *American Economic Review 62* (December 1972): 777–795.

Averch, Harvey, and Leland Johnson. "Behavior of the Firm under Regulatory Constraint. *American Economic Review 52* (December 1962): 1052–1069.

Bishop, Matthew, and John Kay. *Does Privatization Work?—Lessons from the UK.* London: London Business School (1988).

Boardman, Anthony, and Aidan Vining. "Ownership and Performance in Competitive Environments: A Comparison of the Performance of Private, Mixed and State-owned Enterprises." *Journal of Law and Economics 32* (April 1989): 1–33.

Caves, Douglas, and Laurits Christensen. "The Relative Efficiency of Public and Private Firms in a Competitive Environment: The Case of Canadian Railroads." *Journal of Political Economy* (October 1980): 958–976.

Donahue, John. *Public Ends and Private Means.* New York: Basic Books (1989).

Fama, Eugene. "Agency Problems and the Theory of the Firm." *Journal of Political Economy 88* (April 1980): 288–307.

Gilbert, Richard, and David Newbery. "Regulation Games," Discussion Paper 267, Centre for Economic Policy Research, London (1988).

Greenwald, Bruce. "Rate Base Selection and the Structure of Regulation." *RAND Journal of Economics 15* (Spring 1984): 85–95.

Grossman, Sanford, and Oliver Hart. "The Costs and Benefits of Ownership: A Theory of Vertical and Lateral Control." *Journal of Political Economy 94* (August 1986): 297–336.

———. "Takeover Bids, the Free-Rider Problem and the Economics of the Firm." *Bell Journal of Economics 11* (Spring 1980): 42–64.

Hart, Oliver. "The Market Mechanism as an Incentive Scheme." *Bell Journal of Economics 14* (Autumn 1983): 366–382.

Holmstrom, Bengt. "Moral Hazard in Teams. " *Bell Journal of Economics 13* (Autumn 1982a): 324–340.

———. "Managerial Incentive Problems—A Dynamic Perspective." *Essays in Honor of Lars Wahlbeck.* Helsinki: Swedish School of Economics (1982b).

Jones, Leroy, Pankaj Tandon, and Ingo Vogelsang. "Net Benefits from Privatization: A Valuation Methodology." Unpublished paper, Boston University (1988).

Kawalec, Stefan. "Privatisation of the Polish Economy." *Communist Economies 1* (1989): 241–256.

Lipton, David, and Jeffrey Sachs. "Creating a Market Economy in Eastern Europe: The Case of Poland." *Brookings Papers on Economic Activity 1* (1990a): 75–147.

———. "Privatization in Eastern Europe: The Case of Poland." Unpublished paper, Harvard University (September 1990b).

Luders, Rolf. "Chile's Massive SOE Divestiture Program: 1975–1990." Paper presented at World Bank Conference on Privatization and Ownership Changes in East and Central Europe (June 1990).

Molyneux, Richard, and David Thompson. "Nationalised Industry Performance: Still Third-Rate?" *Fiscal Studies 8* (February 1987): 48–82.

Nalebuff, Barry, and Joseph Stiglitz. "Prizes and Incentives: Towards a General Theory of Compensation and Competition." *Bell Journal of Economics 14* (Spring 1983): 21–43.

Peltzman, Sam. "The Control and Performance of State-Owned Enterprises." In MacAvoy, Paul, et al., eds., *Privatization and State-Owned Enterprises.* Boston: Kluwer Academic Publishers (1989), 69–75.

Posner, Richard. "Taxation by Regulation." *Bell Journal of Economics 2* (1971): 22–50.

Sappington, David, and Joseph Stiglitz. "Privatization, Information and Incentives." *Journal of Policy Analysis and Management 6* (1987): 567–582.

Shapiro, Carl, and Robert Willig. "Economic Rationales for the Scope of Privatization." Olin Program Discussion Paper 41, Woodrow Wilson School, Princeton University (1990).

Smith, Adam. *An Inquiry into the Nature and Causes of the Wealth of Nations,* edited by R. H. Campbell and A. S. Skinner. Oxford: The Clarendon Press (1976).

Vickers, John, and George Yarrow. *Privatization: An Economic Analysis.* Cambridge: MIT Press (1988).

———. "The British Electricity Experiment." *Economic Policy 12* (1991).

Williamson, Oliver. *Markets and Hierarchies: Analysis and Antitrust Implications.* New York: Free Press (1975).

———. "Franchise Bidding for Natural Monopolies—In General and with Respect to CATV." *Bell Journal of Economics 7* (Spring 1976): 73–104.

World Bank. *Techniques of Privatization of State-Owned Enterprises* (3 Volumes), Technical Papers 88, 89, and 90. Washington, D.C. (1988).

Yarrow, George. "Privatization and Economic Performance in Britain." *Carnegie-Rochester Conference Series on Public Policy 31* (August 1989): 303–344.

**OPTIMAL GOVERNMENT INTERVENTION**
Topic of Interest:
*Infrastructure*

# S E L E C T I O N     9

Charles R. Hulten and Robert M. Schwab

# Infrastructure Spending: Where Do We Go from Here?

Proponents of public sector infrastructure spending often argue that such capital investments provide the economy with an underlying foundation necessary to generate real growth and to improve international competitiveness. Opponents frequently contend that such government programs are just pork barrel spending, designed only to benefit particular special interest groups. Infrastructure projects are numerous and diverse and include roads, airports, mass transit systems, bridges, dams, the "information superhighway," and even public buildings such as schools and jails. Because each project has political as well as economic dimensions, politics often limits the application of policy recommendations made purely on the basis of economic efficiency.

Charles Hulten and Robert Schwab examine the recent debate in the United States over declining public investment in transportation infrastructure. They conclude that the evidence demonstrates the slowdown in infrastructure spending has had little effect on the slowdown in the performance of the U.S. economy. Public policy suggestions are offered—for instance, greater reliance on cost-benefit analysis and implementation of measures such as the correct pricing of highway services. In general, rather than a massive infusion of infrastructure funding, "a stronger commitment to spend existing resources more efficiently" is needed.

### Questions to Guide the Reading
1. What are the dangers of using the norm of "baby boom" spending to guide infrastructure policy?

Hulten, Charles R., and Robert M. Schwab. "Infrastructure Spending: Where Do We Go From Here?" *National Tax Journal* 46 (September 1993): 261–273.

**Charles R. Hulten** and **Robert M. Schwab** are both Professors of Economics at University of Maryland.

2. What is the evidence that the infrastructure crisis is "specific" rather than "systemwide"?
3. According to studies by David Aschauer, decreased infrastructure investment in the U.S. caused a decline in economic performance. What reasons are given to suggest that this conclusion may be incorrect?*
4. Why might past experience and retrospective studies be poor guides to the economic effects of future infrastructure spending?
5. What are the difficulties inherent in attempting to use infrastructure spending as a short-term policy tool for job creation?
6. According to the authors, what "self-inflicted policy wounds" have contributed to our infrastructure problems?

The infrastructure debate of the 1990s is reminiscent of the debate over supply side economics. In the late 1970s, supply siders argued that the prevailing tax system was responsible for the slowdown in economic growth and the loss of competitiveness, and advocated a dramatic reduction in effective tax rates. This, they argued, would stimulate economic activity to such a degree that it might even lead to higher tax revenues—the famous Laffer curve analysis. The result was the Economic Recovery Tax Act of 1981 (and the subsequent "take-backs" that culminated in the Tax Reform Act of 1986).

Although the vocabulary is different, much the same is now being said of infrastructure investment. Proponents of greater spending have argued that the decline in public investment in the 1970s and 1980s was responsible for as much as 60 percent of the productivity slowdown and that increased spending must play a key role in any plan to revitalize the U.S. economy and improve international competitiveness.[1] Dollar estimates of the investment shortfall have ranged as high as $150–200 billion per year. Some have even pointed to the infrastructure parallel to the Laffer curve—the Aschauer curve, after the economist whose estimates of dramatic returns to public capital investment are widely discussed and cited. With rates of return of the magnitude reported by David Aschauer, an investment in public infrastructure would throw off so much income that the investment would pay for itself in additional tax revenue.[2]

As was the case with supply side economics, many economists and policy analysts are skeptical of the size of the benefits imputed to public capital investment. Many have argued that the infrastructure crisis has been overdramatized

.................................................

* *Editors' note:* Students without a strong background in statistics or econometrics initially may have difficulty with this question. However, even if the econometric arguments are disregarded, the main issues and arguments in the relevant section "Infrastructure Investment and Economic Performance" should be understandable.

and that the public capital problems we do face could be solved largely with redesigned programs funded at roughly current levels. Others have gone further and suggested that any large new infrastructure program should be a low priority use of federal funds in this time of fiscal stringency. Some see infrastructure spending as little more than pork barrel politics.

Conflicts of opinion and disputes over the available evidence are an inherent characteristic of the public policy process. The following remarks are offered in an attempt to sort out the main issues of the infrastructure debate, using the main arguments in favor of greater spending as a framework for the discussion. The case for more public investment rests on four arguments: (1) shortsighted government policies allowed infrastructure spending to fall sharply and the nation's roads and bridges to deteriorate; (2) lower infrastructure spending in the past was a key reason the economy performed so poorly during the last two decades; (3) additional spending in the future will allow the United States to grow much faster and to become more competitive in international markets; and (4) infrastructure spending should be included as a key part of short-term economic policy. We will examine each of these points in turn in the following sections of the paper. We then offer several policy recommendations and a brief summary and conclusions in the final sections.

## INADEQUATE INVESTMENT

The origins of the infrastructure "crisis" can be traced to the precipitous decline in public investment spending after 1968. As can be seen in Figures 1 and 2, state and local government public investment rose more or less continuously from around 2 percent of GDP in the early and mid-1950s to 3 percent of GDP in 1968.[3] Spending declined dramatically after 1968, falling to just over 1.5 percent of GDP in the early 1980s. As a consequence, the state and local capital stock grew roughly 1 percent per year in the late 1970s and the early 1980s as compared to roughly 5 percent per year during most of the late 1950s and 1960s.

Proinvestment advocates have argued that the failure to invest in public capital allowed the country's infrastructure to deteriorate sharply. There is evidence, for example, that pavement quality fell during the 1970s and that congestion increased during the 1980s. A recent study by the Federal Highway Administration (FHWA) (U.S. Department of Transportation 1993) estimates that $46.2 billion was needed in 1992 just to keep highway and bridge performance at its 1991 level but that only $35.9 billion was actually spent. In the same study, FHWA estimates that the cost to maintain 1991 performance and condition will average $51.6 billion per year over the next 20 years and that the cost to improve capacity by 40 percent and eliminate the backlog of highway deficiencies will average $67.3 billion. Other reports, with names such as *America in Ruins* and *Fragile Foundations* that strongly hint that the end is near, have concluded that a massive amount of new spending at all levels of government is required to solve the country's infrastructure problems.

**Figure 1** Investment in State and Local Capital

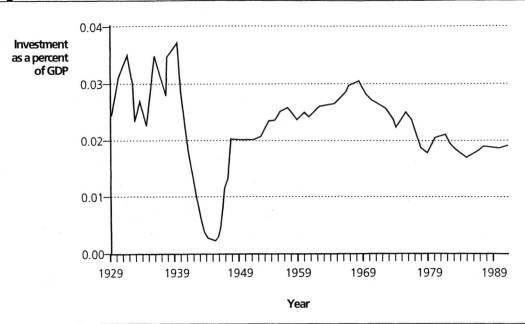

Critics have argued that these estimates are problematic and the argument unpersuasive. A decline in the share of GDP devoted to public capital formation cannot be taken a priori as compelling evidence of inadequate spending. In a dynamic economy, spending priorities are always changing. There was a time when the U.S. economy was predominantly agricultural, and, although the share of GDP originating in agriculture has declined over the decades, no one is talking about a food crisis in the United States.

Moreover, there is a problem with the way the evidence on declining infrastructure investment is framed. The peak spending period (the 1950s and 1960s) was the period in which major portions of the Interstate Highway System were completed and thousands of schools were built to meet the needs of the baby boom. After these programs wound down, it was not surprising that spending declined as the country grew into its newly enlarged capital stock. To accept peak spending as the norm is to frame the problem in a way that implies that anything less than peak spending is inadequate. Such a norm would commit the country to a continuous and endless program of building, regardless of need or voter preferences.

As for the evidence on rising congestion and deteriorating road conditions, critics of a massive new infrastructure program concede that there are indeed problems in many places, particularly in fast growing suburbs and in cities that face difficult fiscal problems. But they also argue that these specific problems

**Figure 2**  Growth Rate of State and Local Capital

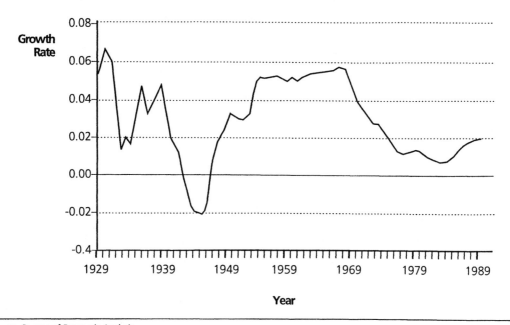

*Source:* Bureau of Economic Analysis

should not be interpreted as evidence of a systemwide crisis in transportation. For example, Sanders (1993) has shown that 40 percent of all bridges that have been classified as deficient are located in just six states. More than half of all bridges in New York State fall into this category as compared to 2 percent of Florida bridges and 6 percent of Oregon bridges. Sanders also shows that a similar pattern emerges in data on pavement quality. According to 1989 data, the average percentage of "poor" quality roads across the states is 11 percent. In most states, the problem is relatively small; in Connecticut, for example, less than 4 percent of the highway pavement is in poor condition. But in a few states the problem is quite serious; more than one quarter of the roads in Idaho, Mississippi, and Rhode Island fall into this category.

As for growing congestion, another FHWA study (U.S. Department of Transportation 1992) found that *mean* travel time to work for the nation as a whole hardly changed between 1980 and 1990—21.7 vs. 22.4 minutes. Of course, the additional 42 seconds is not spread evenly across the population of commuters, and congestion has grown to near crisis proportions in areas like Los Angeles. However, this statistic is a useful reminder that the overall extent of the congestion problem is far less dramatic than the worst-case examples imply. Yet it is precisely these worst cases that get much of the attention in the press and in the policy debate.

Finally, the evidence from FHWA assessment studies must be interpreted with care. These studies are based on the amount of investment needed to maintain or improve average vehicle performance over the highway system. While they provide a framework for assessing the extent and location of possible spending needs, the FHWA warns that "The investment analysis results should not be represented as either preferred or optimal investment strategies. They represent investment and performance benchmarks to support further policy and budget analysis" (U.S. Department of Transportation 1993, 175). In other words, taxpayers may conclude that they have more pressing needs for some of the $51.6 billion needed to maintain vehicle performance at past levels. This conclusion should not be very surprising. People are generally unwilling to spend the money that would be necessary to maintain their car or house in perfect working order and are equally unwilling to spend enough to avoid some degree of congestion and deterioration.

In sum, it is true that during the 1970s spending was allowed to dip significantly below past levels, and it is true that the performance of the transportation system as measured by congestion and pavement conditions did suffer. But it is also true that in a period after any spending boom we will, almost by definition, see reduced construction spending, a deterioration in facility condition as the capital ages, and rising congestion as the country grows into the new capacity. It may well be the case that deterioration and congestion were excessive in certain places. But it must also be recognized that these conditions are currently being addressed. According to a recent Congressional Budget Office study (1992b), real investment measured in constant 1990 dollars in eight important types of infrastructure (highways, mass transit, rail, aviation, water transportation, water resources, water supply, and wastewater treatment) rose an average of 2.4 percent per year from $46.8 billion in 1979 to $63.3 billion in 1989; the Intermodal Surface Transportation Efficiency Act of 1991 (ISTEA) anticipates federal transportation expenditures of more than $150 billion over five years.

## INFRASTRUCTURE INVESTMENT AND ECONOMIC PERFORMANCE

In a series of papers and articles, David Aschauer (see, for example, Aschauer 1989 and 1991) argued that the decline in infrastructure investment was a key factor in the poor performance of the U.S. economy over the last two decades. His work, for example, implies that slower infrastructure investment could explain as much as 57 percent of the productivity slowdown in the 1970s and 1980s. Moreover, he finds the rate of return to infrastructure to be very high—around 70 percent in the following year, according to Robert Reich—and that the gain in output from an additional dollar spent on public capital is two to five times as large as the gain from an additional dollar spent on private capital (Aschauer 1991).

Before Aschauer, most studies of economic growth ignored infrastructure capital and implicitly suppressed any effects due to this type of factor input into a residual category. Aschauer brought infrastructure capital out of the "closet" of neglect and into the light of statistical scrutiny, and he deserves credit for stimulating a huge (and growing) literature on the effect of public infrastructure capital on economic growth. However, while some of the recent contributions to this literature support Aschauer's results (Canning and Fay 1993, Morrison and Schwartz 1991, Fernald 1992), others have reached rather different conclusions.

Aaron (1990), Hulten (1990), Schultze (1990), Jorgenson (1991), and Tatom (1991) have all argued that for a variety of reasons, it is hard to put much faith in the results from aggregate time series studies. One major problem arises from the fact that the U.S. time series data are dominated by two trends: infrastructure investment fell sharply starting in the late 1960s and early 1970s, and the aggregate U.S. economy has performed poorly since roughly 1973. This is sufficient to establish a correlation between infrastructure and output growth. But, while it is clear that the two are associated, it is far from clear that lower infrastructure investment was the *cause* of slower growth. Any variable that fell through the 1960s and early 1970s, like SAT scores, is an equally plausible candidate as the cause of our growth problems.

The following story illustrates this point. The number of storks in a certain region was found to be closely correlated with the number of babies that were born in that region. This might support the conclusion that storks bring babies. But the truth was more mundane. When the harvest was good, families were more likely to have another child and more storks came to the region to take advantage of the available food.

Of course, it is always easy to dismiss any evidence by arguing that correlation does not imply causality. But in this case, there are enough other troubling pieces of evidence to suggest that we truly are dealing with spurious correlation. For example, if infrastructure were an important part of the productivity problem, then we would expect to find a significant slowdown in industries such as manufacturing that are very dependent on infrastructure but little change in other industries, such as services and finance, insurance, and real estate. But, in fact, the exact opposite is true; the productivity slowdown in manufacturing has been very mild. The growth rate of GDP per hour of work in manufacturing was roughly the same in the 1973–1987 period as it was during 1948–1973. In contrast, in the private sector as a whole, GDP per hour grew at a rate only about one-third of the pre-1973 rate.

There is, in addition, an important issue of the direction of causality. Clearly, it is quite plausible to believe that infrastructure causes economic growth when a correlation between the two is observed. It is, after all, impossible to imagine an advanced economy without roads and airports, electricity and telecommunications, etc. However, causality may run in both directions: richer societies can afford to build more infrastructure capital, just as they can afford to have more machines and factories and more human capital. As output increases, there is more total savings to devote to capital formation of all sorts. Thus, infrastructure investment is "caused" by output growth and vice versa.

This leads to the following conclusion: if Aschauer had started with infrastructure on the left-hand side of his regressions instead of the right-hand side and thus used output as an explanatory variable, he would have found a strong correlation. Then the appropriate conclusion would have been that the accelerated growth of output in the 1960s caused the infrastructure boom and the declining growth rate of output in the 1970s caused the drop in public investment. This is an equally valid reading of the evidence, if one believes that correlation implies causality.

Elementary econometrics tells us that this is not true. When an equation like the production function is part of a larger system of equations, the arguments of the function—inputs and output—are all endogenously determined within the system. A simple regression of output on input—or vice versa—will lead to biased results. Moreover, causality does not follow from any observed correlation, since the endogenous variables are jointly determined. There are econometric techniques that try to sort out the direction of causality in single equation models (the Granger causality test). When they are applied to the infrastructure-output regression, they find little evidence that the line of causality runs from output to infrastructure (Ho and Sorensen 1993).

Moreover, it turns out that the time series evidence on this point is very fragile. In Hulten and Schwab (1991b), we found that with slightly different statistical approaches, the same data could lead us to conclude that additional investment in infrastructure could have either a dramatic impact or virtually no impact on the private economy. In his often cited 1989 paper, Aschauer modeled the level of aggregate output as a function of the levels of public capital, private capital, labor, time (as a proxy for technical change), and capacity utilization (to control for the effects of the business cycle). When we estimated models of this type, our results were very similar to his; in particular, we found an elasticity of private output with respect to public capital of 0.21. We then argued that in time series work, there is always the danger of spurious correlation since many variables follow the same time trend. Economists who work with time series data often recast their analysis in terms of whether the *changes* in one variable can explain *changes* in a second variable (that is, they "detrend" the data). When we re-estimate our models after first differencing the data, the impact of public capital vanishes.[4]

Some of the initial regional work found a strong link between productivity and regional economic performance. Munnell (1990b), for example, found an elasticity of public output with respect to public capital of roughly 0.15. Some recent work has also found a strong link between infrastructure and regional output (e.g., Morrison and Schwartz 1991), but other evidence is less encouraging (e.g., Hulten and Schwab 1984). In Hulten and Schwab (1991a), we looked closely at the manufacturing sector in different regions of the country. It is well known that infrastructure investment has been significantly higher in the newer Sun Belt regions as compared to the older Snow Belt. For example, during the 1978–1986 period, the stock of infrastructure essentially did not grow at all in the Northeast and Midwest but grew at an annual rate of about 1.6 percent in the South and West. But, in fact, productivity growth in the Northeast and Midwest was somewhat faster than in the South and West, and this period was not a fluke. We found that throughout the postwar period, productivity growth was roughly the same in all regions; to the extent that we did find differences, in general, productivity grew slightly faster in the Snow Belt.

The work of Holtz-Eakin (1992), Garcia-Mila et al. (1993), Evans and Karras (1991a), and Eisner (1991) identifies another problem with the earlier research on regional and state production functions. All of these papers focus on the appropriate specification of a state level production function that includes public capital as an explanatory variable and find that the appropriate model allows for state specific effects that do not vary over time. That is, they find that the appropriate model is either a fixed effects or random effects model. In such models, they all find that public capital has no impact (at the margin) on private output. They also show that if they ignore these state specific effects, then public capital does appear to have a strong positive effect on output. Munnell does not estimate fixed or random effects models, and thus these four papers strongly suggest that her estimates are subject to an important specification bias.

The evidence from international research is also very weak. There is a substantial literature that has used international data to understand the determinants of growth. Typically, papers in this area use cross section or panel data and a limited set of plausible determinants of growth. Levine and Renelt (1992) present a very careful review of this literature. They found that very few economic variables are robustly correlated with cross-country growth rates or the ratio of investment expenditures to GDP. They did find that while there are many econometric specifications in which policy indicators (taken individually or in groups) are significantly correlated with growth, the cross-country statistical relationship between long-term growth and virtually every policy indicator is fragile. In particular, they found no evidence that public investment is an important determinant of growth.

The Taylor-Lewis (1993) study of the G-7 countries illustrates the Levine and Renelt argument. Taylor-Lewis found that in very simple specifications, there was evidence that infrastructure investment was closely linked to growth. But she also found that this result was not robust. For example, she showed that it disappeared in fixed effects models (Evans and Karras [1991b] reach the same conclusion), in models where she corrected for serial correlation, and in models where she used direct measures of public capital, such as miles of roads and installed electrical capacity. She also found that public capital plays no role in growth once she allowed for convergence; i.e., the possibility that countries with low initial levels of income grow faster than countries with high initial levels of income. Since there is strong evidence that convergence is an important pattern in growth, this result is of particular importance.[5]

Thus, the international evidence strongly suggests that inadequate infrastructure spending is not the source of U.S. competitive problems as some critics have argued. The great success of Japan's auto industry was not due to superior infrastructure capital, nor were Detroit's problems due to a deteriorating American infrastructure. The infrastructure in Japan is, in fact, no better than in the United States and is probably worse; recall that the Japanese hire people to stuff people onto commuter trains at rush hour. Japan auto producers were successful because they pioneered new production techniques, such as quality circles and the just-in-time inventory system. Moreover, the decline in the U.S. steel industry was accelerated when the completion of one piece of infrastructure—the St. Lawrence Seaway—allowed iron ore to be shipped to Japan, made into steel, and sold competitively on world markets.

## THE ECONOMIC EFFECTS OF FUTURE SPENDING

The third argument in favor of higher infrastructure spending suggests that we can safely extrapolate the experience of the past into the future. If the evidence of what happened in the past is problematic, the projections based on this evidence are even more uncertain. Even if past infrastructure investment did yield large returns, it does not follow that future investments will automatically have the same large returns. Indeed, there are reasons to suspect that they might not.

The Congressional Budget Office (1988) has surveyed a collection of cost-benefit studies that look prospectively at the returns available on future investments. They found a very mixed picture. The rate of return on expenditures to maintain highway pavement conditions was quite large, but the return on investments on new roads outside the most congested urban areas and on investments to upgrade roads above minimum standards was typically very low.

Aschauer (1991) and others have argued that cost-benefit studies are flawed, because they are unlikely to recognize important "spillover" benefits. Thus, so this argument goes, while a cost-benefit study might capture the benefits from a particular project that accrue in the city or state in which the project is located, it would likely miss the benefits that accrue elsewhere.

Holtz-Eakin (1992) offers some interesting evidence on this point. If the spillover argument is correct, then one would expect to find that public capital plays a larger role in regional production functions than in state production functions. He tests this hypothesis by estimating both regional and state models and finds no evidence that this is the case.

Moreover, it is also possible that cost-benefit studies may fail to capture some of the diffuse costs associated with infrastructure investment. For example, new road construction may well exacerbate environmental problems (particularly air quality) if it encourages more people to abandon public transportation and drive to work. Also, the Interstate Highway System has encouraged firms and households—particularly upper income households—to forsake central cities in favor of the suburbs and once rural areas and has made the task of rescuing central cities even more difficult. If cost-benefit analysis really does miss significant spillovers, the bias can be negative as well as positive.

Aschauer (1991, 25–26) also argues that projects that should be undertaken will sometimes fail a cost-benefit test for two further reasons: (1) projects with cost-benefit ratios below one should sometimes be undertaken if there are important complementarities between public and private capital, and (2) the federal government has used an unrealistically demanding required rate of return of 10 percent. While point (1) may have some merit, it is important to recognize that the bias built into cost-benefit studies can work both ways. This is the message of Hoehn and Randall (1989), who show that cost-benefit studies are biased toward accepting socially undesirable projects when projects are evaluated sequentially (as is typically the case). Jorgenson (1991) notes that the analyses of public investments are overly optimistic, because they fail to consider the full cost of public funds. He estimates that for every dollar of public spending, the cost is 1 dollar of tax revenue and 46 cents of loss in efficiency in the private sector. The cost of public capital should therefore be multiplied by 1.46 in a cost-benefit study if his estimates are correct.

The argument over the appropriate rate of return will not be very important if Aschauer's estimates of the rate of return on public capital of 50–60 percent are correct. In any event, the issue is now somewhat moot given that the federal government lowered the hurdle rate of return to 7 percent in late 1992.

The second general reason that retrospective studies may be a poor guide to the future is that most types of infrastructure come in the form of interlocking networks of investments. Thus, while initial investments might offer significant benefits, the returns to subsequent investments are much smaller, the returns to a third round smaller still, and so on. Even if we knew with certainty that the first investments in a network have a large payoff, we could not assume automatically that subsequent additions to the network would have the same payoff. Indeed, they probably would not. In other words, while the construction of the Interstate Highway System had a major impact on the growth of American industry—particularly the regional distribution of economic activity—it is hard to imagine that a second interstate system would have nearly the same impact.

The third argument against extrapolation of past success into the future is that changes in the structure of the economy may require new solutions that have little in common with old approaches. The demise of the canals in the face of competition from railroads is but one example. Railroads, in turn, have lost ground to highway transport, and highway and air transport may yield to the telecommunications revolution. In other words, building "information superhighways" may be much more important than building more interstate capacity. But, if this is true, it will not be discovered by studying the past return to road construction and extrapolating the results to other categories of infrastructure.

## INFRASTRUCTURE AND SHORT-RUN ECONOMIC POLICY

Job creation is the final element in the case for more infrastructure spending. The recent recession, combined with the ongoing fiscal distress of many American cities, is seen by many as sufficient reason to enact a public works program to put people back to work. But many have argued that infrastructure spending is a very poor short-term policy tool. Public works projects involve a great deal of planning and long lead times. As a consequence, by the time funds are actually spent, the economy may have recovered and the new spending will come at the peak, rather than the trough, of the business cycle.

This problem has been significant in the past. The U.S. General Accounting Office (GAO) (1986) found that over 2 years after $9 billion was allocated for infrastructure under the Emergency Jobs Act of 1983, only $4.5 billion had been spent. The GAO noted that "funds for public works programs, such as those that build highways or houses, were spent much more slowly" than funds for other programs. A recent Congressional Budget Office memorandum found that, on average, only 17 percent of federal funds for highways are spent in the first year and that more than 30 percent are spent more than 3 years after the money has been allocated. Bartlett (1993), examining job legislation designed to ameliorate the 1949, 1958, 1961–1962, 1971, 1975–1977, and 1983 recessions, found that in each case, the antirecession programs were enacted after a recession had officially ended.

This history is not encouraging for the current "jobs" legislation, which would also be enacted (if passed) after the official end of the recession. The slower than usual recovery of employment, and the recent signs of slower growth, may ultimately propel some form of jobs bill through Congress. At best, given the history of long spending lags, the stimulus for job creation under this legislation may actually come on-line at the beginning of the next recession.

Finally, it should be noted that there is a fundamental conflict between short-term infrastructure programs and longer-run infrastructure objectives. The former stress the "ready to go" aspect of infrastructure projects and their job creating capacity. But it is not at all clear that those projects that are ready to begin in the near term are the best projects to undertake from a long-run growth perspective.

## POLICY ISSUES

Many of the problems with the condition and congestion of America's infrastructure are the result of self-inflicted policy wounds. Far too little attention has been given to the efficient use, design, and management of infrastructure, and too much emphasis has been placed on new construction. This is nowhere more apparent than in the design of federal highway matching grants.

In the early years of the Interstate Highway program, the main problem was to construct a large national network of high speed roads. To achieve this goal, a matching grant system was designed to steer spending to new construction by establishing a federal matching grant rate for Interstate Highway construction of 90 percent and a rate of 75 percent for other federally aided highways. Maintenance and repair expenditures were originally ineligible for matching funds, providing a powerful incentive to states to minimize maintenance spending in order to capture as many nearly free federal construction dollars as possible with available budget resources. The situation has been corrected gradually, but it has left a legacy of poorly maintained bridges and roads in certain areas.

The substitution of political criteria for economic criteria based on cost-benefit analysis or other needs assessments is a second set of self-inflicted wounds. Funds always seem to be available for "demonstration projects" and, as Heywood Sanders has observed, for sports stadiums and arenas. Cost-benefit analysis may be a flawed tool, but it is surely superior to the pork barrel approach to project analysis.

Policymakers at all levels of government have not taken full advantage of a range of management and design decisions that could significantly increase the flow of infrastructure services without necessarily increasing the stock of infrastructure. Winston (1991), for example, argues persuasively that roads should be built much thicker and that road taxes should be based on axle weights in order to provide road users with the appropriate incentives. Others have suggested that computerized traffic signals could yield significant benefits. One recent study of Los Angeles estimated that computerized signals could reduce traffic delays by 30 percent in that city and reduce auto emissions by 13 percent.

Finally, Gramlich (1991) argues that a greater emphasis on pricing infrastructure properly must be a key element of our infrastructure policy. Currently, the price of using most roads is zero. At a price of zero, the demand for any good will almost always greatly exceed supply; if, for some reason, we were to charge nothing for food, the result would almost certainly be chronic food shortages, just as we now seem to have chronic infrastructure shortages in some places. An alternative to spending more on new road construction would be to price the use of roads and other public capital efficiently (i.e., to set the price equal to the costs that users impose on society, particularly the cost of increased congestion). This approach to efficient facility use becomes more attractive as the technology for collecting these user fees evolves.

## Summary and Conclusions

Based on our review of the evidence, we have come to the following conclusions about the adequacy of the nation's infrastructure capital. First, the link between infrastructure and economic performance is, at the margin, very weak. Much of the research that followed David Aschauer's work provides little support for the hypothesis that the slowdown in infrastructure spending caused the economy to perform poorly over the last 20 years.

Second, there is no strong evidence of a broad collapse of the public capital stock. Certainly, there are bridges and roads that are in poor condition and congestion in some urban areas is far above optimal levels, but these problems are localized and should not be confused with a crisis in the transportation system as a whole. These problems can be addressed within existing program parameters, such as those set out in ISTEA.

Third, many of our infrastructure problems can be traced to poor policy decisions rather than inadequate funding. Transportation programs have focused on new construction at the expense of repairs and maintenance. Government has been slow to price infrastructure correctly, thus leading to inevitable congestion. Demonstration projects sometimes demonstrate little more than someone's political clout.

Fourth, it is unwise to use infrastructure spending as a tool to solve short-term economic problems. By their nature, public works projects involve a great deal of planning and long lead times, particularly in a climate when many will be quick to argue that a new road must "not be in my back yard" and are willing to go to court to make their voices heard. As a consequence, by the time funds are actually spent, the economy may have recovered and the new spending will come at the peak rather than the trough of the business cycle.

Finally, future infrastructure programs, like the information superhighway, should be evaluated on their own merits (and demerits). Estimates of the rates of return on past infrastructure programs are largely irrelevant to this assessment.

In sum, the reports of infrastructure's "death" are premature. There are problems that must be addressed, but they do not require a massive infusion of new spending; rather, they need a stronger commitment to spending existing resources more efficiently. In this light, a sound infrastructure policy should include more reliance on cost-benefit analysis, both for future infrastructure projects and for retrospective analyses of past projects. Follow-up analyses can provide valuable insights into where the system has failed in the past and where new procedures are needed. Conversely, broad econometric studies of infrastructure benefits provide little insight into future needs and little reliable evidence of what has happened in the past.

## NOTES

1. The terms "public capital" and "infrastructure" are often used as though they were interchangeable. In fact, a significant part of the nation's infrastructure is located in the private utility sector (much of which is regulated), and public sector capital encompasses much that is not infrastructure (e.g., police cars). The intuition that assigns an importance to public sector investment is based on the strategic role of infrastructure investment in the process of economic development, while "public" investment is the principal unit of public policy. There has also been a tendency in recent years to broaden the definition of infrastructure to include certain human and knowledge capital.

2. Writing in the February 1991 issue of the *Atlantic* magazine, Robert Reich estimated that Aschauer's estimates of the rate of return to public capital imply that a permanent $10 billion increase in the stock public capital would lead to an almost immediate increase in real annual GDP of $7 billion. If 15 percent of this increase is recaptured in higher taxes each year, the original $10 billion investment could be paid off in around 10 years—far less than the useful life of most public capital facilities—with something left over for maintenance and depreciation.

3. Figures 1 and 2 are based on data from the U.S. Bureau of Economic Analysis (BEA). The BEA includes the Interstate Highway System as part of the state and local capital stock.

4. Munell (1992) and others have argued that it is inappropriate to first difference the data, since that would shift the focus from the long-run effects of public capital to the short-run effects. It is hard to understand the logic of this point. If the true model is

$y_t = x_t \beta + \epsilon_t$, then it should not matter if we estimate that model or if we estimate $y_t - y_{t-1} = (x_t - x_{t-1})\beta + \mu_t$; both models should yield unbiased estimates of $\beta$.

5. See Barro and Sala-i-Martin (1992) and Dowrick and Nguyen (1989) for discussions of the convergence hypothesis.

## REFERENCES

Aaron, Henry J. "Discussion of 'Why Is Infrastructure Important?'" in *Is There a Shortfall in Public Capital Investment?* Alicia Munnell, ed., Boston: Federal Reserve Bank of Boston (1990).

Aschauer, David. "Is Public Expenditure Productive?" *Journal of Monetary Economics* (March 1989): 177–200.

––––––. *Public Investment and Private Sector Growth: The Economic Benefits of Reducing America's "Third Deficit."* Washington, D.C.: Economic Policy Institute (1991).

Barro, Robert J., And Xavier Sala-i-Martin. "Convergence." *Journal of Political Economy* (April 1992): 407–444.

Bartlett, Bruce. "Statement Before the Subcommittee on Transportation." Committee on Appropriations, U.S. House of Representatives (February 24, 1993).

Canning, David, and Marianne Fay. "The Effect of Infrastructure Networks on Economic Growth." Unpublished Paper. New York: Columbia University (1993).

Congressional Budget Office. *New Directions for the Nation's Public Works.* Washington, D.C.: U.S. Government Printing Office (1988).

––––––. Internal Memorandum (November, 1992a).

––––––. "Trends in Public Infrastructure Outlays and the President's Proposals for Infrastructure Spending in 1993." *CBO Papers,* Washington, D.C. (1992b).

Dowrick, Steve, and Duc-Tho Nguyen. "OECD Comparative Growth 1950–1985: Catch-Up and Convergence." *American Economic Review* (December 1989): 1010–1030.

Eisner, Robert. "Infrastructure and Regional Economic Performance: Comment." *New England Economic Review* (September/October 1991): 47–57.

Evans, Paul, and Georgios Karras. "Are Government Activities Productive? Evidence from a Panel of U.S. States." Unpublished Paper. Columbus: Ohio State University (1991a).

––––––. "Is Government Capital Productive? Evidence from a Panel of Seven Countries." Unpublished Paper. Columbus: Ohio State University (1991b).

Fernald, John. "How Productive Is Infrastructure? Distinguishing Reality and Illusion with a Panel of U.S. Industries." Unpublished Paper, Cambridge, Massachusetts: Harvard University (1992).

Garcia-Mila, Theresa, Theresa McGuire, and Robert H. Porter. "The Effect of Public Capital in State-Level Production Functions Reconsidered." Institute of Government and Public Affairs Working Paper No. 24. Urbana: University of Illinois (1993).

Gramlich, Edward M. "United States Infrastructure Needs: Let's Get the Prices Right." Paper presented at the American Enterprise Institute Conference on Infrastructure Needs and Policy Options for the 1990s, Washington, D.C. (February 1991).

Ho, Mun S., and Bent E. Sorensen. "Public Capital and Long-Run Productivity in U.S. Manufacturing," Department of Economics Working Paper No. 93-20. Providence, Rhode Island: Brown University (1993).

Hoehn, John P., and Alan Randall. "Too Many Proposals Pass the Benefit Cost Test." *American Economic Review* (June 1989): 544–551.

Holtz-Eakin, Douglas. "Public Sector Capital and the Productivity Puzzle." Working Paper No. 4144. Cambridge: National Bureau of Economic Research (1992).

Hulten, Charles R. "Discussion of 'Infrastructure and Regional Economic Performance,'" in *Is There a Shortfall in Public Capital Investment?* Alicia Munnell, ed., Boston: Federal Reserve Bank of Boston (1990).

Hulten, Charles, and Robert Schwab. "Regional Productivity Growth in U.S. Manufacturing: 1951–1978." *American Economic Review* (March 1984): 152–162.

———. "Public Capital Formation and the Growth of Regional Manufacturing Industries." *National Tax Journal* (December 1991a): 121-134.

———. "Is There Too Little Public Capital in the U.S.?" Paper presented at the American Enterprise Institute Conference on Infrastructure Needs and Policy Options for the 1990s, Washington, D.C., February, 1991b (revised January 1992).

Jorgenson, Dale W. "Fragile Statistical Foundations." *The Public's Capital* (Spring 1991): 6–7.

Levine, Ross, and David Renelt. "A Sensitivity Analysis of Cross-Country Growth Regressions." *American Economic Review* (September 1992): 942–963.

Morrison, Catherine J., and Amy Ellen Schwartz. "State Infrastructure and Economic Performance." Unpublished Paper. Medford, Massachusetts: Tufts University (1991).

Munnell, Alicia. "Why Has Productivity Growth Declined? Productivity and Public Investment." *New England Economic Review* (January/February 1990a): 3–22.

———. "How Does Public Infrastructure Affect Regional Economic Performance?" in *Is There a Shortfall in Public Capital Investment?* Alicia Munnell, ed., Boston: Federal Reserve Bank of Boston (1990b).

———. "Policy Watch: Infrastructure Investment and Economic Growth." *The Journal of Economic Perspectives* (Fall 1992): 189–198.

Reich, Robert. "The Real Economy." *The Atlantic Monthly* (February 1991): 35–52.

Sanders, Heywood T. "What Infrastructure Crisis?" *The Public Interest* (Winter 1993): 3–18.

Schultze, Charles E. "The Federal Budget and the Nation's Economic Health" in *Setting National Priorities: Policy for the Nineties,* Henry J. Aaron, ed., Washington, D.C.: The Brookings Institution (1990).

Tatom, John A. "Public Capital and Private Sector Performance." *Federal Reserve Bank of St. Louis Review* (May/June 1991): 3–15.

Taylor-Lewis, Ruby. "The Role of Infrastructure in Productivity and Output Growth: A Case Study of the Group of Seven." Unpublished Ph.D. Dissertation. College Park, Maryland: University of Maryland (1993).

United States Department of Transportation. *New Perspectives in Commuting.* Washington, D.C.: U.S. Government Printing Office (1992).

————. *The Status of the Nation's Highways, Bridges, and Transit: Conditions and Performance.* Washington, D.C.: U.S. Government Printing Office (1993).

United States General Accounting Office. "Emergency Jobs Act of 1983: Funds Spent Slowly, Few Jobs Created." Report to the Chairman, Subcommittee on Employment and Productivity, Committee on Labor and Human Resources, U.S. Senate (1986).

Winston, Clifford. "Efficient Transportation Infrastructure Policy." *Journal of Economic Perspectives* (Winter 1991): 113–127.

# S E L E C T I O N   1 0

James M. Buchanan

# Public Finance and Public Choice

Early work in public finance economics concentrated primarily on determining the response of private market participants to government tax policies and on developing principles of optimal taxation. Both the expenditure side of the government budget and the public decision-making process were neglected, particularly in the non-European literature. However, modern public finance has substantially broadened in focus and content. Many of the most exciting and influential developments in the field today derive from an ingenious application of micro-economic exchange theory to public choice. James M. Buchanan received the 1986 Nobel Prize in Economics in acknowledgement of his pioneering work in this new branch of public finance.

In this selection, James Buchanan first summarizes late nineteenth-century developments in the European theory of public finance and the related post-World War II evolution of modern public finance. He then introduces what he terms the "public-choice paradigm." In the public-choice paradigm, the behavior of voters, the preferences of politicians and bureaucrats, and perhaps most importantly, the structure of fiscal and political institutions are all recognized to play crucial roles in the ultimate outcome of any policy process.

## Questions to Guide the Reading

1. Post-Marshallian public finance emphasized the positive impact of taxes—e.g., who pays the tax. Post-Pigouvian public finance emphasized the normative nature of taxation—e.g., identifying a "good" tax. What additional areas of study were the focus of nineteenth-century European public economists? What contributions did these economists make?

Buchanan, James M. "Public Finance and Public Choice." *National Tax Journal 28* (December 1975): 383–394.

**James M. Buchanan** is Harris University Distinguished Professor of Economics and General Director of The Center for Study of Public Choice at George Mason University. He received a Nobel Prize in Economics in 1986.

2.  According to Buchanan, what was the importance of Paul Samuelson's seminal paper on public goods?
3.  With respect to the theory of voting, what impact did the works of Duncan Black and Kenneth Arrow have on the research of modern public economists? How is the theory of constitutions related to these and other works? What unique contributions were made by the theory of constitutions?
4.  What important advances in the theory of public-goods supply were made by the scholars Anthony Downs, William Riker, Gordon Tullock, and William Niskansen?
5.  What expansions in the domain of positive economic analysis are made possible by the methodological shift to the public-choice paradigm? What impact might the public-choice paradigm have on an economist's normative discussion?
6.  The social security system continues to be a burning issue in Washington budget debates. How might the public-choice paradigm change the focus of analysis of a government program such as social security? What additional issues might be raised by a public-choice economist?

---

"Public finance," as a quasi-independent subdiscipline in the American academic setting, has been substantially transformed in the thirty years after the ending of World War II, although heritages of the earlier tradition remain, and notably as these affect practical political discussion. From its relatively minor role as one among many fields of applied microeconomic theory—akin to industrial organization, agricultural economics, or labor economics—public finance emerged to become "public economics," which, at least conceptually, is on all fours with "private economics," or, more familiarly, the economics of the private sector. If relative weights are assigned in accordance with relative shares in GNP, "public economics" promises, for better or for worse, to grow still more important in decades ahead.

My purpose in this survey paper is to discuss this transformation of "public finance" from a public choice perspective, one that reflects my own methodological presuppositions. I shall not include reference to the "theory of fiscal policy," which bloomed brightly in the early post-Keynesian environment only to fade somewhat in the face of political realities. The macroeconomic policy emphasis derived from Keynes is a causal element in the relative growth of the governmental sector and, as such, one source of the increasing attention to "public economics." But there is no direct relationship between this emphasis and the fundamental paradigm shift that is the primary subject of my treatment in this paper.

# POST-MARSHALLIAN PUBLIC FINANCE

I can commence by describing the content of "public finance" in post-Marshallian economics, as limited to English-language discourse. Positive analysis was restricted almost exclusively to theories of tax shifting and incidence. And, indeed, as Marshall himself explicitly recognized,[1] the theory of tax shifting becomes almost the ideal instrument for applying the principles of competitive price theory. Comparative statics offered a plausible predictive framework for analyzing tax alternatives. Within limits, and for certain simple forms, the economist could confidently predict the effects of a tax on the behavior of persons and firms in the private economy, and, through this, on the aggregate effects on such variables as relative prices, outputs, profits, and industry structure in particular sectors. For this strictly positive analysis, which could also yield empirically refutable propositions, the economist had no reason to inquire about the political purpose of taxation, no reason to introduce external evaluation of alternative tax instruments.[2] This subarea of public finance, which is essentially applied price theory, has continued to be developed through more sophisticated technical analysis which has now moved beyond the Marshallian partial-equilibrium framework to general-equilibrium settings, including extensions to open economies. No basic paradigm shift has occurred here, but this subarea has necessarily been relegated to a relatively less important role in the larger theory of "public economics" which has emerged.

Alongside this post-Marshallian positive theory of taxation, there existed what I may label as the post-Pigouvian normative "theory" of taxation. This unfortunate and somewhat confused discussion stemmed vaguely from the utilitarian philosophical tradition and had as its purpose the derivation of normative "principles" for taxation. The most sophisticated of these, developed most fully by Pigou,[3] was that of "equi-marginal sacrifice," which was based on a simplistic application of the calculus in a context of assumed interpersonal utility comparability. This normative discussion was much less rigorous intellectually than the positive analysis of tax incidence, and, indeed, the normative treatment of taxation among English-language economists was almost a half-century out of phase from the more sophisticated discussion on the European continent. The normative "principles" of taxation that were seriously discussed may seem bizarre when viewed in a modern post-Wicksellian or public-choice paradigm. But these "principles" assume continuing practical importance as soon as we recognize that observed institutions of taxation find their intellectual origins in these norms, which also, to a large extent, inform modern political criticisms of tax structures, along with continuing calls for tax reform. For example, the most vocal modern advocates for reform, notably Joseph Pechman and Stanley Surrey, base their arguments on presupposed norms for the distribution of tax shares, norms which are derived independently.

There are two related, but quite distinct, gaps in the normative public finance of the post-Marshallian, post-Pigouvian tradition. There is, first, the long-continued, and methodologically inadmissible, neglect of the expenditure side of the fiscal account. The necessary interdependence between the two sides of the public-sector budget must be incorporated into any analysis, even if the purpose is to lay down ideal standards drawn from some external scale of evaluation. Secondly, there is the neglect or oversight of the collective decision structure itself. The shift in paradigm which has occurred involves the incorporation of both these elements.

## THE EUROPEAN THEORY OF THE PUBLIC ECONOMY

Following the central contributions of the early 1870s, the economic theory of markets assumed a unified structure. The simultaneous operation of productive input and final product markets accomplished evaluative allocative, and distributive functions. The European attempts to extend this aesthetically satisfying logic structure to "explain" the operation of a public as well as a private sector now seem to represent predicted increments in scientific progress. The puzzle in intellectual history does not concern these efforts; the puzzle lies in the long-continued failure of English-language economists to make comparable extensions of their basic framework or to acknowledge an interest in the continental efforts.

As early as the 1880s, Mazzola, Panteleoni, Sax, and De Viti De Marco made rudimentary efforts to analyze the public economy within an exchange framework. Sax and Mazzola discussed the demand side of public goods by identifying collective as distinct from private wants. Pantaleoni extended the marginal calculus to apply to the legislator who makes choices for both sides of the budget. De Viti De Marco explicitly constructed a model in which the consumers and the suppliers-producers of the public goods make up the same community of persons.[4]

The most sophisticated contribution was made by Knut Wicksell in 1896.[5] He explicitly identified the fundamental methodological error in the then-orthodox approach, and he combined positive criticism with normative suggestions for reform. Wicksell recognized the necessity of bridging the two sides of the fiscal account, and he noted the indeterminacy of any proposed normative principles that were limited to tax-side considerations. More importantly, Wicksell admonished economists for their failure to recognize the elementary fact that collective or public-sector decisions emerge from a political process rather than from the mind of some benevolent despot. His suggestions for reform were concentrated on the institutional structure for fiscal decision-making, on the institutions of "public choice." The unanimity rule was presented as the normative benchmark for efficiency in public-sector decisions, and a clear distinction was made between those situations where genuine gains-from-trade might emerge and those which involve zero-sum transfers. Despite the essentially normative setting for Wicksell's reform suggestions, the groundwork was laid for subsequent positive analysis of political decision structures.

Subsequent to these early contributions, work was carried forward, notably in Sweden and in Italy. Erik Lindahl's attempt to examine more closely the relationship between standard efficiency norms and the political bargaining process offered a halfway house between Wicksell's seminal effort and modern analyses of public finance in democratic process.[6] Lindahl's proposed solution, the set of so-called Lindahl tax-prices, or Lindahl equilibrium, has come to occupy the attention of several sophisticated analysts who have attempted to extend the modern theory of general competitive equilibrium to include the public sector.[7]

The Italian tradition, following the early work by Pantaleoni and De Viti De Marco, was characterized by an emphasis on the necessary political assumptions required for either a positive or normative theory of the public economy. The Italians devoted much more attention to the implications of nondemocratic political structures for the emergence and viability of fiscal institutions, on both the tax and the expenditure sides, than did their continental counterparts. These aspects, in particular, become helpful in the analysis of the supply institutions of the public economy, an analysis that remains in its formative stages. Apart from these substantive contributions, Barone and Einaudi, in particular, were sharply critical of the naive utilitarian framework of the English-language normative discussion of tax principles.

## THE TRANSITIONAL SETTING

The substantial transformation in American public finance did not spring full blown from some rediscovery of the European theory of the public economy, although it might legitimately be claimed that this theory, appropriately modernized, was sufficiently complete to have allowed for this as an alternative intellectual scenario. The transformation emerged slowly and in bits and pieces, influenced by several sources other than the strict analysis of the continental scholars. Precedence in presenting the central ideas of what he called the "voluntary exchange" theory of the public economy belongs to R. A. Musgrave who, in his first paper, offered a highly critical evaluation.[8] However, Musgrave's analysis was not such as to attract independent and complementary attention to the body of work discussed. And Howard Bowen, in his original and much-neglected 1943 paper, showed no signs of having been influenced by the European analysis.[9] Bowen's paper combined two elements that were to be more fully developed later as separate strands of analysis, the theory of demand for public goods and the theory of voting. Although flawed by minor analytical errors, Bowen's paper was perhaps neglected because it was too much in advance of the analytical mind-set of its time. My own efforts, in my first substantive paper in 1949, one that was also largely neglected, were concentrated in a methodological critique of the post-Pigouvian normative framework. In this, I was influenced almost exclusively by a fortuitous discovery of Wicksell's basic work.[10]

Developments of note came rapidly during the 1950s and 1960s. These may be discussed initially in terms of their independent emergence, with little or no direct interconnection one with another and with the corpus of public finance theory. In what follows, I shall discuss briefly four lines of inquiry or analysis: (1) the theory of demand for public goods; (2) the theory of voting; (3) the theory of constitutions; and (4) the theory of supply of public goods. In each of these, I shall attempt to distinguish positive and normative elements of analysis. After these strands are separately examined, I shall try to integrate these as they relate to modern public finance theory. Finally, I shall use a single example to demonstrate how the modern post-Pigouvian paradigm which, although conceptually flawed, continues to inform some policy discussion.

## THE THEORY OF DEMAND FOR PUBLIC GOODS

As previously noted, there were two gaping holes in the pre-World War II normative analysis of taxation, a neglect of the expenditure side of the fisc and a neglect of the collective decision process. Modern public finance theory incorporates both of these elements, but they remain conceptually distinct and they were, to an extent, independently developed. An internally consistent set of principles for efficiency in the public economy may be elaborated with no attention to the political decision process. This was the framework for Paul A. Samuelson's seminal paper in 1954,[11] in which he laid down the necessary marginal conditions for allocative efficiency in the provision of public or collective goods to a defined community of persons. Samuelson extended the accepted norms of theoretical welfare economics from the private to the public sector of the economy, using individual evaluations as the building blocks. Perhaps his primary contribution lay in his rigorous definition of a "collective consumption" good, embodying both complete nonexclusion and complete efficiency from joint consumption, the two acknowledged attributes of "publicness." Early criticisms of the polarity features of Samuelson's classification were, in my view, misplaced because this initial step seemed essential before the further elaboration of taxonomic detail could take place.

The Samuelson mathematical formulation of the conditions for public sector efficiency did not contain a comparable normative theory of the distribution of tax shares. Income-effect feedbacks of tax-shares on individual evaluations of collective-consumption goods were incorporated in the analysis, but the tax-share distribution itself was arbitrarily selected by resort to a social welfare function. This normative construction is quite different from that which is required for the definition of the allocative conditions for efficiency. Within Samuelson's conceptual framework, resort to the social welfare function for tax-share distribution was an implication of his unwillingness to close the model in a manner analogous to the exchange process of the private sector. He did not conceive the fiscal process as one of "exchange," even at the level of abstraction that the formal statement of the necessary marginal conditions for efficiency required.

Nonetheless, the Samuelson analysis can readily be interpreted positively, which necessarily implies an exchange framework. In this case, the necessary marginal conditions for allocative efficiency become conditions that must be satisfied for an equilibrium solution to the complex "trades" that the political or collective choice process embody. One such solution is the Lindahl equilibrium, which meets the basic Samuelson requirements, although it is arbitrarily restricted in its distribution of the tax shares inframarginally. The more general Wicksellian approach makes no attempt to specify particulars of an equilibrium. Instead this approach concentrates on the institutions for "trading," and implicitly defines efficiency to be present when all gains-from-trade are exhausted. In a setting of zero transactions costs, including bargaining costs, unanimous agreement will be possible on both marginal tax-share distribution and on the quantity of public goods to be purchased, although the position of agreement will not be unique and its characteristics will depend strictly on the path of adjustment.[12]

## THE THEORY OF VOTING

The Wicksellian paradigm for fiscal exchange, ideally operative under a decision rule of unanimity without prior constraints on tax-share distribution, places the "public economy," methodologically, on all fours with the "private economy." The importance of this Wicksellian benchmark or starting point for the developments that have followed cannot be overestimated. But the world is not characterized by zero transactions costs, and these loom especially large when many persons must agree on single outcomes. The two-party dimensionality of private-goods trading, especially as constrained by the presence of numerous alternatives on both sides of exchange, allows the costs of reaching agreement to be minimized, and, because of this, to be largely neglected in analysis. No such neglect is possible for the complex trading process that politics embodies. Necessary departures from the idealized models become much more apparent, and enter analysis even at the level of institutional design. Wicksell himself recognized, in his discussion of qualified majorities, that the ideal political constitution could not embody a strict unanimity rule, even for the legislative assembly. And, of course, historical experience in democratic politics includes a wide variety of voting and decision rules-institutions, only a few of which approximate the unanimity-rule benchmark.

Once the ideal is abandoned, as necessary for the operation of political decision structures in accordance with more inclusive efficiency norms, what rules for collective choice should be chosen? Before this question can be addressed at all, there must be positive analysis of alternative voting rules and institutions. From a current vantage point, in 1975, it sees almost incredible that American public-finance economists completely ignored analysis of voting rules prior to World War II, even though they must have recognized that fiscal outcomes were related directly to the political structure. Aside from the paper by Bowen, noted above, there was no discussion of voting rules prior to the seminal contributions of Duncan Black and Kenneth Arrow, in the late 1940s and 1950s.[13]

Black's earlier efforts had been strictly within the post-Marshallian tradition of incidence analysis.[14] His reading of the Italian works was an acknowledged source of his shift of emphasis to an analysis of voting rules. Black's major work was largely confined to an analysis of majority rule as a means of reaching decisions in collectivities. In his analysis, which included the discovery of precursory work by Borda, Condorcet, and most notably, Lewis Carroll, Black noted the possibility of the majority cycle, but his emphasis was placed on the workability of majority rule rather than the reverse. This emphasis led him to examine restrictions on preference domains that might produce unique majority solutions. He discovered that if all individual preferences could be arrayed over alternatives so as to appear as single-peaked, the majority-rule outcome will always be that which meets the preferences of the median voter in the group. This median-voter construction was to emerge as an important tool in the public-choice theory of the 1960s, and especially in public-finance applications. Single-peakedness in preferences becomes a plausible assumption for many fiscal decision variables.

Kenneth Arrow's work exerted far more influence on economic theory generally than did the closely related work of Duncan Black. However, the specific effects on public-finance theory are less direct. Arrow placed his analysis squarely in the social welfare function discussion that had emerged from theoretical welfare economics, and he demonstrated that there existed no collective decision rule for amalgamating individual preference orderings into a consistent social or collective ordering. This rigorous generalization of the cyclical-majority phenomenon, along with Arrow's emphasis on the impossibility of generating a social ordering meeting plausible criteria, had the effect of putting the analysis of collective decision rules directly on the research agenda of modern economists. Faced with results that they did not welcome, and with their somewhat naive political presuppositions exposed, economists were slowly forced to acknowledge that social welfare functions do not exist. Only two alternatives remained open. They might become public-choice analysts and examine the operation of alternative decision rules, no one of which is ideal. Or, they might revert to the normative post-Pigouvian stance which requires the explicit introduction of private and personal value standards that bear little or no relationship to the decision-determining institutions of the real world.

## THE THEORY OF CONSTITUTIONS (VOTING RULES)

Once positive analysis of the operation of alternative voting rules was placed on the agenda, along with the Wicksellian recognition that no nonunanimity rule could guarantee efficiency in the narrow sense, the way was open for the development of a theory of constitutions, based on an analysis of the choice among a set of less-than-ideal institutions for generating collective outcomes. This was the setting for *The Calculus of Consent*, which I jointly authored with Gordon Tullock, and which was published in 1962.[15] This work carried forward the analysis of alternative decision rules, with emphasis on the political external diseconomies inherent in any less-than-unanimity rule and on the prospects for vote trading as a means of mitigating the results of differential preference intensities. Our central purpose was, however, that of analyzing the choice among collective decision rules, and of deriving criteria for "optimality" at this constitutional level. Our procedure was to shift backwards, to the level of choice among rules, the Wicksellian unanimity or general consensus criterion. The transactions costs barrier to general agreement may be fully acknowledged at the stage of reaching collective decision on specific fiscal (tax and spending) variables. But this need not imply that persons cannot agree generally on the rules or institutions under which subsequent decisions will be made, whether these be majority rule or otherwise. To the extent that individuals' future preference positions are uncertain and unpredictable under subsequent operation of the rules to be chosen, they may be led to agree on the basis of general criteria that are unrelated to economic position.[16]

Our analysis was positive in the conceptual sense, and we made few suggestions for institutional reform. Nonetheless, our discussion was admittedly informed by a vision or model of constitutional process that embodied individualistic norms. This vision was, in its turn, used to "explain" features of existing political structures, features which might, with comparable methodological legitimacy, be "explained" with alternative normative models. Our analysis of constitutions was not sufficiently complete to allow us to discriminate among widely varying explanations for the emergence and existence of observed political institutions.

## THE THEORY OF SUPPLY OF PUBLIC GOODS

This gap in our analysis of the choice among constitutional rules stemmed, in part, from our neglect of the supply side of the public-goods exchange process. The theory of demand for public goods, the theory of voting, and the theory of voting rules—each of these lines of inquiry initially embodied the implicit assumption that individual demands for public goods, once these could be articulated and combined through some collective-choice process, would be efficiently and automatically met. It was as if the alternatives for public choice were assumed to be available independently from some external source; there was no problem concerning the behavior of the suppliers or producers. Governments are, however, staffed by persons who make up only a subset of the community, and any full analysis of fiscal exchange must allow for differences between the behavior of persons in producing-supplying roles and in consuming-demanding roles.

Precursors of supply-side analysis can, of course, be found in the Italian theory of public finance in the nondemocratic or monopolistic state. Models of this political structure were developed in some detail, models in which some ruling group or class collects taxes from the masses who are ruled and utilizes the proceeds to its own maximum advantage. But attention was also paid to the feedback or reaction effects on the behavior of those who were exploited. At the turn of this century, Puviani developed the interesting and still-relevant concept of "fiscal illusion," which he applied to both the tax and the spending side of the fiscal account.[17] However, aside from my own summary of some of these elements, which I did not sufficiently stress, there was no direct linkage between the monopolistic-state analysis of the Italians and the emergence of the modern theory of public-goods supply.

American scholars have operated within a continuing presupposition that their own political institutions remain basically democratic. Even within this structure, however, the demanders and the suppliers of public services must occupy differing economic roles, and the interests of the two groups need not coincide. The seminal American contribution toward the ultimate development of a theory of public-goods supply was made by Anthony Downs. In his book, *An Economic Theory of Democracy*, published in 1957, Downs presented a model of political party competition analogous to the competition among firms in an industry, with vote-maximization serving as the analogue to profit maximization.[18] The predictive power of Downs' model was sharply criticized by William Riker, who introduced a game-theoretic framework to suggest that political parties, even when treated as monolithic decision-taking entities, will seek to organize winning coalitions of minimal size rather than to maximize vote totals.[19] For purposes of this survey, however, the central contribution of these efforts lay not in the explanatory potential of the models themselves but rather in the fundamentally different setting offered for viewing the activities of governments. Once governments came to be viewed as collectivities of persons who were themselves maximizers—whether these persons be party organizers, political representatives, elected officials, judges, or bureaucrats—the emerging paradigm involving the passively efficient supply response to public-goods demanders was dramatically changed in course.

The Downs-Riker models of interparty competition, which have been carried forward and elaborated in more sophisticated forms by other scholars, were paralleled by the development of a theory of bureaucratic behavior, both at the level of the individual member of the hierarchy and that of the agency or bureau itself. Gordon Tullock introduced the maximizing bureaucrat, who responds to his own career incentives like everyone else, and analyzed the implications of this behavioral model for the control problem faced by those at the top of the hierarchy.[20] Even on the extreme assumption that the agency head desires to meet the demands for public goods efficiently, Tullock's analysis suggests that this objective could not be met in organizations requiring personal services.[21]

William Niskanen boldly challenged the orthodox conception of bureaucracy by modeling separate bureaus as budget-maximizing units.[22] The implication of his polar model is that bureaus, acting as monopoly suppliers of public services, and possessing an ability to control the elected political leaders through a complex and interested committee structure in the legislature, fully drain off the potential taxpayers' surplus that might be possible from public-goods provision. Once again, it is not the particular predictive power of Niskanen's analysis that is relevant for our purposes; what is relevant is the contrasting setting within which the operations of agencies and bureaus may be examined.

The theory of public-goods supply has not been fully developed, and efforts to integrate this theory, as it exists, with the theory of demand, including the theory of voting and voting rules, have only commenced.[23]

## THE EXPANDED DOMAIN FOR POSITIVE ANALYSIS

In the four preceding sections of this paper, I have briefly summarized four main lines of inquiry or analysis that have combined to form the still-emerging subdiscipline of "public choice."[24] My purpose has not been that of describing the substantive content of these separate but closely related bodies of analysis; this would have required further treatment of the specific modern contributions in each area.[25] My purpose has been the more restricted one of sketching with a broad brush the separated strands of public choice theory in order to suggest how these have combined to effect the transformation in public finance theory during the decades after World War II.

Methodologically, the central element in this transformation is the dramatic expansion in the scope or domain for positive economic analysis. The subject matter of public finance has shifted outward; the economist now has before him many more questions than his counterpart faced a half-century ago. This expansion in the set of opportunities for applying the economist's tools, both conceptual and empirical, may be discussed in terms of specific categories.

1. *The Effects of Alternative Fiscal Institutions, Existing and Potential, on the Behavior of Persons and Groups in the Private Economy.* As I have noted earlier, this is the only domain for positive economic analysis in post-Marshallian public finance. The results of the public-choice transformation have been to remove this still-important avenue for investigation from its place of exclusive dominance and to put it alongside other significant and equally legitimate applications of economic theory. This does not, of course, suggest that the theory of shifting and incidence, with expenditures added to taxes, has been reduced in absolute importance. The hard questions in incidence theory have not all been resolved, and these will, and should, continue to command the attention of economists.

2. *The Effects of Alternative Fiscal Institutions, Existing and Potential, on the Behavior of Persons and Groups in the Public Economy, in Public Choice.* In a relative sense, however, traditional incidence theory must be reduced in significance because other questions beckon. If the effects of a designated fiscal institution, say a specific excise tax, on the behavior of persons in private markets may be analyzed, what is to deter the intellectually curious and competent economist from examining the effects of this tax on the behavior of persons in "public markets"? If persons pay for public goods through such a tax, might they not be predicted to "purchase" differing quantities than they would do under alternative taxing schemes? Once such questions are raised, the need for answers along with the opportunities for research seem self-evident. An implicit assumption of invariance in fiscal choice over widely divergent institutional structures will simply not stand up to scrutiny.

The whole set of questions raised here stem from the "publicness" of the goods as these are demanded and consumed and as these are supplied through political or governmental institutions. Individuals do not pay "prices" for partitionable units of these goods. They pay "taxes," which are coercively imposed upon them through a political process, and this coercion is, in turn, made necessary by the "free rider" motivation inherent in general collective action. Few persons will voluntarily pay taxes if they expect to receive the benefits of generally available public goods. But what quantity will persons, when they act collectively in public-choice capacities— as voters, actual or potential, as members of pressure groups, as elected politicians, as government employees—choose to provide and to finance? This choice depends on the bridge that is constructed between the benefits or spending side of the account and the costs or taxing side. Differing fiscal institutions influence the weighing of accounts. What are the implications for budgetary size if taxes are spread more generally than benefits? And vice versa? Quite apart from the "true" distribution of tax shares and benefit shares, the "perceived" distribution matters. Fiscal perception becomes an important and relevant area for positive analysis. By necessity, "fiscal psychology" merges with fiscal economics. The research potential for positive analysis seems almost unlimited, and relatively little has been done.[26]

3. *The Effects of Alternative Political or Collective-Choice Institutions, Existing or Potential, on the Behavior of Persons and Groups in the Public Economy, in Public Choice.* A closely related, but somewhat different agenda for positive analysis and one that is more central to what might be called "public-choice theory," as such, involves the choice-making institutions themselves, as these may be predicted to generate fiscal outcomes. This is the public-finance application of the theory of voting, summarized above.

What budget characteristics can be predicted to emerge under simple majority rule? What differences in size and composition might emerge when general-fund budgeting is compared with separate-purpose budgeting, with earmarked tax revenues? What differences in the willingness to issue public debt can be predicted when the effective voting franchise is expanded from local property owners to all members of the local electorate? What will be the comparative levels of public outlay on, say, education, when these services are provided through a set of monopoly school districts and through the market response to educational vouchers provided directly to families? What are the effects of school-district consolidation on budget size? What are the effects of franchising bureaucrats on the level and growth of public spending?

These are only a few of the questions that have been, and are being, asked by those who approach public finance from the general public-choice paradigm. As these sample questions suggest, the domain for positive analysis here includes institutional analysis at a level where explanatory hypotheses are derived deductively from extract models, and also at the level where these hypotheses are tested empirically.[27]

4. *Analysis of the Behavior of Persons and Groups in the Collective Constitutional Choice among Fiscal Institutions.* This area for positive analysis is the direct public-

finance application of the theory of constitutions, previously summarized. As they may be historically observed, certain fiscal institutions take on quasi-permanent or constitutional characteristics. For example, basic changes in the tax code are discussed as if these are expected to endure over a sequence of periods. Neither taxes nor spending programs are chosen carte blanche at the onset of each budgetary period. Indeed one of the primary difficulties in reducing the explosive rate of increase in federal outlays in the 1970s is alleged to be the high proportion of uncontrollable spending in the budget. Once the quasi-permanence of institutions is recognized, the analysis of fiscal choices is modified. Differing criteria for choice must be invoked, criteria which may be less directly identified with self-interest of persons and groups. The models which are designed to derive hypotheses become different in this context.

I shall not attempt to suggest research opportunities that exist in this extension of positive analysis, one that is perhaps less fully developed than the others. My point of emphasis in this listing is to indicate that at least three areas of actual and potential positive analysis now exist over and beyond the severely limited post-Marshallian field of shifting and incidence.

## THE MODIFIED DOMAIN FOR NORMATIVE DISCUSSION

The domain for positive analysis in public finance has been greatly expanded. But what about the domain for normative discourse? So long as the economist proffers his advice as if some benevolent despot is listening to him, he may be much more willing to devote his efforts to persuasion based ultimately on his own personal, private scale of values, even if the argument is couched in quasi-philosophical terms. Despite Wicksell's clearly stated admonitions in 1896, this remains the setting for much of the normative discourse in public finance, even in 1975. If the public-choice paradigm is accepted, however, the assumption of the benevolent despot cannot accompany normative advice, even at the subconscious level. The economist must recognize that collective outcomes emerge from a complex political process in which there are many participants. Almost by necessity, he will be less willing to devote time and effort to persuasion here, even though his own personal convictions about ideal outcomes may be equally as strong as in the despotic paradigm. It should come as no surprise, therefore, that modern public finance is less characterized by normative advice concerning the "best tax" program and more concerned about predicting the effects of alternatives.

The public-choice paradigm does, however, allow for a parallel expansion in the normative realm of discourse. Once it is recognized that fiscal decisions emerge from a complex collective choice process, the economist may concentrate his normative advice on "improvements" in the process itself. He may, for example, say that direct taxation is preferred to indirect taxation, not because direct taxation is likely to be more or less progressive, but simply because direct taxation leads to a more rational choice calculus among voters and their representatives than indirect taxation. Similarly, he may suggest that withholding, as an institution, tends to reduce the rationality of the choice process because it tends to make the taxpayer somewhat less conscious of his costs. These are admittedly normative suggestions that emerge from a paradigm of the political world, one that embodies the democratic-individualistic standard that persons should get what they want so long as each person counts for one. This seems a more secure normative base than that which lays down criteria for choosing among separate persons and groups, in which one man must somehow count for more than another. These comments may, however, reflect my own personal normative biases and I shall not pursue them further in this survey.[28]

## AN EXAMPLE: THE PROVISION AND FINANCING OF SOCIAL SECURITY

I shall conclude this paper by a brief discussion of a single example, one that is of current importance. I shall demonstrate that the transformation in public finance produced by the public-choice paradigm allows different and additional questions to be asked. In the process, policy discussion must be improved, independently of this or that economist's preferred set of norms.

Consider, first, the application of the post-Marshallian theory of shifting and incidence, along with the post Pigouvian norms for taxation. The social security system is financed by payroll taxes, and the shifting and incidence of these, both the employees' and the employers' shares, are proper subjects for inquiry. These taxes are, when viewed in isolation, "regressive," and this characteristic leads the post-Pigouvian to denounce it on normative grounds.

Strictly speaking, this is all that public finance might have contributed to the policy discussion in the methodological mind-set prior to World War II. Straightforward extension of analysis to the other side of the budget, quite apart from the public-choice extension, would have allowed positive analysis of the effects of public pension commitments on the rate of private saving in the economy.[29] Similarly, the effects of the public pensions on retirement behavior might be analyzed. The normative strictures arising from the regressivity of the payroll tax might also have been tempered somewhat by the extension of simple incidence analysis to the benefits side, where progressive elements are significant.

The public-choice paradigm draws direct attention to the bridge between the tax and the spending side of the account. As quoted earlier, this bridge is influenced by perception, and even within the confines of payroll-tax analysis, the effects of the structural features on voter-politician attitudes become important. In the first place, the public-choice analyst would note the earmarking features of the financing; payroll taxes are earmarked for the social security trust fund account. This fact, in itself, strongly suggests that these taxes are viewed differently from other general-fund revenue sources. Secondly, the public-choice theorist would suggest that the withholding feature of the employee share makes payroll taxes less influential on behavior than orthodox incidence analysis might imply. More importantly, he would suggest that the employers' share of payroll taxes, even if ultimately paid by the workers, may not directly influence the attitude of workers. The suppliers of pensions, the authorities of the social security administration, may have been privately quite rational in their early arguments for making this employee-employer tax separation.

The public-choice theorist would try to predict the effects of a proposed shift of the financing of social security, in whole or in part, from earmarked payroll taxes to the sources of general-fund financing, notably to personal and corporate income taxation. Rudimentary analysis would suggest that the direct linkage between tax and benefit sides would be served by such a change, and that both sets of institutions would be subjected to wholly different political criteria. Could pensions be kept related to earnings (and contributions) under such a change? Could a means test for benefits be avoided? Even if the existing structure does not reflect the operation of genuine "insurance" principles, taxpayer-voters, and their political representatives, may acquiesce in its continuance so long as the intergeneration transfer process which the system seems to embody is plausibly acceptable. Young workers who enter the system may not worry when they are told that the present value of tax obligations exceeds manyfold the present value of future pension benefits provided that they continue to expect that future legislatures will insure a reasonable rate of return on their total contributions. Such continuing support may depend, however, on maintaining the separation of the system from the government's general fiscal account and also on insuring that severe limits are imposed on departures from earnings-related benefits.

The public-choice economist, to the extent that he is willing to make suggestions for reform, seems more likely to suggest institutional adjustments designed to insure against the "political bankruptcy" of the system than he is to suggest that the payroll taxes be made more progressive. Whether the discussion takes the form of positive analysis or normative statement, the public-choice economist looks on the fiscal process as a complex exchange, which must involve two sides of the account simultaneously. Those who pay the ultimate costs of public goods need not, of course, be identical with those who enjoy the ultimate benefits. But, in democracies, the intersection between these two sets must be large, especially when the budgets are considered in composite totals and over a sequence of time periods. Regardless of political structure, the proportion of the community's membership that shares in genuine "fiscal surplus" is related inversely to the size and coercive power of the government's police force.

## NOTES

I am indebted to my colleague Gordon Tullock for helpful comments.

1. "... there is scarcely any economic principle which cannot be aptly illustrated by a discussion of the shifting of the effects of some tax...." Alfred Marshall, *Principles of Economics,* 8th ed., London: Macmillan (1930), 413.

2. Beginning attempts were made to extend an analogous positive analysis to the expenditure side of the fiscal ledger (see for example, Earl Rolph, "A theory of Excise Subsidies," *American Economic Review 42*, September 1952, 515–527). But, as noted, the predominant emphasis was, and remains, on taxation.

3. A. C. Pigou. *A Study in Public Finance*. London: Macmillan (1928).

4. For a brief summary discussion of the early continental contributions, see Richard A. Musgrave, *The Theory of Public Finance* (New York: McGraw Hill, 1959), pages 68–80. For a more extended discussion which is, however, concentrated largely on the Italian contributions, see my *Fiscal Theory and Political Economy* (Chapel Hill: University of North Carolina Press, 1960), pages 24–74. For translations of most of the important contributions here, see *Classics in the Theory of Public Finance*, ed. by R. A. Musgrave and A. T. Peacock (London: Macmillan, 1958).

5. Knut Wicksell, *Finanztheoretische Untersuchungen* (Jena: Gustav Fischer, 1896). Major portions of this are translated and included in the *Classics in the Theory of Public Finance*, op. cit.

6. Erik Lindahl, *Die Gerechtigkeit der Besteuerung* (Lund 1919). A central portion of this has been translated and is included in *Classics in the Theory of Public Finance*, op. cit.

7. See, for example, Duncan Foley, "Lindahl's Solution and the Core of an Economy with Public Goods," *Econometrica 38* (January 1970): 66–72; T. Bergstrom, "A Scandinavian Consensus Solution for Efficient Income Distribution Among Nonmalevolent Consumers," *Journal of Economic Theory 4* (December 1970): 383–398; D. J. Roberts, "The Lindahl Solution for Economies With Public Goods," *Journal of Public Economics 3* (February 1974): 23–42.

8. H. A. Musgrave. "The Voluntary Exchange Theory of Public Economy." *Quarterly Journal of Economics 53* (February 1938): 213–237.

9. Howard R. Bowen. "The Interpretation of Voting in the Allocation of Resources." *Quarterly Journal of Economics 58* (November 1943): 27–48.

10. See my "The Pure Theory of Government Finance: A Suggested Approach," *Journal of Political Economy LVII* (December 1949): 496–505, reprinted in my *Fiscal Theory and Political Economy*, op. cit, 8–23.

    I may add here an autobiographical note concerning this discovery that will be familiar to my students and former colleagues but which may deserve wider dissemination. In the summer of 1948, having finished my dissertation and fresh from having passed the German-language requirement, I spent some weeks wandering about the stacks in Harper Memorial Library at the University of Chicago. By chance, I picked up Wicksell's *Finanztheoretische Untersuchungen*, a book that had never been assigned or even so much as mentioned in my graduate courses, and, as I later ascertained, one of the very few copies in the United States. Quite literally, this book was responsible directly for the paradigm shift that I experienced.

11. Paul A Samuelson. "The Pure Theory of Public Expenditure." *Review of Economics and Statistics XXXVI* (November 1954): 387–389.

12. My book, *The Demand and Supply of Public Goods* (Chicago: Rand McNally, 1968), develops public-goods theory in the Wicksellian framework. The book's title is somewhat misleading; the analysis is almost exclusively devoted to the demand side; the supply side is neglected.

13. Their first papers appeared in 1948 and 1950, respectively. See, Duncan Black, "On the Rationale of Group Decision Making," *Journal of Political Economy LVI* (February

1948): 23–34; Kenneth Arrow, "A Difficulty in the Concept of Social Welfare," *Journal of Political Economy LVIII* (August 1950): 328–346.

These were followed by their full-length works. See Kenneth J. Arrow, *Social Choice and Individual Values* (New York: Wiley, 1951); Duncan Black, *The Theory of Committees and Elections* (Cambridge: Cambridge University Press, 1958).

14. Duncan Black. *The Incidence of Income Taxes,* London: Macmillan (1939).

15. James M. Buchanan and Gordon Tullock. *The Calculus of Consent,* Ann Arbor: University of Michigan Press (1962).

16. The setting for our analysis has an obvious affinity to that which is used by John Rawls in his derivation of the principles of justice, a setting that has been made familiar since the publication of Rawls's treatise (John Rawls, *A Theory of Justice* [Cambridge: Harvard University Press, 1971]). Although our approach was independently developed, Rawls had employed the "veil of ignorance" in earlier papers in the 1950s. Other scholars have used essentially similar devices as a means of moving from the individual's short-term interest to that which may be called, in one sense, the "public interest."

17. For a summary discussion of Puviani's contribution, along with a treatment of fiscal illusion more generally, see my *Public Finance in Democratic Process* (Chapel Hill: University of North Carolina Press, 1967), Chapter 10. An English translation of Puviani's basic work will be published in 1976, under the supervision of my colleague, Charles Goetz.

18. Anthony Downs. *An Economic Theory of Democracy,* New York: Harper (1957).

19. William H. Riker. *The Theory of Political Coalitions,* New Haven: Yale University Press (1962).

20. Gordon Tullock. *The Politics of Bureaucracy,* Washington: Public Affairs Press (1965).

21. Tullock's analysis of the bureaucrat represents perhaps the closest that public-choice analysis comes to a parallel, but quite different, development in modern economic theory, that which has been called the theory of property rights. The latter work of Alchian, McKean, Demsetz, Pejovich, and others, has been concentrated on predicting the effects of differing reward-penalty structures, as defined in terms of rights to property, on individual behavior. For a summary, see Eirik Furubotn and Svetozar Pejovich, "Property Rights and Economic Theory: A Survey of Recent Literature" *Journal of Economic Literature X* (December 1972): 1137–1162.

22. William Niskanen. *Bureaucracy and Representative Government,* Chicago: Aldine (1971).

23. Two introductory attempts should be noted: Albert Brenton, *The Economic Theory of Representative Government* (Chicago: Aldine, 1974); and Randall Bartlett, *Economic Foundations of Political Power* (New York: Free Press, 1973).

24. Because of space limits, I have not included a fifth line of analysis, that of locational public choice, or "voting with the feet," which has exerted a significant influence on public finance theory, especially as applied to local governments and to the interrelations among levels of government. The seminal paper which stimulated much of this analysis was that by Charles Tiebout, "The Pure Theory of Local Expenditure," *Journal of Political Economy LXIV* (October 1956): 416–424.

25. For a more extensive survey paper which does have this as its objective, see Dennis Mueller, "Public Choice: A Survey," *Journal of Economic Literature* (forthcoming).

26. My own book, *Public Finance in Democratic Process* (1967), op. cit., is largely a call for such research, along with a summary of some initial efforts, and the provision of a suggested research agenda.

27. Some of the early applications are contained in the separate studies included in the volume, *Theory of Public Choice,* edited by James M. Buchanan and Robert Tollison (Ann Arbor: University of Michigan Press, 1972). For a textbook in public economics that consistently employs a fiscal choice paradigm, see Richard E. Wagner, *The Public Economy* (Chicago: Markham, 1973).

28. My methodological views are developed in several of my books, some of which have been noted. In my most recent book, I try to examine some of the problems that emerge in trying to define "an individual," including the preliminary distribution of rights. See my *The Limits of Liberty: Between Anarchy and Leviathan* (Chicago: University of Chicago Press, 1975).

29. Cf. Martin Feldstein, "Social Security, Induced Retirement, and Aggregate Capital Accumulation," *Journal of Political Economy 82* (September/October 1974): 905–926.

# S E L E C T I O N   1 1

John L. Neufeld, William J. Hausman, and Ronald B. Rapoport*

# A Paradox of Voting: Cyclical Majorities and the Case of Muscle Shoals

Collective decision making is not analogous to individual decision making. Under certain circumstances, a unique political equilibrium cannot emerge under direct majority rule. Thus, while the analogy may be tempting, a public choice system (based on one person, one vote) does not always act like a private market system (based on one dollar, one vote). A perfectly competitive market can reach a unique, Pareto-efficient equilibrium, but if the same market participants vote directly in a political system, there is no guarantee of either uniqueness or Pareto efficiency. Each individual voter may be rational, with decisive and transitive preferences; however, collective or social choices may be intransitive and inconsistent—thus creating the "paradox of voting" known as cycling or the cyclical majority phenomenon.

Although social choice theorists have long investigated the possibility of cyclical majorities, clear examples of its occurrence in the real world have been very hard to find. This infrequency is at least partly due to the fact that legislative rules undermine the unconstrained operation of the lawmaking bodies. However, in this selection, John Neufeld, William Hausman, and Ronald Rapoport identify and explain how a clear-cut instance of cyclical voting occurred during a period of one week in the United States Senate.

### Questions to Guide the Reading
1. What types of voting situations are not subject to cyclical voting?

Neufeld, John L., William J. Hausman, and Ronald B. Rapoport. "A Paradox of Voting: Cyclical Majorities and the Case of Muscle Shoals." *Political Research Quarterly 47* (June 1994): 423–438. Reprinted by Permission of the University of Utah, Copyright Holder.

**John L. Neufeld** is Professor of Economics at University of North Carolina at Greensboro. **William J. Hausman** is Professor of Economics at The College of William and Mary. **Ronald B. Rapoport** is Professor of Government at The College of William and Mary.

2. Why are there so few real-world cases of cyclical majorities?
3. Why might the possibility of maintaining the status quo make it likely that there will be "insufficient evidence to say whether the paradox occurred"?
4. Why is the case of the Muscle Shoals works an important example of the voting paradox? What were the three alternative proposals considered pairwise by the Senate?
5. What finally led to the resolution of this voting cycle in the fifth ballot?
6. What unusual conditions permitted a full voting cycle to occur in the Muscle Shoals case?

Every democratic political system requires procedures for collective decision making, and voting plays a prominent role in those procedures. Social choice theorists have long recognized that when there are multiple proposals (or candidates), situations may arise in which no choice dominates even when individuals are consistent in their preferences.[1] Black (1958, 39) termed the theoretical possibility of cyclical majorities "one of the most surprising and disconcerting features of the theory of committees,"[2] Cyclical majorities occur when social choices are intransitive (i.e., if brought to a vote, proposal A would defeat proposal B, proposal B would defeat proposal C, and proposal C would defeat proposal A), even though individuals have preferences that are transitive (if a voter prefers proposal A to proposal B, and prefers proposal B to proposal C, that voter also prefers proposal A to proposal C). The importance of this result for collective choice is evident, and it has spawned a large literature, based heavily on axiomatic assumptions.[3] It has been difficult, however, to find clear examples of the existence of such cyclical majorities in real-world settings.[4] In this paper we will discuss briefly the conditions for cyclical voting under majority rule and examine previous attempts to identify examples of cyclical voting. We will then present a definitive and significant example of cyclical voting in the U.S. Senate.

Not every situation is subject to cyclical voting. First, the preferences of individuals on at least three policy alternatives must be such as to create a cyclical majority. Second, the rules under which voting takes place must permit all possible pairs of policy alternatives to be considered. Without the second condition, cyclical majorities might exist, but direct evidence of cyclical voting would be absent.

Cyclical majorities will not occur if the preference ordering of individuals is single peaked, i.e., if all voters map the issue in a single dimension or by a single agreed upon criterion (Black 1958, ch. 4). In this case a transitive social ordering will result. The assumption of single-peaked preferences along a common dimension is violated (and the potential for cyclical majorities raised) if voters see the issue in terms of different criteria (or dimensions) of policy concern; but even without a second dimension, voters may lack a common view as to how well respective alternatives meet the agreed upon criterion. Will school busing enhance the goal of integration or will it cause white-flight from public schools? Niemi (1969, 488) suggests that even without multidimensionality, "other factors such as lack of information about, misperception of, and similarity of alternatives as well as simply error make it almost certain that one or more preference orderings will not meet the necessary conditions."

If the possibility for cyclical voting exists, why are there so few examples of it in the literature? Although there is a possibility for a cyclical majority if even one voter deviates from single peakedness, it becomes less likely the fewer the voters who deviate from the dominant criterion. Niemi (1969) shows that with three alternatives, the theoretical maximum percentage of voters that may deviate from a common dimension is one-third, and if three quarters of the voters in a 95-person electorate (the approximate size of the U.S. Senate for most of this century) have a preference ordering along a common dimension, the probability of cyclical majorities diminishes to about 1 percent. This calculation is based on the assumption that all rankings of the three items are equally likely. In a legislative body with dominant issue alignments structuring the socialization of the membership, and common informational resources, single peakedness may be expected to be significantly more likely (and cyclical majorities significantly less likely) to occur than under the assumption of randomness.

The likelihood of cyclical majorities also depends on the number and characteristics of the alternatives being considered. The more alternatives, the stronger the likelihood of cycling (Ordeshook 1986, 58). If cyclical majorities are present, control of the agenda of pairwise votes can create any outcome desired (McKelvey 1976). Given the complicated rules operating in American legislative bodies, there are an abundance of possibilities for agenda manipulation, because some rules limit the possible pairings of alternatives in votes. For example, Ordeshook and Schwartz (1987, 180) cite "'Rule XIV of the House that requires members to perfect an amendment and the substitute amendment before deciding whether to substitute and then whether to amend the bill." However, even with such limitations, the possibility of cyclical majorities does exist. Given the large number of votes taken during a session of Congress even a low probability of cyclical majorities may have a significant effect on public policy.

The failure of alternatives to be paired with all other alternatives frequently prevents cyclical voting and interferes with our ability to identify cyclical majorities. In writing about the U.S. Congress, for example, Bowen (1972) notes that "the system is so constructed that under normal circumstances there is insufficient evidence to say whether the paradox occurred." For example, if a bill (A) that would alter the status quo (C) is introduced, and an amendment to the bill (B) proposed, there are three choices, but it is very unlikely that all three will be paired in sequential votes. If, for example, the bill is proposed and the amendment fails, the vote between the unamended bill (A) and the status quo (C) will settle the matter. The amended bill (B) will not be paired with the status quo. If the unamended bill fails, it is possible that a voting paradox has occurred (i.e., that the original bill is preferred to the amended bill by a majority, and that the status quo is preferred to the original bill by a majority, but that the amended bill actually is preferred to the status quo by a majority). But, in order to know whether the paradox has occurred, it is necessary to know the rank order of the three alternatives for each participant in the votes.[5] With three alternatives there are six possible rank orderings of individual preference, but with only two comparisons (here A vs. B and A vs. C), we usually cannot assign rank orders to all participants with certainty, and we cannot know what the preferences are between the amended bill and the status quo (or, if the amendment passes, between the unamended bill and the status quo).[6] With a tenable status quo as one of the three alternatives, the voting cycle is not likely to be observed.

Because of the theoretical importance of the paradox of voting, and because the choice between the status quo, a bill, and an amended bill is the most common set of legislative options, there have been frequent attempts to discover real-world examples of cyclical majorities when the status quo is an option. Riker (1965) provides two important and widely cited examples of congressional voting that appear to be consistent with the paradox. Both cases, according to Riker, involved attempts by Republicans to exploit the possibility of cyclical majorities by supporting amendments that by passing would doom the amended bill, leaving the status quo in place.[7] The effect of the amendment in both cases was to divide Southern and Northern Democrats over the issue of race. The first example concerns an aid to education bill in 1956 to which Adam Clayton Powell (Democrat, New York) proposed a school desegregation amendment. The amendment passed with Republican support, and the bill then failed. Riker argues that the unamended bill would have passed, but the opportunity for a vote on the original bill never materialized (in keeping with Bowen's contention). Although an unamended bill did pass in the next Congress, changes in circumstances and a significant turnover of members make it impossible to conclude with certainty that a cyclical majority was present the previous year. The second example was a proposal in 1911 for direct election of senators containing a provision prohibiting federal supervision of such elections. An amendment adopted by the House eliminated the prohibition, and this doomed the bill. In neither case, however, were the three alternatives considered pairwise, and, as a result, the full cycle was not observed.

What has been absent from the discussion of cyclical majorities is an example relating to a significant issue in a significant context in which all alternatives are voted on pairwise and sequentially. What circumstances are likely to produce such a situation? If we remove the possibility of a status quo alternative that can be achieved by voting down a bill, cyclical majorities may be easier to observe. If some bill must be passed, then because any proposal can be amended by substitution of another proposal, a straight vote can be taken between any pair of alternatives, and cycles will be evident.

The frequency with which cyclical majorities occur is difficult to determine, but since the literature on cyclical majorities has failed to uncover even a single clear example of cyclical voting, one may surmise that it is small. However, it is just such an example that would be most important in showing clearly the operation of cyclical majorities in non-contrived settings. The example we discuss here was the decision of what to do with Muscle Shoals after World War I. This example fits our requirements because it was a situation in which something had to be done (eventually); it was of major importance at the time (and afterwards); and it pertained to an important legislative body, the United States Senate.

## WHY SOMETHING HAD TO BE
## DONE WITH MUSCLE SHOALS

Muscle Shoals, located near Florence, Alabama, on the Tennessee River is a natural barrier to navigation where the river falls 130 feet in a 37-mile stretch.[8] It has a rich history in the public policy of the nation. In the nineteenth century, numerous efforts had been made to deal with the problem of Muscle Shoals. John C. Calhoun, President Monroe's Secretary of War, had urged a survey of the area in 1824. The survey, taken in 1828, recommended the construction of a canal to permit ships to bypass the area. The state of Alabama completed the canal in 1839, but it proved inadequate. In 1871 the federal government constructed a larger canal that also proved unable to overcome the problem. The arrival of electricity made the "problem" of Muscle Shoals also something of an opportunity, since the drop in the river made it an excellent potential hydroelectric site. Congress passed bills authorizing private development of the site for hydroelectric purposes in 1899, 1903, and 1906. The 1903 bill was vetoed by President Theodore Roosevelt who wanted the economic benefits of electricity production to help pay any costs associated with the improvement of navigation. The other two lapsed when the proposed projects were not constructed. Interest in Muscle Shoals and the Tennessee River continued, and several surveys were taken by the Corps of Engineers. Development did not, however, start in earnest until 1916, when Europe was at war and Congress passed the National Defense Act which directed the President to ascertain the most practical method for producing nitrates (a major component of explosives and fertilizer) and construct such plants and other facilities, including hydroelectric facilities, he deemed necessary for such production. The Act specifically required that the plants be operated solely by the government and not by private industry; it also provided for the facilities' peacetime use for the production of fertilizer.

In 1917 President Wilson chose Sheffield, Alabama, as the site of nitrate plant no. 1, which was to explore the experimental synthetic ammonia (Haber) process for the production of nitrates. Later the same year, he authorized nitrate plant no. 2, a larger cyanamid process plant to be built near Muscle Shoals. In early 1918 the construction of a hydroelectric dam at Muscle Shoals was authorized to provide the electricity required by the cyanamid process. A steam electric plant was also authorized, and the War Department entered into a contract with Alabama Power for the utility to construct additional generating plants. Hostilities ceased within a few months, and the issue of what to do with the works at Muscle Shoals arose immediately. Nitrate plant no. 1 never worked, and all activities at it ceased. Nitrate plant no. 2 had a successful test run, but contributed no nitrates during the war. Work on the hydroelectric facility (Wilson Dam) continued until 1921, but remaining funds were not sufficient to complete the dam, and construction stopped.

A protracted political struggle over the disposition of the Muscle Shoals works including the (initially) uncompleted dam ensued. No other single issue absorbed more of Congress's time in the 1920s.[9] The drama initially involved Henry Ford, who, with Thomas Edison in tow, made a highly publicized visit to the banks of the Tennessee in December 1921. Ford talked of building a new Detroit and of using hydroelectric power to provide farmers with cheap fertilizer. His actions set off a land boom among speculators in the Muscle Shoals area. Ford's offer, however, had several drawbacks that made it controversial. The payment he offered the federal government was low and did not purport to cover most of the expenses the government had already incurred.[10] Ford's commitment to providing fertilizer was a matter of contention, and he apparently had no intention of providing power to others. Finally, Ford demanded exemption from certain provisions of the new Federal Power Act (1920), including the award of an indefinitely renewable 100-year lease. Opposition to Ford arose from several areas, including other private interests (e.g., utilities such as Alabama Power) that might have developed the site. Power Progressives, led by George W. Norris (Republican, Nebraska), lost no opportunity to oppose Ford and push the cause of public ownership and operation of the facility. One of Norris's arguments was that the most efficient use of Muscle Shoals required development of the entire Tennessee River, a position that received support from periodic surveys taken by the Corps of Engineers.

On March 10, 1924, the House approved the Ford proposal by a vote of 227–143, but the controversy continued, and no action was taken by the Senate before it adjourned in June of that election year. In a surprise move in October, Henry Ford withdrew his offer. Norris succeeded in getting the Senate Agriculture and Forestry Committee to substitute his proposal for the now moot House bill. Early in the lame-duck session Senator Oscar W. Underwood (Democrat, Alabama) introduced a Muscle Shoals bill that would have authorized the President to lease the facilities to private interests. Underwood's bill required the lessee to produce fertilizer, a feature designed to win the support of Southern farmers (but which also brought the opposition of fertilizer manufacturers). Underwood's bill was crafted in consultation with the Republican administration, and it appeared to have the solid backing of President Coolidge.[11]

Underwood's bill was fiercely opposed by Norris and others. An argument that seemed particularly effective was the claim that Underwood's proposal was a giveaway to private interests and would result in another Teapot Dome scandal. When a New York *Herald* editorial made this charge, Underwood had the editorial writer hauled before a Senate committee.[12] Norris attacked the proposal with the claim that it was "a concession so great it will make Teapot Dome look like a pinhead" and then went on to criticize the President.[13] These attacks apparently were effective, and Republican senators came from meetings with the President convinced that

Underwood's measure would not pass and that the best disposition of Muscle Shoals was for it to be sent to a commission that would make recommendations to Congress after a year's study.[14] An amendment to the Underwood proposal to create such a commission was prepared by Senator Wesley Jones of Washington, the Republican whip.[15] An editorial in the *New York Times* favored a commission as a means of ensuring that the terms of any concession to private interests would be in the best interests of the public.[16] Senate sentiment appeared to have shifted to support of Jones's proposal.[17] Thus matters stood when the Senate recessed for Christmas. When it reconvened, its consideration of these issues produced a clear example of cyclical voting.

## THE VOTES ON MUSCLE SHOALS

The votes occurred in the Senate during one week between January 8 and January 14, 1925. Three proposals were considered in these votes.[18] One was the proposal for public ownership and development by Norris, which will be referred to as N. The second proposal was that of Underwood to lease Muscle Shoals to private industry. This will be designated U. The third proposal was that of Jones to refer the question of Muscle Shoals to a commission for further study. This will be designated J.

Norris's proposal was put before the Senate on January 8. Underwood offered his proposal as a substitute, and the Senate voted 48 to 37 to accept Underwood over Norris. Thus for the Senate U ≻ N. Jones immediately introduced his proposal as a substitute for Underwood. After debating the issue for several days, the Senate on January 13 voted 46 to 33 to accept the Jones proposal. Thus J ≻ U. Norris then offered his original proposal (with a minor change) as a substitute for Jones. If the Senate's preferences were transitive (and stable), Jones should have won since Jones was preferred to Underwood and Underwood was preferred to Norris. But Norris's proposal won 40 to 39. N ≻ J!

On the same day (January 13), Underwood reoffered his proposal (with a minor change). Norris tried to obtain a ruling that Underwood's resubmission was out of order by noting the cyclical nature of the Senate's voting:

> Now we are in a circle with three points in it. If the Senator [Underwood] should offer his original bill—and, in effect, that is what he has done—and the vote should be the same as it was once before, it is conceivable that his motion would prevail. Then the Senator from Washington [Jones] might offer his proposal, and, if the vote should be the same as it was before, it would prevail. If then I would modify mine just a little and offer it again it would prevail, and it would be back once around, and then the Senator from Alabama could change his bill a little and offer it again, and he would go around the circle again, and we would be just where we started.[19]

Underwood's proposal passed the next day 46 to 33.[20] As Norris predicted, Senator Jones then resubmitted his proposal as a substitute for Underwood. At this point Norris attempted to garner support for Jones by announcing that he would not resubmit his proposal if Jones's won. This time, however, Jones's proposal lost by 43 to 38, breaking the cycle. The Underwood bill then passed 50 to 30.

For those 71 senators who voted on the first three measures, it is possible to rank preferences among the three proposals and determine if each senator's preferences were transitive (assuming that a senator's preferences did not change during the course of the debate and votes). Only one senator (William B. McKinley, Republican, Illinois) exhibited apparently intransitive preferences. McKinley's choice on the fourth vote suggests that his ranking of Norris vs. Underwood changed from Norris preferred to Underwood preferred. Among the remaining senators—those whose preferences appeared transitive—cyclical majorities would have been sustained even more strongly than in the actual Senate votes. Table 1 shows the number of senators with each preference pattern.[21]

In a vote between Norris and Underwood, Underwood would have received the votes of those in groups 2, 5, and 6, and would have won 39 to 31. In a vote between Jones and Underwood, Jones would have received the votes of those in groups 1, 2, and 3, and would have won 40 to 30. In a vote between Norris and Jones, Norris would have received the votes of those in groups 3, 4, and 6, and would have won 37 to 33.

What political positions do these preferences represent? Group 1, the smallest group, was comprised of three Republicans (Couzens, Cummins, and Harreld), at least two of whom had been vehemently opposed to the original Ford proposal.[22] In the Senate debate, Harreld expressed a fear that the Underwood proposal would result in handing over "on a silver platter this magnificent enterprise" to the Ford interests.[23] All three senators in this group voted against final passage of the Underwood proposal. Group 2, the third largest, consisted of eleven Republicans and two Democrats (Cameron and Wadsworth). Their preferences reflected the apparent Administration position on the eve of the Senate recess. Although they favored private over public operation, the preferred option was further study by a commission. Those in Group 2 may have been concerned that a vote for Underwood might result in a scandal like Teapot Dome. It was shifts by members of this group that eventually ended the cycle. Group 3, the largest group, shows the preferences of Norris and others for whom public operation of Muscle Shoals was most important. For this group, the Jones proposal was intermediate because it would at least have postponed any lease to private interests. Groups 4 and 6 have in common that they rank the Jones proposal last. Ten of the thirteen senators in these two groups were either Deep South or border state Democrats.[24] It seems reasonable that these senators were more concerned that their region enjoy the benefits of Muscle Shoals being

**Table 1** Preferences of Senators Voting in First Three Votes on Muscle Shoals

| Group (see text) | Preferences | Number of Senators |
|---|---|---|
| 1. Anti-Ford Republicans | $J \succ N \succ U$ | 3 |
| 2. Jones group | $J \succ U \succ N$ | 13 |
| 3. Norris group | $N \succ J \succ U$ | 24 |
| 4. Southern Democrats | $N \succ U \succ J$ | 4 |
| 5. Underwood group | $U \succ J \succ N$ | 17 |
| 6. Southern Democrats | $U \succ N \succ J$ | 9 |

developed than they were with the question of whether development was best undertaken by public or private operation. Group 5, like Group 3, contained those for whom the issue was primarily one of public versus private operation. Group 5, however, favored private operation, the earlier Administration position.

A remaining question is why Underwood beat Jones in the fifth vote. Eleven senators voted differently that time than they had in the seemingly identical second vote. One of the eleven (Park Trammell, Democrat, Florida) switched from supporting Underwood to supporting Jones. The others switched from supporting Jones to Underwood. Of those ten, four had been absent from either the first or third vote and are not included in the table. The remaining six (five Republicans and one Democrat) were in Group 2, which ranked Norris last. There is evidence that the shift came at the direction of the Coolidge White House. The Republican floor leader shortly before the fifth vote met with the President who was, by this time, reported as favoring Underwood's position.[25] The fact that Group 2 reflected the apparent Administration position lends credence to the idea that it was an Administration shift which ended the cycle. Norris laid the blame on an "unseen power," which was interpreted as a reference to Coolidge.[26]

The votes discussed here did not settle the issue of what to do with Muscle Shoals. Although the Senate passed the Underwood bill, it failed to get House concurrence and the matter eventually went to a commission. The issue continued to consume the time of Congress.[27] A solution remained elusive until the election of 1932 substantially changed the balance of political power. Franklin D. Roosevelt made clear his intention to make Muscle Shoals the seed of a bold plan for the comprehensive development of the entire Tennessee River system. In 1933 Congress enacted the Tennessee Valley Authority Act, ending, finally, the decade-long struggle over the future of Muscle Shoals.

The series of votes on Muscle Shoals exhibited the conjunction of an unusual set of conditions that allowed for the observation of a full cycle of voting. First, there were alternative dimensions under which individuals could evaluate the proposal: the public versus private dimension and the speed of development dimension.[28] Second, the issue was one in which the status quo was not acceptable, and three alternatives to it were proposed. With large amounts of money sunk into the construction of the dam, and the potential for nitrate production already demonstrated, Muscle Shoals could not be ignored. As a result, strategic maneuvers designed to protect the status quo were not utilized and the three alternative proposals were voted on sequentially. The result, in the case of Muscle Shoals, was a real-world example of true cyclical voting, enhanced by the significance of the issue on which it occurred.

This singular example does not tell us how often cyclical majorities exist in democratic political systems. That will depend, among other things, on how often single-peaked preferences are violated. It is clear, however, that in legislative bodies, such as the U.S. Congress, rules inhibit their transparent appearance. To the extent that cyclical majorities exist but are suppressed by rules, setting the agenda in order to generate outcomes that are not actually preferred by a majority becomes extremely important in the voting process.

**Appendix**  Votes on the Disposition of Muscle Shoals

| | Vote#1 U vs N | Vote#2 J vs U | Vote#3 N vs J | Vote#4 U vs N | Vote#5 J vs U | Vote#6 U | Pref Group |
|---|---|---|---|---|---|---|---|
| Ashurst (D, AZ) | N | J | N | N | J | Nay | 3 |
| Ball (R, DE) | U | J | J | U | U | Yea | 2 |
| Bayard (D, DE) | U | U | J | U | U | Yea | 5 |
| Bingham (R, CT) | | J | J | U | U | Yea | – |
| Borah (R, ID) | N | J | N | N | J | Nay | 3 |
| Brookhart (R, IO) | N | J | N | N | J | Nay | 3 |
| Broussard (D, LA) | U | A | A | A | A | A | – |
| Bruce (D, MD) | U | U | N | U | U | Yea | 6 |
| Bursum (R, NM) | U | J | J | U | U | Yea | 2 |
| Butler (R, MA) | U | U | J | U | U | Yea | 5 |
| Cameron (D, AZ) | U | J | J | U | U | Yea | 2 |
| Capper (R, KS) | N | J | N | N | J | Nay | 3 |
| Carraway (D, AK) | U | A | A | A | A | A | – |
| Copeland (D, NY) | N | J | N | N | J | A | 3 |
| Couzens (R, MI) | N | J | J | N | J | Nay | 1 |
| Cummins (R, IO) | N | J | J | U | J | Nay | 1 |
| Curtis (R, KS) | U | U | J | U | U | Yea | 5 |
| Dale (R, VT) | U | U | J | U | U | Yea | 5 |
| Dial (D, SC) | U | U | N | U | U | Yea | 6 |
| Dill (D, WA) | N | J | N | N | J | Nay | 3 |
| Edge (R, NJ) | U | U | J | U | U | Yea | 5 |
| Edwards (D, NJ) | U | A | A | A | A | A | – |
| Elkins (R, WV) | A | A | J | A | A | A | – |
| Ernst (R, KY) | N | A | J | U | J | Yea | – |
| Fernald (R, ME) | U | U | J | U | U | Yea | 5 |
| Ferris (D, MI) | N | J | N | N | J | Nay | 3 |
| Fess (R, OH) | U | U | J | U | U | Yea | 5 |
| Fletcher (D, FL) | U | U | N | N | U | Yea | 6 |
| Frazier (R, ND) | N | A | A | A | A | A | – |
| George (D, GA) | U | U | N | U | U | Yea | 6 |
| Gerry (D, RI) | U | U | J | U | U | Yea | 5 |
| Glass (D, VA) | N | A | A | A | A | A | – |
| Gooding (R, ID) | N | J | N | N | J | Nay | 3 |
| Green (R, VT) | A | U | A | U | U | Yea | – |
| Hale (R, ME) | U | U | J | U | U | Yea | 5 |
| Harreld (R, OK) | N | J | J | N | J | Nay | 1 |
| Harris (D, GA) | N | U | N | N | U | Yea | 4 |
| Harrison (D, MS) | U | U | N | U | U | Yea | 6 |
| Heflin (D, AL) | U | U | N | U | U | Yea | 6 |
| Howell (R, NB) | N | A | N | N | J | Nay | – |
| Johnson (R, CA) | N | J | N | N | J | Nay | 3 |
| Johnson (F-LAB, MN) | A | A | A | A | A | A | – |
| Jones (D, NM) | N | J | N | N | J | Nay | 3 |
| Jones (R, WA) | U | J | J | N | J | Nay | 2 |
| Kendrick (D, WY) | N | U | N | N | U | Yea | 4 |
| Keyes (R, NH) | U | U | J | U | U | Yea | 5 |
| King (D, UT) | U | U | J | U | U | A | 5 |
| Ladd (R, ND) | U | U | N | U | U | Yea | 6 |

**Appendix** Votes on the Disposition of Muscle Shoals *(continued)*

| | Vote#1 U vs N | Vote#2 J vs U | Vote#3 N vs J | Vote#4 U vs N | Vote#5 J vs U | Vote#6 U | Pref Group |
|---|---|---|---|---|---|---|---|
| La Follette (R, WI) | N | J | N | N | J | Nay | 3 |
| Lenroot (R, WI) | A | A | A | A | A | A | – |
| McCormick (R, IL) | U | J | A | U | U | Yea | – |
| McKellar (D, TN) | N | J | N | N | J | Nay | 3 |
| McKinley (R, IL) | N | U | J | U | U | Yea | * |
| McLean (R, CT) | U | U | J | U | U | Yea | 5 |
| McNary (R, OR) | N | J | N | N | J | Nay | 3 |
| Mayfield (D, TX) | N | J | N | N | J | Nay | 3 |
| Means (R, CO) | U | J | J | U | U | Yea | 2 |
| Metcalf (R, RI) | U | U | J | U | U | Yea | 5 |
| Moses (R, NH) | A | J | J | U | U | Yea | – |
| Neely (D, WV) | N | J | N | N | J | Nay | 3 |
| Norbeck (R, SD) | N | J | A | A | A | A | – |
| Norris (R, NB) | N | J | N | N | J | Nay | 3 |
| Oddie (R, NE) | U | J | J | U | U | Yea | 2 |
| Overman (D, NC) | N | J | N | A | J | Nay | 3 |
| Owen (D, OK) | U | A | N | U | U | Yea | – |
| Pepper (R, PA) | U | J | J | U | J | Yea | 2 |
| Phipps (R, CO) | U | J | J | U | U | Yea | 2 |
| Pitman (D, NE) | U | U | N | U | U | Yea | 6 |
| Ralston (D, IN) | A | J | N | N | J | Nay | – |
| Ransdell (D, LA) | N | J | N | N | J | Nay | 3 |
| Reed (D, MO) | A | A | A | A | A | A | – |
| Reed (R, PA) | U | J | J | U | J | Yea | 2 |
| Robinson (D, AK) | U | A | A | A | A | A | – |
| Sheppard (D, TX) | N | J | N | N | J | Nay | 3 |
| Shields (D, TN) | U | U | J | U | U | Yea | 5 |
| Shipstead (F-LAB, MN) | N | J | N | N | J | Nay | 3 |
| Shortridge (R, CA) | U | J | J | U | J | Yea | 2 |
| Simmons (D, NC) | N | J | N | N | J | Nay | 3 |
| Smith (D, SC) | N | J | N | N | J | Nay | 3 |
| Smoot (R, UT) | U | J | J | N | A | Yea | 2 |
| Spencer (R, MO) | A | U | J | U | U | Yea | – |
| Stanfield (R, OR) | U | A | A | A | A | A | – |
| Stanley (D, KY) | U | U | N | U | U | Yea | 6 |
| Stephens (D, MS) | A | A | A | A | A | A | – |
| Sterling (R, SD) | U | J | J | U | J | Yea | 2 |
| Swanson (D, VA) | N | U | N | N | U | Nay | 4 |
| Trammell (D, FL) | N | U | N | A | J | Yea | 4 |
| Underwood (D, AL) | U | U | J | U | U | Yea | 5 |
| Wadsworth (D, NY) | U | J | J | U | J | Yea | 2 |
| Walsh (D, MA) | N | J | N | N | J | Nay | 3 |
| Walsh (D, MT) | N | J | N | N | J | Nay | 3 |
| Warren (R, WY) | U | U | J | A | U | Yea | 5 |
| Watson (D, IN) | U | J | A | U | U | Yea | – |
| Weller (R, MD) | U | A | A | U | J | Yea | – |
| Wheeler (D, MT) | A | A | A | A | A | A | – |
| Willis (R, OH) | U | U | J | U | U | Yea | 5 |

**Appendix** Votes on the Disposition of Muscle Shoals *(continued)*

*Notes:*
Vote #1 = vote on first proposal to substitute Underwood for Norris (U won).
Vote #2 = vote on first proposal to substitute Jones for Underwood (J won).
Vote #3 = vote on first proposal to substitute Norris for Jones (N won).
Vote #4 = vote on second proposal to substitute Underwood for Norris (U won).
Vote #5 = vote on second proposal to substitute Jones for Underwood (U won).
Vote #6 = final vote on Underwood bill (passed).
Pref Group = preference group as shown in the table in the text. All classifications are based on votes 1–3. Senators absent from one or more of those votes were not classified.
N = favored the Norris position.
U = favored the Underwood amendment.
J = favored the Jones Amendment.
A = absent from vote. Note: Bingham did not take his seat until after the first vote.
* = McKinley's votes are consistent with intransitive preferences.
*Source:* U.S. Congress. 1925. *Congressional Record.* 2nd session, 68th Congress. Washington: GPO, pp. 1454, 1726, 1736, 1795, 1805–06, 1808.

# NOTES

We thank Paul Whiteley, Don Campbell, Robert Archibald, David Feldman, and anonymous referees for their comments on earlier versions of this paper.

1. Seminal theoretical contributions have been made by Duncan Black (1958) and Kenneth J. Arrow (1963).
2. Theoretical insights into the paradox of voting have been traced as far back as Jean-Charles de Borda and the Marquis de Condorcet in the 1780s. The Rev. C. L. Dodgson (Lewis Caroll) also recognized the significance of the paradox in the 1870s. Black (1958) presents an historical account of the theory of cyclical majorities.
3. See, for example, McKelvey (1976, 1979); Schofield (1978); Enelow and Hinich (1984); and Mueller (1989). Tullock (1967) argues that while majority voting will always be subject to the paradox of voting, it is of little practical value, particularly when the number of voters is large.
4. The phenomenon has been observed in some experimental settings. McKelvey and Ordeshook (1990) survey recent experimental research on spatial models of committees and elections.
5. The paradox also would have occurred if the amendment had passed (B ≻ A) and the bill failed (C ≻ B) but the unamended bill would have passed if it had been brought to a vote (A ≻ C).
6. If, as suggested, the amendment is voted down and then the unamended bill is voted on, a legislator voting for the amendment (B ≻ A, but against the final bill (C ≻ A) could not be categorized as to whether the status quo is preferred to the amended bill (B ≻ C or C ≻ B). Similarly, a legislator voting against the amendment (A ≻ B) and for the final passage (A ≻ C) cannot be categorized in terms of preference between the amended bill and the status quo (C ≻ B or B ≻ C). Of course, a legislator voting for the amendment (B ≻ A) and then for final passage (A ≻ C) does determine a clear preference ranking as does a legislator voting against the amendment (A ≻ B) and against passage of the original bill (C ≻ A). Scholars such as Bowen (1972), Niemi and Weisberg (1968), Weisberg and Niemi (1972), and Riker (1982) have attempted to

deal with this difficulty by making assumptions about the likelihood of preference ordering for the excluded comparisons in order to ascertain the likelihood of a cyclical majority occurring in Congress.

7. In both of these cases as well as other (Brams 1976, 48; Riker 1990, 52), it is the attempt at manipulation (sophisticated voting by individuals) that creates the effect of cyclical majorities.

8. The primary source of the information given here about the Muscle Shoals issue is Hubbard (1961).

9. Schlesinger (1959, 322).

10. The final cost of the Muscle Shoals works was around $145 million, or nearly $1.5 billion in current dollars.

11. *New York Times,* December 7, 1924, p. 16, and December 8, 1924, p. 3.

12. *New York Times,* December 14, 1924, p. 24, December 15, 1924, p. 2, and December 19, 1924, p.3.

13. *New York Times,* December 18, 1924, pp. 1, 6.

14. *New York Times,* December 20, 1924, p. 7.

15. The commission was to be comprised of the Secretaries of War and Agriculture and a third member appointed by the President.

16. December 22, 1924, p. 16.

17. Lowitt (1971, 253).

18. Senate rules prevented identical proposals from being offered more than once. This was circumvented through the use of minor changes.

19. *Congressional Record,* 68th Congress, 2nd session, Jan. 13, 1925, p. 1737.

20. Three senators switched from supporting Norris on the first vote to supporting Underwood on the fourth vote, and three switched the other way (including Jones).

21. The votes and classification of each senator are shown in the Appendix.

22. Couzens had been Ford's business partner in the early days of the automobile industry and was a top executive with the Ford Motor Company before resigning in 1915 after a heated dispute over Ford's pacifist views. In 1922, Couzens, then Mayor of Detroit, was appointed to the seat Ford had run for and lost in 1918 (Sward 1972, 64; 122–123).

23. *Congressional Record,* 68th Congress, 2nd Session, Jan. 14, 1925, p. 1796. Harreld went on to note that he again was "going to support this amendment of the Senator from Washington [Mr. Jones] if for no other reason than to relieve us from this parliamentary situation into which we have fallen, and which I may say, by the way, is making the Senate look rather ridiculous, in my opinion" (ibid).

24. The exceptions were Kendrick (Democrat, Wyoming), Ladd (Republican, North Dakota), and Pittman (Democrat, Nevada).

25. *New York Times,* January 15, 1925, pp. 1, 6.

26. Ibid.

27. One of Norris' plans for government operation of Muscle Shoals passed in 1928 but was prevented from going into law by President Coolidge's pocket veto. In 1931 Congress again passed a Norris bill. Although President Hoover could have used a pocket veto, he instead sent Congress a forceful veto message opposing a major role for the government in electricity generation.

28. Speed of development was almost certainly the dominant dimension for the thirteen senators in Groups 4 and 6, and perhaps also for those in Groups 1 and 2.

## REFERENCES

Arrow, Kenneth J. *Social Choice and Individual Values*, (first ed., 1951). New Haven: Yale University Press (1963).

Black, Duncan. *The Theory of Committees and Elections*, Cambridge: Cambridge University Press (1958).

Bowen, Bruce D. "Toward an Estimate of the Frequency of Occurrence of the Paradox of Voting in U.S. Senate Roll Call Votes," in Richard G. Niemi and Herbert F. Weisberg, eds., *Probability Models of Collective Decision Making*, Columbus, Ohio: Merrill (1972), 181–202.

Brams, S. J. *Paradoxes in Politics*, New York: Free Press (1976).

Enelow, James M., and Melvin J. Hinich. *The Spatial Theory of Voting*, Cambridge: Cambridge University Press (1984).

Hubbard, Preston J. *Origins of the TVA: The Muscle Shoals Controversy 1920–1932*, Nashville, Tennessee: Vanderbilt University Press (1961).

Lowitt, Richard. *George W. Norris: The Persistence of a Progressive*, Urbana: University of Illinois Press (1971).

McKelvey, Richard D. "Intransitivities in Multidimensional Voting Models and Some Implications for Agenda Control." *Journal of Economic Theory 12* (June 1976): 472–482.

———. "General Conditions for Global Intransitivities in Formal Voting Models." *Econometrica* (September 1979): 1085–1101.

McKelvey, Richard D., and Peter C. Ordeshook. "A Decade of Experimental Research on Spatial Models of Elections and Committees," in James N. Enelow and Melvin J. Hinich, eds., *Advances in the Spatial Theory of Voting*, Cambridge: Cambridge University Press (1990), 99–144.

Mueller, Dennis C. *Public Choice II*, Cambridge: Cambridge University Press (1989).

Niemi, Richard G. "Majority Decision-Making with Partial Unidimensionality." *American Political Science Review 63* (June 1969): 448–498.

Niemi, Richard G., and Herbert F. Weisberg. "A Mathematical Solution for the Probability of the Paradox of Voting." *Behavioral Science 13* (July 1968): 317–323.

Ordeshook, Peter C. *Game Theory and Political Theory*, Cambridge: Cambridge University Press (1986).

Ordeshook, Peter C., and Thomas Schwartz. "Agendas and the Control of Political Outcomes." *American Political Science Review 81* (June 1987): 170–200.

Riker, William H. "Arrow's Theorem and Some Examples of the Paradox of Voting," in John M. Claunch, ed., *Mathematical Applications in Political Science*, Dallas, Texas: Arnold Foundation of Southern Methodist University (1965), 41–60.

———. *Liberalism against Populism*, San Francisco, California: Freeman (1982).

————. "Heresthetic and Rhetoric in the Spatial Model," in James N. Enelow and Melvin J. Hinish, eds., *Advances in the Spatial Theory of Voting,* Cambridge: Cambridge University Press (1990), 46–65.

Schlesinger, Arthur M. *The Coming of the New Deal,* Boston: Houghton Mifflin (1959).

Schofield, Norman. "Instability of Simple Dynamic Games." *Review of Economic Studies* 45 (October 1978): 575–594.

Sward, Keith. *The Legend of Henry Ford,* New York: Antheneum (1972 [originally published in 1948]).

Tullock, Gordon. "The General Irrelevance of the General Impossibility Theorem." *The Quarterly Journal of Economics* 81 (May 1967): 256–270.

Weisberg, Herbert F., and Richard G. Niemi. "Probability Calculations for Cyclical Majorities in Congressional Voting," in Richard G. Niemi and Herbert F. Weisberg, eds., *Probability Models of Collective Decision Making,* Columbus, Ohio: Merrill (1972), 204–231.

# S E L E C T I O N   1 2

Robert D. Tollison

# Rent Seeking: A Survey

Rent seeking occurs as parties compete for profits that have been artificially contrived by government policies. For example, rent seeking can take the form of special interest groups lobbying for favorable treatment. In general, any policy which restricts free market competition can generate rents and cause rent seeking: international barriers to trade such as tariffs and import quotas, domestic market interventions such as command-and-control pollution regulations or barriers to entry such as cellular telephone licenses awarded by the Federal Communications Commission (FCC), and state or local economic development efforts such as special tax abatements and low-interest loans to attract new businesses.

In this selection, Robert Tollison first clarifies the important differences between profit seeking and rent seeking. The rent-seeking literature has focused on the explanation of contrived rents, the analysis of how individuals and groups compete for such rents, and dollar estimates of the amount of income redistribution engendered by these activities. Tollison demonstrates how rent seeking can be wasteful by focusing on rivalry in the political arena for a government-protected monopoly franchise or license. In this case, rent seeking can result in a social waste of resources exceeding the welfare cost of monopoly.

### Questions to Guide the Reading
1.  How does the existence of economic rents lead to a more efficient allocation of resources in a competitive market system?
2.  How does profit seeking in the competitive market system differ from competition for government-contrived or "fake" rents? Why

Tollison, Robert D. "Rent Seeking: A Survey," *Kyklos 35* (Fasc. 4, 1982): 575–602. This selection is an abridged version of the original article.

**Robert D. Tollison** is the Duncan Black Professor of Economics and Director of The Center for Study of Public Choice at George Mason University.

are there additional costs associated with rent seeking? Why are these costs considered wasteful?

3. How can rent seeking be seen as a "transfer" or redistribution of income?

4. According to Tullock, under what circumstances will the conventional model of the welfare loss from monopoly be incomplete?

5. What are possible public policy implications of ignoring consumer lobbying in analyses of rent seeking?

## I. INTRODUCTION

The purpose of this essay is to survey the emerging theory of the rent-seeking society. The initial problem is to clarify terminology. Rent is a venerable concept in economics. Defined as a return in excess of a resource owner's opportunity cost, economic rent has played a prominent role in the history of economic analysis ("corn is not high because rent is paid, rent is paid because corn is high"). In this sense it is a fair guess that most economists would consider "rent seeking" to be equivalent to "profit seeking," whereby it is meant that the expectation of excess returns motivates value-increasing activities in the economy. Such excess returns (positive *and* negative) are typically viewed as short-lived (quasi-rents) because competition will drive them to normal levels.

The competitive dissipation of rents, however, is not what is meant by "rent seeking." Rents emanate from two sources. They arise *naturally* in the price system by, for example, shifts in demand and supply curves. The pursuit of rents under these circumstances is the sense in which rent seeking is equivalent to profit seeking. Rents can also be contrived *artificially* through, for example, government action. The fact that rents are contrived, however, does not mean that they are exempt from competition, and this is where rent seeking comes into play.

Consider the example of monopoly rents. The typical discussion depicts such returns as a transfer from consumers to a monopolist. Treated as such, monopoly rents embody no social costs. Yet if the process by which monopoly rents are contrived is subject to competition (e.g., lobbying), the analytical fiction of these rents as a pure transfer vanishes because resources spent in the pursuit of a transfer are *wasted* from society's point of view. These expenditures add nothing to social product (they are zero-sum at best), and their opportunity cost constitutes lost production to society.

The theory of rent seeking involves the study of how people compete for artificially contrived transfers. Like the rest of economic theory, rent seeking has normative and positive elements. Normative rent-seeking theory refers to the specification and estimation of the costs of rent-seeking activities to the economy. Are contrived rents dissipated by competition to capture them? Are they exactly dissipated by competitive rent seeking, or are there imperfections in rent-seeking processes such that expenditures to capture monopoly positions either exceed or fall short of the rents that inhere in them? What role does the consumer play in the theory of the rent-seeking society? What is the domain of rent-seeking behavior, that is, is government required for rent-seeking theory to be applicable or can rents be contrived and dissipated in private settings?

The positive side of rent-seeking theory is directed to the question of what explains the sources of contrived rents in a society. For example, in normal text-book presentations monopoly is introduced by drawing a downward sloping demand curve and its associated marginal revenue curve. The effects of monopoly are explained, but the issue of why some industries consist of pre-takers and others consist of price-searchers is largely begged. Positive rent-seeking theory goes behind the facade of microeconomic theory and attempts to explain why some sectors of the economy are sheltered and some are not.

This essay will survey the economic theory of rent seeking. In Section II, a more detailed discussion of the differences between rent seeking and profit seeking is given. In Section III, normative rent-seeking theory and empirical measures are discussed. . . . Some concluding remarks are offered in Section V.

## II. RENT SEEKING VERSUS PROFIT SEEKING

In economic analysis the definition of economic rent is a payment to a resource owner above the amount his resources could command in their next best alternative use. An economic rent is a receipt in excess of the opportunity cost of a resource. It has been observed that it is not necessary to pay economic rents in order to procure an efficient allocation of resources. This argument, however, is based on a faulty perception of the dynamics of the competitive market process. Over time, the presence of economic rents provides the incentive for resource owners to seek out more profitable allocations of their resources. When competition is viewed as a dynamic, value creating, evolutionary process, the role of economic rents in stimulating entrepreneurial decisions and in prompting an efficient allocation of resources is crucial (Kirzner 1973) "Rent seeking" or "profit seeking" in a competitive market order is a normal feature of economic life. The returns of resource owners will be driven to normal levels (on both the intensive and extensive margins) by competitive profit seeking as some resource owners earn positive rents which promote entry and others earn negative rents which cause exit. Profit seeking and economic rents are inherently related to the efficiency of the competitive market process. Such activities drive the competitive price system and create value (e.g., new products) in the economy.

The task at hand is to distinguish what is meant by rent seeking from profit seeking. Consider a simple example in which the king wishes to grant a monopoly right in the production of playing cards. In this case artificial scarcity is created by the state, and as a consequence, monopoly rents are present to be captured by monopolists who seek the king's favor. Normally, these rents are thought of as transfers from playing card consumers to the card monopolist. Yet in the example, this can only be the case if the aspiring monopolists employ no real resources to compete for the monopoly rents. To the extent that real resources are spent to capture monopoly rents in such ways as lobbying, these expenditures create no value from a social point of view. It is this activity of wasting resources in competing for artificially contrived transfers that is called rent seeking. If an incipient monopolist hires a lawyer to lobby the king for the monopoly right, the opportunity cost of this lawyer (e.g., the contracts that he does not write while engaged in lobbying) is a social cost of the monopolization process. Moreover, the deflection of lawyers from productive to transfer-seeking pursuits will generate a disequilibrium in the market for lawyers, with the implication that there will be excessive entry into the legal profession. As will be presented in more detail in Section III, such rent-seeking costs must be added to the standard welfare-triangle loss associated with monopoly to obtain an estimate of the total social costs of monopoly and regulation.

"Real" rents are different from "government" or "fake" rents because rent seeking has productive implications in the first case but not in the second. Just to drive the point home, consider the following example. The return to professional baseball players includes some (inframarginal) rents which leads young children to play baseball rather than practice the piano. This increases the supply of baseball players tomorrow (because young children practiced today), and the amount and quality of baseball is altered (improved?). In the case of monopoly rents lobbying is the analogy to practicing, and lobbying does not increase output because output is fixed by definition. It is the restricting of output artificially that creates the rents.

Rent seeking is the expenditure of scarce resources to capture an artificially created transfer. The implications of the economic wastefulness of rent-seeking activity are difficult to escape once an artificial scarcity has been created (Buchanan 1980). At one level the king can allow individuals to compete for the playing card monopoly and waste resources through such activities as bribery. Such outright venality is perhaps the simplest and most readily understood level of rent seeking. At a second level the state could sell the monopoly right to the highest bidder and put the proceeds at the disposal of government officials. In this case the monopoly rents will most likely show up in the wages of state officials, and to capture rents at this level individuals will compete to become civil servants. This competition might be thought of in terms of excess returns to bureaucratic agents where these returns are competed away by excessive expenditures on education to prepare for civil service examinations (Tullock 1980). At still another level should the monopoly right be sold to the highest bidder and the resources dispersed through the state budget in terms of expenditure increases and/or tax reductions, rent-seeking costs will be incurred as individuals seek to become members of the groups favored by the tax-expenditure program. Rent-seeking costs are incurred in each case, and only the form that such costs take is influenced by how the government transacts its business in artificially contrived scarcity values.

## III.   THE WELFARE ANALYSIS OF RENT SEEKING

The welfare analysis of rent seeking concerns the issue of how costly such activities are to the economy. It was, in fact, through an effort to assess the nature of these costs that Tullock (1967) first analyzed the concept of rent seeking. Subsequent research has concentrated on expanding Tullock's theoretical insight and on developing empirical measures of rent-seeking costs.

## 1. Competitive Rent Seeking

In Figure 1 a simple monopoly diagram is drawn ($Q_m = 1/2 Q_c$). This model is sufficient to yield all of the insights generated by competitive rent-seeking theory.

In the standard analysis of monopoly a competitive industry is *costlessly* transformed into a simple monopoly. This analysis is developed as if a snapshot of equilibrium conditions were taken at two instants of time. One photograph reveals $P_c Q_c$ as the market equilibrium and the other $P_m Q_m$. In this conceptual experiment the welfare cost is the lost consumer surplus given by *ABC*. In its modern form this partial equilibrium analysis was pioneered by Harberger (1954), who developed a reduced-form equation for *ABC* and used it to measure the extent of such losses in the U.S. manufacturing sector circa 1929. His empirical results showed the welfare loss from monopoly to be a negligible proportion (less than 1 percent) of GNP. By modifying the assumptions underlying the reduced-form for *ABC* (e.g., the elasticity of demand), a variety of subsequent estimates of welfare losses from monopoly have been published. These estimates generally follow the Harberger result in not constituting monopoly as an overwhelming social problem.[1]

Commenting upon the relatively low estimates of the welfare costs of monopolies and tariffs, Mundell (1962, 622) observed that "unless there is a thorough re-examination of the validity of the tools upon which these studies are founded... someone will inevitably draw the conclusion that economics has ceased to be important." Tullock rose to this challenge in a 1967 paper in the *Western Economic Journal* (now *Economic Inquiry*).[2] Tullock's insight was simple and straightforward. He argued that any resources spent to capture $P_m P_c AB$ were *also* a social cost of monopoly and that the conventional model of the welfare loss from monopoly, in which monopoly profits are treated as a lump-sum transfer from consumers to the monopolist, was incomplete if potential monopolists spent resources to capture the monopoly right. Since economists typically believe that competition is ever present, the relevance of Tullock's argument is apparent—monopoly rights will not generally be exempt from competition and expenditures to capture such contrived transfers are a social cost. The earlier application

## Figure 1

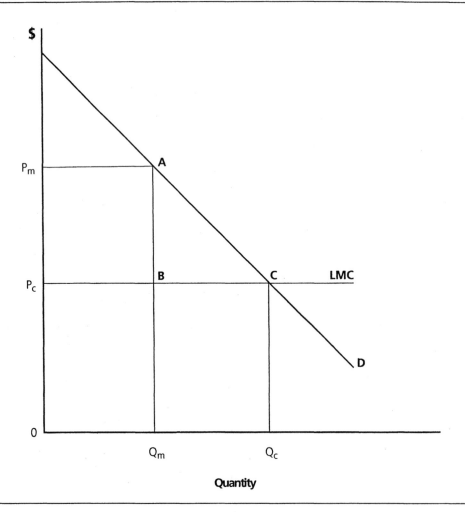

of this discussion to the employment of lawyer-lobbyists resources by monopoly-seekers need not be repeated here.[3]

What can be termed competitive rent seeking implies that the monopoly rents in Figure 1 ($P_cP_mAB$) are exactly dissipated. Tullock's original formulation of the problem was in these terms, as were the subsequent contributions by Krueger (1974) and Posner (1975). Consider Posner's example of how competitive rent seeking might work in practice. A monopoly right is worth $100,000. There are ten risk-neutral bidders among whom there is no collusion. Each will bid $10,000 for the right, an expenditure which cannot be returned if theirs is not the winning bid. The result is that the monopoly returns are dissipated at a social level—$100,000 is spent to capture a transfer of $100,000.

Empirical work with the competitive rent-seeking model is relatively easy to implement. In effect the analyst must estimate the area of a trapezoid rather than just a triangle. Both Krueger (1974) and Posner (1975) have applied variations of such a model to derive estimates of rent-seeking costs. Krueger estimated that the value of rents in various parts of the Indian public sector constituted 7.3 percent of national income. She also estimated the rents in Turkish import licenses in 1968 to be approximately 15 percent of GNP. Posner has presented measures of rent-seeking costs in the U.S. economy. He asserts that such costs constitute roughly 3 percent of GNP, an amount which would have to be added to Harberger-type losses in the economy to obtain an estimate of the total social costs of monopoly and regulation. Rent-seeking analysis tends to magnify the problem of monopoly over and beyond the traditional measurements made by Harberger, rising to the challenge laid down by Mundell.

## 2. Rent Seeking and Consumers

In the usual presentation of the welfare costs of monopoly, whether of the Harberger- or the Tullock-Posner–type, the role of the consumer is entirely passive. No account is made of potential consumer activities to counter monopolization efforts by producers. This assumption of economic importance is typically made on the basis of stylized facts which portray consumers as an unorganized, widely dispersed group without incentive to try to restrain the political monopolization process.

Two things can be said about this nontreatment of consumers. First, as an empirical issue, it is surely wrong. Since the 1960s there has been a rapid growth in the number and size of organized consumer groups; Evans (1980, 5) lists twenty-one major consumer organizations active in the U.S., including such familiar groups as Common Cause, the American Farm Bureau Federation, and the network of Nader organizations. The major groups concentrate on lobbying Congress and state legislatures, but there are also many smaller local groups which regularly appear in such mundane places as rate hearings to lobby for lower prices. Second, to the extent that welfare analysis does not include a role for consumer lobbying, it is lagging behind developments in the positive economic theory of rent seeking. Peltzman (1976), for example, offers a model in which a vote-maximizing regulator trades-off industry price and profits between consumer and producer forces. This formulation is squarely based on the idea that consumers impinge on political prices. As a corollary to Peltzman's contribution, it seems useful to expand the normative theory of rent-seeking to include a role for consumers.

\* \* \*

## V. CONCLUDING REMARKS

Economic rent is not new to economists. Yet as this essay hopefully demonstrates, the full implications of the role of rents in the economy are just starting to emerge. In this sense rent seeking is an interesting intellectual innovation. As a rereading of Tullock's 1967 paper would convince virtually anyone, the insight that brought about the idea of rent seeking was exceedingly simple. Rents are competed for, and where rents are contrived, this competition has important normative and positive implications for economic analysis. The moral is perhaps that important advances in economics do not naturally have to flow from a highly mathematical or statistical approach to the subject. In this regard Tullock's original paper on rent seeking calls to mind Coase's (1960) seminal work on social cost.

## NOTES

Thanks go to James Buchanan, Robert McCormick, and Dennis Mueller for helpful comments. The usual caveat applies.

1. Since this paper is concerned with rent seeking and not with the conventional welfare loss from monopoly, a review of the efforts to improve upon Harberger's original formulation of the latter problem is not pursued here. The interested reader may consult Scherer (1980, ch. 17) and the references cited there.
2. Also see Tullock (1971, 1974) and Browning (1974).
3. One immediate implication of Tullock's insight, noted by Posner (1974), is that studies of the distributional effects of monopoly are misleading (e.g., Comanor and Smiley [1975]). Monopoly rents are *dissipated* (provided that lawyer-lobbyists earn normal returns) not *transferred*.

## REFERENCES

Browning, Edgar K. "On the Welfare Cost of Transfers." *Kyklos 26* (April 1974): 374–377.

Buchanan, James M. "Rent Seeking and Profit Seeking," in *Toward a Theory of the Rent-Seeking Society,* Buchanan, Tollison, and Tullock, eds., College Station, Texas: Texas A&M University Press (1980), 3–15.

Coase, Ronald H. "The Problem of Social Cost." *Journal of Law and Economics 3* (October 1960): 1–44.

Comanor, William S., and Smiley, Robert H. "Monopoly and the Distribution of Wealth." *Quarterly Journal of Economics 89* (May 1975): 177–194.

Evans, Joel R. (ed.). *Consumerism in the United States,* New York: Praeger (1980).

Harberger, Arnold C. "Monopoly and Resource Allocation." *American Economic Review 44* (May 1954): 77–87.

Kirzner, Israel. *Competition and Entrepreneurship,* Chicago: University of Chicago Press (1973).

Krueger, Anne O. "The Political Economy of the Rent-Seeking Society." *American Economic Review 64* (June 1974): 291–303.

Mundell, Robert A. "Review of Jansenn's *Free Trade, Protection and Customs Union.*" *American Economic Review 52* (June 1962): 621–622.

Peltzman, Sam. "Toward a More General Theory of Regulation." *Journal of Law and Economics 10* (August 1976): 211–240.

Posner, Richard A. "Theories of Economic Regulation." *Bell Journal of Economics and Management Science 5* (Autumn 1974): 335–358.

————. "The Social Costs of Monopoly and Regulation." *Journal of Political Economy 83* (August 1975): 807–827.

Scherer, F. M. *Industrial Market Structure and Economic Performance,* Chicago: Rand McNally (1980).

Tullock, Gordon. "The Welfare Costs of Tariffs, Monopolies, and Theft." *Western Economic Journal 5* (June 1967): 224–232.

Tullock, Gordon. "The Cost of Transfers." *Kyklos 24* (December 1971): 629–643.

Tullock, Gordon. "More on the Cost of Transfers." *Kyklos 27* (April 1974): 378-381.

Tullock, Gordon. "Rent Seeking as a Negative-Sum Game," in Buchanan, Tollison, and Tullock, eds., *Toward a Theory of the Rent-Seeking Society,* College Station, Texas: Texas A&M University Press (1980), 16–36.

# S E L E C T I O N  1 3

David E. Bloom and Sherry Glied

# Benefits and Costs of HIV Testing

To an economics student, the activity implied by "cost-benefit analysis" probably seems noncontroversial and straightforward: determine costs, determine benefits, compare. So straightforward, in fact, that it may be hard to imagine why cost-benefit analysis has been referred to (among other things) as an "insidious poison in the body politick." The answer is equally simple—it is often hard to identify and value all relevant costs and benefits. And when this is the case, economic analysts may differ considerably in their estimates, and thus, in their policy recommendations. However, even if no definitive answer is found, cost-benefit analysis can help to clarify the issues at the heart of the disagreements, and thus at the very least, help to ensure more informed choices.

Cost-benefit analysis has been applied to a wide and fascinating range of activities, such as: imprisonment, abortion, endangered-wildlife recovery, urban air pollution, recycling, enforcement efforts to reduce DWIs (citations for driving while intoxicated), air bags and automatic seat belts, tax farming in lesser-developed countries (use of private collection agencies), welfare-to-work programs, and even, economic statistics (see Suggested Further Readings). In the following selection, David Bloom and Sherry Glied apply cost-benefit analysis to examine employers' incentives to require tests for human immunodeficiency virus (HIV) as a condition of employment. (Most of us have probably had either first-hand experience with drug testing for employment, or know someone who has. HIV testing is viewed as an extension of this practice.) Bloom and Glied find that, in general, employers will not be interested in HIV testing since it yields private benefits less than costs.

Reprinted with permission from David E. Bloom and Sherry Glied. "Benefits and Costs of HIV Testing." *Science 252* (June 28, 1991): 1798–1804. Copyright 1991 American Association for the Advancement of Science.

**David E. Bloom** is Professor of Economics at Columbia University. **Sherry Glied** is Assistant Professor of Public Health and Economics, School of Public Health and Department of Economics at Columbia University.

However, the social benefits of HIV testing in the workplace may exceed private benefits. Thus, private behavior in labor markets will not necessarily result in a socially-optimal level of HIV testing.

### Questions to Guide the Reading

1. What explains "the growing use of health-related tests in employment settings"? How do these factors relate to the HIV epidemic?
2. Why are the costs to a firm of hiring an HIV-positive individual much higher than for most other medical conditions?
3. What are the direct costs to employers of HIV testing? Why might these costs vary across firms?
4. What are some of the indirect costs associated with HIV testing? According to the authors, how might the existence of these costs affect the results of their study?
5. Why do the private (employers') benefits of HIV testing differ from the social benefits?

In making hiring decisions, employers typically pay great attention to characteristics thought to predict a worker's productivity, such as education, previous work experience, and various physical and psychological attributes. Increasingly in recent years, this information has been supplemented by results from tests for a variety of existing and potential health conditions, and for drug and alcohol use.[1-3] These test results may provide further indications of likely productivity. They may also help in assessing the cost that a prospective employee will impose on a firm, especially on the firm's cost of providing health-contingent benefits.[4] Hiring an employee who imposes significant costs on a firm will diminish the firm's performance in the same way as would hiring a relatively unproductive employee.

The growing use of health-related tests in employment settings has its roots in three developments: (i) the increasing cost of health-contingent benefits offered by employers, (ii) the existence of relatively inexpensive biomedical tests designed to predict or assess health conditions, and (iii) the concern that firms with the most liberal compensation plans will attract a disproportionate share of individuals who place relatively sizable burdens on such plans (that is, the problem of adverse selection in response to health-related information that is not normally available to employers).[5] Each of these developments is well illustrated in the context of the human immunodeficiency virus (HIV) epidemic: the direct medical care costs associated with cases of HIV infection are substantial,[5-6] tests for HIV infection are readily available,[7] and individuals are likely to have better information about their own HIV status than are their employers—information that they may use in choosing an employer, or in making fringe benefit selections.[8]

For these reasons, the HIV epidemic provides a natural context in which to explore the general issues that arise when employers screen prospective employees on the basis of their current and predicted future health. HIV testing is also important in its own right, given the large number of working-age Americans who may be infected with HIV and the growing number of firms who report having at least one HIV-infected employee.[9] In this article, we attempt to shed some light on these issues by examining the incentives employers have to require negative HIV test results as a condition of employment. We also examine the extent to which the public interest in HIV testing will be adequately served by the decisions made by private employers.

A fundamental premise of the ensuing analysis is that a firm will test its employees for HIV infection when the firm's expected benefits of testing outweigh its expected costs. We discuss the benefits and costs of HIV testing in employment settings that are free of legal constraints on testing. We also report estimates of the magnitudes of these private benefits and costs. We compare these magnitudes in order to assess the conditions under which employers would tend to favor HIV testing in a competitive market economy. Finally, we consider whether society would benefit from adopting policies designed to influence the level of HIV testing in employment settings and discuss current legislation related to HIV testing in this area. In summary, we find that (i) the social benefits of HIV testing in employment settings are fundamentally different from the private benefits, implying that private behavior in the labor market will not necessarily result in a socially optimal level of HIV testing; and (ii) from the point of view of most employers, HIV testing is not cost beneficial given relevant estimates of the prevalence of HIV infection. In addition, the incentives not to test for HIV are reinforced by legal prohibitions against testing in most jurisdictions, and especially in those in which the incidence of AIDS is relatively high.

## INCENTIVES FOR EMPLOYERS TO REQUIRE HIV TESTS

Consider an employer who is trying to fill a job vacancy by deciding between two applicants who have identical productivity-related characteristics. Assume it is known that one applicant is HIV-positive and the other is not. Assume further that the employer and his workforce and customers are "informed," in the sense that they recognize that HIV is not spread through casual contact. In the absence of any legal restrictions on the employer's hiring process, even this "informed" employer is likely to prefer the applicant who tested negative. As we argue below, this preference is mainly due to the increased probabilities of morbidity and mortality of the HIV-positive applicant, which suggest that he or she is likely to impose relatively larger costs on the firm than would the HIV-negative applicant.

An employer might be able to avoid certain employment costs by rejecting job applicants who test positive for HIV. These avoided costs, which represent the expected benefits to an employer of HIV testing, are set forth in Table 1. There are

**Table 1**  Expected Value of Costs Avoided by Hiring an HIV-Negative Individual Instead of an Otherwise Identical HIV-Positive Individual

Low-cost city estimates are based on health care cost data for San Francisco. High-Cost city estimates are based on health care cost data for New York City. Small-firm estimates are based on the degree of experience rating and the benefits offered by a firm with about 50 employees. Large firm estimates are based on the degree of experience rating and the benefits offered by a firm with about 1000 employees. We assume that all costs are incurred at the end of each period. All estimates are in 1987 dollars, rounded to the nearest 100 dollars. The estimates represent simulations of the experience of "average" firms in different cities and employment size categories. The experience of a particular firm will depend on its specific characteristics.

| Sources of avoided costs | Large firm | | Small firm | |
|---|---|---|---|---|
| | High-cost city | Low-cost city | High-cost city | Low-cost city |
| | *Health insurance**  | | | |
| Health care cost | $ 80,000 | $40,000 | $80,000 | $40,000 |
| Degree of experience rating (%) | 100 | 100 | 50 | 50 |
| Firms offering (%) | 100 | 100 | 80 | 80 |
| Cost to firm | $ 80,000 | $40,000 | $32,000 | $16,000 |
| | *Life insurance†* | | | |
| Death benefit | $ 23,200 | $ 23,200 | $23,200 | $23,200 |
| Degree of experience rating (%) | 100 | 100 | 10 | 10 |
| Firms offering (%) | 94 | 94 | 40 | 40 |
| Cost to firm | $ 21,800 | $ 21,800 | $    900 | $    900 |
| | *Disability insurance‡* | | | |
| Sick leave | $   1,200 | $  1,200 | $  1,200 | $  1,200 |
| Firms offering (%) | 91 | 91 | 36 | 36 |
| Long-term disability | $ 17,800 | $17,800 | $17,800 | $17,800 |
| Degree of experience rating (%) | 100 | 100 | 10 | 10 |
| Firms offering (%) | 69 | 69 | 10 | 10 |
| Cost to firm | $ 13,400 | $13,400 | $    600 | $    600 |
| Total insurance cost to firm | $115,200 | $75,200 | $33,500 | $17,500 |
| | *Pension§* | | | |
| Value of offset | –$   4,000 | –$  4,000 | – $  1,100 | –$  1,100 |
| Firms offering (%) | 61 | 61 | 33 | 33 |
| Pension offset received by firm | –$   2,400 | –$  2,400 | –$     360 | –$     360 |
| Present value discount factor‖ | 1.25 | 1.25 | 1.16 | 1.16 |
| Discounted hiring and training cost** $ | 700 | $      700 | $      680 | $      680 |
| Total discounted differential cost if individual develops AIDS | $  90,900 | $58,900 | $29,300 | $15,500 |
| Probability that an HIV-positive individual develops AIDS†† | 0.35 | 0.35 | 0.15 | 0.15 |
| Expected value of costs avoided | $  31,800 | $20,600 | $  4,400 | $  2,300 |

\* Sources of data used in calculations: Bloom and Carliner[5] for health care costs; Tewksbury[11] for experience rating; ICF Incorporated[10] for benefits offered. Figures on the cost of treating AIDS patients are used as estimates of the cost of treating seropositive individuals because there is no direct information on the latter. Although this procedure may introduce some bias, its direction is unclear and its magnitude is not likely to be large. See Bloom and Glied[6] especially pages 190 to 191 for some discussion relevant to this point.
† Forty-five percent of life-insurance policies pay annual earnings, 34% pay twice annual earnings, and the remainder pay a lump sum, usually about $10,000.[43] We ignore the probability of death from other causes because death rates from other causes in the 25 to 44 age group

**Table 1** Expected Value of Costs Avoided by Hiring an HIV-Negative
Individual Instead of an Otherwise Identical HIV-Positive Individual *(continued)*

are less than 0.3% per year.[44] Sources of data: *Statistical Abstract*[12] for average annual earnings; Tewksbury[11] for experience rating; ICF Incorporated[10] for benefits offered.

‡ The disability cost is calculated on the basis of the following assumptions: (i) people with AIDS work for 40% of the available work days during the first year after diagnosis and do not work during their second year after diagnosis;[45] (ii) sick leave is available for 15 days in firms with disability policies;[43] (iii) individuals who are not HIV-infected do not use any sick days (if such individuals do take sick days, the estimate reported here will be an overestimate of the true cost of sick leave); (iv) long-term disability policies replace about 60% of income.[43] Sources of additional data: *Statistical Abstract*[12] for average annual earnings; Tewksbury[11] for experience rating; ICF Incorporated[10] for benefits offered.

§ Pension offset is calculated based on the following assumptions: (i) pensions replace on average 21% of income;[46] (ii) individuals collect pensions for 14.5 years after retirement at age 65;[46] (iii) in 1983, among firms offering pensions, 35% of small firms and 79% of large firms offered defined benefit pension plans[47] (Defined benefit plans, which are a declining proportion of all benefit plans, are primarily funded by employer contributions and do not usually pay benefits to a decedent's estate. On average, defined benefit pensions are fully vested after 10 years);[47] (iv) 50% of employees at small firms and 80% of employees at large firms remain at the firm for 10 years; (v) the probability that a 35-year-old male will survive to collect his pension at age 65 is 77%.[46] The source of data on the percentage of firms offering this benefit is ICF Incorporated.[10]

‖ The discount rate is calculated by assuming equal probabilities of becoming ill during each year of job tenure and a real interest rate of 5%. The calculations are relatively insensitive to variations in the real interest rate.

** Average hiring and training costs are $1750.[48] The procedure for calculating the added cost of hiring and training an individual who subsequently develops AIDS is described in Glied[15] based on job tenure data from Brown, Hamilton, and Medoff.[49]

†† The probability of developing AIDS during an individual's expected tenure at the firm is calculated on the basis of the following: (i) average job tenure is 5 years at small firms and 8 years at large firms[49] and (ii) the individual is assumed to have become infected on the day he begins work. The source of data on the probability of developing AIDS is Rutherford.[13]

three main items to note with respect to Table 1. First, the benefits of not employing qualified applicants who test positive for HIV vary substantially among firms in different cities and different employment size categories. Because the lifetime medical care costs of treating AIDS patients are substantially lower in some cities than in others, and because health care costs are a sizable fraction of total avoided costs, firms located in cities with high health care costs for AIDS patients (for example, New York City)[5] will perceive, other things equal, the benefits of testing to be much greater than will firms located in low cost cities (for example, San Francisco).[5] Large firms are also likely to face higher costs of employing an HIV-positive individual than are small firms, because large firms are more likely to offer health-contingent fringe benefits, and to pay insurance premiums for those benefits that are more closely linked to the firms' claims experience.[10-11]

Second, the expected present value of the avoided costs (reported in the last row of Table 1) is less than the lifetime medical care cost of treating an individual of AIDS. This result occurs because most of the costs associated with hiring an individual who develops AIDS are incurred in the future (and therefore must be discounted to reflect their burden at the time employment decisions are made), and because not all HIV-infected individuals will develop AIDS during their expected tenure at a firm.

Third, the costs avoided (in present value terms) by hiring an HIV-negative individual instead of an HIV-positive individual range from small, but nontrivial sums, to quite sizable amounts (for example, between 11 and 160 percent of median annual earnings received by a male worker in the United States in 1987).[12] These figures are much higher than they would be for most other illnesses primarily because (i) the lifetime medical care costs of treating AIDS patients are considerable, both absolutely and relative to other serious diseases and disabilities;[5] (ii) the probability that a seropositive individual develops AIDS during his expected employment tenure is relatively high (15 to 35 percent);[13] and (iii) AIDS tends to strike individuals during their prime working years when the risk of disability or death due to other causes is low, and long before the age at which they would become eligible to receive pension benefits from defined benefit plans.[14] For example, the present value of the costs avoided by rejecting a job application from a 55-year-old smoker (and instead hiring a 55-year-old nonsmoker who is otherwise identical to the smoker) have been estimated to be between $600 and $3500.[15] This differential is much smaller than that for an HIV-positive individual employed in a comparable firm because the smoker's expected medical care costs are lower, because a 55-year-old is more likely to succumb to nonsmoking-related diseases, and because a smoker who dies will forego a pension that he or she was closer to receiving.

We thus conclude that employers have well-defined, easily measurable, and non-trivial incentives to use HIV test results in making employment decisions, although there is considerable variation across employers in the strength of those incentives.

## THE COSTS OF HIV TESTING

The two main HIV tests currently in use in the United States are the enzyme-linked immunosorbert assay (ELISA) and the Western blot (WB) blood tests[7, 16] (Table 2). The former is relatively simple and inexpensive while the latter is somewhat more complex and costly to perform and more difficult to interpret. Although both tests are quite accurate, neither is entirely free from error. For example, both have a nonzero probability of misclassifying individuals who are not truly HIV-infected as well as of misclassifying individuals who are truly HIV-infected.

Table 2 shows two estimates for the overall price of an HIV test.[17] The low estimate is the Department of Defense's negotiated contract price for an ELISA/WB package.[7, 18] The high estimates are the average prices for HIV tests paid by individuals tested under Illinois' mandatory premarital testing law during 1988.[19] These estimates differ primarily because the quoted price for the Department of Defense does not account for the costs of taking a blood sample and of post-test counseling and because the Department of Defense effectively receives a quantity discount on HIV test kits (for example, 1.2 million individuals were tested for HIV infection by the Department of Defense between October 1985 and July 1987).[18] Similarly, the small difference between the price of a WB test kit and the overall price of a WB test reflects the fact that a WB test can be performed on the same blood sample as the initial ELISA test (that is, it is not necessary to incur the cost associated with drawing a new blood sample).

The estimates in Table 2 suggest that the cost of HIV testing is much lower for large firms that can negotiate quantity discounts and that routinely require blood tests among their employees than it is for other firms. Indeed, large firms are more than six times as likely to require medical exams among their employees as are small firms.[20]

**Table 2**  Selected Facts about HIV Tests

The ELISA is a simple test in which antibodies contained in blood that has been exposed to the HIV bind to HIV proteins in the test kit. The interpretation of results can be automated. The Western blot (WB) test is a complex test that identifies antibodies to the three major groups of proteins of the HIV. Test results must be interpreted by a skilled technician. An ELISA/WB package refers to a testing protocol in which individuals are initially tested using an ELISA test. Positive results are checked using a WB test, sometimes after a confirmatory ELISA test. All prices are in 1987 dollars.[7]

| Test characteristic | ELISA | WB | ELISA/WB package |
|---|---|---|---|
| Price of test materials* | $ 3.50 | $55 | |
| Price per test performed | | | |
|    Illinois Premarital† | $30 | $60 | $35 |
|    Department of Defense | | | $ 4.40 |
| False positive rate (%)‡ | | | |
|    Under ideal conditions | 1.0 | 0.5 | 0.005 |
|    In actual use | 1.7 | 4.7 | 0.08 |
| False negative rate (%)‡ | | | |
|    Under ideal conditions | 0.4 | 0.4 | 0.4 |
|    In actual use | 0.6 | 9.3 | 0.6 |

*Western blot price is for an FDA-approved test kit (DuPont Chemical, December 1989).

†ELISA and Western blot prices are averages from Illinois hospitals that offer the test. The test package price is from the State of Illinois testing program. These prices include the drawing of a blood sample.[19]

‡"In actual use" estimates are based on studies by the College of American Pathologists. The estimated false positive rate for the test package is based on the assumption that the test results are independent. Estimates of the false negative rate for the test package are based on an assumed population seroprevalence of less than 1%.[7] The Department of Defense follows a testing protocol in which a Western blot test is only performed after two positive ELISA tests. A positive Western blot is then checked by performing another Western blot test on a new blood sample. The Department of Defense finds a false positive rate of 0.0007%.[18]

Both the false positive and false negative rates associated with HIV tests are quite low for the practical purposes for which employers might use such tests. For example, suppose the true prevalence of HIV were 0.012% in a firm that employed 100,000 individuals. Suppose further that the firm decided to perform an ELISA test on all of its workers and a WB test on those workers who tested positive with ELISA. On the basis of these assumptions and the figures in Table 2, this testing protocol would yield seventeen seropositive individuals (that is, individuals who tested positive on both the ELISA and the WB tests), of whom twelve would be true positives and five would be false positives. There would be essentially no false negatives in this firm (that is, 0.07 individuals).[7]

If it were legal, and if a firm followed a policy of not hiring (or dismissing) individuals who tested positive for HIV on both the ELISA and WB tests, the cost to the firm of type I and type II test errors would be small. As illustrated by the preceding example, false negatives, each of which could be quite costly to a firm (based on the results of the preceding section), almost never occur. On the other hand, false positives, whose occurrence is also rather infrequent in absolute terms (though far less so in relative terms in a low prevalence population), may impose only a minimal cost on employers who are not negligent in the administration of HIV tests and who can readily hire other workers.

Estimates of the cost an employer would expect to incur to identify an individual who is truly HIV positive are summarized in Table 3. The estimates are constructed from the two measures of the cost of HIV testing described in Table 2: (i) the Department of Defense estimate of $4.40 for an ELISA/WB package (which is a lower bound for larger firms that normally require blood examinations as a condition of employment); and (ii) the Illinois premarital testing estimates for the ELISA and WB tests (which represent upper bounds for firms that do not normally require blood tests among their employees). The estimates are also constructed under varying assumptions about the true prevalence of HIV infection among the group of individuals from which a firm's workforce is drawn. These estimates of HIV prevalence range from a low of 0.01% (which represents the percentage of blood donors to the Red Cross in 1988 who were HIV-infected) to a high of 0.86% (which represents the Centers for Disease Control's 1989 upper bound estimate of the percentage of the adult U.S. population that has tested positive for HIV).[14]

The figures in Table 3 make it clear that the cost a firm would expect to incur to identify a seropositive individual depends importantly upon whether the firm normally requires blood examinations and receives quantity discounts on HIV test kits. The cost of HIV testing is roughly seven times lower for such firms than for small firms that do not normally require blood tests. The figures in Table 3 also indicate that the cost of HIV testing varies even more sharply across the range of prevalence estimates. To illustrate, for a firm that does not normally require its employees to undergo blood tests, it will cost an average of $3,700 to identify a single seropositive employee if the relevant rate of HIV prevalence is 0.86%; but if the prevalence rate facing that firm is 0.01%, the cost rises by a factor of 80 to $310,300, primarily because the firm has to test many more employees to identify someone who is truly seropositive.

Although the expected costs of identifying one truly HIV-positive individual range from $500 to $310,300, very few firms are likely to face testing costs at the

**Table 3** Costs of Identifying One Truly HIV-positive Individual under Alternative Assumptions about the Prevalence of HIV and the Cost of HIV Testing

These figures are based on "in actual use" (Table 2) estimates of the false positive and false negative rates associated with the different HIV tests. The figures change little if they are based on the "under ideal conditions" estimate. All figures are 1987 dollars.

| Price of test | Cost for various prevalence estimates: | | | |
|---|---|---|---|---|
| | U.S. upper limit* (0.86%) | U.S. lower limit[†] (0.29%) | U.S. military[‡] (0.14%) | Blood donors[§] (0.01%) |
| $4.40 package | $ 500 | $ 1,500 | $ 3,200 | $ 44,000 |
| $30 ELISA, $60 WB (if necessary) | $3,700 | $10,800 | $22,400 | $310,300 |

*Assumes that 1.5 million Americans are truly HIV-positive in an adult population of 174 million people. This prevalence estimate is roughly the upper limit estimate by the Centers for Disease Control in 1989.[14] The numbers in parentheses represent the percentage of the population infected.
† Assumes that 500,000 Americans are truly HIV positive. See Hay et al.[50]  ‡Estimate based on Department of Defense testing of new recruits.[14]
§ Estimate based on testing donors of blood to the Red Cross in 1988.[14]

lower end of this range. About two-thirds of firms do not require any of their employees to undergo blood tests.[20] In addition, the two highest prevalence rates in Table 3 are likely to be well above those faced by most employers because those rates are calculated for a population that includes (i) a substantial number of "heavy drug abusers" (that is, about 225,000, or 15 to 23% of all those estimated to be HIV infected)[21] who are relatively unlikely to be active participants in the formal labor market and (ii) a non-negligible number of individuals who are too young, too old, or too sick (because they have AIDS) to participate actively in the labor market. In addition, most firms presumably recruit workers from a population with a lower rate of HIV prevalence than that found in the U.S. military. Indeed, the military draws a disproportionately large number of recruits from demographic groups among whom the prevalence of HIV infection is known to be relatively high: young males, blacks, and Hispanics.[14]

In addition to the direct costs of HIV tests noted above, employers may also bear certain indirect costs associated with testing. These costs can arise if the practice of testing for HIV makes it more difficult for an employer to recruit or retain employees. This situation might occur if actual or prospective employees have strong preferences against testing. For example, employees may find the blood test procedure unpleasant, or may fear that a positive test result (which may be a false positive) will lead to discrimination, or to a loss of eligibility for nongroup health and life insurance benefits.[22] In addition, employees may prefer not to know whether they are infected.[23] Under these circumstances, firms that hire workers in competitive labor markets and that require HIV tests will have to offer greater compensation to actual or prospective workers than will otherwise identical firms who do not require HIV tests. The cost estimates reported in Table 3 should thus be viewed as lower bound estimates of the actual cost that employers will incur to identify truly HIV-positive individuals, because our calculations do not account for (i) these indirect costs to employers of HIV testing and (ii) other costs related to maintaining the confidentiality of test results, such as providing counseling for individuals.

## COMPARING THE BENEFITS AND COSTS OF HIV TESTING

It is natural for firms to compare the cost of identifying an individual who is seropositive (the figures in Table 3) with the benefit of having that information (the costs it can expect to avoid by not hiring or by dismissing that individual [see Table 1]). This comparison suggests that HIV testing is not cost-beneficial for most small firms. The expected benefit of $2,300 to $4,400 is far below the expected cost of identifying a seropositive individual in a low-prevalence working population: $22,400 to $310,300.[20] Similarly, HIV testing is not likely to be cost-beneficial for most large firms, although it may be cost-beneficial for some large firms that recruit workers from populations with a relatively high HIV prevalence. For example, the costs large firms can expect to avoid by identifying a seropositive individual ($20,600, $31,800) exceed the costs they will incur to identify such an individual if the true prevalence of HIV infection is 0.14% and the firm faces the lower cost of HIV testing. But, the expected benefits of HIV testing (the cost savings) fall far short of the expected cost of HIV testing if the true prevalence is closer to 0.01%, a more reasonable assumption for most large firms, as argued above.[24]

Thus, most profit-maximizing employers are not likely to find HIV testing to be a cost-beneficial personnel policy, even if they are permitted to use test results in making employment decisions. This conclusion is strengthened insofar as the cost calculations upon which this analysis is based underestimate the true cost of HIV testing (for reasons noted in the preceding section). This conclusion is further strengthened by the fact that our analysis does not account for the possibility that an individual who tests negative for HIV at the time he is hired will become infected with the virus during his tenure with an employer. If this situation were common, it might be appropriate to consider a protocol of testing employees periodically. However, retesting individuals who were previously found to be seronegative is especially unlikely to be cost-beneficial because the prevalence of HIV infection in such a population is likely to be very low (lower than the lowest prevalence estimates in Table 3). In the context of a single test protocol, the possibility that a previously unidentified individual will become infected leads to a reduction in the benefits of testing.

## THE PUBLIC INTEREST IN HIV TESTING

In a decentralized market economy, profit-maximizing employers will decide whether to require HIV tests as a condition of employment primarily on the basis of the benefit-cost calculations described above (absent any legal restrictions on HIV tests). The expected benefits of HIV testing will fall short of the costs for most firms, though some large firms that recruit workers from high HIV prevalence populations may find HIV testing to be cost-beneficial.

Society can benefit from HIV testing in employment settings if HIV testing reduces the total cost of the epidemic or leads to a distribution of the cost that is more desirable from society's standpoint. According to economic theory, the testing outcomes that emerge from the voluntary interactions of firms and workers will reduce the total costs of the epidemic if two conditions hold: (i) the social and private costs of HIV testing are equal and (ii) the expected social and private benefits of HIV testing are equal. In such a case, government policies that either promote or discourage HIV testing in employment settings can only be socially beneficial if they sufficiently improve the distribution of these (now larger) costs.

The first of the above two conditions does not appear to be violated. The social cost of HIV testing includes the cost of conducting and analyzing an HIV test and the amount that a representative individual would be willing to pay to avoid undergoing an inherently unpleasant test. Because there is no reason to think that the market for HIV tests is noncompetitive, or that the labor market will not fully account for workers' attitudes toward being tested, the social and private costs of HIV testing are likely to correspond closely.

By contrast, there is no reason to believe that the social and private benefits of HIV testing will be equal. The private benefits of testing are enjoyed by firms to the extent that testing allows them to shift the cost of the epidemic away from themselves (and onto other economic agents). While cost-shifting would not be expected to influence the overall magnitude of the epidemic, it may lead to a more desirable distribution of society's economic resources. These distributional benefits, however, do not enter the decision-making process of most firms. Furthermore, it is uncertain whether employment testing improves the distribution of economic resources, largely because so little is known about the final incidence of the costs of the epidemic (that is, the extent to which these costs will ultimately be borne by HIV-infected individuals and their families, other users of the health care system, employees and shareholders of firms that do not test for HIV, and taxpayers).[5]

There are several other potentially large sources of social benefits associated with HIV testing that are distinct from the private benefits described earlier and the cost-shifting benefits described immediately above. These benefits, which are considerably more difficult to estimate than the private benefits defined above, can arise because informing individuals of their HIV status has the potential to (i) prolong the lives of those already infected with HIV (through the prophylactic use of certain drug therapies); (ii) resolve many individuals' uncertainty about their health status; and (iii) control the future spread of the disease (through the impact of HIV test results on behavior).[25]

First, the extent to which the lives of HIV-infected individuals can be prolonged by the prophylactic use of drug therapies (such as AZT and aerosolized pentamidine) is still largely unknown. In addition, the impact of these drug therapies on the direct medical costs of HIV-infected individuals is also uncertain and will depend on the changing cost of these drug therapies, the costs associated with any side effects due to the use of the drugs, and the extent to which medical costs are incurred further in the future.[6] To the extent that these prophylactic drug therapies prolong or enhance the quality of life—for which there is some evidence—the indirect cost associated with an HIV infection, that is, the value of the years of life lost, will unambiguously fall, though by a magnitude that would be difficult to estimate.[26, 27]

Second, in most models of economic behavior, individuals would pay to resolve uncertainty. Based on these models, one might conclude that HIV test results confer benefits upon individuals (and therefore upon society) because they reduce individual uncertainty. This conclusion might be qualified, however, by the results of recent studies that suggest that some individuals may prefer to delay the resolution of certain sources of uncertainty.[23] These benefits (or negative benefits) are not readily measurable.

Third, changes in individual behavior related to HIV transmission can have a profound impact on the future magnitude of the epidemic. If each seropositive individual infects other individuals, who in turn infect others, then even a small change in transmission rates can have a large cumulative effect on the total number of individuals who ultimately contract the disease and on the cost of the epidemic. The effect of changes in HIV transmission rates on the economic impact of the epidemic will depend on the cost of each AIDS case, the transmission rates among individuals, and the magnitude of changes in those rates.

Suppose, for example, that each seropositive individual in some population infects, on average, 0.8 other individuals per year,[28] and that the present value of direct and indirect costs to society of an individual newly infected with HIV is $600,000.[5] If just one seropositive person reduced the number of individuals he infects per year by 10 percent, to 0.72 persons per year, the present value of the cost savings over an 11-year period (that is, the expectation of life of a newly infected individual)[29] would amount to nearly $25 million.

Under the above assumptions, testing would appear to be unambiguously socially beneficial because the magnitude of social benefits considerably exceeds the private (and social)cost of HIV testing in all of the populations examined in Table 3. However, the social benefits of testing would be smaller if the annual rate of new infections per seropositive individual were lower than 0.8; they would also be lower if the relative reduction in risk behavior were less than 10 percent (which is consistent with several studies that report very little behavioral response to HIV test results).[30-32] For example, if each seropositive individual infected only 0.08 other individuals per year, and if the reduction in the transmission rate of the seropositive individual who was informed of his seropositivity were only 3 percent, then the economic benefits of testing over 11 years would be less than $18,300, or less than the cost of testing in the low-prevalence populations in Table 3. In fact, in some studies, individuals who were informed of their HIV status actually increased their high-risk behavior.[33, 34] In such cases, this component of the social benefits of testing is negative.

The ability to generalize from the above simulations is limited because all of the parameters used are estimates based on self-selected samples of individuals who voluntarily underwent confidential or anonymous HIV tests in nonemployment settings. In addition, the social costs and benefits of HIV testing will be affected by the false positive and false negative rates of the HIV tests. For example, false positive results can diminish the social benefits of testing by creating mental stress and by leading to unnecessary changes in behavior, including the inappropriate use of prophylactic drug therapies. False negative results can also diminish the social benefits of testing by leading individuals to delay changes in their behavior or in their use of prophylactic drug therapies. These considerations magnify our already considerable uncertainty about the net social benefits of HIV testing.

## THE LEGAL ENVIRONMENT

The divergence of the private and social benefits of HIV testing in employment contexts suggests that the testing policies of unregulated employers are not likely to yield socially optimal economic outcomes. Unfortunately, existing information does not permit one to determine whether these policies result in too much or too little testing from a social point of view. Thus, there is little basis for arguing that policies that promote or discourage HIV testing are desirable on grounds that they will reduce the total cost of the epidemic. Yet, policymakers have been and continue to be active in crafting regulations in this area. Current state legislation governing HIV testing is summarized in Table 4 along with annual rates of AIDS incidence in each state (per 100,000 population) for the period November 1988 to October 1989.[35] States are divided into those in which HIV testing is currently prohibited in virtually all employment contexts and those in which HIV testing is not explicitly prohibited; the latter is subdivided into states in which employers are prohibited from discriminating against employees on the basis of their HIV status and those in which such discrimination is not prohibited.

**Table 4**  State Laws Pertaining to HIV Testing in Employment Settings and AIDS Annual Incidence Rates Per 100,000 Population from November 1988 to October 1989[35]

| Testing prohibited* | Testing permitted | |
| --- | --- | --- |
| | **Cannot discriminate**[†] | **Can Discriminate**[‡] |
| District of Columbia 81 | New York 36 | Georgia 18 |
| Florida 27 | New Jersey 29 | Texas 15 |
| California 22 | Maryland 15 | Hawaii 15 |
| Massachusetts 13 | Nevada 15 | Louisiana 11 |
| Washington 10 | Connecticut 13 | Virginia 7 |
| Rhode Island 8 | Delaware 12 | Mississippi 6 |
| Utah 5 | Colorado 11 | North Carolina 6 |
| Wisconsin 3 | Illinois 10 | Alabama 6 |
| Vermont 3 | South Carolina 9 | Tennessee 5 |
| Iowa 2 | Pennsylvania 9 | Ohio 5 |
| | Oregon 9 | Kansas 4 |
| | Arizona 8 | New Hampshire 4 |
| | Missouri 8 | Arkansas 3 |
| | Michigan 6 | Kentucky 3 |
| | New Mexico 6 | Nebraska 3 |
| | Oklahoma 5 | Wyoming 3 |
| | Indiana 5 | North Dakota 1 |
| | Maine 5 | South Dakota 1 |
| | Minnesota 4 | |
| | Alaska 3 | |
| | West Virginia 3 | |
| | Idaho 2 | |
| | Montana 2 | |

*Sources for state laws on testing are Leonard[51] and Bowleg and Bridgham.[52] These laws state, in general, that an employer may not require an HIV test as a "condition of employment."
†State regulation of discrimination on the basis of HIV status is based on the judicial review of existing statutes that prohibit discrimination against individuals perceived to be handicapped [see National Gay Rights Advocates].[36]
‡This category includes states without prohibitions against handicap discrimination in employment, or in which statutes that prohibit discrimination only apply to individuals who have an actual handicap, or that have anti-discrimination statutes that exclude communicable diseases.

Although HIV testing as a condition of employment is only specifically illegal in ten states, it is effectively illegal for most firms in the twenty-four other states in which discrimination on the basis of an individual's HIV status is prohibited. Firms governed by federal law (for example, firms that hold federal contracts or that receive federal funds) also fall into this category.[36] Even in states in which testing is permitted, a policy of testing only those individuals who have characteristics that are correlated with being seropositive (for example, gender, race, ethnicity, age, marital status, sexual orientation, and so on) may violate broader antidiscrimination statutes.[37]

Legal restrictions on HIV testing or on the use of HIV test results in making personnel decisions thus reinforce the economic incentives against testing in most jurisdictions (that is, in thirty-three states and the District of Columbia) and in firms that must comply with federal laws. It is interesting to note that the incidence of AIDS in these jurisdictions (that is, the rate per 100,000 population at which new AIDS cases were diagnosed from November 1988 to October 1989) is nearly twice as high as in the seventeen states in which HIV testing and discrimination based on HIV test results are permitted. Coupled with the economic incentives against testing in low-prevalence settings, these legal prohibitions against testing in most high-prevalence settings result in there being a very limited level of testing in the U.S. economy. Indeed, even in jurisdictions where HIV testing is not legally prohibited, fewer than one in sixteen firms require HIV tests as a condition of employment.[38]

In July 1990, President Bush signed the Americans with Disabilities Act (Public Law 104–327), the employment provision of which will take effect in July 1992. Those provisions prohibit virtually all U.S. employers of twenty-five or more employees from discriminating in their employment practices on the basis of whether an individual has an actual disability or is perceived to have a disability (starting in July 1994, the act will cover firms employing fifteen or more employees). The act also contains an explicit prohibition on pre-employment medical screening. Assuming that employers comply with this act (which can reasonably be expected in the case of HIV testing, based on the foregoing analysis), HIV and other forms of medical testing in employment settings will effectively be eliminated among medium and large employers.[39] Because the preceding analysis suggests that small employers are least likely to find HIV testing cost-beneficial, their exemption from the provisions of the act should be relatively inconsequential.[40]

Given the absence of evidence to justify social policies regulating HIV testing in employment contexts on grounds that it would reduce the total (present and future) cost of the epidemic, equity considerations have presumably governed the design of the state and federal laws promulgated in this area. Indeed, this observation is consistent with the form and substance of the Americans with Disabilities Act, which treats individuals with potential health risks similarly to other categories of individuals who are protected from the outcomes generated by markets (for example, individuals with handicaps, older workers, women, and minorities). In addition, the passage of laws that prevent employers from testing for HIV (or from using test results as a basis for making employment decisions) may affect the distribution of economic resources by deflecting some of the costs of the epidemic away from public hospitals and taxpayers and concentrating them on workers and firms' shareholders.[41]

## CONCLUSION

Employers who offer the most generous fringe benefit packages and who recruit workers from populations that have a high prevalence of HIV infection are the ones most likely to find that the benefits of HIV testing exceed the costs. Changes in the benefits and costs of HIV testing (for example, in the price of test kits or in the lifetime cost of treating HIV infection) will change the number of employers in this category. These employers will have incentives to circumvent the spirit of the legislative prohibitions on testing, such as those that will take effect under the Americans with Disabilities Act. For example, they may screen prospective employees on the basis of characteristics that they believe are correlated with the outcomes of HIV tests. They may also limit the eligibility or generosity of their health-contingent benefits. (They are especially likely to do this if individuals who either suspect or know that they are HIV-positive elect, on the basis of that information, to work for employers who offer generous benefit packages.)[42] The latter practice will leave many employees who test negative in those firms with less than optimal levels of health-contingent benefits—a real social cost of achieving the distributional objectives that presumably led to the legal prohibitions on testing.

The net social benefits of testing may also change in the future (though not necessarily in the same direction or to the same extent as the net benefits to employers). If they increase, society could potentially benefit from additional testing. In order to realize these potential benefits, society may adopt policies that promote or permit HIV testing. However, to the extent that society continues to be concerned over the distributional implications of HIV testing, it may limit the contexts in which test results can be used (for example, by only promoting confidential HIV testing). Alternatively, society may permit HIV testing in a broad set of contexts and use other policy instruments (such as national health insurance or expanded welfare eligibility for seropositive individuals) to further its distributional objectives.

It may seem callous, or irrelevant, to think of HIV testing as an economic issue. However, a failure to recognize the likely response of the labor market to the epidemic and to HIV testing will not make that response disappear. Compassionate societies may wish to divert some of the costs of the AIDS epidemic away from those who are already HIV-infected. However, social policies are more likely to succeed in reducing the magnitude of those costs and distributing them more broadly if they explicitly account for the response of rational individuals and firms to the incentives created by the epidemic.

# REFERENCES AND NOTES

1. W. F. Banta and F. Tennant. *Complete Handbook for Combating Substance Abuse in the Workplace,* Lexington, Massachusetts: Lexington Books (1989).

2. R. DeCresce, A. Mazure, M. Lifshitz, and J. Tilson. *Drug Testing in the Workplace,* Chicago: American Society of Clinical Pathologists Press (1989).

3. L. J. Boden. *Journal of Occupational Medicine 28* (1986): 751.

4. The term "health-contingent benefits" refers to such benefits as health, life, and disability insurance, whose cost to an employer and value to an employee depend upon the employee's current and future health. Such fringe benefits have expanded dramatically in magnitude and scope in the post-World War II era (J. Long and F. Scott, *Review of Economics and Statistics 64* [May 1982]: 211).

5. D. E. Bloom and G. Carliner. *Science 239* (1988): 604.

6. D. E. Gloom and S. Glied. *Health Policy 11* (April 1989): 187.

7. L. Miike. Testimony Before the House Committee on Small Business, 19 October 1987, Committee Serial No. 100-32, Washington, D.C.: Government Printing Office (1988).

8. In some voluntary testing programs, over 70 percent of individuals who tested positive had correctly anticipated their test results (see, for example, D. G. Ostrow et al., *AIDS Education and Prevention 1,* [spring 1989]: 1; L. J. Fehrs et al., *Lancet ii* [1988]: 379).

9. "Business Response to AIDS." *Fortune.* New York: Time Inc. (1988).

10. ICF Incorporated. "Health Care Coverage and Costs in Small and Large Businesses." Washington, D.C.: Final Report for the Office of Advocacy, Small Business Administration (April 1987).

11. R. L. Tewksbury, in *The Handbook of Employee Benefits: Design, Funding and Administration,* J. Rosenbloom, ed., Homewood, Illinois: Dow Jones-Irwin (1984), 678–703.

12. *Statistical Abstract of the United States.* Washington, D.C.: Government Printing Office (1990).

13. W. Rutherford, testimony presented to the Presidential Commission on the Human Immunodeficiency Virus Epidemic, 10 December 1987.

14. Centers for Disease Control, *Morbidity and Mortality Weekly Report 38 S-4* (12 May 1989).

15. S. Glied, thesis, Harvard University (1990).

16. Urine and saliva tests for HIV infection are currently under development. Although these tests are promising, information about their cost, and their sensitivity and specificity in actual use is rather limited (Briefings, *Science 249* [1990]: 20).

17. These prices include the cost of test kits (which contain all of the necessary materials and reagents to perform the particular test) and the costs associated with obtaining and processing a blood sample, and any record-keeping, communication, and follow-up counseling that may be provided.

18. D. Burke et al., *New England Journal of Medicine 319* (1988): 961.

19. B. J. Turnock and C. J. Kelly, *Journal of the American Medical Association 261* (1989): 23.

20. J. M. Ratcliffe et al., *Journal of Occupational Medicine 28* (1986): 907.

21. Centers for Disease Control. *Morbidity and Mortality Weekly Report 36 S-6* (December 1987).

22. J. Eden. *AIDS and Health Insurance.* Washington D.C.: Office of Technology Assessment (February 1988).

23. For example, in one study, 59 percent of individuals who were voluntarily tested for HIV never inquired about their test results (H. F. Hull et al., *Journal of the American Medical Association 260* [1988]: 935).

24. In order to make it cost-beneficial for small firms in low-cost cities to test in the lowest prevalence populations, a test with the sensitivity and specificity of the ELISA/WB combination test would have to cost 25 cents, less than 1 percent of the current cost.

25. These effects will be muted (or perhaps nonexistent) if individuals correctly anticipate their HIV status.[8]

26. P. A. Volberding et al. *New England Journal of Medicine 322* (1990): 941.

27. J. A. Golden, D. Chernoff, H. Hollander, D. Feigal, J. Conte. *Lancet i,* (1989): 654 .

28. M. H. Gail, D. Preston, S. Piantadosi. *Statistics in Medicine 8* (1989): 59.

29. G. F. Lemp et al. *Journal of the American Medical Association 263* (1990): 1499.

30. J. McCusker et al. *American Journal of Public Health 78* (1988): 462.

31. R. O. Valdiserri et al. *Ibid.,* 801.

32. J. A. R. van den Hock, H. J. A. van Haastrecht, R. A. Coutinho. *Ibid. 79* (1989): 1355.

33. G. van Griensven et al. *American Journal of Epidemiology 129* (1989): 596.

34. W. Cates, Jr., and H. Handsfield. *American Journal of Public Health 78* (1988): 1533.

35. Centers for Disease Control. *HIV/AIDS Surveillance* (November 1990).

36. National Gay Rights Advocates, *Protection Against AIDS-Related Discrimination Under State Handicap Laws: A Fifty State Analysis.* San Francisco: National Gay Rights Advocates (1989).

37. For example, Title VII of the Civil Rights Act of 1964 prohibits employment practices that would discriminate on the basis of race or gender.

38. Estimate based on data contained in *Fortune* (Note 9: 72–76) and the Statistical Abstract of the United States.[12]

39. There are some exceptions to this act, among them a provision permitting employment decisions to be made on the basis of disabilities that crucially relate to the performance of work (for example, poor eyesight for a potential pilot).

40. Employees in firms with fewer than 25 employees account for about 25 percent of the U.S. labor force, whereas employees in firms with fewer than 15 employees account for slightly less than 18 percent of the U.S. labor force (S. Dixon, personal communication).

41. Our analysis does not rule out the possibility that public policymakers may promote social equity and economic efficiency through policies that restrict testing in employment contexts and encourage testing in nonemployment contexts.

42. Firms may also respond to the costs of the HIV epidemic by limiting their health-contingent benefits, although they are less likely to do so if HIV testing is permitted.

43. Bureau of Labor Statistics. *Bureau of Labor Statistics Bulletin 2262* (July 1986).

44. National Center for Health Statistics. *Health, United States, 1987.* Washington, D.C.: Government Printing Office (1988).

45. A. A. Scitovsky and D. P. Rice. *Public Health Report 102* (1987): 5.

46. Current Population Reports. *Household Economic Studies, series P-70* (no. 12) (1987).

47. L. J. Kotlikoff and D. E. Smith. *Pensions in the American Economy,* Chicago: University of Chicago Press (1983).

48. D. O. Parsons, in *Handbook of Labor Economics,* O. Ashenfelter and R. Layard, eds. Amsterdam: North-Holland (1986), vol. 2, 789–848.

49. C. Brown, J. T. Hamilton, and J. Medoff. *Employers Large and Small,* Cambridge: Harvard University Press (1990).

50. J. W. Hay et al. *Journal of AIDS 1* (1988): 466.

51. A. S. Leonard, in *AIDS and the Law: A Guide for the Public,* H. L. Dalton, S. Burris, the Yale AIDS Law Project, eds., New Haven: Yale University Press (1987), 109–125.

52. I. Bowleg and B. Bridgham. "A Summary of AIDS Laws from the 1988 Legislative Sessions." Washington, D.C.: George Washington University Intergovernmental Health Policy Project (April 1989).
53. Financial support was provided by NIH grant HD25914-01. L. Dynan provided helpful research assistance. Helpful comments were received from two anonymous referees.

.......................................................................................
**DISTRIBUTION OF INCOME**
Topic of Interest: *Changing Definitions of
Income at the Census Bureau*

.............................
| S E L E C T I O N     1 4 |

Charles T. Nelson and John F. Coder

# Measuring the Effects of Benefits and Taxes on Income and Poverty

Poverty and welfare, distribution of income, taxes on income—these and related issues engender some of today's most critical and controversial public policy debates. The titles of numerous articles and books ask: What is poverty? Who are the nation's truly poor? Is welfare really the problem? Inequality in America: Where do we stand? How should we measure distribution? How rich is too rich? Can America afford to grow old? Who bears the lifetime tax burden? Taxes and transfers: How much economic loss? Family tax burdens: How do the states compare? Is tax reform in the public interest? (See Suggested Further Readings.) But in order to address any of these questions, "income" must be defined—and differences in "income" exclusions, inclusions, and dollar-valuations can change the answers dramatically.

    Charles Nelson and John Coder report on over a decade's worth of efforts to construct more accurate definitions of household income at the U.S. Bureau of the Census. Surprisingly, the United States has no official statistical definition of income. And as part of the U.S. Department of Commerce, the annual income surveys issued by the Census Bureau provide data for all branches of government—data which are used to formulate and propose changes in legislation affecting almost every aspect of our lives (e.g., tax laws, social security rules, welfare programs). As this reading demonstrates, the move from theoretical definitions of income to practical, working measures of income is not straightforward. While Nelson and Coder report that major advances have been made, the authors conclude by describing the Census Bureau's continuing

.......................................................................................................
Nelson, Charles T. and John F. Coder. "Measuring the Effects of Benefits and Taxes on Income and Poverty." *Journal of Economic and Social Measurement 19* (Spring 1993): 41–58. This selection is an abridged version of the original article.

**Charles T. Nelson** is Assistant Division Chief for Economic Characteristics and **John F. Coder** is Economic Statistician at the Housing and Household Economic Statistics Division, U.S. Bureau of the Census, U.S. Department of Commerce.

research plans to improve the accuracy and relevance of income measurement for policymakers, analysts, and voters.

### Questions to Guide the Reading

1. Previous to 1980, the Census Bureau used a pretax, posttransfer definition of personal income. What are the three major weaknesses of this definition?
2. Even after the deficiencies had been recognized, the Census Bureau was not quick to reform the pre-1980 definition of income. Why? Are these reasons still relevant today? Explain.
3. What does the lack of an official definition of income (and the existence of alternative definitions) imply about the type of household income data available to researchers?
4. Why did "noncash valuation" become an important issue? How do the three alternative valuation methods differ—in general, and specifically, in their treatment of medical benefits?
5. What major changes occurred as a result of the Bureau's 1988 research project? How have these changes affected the measurement of employer-provided benefits? Benefits of home-ownership? Food benefits?
6. Why were the three original noncash valuation methods considered inadequate in their treatment of medical benefits? What new valuation method was adopted for this purpose, and how does it work?

## 1. INTRODUCTION

Measures of economic well-being, income inequality, and the extent of poverty the United States have, for the most part, been based on data collected in household surveys. One such survey, that is generally considered to be the official source of estimates of household income and poverty, is the March Current Population Survey (CPS). It has provided income statistics annually since 1947 and has been the official source of data used to estimate the number of persons living below the poverty level since these estimates were first published in 1968.

During the period from 1947 through 1979, the collection of income data in the March CPS was aimed directly at a definition based on calendar-year, pretax, posttransfer cash income. Despite its obvious shortcomings and the fact that the tax and transfer system in the U.S. was changing dramatically over this period, there was little movement to collect additional data needed to estimate income based on alternative definitions until the late 1970s.

The pretax, posttransfer cash income definition has three major weak points. It failed to account for the effects of major new government noncash programmes providing medical, housing, and food benefits that emerged during the 1960s and grew rapidly during the decade of the 1970s. It failed to reflect the effect of personal income taxes on the distribution and redistribution of household income. Finally, it failed to include private noncash benefits, mainly in the form of employer-provided health insurance and other fringe benefits.

Even though it was quite evident that the pretax, posttransfer cash income concept was becoming more and more obsolete, the data collection system was slow to adjust for a number of practical reasons. First, a change in the definition of income would end the long time series that had been constructed. Second, any change in the questionnaire to accommodate queries about new sources of income would require major revisions to data collection and computer processing systems. Third, the added respondent burden resulting from additional questions might reduce levels of cooperation in the CPS which relies on voluntary cooperation. Fourth, physical size of the questionnaire was limited since all coded entries are optically read by machines with limits on the number of pages.

Changes to the data collection were introduced, however, in the March 1980 CPS. These changes were made mainly in reaction to the growth of the government noncash benefit programmes whose benefits, while largely targeted to the poor, were ignored in the definition of income used to measure poverty. Included in the expanded questionnaire were questions covering the Medicare and Medicaid programs, residence in subsidized housing, food benefits, and energy assistance. Questions concerning employer-provided health insurance and pension plans were also added. Stemming from concerns about respondent burden, presumed difficulty in providing responses, and perceived sensitivity, no attempts were made to collect information about personal income or payroll taxes.

Even though the data collection procedures had been expanded to include information about some of these new sources of income there were difficult issues to be confronted. What are the viable alternative income definitions that should be generated from the existing set of survey data? Which of these definitions is best for the measure of the level of household income, the measure of income inequality, and the measure of poverty? And which methods should be used to assign values for noncash benefits?

The main purpose of this paper is to describe the evolution of a research programme at the Bureau of the Census to expand the definition of income from the original pretax, posttransfer concept. It begins with a general discussion of some of the issues surrounding the definition of household income and a brief look at the evolution of data collection and definitions prior to the decade of the 1980s. Second, it describes our attempts to assign values to noncash government transfers. Conceptual, methodological, and technical issues are examined. The third section describes development of systems for simulating income and payroll taxes using data collected in the survey and independent data from tax returns. . . . The final section summarizes the paper and looks to the future.

## 2. DEFINING INCOME

One basic issue which seems to receive less attention than it deserves is the definition of income. The manner in which it is defined can have profound effects on conclusions about the distribution of income and the measure of poverty. Ideally, the income definition should fit the specific topic under investigation, however, this as we know is the exception rather than the rule. The choice of a definition can be a complex process, one can touch both conceptual and empirical grounds. Often the choice is constrained by the existing survey questions, a situation over which researchers often have little control. And in almost all cases, survey questions have been or will also be constrained. Restrictions include cost of interviews, limits on perceived respondent burden, competing interests for a finite amount of questionnaire space and interviewing time, and the likelihood of obtaining sufficiently accurate responses. In this section of the paper we discuss these issues in general and as they relate directly to the March CPS and income statistics derived from this long-standing survey.

### 2.1. Lack of Consensus on Household Income Definition

There is no general consensus concerning the preferred definition of household income contained in Chapter VIII of the "Handbook of Household Surveys" published by the United Nations.[1] Principles enumerated in this document, which were developed by the International Labour Organization (ILO), are very general in nature. They are aimed mainly at the operational issues related to the survey and not at more conceptual issues related to the income measurement. The recommendations include use of a pretax, posttransfer definition that counts income from both cash and noncash sources. It calls for the exclusion of "lump-sum" and "one-time" receipts of income, income from the sale of real property, and withdrawals from personal savings, and income received in the form of loans from others. No specific definition of noncash income is given. The report recommends a one-year accounting period for measuring the income received.

A second widely accepted definition of income which is not directly related to household income and surveys, is provided by international guidelines regarding national income and product accounts (NIPA).[2] While a strong case can be made for this definition for the purpose of establishing a system of social accounts, thereby linking macro and micro statistical systems, the costs and data collection problems are enormous and, at this time, prohibit serious, comprehensive efforts in this direction. Work in the early 1970s toward integrating the March CPS and the personal income of the NIPA by Budd and Radner proved to be extremely difficult and their work was discontinued.[3] Nonsampling errors related to survey data and lack of detailed information from the survey for many income sources included in the NIPA were problems that proved too difficult to overcome with the resources available.

Even if data were available to define household income according to NIPA accounts some definitions of income could lie outside this broad domain. For example, NIPA excludes realized capital gains (or losses), an income source that is highly concentrated and thus potentially important to measure of income inequality. (We will ignore perhaps a more fundamental issue of unrealized capital gains.) The accounts also exclude, for the most part, home production, other than food and fuel produced and consumed on farms. While it may be at the fringes of what most economists would consider as income, a case could be made for specific purposes to include government expenditures, such as those for education (or at least some part) as income for those households with children in school.

## 2.2 Absence of an Official Income Definition for the United States

At present in the United States we have no official definitions of income for statistical purposes. The statistical agency responsible for collecting and disseminating household income and poverty statistics is the Bureau of Census, an organization within the Department of Commerce. The Bureau of the Census, in consultation with other government agencies, is responsible for the questionnaire content, maintenance of the sampling frame, selection of the sample households, collection and processing of the survey data, and release of statistics and other data products. These include a publicly-available microdata file containing detailed data for each sample household (with all personal identification removed). Those persons working with this microdata file are able to define income as they choose, either within the limits defined by the questionnaire or by expanding the definition through simulation, etc.

## 2.3 Data Collection and Income Definition: 1947–1979

As no official definitions of income have been established for statistical purposes, definitions now used are historical products beginning with the initial survey for 1947. For the period from 1947 to 1979, the March CPS contained questions pertaining solely to sources and amounts of pretax, posttransfer income using the calendar year as the accounting period. During this 32-year span the income definition was precisely the cash component of the definition that was later adopted by the ILO and outlined in the U.N. handbook.

While a number of significant revisions to the questionnaire occurred during the 1947–1979 period, the first changes designed to extend the definition of income into the noncash area did not take place until 1980. In that year the questionnaire was expanded to provide information on coverage under the Medicare and Medicaid programmes, benefits from subsidized public housing for the low-income population, food stamps, free and reduced-price school lunches, home energy assistance, employer-provided health insurance benefits, and employer-sponsored pension plans.

Collection of this information was, in all cases except food stamps and energy assistance, limited to the goal of identifying persons who were either enrolled in these programmes or who had actually received benefits. In the cases of food stamps and energy assistance, there were also questions concerning the value of the food stamps received during the year.

There were several reasons for limiting data collection to the identification of enrollment or receipt. First, as this was the first attempt to collect this information we were unsure about the results and, therefore, approached the effort cautiously. Second, with the exception of food stamps and energy assistance, we saw conceptual and practical issues that made it extremely difficult to design questions to collect meaningful responses for the values or amount of benefits received. Finally, we were limited by the usual concerns of respondent burden, questionnaire space, interviewing time, etc. This questionnaire revision established the questionnaire structure as it is in use until now with some minor changes. No major new initiatives have been undertaken since that time.

Collection of this new data covering major sources of noncash income was not undertaken to provide specific information for a predetermined, new definition of income or a set of income definitions. It was driven solely by the need for more information. Use of this new data for developing alternative income definitions came later.

## 2.4 Developments During the 1980s

During the 1980s there were three major events shaping the continued evolution of the income definition. The first was a research effort to investigate methods for assigning values to noncash benefits from the major government noncash programmes. The second was development of tax simulation models which used cash income data to estimate the income and payroll tax liabilities of households. The third, occurring later in the decade, was a combined effort to revise the noncash valuation techniques, to expand the valuation techniques to cover noncash benefits not considered in previous efforts, and to integrate values of noncash income and the pre- and post-tax and pre- and post-transfer incomes to produce a wide choice of income definitions.

## 3. ASSIGNING VALUES TO GOVERNMENT NONCASH BENEFITS

The major question leading up to the expansion of the data collection operation was how would changing the definition of income affect the measure of poverty (based strictly on the pretax, posttransfer cash income). In 1981, soon after the computer processing of the new data had been completed, the Census Bureau was formally directed by the U.S. Congress to report on the effect noncash government transfers have on estimates of the number of families and individuals below the poverty level.

By the time the official directive had been received the research on valuation techniques had already begun. There were two objectives of this research. The first was to assign dollar values to represent benefits received as a result of participation in those programmes. The second was to provide alternative estimates of the poverty population based on income definitions that include these values. Dr. Timothy Smeeding, the principal researcher, agreed to work on the project as part of the joint Census Bureau–American Statistical Association fellowship programme funded by the National Science Foundation.

The reference year for the study was 1979, the first year for which the noncash benefit data were collected. The data collection took place in March 1980 using the modified income supplement which asks retrospective questions about income and work experience during the previous calendar year.

Noncash benefit programmes had grown enormously during the 15-year period between 1965 and 1980. In 1965 noncash benefit programmes amounted to only about $2.2 billion but grew to $72.5 billion by 1980 when more than two-thirds of all means-tested government assistance was in the form of in-kind (used here interchangeably with the term "noncash") medical, food, housing, and energy assistance benefits. Programmes providing medical benefits were Medicare (for the aged and disabled) and Medicaid (for the low-income population) and these accounted for 75 percent of the 1980 noncash expenditure total. Food benefit programmes included one providing vouchers used to purchase food in the private market (the Food Stamp Programme) and another providing free and reduced-price lunches at public schools (the National School Lunch Programme). Housing benefits were provided mainly in the form of rent subsidies (through several major federal, state, and local public programmes). Finally, assistance in paying for energy costs, mainly involving winter household heating expenses, was provided by the Low-Income Home Energy Assistance Programme. Data collection for this last programme did not begin until 1982.

## 3.1. Valuation Techniques

Three alternative noncash valuation techniques were explored. The investigation of alternatives reflected both the general unsettled nature of economic research in this area and, as is the case with income definitions, that different valuation techniques may be needed depending on the purpose and the nature of the benefit. The three alternatives concepts were: (1) the market value, (2) the recipient (or cash equivalent) value, and (3) the poverty budget share value. The market value concept refers to the private market cost of the goods and services transferred to the recipient. The recipient value concept represents the "cash" amount for which the recipient would be willing to trade for the in-kind benefit given their current income level. The poverty budget share value is a concept linked directly to the official U.S. poverty line and represents the amount of money usually spent on that commodity by households with incomes at the poverty line. More details of these techniques and how they were applied to each type of benefits are described in the following sections.

**3.1.1. Market Value.** The market value represents the private market cost of the good or service. The rationale behind market value is that an in-kind transfer presents beneficiaries with control over some amount of resources that can be purchased and thus have an explicit value in the private market. Procedures used to assign a market value require first the identification of a good or service in the private marketplace which is analogous to the in-kind benefit and then estimation of the cost of that good or service. This is easier said than done for some types of noncash benefits whose true analogies are difficult or impossible to locate.

In the case of *food stamps* establishment of a market value was relatively clear. Recipients use food stamps as a substitute for cash to purchase food in the private marketplace. Their market value was assigned to be the same as the face value of the stamps as reported on the survey.

Procedures for estimating the market value of *school lunches* did not follow the general definition as stated above. As no real analogue exists in the private market for school lunches, market value was defined to be the difference between the cost of preparing the lunches and the cost paid by the students for the lunches. While the cost of preparing the lunches is fixed for all students, the price paid by students is not. All students receive the lunches at a cost below that of preparation. Low-income students may receive lunches for free or at a "reduced" price while others pay the regular or full price. Aggregate government statistics were used to compute the preparation cost per meal. Various assumptions were made about school attendance and meal consumption to arrive at the final estimates of market values per student.

*Medical benefits* were, by far, the most important component of the noncash programmes, totaling $54.5 in government expenditures in 1980. A number of important issues arose in the development of market values for these benefits. Among them were (1) the basic conceptual choice between assignment of an insurance value of the benefit or assignment of a value equal to the actual amount of health care consumed and (2) the method for handling the institutionalized population.

The estimation of market value could be made based on either the cost of the equivalent private health insurance policy or as the direct amount of health care consumed. Methods based on the direct amount of health care consumed were rejected for purposes of this study for several reasons. First, those persons consuming more health care, that is, those in the poorest state of health, would be considered "better off" using the income and poverty measures normally referenced. Second, reliable information concerning consumption of health care was difficult to obtain and that which was available was out of date.

The issue of the institutionalized population is important because the CPS survey universe is restricted to the noninstitutionalized population. Since a very large proportion of total government medical expenditures go to aged and disabled persons living in institutions one must consider alternative methods within the market value concept itself.

In a strict sense the private market analogue of the type of health insurance coverage provided by Medicare and Medicaid do not exist. In the case of

Medicare, distortions resulting from the existence of this programme and the near universal coverage for the aged make the market value of a private plan for this group unavailable for our purposes. The same is largely true for the Medicaid programme which serves two main low-income groups: nonworking, single women with children and the aged.

As a substitute for the private market, the assumption was made that the government acts as a large, nonprofit insurance company. The population was separated into "risk" classes based on age, disability status, family status, and state of residence. The market value was computed as the total government expenditure on health care within each risk class (with some overhead costs included) divided by the total number of persons within each risk class. In addition, separate estimates based on expenditures including and excluding that portion spent on the institutionalized population were made. It was also difficult to find the true market analogue for public or subsidized housing since the location and quality of public housing may differ from other housing available in the private market. Despite these problems the market value of this programme was determined by simulating the market rent of public housing based on housing characteristics and then subtracting any rent paid. The resulting difference was the market value of the housing subsidy. As no information was collected on rents paid or on housing characteristics on the March CPS, all of the above relationships were developed using data from another survey, the American Housing Survey (AHS) and then added to the CPS household using variables common to both.

**3.1.2. Recipient Value.** The receipt of noncash benefits may distort consumption patterns, and thus add less to a recipient's well-being than an equal dollar value cash transfer. If so, in theory, benefits should be discounted from their market value to reflect this difference. Recipient value should reflect the programme beneficiary's own valuation of the benefit in that it measures the amount of cash which would make the recipient feel just as well off as the noncash benefit. By definition the recipient value cannot exceed the market value.

While this concept is relatively clear to economists from the conceptual standpoint there are no data available directly reflecting individual assessments of the cash equivalent values for noncash benefits. As a proxy, the recipient value for a specific noncash benefit was assumed to be equal to the normal or average expenditure of "similar" households not receiving the noncash benefits. The term "similar" was defined in terms of variables such as income level, number of members, age, etc.

The normal expenditure approach presented some serious problems related to the availability of household consumption data. Though this information was needed to develop normal expenditure estimates by household characteristics, no such information was collected in the March CPS. The latest available data for food and medical expenditures were from a 1972–1973 Consumer Expenditure Survey (CEX). Current data were available from the AHS for estimation of housing expenditures. Both of these data sources, despite their problems, were the best available at the time and were, therefore, used in the estimation process. Estimates from the 1972–1973 period were adjusted for price and income changes to the 1979 reference year.

The recipient values for *food stamps* and *school lunch* benefits aligned closely with the market values assigned in the previous step. Overall, the normal expenditure estimates of food expenditures for households receiving these benefits averaged about 96 percent of the market value of the benefits received. If one assumes that the normal expenditure is a good approximation of the recipient value, the conclusion can be reached that these benefits are very nearly equivalent to cash income.

Recipient value estimates for *public housing subsidies* were somewhat lower with respect to the estimated market value for these subsidies. On average, these values were about 81 percent of the market value. The process of estimating normal expenditure values involved computation of market rent values for nonsubsidized rental housing whose incomes were below $20,000 using the AHS data and then assigning these rents to "similar" households from the March CPS.

Estimation of the normal expenditures for *medical care* presented yet more conceptual and empirical problems. First, the analogue chosen for market value, that of defining the government as a nonprofit insurance company, avoided the problem that is difficult to avoid here. This is the lack of an adequate universe from which to compute normal expenditures, especially for the aged where almost all persons are covered by Medicare. Expenditure information on health care were tabulated from the 1972–1973 CEX are treated as normal expenditures even though the levels would be clearly biased downward. These normal expenditure values were then assigned to each March CPS household with members covered by Medicare and/or Medicaid. The average recipient value for medical benefits was 47 percent of the market value including expenditures for the institutionalized and 57 percent excluding expenditures for that universe. Since the method used to compute normal expenditures seemed biased downward, caution was advised with regard to these values.

**3.1.3. Poverty Budget Share Value.** This concept was developed as a variant to the recipient value concept. It is linked directly with the official measure of poverty. For this valuation technique, normal expenditures were computed only for households with incomes at or near the official poverty line. These normal expenditures were defined as the poverty budget share values. This approach assumes that the value of in-kind benefits for the purpose of measuring poverty should be limited to no more than the amounts implied by consumption patterns of those with incomes at the poverty level. This assumption does not presume that benefits above that amount have no worth, though it does presume that recipients have little ability to use the excess amounts of one noncash benefit to fulfill other needs.

In practice, the actual poverty budget share values were used as limits in the calculation process. If the previously computed market value of a noncash benefit was less than the poverty budget share value for that type of household, then the market value was assigned as the poverty budget share limit. If the market value was greater than the poverty budget share limit, then the poverty budget share limit was assigned as the poverty budget share value.

The estimation of poverty budget share values was based on data from the 1960–1961 CEX. This older source of data was chosen mainly because the time period covered was very close to when the official poverty definition was derived and because distortions resulting from the introduction of noncash benefits programmes occurred later in the decade. The 1960–1961 data were used to compute the share of income spent on housing and medical care by size and age of household. These shares or proportions were then applied directly to the poverty line for 1979 to arrive at the poverty budget share limits.

Since poverty thresholds in the U.S. were developed assuming that one-third of household income is spent on *food*, the poverty budget share value limits for food were set at one-third of the household's poverty threshold. The market values of both food stamps and school lunches were summed to obtain a total market value for food in order to derive the poverty budget value.

Poverty budget share limits for *housing subsidies* were obtained by averaging the share of income spent on housing and the share of consumption spent on housing. This technique was used because measures of consumption often exceed measures of income for the lower end of the income distribution.

Values for *medical benefits* were also computed by averaging shares based on consumption and income.

\* \* \*

## 5. REVISION AND INTEGRATION

The period between 1982 and 1987 saw a breakout from the previous reliance on the pretax, posttransfer income definition. Throughout this period, however, estimates of income based on these new definitions were maintained separately. Statistics were released independently, in separate reports, at different times. In addition, the pretax, posttransfer measures of income and poverty continued to dominate.

In 1988, a new research project began which focused on the next step in the process of income definition evolution. There were three basic objectives of this project: (1) to expand the valuation of noncash benefits to include private sector in-kind benefits, (2) to integrate the processes of estimating noncash benefit values and income and payroll taxes, and (3) to introduce revisions to the valuation techniques for government noncash benefits used in the past and reduce the previous alternative valuations to a single "preferred" valuation. The base year chosen for the research was 1986.

Expansion to include the value of private sector in-kind benefits was restricted to employer-provided health insurance and the value of services from owner-occupied housing. Integration of the noncash values and the posttax, posttransfer cash definitions required the relatively simple integration of computer simulation systems and production of a single data file. Introduction of revisions to the noncash valuation techniques and acceptance of a single valuation method for each type of noncash benefit required significant new research and development.

In terms of employer-provided benefits, the March CPS collected data on coverage by *employer-provided health insurance plans* and participation in employer-provided retirement plans. While both of these benefits could be considered as income under certain definitions, pension-plan participation was not considered as income since the recipient's current command over the benefit is very limited. Data available from the National Medical Care Expenditure Survey for 1977 were used to estimate the value of employer-provided health insurance benefits. Relationships developed between employer cost for health insurance and employee characteristics were modeled and used to assign values to persons in the CPS reporting coverage.

The benefits of home-ownership, that is, the imputed rent or services provided through *home-ownership* is considered as income in the NIPA accounts and is sometimes included in definitions of household income. The approach taken in this research was to value these services at the opportunity cost of the owner's equity in the home less the amount of income paid in property taxes. Complex issues related to the deductibility of mortgage interest, depreciation, and other housing costs were ignored. Relationships between home equity and household characteristics were developed from the AHS. These relationships were when applied to owner-occupied households identified on the March CPS.

Revision and simplification with regard to the techniques for valuing government noncash programmes affected food, housing, and medical benefits to varying degrees. For food benefits the market value approach was selected as the only valuation method. The technique used to assign market value remained unchanged. For housing benefits the market value technique was also selected as the single valuation concept. Valuation procedures were updated and modified, though the AHS continued to be used as the source of rents for public or subsidized housing units and the simulation of the market rent for these units.

It was the method for computing the value of noncash medical benefits that had received the most criticism and, therefore, the most attention when the revision process was undertaken. The market value technique based mainly on government expenditures within risk groups often resulted in values for medical benefits that, on their own, exceeded the poverty threshold. This resulted in a poverty rate for the elderly of virtually zero when using the market value of medical benefits. The data needed to estimate the recipient value and poverty budget share value had always been inadequate, making even the conceptually preferred methods difficult to support.

An important new valuation technique was adopted for medical benefits to overcome the problems described above. The concept called fungible value was introduced for valuation of medical benefits. Benefits are counted as income to the extent that they free up resources that could have been spent for other goods and services, in this case on medical care. Fungible values were assigned using the following criterion:

1. Government medical benefits have no value if a household lacks the resources to meet basic food and housing needs or if the family has no remaining resources after meeting basic food and housing requirements.
2. Medical benefits have full market value if the resources of the household after deducting amounts required for food and housing needs are equal or greater than the market value of the government medical benefits.
3. Medical benefits have partial value if the resources of the household are between zero and the market value of medical benefits after deducting basic food and housing requirements.

The major advantage of this approach is that it eliminates the distortion of removing persons from poverty who lack the resources to meet their basic food and housing needs.

## 5.1 Release of Reports

Results of this research were published by the Bureau of the Census in 1988.[4] A new category of report, the research and development series, was created in order to accommodate these expanded measures of income. For the first time both general income distribution statistics and measure of poverty were brought together in a single report. The report contained information for a total of twelve different definitions of income. These definitions were derived through logical combinations of cash and noncash income with pretax and posttax and pretransfer and posttransfer bases. The first report, which contained data for 1986 has been followed by reports covering 1987 through 1989.[5] Annual release of these estimates is now a permanent part of the statistical programme.

## 6. PLANS FOR THE FUTURE

Throughout this paper we have attempted to describe efforts at the Census Bureau over the last ten years to expand the definition of income beyond the original pretax, posttransfer income concept. This effort began with an expansion of the CPS income supplement to include questions about the receipt of noncash benefits. Research in the early 1980s resulted in a series of exploratory reports that focused on the effect of government noncash benefits on the number of families and persons living below the poverty level. A second series of studies examined the effect of taxes on the distribution of income. Research efforts were expanded and integrated in the late-1980s to create a new series of reports that have provided a comprehensive picture of the effect of taxes and noncash benefits (from both the public and private sectors) on income distributional measures and the prevalence of poverty.

Though this new report series represents a significant achievement at the Census Bureau, our efforts in the area of income research are far from over. Census Bureau noncash benefits research in the 1980s was the result of a realization that the growth in in-kind benefit programmes had seriously eroded the relevance of the money income definition first developed in the 1940s. Income underreporting is another critical problem limiting the usefulness of surveys such as the CPS for policy-making and analytic purposes. The Census Bureau has embarked on a major research initiative to explore the issue of income underreporting. The ultimate goal of this research is an integrated data set that will (1) reflect income concepts truly relevant for policymakers and analysts, and (2) utilize a combination of survey and administrative data to derive an adjusted set of income and poverty estimates which provide a much more accurate portrayal of economic status than survey data alone. As research into the valuation of noncash benefits and tax simulations were perhaps the most important Census Bureau income research issues of the 1980s, income underreporting and the integration of survey and administrative data may well become the critical research issues of the 1990s.

## NOTES

1. United Nations. "Handbook of Household Surveys," New York (1984).
2. Organization for Economic Cooperation and Development. *National Accounts: Main Aggregates,* Vol. 1: 1960–1989, Paris (1991).
3. E. Budd, D. Radner, and J. Hinrichs. "Size Distribution of Family Personal Income: Methodology and Estimates for 1964." *Bureau of Economic Analysis Staff Paper No. 21* (1973).
4. U.S. Bureau of the Census. *Current Population Reports,* Series P-60, no. 164-RD-1. "Measuring the Effects of Benefits and Taxes on Income and Poverty: 1986." Washington, D.C.: U.S. Government Printing Office (1988).
5. U.S. Bureau of the Census. *Current Population Reports,* Series P-60, No. 176-RD. "Measuring the Effect of Benefits and Taxes on Income and Poverty: 1990," Washington, D.C.: U.S. Government Printing Office (1991).

# S E L E C T I O N    1 5

Robert Haveman and Barbara Wolfe

# Children's Prospects and Children's Policy

Government programs affecting the status of children in the United States are numerous and include most major social welfare programs. The eight largest programs assisting children are: Aid to Families with Dependent Children, Food Stamp Program, various housing assistance programs, Medicaid, Earned Income Tax Credit, National School Lunch Program, Special Supplemental Feeding Program for Women, Infants, and Children, and Head Start (see Suggested Further Readings, Currie 1994). But recent downward trends in the status of many of America's children have raised controversial questions concerning what government policy towards children should be. The gap between income levels of rich and poor families with children is increasing. Child poverty rates are high—the U.S. rate has been found to be at least twice that of comparable industrialized nations. Basic health care needs, such as polio and measles vaccinations, are not universally met. Teen suicides have more than doubled since the 1960s.

In this selection, the authors survey the available data and offer general guidelines for the development of policy directed towards children. After surveying the current conditions challenging childhood in America, Haveman and Wolfe address the possible reasons behind the rising public concern. They then present an economic framework which can be helpful in determining efficient public investment in children. The authors summarize the current state of research about the determinants of children's success, and conclude that, although there is much we do not know, certain reasonable policy suggestions can be made.

Haveman, Robert, and Barbara Wolfe. "Children's Prospects and Children's Policy." *Journal of Economic Perspectives 7* (Fall 1993): 153–174.

**Robert Haveman** is John Bascom Professor of Economics and Public Affairs at the University of Wisconsin at Madison.
**Barbara Wolfe** is Professor of Economics and Preventive Medicine and Director of the Institute for Research on Poverty at the University of Wisconsin at Madison.

**Questions to Guide the Reading**
1. The authors state that children have lost ground in particular areas while improving in others. How have children's conditions improved or worsened?
2. What possible explanations are given for the current public concern?
3. Describe the economist's "human capital" perspective as it pertains to investment in children.
4. What economic factors might contribute to societal underinvestment in children?
5. What issues are raised by the question "which children"?
6. What factors have research studies identified as fundamental determinants of children's success?

The nation's concern for the well-being, education, and development of its children is again on the rise, reaching a level not seen since at least the 1950s, which brought passage of the National Defense Education Act. The concern is to some extent caught up in broader questions regarding the nation's lagging economic performance. Claims that America is neglecting its future often begin by citing the sagging indicators of children and youth attainments, followed by evidence on low rates of saving and investment, high and persistent public deficits, and deteriorating public infrastructure. Discussions of poverty in America inevitably include statistics on child poverty rates, which are higher than those of other groups, higher than they have been in the past, and higher than they are in other developed countries. These statistics also show an increasing share of the nation's children growing up in mother-only households, in dysfunctional neighborhoods, and dependent on welfare. Discussions of Social Security often include statements concerning how we have done well by our older citizens, while neglecting children.

Children also are brought into policy debates over other issues. To many, welfare support for unmarried women who care for children at home seems inconsistent with the fact that well over half of married women with children are now working. Debates over housing policy reflect the belief that past policies bear much of the responsibility for concentrating children in neighborhoods that foster joblessness, school failure, drug use, and crime. The debate over education reform—school choice, magnet schools, busing—starts from a common judgment that neither schools nor families are serving children well.

Within the last five years, a number of prominent commissions and task forces have reported on the status of children, and most of them have called for sizable new interventions.[1] One recent and highly publicized report is that of the National Commission on Children (1991), which was established by the Congress and appointed by the President. In *Beyond Rhetoric: A New American Agenda for Children and Families*—a title that reflects some of the frustration over the paucity of policy responses to the previous reports—the commission discusses numerous policies targeted at children and recommends adoption of a far-reaching package of initiatives, at a cost of over $50 billion in 1992. These include a $1,000 per child refundable tax credit; a play-or-pay public-private health insurance plan; major expansion of early childhood education (Head Start) and women's and children's nutrition programs; educational reform (including school choice); and demonstration projects to assure child support payments for the custodial parent. Some common proposals from other reports are listed in Table 1.

This paper offers some facts on trends in children's economic status and an economic perspective for thinking about public policy toward children. Throughout, we will attempt to make clear what is known and what is not known empirically about the relationships that are embodied in our perspective.

## HOW, IN FACT, ARE CHILDREN FARING?

No single metric exists to compare the status of children over time, but American children appear to have lost ground relative to those in earlier decades in most (but not every) dimension. We will mention a few of the measures here, and present facts on several others in tables that follow.

The nature of the families in which children are raised is perhaps the most vivid indication of the deterioration in the status of children, and some information on demographic and parental factors is presented in Table 2. Because of soaring birth

**Table 1**  Some Common Proposals for Assisting Children

Increase the earned income tax credit for families with children.
Expand the Head Start program.
Encourage school "choice" plans.
Increase teacher salaries to attract more able faculties.
Impose standard child support obligations on noncustodial parents, and enforce them.
"Sanction" welfare recipients for unapproved behaviors.
Mandate Norplant implants for welfare recipients to limit increases in family size.
Impose work requirements on welfare recipients.
Reorient welfare programs toward short-term relief providing a temporary safety net, including time limits on eligibility.
Increase job training, education, and community employment opportunities as transitional assistance for welfare recipients who have exhausted time-limited welfare benefits.
Provide employment subsidies on both the demand and supply side of the labor market.
Initiate youth capital accounts for education and training.
Create "enterprise zones" for development in urban areas.
"Empower" poor people through home ownership programs and subsidized asset accumulation.
Sponsor ghetto task forces composed of released military personnel.
Provide college scholarships based on future service in low-income communities.
Establish universal health insurance for pregnant women and children.

**Table 2** Demographic and Parental Factors Influencing Children's Well-Being

|  | Total | White | African-American |
|---|---|---|---|
| Percentage of Population under 15[a] |  |  |  |
| 1960 | 31.1 | 30.3 | 37.7 |
| 1970 | 28.4 | 27.6 | 35.4 |
| 1989 | 21.7 | 20.7 | 27.2 |
| Birth Rates (per 1000) of Unwed 15–19-Year-Old Mothers[c] |  |  |  |
| 1970 | 22.4 | 12.2 | 97.3 |
| 1980 | 27.6 | 16.2 | 89.2 |
| 1989 | 40.6 | 27.5 | 106.7 |
| Percentage of Births to Mothers with Less than 12 Years Education |  |  |  |
| 1970 | 30.8 | 27.0 | 51.0 |
| 1987 | 20.2 | 17.3 | 31.3 |
| Average Number of Children per Family with Children[a] |  |  |  |
| 1970 | 3.58 | 3.52 | 4.13 |
| 1988 | 3.16 | 3.11 | 3.43 |
| Percentage of Children Living with Single Parent[c] |  |  |  |
| 1960 | 9.1 | 7.2 | 21.9 |
| 1970 | 11.9 | 9.7 | 31.8 |
| 1990 | 24.7 | 19.2 | 54.8 |
| Percentage of Children Under 18 Living with Never-married Mothers[c] |  |  |  |
| 1970 | 0.1 | 0.02 | 4.5 |
| 1990 | 7.6 | 3.7 | 28.3 |
| Percentage of Children Under Age 6[d] (18)[b] with Mother in Labor Force |  |  |  |
| 1970 | 29 (39.2) |  |  |
| 1987 | 51 (61.7) |  |  |

*Source:* See notes following Table 5.

rates to unmarried teens, about 25 percent of today's children have been born to an unwed mother, and less than 75 percent of them live with two parents. For African-American children the situation is more extreme: nearly two-thirds of them were born to a nonmarried mother and less than 50 percent of them live with two parents. The high birth rate among African-American teens and the increasing rate among whites suggest the proportion is likely to increase.

Moreover, with increasing numbers of mothers in the labor force, the amount of parental time for child care has been reduced. Whereas in 1965 the average child spent about 30 hours per week interacting with a parent, by the late 1980s this figure had dropped to about 17 hours.[2]

The rising rate of marital dissolution—an increase of more than 30 percent from 1970 to 1987—has enlarged the extent to which children are exposed to this form of stress. Whereas 19 percent of American children experienced dissolution of their parents' marriage during the 1960s, this rate increased to 30 percent in the 1980s.

Table 3 shows the adverse trends in factors such as vaccinations and insurance that are related to children's health, also suggesting deterioration in this important aspect of children's well-being. The rate of child maltreatment (including abuse) now stands at more than 300 per 10,000 children, up from about 100 per 10,000 two decades ago. (While a portion of this increase may be due to improved statistical reporting, surely not all of it is.) The suicide rate among those aged 15–19 is rising, and now stands at more than 11 per 100,000, or nearly the 11.9 overall rate for the entire population.

There have also been important changes in both the income available to children and in the sources of that income, as shown in Table 4. The average cash income of families in the lowest fifth of the income distribution has dropped from more than $10,000 in 1973 to less than $8,000 in 1989 (in 1989 dollars). In part, this reflects the relative and absolute decline of earnings for younger men and those with limited education over this period (Levy and Michel 1991). It also partly

**Table 3**  Health Factors Reflecting Children's Well-Being

| Changing Factors | Total | White | African-American |
|---|---|---|---|
| Percentage of Children ages 1–4 Vaccinated against Polio (DPT)[e] | | | |
| 1965 | 74 | | |
| 1970 | 77 (76) | 81 (80) | 63 (59)* |
| 1985 | 55 (65) | 59 (69) | 40 (49)* |
| Percentage of Children under 15 without Health Insurance[f] | | | |
| 1980 | 12.8 | | |
| 1989 | 15.9 | | |
| Percentage of Young Adults (18-25) Ever Used Cocaine (Heroin)[a] | | | |
| 1974 | 53 (4.5) | | |
| 1988 | 56 (0.4) | | |
| Reported Child Maltreatment (per 10,000)[a] | | | |
| 1976 | 101 | | |
| 1980 | 181 | | |
| 1986 | 328 | | |
| Suicide Rate, Ages 15–19 (per 100,000)[a] | | | |
| 1970 | 5.9 | 9.4[†] | 4.7[†] |
| 1980 | 8.5 | 15.0[†] | 5.6[†] |
| 1988 | 11.3 | 19.6[†] | 9.7[†] |

*Nonwhite.
†Males only.
*Source:* See notes following Table 5.

**Table 4**  Income, Poverty, and Welfare Factors Reflecting Children's Well-Being

| Changing Factors | Total | White | African-American |
|---|---|---|---|
| Percentage of Children under 19 below the Poverty Line[e] | | | |
| 1959 | 26.1 | 18.8 | 63.3 |
| 1969 | 15.6 | 10.4 | 41.1 |
| 1979 | 17.1 | 11.7 | 36.1 |
| 1990 | 20.6 | 15.9 | 44.8 |
| Average Cash Family Income, Families with Children, Lowest Quintile, 1989$[c] | | | |
| 1973 | $10,529 | | |
| 1989 | 7,714 | | |
| Percentage of Mother (Father)-only Families with Children Who Are Poor[c] | | | |
| 1979 | 39.7 (6.4) | | |
| 1990 | 45.3 (8.5) | | |
| AFDC Child Recipients as a Percentage of Children in Poverty[c] | | | |
| 1970 | 58.5 | | |
| 1990 | 59.9 | | |
| Average AFDC and Food Stamp Benefits for Mother with 2 Children and No Earnings, 1991$[c] | | | |
| 1972 | $10,169 | | |
| 1991 | 7,471 | | |
| Percentage of Total Income from AFDC, SSI and General Assistance, Poor Female-Headed Families[c] | | | |
| 1979 | 38.1 | | |
| 1990 | 31.7 | | |

*Source:* See notes following Table 5.

reflects a decline in the real value of public income support programs. As of 1990, real AFDC benefit levels for the average mother and two children were less than $7,500, down from more than $10,000 in 1972. To characterize it another way, among poor families headed by a female, the proportion of total income from AFDC, SSI, and general assistance declined from 38 to 32 percent from 1979 to 1990. In addition, the effectiveness of these government programs in moving working-age, earnings-poor families out of poverty has fallen significantly; the last 20 years have been an era of retrenchment.[3]

Many of these troubling indicators of children's status can be summarized by the nation's official poverty statistics. More than 20 percent of all children now live in poor families, up from less than 15 percent in 1973.[4] The incidence of children's poverty is above 40 percent in minority families.[5] Nearly 12 percent of families with children younger than 18 fail to escape from poverty even though someone in the family works; about 7 percent of these families remain in poverty even though there was at least one person working at least three-fourths time. Using data from the Luxembourg Income Study and a common poverty standard similar to the official U.S. norm,[6] Smeeding (1992) found the children's poverty rate in the U.S. to be about three times that in other OECD countries, and trending in the opposite direction.

Growing up in a family with low income conveys only a portion of the deprivation that is experienced. Children who grow up in poor families have relatively low health status and are less likely to be immunized against common preventable diseases. Today, the percentage of children who are vaccinated against rubella, DPT (diphtheria-tetanus-pertussis), polio, or mumps is lower than during the late 1970s or early 1980s, and the percentage of minority children living in inner cities who are vaccinated against these diseases hovers at about 53 percent. Children of poor families tend to live in neighborhoods with high rates of crime, drug dependence, and drug trafficking (Case and Katz 1991), to attend schools with diminished capacities to convey education or inspire learning (Mayer, 1991), and to live in families with no working adult. They are more likely to give birth out of wedlock and—by their own testimony—find unrewarding the traditional norms of hard work, creativity, diligence, organization, stability, and loyalty. To make matters worse, all of these correlates of living in a poor family are substantially higher if the children are African-American or Hispanic.

The picture in terms of children's educational attainments is more mixed, as shown in Table 5. Teens continue to drop out of high school at a 15 percent rate, with higher rates for minorities; however, the overall dropout rate is declining. Scores on reading and mathematics proficiency tests given to nine-year-olds show no overall deterioration, but no progress either. However, in a National Education Goals report, the mathematics and science test scores of U.S. 13-year-olds fell below those of children of the same age in the United Kingdom, Spain, Korea, and Ireland, the four other countries studied (U.S. House of Representatives 1992, 1143). For those who stay in high school and take the Scholastic Aptitude Test, the average combined score of slightly more than 900 is judged to be low by nearly all observers, although the increase in the proportion of high school students taking the test may account for all or most of the decline since 1970.

Not all factors contributing to child well-being have deteriorated, however, On average, today's parents are better educated than those of any previous cohort. Somewhat more than 30 percent of children born in 1970 had mothers with less than a high school education: as of 1987, this figure had declined to about 20 percent. In 1970, 61 percent of the parents of elementary school children had completed high school; by 1987 this figure had increased to 73 percent. Among African-American children, the increase in this percentage is even more dramatic: from 36 to 67 percent (National Commission on Children 1991, 32). Although there is no guarantee that more educated parents are better parents, there is some evidence—and a common presumption—that parents with more education are more able to make choices that enhance the quality of life for their children.

**Table 5** School Performance Factors Influencing Children's Well Being

| Changing Factors | Total | White | African-American |
|---|---|---|---|
| National Assessment of Education Progress Reading (Math) Test Scores, 9-Year-Olds[a] | | | |
| 1979–80 | 215 (219) | 221 (224) | 189 (192) |
| 1987–88 | 212 (222) | 218 (227) | 189 (202) |
| Percentage of 18–21-Year-Olds Who Are High School Dropouts[a] | | | |
| 1970 | 16.4 | 14.3 | 30.5 |
| 1980 | 15.8 | 14.7 | 23.0 |
| 1989 | 15.0 | 14.6 | 17.4 |
| Average SAT Scores Vebal (Math)[h,c] | | | |
| 1960 | 477 (498) | | |
| 1970 | 466 (488) | | |
| 1980 | 424 (466) | | |
| 1991 | 422 (474) | | |

[a]*Statistical Abstract of the United States,* 1991. Population under 15, p. 13; children with children, p. 51; suicide rate, p.126; cocaine/heroin use, p.121; child maltreatment, p.182; NAEP scores, p. 155; dropouts, p. 156.
[b]Bianchi (1990). Children living with two parents, p. 10; children under 18 with mother in labor force, p. 17.
[c]*1992 Green Book.* Birth rates, p. 1076; children living with never-married mothers, pp. 1080–83; cash family income, p. 1371; AFDC child recipients, p. 663; AFDC, Food Stamp benefits, p. 1190; poverty rate and living arrangements, p. 1182; SAT scores, p.1073.
[d]*Kids Count Data Book,* 1992, p. 39.
[e]Wolfe (1991). Vaccinations, p. 53; children below poverty line, p. 45.
[f]National Center for Health Statistics (1991). Vaccinations, p. 186; children without insurance, p. 291.
[g]Long (1988), p. 51.
[h]Fuchs and Reklis (1992), p. 42.

Similarly, average family sizes have decreased over the past quarter century. The average number of births per 1,000 women aged 15–44 declined from 122.7 in the mid-1950s to 67.8 in the mid-1980s, and has increased only slightly since that time. As a result, the average child has fewer siblings today than in earlier decades, and less competition for parental attention and resources. This decline in the average number of children per family has been greater among African-American and Hispanic families than white families, although the average remains higher among minority families.

While these statistics are discouraging, they clearly do not apply to all children. As in other cases, beware of the mean! While the average values of many of these indicators of children's well-being may be falling over time, they often reflect drastic declines for children at the bottom of the distribution, who are largely minority children living in large cities, or children in isolated rural circumstances. Many of these children confront multiple risks—poor education, poverty, single and unstable families, dysfunctional neighborhoods—and the nation's failure to improve these circumstances affects the trend in the means that we have observed.

In sum, along many dimensions the problem of children's status is rooted in growing differences among children; some of these differences are far larger today than they have been since statisticians began keeping track. In this sense, the nation's "children problem" stems from the drift of the bottom tail away from the median, and the corresponding need is for measures targeted on specific children, rather than an overall increase in resources allocated to children.

## WHY THE CURRENT PUBLIC CONCERN?

It is interesting to speculate for a moment on the basis for the current surge of interest in children's well-being and attainments. Children themselves do not vote; they are not politically organized; and the number of voting households containing children is smaller now than it has been in decades. Given these political realities, the trends and facts just cited may not be the true reason why children are so high on today's policy agenda. Is the recent surge of concern for children due to the self-interest of the voting population, or to its altruism?

Self-interest is not irrelevant here. For one thing, it remains true that many in the voting-age population have children of their own. If their well-being is determined in part by the future prosperity and prospects of their children—if utility functions are generationally interdependent—their own self-interest implies support for public measures to improve children's status and attainments. However, given that the nature of those public interventions most discussed tend to target resources on children concentrated in families who neither vote regularly nor have political influence apart from their votes, general support for such policies would not rest primarily on this form of self-interest. Moreover, if adults are concerned about the future prospects of their *own* children, private reallocations— either *inter vivos* transfers or the bequeathing of assets upon death—would seem to be the more rational response, rather than public interventions.

Self-interest resting on a more dynamic view of the determinants of that public good called "future prosperity" could play a more important role. Clearly, the future well-being of today's middle-aged and older population—their wage rates and the safety of their retirement pensions and health care benefits—rests on future productivity and economic growth, and hence the quality of the nation's future workforce.[7] Moreover, to the extent that children and youth exhibit more threatening incidents of grossly dysfunctional behavior like violence, drug use, and weapons possession, it is in the general interest to support public action to reduce the alienation that induces such behavior. However logical this case in theory, in practice the advocates for the politically powerful older population are well aware of the implications for them of arguments for intergenerational redistribution.

Largely because other arguments are so unconvincing, we conclude that some form of altruism must be driving the current support for public action on behalf of children. While the nature of this "concern with others" could take many forms, we suggest that there is a long tradition of willingness of Americans to provide benefits to those viewed as innocent victims. The discussions that led to the passage of public assistance legislation, for example, focused on widows and their children. Today, the image of children as innocent victims appears to be the most powerful source of support for public measures on their behalf.

The cohort of people currently younger than age 18 is saddled with poor economic prospects. Since the early 1970s, growth in real earnings and income has fallen to near zero, and few forecast a return to pre-1970 levels of economic growth. Even though the current cohort of children is small, there is little expectation that it will experience the rising relative wages and falling housing prices that benefited earlier small cohorts. Moreover, because of rapid increases in life expectancy, children today face the prospect of supporting a large and growing elderly population to which huge implicit pension and health care commitments have been made. Estimates of the income and health care requirements of the dependent population relative to the earnings of the working-age population in the early twenty-first century—when today's young cohort will be the workers—are at an all-time high.[8] As a result, today's children are not likely to be better off than their parents, and this turnabout in a long tradition of growing children's prospects is viewed as unfair.

Feelings of altruism are also likely to extend to particular groups of children whose future looks dim. Those children growing up in poor and typically mother-only families, coping with dysfunctional neighborhoods and schools, are seen as innocent victims of some ill-understood breakdown in family and community performance. The earlier tables offer considerable evidence both that such children exist and that their experience deviates more from that of the median American child today than at any time in this century (on these points, see also Aspen Institute 1993; Fuchs 1990). The character of the upbringing these children receive is seen as violating minimally acceptable standards; through no fault of their own, they face a tremendous handicap in the economic race.

Although it is theoretically possible, of course, that future expected bequests from parents to children will be increased—or future expected commitments to parents from their children will be decreased—neither logic nor evidence suggests that the magnitude of such responses will be sufficient to offset the expected generational inequities. For one thing, few parents or grandparents of today's poor children have assets available for transfer. Moreover, there is little reason to believe that the level of public support for the elderly will be seriously eroded, or that tomorrow's children will reverse the trend of substituting public for private responsibility for the well-being of aged parents with few resources (Lampman and Smeeding 1983).

In short, we believe that the rise in support for public policies targeted on children stems mainly from the perception that our society is handing on a relatively unattractive future to many of its children, that this is not fair, and that private responses will not compensate for the shortfall.

## CHILDREN AS HUMAN CAPITAL: AN ECONOMIC FRAMEWORK

We view children's success as determined by three primary factors: social (primarily government) investment in children; parental investment in children; and choices that each child makes. This way of characterizing the situation of children suggests a sequential view of the world. Society (government) acts first, according to its own interests, making some direct investments on behalf of children (like public education or Head Start) and families (AFDC), and setting the economic environment in which both parents and children operate. Given this environment, parents choose how much to work and earn (given their talents) and how much time to spend with their children, and then, given their income, they decide how much to devote to their children.[9] They also make decisions about family structure and location that serve their own interests, but which also have an effect on their children. Finally, given their own talents, the resources that have been invested in them, and the incentives that they confront, children make choices about their education, their peers, their fertility, and their work effort. We observe the outcome of these choices—children's well-being and their attainments.

Of course, this perspective is more deterministic and rational than the decisions which we all take and observe. It assumes that children are utility maximizers, and while this may be reasonable for those older than, say, 15 years, it hardly holds true for younger children. It neglects important factors such as information, liquidity constraints, stigma, and just plain luck; moreover, it does not explicitly recognize the potential contributions of "social capital" to children's success (Coleman 1988).[10] Notwithstanding these reservations, this economic framework is helpful for thinking about public, family, and personal investments in children; it raises a variety of questions regarding the level and composition of investments in children, many of which have policy import.

## IS AMERICA "UNDERINVESTING" IN CHILDREN?

Determining the "optimal" level of investment in children is an issue with which economists are equipped to deal, at least in principle.[11] The pat answer is clear: keep allocating resources to children until the value of social benefits produced by the last unit of investment is just equal to the value of what could be produced by those resources if they were used in some other way, or until the "social rate of return" on investments in children is equivalent to that on other allocations. But that response raises as many questions as it answers.

For example, how can economists measure the returns from the use of resources in activities that are alternatives to investment in children? One confronts assertions every day about social needs to which resources could be efficiently allocated—caring for the homeless, improving the nation's infrastructure, finding a cure for AIDS, increasing investment in private plant and equipment. While many would feel more comfortable advocating greater investment in children if we knew the resources were coming from, say, New Year's Eve celebrations costing $300 per person at New York's Plaza Hotel, rather than from investments in new technology yielding a high social rate of return, such a presumption is difficult to sustain in the absence of estimates of the social payoff from alternative activities.

Apart from this issue, there is the question of determining the economic payoff to investment in children. This, of course, involves assessing the benefits from resources allocated to children. There are several reasons why society's investment budget is likely to be biased against allocations to children.

First, there are external or spillover effects of investments in children, and they may be substantial. A review of the literature on the nonmarketed benefits of education, an important form of investment in children, is found in Haveman and Wolfe (1984) and Wolfe (forthcoming). They estimate these external effects to be a significant portion of total social benefits derived from this form of investment in children. Because both parents and the government are likely to ignore these potential effects, as a nation we probably underinvest in our children.

Capital market imperfections also suggest such underinvestment. For example, it might be socially efficient for a talented child to attend a special, costly school to nurture a unique musical talent. Such an investment might have a social payoff which is greater than that of the alternative use of the required resources— say a business desiring a new office computer system. Yet, while the business will be able to obtain loan financing for its investment, neither the child nor the parents will be able to arrange bank financing for the music training. Because human capital cannot be "secured" by the bank, and the payout from the investment may be uncertain, long delayed, and (in some cases) not marketed, insufficient investment in children is likely.

A final reason suggesting underinvestment in children is the dominance of state and local governments in the provision of public education. Given geographic mobility, lower levels of government will not be able to capture that portion of the benefits of investments in children reflected in increased future taxes or better citizenship. From the perspective of these investors, underinvestment is the optimal strategy.

Taking these factors into consideration, the case that society is dedicating sufficient resources to children seems a difficult one to make.

## IN WHAT DIRECTION SHOULD INVESTMENTS IN CHILDREN FLOW?

Even if it is decided that particular investments in children would have a very large payoff relative to other investment options available in the economy, it does not follow that society is investing too few resources in children in the aggregate. Perhaps rather than increasing the resources for children, we should be reallocating the current commitment of resources. For example, a common assertion is that in attempting to increase the quality of education, school systems have added administrators and special programs that may serve only to bureaucratize and stifle teacher creativity and spontaneity. If this assertion is true, children's attainments could be increased by reallocating resources away from this form of investment in children to other more productive investments in them.

This issue of the "best" mix of investments in children is an important one, given that investment activities can be undertaken by the government, by parents, and by children themselves. At the margin, where is the largest payoff in terms of children's attainments: formal schooling, enriched early education, more and more effective parental time, higher family income, better adjusted and mature parents, improved neighborhood quality, or increased counseling to assist children in coping with stressful events or avoiding destructive behaviors? From the perspective of public policy, the trick is to identify those specific investments in children that have the greatest payoff relative to their cost. Stating this rule is easy; implementing it is the difficult part. Several complexities immediately arise.

First, many investments in children—parental education, family income, neighborhood or school quality, parental time—are likely to have declining marginal benefits, so measuring the average benefit accomplished by the current level of investment will not suffice. In much the same way, the marginal benefit of the same investment may vary with the level of other investments with which it is associated. An increase in parental time devoted to children may have a quite different effect on their attainments if the family moves from an "underclass" neighborhood than if it stays in the same house or neighborhood.

Moreover, some investments may only influence children's attainments via other factors that can then be said to mediate the impact of the investment. For example, parental participation in an adult education program designed to improve their job prospects might simultaneously increase their expectations for children's success, thereby increasing their monitoring of children, or improving family life. As a result, their children may perform better in school or be better equipped to cope with stressful events related to family or peers.

Finally, "children's attainments" are multidimensional, and include educational success, fertility behavior, occupation and earnings, dependence on welfare, the quality of personal and family relationships, attitudes toward accepted rules and customs, and more.

Somehow, for each child in differing proportions, these elements combine to form "success." But for society and the family, decisions about investment must include some judgment about the relative importance of each of these attainments.

## TO WHICH CHILDREN SHOULD INVESTMENTS BE DIRECTED?

On efficiency grounds, there is no particular reason that investments in children should be equal. Society may reap substantial benefits from additional education resources devoted to some children, but not to others. An efficient pattern of investment would concentrate education spending on the former group. This optimally unequal treatment of children could extend even into the family. Conversely, if equal treatment of children is desired, families (and society) should find other ways of assisting those children who do not receive as much schooling investment. Yet a third possibility would be greater equality of outcomes, perhaps measured by income. For this goal, families (and society) should concentrate investments on children whose expected earnings and income lie at the bottom of the distribution.

In many circumstances, these three objectives need not suggest conflicting policies. For example, the "underinvestment" case is clearly the strongest in the case of children growing up in poor families, minority families, and mother-only families. These children tend to have fewer resources available to them along a whole spectrum of dimensions than do children from middle- and upper-class families. Because of the constraints on the allocation of resources to them—both budget constraints and the "bite" from capital market imperfections—it is likely that the social return on the marginal dollar invested in them is high, relative to investments in nonpoor children. Moreover, since the level of family resources they receive is relatively low, the equal treatment argument also would support greater public investment in this group. Finally, since adult prospects also look less promising for this group, relatively more investment in the group could be justified in the interests of greater equality of outcomes.[12]

The "to which children" question is also relevant in considering the ages of those in whom investments are to be made. Is the return at the margin greater for investments in prenatal care, in enriched early childhood programs, in elementary and secondary school years, or in adolescence and beyond? There appears to be a growing consensus among child development experts and researchers that the United States is overinvesting in children who have graduated from high school (and who go on with their education) relative to younger children (Hamburg 1992). However, in the absence of reliable estimates of the total social return to investments in young children, these conclusions are open to dispute.

## WHO SHOULD BE INVESTING?

Government can either provide services directly to children (through improved school, nutrition, or children's health programs, or through enriched day-care programs, for example), or it could provide parents with adequate resources and incentives to better nurture their children. How should scarce resources be allocated between these two strategies? The answer rests on considerations of both cost-effectiveness and values.

Consider, first, the efficiency questions that need answering in developing effective policy. Are families or the state most effective in providing services to children? Can the state, through assistance to parents, assure that the resources are invested in children; or is direct provision the only feasible vehicle?

Beyond these questions are issues of values: Should the nurturing of the nation's children be the primary responsibility of families, or should the state take a more active role in the shaping of children? Debate over these questions plays itself out in issues such as the "choice" controversy in education; the question as to whether day-care should be subsidized through refundable tax credits or publicly funded day-care centers; whether a children's allowance should be provided to families, or free lunches offered at schools; and whether additional support for higher education should be provided with direct government support to institutions, or special capital accounts for individuals.

## THE DETERMINANTS OF CHILDREN'S SUCCESS

Hundreds of research studies by economists, sociologists, and developmental psychologists have attempted to identify the determinants of children's success and to measure the impacts on children's attainments of changes in these factors. Because of differences in disciplinary perspectives, data, and empirical methods, the findings are nearly as disparate as they are voluminous. Moreover, because the complexity of the attainment process far exceeds both the data and the causal modeling methods available to researchers, many of the estimated relationships need to be interpreted as correlations rather than as causal linkages. Nevertheless, if one were to summarize what we do know in a few sentences (Haveman and Wolfe, forthcoming 1994, offer a more complete discussion), the story would run something as follows.

Consider first family-based investments in children. The most important determinant of children's success—their education, earnings, and avoidance of destructive behaviors—appears to be the education of their parents, especially the mother's education.[13] In some studies, but not all, this relationship seems to be stronger for white children than for racial minorities.

The number of siblings in the family has a persistently negative effect on children's success, perhaps because family economic and time resources need to be spread more thinly when more children are present. Exposure to values also seems important: children from religious families tend to do better; those whose parents (and siblings) divorce, become arrested, or choose nonmarital childbearing tend to do worse.

Economic circumstances, like the level of family income relative to needs, have a persistently positive effect on children, though this linkage does not appear to be quantitatively large. The intergenerational transmission of welfare dependence, while found in several studies, does not appear to be large in magnitude.[14] Holding constant the level of family income, there is some hint that the proportion of total income that comes from earnings (rather than welfare) is positively related to children's attainments.

In several studies (but not all), the amount of time a mother works in the paid labor market appears to have a positive and substantial effect on children's attainment, as measured by their education and economic activity. Because this effect appears larger than one would expect from the increased family income from mother's work, something of a "role model" effect may be at work (Haveman and Wolfe, forthcoming 1994). Independent of mother's work time, there is recent evidence that the amount of parental time spent nurturing or monitoring children also has a payoff in terms of their success.

Children also appear to be adversely affected by stressful events and circumstances in their childhood, such as changes in geographical location or family structure. The findings on the effects of family location moves are recent, but consistent with research by psychologists on the negative impacts of instability and stress on children (Haveman and Wolfe, forthcoming 1994). Changes in family structure—separations, divorces, remarriages—are also found to have persistently negative effects on children. The negative influence of remarriages is perhaps unexpected, but may reflect the limited access by the child to the stepparent's economic resources or time, or the stress associated with the introduction into the family of a competitor for the mother's attention.

These "stressful event" effects seem to hold even when the number of years that children spend in a family with but one adult (typically, the mother) is taken into account. The single-parent effect—often interpreted as the effect of divorce on children—is regularly found, in studies from several disciplinary perspectives, to have a deleterious effect on children. McLanahan and Booth (1989) offer a review of this research.

Next, consider public investments in children. The dollar value of school resources per child does not seem to have much of a value-added effect on cognitive achievements, though some recent evidence suggests a positive correlation with the number of years of schooling (and, hence, earnings). There are suggestions in the research literature that the small measured effects on cognitive achievements are attributable to the allocation of resources within schools. This conjecture is supported by recent, more disaggregated studies of school performance that have found positive effects from increments of certain school inputs, such as teacher skills, parental involvement, small class sizes, and the socioeconomic composition of the student body.

Early childhood education programs, such as the Head Start program, appear to increase cognitive test scores while children are enrolled in them; the duration of the impact is strongly debated. Claims made in policy discussions regarding the benefits of enriched day-care programs cry out for more reliable evidence.

The quality of the neighborhood in which children grow up, as measured by factors like the incidence of single mothers, high school dropouts, and crime, and hence the characteristics of their peers, appears to affect children's attainment, apart from other factors. Again, however, the measures of neighborhood quality may be standing for some family and school characteristics that are not otherwise measured. Access to community services, like family-planning services, seems to reduce destructive behaviors such as the propensity of teens to choose a nonmarital birth.[15]

Finally, children and youths themselves tend to respond in expected ways to the opportunities and constraints they face. For example, the existence of employment opportunities in the community seems to reduce the probability that a teen girl will give birth out of wedlock.

These findings are clues to the sorts of social and parental investments that might yield increased children's attainments. While many of them appear robust over several studies, their quantitative impacts are quite uncertain. For example, we know little regarding the pattern of marginal returns to individual interventions. Some of these interventions may yield effects on children that are realized only after a long lag, and the length and structure of the lags are unknown. In some cases, individual interventions may be unproductive if undertaken alone, but have a very large impact if implemented in concert with a constellation of other interventions. We know little about such synergies and interdependencies.

Perhaps most seriously, while some results exist regarding the effectiveness of proposals now attracting substantial attention among policymakers, the reliability of these findings is open to question. Program strategies for reducing drug usage among youths, or for improving the safety of neighborhoods, come immediately to mind. In some cases, we have studied the linkages between investments in children and their attainments, but have neglected important spillover effects. For example, while incarceration of lawbreakers designed to reduce crime in ghetto neighborhoods may contribute to that objective, there may be a negative effect of jailed fathers, mothers, or siblings on the children most directly affected, or perhaps a positive effect on other children in the neighborhood less affected by crime.

In sum, our knowledge of the full impact of both public sector and parental investments on children's attainments is more broad than deep. Moreover, the full economic costs associated with securing either public or family increases in children's investments are often murky. For example, apart from its effects on neighborhood crime or drug usage, what would be the value of the forgone labor of, say, a program which trained and placed 100,000 released military personnel as monitors and counselors in inner-city neighborhoods? Or of a reallocation of education expenditures designed to increase the test scores in the nation's poorest schools by 10 percent? Or of a specified reduction in the detrimental effects of a variety of family-based stressful circumstances or events?

## A PROPOSED COURSE OF ACTION
## FOR INVESTING IN CHILDREN

Based on the existing evidence, what would be some responsible approaches for policy to follow? While this question is fraught with pitfalls, the billions of dollars of public resources that have been spent on studies of this issue would seem to require some answer by the research community. Some general approaches would seem to have basis in the research findings that are now available. Sawhill (1992) also discusses the policy implications of research on children's success.

First, increases in years of school completed—apart from any fundamental change in the education process—seem to have potential for improving the success of, at least, the next generation of children. Efforts to reduce high school dropout rates and to increase post secondary training and schooling would appear to be among the more justifiable interventions.

Second, substituting earned income for welfare income through both workfare mandates and work subsidization (through, say, expansion of the earned income tax credit) could increase the incomes of families and alter expectations regarding how income should be obtained. Evidence suggests that both the income and role-model effects of work-related subsidies could improve children's attainments; other evidence suggests that well-designed workfare programs meet a benefit-cost test (Gueron and Pauly 1991).

Third, to increase the nonwelfare financial resources available to mother-only families, policies designed to increase child support collections from noncustodial parents, including a universal child support program, should be considered (Garfinkel 1992).

Fourth, in the absence of any direct public means of reducing the family-based stressful events that appear to strongly prejudice children's attainments, increased resources for improving the effectiveness of counseling and adjustment programs would appear justified.

Fifth, since there is little evidence that children who grow up with mothers who work have lower levels of success and attainments than those whose mothers stay at home (indeed, the opposite effect seems to predominate), policy should not discourage, but perhaps encourage, opportunities for women to work outside the home.

Sixth, altering the functioning of the low-skilled segment of the labor market through both supply- and demand-side subsidization would appear worthy of large-scale testing. Options would include marginal employment subsidies favoring low-skilled hiring offered to firms and a wage rate subsidy for accepting employment at market wages below some target rate (Haveman 1988).

Seventh, providing health care coverage to children regardless of their family's income would decrease the incidence or severity of preventable diseases among children, encourage parent's labor force participation, and increase labor mobility.

Finally, because of the multiple and interconnected problems which impede successful child and youth development in central city ghettos—lack of jobs, rampant crime and drug use, substandard housing, nonfunctioning schools, and the absence of role models—experimenting with multipronged intervention programs would be desirable (Aaron 1992). Only in this way can we learn about the potential synergistic effects of interventions that, taken one at a time, appear to have only minimal benefits.

# NOTES

The authors thank Henry Aaron, Sheldon Danziger, Victor Fuchs, Alan Krueger, Robert Plotnick, Gary Sandefur, Isabel Sawhill, Joseph Stiglitz, and Timothy Taylor for helpful comments.

1. Some recent committees, commissions, task forces, and study groups that have reported on the status of children include: *The Unfinished Agenda: A New Vision for Child Development and Education* (Committee for Economic Development 1991); *U.S. Children and Their Families: Current Conditions and Recent Trends* (U.S. Congress, House of Representatives, Select Committee on Children, Youth, and Families 1989); *Who Cares for America's Children? Child Care Policy for the 1990's* (Hayes et al., [National Academy of Science] 1990); *Risking the Future: Adolescent Sexuality, Pregnancy, and Childbearing* (Hayes, ed. 1987); *The Forgotten Half: Pathways to Success for America's Youth and Young Families* and *The Forgotten Half: Non-College Youth in America* (William T. Grant Foundation Commission on Work, Family and Citizenship 1988); *Turning Points: Preparing American Youth for the 21st Century* (Carnegie Council on Adolescent Development 1989); *S.O.S. America! A Children's Defense Budget* (Children's Defense 1990); *Putting Children First: A Progressive Family Policy for the 1990s* (Kamarck and Galston, [Progressive Policy Institute] 1991); *Troubling Trends: The Health of America's Next Generation* (National Commission to Prevent Infant Mortality, 1990); *Schools That Work: Educating Disadvantaged Children* (U.S. Department of Education 1988); *A Commitment to Change* (National Commission on Child Welfare and Family Preservation [American Public Welfare Association] 1991); *The Aspen Institute Quarterly*, Special Issue on Children and Families (Aspen Institute 1993).

2. These data are from a time-diary study by John Robinson, a sociologist from the University of Maryland, cited in Mattox (1991). Mattox also cites a 1990 *Los Angeles Times* poll which reported that over 55 percent of fathers and mothers feel guilty about spending too little time with their children.

3. The *1991 Green Book* (U.S. House of Representatives 1991) provides a comparison of federal programs targeted on children in 1978 and 1987. In constant dollars, the value of all programs decreased by 4 percent (from $50.7 to $48.9 billion). This includes a decrease in income programs to 10 percent (from $20.6 to $18.6 billion) and an increase in nutrition programs of 11 percent (from $13.1 to $14.5 billion), an increase in health programs of 10 percent (from $3.4 to $3.75 billion), a decrease in educational programs of 8 percent (from $7.6 to $7 billion), and a 44 percent drop in training and employment programs (from $3.0 to $1.65 billion). (See Table 3, Appendix L.) This decrease occurred during a period in which pretax and pretransfer incomes of families with children were declining on average—and poverty rates were increasing. The declining impact of public income support programs in removing children from poverty is reviewed in Danziger (1990).

4. Danziger and Gottschalk (1986) explore the changes in income available to families with children, and conclude that the increase in children's poverty rates is due to the increased incidence of female-headed families, the increased incidence of low earnings among male family heads, and the decline after 1973 in the real value of per family cash transfers.

5. The poverty rate for Hispanic children was 38.4 percent in 1990, more than twice that of white children, but below that of African-American children. Note, however, that adjusting for food stamps and housing benefits reduces these poverty rates. Duncan and

Rodgers (1991) calculate that the poverty rate for African American children in 1986 would decline from 43.1 to about 37 percent if these two adjustments were made.

6. The poverty definition in this study is a line equal to 40 percent of median income; the U.S. line has amounted to 41 percent of median income in recent years. The line is adjusted for family size.

7. The possibility that immigration could provide the new workers to support future productivity growth would blunt this self-interested concern with our own children.

8. See Kotlikoff (1992) for estimates of the net burden on today's and tomorrow's children because of the demographic structure of the population and the intergenerational commitments that have been made through public fiscal measures.

9. While our production function for quality of children is sequential, in some cases the relationship among the primary input-suppliers to the process may be iterative. For example, decisions of parents may "induce" government to intervene on behalf of children: to provide vaccinations if parents have not, or to offer after-school programs if parents fail to provide such care. This framework also abstracts from the effects of children on family decisions (Browning 1992).

10. Coleman (1988) emphasizes that both society (government) and families can create a structure of support, trust, expectations, and nurture based on the character of social relations—social capital—that contributes to children's attainments apart from more explicit and measurable inputs such as school expenditures, neighborhood police patrols, parental economic resources, or parental human capital. In this view, not only are the resources devoted to a school relevant inputs but also the supportive character of teachers and students in the school; not only the time parents spend with children, but what they do with that time. This perspective has clear implications for empirical sutdies of the determinants of children's success.

11. The discussion in this and the following section draws from an insightful paper by Fuchs (1990).

12. To the extent that investments in children by governments and parents are substitutes, there may be a further argument for directing public investments toward children in low-income families. If public investment in certain services for children—for example, music training—simply substitutes for similar parental investments in high-income families, but such parental investments are seriously budget-constrained in poor families, there is a presumption that such public investments should be concentrated on children from low-income families.

13. It should be noted that parental schooling may capture unmeasured characteristics of parents: motivation, intelligence, values. As a result, empirical estimates of the relationship of parental education and children's attainment may be biased upward.

14. This overall finding cannot be generalized across racial groups, and some studies fail to reveal such a relationship.

15. For example, see Corman, Joyce, and Grossman (1987) on the importance of community resources in decreasing infant mortality rates, and Lundberg and Plotnick (1990) on their importance in the nonmarital birth decisions of teens.

## REFERENCES

Aaron, Henry. "Designing a Social Policy Strategy." Washington, D.C.: The Brookings Institution, mimeo (1992).

Aspen Institute. *The Aspen Institute Quarterly 5,* Special Issue on Children and Families (Winter 1993): 1.

Bianchi, Suzanne. "America's Children: Mixed Prospects." *Population Bulletin 45*:1 (June 1990): 1–42.

Browning, Martin. "Children and Household Economic Behavior." *Journal of Economic Literature, 30*:3 (September 1992): 1434–1475.

Carnegie Council on Adolescent Development. *Turning Points: Preparing American Youth for the 21st Century.* New York: Carnegie Corporation (1989).

Case, Anne, and Lawrence Katz. "The Company You Keep: The Effects of Family and Neighborhood on Disadvantaged Youths." Cambridge: National Bureau of Economic Research, Working Paper No. 3075 (1991).

Casey Foundation, Annie, E. *Kids Count Data Book.* Washington, D.C.: Center for the Study of Social Policy (1992).

Children's Defense Fund. *S.O.S. America! A Children's Defense Budget.* Washington, D.C.: Children's Defense Fund (1990).

Coleman, James S. "Social Capital in the Creation of Human Capital." *American Journal of Sociology 94* (1988) Supplement S95–S120.

Committee for Economic Development. *The Unfinished Agenda: A New Vision for Child Development and Education.* New York: Committee for Economic Development (1991).

Corman, Hope, Theodore Joyce, and Michael Grossman, "Birth Outcome Production Function in the United States." *Journal of Human Resources 22*:3 (Summer 1987): 339–360.

Danziger, Sheldon. "Anti-Poverty Policies and Child Poverty." *Social Work Research and Abstracts 26*:4 (1990): 17–24.

Danziger, Sheldon, and Peter Gottschalk. "How Have Families with Children Been Faring?" Institute for Research on Poverty, Discussion Paper 801-886, University of Wisconsin-Madison (1986).

Duncan, Greg, and Willard Rogers. "Has Children's Poverty Become More Persistent?" *American Sociological Review 56* (1991): 538–550.

Fuchs, Victor. "Are Americans Underinvesting in Children?" in Blankenhorn, D., S. Bayme, and H. B. Elshtain, eds., *Rebuilding the Nest,* Milwaukee: Family Service America (1990), 53–70.

Fuchs, Victor, and Diane Reklis. "America's Children: Economic Perspectives and Policy Options." *Science 255* (January 3, 1992): 41–46.

Garfinkel, Irwin. *Assuring Child Support: An Extension of Social Security.* New York: Russell Sage Foundation (1992).

Gueron, Judith M., and Edward Pauly. *From Welfare to Work.* New York: Russell Sage Foundation (1991).

Hamburg, David. *Today's Children: Creating a Future for a Generation in Crisis.* New York: Times Books, Random House (1992).

Haveman, Robert. *Starting Even: An Equal Opportunity Program to Combat the Nation's New Poverty.* New York: Simon and Schuster (1988).

Haveman, Robert, and Barbara Wolfe. "Schooling and Economic Well-Being: The Role of Nonmarket Effects." *Journal of Human Resources 19*:3 (Summer 1984): 377–407.

———. *Succeeding Generations: On the Effects of Investments in Children.* New York: Russell Sage Foundation (forthcoming 1994).

Hayes, C. D., ed. *Risking the Future: Adolescent Sexuality, Pregnancy, and Childbearing.* Washington, D.C.: National Academy Press (1987).

Hayes, C. D., J. L. Palmer, and M. J. Zaslow, eds. *Who Cares for America's Children? Child Care Policy for the 1990's.* Washington, D.C.: National Academy Press (1990).

Kamarck, E. C., and W. A. Galston, eds. *Putting Children First: A Progressive Family Policy for the 1990s,* Washington, D.C.: Progressive Policy Institute (1991).

Kotlikoff, Laurence J. *Generational Accounting: Knowing Who Pays, and When, for What We Spend.* New York: The Free Press (1992).

Lampman, Robert, and Timothy Smeeding. "Interfamily Transfers as Alternatives to Government Transfers to Persons." *Review of Income and Wealth 29*:1 (March 1983): 45–66.

Levy, Frank, and Richard Michel. *The Economic Future of American Families.* Washington, D.C.: Urban Institute Press (1991).

Long, Larry. *Migration and Residential Mobility in the United States.* New York: Russell Sage Foundation (1988).

Lundberg, Shelley, and Robert Plotnick. "Effects of State Welfare, Abortion, and Family Planning Policies on Premarital Childbearing among White Adolescents." *Family Planning Perspectives 22*:6 (1990): 246–251.

Mattox, Jr., William. "The Parent Trap: So Many Bills, So Little Time." *Policy Review* (Winter 1991): 6–13.

Mayer, Susan. "How Much Does a High School's Racial and Economic Mix Affect Graduation Rates and Teenage Fertility Rates?" in C. Jencks, and P. Peterson, eds., *The Urban Underclass,* Washington, D.C.: The Brookings Institution (1991): 321–341.

McLanahan, Sara, and Karen Booth. "Mother-Only Families: Problems, Prospects and Politics." *Journal of Marriage and the Family 51*:3 (August 1989): 557–580.

National Center for Health Statistics. *Health United States 1990.* Hyattsville: Public Health Service (1991).

National Commission on Child Welfare and Family Preservation. *A Commitment to Change.* Washington, D.C.: American Public Welfare Association (1991).

National Commission on Children. *Beyond Rhetoric: A New American Agenda for Children and Families.* Washington, D.C.: U.S. Government Printing Office (1991).

National Commission to Prevent Infant Mortality. *Troubling Trends: The Health of America's Next Generation,* Washington, D.C.: National Commission to Prevent Infant Mortality (1990).

Sawhill, Isabel V. "Young Children and Families," in H. J. Aaron and C. L. Schultz, eds., *Setting Domestic Priorities: What Can Government Do?* Washington, D.C.: The Brookings Institution (1992), 147–184.

Smeeding, Timothy. "Why the U.S. Antipoverty System Doesn't Work Very Well." *Challenge 35*:1 (January/February 1992): 30–35.

*Statistical Abstract of the United States, 1991.* Washington, D.C.: U.S. Department of Commerce, Bureau of the Census (1991).

U.S. Congress, House of Representatives, Select Committee on Children, Youth, and Families. *U.S. Children and Their Families: Current Conditions and Recent Trends, 1989.* Washington, D.C.: Government Printing Office (1989).

U.S. Department of Education. *Schools That Work: Educating Disadvantaged Children.* Washington, D.C.: U.S. Government Printing Office (1988).

U.S. House of Representatives, Committee on Ways and Means. *1991 Green Book.* Washington, D.C.: U.S. Government Printing Office (1991).

———. *1992 Green Book.* Washington, D.C.: U.S. Government Printing Office (1992).

William T. Grant Foundation Commission on Work, Family and Citizenship. *The Forgotten Half: Non-College Youth in America.* Washington, D.C.: William T. Grant Foundation (1988).

———. *The Forgotten Half: Pathways to Success for America's Youth and Young Families.* Washington, D.C.: William T. Grant Foundation (1988).

Wolfe, Barbara. "The Deteriorating Economic Circumstances of Children" in Emily Hoffman, ed., *Essays on the Economics of Discrimination.* Kalamazoo: Upjohn Institute (1991): 43–66.

———. "External Benefits of Education." *International Encyclopedia of Education,* forthcoming.

## S E L E C T I O N   1 6

Alan B. Krueger and William G. Bowen

# Income-Contingent College Loans

In the early 1970s, Yale University experimented with an innovative student loan program: students would repay loans by contributing a fixed percentage of their after-college income for a predetermined number of years. Such "income-contingent loans" for financing higher education were proposed by Nobel laureate Milton Friedman in 1955 (see Suggested Further Readings). More recent plans (such as those put forth during the Clinton Administration) would create a national trust fund from which individuals could borrow, and would also let borrowers choose whether to repay the loans from future earnings or through community service.

In this selection, Alan Krueger and William Bowen consider the necessary elements for a workable national income-contingent loan plan for students. Income-contingent loans (ICLs) have a major advantage over conventional loans: ICLs can provide protection against high debt burdens for low income earners, while at the same time, increase the amount of national funding available to finance college education. However, implementation problems exist. The most severe one involves "adverse selection"—a problem of asymmetric information typically found in insurance or loan markets where buyers have more information than sellers (and the information is crucial to determining appropriate insurance rates or default probabilities). Krueger and Bowen find that realistic repayment rates may be considerably higher than is often assumed, and could lead to distortions in labor supply decisions.

Krueger, Alan B., and William G. Bowen. "Income-Contingent College Loans." *Journal of Economic Perspectives 7* (Summer 1993): 193–201. This selection is an abridged version of the original article.

**Alan B. Krueger** is Professor of Economics at Princeton University. **William G. Bowen** is President of the Andrew W. Mellon Foundation.

**Questions to Guide the Reading**

1. What economic justifications are given to support government intervention in the student loan market?
2. Why does the incentive structure of a typical ICL program create an adverse selection problem?
3. What alternative definitions of income have been proposed for the purposes of an ICL plan? What specific difficulties might be caused if adjusted gross income (AGI) were used?
4. What impact does the inclusion of adverse selection have on Krueger and Bowen's estimates of the required payback tax rate? How might the effects of adverse selection be mitigated?
5. What complications might be introduced by a "community service" option?

# INTRODUCTION

A central part of President Clinton's higher education program was an "income-contingent loan" (ICL) plan. Congress would establish a national trust fund from which students could borrow money to finance the cost of attending "college" (short-hand for any institution of higher learning); students would repay these loans by contributing a fixed proportion of their subsequent income for a specified number of years. The Clinton-Gore (1992) plan also gave borrowers the option of repaying their loans "through community service as teachers, law enforcement officers, health-care workers, or peer counselors." Two ICL bills were proposed in Congress, one by Senator Bill Bradley and one coauthored by Congressman Thomas Petri and Senator Paul Simon.[1]

The motivation behind these proposals is easy to understand, given the evident problems faced by families, educational institutions, and the government in financing the costs of college attendance. Moreover, the conventional loan component of student aid programs has increased sharply over the last ten years, existing guaranteed loan programs have become very large (with estimated outlays of nearly $14 billion in 1991–1992), default rates and administrative costs are high, and subsidies are substantial (The College Board 1992; Reischauer 1991).

Some commonly cited economic rationales for government intervention in the student loan market are that investment in human capital is risky, nondiversifiable, and not easily collateralized. The private market, therefore, will fail to provide sufficient capital for student loans. Other justifications for government loan programs include possible positive externalities from education, both economic and noneconomic (including concern for equal access to education and other social policy considerations). These are valid reasons for government involvement, but they do not of course imply that an income-contingent loan program is the optimal response.

## DISCOUNTING FUTURE EARNINGS

One key issue is whether proposed income-contingent loan plans will be self-financing; that is, will the value of loan repayments cover the initial cost of providing the loan? Because loan repayments are based on future earnings, the present value of payments depends critically on the timing and level of future earnings.

Figure 1 displays average annual earnings by age and gender for college and high school educated workers in 1990. The figure illustrates several important features of earnings profiles.[2] First, college graduates earn substantially more than high school graduates. Second, earnings rise with age, especially for male college graduates. Third, the average male worker earns substantially more than the average female worker, at each level of education and age. Fourth, earnings rise less with age for female college graduates than for male college graduates.

**Figure 1** Age-Earnings Profiles, 1990. High School (HS) and College Graduates.

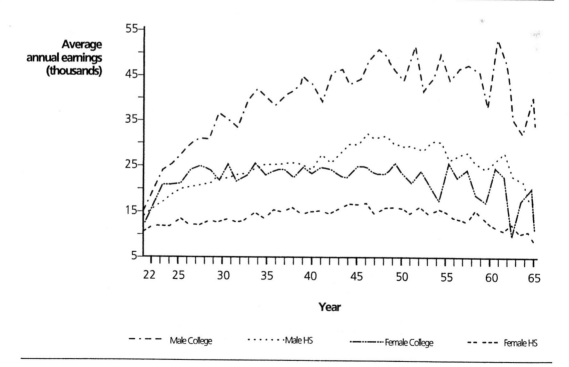

These findings have significant implications for income-contingent loans. In particular, it is necessary to take account of the upward-sloping nature of the age-earnings profile to evaluate the revenue collected by an ICL plan. In addition, if the plan is the same for men and women, the program will be far more attractive for women, on average, since women tend to have lower earnings than men.

## ADVERSE SELECTION

The typical income-contingent loan program requires borrowers to pay a proportion of their income to repay their loan. Students who expect to earn a high income have less incentive to participate in the program because their payments may exceed the cost of a conventional loan. On the other hand, students who expect to have low income will consider ICL plans very generous. Thus, if students can accurately forecast their future earnings, the incentive structure of the typical ICL plan creates a classic adverse selection problem, with lower participation by high-income students and higher participation by low-income students.[3]

For adverse selection to be a problem, a substantial number of potential borrowers must be able to forecast their future income accurately. We have investigated how well students can forecast their future income by analyzing data from the National Longitudinal Study of the High School Class of 1972. Specifically, we used characteristics of high school students to explain their (log) weekly earnings in 1986.[4] By 1986, most students in the sample would have been out of school for around 10 years, so their earnings would be approximately in the middle of the payback period. Because our purpose is to explain as much earnings variability as possible, we included an embarrassingly long list of explanatory variables: a total of 108 explanatory variables, including sets of variables measuring family income, parents' education, parents' occupation, students' expected occupation, race, sex, age, religion, and achievement test scores. Perhaps surprisingly, an ordinary least squares regression with these variables accounted for only one-quarter of the variability in earnings.

We also examined whether individuals who have *high* earnings might be able to predict that in advance, since participation of high-salary workers in an income-contingent loan plan is of particular concern. Specifically, we estimated a logit equation in which the dependent variable equaled 1 if the individual's salary is in the top 10 percent of the cohort, and 0 otherwise. We used the same explanatory variables described above. The logit estimates indicate that fully 40 percent of workers who are in the top 10 percent of the earnings distribution have fitted values in the top 10 percent of the cohort.

Since earnings in 1986 are a noisy measure of income due to transitory earnings fluctuations and reporting errors, and since there are many characteristics of students (like motivation) that we do not observe but of which students are aware, our estimates of students' ability to predict their earnings are an understatement. On the other hand, our estimates may overstate students' ability to predict their earnings because high school students may not be as adept at finding the "best fitting line" as an econometrics software package is. We conclude from this analysis that students have some ability to forecast their subsequent earnings, especially those who ultimately have high earnings, which suggests adverse selection will be a problem.

## DEFINING INCOME

How should income be defined for purposes of an income-contingent loan plan? Friedman (1955) initially proposed that the relevant income for ICLs is earnings *in excess* of the level of earnings the individual would have received without the extra investment in human capital. This income measure is attractive because it provides individuals the proper incentives for optimal investment in education. In practice, however, it is unmanageable to calculate base earnings on a case-by-case basis.[5]

Proposed income-contingent loan programs typically use adjusted gross income (AGI) as the income measure. Because these proposed plans often have the Internal Revenue Service collect loan payments, AGI is a convenient income measure. Although the IRS has been reluctant to be a collection agency for nontax programs in the past, a great advantage of using the IRS is that the default rate will be low.[6]

Nevertheless, the AGI concept creates several problems. First, taxing total AGI reduces the incentive to invest in higher education, because AGI includes more than the return on the investment in higher education. Second, AGI creates difficult issues for married couples and joint filers. The ICL would impose a severe marriage tax if working spouses who had not participated in the ICL have their income taxed to repay the loan taken out by the other spouse. An alternative to AGI is personal wage and salary earnings, which avoids the joint filing and nonlabor income issues, and could be collected by the IRS or by an addition to the Social Security payroll tax.

## ILLUSTRATIVE CALCULATIONS

Although proposed legislation is complex, in essence the typical income-contingent loan proposal involves three parameters: the amount of the loan, the period over which income is "taxed," and the rate at which income is taxed. Proposed bills typically require students to pay a proportion of income for 10 to 25 years. Our benchmark is to calculate what proportion of income must be collected, given various assumptions on interest rates, students' future income, and who participates in the loan program, to pay for each $10,000 loan increment. In other words, at what level must the tax rate be set for an ICL plan to be self-financing? We present several estimates that might be useful to those who wish to evaluate various proposals.

To simplify the calculations, assume the loan is made to a student at age 18, the student attends college for four years, and that the student begins payments at age 22. Wage and salary earnings, not AGI, is the measure of income used in our calculations. We begin by assuming a real interest rate of 3 percent and that real earnings will be constant in the future. The latter assumption is more or less consistent with the experience of the last decade. Given these assumptions, one can calculate the tax rate required to collect a present value of $10,000 in revenue from an income-contingent loan.

We first assume there is no adverse selection, so a random sample of individuals is presumed to participate in the program. Specifically, we assume the average participant will have earnings equal to the average person who acquires at least one year of education after high school.[7] An estimate of participants' average annual earnings at each age was made from the March 1991 Current Population Survey.

Table 1 presents estimates of the required tax rate for an income-contingent loan plan to be self-financing, under three alternative payback periods. For a 10-year plan, for example, the participant must incur an additional 7.1 percent earnings tax for the loan to break even. Moreover, the results indicate that a much higher proportion of income is required of women than of men for the plan to be self-financing. If a single rate is set for men and women, men will highly subsidize women.

Naturally, our calculations are sensitive to the interest rate and the rate of wage growth. If we discount revenues at a 4 percent interest rate (instead of 3 percent), the self-financing tax rate would increase to 7.8 percent for a 10-year plan

**Table 1** Required Percentage of Earnings Per $10,000 Loan for Worker with Average Earnings or with 25th Percentile Earnings

|  | Payback Period | Average Earnings | 25th Percentile Earnings |
|---|---|---|---|
| A: Men and Women with Some Post-High School Education |  |  |  |
|  | 10 years | 7.1 | 17.7 |
|  | 20 years | 3.5 | 10.1 |
|  | 25 years | 2.8 | 8.4 |
| B: Men with Some Post-High School Education |  |  |  |
|  | 10 years | 6.0 | 11.5 |
|  | 20 years | 2.8 | 5.3 |
|  | 25 years | 2.3 | 4.3 |
| C: Women with Some Post-High School Education |  |  |  |
|  | 10 years | 16.1 | 59.1 |
|  | 20 years | 6.3 | 32.1 |
|  | 25 years | 5.0 | 27.4 |

*Note:* Estimates assume a 3 percent real interest rate and constant real wages. See text for further details.

and 3.3 percent for a 25-year plan. On the other hand, if real annual earnings grow by 1 percent per year, the required tax rate would fall to 6.5 percent for 10 years and 2.4 percent for 25 years (assuming a 3 percent interest rate).

Because the interest rates are compounded over many years, small deviations in the proportion of income charged can have a substantial effect on the subsidy required by an income-contingent loan plan. For example, it is common for proposed plans to specify a 2.5 percent income tax rate for 25 years for each $10,000 loan increment. Even ignoring adverse selection problems, after 25 years a 2.5 percent tax would return only $8,780 in principal (present value). According to the estimates in Table 1, a tax rate of 2.8 percent is required for the ICL plan to be self-financing.

In 1989–1990 the average tuition and room and board for four years at four-year colleges was $28,976, and the corresponding figure was $49,392 at private colleges (National Center for Education Statistics 1991). If we suppose a participant borrows $25,000, the required supplementary tax rate to repay the loan would be 17.75 percent over 10 years or 7 percent over 25 years, again assuming no adverse selection.

Because of adverse selection, the average program participant will probably have lower earnings than the average eligible person in the population. As a rough approximation, we have made additional calculations assuming that the average participant will have earnings equal to that of a worker occupying the 25th percentile of the earnings distribution. These calculations indicate that the proportion of income required for a $10,000 loan would almost double for men, and increase five-fold for women, as compared to the situation where there is no adverse selection. Clearly, adverse selection could have a great effect on the viability of an ICL program

One way to mitigate the effects of adverse selection is to set a minimum and a maximum payment for participants.[8] Alternatively, in Senator Bradley's plan, an interest rate is established when the loan is made.[9] Individuals are required to pay 7 percent of their income for 25 years toward repaying the loan. However, individuals are freed of future payments as soon as the principal and interest are repaid. If the loan and interest have not been fully repaid at the end of 25 years, the individual is forgiven the remaining obligation. In essence, Senator Bradley's plan is an attractive hybrid, combining an income-contingent loan program and a conventional loan program.

The "community service" feature of the Clinton-Gore income-contingent loan plan complicates this picture, but is difficult to evaluate. Since students can choose to perform community service or to pay a higher income tax, rational decision-making presumably would lead participants to be no worse off than if there were no option for community service. However, allowing students to elect community service would reduce repayments, thereby requiring either a larger government subsidy or a higher tax rate. Whether the additional community service encouraged by the plan is worth the foregone revenue (or higher tax rate) is a separate question.

## CONCLUSIONS

1.  A well-conceived income-contingent loan plan would increase the capital available to students for financing their education, and it would do so in a way that simultaneously provides "insurance" against the debt-burden consequences of ending up as a low earner and schedules repayments to fit the individual's changing ability to pay. These are the principal advantages relative to conventional loans. Reductions in defaults and in administrative costs would be welcome, but these advantages stem from IRS administration of the plan, and presumably could also be obtained while using conventional guaranteed loans.

2.  Unless a conscious decision is made to provide a large subsidy to participants, repayment rates must be set at realistic levels from the beginning. Our calculations suggest that these rates could be appreciably higher than often supposed.

3.  Much depends on whether a plan contains provisions that would minimize adverse selection. Senator Bradley's variant is an improvement over simpler plans in the way in which it caps repayments, thereby providing another kind of "insurance"—protection against being penalized for earning too much. To the extent that other government-sponsored borrowing options continue to exist, the risk of considerable adverse selection is increased.

4.  Any income-contingent loan plan is likely to distort labor supply incentives by raising marginal tax rates, perhaps substantially.

5.  A workable ICL plan would almost certainly involve government subsidies to minimize adverse selection problems. Therefore, thought must be given to the effects of an income-contingent loan plan on the willingness of parents to continue to finance the education of children. For traditional college-age students attending undergraduate programs, we believe there is much to be said for continuing to expect families to invest in education consistent with their ability to do so. Thus, we believe that an ICL plan is particularly suitable for "independent" students—and especially those enrolling in college at a later age. Eligibility criteria should be considered carefully.

## NOTES

1.  Income-contingent loans have been proposed numerous times in the past. Indeed, the idea dates back at least to Milton Friedman (1955). See Karl Shell et al. (1968) for a detailed analysis of the Educational Opportunity Bank, which was proposed in 1967. Martin Feldstein (1988) offers a critical evaluation of Michael Dukakis' ICL program. Yale University experimented briefly with its own version of an ICL program in the early 1970s.

2.  The data underlying the figure were calculated by the authors from the March 1991 Current Population Survey. A high school graduate is defined as having exactly 12 years of completed education, and a college graduate as having exactly 16 years of completed

education. These estimates are based on workers with positive earnings in 1990, but later calculations include (as they must) zero earners as well. Although the earnings profilesin Figure 1 are based on a cross section of workers, and thus may confound cohort and age effects, longitudinal estimates of earnings profiles have similar features.

3. See Michael Rothschild and Joseph Stiglitz (1976) for an analysis of the insurance industry in the presence of adverse selection.

4. We are grateful to Michael Boozer for providing assistance on this analysis. To limit the sample to potential participants in an income-contingent loan program, we restricted the sample to individuals who graduated from high school and attended at least one year of school after high school.

5. An alternative scheme would be to tax earnings in excess of the average earnings of high school graduates, which would make the financing more progressive.

6. Of course, one may be concerned that using the IRS as a collection agency may adversely affect income tax filings.

7. The sample underlying these estimates includes individuals who had zero earnings during the year.

8. The Petri-Simon income-contingent loan plan has exactly the opposite effect of a minimum payment—if individuals' income falls below a certain level, their repayments are set to zero.

9. The interest rate could be set above the conventional student loan interest rate so individuals pay a premium for "insurance" provided by the ICL.

# REFERENCES

Clinton, Bill, and Al Gore. *Putting People First.* New York: Times Books (1992).

The College Board. *Trends in Student Aid: 1982 to 1992* (September 1992).

Feldstein, Martin. "Dukakis Tuition Plan Flunks Its Tax Test." *The Wall Street Journal* (September 1988): 36.

Friedman, Milton. "The Role of Government in Education," in Robert A. Solo, ed., *Economics and Public Interest.* New Brunswick: Rutgers University Press (1955); reprinted in *Capitalism and Freedom* by Milton Friedman, Chicago: University of Chicago Press (1982): 85-107.

National Center for Education Statistics. *Digest of Education Statistics, 1991.* Washington, D.C.: U.S. Department of Education, Table 291.

Rothschild, Michael, and Joseph Stiglitz. "Equilibrium in Competitive Insurance Markets: An Essay on the Economics of Imperfect Information." *Quarterly Journal of Economics* 90:4 (November 1976): 630-649.

Reischauer, Robert D. "Statement Before the Committee on Labor and Human Resources, United States Senate," mimeo, Congressional Budget Office (October 29, 1991).

Shell, Karl, et al. "The Educational Opportunity Bank: An Economic Analysis of a Contingent Repayment Loan Program for Higher Education." *National Tax Journal 21* (March 1968): 2–45.

# S E L E C T I O N  1 7

Barry Bosworth

# Putting Social Security to Work: How to Restore the Balance between Generations

Social Security is the most expensive U.S. federal government program, surpassing national defense for the first time in 1993. One of every five dollars spent by the federal government goes to provide social security pensions. The "pay-as-we-go" system requires today's workers to finance today's retirees, i.e., current payroll taxes fund current social security retirement benefits. In the next century, as the proportion of the population eligible for such pensions rises, the amount spent on social security is predicted to grow rapidly—if tomorrow's workers are able to finance tomorrow's retirees. Understandably, the financial solvency of the Social Security System is an issue of great concern to all generations. The prospect of increasing payroll taxes and diminishing benefits makes young voters particularly uneasy. Not surprisingly, politicians seem to tread very carefully when Social Security reform becomes part of public policy debate.

In this selection, Barry Bosworth considers the financial outlook for the Social Security System and proposals for reform. Because a real increase in national saving is needed, Social Security surpluses should not be allowed to finance other federal programs. Also, Bosworth argues that a serious commitment to surpluses (a partially funded system) could help reduce the System's looming shortfall and avoid potentially destructive "battles between generations." Bosworth proposes allowing the fund to invest a portion of its assets in private securities—thus, helping the Social Security System meet retiree benefit payments more through investment income and less through taxes. However,

.................................................................................................
Bosworth, Barry. "Putting Social Security to Work: How to Restore the Balance between Generations." *The Brookings Review 13* (Fall 1995): 36–39.

**Barry Bosworth** is Senior Fellow in the Economic Studies Program at The Brookings Institution.

Bosworth emphasizes that more aggressive investment policy alone cannot ensure long-term solvency for the Social Security System: both a payroll tax increase and a higher rate of return are essential.

### Questions to Guide the Reading

1. How is the bulge in the baby-boom generation actually delaying an inevitable spiral in social security costs?
2. Why was "pay-as-you-go" financing for Social Security attractive in the decades after World War II?
3. What were the perceived disadvantages of the alternative "funded" system, and why does a funded system seem more attractive now? How might a funded Social Security System "help reverse the deteriorating rate of wealth accumulation" in the United States?
4. Why would instituting a "fully funded" system be unfair to today's workers? What compromise is available?
5. According to Bosworth, Social Security surpluses must raise national saving. What suggestions does Bosworth provide to help guarantee this? What are the advantages and disadvantages of a move toward privatization of Social Security?
6. Why would shifting Social Security investments from government to private securities strengthen the system? Why would such a shift not, in itself, increase national income?

How secure is social security? More and more Americans are beginning to wonder. Many younger Americans, in particular, profess to believe that they will never collect any benefits. And the 1994 trustee report on the Social Security system would seen to bear out those fears. Spending on Social Security benefits is likely to exceed payroll tax revenues by 2013. Although interest income on the system's built-up assets will cover the shortfall for another six years, the fund will have to draw on its assets beginning in 2020. And those assets will be gone by 2030.

Most suggestions for reform call for reducing future benefits or increasing tax rates. And, indeed, the system could be brought back into actuarial balance with a combination of tax increases or benefit reductions of a bit more than 2 percent of taxable payroll. But that balance would be only temporary. To *maintain* the system's solvency, taxes would have to be increased, or benefits cut, between one-half and 1 percent every 10 years. By the time today's young workers retire, the payroll tax rate needed to finance planned benefits will have roughly doubled from today's 12.4 percent.

The prospect of ever-increasing taxes is unacceptable to most Americans. And the prospect of ever-diminishing benefits is no better. Social Security benefits are already low by world standards. Workers earning half the average wage received benefits that put a couple at the poverty threshold, a single person below it.

But there is another option for policymakers. Instead of trying to mediate battles between generations over the distribution of future income, they could use the Social Security system itself to expand the pool of income from which benefits would be paid.

## THE CURRENT OUTLOOK

Projecting Social Security costs several decades into the future is a highly uncertain exercise. But planning for the retirement of youthful Americans requires a long-term view. What is a certain is that demographic factors (lower birth rates, immigration, mortality), as well as retirement patterns (lengthening retirement as Americans live longer and retire earlier), are driving Social Security costs up far faster than planners anticipated when, in 1983, they approved payroll tax increases and other measures that placed the system (they thought) in actuarial balance over 75 years.

The rising costs are often blamed on the looming retirement of the baby-boom generation, beginning in 2010. But the bulge of the baby-boom generation is actually delaying an inevitable upward spiral of costs. In part, costs are rising because life expectancies are growing while the retirement age remains unchanged. In 1940 a man aged 65 could expect to live 13 more years; today, he could expect to live 17 years. By 2030, the average worker will be retired about half as long as he works.

Growth in the number of retirees will actually slow, from an annual rate of 2.2 percent during 1970–1995 to 1.8 percent between now and 2030 to only 0.4 percent between 2030 and 2070. What is really pushing up costs is the slowing of growth in the working-age population—from 1.6 percent a year during 1970–1995 to 0.45 percent in 1995– 2030 to 0.1 percent in 2030–2070. The "dependency rate," the ratio of beneficiaries to covered workers, will continue to rise even after the baby-boomers are gone.

And the dependency rate is the key to the problem. For, like most industrial countries, the United States runs a "pay-as-you-go" social insurance program, with each generation paying for the benefits of retirees, in return for the same support during its own retirement. Pay-as-you-go depends on rapid growth in the tax base—more workers at steadily rising wage rates. Without that rapid growth, higher costs must lead to higher tax rates.

In the decades after World War II, pay-as-you-go was attractive, not only for the first generation of retirees, who paid little in return for their benefits, but for subsequent generations too. With expectations of a rapidly expanding workforce and continued wage growth, each generation could look forward to an ever-larger pool of wages from which to finance its own benefits. In effect, workers would earn a real rate of return of 3–4 percent even if tax rates were held constant. The alternative—a "funded" system—would have invested each worker's contributions to Social Security in government securities, with income designated to pay benefits at retirement. At the time the annual return on such an investment was thought to be only about 1 percent. Furthermore, a funded system would have delayed for many years the effort to reduce poverty among the elderly.

Today's picture is far different. Employment growth is projected to fall. Real wages, stagnant for the past two decades, leave little obvious reason for optimism. For young workers, faced with paying for the retirement of the baby-boom generation, the projected rates of return of a pay-as-you-go system are not very attractive. The success of private pension funds, which invest in bonds and equities and earn a real rate of return of 4–5 percent, has made a funded system look far better.

## THE BENEFITS OF INCREASED SAVING

Discussion of the merits of funded and pay-as-you-go systems has been skewed by the use of the government bond rate to measure the return of a funded system. That rate is the right one to use to evaluate the financial condition of a Social Security fund that invests only in government securities, but it greatly underestimates the benefits of a funded system. True, the Social Security fund itself earns only about 2 percent on its investments in government securities; but in buying those securities, it frees up resources that pass through capital markets to be used by others willing to make riskier investments with higher returns. In particular, if the saving of Social Security (the excess of its tax and interest income above its outlays) adds to national saving, it can finance an increase in the nation's stock of physical capital. And increased capital can benefit future generations in two ways—both by the income earned on it and by the higher wages paid workers whose productivity it enhances. Historically, the inflation-adjusted rate of return on capital invested in the U.S. economy has averaged 6–7 percent, and the large stock of capital per worker has helped keep American incomes higher than those of other countries.

Today, Americans are trying to compete in a rapidly expanding global economy with rates of national saving and capital accumulation equivalent to those of the poorest economies. The nation now must rely on foreign funds to finance about half its net investment in new capital. A funded social insurance system, financed in a manner similar to private pension funds, could help reverse the deteriorating rate of wealth accumulation—but *only* if it translates into increased saving and investment, not a substitute source of financing other government programs.

## FUNDING SOCIAL SECURITY

Replacing today's pay-as-you-go system with a *fully* funded system would not be fair to today's workers, who would have to pay twice for retirement—once for their own retirement through a fully funded system and once for the retirement of the currently and near-retired through the old pay-as-you-go system.

What might be possible instead would be a compromise—advance funding only of the added costs projected for the future. Today's older workers have a particularly good deal because they support a smaller population of retirees for a shorter period of retirement than will be the case when they retire. The burden on future workers will be far heavier, but it could be much eased if today's workers were to agree to meet the *added* cost of their own retirement by increasing their own saving. The result would be a larger future stock of capital, a more productive, higher-wage workforce, and a bigger pool of income from which to pay future benefits. In addition, a large portion of those benefits would be paid out of the interest earned on the Social Security funds, rather than relying solely on the contributions of future workers.

In fact, Congress has already begun to move away from a pay-as-you-go system. When it adopted the amendments to Social Security in 1977 and 1983, it tried to stabilize the system by means of some advance funding and a buildup of reserves. Had Congress kept the commitment to actuarial balance it made then— and had it ensured that the reserve thus built up would be set aside to add to national saving—the advance funding it approved could have increased aggregate income more than enough to compensate future generations for the added taxes they would pay. But Congress did not keep that commitment, and the reserve buildup, and thus the pool of potential saving, has been smaller than expected. Nor has the advance funding added to national saving.

## THE EFFECT ON NATIONAL SAVING

A partial funding of Social Security can offset the increased burden on future workers *only if* the resulting surpluses increase national saving. Between the end of World War II and 1980, U.S. saving averaged about 8 percent of national income. A private-sector saving rate of 8.5–9 percent was offset by a public sector *dis*saving, or deficit, of 0.5–1 percent. Then, during the 1980s, national saving fell precipitously. Over the past five years, national saving has been only about 2 percent—6 percent for the private sector less a roughly 4 percent dissaving in the public sector.

Although Social Security is officially an off-budget agency, nearly all public discussion of the federal budget focuses on the total, inclusive of Social Security. Any surplus in the Social Security fund thus lessens the budget deficit and leads Congress to tolerate larger deficits in other programs. Though it comes as a surprise to most Americans, who view Social Security as a retirement program, surpluses in the Social Security fund now finance other federal programs.

If Social Security is to raise national saving, the retirement accounts and the government's operating budget must be kept separate. Most states already exclude their retirement programs from their budgets, and nearly all fund those liabilities to some degree. A few state constitutions expressly forbid increased borrowing as an offset to pension reserves, but for the most part states have been able to resist that temptation without such constitutional props. And while the annual state retirement fund surpluses have steadily grown, to more than 17 percent of GDP, the nonretirement budget balance of the states has hovered around zero with no clear tendency to rise or fall. That most states can make rational decisions about their pension programs suggests that the federal government is at least capable of doing so.

Congress could, for example, make Social Security an independent agency and remove its revenues and outlays from budget documents and the annual congressional budget process. Congress and the administration could exercise oversight responsibilities, while the Board of Trustees maintains the fund's actuarial balance and manages the investments. As a minimum, the change would ensure accurate public discussion of the federal budget deficit and would approximate the states' treatment of their retirement accounts.

As a more drastic step, Congress could shift the funded portion of the system to the private sector. It could allow workers to move some of their contributions to a privately managed defined-contribution program that permits them to choose among several funds with strong regulatory supervision by the Social Security system. Creating so many small accounts, however, would be administratively costly. And most workers may not have the knowledge or inclination to manage their own accounts. Such a step would also invite complex and divisive debates about how to reduce the promised benefits of workers who opt out of the system in a way that could maintain the current commitment of adequate retirement income to the lowest-wage workers.

## MANAGING THE SOCIAL SECURITY FUND

Allowing the Social Security fund to invest a portion of its assets in private securities would be a less radical approach but could accomplish two important goals. First, it would strengthen the distinction between the retirement accounts and the rest of the budget. Reserves are now invested in Treasury securities that earn the average yield on government bonds in excess of four years. Bonds are purchased directly from the Treasury. Brokerage fees are thus saved, but the transactions are treated as pure government bookkeeping with no real consequences. (The average real rate of return, about 5 percent over the past 10 years, is expected to fall to 2 percent, more nearly the average historical yield.) If Social Security did not purchase the bonds through an internal transfer, the Treasury would have to borrow more in the private market, highlighting the costs of deficit finance and further breaking the link between the retirement accounts and the federal budget.

Second, the higher rate of return from a more diversified investment strategy would allow the funds to capture more of the benefits that their saving actually contributes to the nation. It would make more evident to the public the benefits of saving in preparation for retirement rather than relying on pay-as-you-go.

Shifting to investments in private securities would not, in itself, increase national income. Imagine, for example, that the Social Security system sold $1 trillion of Treasury securities, replacing them with private securities with a higher yield, presumably reflecting the higher degree of risk. But the private sector would hold the Treasury securities now held by Social Security. A simple swap of public and private debt between the trust fund and private markets would not appreciably affect total saving, the stock of physical capital, or output. The trust fund would report a higher rate of return, while the private sector would hold the lower-yield Treasury securities once held by the fund. But the yields on private and public securities would remain essentially unchanged—particularly in the context of a huge global capital market.

Investing funds in private securities would, however, strengthen the Social Security system by allowing it to meet retiree benefit payments more through interest and less through taxes. That would soften the discontent of younger workers who feel that they are paying all the added costs of retirement for current and soon-to-be retirees.

## HOW MUCH?

The Social Security trust fund now faces an actuarial deficit of about 2 percent of taxable payroll. If that deficit were closed through higher taxes, the fund would build up its reserve until about 2023, but it would begin to run deficits again around 2055, and the reserve would be gone in about 75 years (Figure 1).

**Figure 1**  Assets of the Social Security Trust Funds

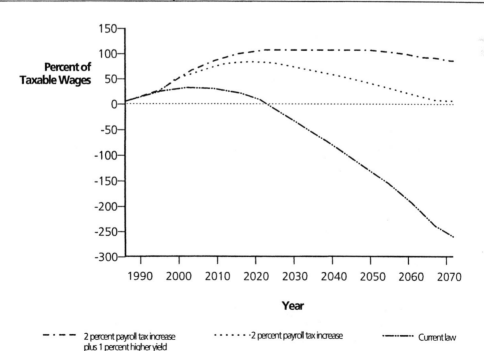

Legend:
- — · — — 2 percent payroll tax increase plus 1 percent higher yield
- · · · · · · 2 percent payroll tax increase
- —·—·—· Current law

Increasing the payroll tax *and* changing the investment policy to allow the fund to earn just 1 percent more than the rate on government securities would provide a far more durable solution. It would stabilize the reserve at a level roughly equal to the taxable wage base—and represent an increase in the long-run capital stock from about the present 3 times GDP to about 3.5. Figure 1 itself actually greatly understates the longer-term gains because it does not incorporate the increase in national income and tax receipts that would follow from expanded saving and investment. The increase in national saving would represent 3-4 percent of national income at its peak, and about 1–2 percent in the long run. While the saving of the fund tends to decline somewhat as a share of taxable wage near the end of the forecast period, it nevertheless remains strong.

To repeat. By itself, a payroll tax increase cannot ensure long-term solvency for Social Security. And by itself, a more aggressive investment policy can do little. It does not help to aim to earn a higher rate of return if there is no saving to begin with. Both a tax increase and the higher rate of return are essential. Together, they could stabilize the Social Security fund and eliminate the need for further tax increases or cuts in benefits for the foreseeable future.

# S E L E C T I O N   1 8

Martin Feldstein

# The Economics of Health and Health Care: What Have We Learned? What Have I Learned?

In recent years, Americans have become increasingly concerned about their health and the costs of health care. As a nation we do not enjoy the best health status in the world, even though we have the world's highest per capital health expenditures. Government has played a significant role in financing health care for the poor and elderly since Medicaid and Medicare were created in 1965 (as amendments to the Social Security Act). Based on 1992 policies, the Congressional Budget Office has forecast that the share of the federal budget devoted to health care will be 25 percent in the year 2000, up from 7.1 percent in 1970 and 14.1 percent in 1991 (see Suggested Further Readings). Not surprisingly, proposals for health care reform are both numerous and common topics for debate.

Any successful reform of health care in the United States must take into account the unique features affecting the operation of this market. In this selection, Martin Feldstein examines what he and the economics profession have learned about health care during the last three decades. Compared to other nations, spending per capita and quality of service are high, as is the degree of consumer choice. Feldstein focuses on the causes of the rapid rise in costs, and on the challenge to make our health care system more efficient.

Feldstein, Martin. "The Economics of Health and Health Care: What Have We Learned? What Have I Learned?" *American Economic Review* 85 (May 1995): 28–31.

**Martin Feldstein** is Research Associate and President of the National Bureau of Economic Research and Professor of Economics at Harvard University.

### Questions to Guide the Reading

1. According to Feldstein, what changes have occurred in the "style" of health care in the United States? Why have these changes led to cost increases?
2. Besides subsidizing health insurance as a tax-exempt fringe benefit, what other ways could the government "use its scarce dollars to improve the health of target populations"?
3. What role does the uncertainty of health technology play in the high cost of care?
4. How do individual differences in attitudes toward risk affect the demand for health insurance?
5. If writing today, what primary change in focus would Feldstein make in his doctoral thesis?

Victor Fuchs and I have been talking with each about the economics of health and health care since we met nearly 30 years ago. I was pleased therefore when he asked me to organize this session of his American Economic Association annual meeting but then rather dismayed by his suggestion that, as one of the papers in the session, I offer an overview of what I have learned about the subject during those 30 years.

As a profession, we have indeed learned a great deal in these three decades. The rapid growth of health care spending that doubled its GDP share to one-seventh of the economy and the 1966 Medicare and Medicaid programs that have made federal health care spending exceed the combined total of all domestic discretionary federal outlays have attracted a generation of researchers to a subject that had been largely neglected by economists before the 1960s.[1] Econometric research and conceptual developments have been mutually reinforcing, helped by advances in econometric theory and by the government's creation of a rich array of detailed data. Although there remains substantial controversy about many issues in this field (as in most other parts of economics), there is no doubt that anyone setting out to teach a course on health economics or to do policy analysis in this area would start from a very different base today than 30 years ago.

## I. WHAT HAVE WE LEARNED?

It is of course impossible in the short space of these remarks to summarize the key findings of dozens of researchers during a 30 year period. I will limit myself to noting the issues on which I think significant improvements in our understanding have occurred.[2] I will then return to Victor's question and comment briefly on the change in my own thinking over these years.

Much of the research was motivated by the rising cost of care, particularly of hospital care. The microeconomic studies of hospital production and costs that helped us to understand some of the reasons that hospitals differ in their costs are now attracting attention among hospital officials who are being forced by new competitive pressures to seek greater management efficiencies. But these cross-sectional cost differences are small relative to the dramatic increases over time that have raised the average cost per patient day from $22 in 1960 to more than $700 in the early 1990s, an increase of more than 600 percent even after adjusting for the general rise in consumer prices.

Thirty years ago it was not uncommon to hear such cost increases explained in terms of inelastic supplies or monopolistic rents. Now we understand that the rising cost of hospital care has been driven by changes in the technology or style or quality of care, characterized by more inputs per patient day rather than by higher prices for given inputs.

A key research challenge has therefore been to understand why the style of health care has become so much more expensive. Although some of the explanation may lie in the exogenous path of basic medical science, it seems more likely that the technologies that are chosen, and indeed even those that are developed, reflect the impact of insurance on the willingness of patients to pay for expensive care. With private and government insurance now paying more than 90 percent of hospital bills—so that patients pay only about 10 percent of the cost of hospital care at the time of illness—it is not surprising that patients and their doctors seek ever more sophisticated treatments.

The central role of insurance in the finance of health care has also made insurance a central subject for researchers. Developments during the 1960s in the general theory of risk-bearing were soon followed by applications to health insurance, with a number of studies on the optimal design of health insurance. The analogy between optimal insurance and optimal taxation was also not lost on economists who saw the trade-off between redistribution and distortion in the theory of income taxation paralleled in the health insurance trade-off between protection against large expenses and distortion of the demand for medical care. The theory of optimal taxation could therefore help us to think about optimal insurance.

But insurance markets differ from taxation in a fundamental way: insurance is voluntary. Individuals and groups choose the kind of insurance that they will buy, and private companies choose the insurance that they are willing to sell. Opportunities for adverse selection can in theory destroy the insurance market, although in practice the combination of the large individual gains from insurance, the use of large group purchases, and the tax subsidy has supported a thriving, perhaps too thriving, market for insurance. The role of the implicit income tax subsidy in expanding the demand for health insurance has been an important issue both in research and in discussions of policy reform.

The growth of the Medicare and Medicaid programs has led to significant research on the effects of those programs on the utilization of care by the target populations and on health-care outcomes. Some recent analyses have emphasized that government programs to finance or provide health care displace private efforts, much as social security displaces private saving.

Now that health care has become the most expensive fringe benefit, with employer-financed health insurance costing several thousand dollars per employee, researchers have begun important studies of the impact of health-insurance benefits on the labor market, including the effects on wages, on job mobility, and on retirement.

A somewhat separate group of researchers, building on the theory and econometrics of consumer demand, have been studying consumers' demand for products and services that affect individual health. Studies of smoking, drinking, and the use of narcotics show that such behavior is amenable to economic analysis and sensitive to prices. Other studies have looked at the demand for prenatal care and for other services that can be expected to improve health. We can anticipate future studies that help us to understand the relative importance of tastes, information, and opportunity costs on such lifestyle choices as diet and exercise that affect health. With such information, it would be possible to ask whether the government could use its scarce dollars to improve the health of target populations more effectively through specific health education or even through subsidies to particular kinds of food or activities rather than through subsidies to health insurance or health care.

An exciting new generation of researchers has begun studying the economics of health and health care. They will build on what has been done in the past but they will also criticize it and go beyond it. It is to them that we can look to learn more about such important issues as why 35 million people remain uninsured, how the recent innovations in health-care delivery and finance are affecting the efficiency of the health-care system, and why different individuals make the specific lifestyle choices that affect their health outcomes.

## II. WHAT HAVE I LEARNED?

Reviewing what we as a profession have learned about the economics of health and health care over the past three decades has led me to think about the fundamental way in which my own views have changed since Victor Fuchs and I first discussed these issues. I can summarize the change most succinctly by saying that back then I gave too little weight to two very important things: the uncertainty of health care technology and the heterogeneity of individual preferences.

As a graduate student beginning to think about health care, I thought in terms of nonstochastic production function in which a multidimensional product ("health") was the output produced by inputs of various health services. Selecting an optimal allocation of resources therefore required only specifying this technology and evaluating the costs and benefits. Benefit evaluation involved issues of discounting future consumption and of valuing the nonpecuniary aspects of good health. Once these issues were resolved, the government would know how much to spend on health care, what health care to produce, and how to produce it.

In retrospect, I now recognize the fundamental importance of the *uncertainty* of health technology that my early view ignored. Although doctors know a great deal, uncertainty is ubiquitous in health care. That uncertainty drives the cost of care and creates a very different problem for public policy than the nonstochastic technology that I imagined 30 years ago.

Much of the spending on medical care is designed to reduce uncertainty: tests aimed at resolving uncertain diagnoses, procedures aimed at reducing the risks to hospital patients, and treatments aimed at improving patient's uncertain long-term prospects. Decisions about how much to spend on health care and what to buy are therefore generally about spending to reduce uncertainty. Even after diagnosis and treatment, uncertainty remains. In health care, we pay not only for the improved expected value of outcomes, but also for reductions in the uncertainty that remains with us throughout our lives. (If all this seems very abstract, think about the diagnosis and treatment of someone who has had a heart attack or cancer of the breast or prostate. Treating such a patient is really an exercise in the management of uncertainty that lasts the rest of the patient's life.)

More generally, health care includes not only professional medical treatments, but also the treatment that we give to ourselves in the lifestyles that we choose. Here too the link between actions and outcomes is uncertain. Even when health science tells us how particular kinds of behavior influence the probabilities of health outcomes in certain populations groups, for each of us the link between behavior and outcomes is stochastic. Moreover, even the aggregate probabilistic relation between behavior and outcomes is itself often very uncertain.

As individuals, we differ substantially in our attitudes about uncertainty and in our willingness to take health risks. We see this clearly in the choice of lifestyles that affect health prospects. We have all heard about the advantages of not smoking, of getting regular exercise, of eating certain types of low-fat diets, of wearing seat belts, of avoiding various risky activities, and of a variety of other low-cost ways in which we can improve the probability distribution of our future health and survival. Some of us take more of this advice than others, not because of ignorance or inability to pay, but because of differences in our willingness to trade off health risks for the various pleasures and conveniences of daily life, and because of differences in our willingness to make sacrifices in order to reduce the uncertainty with which we live from day to day or to reduce the probability that we might later regret not having acted in certain ways.

Although there was no place in my early thinking about the optimal provision of health care for the heterogeneity of tastes and of attitudes toward risk, I now regard that heterogeneity as central. Two individuals with the same income and the same insurance may choose very different medical care just as they choose different lifestyles because of differences in their attitudes toward health risks. As long as medical care involves a balancing of the various risks, patients who are medically identical are likely to have different desired treatments.

Differences in attitudes toward financial risks that manifest themselves in different portfolio preferences also affect the kind of insurance that individuals choose and would do so even more if they could select their own coverage and were not influenced by tax subsidies. And differences among individuals in attitudes about risk and about regret and about the psychological costs of making health-care decisions will influence individuals' choices in the continuum between traditional fee-for-service arrangements and fully prepaid group-practice HMOs.

Tastes are not compartmentalized. Just as individuals make different choices about lifestyles that affect their health, individuals with the same incomes may also differ substantially in the amount that they want to spend to reduce the risks associated with illness. As a result, they will want to have different kinds of insurance and, given any schedule of deductibles and copayments, will choose to spend different amounts.

All of this now seems natural and appropriate to me. Instead of ignoring uncertainty and seeking a technological solution to health-care spending, the appropriate starting point for government policy is a recognition of the uncertainty of technology and of the heterogeneity of individual attitudes about health-care risks.

## III. A LESSON FROM ENGLAND

Victor Fuchs and I first met in England. I had gone there after graduating from college to study the National Health Service as a possible model of the rational management of health care. I soon discovered that there was no "rational management" and that there was no research aimed at achieving an optimal use of health-care resources. Instead, the allocation of resources perpetuated historic patterns of care and historic class differences in health outcomes. I wrote a doctoral thesis trying to show how economic analysis and econometric methods could be used to reduce hospital costs and to provide government planners with information on how changes in the availability of services would affect the patterns of care.

What was missing in that dissertation, and in the British health-care system itself, was any way for the total level of health-care spending and its allocation among different kinds of services to respond to the preferences of the British people. Since all health care was free, there was always excess demand and rationing by queues or local capacity. The British system lacked a mechanism by which individuals could indicate their different tolerances for risks and their willingness to sacrifice other goods and services in order to obtain more health care. In short, it lacked a price mechanism.

As I look back over the past three decades, I realize that the most fundamental challenge to any health-care system is to make the pattern of care responsive to individual preferences without imposing excessive financial burdens on individuals or denying necessary care because of an inability to pay. The task for future research on the economics of health and health care is therefore to increase the information that can help us as a nation to meet that challenge.

# NOTES

1. There was of course an earlier literature dating back to the seventeenth century economist William Petty and including such other distinguished contributors as Simon Kuznets and Milton Friedman who did a 1945 study of physicians' incomes. Several other economists, including Rashi Fein and Herbert Klarman, had written extensively about health policy issues. Nevertheless, it has only been in the past three decades that health economics has attracted a substantial number of economists using modern tools of economic analysis.
2. Rather than slight the contribution of any particular researcher in this necessarily brief review, I will not provide any references to particular individuals or particular studies.

# SELECTION 19

James M. Buchanan

# The Bridge between Tax and Expenditure in the Fiscal Decision Process

Governments spend. Governments tax. From an individual perspective, these government activities are commonly viewed as separate—a split which causes problems for public choices that do not exist for private market choices. When government expenditure and revenue decisions are made separately, the resulting choices are apt to be inefficient as well as more uncertain. The debate over more government versus less government, while often explained by differing ideologies, may be attributed more to the lack of a "bridge" between these two basic government activities. For instance, an individual may vote in favor of a new public service program. Yet if the institutional setting isolates the financing decision, this same person may vote against new tax legislation to raise the necessary funds to support the program.

In this selection, Nobel laureate James Buchanan explores the implications of isolating spending and taxing choices. How do the institutional organizations of government affect the ways in which individuals respond to fiscal or public choices? What are the policy implications of splitting the expenditure and revenue decisions? What are the benefits of integrating or "bridging" the different types of choices? What different methods can be used to link these choices? Buchanan has argued that public finance must incorporate what he refers to as "fiscal psychology"—in this case, how the voter perceives the fiscal connection (or bridge) between the spending and the taxing sides of the fiscal process.*

Reprinted from *Public Finance in Democratic Process: Fiscal Institutions and Individual Choice,* by James M. Buchanan. Copyright ©1987 by the University of North Carolina Press. Used by permission of the publisher.

**James M. Buchanan** is Harris University Distinguished Professor of Economics and General Director of The Center for Study of Public Choice at George Mason University. He received a Nobel Prize in Economics in 1986.

*Editors' note:* "Fiscal psychology" is discussed in "Public Finance and Public Choice" by James Buchanan (selection 10 of this volume). In *Public Finance in Democratic Process* (1967, p. 185), from which this reading is excerpted, Buchanan credits Professor Günter Schmölders of the University of Cologne, Germany with coining the term "fiscal psychology."

**Questions to Guide the Reading**

1. Why is it absurd to consider private market choice as two separate decisions?
2. In public choice, what is the "necessary real bridge" between the tax decision and the spending decision?
3. How do the institutional characteristics of political decision-making processes tend to cause a "gap between approved spending and approved taxes"? What is the nature of the deficit implied by this gap?
4. What does Buchanan mean when he states that "rational behavior need not reflect full information"? How might this influence the individual's choice of a preferred level of spending? Of a preferred level of taxes?
5. Historically, how have political institutions attempted to address the potential conflict between spending and taxing decisions?
6. What public policy implications might Buchanan's thesis have for the merits and structure of balanced-budget requirements?

# INTRODUCTION

To the individual taxes are the "prices," the "costs," of the goods and services that the government supplies for his benefit. This conception of the fiscal structure is central to this study, and our procedure has compared the individual's behavior in fiscal choice with that in market or private choice. In the market, the individual selects a preferred quantity at a given price per unit, or, alternatively, he allocates a specific outlay to the purchase of a specific good, which, at the given price, results in a determinate quantity being taken. The selection of a preferred physical quantity automatically determines total outlay, or, conversely, the selection of an amount to be spent automatically determines the physical quantity. In either case, the purchaser is assumed to make only *one* decision. It is absurd to think of his making two separate decisions, one as to the physical quantity of the good to be purchased and the other as to the total outlay to be made. Given the availability of a good or service at an invariant market price, these two decisions reduce to one and the same.

Institutionally, it is possible for the individual to make market purchases in either of these two ways. I may drive my automobile to a gasoline pump and order five gallons, or I may, alternatively, order two dollars' worth. In the first instance, my outlay is residually determined by my decision on quantity; in the second, the quantity is determined by outlay. If I am faced with some uncertainty as to price, there need be no unique relationship between quantity and outlay at the moment of my decision. If I order five gallons of gasoline, knowing only that the price falls somewhere between thirty and fifty cents per gallon, total outlay may be anything from $1.50 to $2.50. Or, conversely, if I order $2.00 worth in this situation, I may get anything from four to six and two-thirds gallons.

From our earlier discussion, it is evident that individual fiscal choice resembles the price-uncertainty case here. In that discussion, however, we continue to assume that fiscal choice remained analogous to market choice in that only one decision is taken, with residual determination of either tax rate or total outlay (public goods quantity). Given a specific tax institution, other than that with invariant tax-price, some residual uncertainty must remain in any individual fiscal choice. The group decision may, for example, be stated in terms of a specified expenditure on public education. This will imply, in its turn, a certain rate of tax on local real property, and this rate is assumed to be residually set by the decision on spending. Or, conversely, the specifically chosen mill rate of tax for education implies a certain revenue total available for spending.

Casual observation of actual fiscal processes, at almost any governmental level, suggests that the "bridge" between the tax decision and the spending decision is not nearly so direct as these earlier models have implied. In many instances, the fiscal process appears to embody a double choice; one a choice or decision as to the size of the public spending program and the other a choice or decision on the rates of taxation. Clearly, the institutional setting that allows this apparent splitting of the fiscal decision into two parts can influence the outcome of decision.

## THE NECESSARY REAL BRIDGE

In some *real* sense, there can be only one independent fiscal decision. To simplify discussion, let us again limit consideration to a single public good or service. Observed ex post, there is a specific quantity of this good or service provided. In the collective decision to supply this quantity, economic resources were committed and these were drawn from other potential employments. What these resources could have produced in alternative uses is the *real* cost of the public goods or services supplied, and this cost is directly related to the number of units. To the extent that resources are employed in the private sector, any decision to spend publicly directly implies "taxation" that is at least equal in magnitude to the money value of the spending, the measure of the value of alternative product.

The notion that the real cost of public goods or services arises from the decision to commit resources, to spend publicly, is not inconsistent with the earlier point that this decision can be made in two ways. A specific tax of X percent can be levied with the proceeds dedicated to the provision of the public good or service. Or, Y dollars can be appropriated for spending on the good or service, with a tax sufficient to raise this amount being levied, which may be X percent. But the logical extension of the real-cost principle suggests that taxation, in and of itself, cannot impose a real cost since there is no implication that the revenues collected are to be spent in providing public services.[1] If distributional considerations are entirely left out of account, this extension is a valid one. Within the framework of this study, the real-value approach tends to be misleading, however, because attention here is focused on the choice behavior of the individual and not on aggregative results. To the individual taxpayer, or potential taxpayer, who ultimately makes fiscal choices, the imposition of any tax implies that he will, personally, undergo some cost. He will be largely unconcerned with the macroeconomic real variables of the economist. To the extent that a tax is imposed, and the funds are not spent, the only institutional means of eliminating distributional elements entirely would be that of refunding the tax revenues, in the same manner as these are received. In this case, however, no decision to tax could really be said to have been made.

Despite the necessary real bridge that must be present for the whole community between any decision to spend publicly and to impose taxes, the individual as a participant in political choice may not consider proposals to spend funds and proposals to raise taxes as directly interdependent. The degree to which he senses the underlying real interdependence will depend partially upon the institutions through which fiscal choices are made.

## THE SETTING FOR INDIVIDUAL CHOICE

We have noted that the individual who participates in collective choice can never be placed in a position that is fully analogous to that which he faces in market choice. He cannot confront a one-to-one correspondence between his own choice behavior and a result or outcome. At best, in collective choice the individual can know only that, if a sufficient number of his fellows agree with him, an outcome will follow from a choice. It will be useful to specify carefully that institutional setting under which the individual's position with respect to the two-sidedness of the fiscal decision most closely resembles his position in the marketplace. If the group is faced with a decision as to the quantity of a single public good to be provided from the proceeds of a single specified tax, the individual participant should not find it impossible to construct for himself a personalized real bridge between the benefits side and the cost side of the account. In this limiting case, the residual nature of one or the other sides will be recognized. This is not, of course, to suggest that the community outcome will tend to be "efficient," even in such limiting cases. This will depend in part on the nature of the collective decision rules and upon the relative generality of taxes and of benefits among members of the community.[2]

Let us now examine the more familiar setting in which proposals are made to spend public funds *without* specifying the tax sources that are to provide these funds, and, conversely, that in which proposals are made to levy taxes *without* specifying the public-goods and services mix that is to be financed with revenues raised. How will the individual behave in this situation? Consider first his reaction to a proposal to spend on a public good that promises to yield him some measurable benefits. If he wholly divorces the spending decision from the tax decision, he will "vote for" an expansion in outlay to the point at which his own marginal evaluation of the good or service becomes zero. Such a conceptual separation of the two sides of the account will tend to be present insofar as the individual considers both the amount and the distribution of taxes to be settled in a decision process wholly apart from the spending decision. Choice behavior of this sort is not so foreign to real-world experience as it might initially appear. There is much discussion, both in the popular press and in quasi-intellectual circles, concerning "needs" for various public services. Almost universally, these "needs" are measured or estimated independently of costs. This "needs" approach to budgeting is based on precisely the model that is here discussed.[3]

At the same time that the individual "votes for," or otherwise supports, public spending programs without substantive regard for costs, the same individual, in yet another capacity, may refuse to support any new tax legislation. This half of the extreme independence model is less familiar to everyday experience, because most individuals are normally aware, at least to some vague extent, that they must accept taxes in order to secure the benefits of public goods. Nonetheless, if the individual treats the two decisions as wholly independent, one from the other, he will refuse to vote for any tax legislation.

A somewhat more realistic model is one in which some cost consciousness informs the expenditure decision, while some benefit consciousness informs the separate tax decision, but in which the two sides of the account are differently weighted. Empirical research might reveal isolated instances, but surely cases are few and far between where legislative assemblies have intentionally voted separately for a level of taxes that is more than sufficient to finance the level of spending separately chosen, debt amortization included. The direction of bias seems evident. The splitting of the fiscal decision into two parts tends to cause a "deficit" between approved spending rates and approved tax rates. Insofar as the expenditure decision fails to take into account the cost side, public services provided will tend to be extended beyond that level which fully informed consideration of alternatives would produce. Conversely, in so far as the tax decision fails to incorporate the benefit side, total revenues will fall short of the amount needed to finance that level of public services that an informed consideration of alternatives would provide. In other words, the gap between approved spending and approved taxes, in such a democratic decision model, will tend to "straddle" the unique tax-spending solution that an "efficient" fiscal decision might produce.

It is to be emphasized that the probable gap between approved spending and approved taxation that is discussed here emerges from the choices of a single individual in an institutional setting that splits fiscal choice into two parts. To this point, we have left out of account the interaction of separate individual decisions in producing a group or community outcome. Our central concern is with the individual calculus, and the gap suggested is between the individual's preferred level of spending, as this might conceptually be expressed in a voting choice, and his preferred level of taxation, as this might be similarly expressed. Does not the existence of such a gap, regardless of the institutions of choice, reflect irrational behavior on the part of the individual? If he chooses "rationally" should he not "cut through" the possible institutional maze, regardless of complications, and recognize the underlying real interdependence between the separate decisions? To answer these questions, it is necessary to recall the provisional definition of "rational behavior" suggested earlier. To the individual chooser, rational behavior need not reflect full information for the simple reason that the securing of information is a costly process. In any specific choice situation, there is some "optimal" investment in information-gathering which seldom, if ever, will result in perfection. The institutions through which choice must be made can evidently affect this level of optimal investment as well as the degree of perfection in results.

It is useful to look at the apparent splitting of the fiscal decision in this context. Suppose that the individual faces a choice as to his preferred level of spending on a single public good or service or on some designated package of services. He is aware, within limits, of the potential benefits that these goods and services will yield to him. He chooses, of course, under conditions of high uncertainty since he cannot know the outcome of the political process, but he probably can make reasonable accurate estimates for his own personalized share in the benefits from incremental changes in the level of public-goods supply. He will sense that these services must be financed, and he may be able to make some translation into tax-cost terms. But this step will clearly require more investment in information than the comparable estimate on the benefit side. The form of the decision process in effect partially solves his information problem on one side but not on the other. The issue is presented to him in public spending terms. He must make his own translation into tax-costs.

Contrast this situation with that where the same individual confronts a choice concerning the level of taxes to be imposed, without connection to spending levels. In the case, the calculus is reversed. The institution of decision itself partially assists the individual in computing tax-costs but wholly obscures public-goods benefits. It is surely plausible to expect that most individuals will behave differently in the two cases, and, as a result, the gap suggested above will tend to emerge. In the one case the individual is reasonably well informed as to benefits, in the other case as to costs.

## CLOSING THE GAP

To shift from an analysis of the individual decision calculus to that of the group requires that some consideration be given to the processing of individually expressed desires through a set of political decision rules. The effects discussed here are surely accentuated when it is recognized that each person in his spending decision will hope that the tax-costs will be shifted onto the other members of the group, and vice versa for taxing decisions. It is useful to leave this whole question of group decision-making until a later chapter, however, even though some reference to political outcomes seems necessary. To do this, we may simply assume that the individual that we are discussing is the "median" or "representative" man in the many-person community.

In the aggregate, the potential gap between approved levels of spending and approved levels of taxation must be closed. Throughout this chapter, we are assuming that there exists an over-all restriction of budget balance. And lest the discussion here appear overly abstract, it is worth noting that conflicts of the sort mentioned here are familiar occurrences in real-world fiscal systems. Newspapers carry stories of financial "crises" faced by states and local governments; school teachers do not get paid; road contracts do not get let. How are these conflicts, actual or potential, resolved, and how can some prediction as to the manner of resolution be made? There seems to be no general direction of effect that is predictable. In the face of a potential excess of spending over tax revenues, will taxes be increased to meet the deficit, or will spending be cut? The outcome will, in each instance, be determined by the stronger set of rules, dictated in part by constitutional provisions. It is the financial conflict that brings to the surface the necessary final interdependence between spending and tax decisions and makes some resolution of the contradiction essential. This will generate a reevaluation of both choices, and no general pattern of results can be predicted.

We know that political structures, as they operate, do incorporate institutions that tend to produce this apparent splitting of the fiscal decisions into the two parts. These same structures contain, however, other institutions that have been developed to resolve the potential conflict. Historically, legislative bodies, through which the preferences of individual citizens are most directly represented, have exercised more control over revenue or tax decisions than they have over expenditure decisions. In part this asymmetry has its origin in the development of democratic political institutions out of monarchial institutions. Representative bodies, parliaments, first achieved the power to restrict the tax-gathering privileges of the kings. Before taxes could be levied on the people, representative bodies were given the right to grant their approval. No consideration was given to the spending side of the account because public expenses were assumed to benefit primarily the royal court, at least in the early days of constitutional monarchy. Taxes were viewed as necessary charges on the people, but they were not really conceived as any part of an "exchange" process from which the people secured public benefits. It was out of this conception of the fiscal process that both the modern institutions and the modern theory of public finance developed.

The emerging of modern democratic states dramatically modified the setting for the fiscal process, but only recently has attention been paid to the necessity of revising age-old norms. As royal courts came to be replaced by executives, and monarchies by republics, taxes continued to be viewed as necessary to sustain the expenses of "government," with the burden of these taxes to be minimized to the maximum extent possible. Surprisingly little recognition has been given, even yet, to the idea that taxes must, in the final analysis, be considered as the "costs" of those public goods and services which provide benefits to the same people who pay taxes.

With the development of modern executive structures, the traditional asymmetry has remained, but, partly because of these structures, the decision conflict discussed above has been mitigated. The executive normally exercises greater control over the budget, over the expenditure plans, than it does over the revenue side of the account. Being somewhat less responsible to the desires of individual citizens than the legislature, in a compartmentalized, differentiated sense, the executive utilizes the expenditure budget as a means through which revenue projections and spending projections are reconciled. And in part it was the prevalence of just such conflicts as those discussed which provided the impetus for the development of modern budgetary institutions. These generalizations are relevant largely to the American political structure, and they are somewhat less applicable to genuine parliamentary systems.

## DO GOVERNMENTS ADJUST INCOME TO MEET SPENDING NEEDS?

It was concluded above that no general direction of adjustment could be predicted when the split-decision conflict arises in democratic political structures. This runs contrary to a time-honored notion in public finance. In some of the earlier works especially, the difference between the government account and the private account was emphasized in a manner that suggested one particular resolution of the conflict. "Whereas the individual or family tends to adjust its expenditures to meet its income, the government adjusts its income to meet its expenditure needs." If this "principle" has any general validity, there is a basic difference in the way in which the individual behaves in family and in public accounting structures. But does the false-analogy notion here have any claim to validity, especially in representative democracy, where, ultimately, all fiscal choices are made by the individual, directly or indirectly, and not by "government," as some entity wholly divorced from the citizens? The individual in "voting for" public outlays is "spending" in a manner that is analogous to his spending for private goods. His decision to cover this spending with tax revenues, to approve the levy of taxes on himself and others, is made in order to finance these "purchases" from the public sector. Ultimately, the income constraint applies here just as it does in private spending. What the individual does is to adjust his total spending, private and public, to his income, which itself is adjustable only within relatively narrow limits in the normal case. The traditional generalization concerning the relevance of the income constraint is restricting private spending and its irrelevance in restricting public spending is not applicable. There is no reason why tax revenues should necessarily be adjusted to meet approved patterns of public spending, as implied, rather than spending levels adjusted to meet approved levels of tax revenues. The direction of adjustment will surely depend on the particulars of each situation of conflict.

## CONCLUSION

The primary sources of pressure on democratic legislatures, those for reduced taxation on the one hand and for expanded public spending on the other, arise because of the differentiation among groups in the political community. This distributional aspect of fiscal choice has been deliberately neglected here. The purpose of this chapter is to suggest that, quite apart from the intergroup or distributional conflicts that may arise, the organization of the decision-making institutions themselves may be such that the interdependent fiscal accounts are treated as embodying two apparent choices, the results of which may conflict, even in an individual calculus. It is impossible to predict with accuracy the direction of effect that this institutional influence will impose on fiscal outcomes, or to measure its over-all importance. What can be said is that this apparent splitting of decision, insofar as it is present, tends to create greater uncertainty in fiscal choice than seems necessary. In a balanced-budget context, a decision to spend publicly implies a decision to tax, and a decision to tax implies a decision to spend. Only if the actual institutions of fiscal choice are organized in such a way that this basic truism is reflected in the alternatives confronting the individual participant can these uncertainties be minimized. Much of the modern criticism of the United States Congress is directed at its failure to allow simultaneous consideration of expenditure and tax decisions. Differences of opinion may, of course, arise concerning the most appropriate means of introducing the desired symmetry in the fiscal decision process, in repairing the bridge between taxes and spending. But greater rationality in choosing the mix between public and private goods, on the part of the individual citizen as reflected through the legislative processes, depends critically on some correction of inherited error, both intellectual and institutional.

## NOTES

1. This point has been stressed effectively by Earl Rolph. See *The Theory of Fiscal Economics* (Berkeley: University of California Press, 1954).
2. If both taxes and benefits are general throughout the community, simple majority decision rules will not distort the outcomes. However, if one side or the other should be differentially general, distortion is introduced. If benefits are specific to particular subgroups in the community, while taxes are general over the whole community, there will be a tendency to expand spending beyond "optimal" levels. The supporting analysis for this conclusion is developed in James M. Buchanan and Gordon Tullock, *The Calculus of Consent* (Ann Arbor: University of Michigan Press, 1962).
3. For effective criticism, see Charles J. Hitch and Ronald N. McKean, *The Economics of Defense in the Nuclear Age* (Cambridge: Harvard University Press, 1960), pp. 46–49.

**TAXATION**
**Topic of Interest:**
*Excess Burden of "Green" Taxes*

# S E L E C T I O N   2 0

Wallace E. Oates

# Green Taxes: Can We Protect the Environment and Improve the Tax System at the Same Time?

The issue of optimal pollution or "green" taxes lies at the intersection of two areas of public finance economics. In one area, public finance economics treats pollution taxes in the context of market failures and externalities. In the other area, a pollution tax is a revenue source, and as such, the focus becomes how much revenue is raised and who pays the tax as well as whether (and how) the tax changes behavior. Connecting these two areas of analysis is crucial to developing effective policy. A complete investigation of the ramifications of any proposed government policy should also include the potential impact on other related activities. The consequences of environmental and other regulatory activities in the real world are complex and far-reaching. Rigorous research and testing must be integral to the process; intuition can be a poor guide.

In this selection, Wallace Oates cautions against relying too heavily on what might be considered the wishful thinking of those who believe the revenues from green taxes can replace or reduce other types of taxation. Specifically, green taxes have been claimed to yield a "double dividend." The ability of the taxes to reduce pollution activities to efficient levels yields the first dividend. And a "revenue-recycling effect," whereby the tax revenues permit reductions in the levels of efficiency-distorting taxes (such as on labor income), yields the second dividend. But as Oates points out, recent research based on sophisticated computerized

Oates, Wallace E. "Green Taxes: Can We Protect the Environment and Improve the Tax System at the Same Time?" *Southern Economic Journal* 61 (April 1995): 915–922.

**Wallace E. Oates** is Professor of Economics at University of Maryland and Fellow at Resources for the Future.

general equilibrium (CGE) models casts serious doubt on the existence of the circumstances necessary to guarantee this double dividend. Intuition may have built a false linkage between the provision of environmental protection through penalty green taxes and the disposition of the resulting tax revenues.

### Questions to Guide the Reading

1. Under what circumstances would pollution taxes generate a "double dividend"?
2. Why do many CGE models find substantial additional distortions or excess burdens from green taxes?
3. Why does a tax on gasoline fail to provide the proper incentives to decrease automobile emissions?
4. How would a "Leviathan" determine green taxes? Why might the Leviathan be "either a friend or foe of the environment"?
5. What is wrong with the common practice of setting environmental taxes at levels to raise the required funding for certain environmental programs?
6. What are the possible advantages of including green taxes in a revenue-neutral tax package?

## I. INTRODUCTION

On a cursory inspection, public economics appears to provide a straightforward and compelling answer of YES to the question posed in the title to this paper. As economists have long argued, appropriately designed taxes can, in principle at least, efficiently restrain levels of polluting activities. And, in addition, such taxes will generate revenues so that we can reduce rates on other forms of taxation that distort the functioning of the economy. Green taxes, in short, promise a "double dividend": they can both reduce excessive levels of pollution and increase the efficiency of the overall tax system. At least, so several economists have argued recently (Oates 1993; Repetto et al. 1992).

But is this really so? With the growing recognition of the enormous revenue potential of certain environmental taxes (especially carbon taxes to address the problem of global warming), public economists have returned to this question with a new round of research efforts directed both to understanding the properties of pollution taxes *as revenue sources* and to estimating their revenue potential and the magnitude of their effects on the economy. And the newly emerging literature is producing some quite astonishing and very troubling findings.[1]

In this paper, I want to review this work and explore its implications. When viewed in relation to some other research, it appears to suggest that most forms of regulatory activity (at least those that increase the costs of the regulated activities) may have hitherto unappreciated costs of a stunning magnitude. What many of us would have taken to be "second-order side effects" of environmental and other regulatory policies can be of a magnitude that compromises to a significant extent their welfare-enhancing properties. Having reviewed this body of work, I wish also to explore some issues in the political economy of green taxes. It is helpful to begin by briefly putting the issue in historical perspective.

## II. SOME BACKGROUND

The early work on Pigouvian taxes or charges essentially ignored the revenue issue. The assumption, either explicit or implicit, was that the revenues would somehow be returned to the economy in lump-sum fashion so as not to cause any distortions in economic activity. The one qualification in this literature is that the revenues must not be used to compensate victims for the damages they suffer from polluting activities, for such compensation would compromise the incentives for efficient levels of defensive activities by victims. But, for our purposes here, the essential point is that the early literature (with the important exceptions of Agnar Sandmo [1975; 1976] and Yew-Kwang Ng [1980]) gave little serious attention to Pigouvian taxes as a source of public revenues.[1]

A later strand in the literature took up this issue. David Terkla (1984) actually estimated the potential efficiency gains from substituting revenues from a hypothetical set of nationwide taxes on particulate and sulfur oxide emissions for revenues from federal income (or alternatively corporate income) taxes. Using an optimal tax framework, Dwight Lee and Walter Misiolek (1986) explored the determination of pollution tax rates to maximize the efficiency gains. Drawing on such work, observers advanced the seemingly compelling intuitive case for a "double dividend" from pollution taxes. Not only can such taxes raise social welfare by reducing polluting activities to (or at least toward) their efficient levels, but they can give us an improved revenue system by reducing reliance on income, sales, and other distorting taxes. Pollution taxes, in short, can give us both enhanced environmental quality and a better tax system.

## III. IS THERE A DOUBLE DIVIDEND?

But things do not turn out to be quite this simple. As often happens when we enter the murky waters of the second-best, our economic intuition is not a very reliable guide. In this instance, we find that, in the presence of existing distortions, the introduction of pollution taxes can itself exacerbate these distortions with a resulting increase in the level of excess burden. And the striking result in the new literature is that this effect can easily outweigh the efficiency gains from recycling the revenues so as to reduce rates on existing taxes. Thus, there *may* be no double dividend.[3]

There are certainly instances where a double dividend exists. Sandmo (1994) cites an especially transparent case. Suppose that the revenues from pollution taxes set equal to marginal social damage provide sufficient funds to finance the entire public budget. Then, of course, all distorting taxes can be done away with. And we will achieve both efficient levels of externality-generating activities and a revenue system with no excess burden. Here there is clearly a double dividend from the introduction of environmental taxes. But, more generally, where pollution taxes must exist alongside distorting levies, the various economic linkages between the demands for different goods and in their production will typically be the source of additional excess burden.

To get a better sense of this, consider a case where there exist taxes on labor income (as in the seminal paper by Bovenberg and de Mooij [1994a]). There is thus a distortion in the work-leisure choice (assuming that the compensated labor supply function is not perfectly inelastic). A tax on polluting waste emissions in the production of various goods will raise the price of these goods, thereby reducing the return to work effort and inducing a substitution of additional leisure for consumption. Lawrence Goulder (1994b) calls this the "tax-interaction effect." And as Ian Parry (forthcoming) shows, so long as the output of polluting industries exhibits a (roughly) average degree of substitution for leisure, this effect will operate to increase the excess burden associated with the undersupply of work effort.

Note that although the induced change in work effort (employment) may be small, the incremental distortion in the labor market can be quite large because the welfare loss *per unit of employment* at the margin is large reflecting the large difference between the gross and net wage.[4] In terms of our usual diagrams, the point here is that the incremental distortions take the form of "tall" rectangles so that their area can be substantial even though their base is relatively small. These incremental distortions can be offset to some extent by using the revenues from the pollution taxes to reduce the rate of taxation of labor income (the "revenue-recycling effect"), but the conditions required for the revenue-recycling effect to offset fully the tax-interaction effect are stringent as Parry (1994; forthcoming) shows in his simple and very helpful analytical models.[5] Existing distortions in the labor market, incidentally, are by no means the only source of additional excess burdens. Programs, especially those that affect the prices of intermediate goods, can produce a wide range of incremental excess burdens in other markets.

We find, more generally, in the large CGE models that are being used to simulate hypothetical carbon taxes, that the incremental distortions from pollution taxes can be substantial (Bovenberg and Goulder 1994; Jorgenson and Wilcox 1992). The distortions introduced by these taxes often exceed the reductions in excess burden from revenue recycling with the implication that the optimal Pigouvian tax is something less, not more, than marginal social damage. Bovenberg and Goulder (1994), for example, in their seminal work on this issue find that their model suggests rates of pollution taxation significantly below Pigouvian levels. Likewise, in his simpler but more transparent analytical model, Parry (forthcoming) turns up tax rates on pollution that, for certain cases, are roughly 70 percent of marginal environmental damages.

These results are admittedly quite sensitive to the structure of the models, the values of key parameters (including the elasticity of labor supply, the elasticity of substitution between polluting goods and leisure, the tax elasticity of waste emissions, etc.), and the assumptions concerning the form of revenue-recycling. It is certainly possible (although not typical in these models) for there to exist a double dividend—that is, instances where the gains from revenue-recycling exceed the losses from the distorting effects associated with the introduction (or increase) in pollution taxes. But the general thrust of the findings seems to run in the opposite direction, thus undermining the case for a double dividend.

The cases in which we find a double dividend are typically those where there is some highly distorting tax in the system (as taxes on capital may be under certain circumstances) so that the revenues from the green taxes result in major reductions in existing excess burden (as, for example, in Jorgenson and Wilcoxen [1992]). But this is a somewhat contrived result in that such efficiency gains could presumably be achieved through tax reforms of other kinds.

I don't wish to suggest that the double-dividend issue is resolved at this juncture. The outcomes vary significantly across different models and different assumptions concerning key parameter values. And they are especially sensitive to the form that revenue-recycling takes. But the basic point seems well founded; in particular, the simpler analytical models (like those of Bovenberg and de Mooij [1994a] and of Parry [1994; forthcoming]) generate outcomes with no double dividend in a comprehensible and compelling way. The case for the double dividend appears shaky at best.

## IV. SOME FURTHER IMPLICATIONS OF THE NEW LITERATURE ON POLLUTION TAXES

The insight that first-best policy measures may have their efficiency-enhancing properties compromised by existing distortions is obviously not a new idea; the second-best has been with us for many decades. In the field of environmental economics, for example, Albert McGartland (1987) among others has shown that measures of control pollution in agriculture will have very different effects in the presence of U.S. farm programs than in an unregulated farm sector. But such cases involve policy measures with direct effects on distorted markets.

What is striking here is that apparently secondary effects operating through linkages with other markets can be of such magnitude. This same result is emerging in other sorts of studies. Edgar Browning (1994b), for example, has reexamined the issue of the welfare losses from monopoly. The traditional Harberger results based on the distortion in output markets suggest quite small losses. But when Browning integrates this analysis into a setting with a large existing distortion at the margin in the labor market, he finds that the welfare losses from monopoly are from 5 to 15 times higher than when the effect on the labor market is ignored!

This suggests that regulatory programs that raise prices of regulated outputs may have hitherto unimagined costs resulting from the incremental distortions they generate in other markets. Returning to environmental policy, consider the case of systems of tradable emissions permits where the permits, rather than being sold to sources at auction, are simply distributed without charge (perhaps under a grandfathering scheme—like that of the acid-rain provisions in the 1990 Clean Air Act Amendments). Such programs generate no revenues; hence, there is no revenue-recycling effect to offset (at least in part) the tax-interaction effect. Parry (1994) finds that for such programs, it is quite possible for the distortions from the tax-interaction effect to exceed the entire welfare gain from pollution control!

The findings in this newly emerging body of research must certainly be taken as preliminary at this juncture. Much remains to be understood. But this work suggests strongly that we must be cautious in drawing policy conclusions from partial-equilibrium analyses—or from general-equilibrium analyses that ignore preexisting distortions in the system. The effects operating through the linkages between distorted markets in a general-equilibrium system appear to have far greater implications for policy design than we have appreciated. And I suspect that we have just scratched the surface of this issue.

## V. ON THE POLITICAL ECONOMY OF POLLUTION TAXES

For the remainder of this paper, I shift the focus to a set of important issues in the actual design and implementation of pollution taxes. In the course of legislative debate and compromise, it is easy for environmental tax programs to become emasculated in ways that undermine their basic economic rationale. In this section, I want to comment briefly on what I see as some central matters in the actual design of pollution tax legislation.

### The Tax Base

Economic theory is clear on this issue: taxes on externalities should be levied directly on the activity that generates the external cost. If the process of production of some commodity involves the emissions of damaging wastes, it is the emission of the wastes that should be the subject of a unit tax, not the commodity itself (aside from the unusual case of fixed coefficients of production). A tax on the output or profits of a polluting industry is not, in general, a good substitute for a tax on the offending activity itself.

There are, of course, cases where because of difficulties of monitoring waste emissions, we may have no alternative but to tax an activity closely related to the emitting of the damaging wastes. But *wherever possible* we should design the tax to address directly the polluting act. This may in some instances require some ingenuity. To take one example, automobile emissions are a primary source of urban air pollution in many countries. It is tempting to regard such emissions

**Wallace E. Oates** .................. **305**

Green Taxes: Can We Protect the Environment and Improve the Tax System at the Same Time?

from a particular vehicle as beyond our monitoring capacities and to settle for a tax on gasoline. But such a tax, while perhaps discouraging driving to some extent, fails to provide needed incentives to purchase automobiles with desirable emissions characteristics and, equally important, to maintain them in ways to keep pollutant emissions at low levels. But there are taking place important advances in monitoring technology. It may soon be possible through periodic inspections (or perhaps even remote detection devices) to measure the levels of emissions from individual vehicles and then, with some measure of miles driven, to fashion tax bills that reflect reasonably accurately actual emissions.

Auto emissions is obviously a difficult case. It is clearly easier to levy pollution taxes on sulfur emissions from power plants or the carbon content of various fuels, but my point here is that in designing these measures, it is important to be sure that, as closely as possible, we are taxing the right thing.

## Setting the Tax Rate

As Sandmo's (1975) earlier paper and the ongoing research makes clear, the determination of the second-best optimal tax rate on polluting activities is a complicated enterprise. In particular, it involves elements that reflect both the environmental costs associated with the pollution and the way the tax measure interacts with the rest of the revenue system. In practice, this suggests that the actual design of environmental taxes will involve two distinct sets of policy makers: environmental regulators and fiscal managers. And the setting of the rates of pollution taxes will entail some sort of compromise reflecting environmental objectives and revenue needs.

This is a tricky legislative and administrative issue. While effective cooperation between environmental and fiscal agents is certainly possible in some settings, it is also easy to think of cases where one authority or the other will determine the levels of pollution taxes. Taking a public-choice perspective on this matter, suppose that the public revenue authority (e.g., Treasury officials or a tax committee in the legislature) sets tax rates. To take an extreme case, Geoffrey Brennan and James Buchanan (1980) have argued that we can view the public sector as a revenue-maximizer, a "Leviathan" that seeks to extract the most it can in public revenues from the economy. For this polar case, the authority would seek tax rates on polluting activities that maximize the inflow of revenues—rates that would get us to the top of the Laffer curve.

What would be the environmental consequences of such behavior? Some environmentalists have expressed the concern that tax rates are likely to be set too low from an environmental perspective; such rates they fear would not provide an adequate incentive to reduce waste discharges. Is this a legitimate concern or would Leviathan set rates that are too high? Or put differently, how would the revenue-maximizing rate compare with the Pigouvian tax rate? There appears not to be a general answer to this question, for it depends on the elasticity of the tax base. Suppose that *given* an existing set of other taxes, the environmental authority, following the dictates of some environmental economists, were to set pollution taxes such that marginal abatement costs equal marginal social damages (although this is admittedly not, in general, optimal in a distorted setting). Next, suppose that rate-setting authority were transferred to a Leviathan fiscal agent. Would this agent raise or lower the tax rates on polluting activities? The answer is that it could go either way, depending on the elasticity of the tax base (at the Pigouvian rate). If the base is revenue elastic, our Leviathan agent would lower the tax rate and vice versa. Moreover, as Lee and Misiolek (1986) suggest, there is no strong presumption here; their estimates of the elasticities of the tax base for a number of pollutants in the United States exhibit considerable variation, some well below unity and others above unity. Thus, Leviathan could turn out to be either a friend or foe of the environment!

Note further that for the Leviathan case, there would be no welfare gains from revenue-recycling; the added revenues would simply go to swell the size of the public budget. This is admittedly a contrived case. More realistically, we might expect even a revenue authority to give some weight to the environmental and other economic effects of these taxes in the setting of rates. But there are potential problems associated with the locus of tax authority. If, incidentally, it comes to a choice of placing pollution taxes under the aegis of either a fiscal authority or an environmental regulator, my preference would go to the latter. Pollution taxes are a potentially quite powerful tool for environmental management, one of a quite limited set of efficient policy instruments. To place such taxes in the fiscal domain is likely to discourage environmental regulators from shifting away from their traditional command-and-control instruments for pollution control.

## On Environmental Trust Funds

Environmental taxes have not been widely employed. Moreover, as Robert Hahn (1989) and others have pointed out, environmental authorities that have used such taxes have typically employed them not so much as instruments for regulating levels of polluting activities, but rather as devices to raise funds for environmental projects. Rates have often been set at levels that will raise the requisite monies for certain environmental programs, not to regulate waste flows.

This is an important issue in the political economy of environmental taxes. Various proposed bills in the United States for pollution taxes have contained within them special provisions for the creation of a "trust fund" into which the revenues would flow. The funds would then be allocated to certain kinds of environmental projects. Such earmarking of funds has a certain appeal. And in the political process it can be an effective way to coalesce the support of environmental (and other interested) groups in support of such measures.

But such inclinations, I want to argue, should be resisted. If revenues from pollution taxes are siphoned off into trust funds, they will result in increased spending, and there will obviously be no opportunity to realize the welfare gains from revenue-recycling. Moreover, it will mean that certain environmental projects are likely to be undertaken simply because there are unused monies in the trust fund. Environmental projects should have to meet the same economic and budgetary tests as other projects; they should not be undertaken simply by virtue of the availability of some earmarked funds.

## Revenue-Neutral Tax Reform and Equity

A more appealing approach to the introduction of pollution taxes is as part of a revenue-neutral tax package that realizes the potential gains from revenue-recycling. This approach has considerable political potential, for the new taxes on pollution can be combined with welcome reductions in other taxes that will generate support for the proposed reform.

The Swedish Tax Reform of 1991 is instructive in this respect (Bohm 1994; Sterner 1994). Among other elements, the reform act included the introduction of taxes on carbon-dioxide and sulfur emissions. The revenues from these new levies were part of a package involving reductions in other tax rates. In particular, to reduce distortions in the labor-leisure choice, the top marginal income tax rates were dramatically reduced: these rates were reduced to about 30 percent for 80 to 90 percent of income earners and to about 50 percent for the remaining high income earners (from a top marginal rate of 73 percent in 1989 and 85 percent a few years earlier).[6]

Such revenue-neutral reforms can also address equity issues. There is concern that broad-based pollution taxes are likely to be somewhat regressive in their pattern of incidence. And some evidence (Robinson 1985) exists to support this contention. But in a revenue-neutral tax reform, it is possible to increase progressivity elsewhere in the tax system so as to offset (or more than offset) the regressivity inherent in the new taxes on pollution. Reductions in the lowest tax rates under the income tax or perhaps tax credits for low-income households can address this objective.

## VI. SOME CONCLUDING REMARKS

Pollution taxes can play a significant and constructive role in the revenue system. And the work described in this paper should not, in my view, be interpreted as a serious challenge to this basic claim. Not only do such taxes serve to reduce levels of polluting activities, but, as environmental economists have emphasized repeatedly, compared to their command-and-control counterparts, they provide important incentives for research efforts into new and improved abatement technologies.

The theme of this paper is that the design of these measures must be undertaken with care. The tax base, wherever possible, should be the polluting activity itself—not some related activity. Moreover, there is a strong case to introduce these measures in (approximately) revenue-neutral ways so that the recycling of the revenues can be used to reduce some of the more damaging features (in both efficiency and equity terms) of the existing tax system. The ongoing research on this issue has much to contribute to our understanding of how best to do all this.

## NOTES

Presidential Address delivered at the sixty-fourth annual meeting of the Southern Economic Asssociation, Orlando, Florida, November 21, 1994. I am grateful to Ian Parry and Robert Schwab for valuable comments on an earlier draft and to the National Science Foundation for its support of this research.

1. There is much current research addressing this important issue (most, at the writing of this paper, still in draft form). For a small sampling, see Bovenberg and Goulder (1994), Bovenberg and de Mooij (1994a; 1994b), Boyd, Drutilla, and Viscusi (forthcoming), Goulder (1994a; 1994b), Johansson (1994), Jorgenson and Wilcoxen (1992), Parry (1994; forthcoming), and Schob (1994).

2. I am somewhat puzzled why the work on optimal taxation in the presence of externalities by Sandmo (1975; 1976) and Ng (1980) was overlooked. It certainly did not appear in obscure places. Ian Parry has suggested that the rather complicated optimal tax formulas may have masked the interpretation of the results and that their work had no empirical counterpart to give some sense of its likely importance. But for whatever reason these papers had no real impact on the environmental economics literature.

3. See Goulder (1994b) for a careful treatment of the concept of the double dividend. The literature employs this term with somewhat different meanings.

4. See Edgar Browning (March 1994a) for an illuminating treatment of the sources (both tax and non-tax) and the magnitude of the "wedge" at the margin between the gross and net wage.

5. Note that the revenue-recycling effect is itself offset to some extent by a loss in revenues from the tax on labor resulting from the reduction in work effort induced by the pollution tax. This is a kind of "tax-erosion" effect.

6. Is is hard to believe that the efficiency gains from revenue-recycling were not quite sizable here!

## REFERENCES

Bohm, Peter. "Environment and Taxation: The Case of Sweden," in *Environment and Taxation: The Cases of the Netherlands, Sweden, and the United States.* Paris: OECD (1994), 51–101.

Bovenberg, A. Lans, and Lawrence H. Goulder. "Integrating Environmental and Distortionary Taxes: General Equilibrium Analyses." Unpublished paper (1994).

Bovenberg, A. Lans, and Ruud A. de Mooij. "Environmental Levies and Distortionary Taxation." *American Economic Review* (September 1994a): 1085–1089.

———. "Environmental Tax Reform and Endogenous Growth." Unpublished paper (1994b).

Boyd, Roy, Kerry Krutilla, and W. Kip Viscusi. "Energy Taxation as a Policy Instrument to Reduce $CO_2$ Emissions: A Net Benefit Analysis." *Journal of Environmental Economics and Management* (forthcoming).

Brennan, Geoffrey, and James Buchanan. *The Power to Tax: Analytical Foundations of a Fiscal Constitution.* Cambridge: Cambridge University Press (1980).

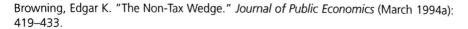

**Wallace E. Oates** ................ **309**
Green Taxes: Can We Protect the Environment and Improve the Tax System at the Same Time?

Browning, Edgar K. "The Non-Tax Wedge." *Journal of Public Economics* (March 1994a): 419–433.

———. "The Welfare Cost of Monopoly and Other Output Distortions." Unpublished paper (1994b).

Goulder, Lawrence H. "Effects of Carbon Taxes in an Economy with Prior Tax Distortions: An Intertemporal General Equilibrium Analysis." Unpublished paper (1994a).

———. "Environmental Taxation and the 'Double Dividend:' A Reader's Guide." Unpublished paper (1994b).

Hahn, Robert W. "Economic Prescriptions for Environmental Problems: How the Patient Followed the Doctor's Orders." *Journal of Economic Perspectives* (Spring 1989): 95–114.

Johansson, Olaf. "Optimal Indirect Taxation in a Second-Best Perspective with Regard to Externalities, a Public Budget Restriction and Distribution Effects." Unpublished paper (1994).

Jorgenson, Dale W., and Peter J. Wilcoxen. "Reducing U.S. Carbon Emissions: An Econometric General Equilibrium Assessment." Unpublished paper (1992).

Lee, Dwight R., and Walter S. Misiolek. "Substituting Pollution Taxation for General Taxation: Some Implications for Efficiency in Pollution Taxation." *Journal of Environmental Economics and Management* (December 1986): 338–347.

McGartland, Albert M. "Implications of Ambient Ozone Standards for U.S. Agriculture: A Comment and Some Further Evidence." *Journal of Environmental Management,* No. 2 (1987): 139–146.

Ng, Yew-Kwang. "Optimal Corrective Taxes or Subsidies When Revenue Raising Imposes an Excess Burden." *American Economic Review* (September 1980): 744–751.

Oates, Wallace E. "Pollution Charges as a Source of Public Revenues," in *Economic Progress and Environmental Concerns,* Herbert Giersch, ed., Berlin: Springer-Verlag (1993), 135–152.

Parry, Ian W. H. "Environmental Policy in a Second Best World." Unpublished paper (1994).

———. "Pollution Taxes and Revenue Recycling." *Journal of Environmental Economics and Management* (forthcoming).

Repetto, R., R. C. Dower, R. Jenkins, and J. Geoghegan. "Green Fees: How a Tax Shift Can Work for the Environment and the Economy." World Resources Institute Document, Washington, D.C. (1992).

Robinson, H. David. "Who Pays for Industrial Pollution Abatement?" *Review of Economics and Statistics* (November 1985): 702–706.

Sandmo, Agnar. "Optimal Taxation in the Presence of Externalities." *Swedish Journal of Economics* (March 1975): 86–98.

———. "Direct versus Indirect Pigouvian Taxation." *European Economic Review* (1976): 337–349.

————. "Public Finance and the Environment." Unpublished paper (1994).

Schob, Ronnie. "Evaluating Tax Reforms in the Presence of Externalities." Unpublished paper (1994).

Sterner, Thomas. "Environmental Tax Reform: The Swedish Experience." Unpublished paper (1994).

Terkla, David. "The Efficiency Value of Effluent Tax Revenues." *Journal of Environmental Economics and Management* (June 1984): 107–123.

# S E L E C T I O N      2 1

Don Fullerton and Diane Lim Rogers

# Lifetime versus Annual Perspectives on Tax Incidence

Tax incidence is concerned with the distribution of the burden of taxation: Who pays taxes? However, traditional incidence analysis most often focuses on distinguishing between who has legal responsibility for payment of a tax and who actually ends up paying the tax—in a single year. But as most taxpayers are keenly aware, April 15th recurs year after year—as do property tax deadlines, motor vehicle registration renewals, and so on. (An addendum to Benjamin Franklin's famous saying might be that only death stops taxes.*) Thus, many tax incidence researchers—themselves taxpayers—have been asking a different question: Do studies of annual burdens accurately capture lifetime burdens of taxation, and if not, how does lifetime incidence differ from annual incidence? Not surprisingly, some of the answers have already generated a great deal of controversy.

Two of the leading investigators of lifetime tax burdens are Don Fullerton and Diane Lim Rogers. In this selection, Fullerton and Rogers first explain the reasoning behind lifetime tax-incidence analysis, and then discuss the new problems brought about by attempting to classify individuals by lifetime-income groups. Preliminary conclusions regarding differences in lifetime versus annual burdens of specific taxes are presented. The authors believe that the available empirical evidence invalidates any presumption that annual burdens will always mirror lifetime burdens—thus,

Fullerton, Don, and Diane Lim Rogers. "Lifetime versus Annual Perspectives on Tax Incidence." *National Tax Journal 44* (September 1991): 227–287. This selection is an abridged version of the original article.

**Don Fullerton** is Professor of Economics and Public Policy at Carnegie-Mellon University. He served as Deputy Assistant Secretary of the Treasury for Tax Analysis from 1985 to 1987. **Diane Lim Rogers** is Assistant Professor of Economics at Pennsylvania State University.

* *Editors' note:* In a letter to M. Leroy in 1789, Benjamin Franklin wrote: "Our Constitution is in actual operation; everything appears to promise that it will last; but in this world nothing is certain but death and taxes."

underscoring the importance of supplementing annual incidence analysis with independent studies of lifetime burdens of taxation.

### Questions to Guide the Reading

1. How might "hump-shaped" income patterns and income volatility affect lifetime versus annual measures of tax incidence?
2. How do the lifetime and annual perspectives differ in their measures of income? How does capital income affect lifetime tax burdens?
3. What are the basic differences between the ways in which income groups might be classified for (*i*) an annual incidence study and (*ii*) a life-cycle incidence study? In annual incidence studies, households are often grouped into income categories, treating all members of the same household as a single consumer. Why, in contrast, might the use of household income be unreasonable in a lifetime incidence study?
4. What conclusions do the authors draw from their classification analysis of the Panel Study of Income Dynamics?
5. According to the authors, why is the personal-income tax incidence likely to be less progressive from a lifetime perspective than from an annual perspective?
6. Proposals to substitute a consumption-type valued-added tax for the federal income tax have received strong support. While critics have argued that such a tax system would be highly regressive, some researchers hypothesize that the incidence of consumption taxes should be proportional when viewed over a lifetime. However, Fullerton and Rogers believe the lifetime incidence of consumption taxes might still be regressive. Why?
7. How is lifetime incidence analysis likely to impact tax policy formation?

## I. INTRODUCTION

Recent academic research on tax incidence has shifted from an emphasis on static and annual perspectives to examinations of dynamic and lifetime issues. Meanwhile, policy economists are forced to rely on annual data and hence annual analyses. The purpose of this paper is to discuss the nature and analysis of lifetime tax incidence, and to compare and contrast this lifetime perspective with the more familiar annual perspective. In our comparison, we find that (i) the lifetime perspective requires much more data over longer periods of time, because results depend critically on the whole shape of the lifetime earnings profile, (ii) individuals classified by annual income decile are often reclassified into very different lifetime income deciles, (iii) the personal income tax and corporate income tax appear less progressive on a lifetime basis, while consumption taxes appear less regressive on a lifetime basis, and (iv) despite the different approaches and the different reasons underlying the incidence of each particular tax, the lifetime incidence of the entire U.S. tax system is strikingly similar to the annual incidence.

Studies of the distributional effects of tax policy have progressed from the Harberger (1962, 1966) tradition of small theoretically-based analyses of incidence using relatively few sectors and consumers. Another approach, best exemplified by Pechman and Okner (1974), is to use the results of these theoretically-based models to allocate the burden of each tax across a large sample of households classified into annual income categories. The corporate income tax, for example, is distributed according to receipt of corporate-source income or according to receipt of capital income generally. More sophisticated general equilibrium models such as Ballard et al. (1985) still divide households into groups based on current income.

In contrast, life-cycle simulation models such as Auerbach and Kotlikoff (1987) examine the intergenerational distribution of tax burdens. They compare different age groups, but not different lifetime income groups. Other data-oriented studies examine incidence across lifetime income categories, including Menchik and David (1982), Davies et al. (1984), and Poterba (1989). Most recently, Lyon and Schwab (1990) compare the lifetime annual incidence of alcohol and cigarette taxes, and Fullerton and Rogers (1991) employ a general equilibrium model to examine the distribution of the U.S. tax burden across lifetime income categories.

The distinction between annual and lifetime perspectives may be important for measuring income, as discussed in section II below. Annual income may be volatile, or it may rise and then fall in a predictable pattern. Lifetime income takes a long-run perspective and accounts for both these kinds of changes. We also discuss the use of data, and the choice of model. The distinction also is important for classification, as discussed in section III below. The typical annual incidence study would lump together individuals of different ages who happen to have the same annual income, and the typical life-cycle study would lump together individuals with different incomes who happen to be the same age. We outline a lifetime incidence study that distinguishes individuals by both age and income. Finally, the distinction between annual and lifetime perspectives may be important for measuring tax burdens, as discussed in section IV below. Individuals of different ages consume different goods, supply different factors, and bear different annual tax burdens. If everyone bears each of these burdens during the course of life, then overall burdens can look very different in the lifetime perspective.

These three distinctions are related, since tax burdens are usually divided by a measure of income. In either the annual or lifetime perspectives, the measure of income used as denominator in this ratio should be the same as the measure of income used in classification of households.

Given the desirability of lifetime tax incidence analysis, and given its obvious practical limitations, a natural question is how the annual perspective compares to the lifetime one: if policy economists are forced to rely only on annual measures of tax incidence, how different are their conclusions from those that would come out of a lifetime analysis? According to the preliminary results of our book (Fullerton and Rogers 1991), the patterns of lifetime tax burdens are often quite similar to the familiar annual incidence results. Often a tax that is progressive in an annual sense is also progressive (although less so) in the lifetime perspective. Similarly, annually regressive taxes are merely less regressive on a lifetime basis. While the "bottom lines" are often similar, however, the stories underlying these incidence patterns are typically quite different.

## II. LIFETIME VS. ANNUAL INCOME

The distinction between lifetime and annual perspectives would be unimportant if each person's income did not change over the course of his or her lifetime. In that case annual income would accurately reflect permanent income, and individuals would not change annual income categories. Income paths would be flat, and the poorest annual income category would include the same individuals as the poorest lifetime category.

The first difference between the two perspectives therefore arises from hump-shaped income profiles. Many studies confirm that incomes rise during early years, level off during later working years, and fall during retirement. This pattern puts young and old lifetime-rich individuals into low annual-income groups. It thereby affects incidence results.

A second difference can arise simply with income volatility. Self-employed individuals with an average permanent income might be placed into a high-annual income category, or a low-annual-income category, depending on the year taken for study. Employed workers subject to temporary layoffs may experience similar fluctuations in annual incomes.

A third distinction involves "ability to pay." A misconception is that the lifetime perspective takes lifetime income as a superior measure of current ability to pay. Not so. Instead, the lifetime perspective takes two individuals with similar lifetime incomes as similar on a lifetime basis. For the tax system to be horizontally equitable, these two individuals should pay similar taxes over their lifetimes. In addition, for vertical equity, higher lifetime incomes could be associated with higher lifetime tax burdens. It does not matter when those taxes get paid. There is no presumption that lifetime income measures current ability to pay, only that lifetime income measures lifetime ability to pay. Whether or not actual taxes are based on an annual accounting system policymakers should be concerned with both "short run equity" and "long run equity." With borrowing constraints, for example, the timing of tax payments can be important. Still, the fairness of a tax should be evaluated both on how current taxes reflect current ability to pay and on how lifetime taxes reflect lifetime ability to pay.

Other differences are more subtle. A fourth distinction concerns what to include in the measure of income. In the annual perspective, income includes wages and salaries, entrepreneurial income, and all forms of capital income such as interest, dividends, and capital gains. One might impute all corporate-source income through to shareholders. Annual income may be realized or accrued, and it may be before or after taxes and transfers. Similarly, annual taxes may be realized or accrued. In contrast, a lifetime measure of income requires no capital income at all. Lifetime income would include only gifts and inheritances received plus labor income, although these would be discounted by the net rate of return to capital. Any capital income received at any point during the lifetime would then reflect not different levels of well-being, but simply different choices about when to consume: two individuals with identical paths for labor incomes and inheritances will have the same lifetime income, even if one prefers later consumption and thus has higher initial savings and capital income.

We note, however, that while lifetime income is independent of capital income, lifetime tax burdens are not. The lifetime burden of our tax system will be affected by consumption and savings behavior, since capital income is included in the income tax base. For two individuals with the same lifetime income, the current system places a larger burden on the one with more savings and delayed consumption.

*  *  *

## III. LIFETIME VS. ANNUAL CLASSIFICATION

To illustrate the classification problem, suppose that the economy included only the two types of individuals depicted in Figure 1. One has relatively poor lifetime prospects, advancing with age through points A, B, C, and D. The other has relatively rich prospects, and advances with age through points E, F, G, and H. The typical annual incidence study would take individuals at point G as the highest-income group, lump together individuals at points F and C for the second group, those at points E, B, and H for a third group, and those at points A and D for the poorest group. The typical life-cycle study would lump together individuals at points A and E as one youngest group, those at B and F as another group, C and G as the next group, and D with H as the oldest group. The model could then calculate redistributions between the old, the young, and later generations. Neither of these analyses captures the fundamental distinction between the two types of individuals in this economy. We report below on a preliminary attempt to distinguish groups by lifetime income.

In order to classify consumers into groups, however, we must first specify who is being classified. That is, we must choose the unit of analysis. In annual studies such as Pechman (1985), consumers are categorized according to household income. This makes good sense, since the well-being of an individual depends not simply on his or her own income or wealth, but rather on the income or wealth of the entire household. Our income tax system uses the household as the unit of analysis for similar reasons. In the lifetime perspective, however, it becomes extremely difficult to think about the "lifetime" of a household. Household compo-

## FIGURE 1

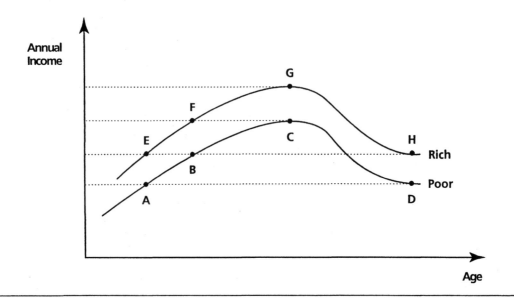

sition varies tremendously over an individual's lifetime due to marriage, births, divorce, deaths, and the moving out of adult children. The concept of "lifetime household income" is very complicated even in theory, but especially in practice. For this reason, the lifetime perspective may typically examine burdens across individuals rather than households. Still, however, one can assign shares of total household labor income or inheritances to the different individuals in the household.[1]

\* \* \*

In our model, we adopt the leisure-inclusive definition of lifetime resources both for the classifier of individuals and for the denominator of the burden measure. This choice will affect classifications if, for example, two individuals with the same earned income differ with respect to the value of leisure taken. It will affect relative tax burdens if, for example, income groups vary systematically with respect to the leisure/endowment ratio. In the next section we discuss incidence results from a model where high income groups take relatively more leisure, a good that is excluded from any tax on labor, on capital, or on consumption. As a consequence, all U.S. taxes look more regressive. An immediate implication is the importance of measuring differences in leisure/endowment ratios by group, despite the obvious difficulties.

Thus lifetime income and classification may differ from the annual perspective because of hump-shaped earnings profiles, volatility in annual income, the exclusion of capital income, the use of a lifecycle model, the individual as the unit of account, and the decision to include leisure in the total value of endowment. The next logical question, therefore, is whether these issues really matter. How different is a lifetime classification from the standard sort of annual classification?

To address this question, we estimate lifetime wage profiles for individuals in the Panel Study on Income Dynamics (PSID). Using simple econometric techniques with all individuals and years together, we first estimate the wage rate as a function of time, age, age-squared, age-cubed, and various demographic characteristics. Then we return to each individual in the sample, take actual wage rates for available years, and use the estimated regression coefficients to predict wage rates in other years. The estimated wage profile for each individual allows us to calculate potential lifetime earnings, that is, the total value of the endowment used for classification into deciles. (A later step involves reestimating the wage profile for each group separately, but the step is not relevant for the classification issue discussed here.)

Then, for the same individuals in the PSID, we take annual income for 1984, including labor and capital income (but excluding transfers). Thus the same individuals can be classified into annual income deciles.

Table 1 shows the percentages of each annual income decile that fall into each of the lifetime income deciles. For the poorest annual income group, for example, the first row shows that 47.5 percent are also in the poorest lifetime decile and 20.1 percent are in the second decile. The weighted number of observations is in parentheses.

Few observations are grossly reclassified. The upper right corner of the table indicates that nobody from the poorest annual group is placed into the richest lifetime group. The lower left corner indicates that one observation from the richest annual group is placed into the poorest lifetime group. Yet the diagonal from upper left to lower right indicates that few observations are similarly reclassified, either. The top and bottom annual deciles have about half their members in the same lifetime category, but annual groups 2 through 9 have only 15 to 20 percent of members placed in the same lifetime group.

Percentages away from the diagonal may be small, but the reclassification may be important. For example, column 10 of row 2 indicates that 2.3 percent of individuals from the second-poorest annual income decile are actually in the richest (10th) lifetime income decile. These are largely very young and very old lifetime-rich individuals at the low points in their age-income profiles. Column 2 of row 7 indicates that 4.2 percent of individuals from annual income decile 7 (fairly high annual income) are only in the second poorest lifetime income decile. These are mainly middle-aged lifetime-poor individuals, at the peaks of their age-income profiles.

Overall, 24.8 percent of individuals are in the same annual and lifetime income decile. Only 56.1 percent are in a lifetime decile within plus-or-minus one of their annual decile. If the same calculations are performed including transfers in annual income, then 23.3 percent of individuals are in the same annual and lifetime

**Table 1** Annual Income Decile by Lifetime Income Decile (Percent of Each Annual Income Decile Falling in the Various Lifetime Income Deciles; Weighted Number of Observations in Parentheses; Diagonal Underlined)

| | | | | | **Lifetime Decile** | | | | | |
|---|---|---|---|---|---|---|---|---|---|---|
| | **1** | **2** | **3** | **4** | **5** | **6** | **7** | **8** | **9** | **10** |
| **1** | 47.5 (3,993) | 20.1 (1,690) | 14.7 (1,236) | 9.0 (754) | 2.5 (214) | 2.9 (245) | 1.3 (108) | 0.5 (40) | 1.4 (121) | 0.0 (0) |
| **2** | 23.3 (1,967) | 16.7 (1,417) | 12.2 (1,032) | 13.4 (1,131) | 8.5 (723) | 10.0 (847) | 6.1 (515) | 5.5 (462) | 2.0 (172) | 2.3 (194) |
| **3** | 14.2 (1,192) | 18.2 (1,527) | 15.7 (1,313) | 14.1 (1,182) | 9.5 (798) | 8.2 (688) | 7.6 (638) | 5.2 (438) | 3.6 (303) | 3.6 (300) |
| **4** | 11.7 (994) | 17.7 (1,507) | 17.1 (1,457) | 14.6 (1,246) | 15.3 (1,307) | 8.3 (705) | 5.1 (431) | 3.9 (334) | 5.5 (466) | 1.0 (85) |
| **5** | 2.6 (215) | 16.0 (1,337) | 17.3 (1,444) | 12.8 (1,067) | 16.3 (1,364) | 14.8 (1,234) | 6.5 (541) | 8.6 (714) | 4.7 (395) | 0.4 (34) |
| **6** | 0.5 (39) | 6.2 (527) | 13.7 (1,161) | 11.2 (952) | 16.2 (1,379) | 18.6 (1,584) | 11.9 (1,008) | 9.1 (773) | 8.0 (680) | 4.6 (394) |
| **7** | 0.0 (2) | 4.2 (341) | 6.6 (540) | 12.5 (1,018) | 10.1 (820) | 18.2 (1,483) | 19.4 (1,582) | 10.8 (879) | 15.9 (1,292) | 2.4 (193) |
| **8** | 0.0 (2) | 0.0 (0) | 1.5 (125) | 7.5 (642) | 8.5 (734) | 13.6 (1,169) | 22.3 (1,921) | 21.9 (1,890) | 17.6 (1,514) | 7.2 (618) |
| **9** | 0.5 (39) | 0.9 (80) | 1.1 (91) | 4.3 (374) | 8.3 (715) | 3.8 (328) | 13.2 (1,133) | 25.0 (2,155) | 20.5 (1,768) | 22.4 (1,929) |
| **10** | 0.0 (1) | 0.0 (0) | 0.6 (48) | 1.6 (137) | 4.3 (367) | 1.8 (153) | 6.7 (574) | 8.9 (756) | 20.5 (1,747) | 55.6 (4,743) |

*(Left vertical axis label: Annual Decile)*

deciles, while 55.5 percent are within plus-or-minus one of the same decile. We conclude that the annual and lifetime classifications are too different to assume that lifetime incidence will be similar to annual incidence.

## IV. LIFETIME VS. ANNUAL TAXES

Theoretical models and common sense agree that tax burdens can be shifted by changes in behavior. Corporate taxes, for example, can be borne on the "sources side" through changes in the wage rate or through changes in the net rate of return to all capital owners, and they can be borne on the "uses side" through changes in product prices. These considerations have led to two approaches. First, the researcher may choose among alternative assumptions about the shifting of each tax instrument, and then add up the burdens for each group. The approach is not necessarily "partial equilibrium," because it may assume particular general equilibrium effects on factor returns or product prices. This first approach has been used in annual incidence calculations by Pechman and Okner (1974), and in lifetime calculations by Davies et al. (1984). Second, the researcher may specify all demand and supply behaviors in an explicit general equilibrium model and then "compute" the ultimate burdens on each group. This approach has been used in annual incidence calculations by Ballard et al. (1985), and in lifetime calculations by Fullerton and Rogers (1991).

The main advantage of the first approach is that it can employ detailed micro-data on thousands of households. The computer program makes one pass through each household, calculates income, allocates it to an income group, and adds its taxes to that group's burden. In contrast, a general equilibrium model might take many iterations to find an equilibrium price vector, so the sample must be reduced or aggregated for repeated calculations.

The main advantage of the second approach is that it employs a structural model with demand and supply behaviors derived from explicit production functions and utility functions. The advantage is not that tax incidence is "calculated rather than assumed," because the structural model itself requires many assumptions about functional forms and elasticity values. Varying the elasticity of substitution in production will generate different amounts of burden shifting, the same way that the first approach may assume different amounts of burden shifting. Rather, the advantages are more subtle. First, the analyst can see explicitly how results are tied to a particular elasticity parameter that might be estimated. Second, incidence results are consistent in that all tax burdens interact simultaneously rather than being assumed independently. Results can include small effects on unrelated markets, and they can include implicit taxes such as the difference between the market rate of return on tax-free bonds and taxable bonds.[2] Third, results can be stated in terms of an "exact" utility-based welfare measure such as an equivalent variation (in either the annual or lifetime perspective).[3] Fourth, this utility-based welfare measure can include excess burdens or deadweight loss. Whereas the first approach allocates burdens across households that sum to total taxes paid, the second approach calculates changes in consumer surplus that may sum to a figure larger than total taxes paid.

This last effect may be small, especially in one-period models such as that of Harberger (1966), where excess burden remains only 0.5 percent of income. Incidence analysis by definition is concerned with distributional effects rather than the overall efficiency of the tax system. Excess burdens may differ across income categories, however, if higher-income individuals have different factor supply elasticities or face different marginal tax rates. However, efficiency effects may be much larger in dynamic models with intertemporal effects on savings, capital formation, and growth (Judd 1987). Thus, utility-based measures may be more important in the lifetime perspective. For these reasons, we use an applied general equilibrium framework, specify a lifetime utility function, and compute tax burdens according to a lifetime equivalent variation.

Now we turn to specific tax instruments and discuss likely differences between tax incidence in the annual and lifetime perspectives. First, for the personal income tax, economic incidence is often assumed equal to statutory incidence. Even general equilibrium models do not find much shifting of this tax (Devarajan et al. 1980). The progressivity of the personal income tax affects annual incidence more than lifetime incidence, however as confirmed in Davies et al. (1984), and Fullerton and Rogers (1991). Both of these studies find that personal income taxes remain progressive in the lifetime perspective, but that they are less progressive than in annual studies. As we saw in the previous section, many annually-poor individuals are actually young or old lifetime-rich individuals, so their temporarily low taxes do not represent low taxes on low lifetime income. Similarly, some middle-aged lifetime-poor individuals may have a current annual income that is fairly high, so their temporarily high taxes do not represent high taxes on high lifetime income. The lifetime income distribution exhibits much less inequality than the annual income distribution, and the lifetime incidence of the income tax appears less progressive than the annual incidence.

Second, consider taxes on income from capital such as the property tax, corporate income tax, and the personal income tax on interest and dividends. These taxes may have "uses side" effects on the prices of consumption goods, but we discuss such effects later. For now, just consider a tax that reduces the net rate of return on the "sources side."

In the annual perspective, capital income taxes burden those who own capital. They clearly redistribute from "rich" to "poor," if households are categorized by wealth. If households are categorized by annual income, however, Devarajan et al. (1980) find that the ratio of capital income to labor income is U-shaped. The low income group includes many retirees with accumulated savings and no labor income. Middle-income households are in their high-earnings years, and the highest income households again hold more wealth. Thus the distributional burden of capital taxes also is U-shaped across annual income groups. In other words, capital taxes appear to burden some low-annual-income individuals who may not have low-lifetime-income.

In the lifetime perspective, very different considerations come into play. The burden of capital taxation depends very much on the whole shape of the estimated profile for the lifetime endowment. First, the burden of capital taxes depends on the height of the peak. In the life-cycle model, individuals wish to achieve smoothly increasing consumption over the lifetime (if the interest rate is higher than the rate of time preference). A steeper earnings profile would therefore induce them to save and then dis-save, earning more capital income and paying more capital taxes.

Who has steeper profiles? After all of the PSID individuals were classified into lifetime income deciles as described in the previous section, we reestimated the profile separately for each decile as a function of age, age-squared, and age-cubed. As it turns out, our estimated profiles are flatter for low-lifetime-income groups and more steeply peaked for high-lifetime-income groups. Thus life-cycle savings behavior generates higher capital-labor ratios for the lifetime-rich than for the lifetime-poor, and the lifetime-rich bear more sources-side burden of capital taxes. The lifetime-rich tend to be "capitalists" just as in the annual perspective, but for a different reason. While property and other capital taxes tend to be lifetime progressive for this reason, payroll taxes tend to be lifetime regressive. These results are similar to those of annual studies.

Second, the burden of capital taxes depends on the timing of the peak. If individuals achieve high earnings early in the life-cycle, and desire smoothly rising consumption, then they will have more savings and bear more burden from capital income taxes. Unfortunately, however, the estimated profiles demonstrate no clear tendency to peak early or late in the lifetimes of those with high or low lifetime income. This effect is difficult to measure, however, and deserves much more study.

Third, the burden of capital taxes depends on the extent and timing of gifts and inheritances. If such gifts are larger or received earlier in life for those with high lifetime income, then their capital income and the burden of capital taxes will be greater. Again this issue deserves greater study.

Finally, consider taxes on consumption. In this category we include the effects of any tax on the "uses side," that is, effects on the prices of consumption goods. In the annual perspective, consumption taxes are regressive because the annual-poor have a high ratio of consumption to income. Consumption may even be higher than income for the very young, for retired generations, and for anyone with volatile income in a bad year. In contrast, the lifetime perspective eliminates these age specific effects, so that the overall lifetime ratio of consumption to income is more similar across lifetime income categories. Poterba (1989) points out that if individuals consume according to the life-cycle hypothesis with no intergenerational transfers, then the present value of consumption must equal the present value of labor income. Thus a proportional tax on all consumption would be strictly proportional to lifetime income.

Consumption taxes may still be regressive in the lifetime perspective, however, for three kinds of reasons. First, actual consumption taxes are not strictly proportional. In preliminary work, we find that lifetime income categories differ in the types of goods consumed. The lifetime-poor spend larger fractions of their income on highly taxed goods, such as cigarettes, alcohol, and gasoline. As a result, U.S. sales and excise taxes are still lifetime regressive.

Second, even if consumption tax rates were strictly proportional, the tax base excludes bequests given. Menchik and David (1982) find that low-lifetime-income groups may bequeath a low fraction of a lifetime income measure that includes both earnings and public transfers. They would thus bear a relatively high burden from consumption taxes.

Third, consumption taxes do not apply to consumption of leisure. If high-lifetime-income groups consume proportionately more untaxed leisure than low-lifetime-income groups, then even a proportional consumption tax is regressive.

This simple point does not appear in existing incidence literature, possibly because no study has estimated the ratio of leisure to income on a lifetime basis. Also, discussion of leisure has been oriented toward efficiency issues, focusing on the second-best problem of minimizing excess burden given that leisure must be left untaxed. We note that leisure is important for distributional issues, however, whether lifetime or annual in nature. If any individuals enjoy relatively high amounts of leisure as a fraction of the full value of their endowments, then those individuals bear proportionately less of the consumption tax burden.

As illustration of this effect, the lifetime-rich in our model choose higher leisure-to-endowment ratios than do the lifetime-poor. Thus all consumption-based or labor-based taxes look more regressive.[4] Whether doing annual or lifetime incidence analysis, economists might therefore want to consider more carefully the intensity of labor across income categories.

Finally, we use the lifetime incidence model to evaluate the entire tax system, i.e., the combination of personal income taxes, corporate taxes, property taxes, payroll taxes, and sales and excise taxes. Overall, U.S. taxes are close to proportional in lifetime incidence, with slightly heavier burdens in the upper and lower tails of the lifetime income distribution. Interestingly, this overall incidence pattern is similar to that found by Pechman and Okner (1974) in their well-known annual incidence study.[5]

This overall similarity derives from off-setting effects. The lifetime incidence of personal income taxes is less progressive, and that of consumption taxes is less regressive, but the combined pattern is similar to annual incidence. We emphasize, however, that while the lifetime and annual perspectives come to similar overall conclusions, they provide very different explanations and somewhat different conclusions for the incidence of each particular tax.

## IV. CONCLUSION

Annual incidence analysis will remain a basic tool for detailed tax studies and specific policy analyses. Yet lifetime incidence provides us with a longer-run view of the distributional effects of taxes. The lifetime perspective does not substitute for, but rather supplements, the annual perspective. Especially with liquidity constraints, annual tax burdens should increase with annual abilities to pay, while lifetime tax burdens still reflect lifetime abilities to pay.

The earliest of lifetime studies indicate that the lifetime incidence of the overall tax system is close to proportional, similar to conclusions from annual studies. The underlying factors under the two perspectives differ, however. For example, the progressivity or regressivity of each type of tax tends to be reduced in adopting the lifetime perspective, due to the humped nature of age-income or age-endowment profiles. Whereas age itself affects capital-labor income ratios in the annual perspective, it is the whole shape of the life-time profile that determines savings and thus capital-labor income ratios in the lifetime perspective.

While practical considerations presently limit the widespread use of lifetime analysis as a routine procedure, academic studies of lifetime tax incidence can still provide policy economists with insights into the differences and similarities between the annual and lifetime perspectives. Any discussion about equity that is based on annual calculations could be supplemented, wherever possible, with potential lifetime effects. Until better data are available, however, the lifetime perspective will most likely be used as a qualitative rather than quantitative input into tax analysis.

# NOTES

We are grateful for suggestions from Jane Gravelle, Jon Hakken, Paul Menchik, and Jon Skinner. This paper is part of the NBER's research program in Taxation. Any opinions expressed are those of the authors and not those of the National Bureau of Economic Research.

1. For example, husband and wife could each be assigned one-half of their combined incomes or inheritances in each year.
2. An individual holding municipal bonds would not explicitly pay taxes on the return to these bonds and yet would implicitly be bearing a burden of taxation in the form of a reduced return.
3. "Equivalent variation" is the money-metric equivalent of a utility change, based on ex ante prices. Based on the Hicksian (compensated) demand system, this is an exact measure of welfare change, whereas Marshallian consumer surplus is not. Another exact measure is the "compensating variation," which measures the utility change in terms of ex post prices. See Tresch (1981, 64–69).
4. Incidence results are affected only quantitatively and not qualitatively. Our differences in leisure-to-endowment ratios affect only the degree to which consumption taxes and payroll taxes are regressive, and the degree to which income taxes are progressive.
5. An updated version of annual incidence analysis is Pechman (1985). The later version does not find the same curling up at the high end of the income distribution as was found in the earlier study.

# REFERENCES

Auerbach, Alan J., and Laurence J. Kotlikoff. *Dynamic Fiscal Policy*, New York: Cambridge University Press (1987).

Ballard, Charles, Don Fullerton, John Shoven, and John Whalley. *A General Equilibrium Model for Tax Policy Evaluation.* Chicago: University of Chicago Press (1985).

Davies, James, France St-Hilaire, and John Whalley. "Some Calculations of Lifetime Tax Incidence." *American Economic Review 74* (September 1984): 633–649.

Devarajan, Shantayanan, Don Fullerton, and Richard Musgrave. "Estimating the Distribution of Tax Burdens: A Comparison of Alternative Approaches." *Journal of Public Economics 13* (April 1980): 155–182.

Fullerton, Don, and Diane Lim Rogers. *Who Bears the Lifetime Tax Burden?*, manuscript prepared for the Brookings Institution, Washington, D.C. (1991).

Harberger, Arnold C. "The Incidence of the Corporation Income Tax." *Journal of Political Economy 70* (1962): 215–240.

———. "Efficiency Effects of Taxes on Income from Capital," in M. Krzyzaniak, ed., *Effects of Corporation Income Tax,* Detroit: Wayne State University Press. (1966).

Judd, Kenneth. "The Welfare Cost of Factor Taxation in a Perfect-Foresight Model." *Journal of Political Economy 95* (August 1987): 675–709.

Lyon, Andrew B., and Robert Schwab. "Consumption Taxes in a Life-Cycle Framework: Are Sin Taxes Regressive?," paper presented at the American Economic Association meetings, Washington, D.C. (December 1990).

Menchik, Paul L., and Martin David. "The Incidence of a Lifetime Consumption Tax." *National Tax Journal 35* (June, 1982): 189–203.

Pechman, Joseph A. *Who Paid the Taxes, 1966–85?* Washington, D.C.: Brookings Institution (1985).

Pechman, Joseph A., and Benjamin A. Okner. *Who Bears the Tax Burden?* Washington, D.C.: Brookings Institution (1974).

Poterba, James M. "Lifetime Incidence and the Distributional Burden of Excise Taxes." *American Economic Review 79* (May 1989): 325–330.

Tresch, Richard W. *Public Finance: A Normative Theory.* Plano, Texas: Business Publications, Inc. (1981).

## S E L E C T I O N    2 2

Joseph A. Pechman

# The Future of the Income Tax

The search for an optimal tax system is probably the longest lived of all research efforts in public finance economics, and is showing no sign of concluding. Many criteria for judging tax policy have been used over the years, including efficiency, equity, ease of compliance, and administrative cost. However, even agreement on the criteria does not imply agreement on the relative importance of each standard. In addition, the validity of most conclusions from optimal tax research depends upon the assumptions made about markets and individual behavior, and unanimity has yet to be reached on these assumptions as well. Although major changes have been instituted in the last decade, tax reform remains a controversial and important topic for current public policy debate.

This selection is the Presidential address for the one-hundred second meeting of the American Economic Association. In this address, Joseph Pechman provides a strong and general defense of the progressive federal income tax, comparing it to both a flat-rate (or proportional) tax and a personal expenditure (or consumption) tax—two of the most frequently proposed alternatives to the income tax. Although he passed away in 1989, Joseph Pechman was a well-known and long-time supporter of progressive and comprehensive income taxation, and his fundamental arguments are still relevant today.

### Questions to Guide the Reading

1. In general, what changes occurred in the distribution of income during the last decade? Why did the before-tax income share of the top 1 percent rise in the 1980s after remaining constant for three decades?

Pechman, Joseph A. "The Future of the Income Tax." *American Economic Review 80* (March 1990): 1–20.

**Joseph Pechman** passed away on August 19, 1989. His Presidential address was delivered posthumously on December 29, 1989. At the time of his death, Joseph Pechman was Senior Fellow, Emeritus, in the Economics Studies Program at The Brookings Institution.

2. How did the Tax Reform Act of 1986 change the distribution of tax burdens in the United States? Who is financing the transfer system in the United States (and what evidence is presented to support this conclusion)?

3. One policy alternative to the progressive income tax is a flat-rate income tax, i.e., an income-based tax with a single proportional rate. Why does Pechman argue instead for income tax progressivity?

4. What evidence is presented regarding the effects of income taxation on economic incentives to work and save?

5. Why does Pechman conclude that "substituting an expenditure tax for an income tax cannot be justified on theoretical or practical grounds"?

6. How did the Tax Reform Act of 1986 "greatly improve the fairness and efficiency of the tax system"? Specifically, how did the Act broaden the income tax base?

7. What major additional reforms in federal income taxation does Pechman advocate? How would these reforms make the federal income tax more progressive and comprehensive?

---

The federal income tax has been under attack by the economics profession for more than a decade. The attack comes from two directions: supply-siders who believe that progressive income taxation impairs economic incentives,[1] and more traditional economists who would substitute a progressive expenditure tax for the income tax.[2] At one time, support for the expenditure tax was confined to a few members of our profession, including such distinguished names as John Stuart Mill, Irving Fisher, Nicholas Kaldor, and James Meade. Today, it is fair to say that many, if not most, economists favor the expenditure tax or a flat rate income tax. This group has joined the opponents of progressive taxation in the attack on the income tax.

Despite an incessant barrage from both groups, no country in the world is planning to abandon the income tax or is even considering a personal expenditure tax. A wave of tax reform, beginning with the U.S. reform in 1986, has been sweeping the world, aimed at improving the income tax, not at eliminating it. Tax preferences formerly regarded as sacrosanct are being removed and there is a distinct movement toward comprehensive income taxation.[3] However, individual income tax rates are being cut, tax progressivity has been declining almost everywhere, and reliance on the income tax has been diminishing.

It will come as no surprise to this audience that I approve of the base-broadening feature of the current tax reform movement, but I believe that the reduction in the redistributive effect of the income tax has gone too far. In this paper, I shall show that the progressivity of the U.S. tax system—never very pronounced, except during and immediately after the two world wars—has been declining for more than two decades and that the Tax Reform Act of 1986 reversed this decline, but only slightly. Consequently, we have a long way to go to improve the equity of the tax system. I believe this can be done without punitive tax rates that will hurt economic incentives.

I begin with a brief review of recent changes in the U.S. distribution of income and follow this with an analysis of the effect of taxes on the income distribution. I next examine arguments for and against the income tax, with particular emphasis on its effects on economic incentives and its merits when compared with the expenditure tax. I then evaluate the income tax as it emerged from the 1986 tax reform and conclude with an agenda for further reform in the context of the current fiscal crisis. I believe that, when the nation gets around to eliminating or substantially reducing the federal deficit, the income tax should play an important role.[4]

## DISTRIBUTION OF INCOME AND TAX BURDENS

It is well known that, after several decades of relative stability, the U.S. pretax income distribution has become much more unequal in the last ten years. Official statistics understate the increasing inequality. At the same time, the tax system as a whole—and the income tax in particular—has become less equalizing, so that the trend toward inequality is even more pronounced after tax than before tax.

### Distribution of Income

The longest continuous and comparable income distribution series available to us comes from the annual Current Population Survey (CPS) of the Census Bureau. The figures show that the share of total income received by the highest fifth of the nation's families fell from 1948 to 1952, remained unchanged between 1952 and 1981, and then rose from 1981 to 1988. By 1988, the share of the top fifth was the highest ever recorded. The figures for the top 5 percent are similar, except that their share in 1987 had not quite recovered to the 1952 high (Table 1).

It is well known that very high incomes are virtually unrepresented in the CPS distribution and that the official census statistics greatly understate income inequality in any year. What is not recognized is that the CPS data greatly understate the *increase* in inequality that has occurred during the 1980s because very high incomes have been increasing much faster than the incomes in the lower part of the distribution.[5] This can be seen by examining changes in the shares of the top income recipients reported in the annual *Statistics of Income* published by the Internal Revenue Service (Table 2).[6]

Like the CPS data, the tax data show that the very rich in the United States—defined as either the top 1 percent or the top 5 percent of the income distribution—enjoyed about the same income increases as the average income recipient in the 1950s, 1960s, and 1970s, but their share of total income has been rising in the

**Table 1** Before-Tax Income Shares, Census Data, Selected Years, 1948–1988, Percent

| Year | Top 5 percent of families | Top 20 percent of families |
|------|---------------------------|----------------------------|
| 1948 | 17.1 | 42.4 |
| 1952 | 17.4 | 41.5 |
| 1957 | 15.6 | 40.4 |
| 1962 | 15.7 | 41.3 |
| 1967 | 15.2 | 40.4 |
| 1972 | 15.9 | 41.4 |
| 1977 | 15.7 | 41.5 |
| 1981 | 15.4 | 41.9 |
| 1987 | 16.9 | 43.7 |
| 1988 | 17.2 | 44.0 |

*Source:* Bureau of the Census. Income includes transfer payments (for example, Social Security benefits, unemployment compensation, welfare payments, etc.) but excludes capital gains. Distribution includes only families and excludes single persons living alone.

1980s. From 1952 to 1981, the share of the top 1 percent of the tax units remained in a very narrow range—between 8 and 9 percent of the total income reported on tax returns. Since 1981, their share has skyrocketed to 14.7 percent in 1986. The same trends are shown by the top 2, 5, 10, and 15 percent of the tax units.

Much of the increase in the share of the top tax units reflects the large increase in realized capital gains that accompanied the bull market of the 1980s. But salaries and other incomes of the top units have also been increasing faster than average.[7] In fact, the movement toward inequality must have been even greater than the tax data show because they do not include the large amounts of income taxpayers were able to shelter before the enactment of the Tax Reform Act of 1986.

Many economists and statisticians have examined these trends, but nobody has been able to explain them fully. The declining share of incomes received by the lower income classes has been attributed to the increase in the number of sin-

**Table 2** Before-Tax Income Shares, Tax Data, Selected Years, 1948–1986, Percent

| Year | Top 1% of Tax Units | Top 2% of Tax Units | Top 5% of Tax Units | Top 10% of Tax Units | Top 15% of Tax Units |
|------|---------------------|---------------------|---------------------|----------------------|----------------------|
| 1948 | 9.8 | 13.4 | 20.2 | 27.9 | 34.3 |
| 1952 | 8.7 | 12.1 | 18.7 | 26.7 | 33.4 |
| 1963 | 8.8 | 12.3 | 19.4 | 28.2 | 35.5 |
| 1967 | 8.8 | 12.3 | 19.6 | 28.3 | 35.5 |
| 1972 | 8.0 | 11.4 | 18.7 | 27.8 | 35.4 |
| 1977 | 7.8 | 11.3 | 18.9 | 28.3 | 36.1 |
| 1981 | 8.1 | 11.5 | 19.0 | 28.6 | 36.5 |
| 1986 | 14.7 | 18.2 | 26.6 | 36.8 | 45.1 |

*Source: Statistics of Income. Income* excludes transfer payments, but includes realized capital gains in full.

gle-parent families, slow growth in earnings of production workers, the disappearance of middle-income jobs, and other factors.[8] But these explanations do not account for the recent explosion of earned and property incomes of those in the top tail of the distribution.

The trend toward greater inequality has developed despite the existence of an income tax in the United States for seventy-six years and of an estate tax for eighty years. Clearly, the tax system never reduced inequality very much and other forces in the 1980s have swamped whatever equalizing effect it may have had earlier. I turn now to an examination of the burdens imposed by the tax system and how they have affected the distribution of income after tax.

## Distribution of Tax Burdens

I have been estimating federal, state, and local tax burdens by income classes for the last two decades on the basis of the Brookings MERGE files.[9] These files are based on the CPS surveys, modified at the top by the incomes reported on federal individual income tax returns. As shown in Table 3, the tax burdens of the bottom 90 percent of the income distribution did not change very much from 1966 to 1985. By contrast, the

**Table 3**  Effective Rates of Federal, State, and Local Taxes, by Population Percentiles, Selected Years, 1966–1988[a]

| Population Percentile[b] | Percent | | | | | |
|---|---|---|---|---|---|---|
| | 1966 | 1970 | 1975 | 1980 | 1985 | 1988[c] (est.) |
| 1st Decile[d] | 16.8 | 18.8 | 19.7 | 17.1 | 17.0 | 16.4 |
| 2nd Decile | 18.9 | 19.5 | 17.6 | 17.1 | 15.9 | 15.8 |
| 3rd Decile | 21.7 | 20.8 | 18.9 | 18.9 | 18.1 | 18.0 |
| 4th Decile | 22.6 | 23.2 | 21.7 | 20.8 | 21.2 | 21.5 |
| 5th Decile | 22.8 | 24.0 | 23.5 | 22.7 | 23.4 | 23.9 |
| 6th Decile | 22.7 | 24.1 | 23.9 | 23.4 | 23.8 | 24.3 |
| 7th Decile | 22.7 | 24.3 | 24.2 | 24.4 | 24.7 | 25.2 |
| 8th Decile | 23.1 | 24.6 | 24.7 | 25.5 | 25.4 | 25.6 |
| 9th Decile | 23.3 | 25.0 | 25.4 | 26.5 | 26.2 | 26.8 |
| 10th Decile | 30.1 | 30.7 | 27.8 | 28.5 | 26.4 | 27.7 |
| Top 5 Percent | 32.7 | 33.0 | 28.4 | 28.9 | 26.0 | 27.4 |
| Top 1 Percent | 39.6 | 39.0 | 29.0 | 28.4 | 25.3 | 26.8 |
| All Deciles[e] | 25.2 | 26.1 | 25.0 | 25.3 | 24.5 | 25.4 |

*Source:* Brookings MERGE files.

[a] Assumes corporate income and property taxes are borne by capital income.

[b] Arrayed by comprehensive income which includes transfer payments, employee fringe benefits, net imputed rent, and corporate earnings allocated to shareholders.

[c] Projected from 1985 on the basis of CBO estimates of changes in effective federal tax rates. Assumes no change in effective state-local tax rates between 1985 and 1988.

[d] Includes only units in the sixth to tenth percentiles.

[e] Includes negative incomes not shown separately.

tax burdens of the top ten percent of income recipients fell, especially those of the top 5 percent and 1 percent. Effective tax rates of the top 5 percent dropped by one-fifth between 1966 and 1985 (from 32.7 percent to 26.0 percent); for the top 1 percent, the reduction was more than one-third (from 39.6 percent to 25.3 percent).

Tax burdens of the highest income recipients fell because top federal individual tax rates were reduced throughout this period, from 70 percent in 1966 to 50 percent in 1985. Furthermore, the federal corporation income tax dwindled to relative obscurity, falling from 4.1 percent of GNP in 1966 to 1.6 percent in 1985. The proliferation of personal deductions (for example, state and local taxes, interest payments, and IRAs), tax-exempt bonds, and tax shelters were also major factors in the reduction of the tax burdens in the top part of the income distribution. The reduction in the corporate tax reflected primarily the investment incentives introduced in the 1960s and liberalized in the 1970s and 1980s, as well as a reduction in the profitability of the corporate sector.[10]

Since 1985, the distribution of tax burdens has changed largely because of the enactment of the landmark Tax Reform Act of 1986. This act increased the progressivity of the tax system, most notably by raising the personal exemptions, standard deductions, and the earned income credit, and by shifting about $25 billion of tax annually from individuals to corporations. However, this change in tax policy restored only a small fraction of the progressivity lost in the preceding two decades. At the very top of the income distribution, the 1986 federal tax reform restored about half the reduction in effective tax rates between 1980 and 1985, but left them far below the 1966 levels: the top 1 percent paid only 26.8 percent in taxes in 1988 as compared with 39 percent in 1970 (Table 3).

The inescapable conclusion from these figures is that the well-to-do in our society had very large reductions in tax rates in recent years, while the tax rates at the low and middle income levels have not changed much. Since the before-tax distribution has become much more unequal in the 1980s, it follows that inequality has increased even more on an after-tax basis.[11]

## Transfer Payments

The only major element of government policy affecting the distribution of income is the system of transfer payments, or negative taxes. This system includes programs of public assistance that are designed explicitly to help the poor, but it also includes others that are not designed primarily for this purpose (for example, retirement and unemployment benefits and health insurance). To evaluate the impact of the tax-transfer system on the distribution of income, cash and in-kind transfers must be added to market incomes while taxes are deducted.

While I cannot separate the effects of transfer payments and of taxes on the recent changes in the after-tax income distribution,[12] a snapshot for a recent year— 1985—suggests what happened (Figure 1). When family units are arrayed by their incomes from market production (wages, salaries, interests, dividends, etc.), the U.S. tax system is only mildly progressive. On the other hand, transfer payments

**Figure 1** Federal, State, and Local Transfers and Taxes as a
Percent of Market Income by Income Percentile, 1985

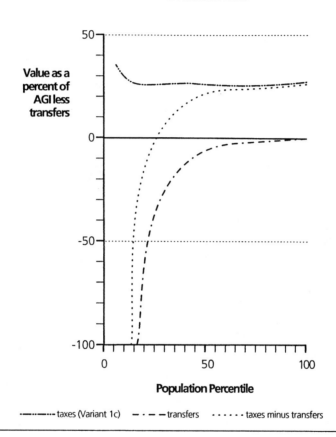

**Tax-Transfer Table**

Value as a percent of AGI less transfers (y-axis)

Population Percentile (x-axis)

------- taxes (Variant 1c)   — · — transfers   · · · · · taxes minus transfers

are highly progressive. Taxes in 1985 were regressive in the lowest deciles and proportional thereafter, while transfer payments declined from over 200 percent of market incomes in the lowest decile to 1.4 percent in the highest. On balance, families in the lowest three deciles received more in transfers than they paid in taxes, while those in the top seven deciles paid more in taxes than they received in transfers.

Clearly, the tax-transfer system is progressive, mainly because of transfers, not taxes. What we are doing in the United States is financing redistributive transfers with taxes that are roughly proportional to incomes. Moreover, the tax system has been getting less progressive in the last two decades, while the ratio of transfers to income has been increasing.[13] In other words, the recent increases in transfer payments in the United States have been financed by the low and middle income groups, while the rich have been getting tax cuts.

## WHAT ROLE FOR THE INCOME TAX?

Most people support tax progressivity on the ground that taxes should be levied in accordance with ability to pay, which is assumed to rise more than proportionately with income. Economists have long had trouble with the "ability to pay" concept. In recent years they have revived the old notion that consumption measures ability to pay better than income does. I believe that the person in the street is right and that we should continue to rely on the income tax to raise revenue in an equitable manner.

### Ability to Pay

In the latter half of the nineteenth century, progressive income taxation was justified by "sacrifice" theories that emerged from discussions of ability to pay. Under this doctrine, ability to pay is assumed to increase as incomes rise, and the objective is to impose taxes on a basis that would involve "equal sacrifice" in some sense. If the marginal utility of income declines more rapidly than income increases and the relation between income and utility is the same for all taxpayers, equal sacrifice leads to progression.[14] Whether or not one believes in sacrifice theory, the ability to pay idea has been a powerful force in history and has doubtedly contributed to the widespread acceptance of progressive taxation.[15] Young has found that the equal sacrifice model fits most U.S. tax schedules in the postwar period, with the notable exception of the schedule adopted in 1986. Similar results hold for Italy, West Germany, and Japan.[16]

Henry Simons vigorously attacked sacrifice theory although he argued strongly that the purpose of the progressive income tax is to reduce economic inequality.[17] Simons was vague on how far progression should be pushed, but he clearly felt that it had not yet gone too far in most countries. His prescription was the pragmatic one that the tax rates should not impair economic incentives. In his policy statements, he argued in favor of a broad base and graduated rate schedule that rises to a maximum of 50 percent.[18]

I agree with Simons that the income tax should be used to reduce the great disparities of welfare, opportunity, and economic power arising from the unequal distribution of income. I also recognize that this view is not widely held and has probably not been the major rationale for income tax legislation in the United States or in most other countries. The income tax is widely used primarily because it raises large amounts of revenue in a moderately progressive way. Recent income tax reforms have concentrated mainly on eliminating tax preferences to improve horizontal equity; where income tax rates had been pushed to very high levels, they are being moderated. Curiously, the world appears to be moving toward a consensus on the Simons' view that the income tax should be levied on a broad base with graduated rates reaching a maximum of 50 percent or less, though not for his reasons.

## Economic Incentives

The effects of the progressive income tax on incentives to work and to save are hard to measure. As is well known, the substitution and income effects of taxation work against each other, and the net result cannot be predicted.

Sample surveys have revealed that professional personnel do not vary their hours of work in response to high tax rates.[19] However, recent econometric studies suggest that the pre-1986 income and payroll taxes reduced the work effort of primary earners in the United States by about 8 percent, while secondary earners—who have a greater opportunity to vary their labor input—reduced their work effort by as much as 30 percent.[20] According to this approach, the 1986 reform may have increased labor supply of married men by only 1 percent and of married women by less than 3 percent, largely because the marginal tax rates of most workers were not reduced very much.[21] Burtless estimates that the Reagan tax and transfer policies increased average annual taxes of men aged 25–54 by no more than 2–4 percent and of women in the same age group by no more than 3.5 percent.[22]

Historical trends in U.S. labor supply are not consistent with the finding that taxes have reduced work effort. Adult males have been reducing their labor supply over the last forty years, largely through earlier retirement little of which is the effect of tax rates. The labor force participation of women has risen sharply in recent years, despite high marginal rates resulting from the requirement that married couples must file joint returns to benefit from income splitting. Studies in other countries are not reliable enough to support conclusions about the relationship between taxes and labor supply.

The effect of taxes on saving is even more ambiguous. A few studies claim that they have found a significant response to an increase in the real after-tax return on saving; others find that the response, if any, is close to zero.[23] The reduction in the personal saving rate in the United States in the 1980s confounded most economists in view of the reductions in the marginal tax rates, the incentive provided by individual retirement accounts (IRAs), and the high real interest rates, all of which should have increased the incentive to save.

The strongest conclusion one can draw from the available evidence is that the incentive effects of taxation have been relatively small. Yet the supply siders were convinced that the incentive effects were so large that rate cuts would increase revenues when tax rates are reduced.[24] U.S. tax rates were cut sharply in 1981 and 1986, but these cuts had little effect on labor supply and no effect on saving. Under the circumstances, so long as tax rates are not pushed to punitive levels, incentive considerations do not justify neglect of the distributional objective of tax policy.

## Income vs. Expenditure Tax

The revival of interest in the expenditure tax can be traced to the difficulties of taxing income from capital under the income tax. However, economists and tax lawyers have also found efficiency reasons to prefer the expenditure tax and these need to be addressed.[25]

A basic difference between the income and expenditure taxes is in the time perspective of the two taxes. The perspective of the income tax is relatively short-run—a year or several years to allow for short-run income fluctuations. Consumption is more stable than income and is alleged, therefore, to be a better measure of long-term well-being. In fact, under certain simplifying assumptions, the *bases* of taxes on the discounted present value of income and expenditure are the same over a lifetime. Assuming perfect capital markets, constant discount rates that apply equally to all people under all circumstances, tax rates that are constant and proportional, and no gifts and bequests, the present values of lifetime expenditures of people with the same (discounted) lifetime incomes are the same regardless of when the incomes are consumed.[26]

Advocates of the expenditure tax regard the lifetime perspective as a major advantage because it permits them to pretend that taxing consumption is equivalent to taxing personal endowments. A tax on endowments, if they could be measured, would avoid the distortionary effects of either an income tax or an expenditure tax. If it is assumed that lifetime consumption approximates endowment, then taxing consumption at flat and constant rates treats equally all taxpayers with the same endowment.[27] The totally unrealistic assumptions underlying this line of reasoning strain credulity, but it does seem to lie behind the strong support for the expenditure tax by many economists.

The lifetime perspective has little merit even without the endowment rationale. In my view, it is difficult enough to measure economic circumstances over relatively short periods. Taxation of lifetime consumption (or income) hardly seems appropriate in a world of changing tax rates, substantial family instability, economic and political change, and uncertainty. Except for the attractiveness of the arithmetic, lifetime economic circumstances as measured by discounted lifetime incomes or consumption cannot be regarded as satisfactory indexes of ability to pay.[28] Moreover, taxation of annual consumption expenditures at graduated rates would destroy the identity of lifetime taxes of taxpayers with the same (discounted) lifetime incomes.

The expenditure tax is alleged to be superior to the income tax on the additional ground that the income tax reduces the return on saving and therefore encourages current as against future consumption. Even if saving remained unchanged, the distortion generates a welfare loss for consumers. It has been pointed out by many economists that this effect must be balanced against the welfare cost of further distorting the choice between labor and leisure. There is no theoretical basis for judging whether the welfare gain from eliminating the intertemporal distortion of consumption would exceed the welfare loss from increasing the intratemporal distortion of the labor-leisure choice.[29]

A tax that omits saving from the tax base can be shown to be the same as a tax applying only to labor income and exempting all property income.[30] Several expenditure tax advocates have, in fact, proposed a tax on labor income on grounds of simplicity and administrative feasibility.[31] Most people would be appalled by a proposal to substitute a wage tax for income tax, yet that is essentially what expenditure tax proponents are advocating.

Many economists are attracted to the expenditure tax because it would not tax income from capital and would thus eliminate all the income tax problems arising from the use of the realization principle for calculating capital gains and losses and from the accounting conventions for inventories, depreciation, and depletion used in arriving at net business profits. There would also be no need to adjust the tax base for inflation, as consumption would be measured appropriately in current dollars. These are serious problems for income taxation and I shall deal with them later, but it would be unfortunate to abandon the income tax for administrative and compliance reasons alone.

The transition from the income tax to an expenditure tax would be troublesome. The retired elderly would draw down assets, some of which had previously been taxed under the income tax, to finance current consumption that would be taxed yet again. To avoid this double tax, some method would need to be devised to identify consumption from previously taxed accumulations. Grandfathering all assets at the time an expenditure tax is initiated would leave a big loophole for people with large amounts of untaxed accrued capital gains. But I have not seen any practical method of making the necessary distinctions in order to prevent wholesale tax avoidance and to achieve equity.[32]

Under an expenditure tax, taxpayers who save could accumulate large amounts of wealth over a lifetime. Many, but by no means all, expenditure tax advocates support wealth or estate and gift taxes to prevent excessive concentrations of wealth. But the history of transfer taxation in this country and abroad provides little assurance that effective death and gift taxes would be levied to supplement an expenditure tax.

Proponents of expenditure taxation often compare the merits of a comprehensive expenditure tax with the income tax as it has developed. It is hard to believe that an expenditure tax would be enacted without numerous exemptions and exclusions. In fact, most of the eroding features of the income tax (for example, preferences for housing, fringe benefits, child care, state-local borrowing, etc.) might be carried over to the expenditure tax. Thus, an expenditure tax is no less immune to erosion than the income tax and, in such circumstances, it loses much of its attractiveness.

I conclude that income is a better indicator of ability to pay than consumption and that the major upheaval of substituting an expenditure tax for an income tax cannot be justified on theoretical or practical grounds.

## How Much Progression?

The effective degree of progression of the income tax depends on the comprehensiveness of the tax base as well as on the tax rates. We have learned from experience that high, graduated tax rates do not assure progressivity of the income tax. For most of the period since the end of World War II, the top U.S. income tax rates were 70 percent or higher. Yet little equalization resulted because of the erosion of the base of the individual and corporate income taxes and because of increases in the payroll tax for Social Security.[33] According to estimates of the Congressional Budget Office (CBO), in 1977, when the top income tax rate was 70 percent and the general corporate tax rate was 48 percent, the Gini coefficient of inequality was 0.4502 before tax and 0.4185 after federal taxes (more than half of which were individual and corporate income taxes). In 1980, when the top tax rate was still 70 percent (though only on unearned income) and the corporate rate was 46 percent, the Gini coefficient was 0.4627 before tax and 0.4320 after the same taxes. Thus, as measured by the Gini coefficient, the equalization achieved by the federal tax system declined from a modest 0.0317 points (7.0 percent) in 1977 to an even more modest 0.0307 points (6.6 percent) in 1980 (Table 4).

Two major pieces of tax legislation were enacted during the 1980s. One increased inequality, the other reduced it. The 1981 Act, enacted after Ronald Reagan's sweeping victory in the 1980 presidential election, increased inequality by reducing income tax rates by 23 percent across the board (with a top rate on ordinary income of 50 percent), lowering the capital gains rate to a maximum of 20 percent, introducing generous deductions for individual retirement accounts, and providing very liberal depreciation allowances for business investment on top of the previously enacted investment tax credit. The Tax Reform Act of 1986 reduced inequality by increasing personal exemptions and the standard deduction, equalizing the tax rates on capital gains and ordinary income, and closing numerous loopholes. At the same time, income tax rates were reduced to a maximum of 33 percent on individuals and 34 percent on corporations.

Despite the large rate cuts at the top of the income scale, the 1986 act increased income tax progression, though not to the 1980 level. By 1984, the equalization provided by the federal tax system had declined to 0.0184 points (3.8 percent) in terms of the Gini coefficient. As a result of the 1986 act, the degree of equalization increased to 0.0218 points (4.4 percent) in 1988 (Table 4). While this change is modest, it is noteworthy as the first movement toward greater income tax progressivity at least since 1964, when the Kennedy-Johnson tax cut was enacted.

**Table 4**  Gini Coefficients of Inequality Before and After
Federal Taxes, Selected Years, 1977–1988

| Year | Gini Coefficients | |
| --- | --- | --- |
| | **Before Federal Taxes** | **After Federal Taxes** |
| 1977 | 0.4502 | 0.4185 |
| 1980 | 0.4627 | 0.4320 |
| 1984 | 0.4884 | 0.4700 |
| 1988 | 0.4940 | 0.4722 |

*Source:* Congressional Budget Office, *The Changing Distribution of Federal Taxes: A Closer Look at 1980* (July 1988): 98.

I suggest that a minimal goal of federal tax policy in the next several years should be to restore the equalization achieved by the federal tax system in the mid-1970s.[34] While this may appear to be a modest goal, it turns out to be a rather ambitious undertaking, particularly if income tax rates are to be kept to moderate levels. Before calculating the tax rates, it is necessary first to establish the appropriate tax base for a modern income tax.

## REFORM OF THE INCOME TAX

The proper base for the income tax was described fifty years ago by Henry Simons, who argued that it should conform with an economic definition of income.[35] Admittedly, the use of a comprehensive income tax contradicts the principle of optimal taxation that tax rates should vary with a number of elasticities. However, the optimal tax models are based on strong assumptions that are often implausible or virtually impossible to validate. Consequently, there is no empirical basis for determining how different commodities and sources of income should be taxed. Moreover, the compliance and enforcement costs of such a system could be large enough to more than offset the potential inefficiencies of a uniform tax. In the absence of reliable data, it is safer to rely on the comprehensive approach rather than to introduce tax differentials that will generate their own distortions.[36]

According to Simons and others, income is the sum of an individual's consumption and change in net worth during a particular time period. For a long time, the federal income tax base was a far cry from a comprehensive definition of income. In 1986, however, Congress reversed its previous practice and enacted a wholesale tax reform that moved the income tax a long way toward the Simons' ideal. This remarkable piece of legislation can provide the basis for achieving the distributive objectives discussed earlier with moderate tax rates.

### The 1986 Tax Reform[37]

The Tax Reform Act of 1986, a major step toward comprehensive income taxation, greatly improved the fairness and efficiency of the tax system. The major accomplishments of the act are as follows:

By doubling personal exemptions and increasing the standard deduction, the act relieved about 5 million poor people from paying any income tax. This step restored the principle (abandoned by Congress in 1978) that people who are officially designated as "poor" should not be required to pay income tax. The principle was perpetuated by the resumption in 1989 of an automatic annual adjustment of the exemptions and standard deduction of inflation.

Significant increases were made in the earned income credit for wage earners with families. These increases eliminated almost the entire Social Security payroll tax (including the employer's share) for those eligible for the full credit and reduced the tax burden for many low-income workers.

For the first time since 1921, realized capital gains were made taxable as ordinary income. This is the keystone of comprehensive tax reform: it reduces the incentive to convert ordinary income into capital gains and removes one of the major elements of tax shelter arrangements. Moreover, this change made it possible to reduce tax rates without reducing the progressivity of the income tax.

A good start was made to reverse the erosion of the individual income tax base. For example, unemployment benefits, which were previously taxable only if a married taxpayer's income exceeded $18,000 ($12,000 if single), were made taxable regardless of the size of income. Deductions for state and local sales taxes were eliminated and those for consumer interest were phased out. For administrative reasons, deductions for unreimbursed business expenses, costs incurred in earning investment income, and other miscellaneous expenses were allowed only to the extent that they exceed a floor of two percent of income.

Some of the most egregious loopholes and special tax benefits were eliminated. Many tax shelters were rendered unprofitable by denying deductions for losses from passive activity against income from anything but passive activities.[38] Tax subsidies for borrowing (other than for mortgages) were eliminated by another limitation on the deduction for interest expenses to the amount of investment income reported on the individual's tax return.[39] Deductions for contributions to individual retirement accounts were curtailed. Deductible business expense accounts for meals, travel, and entertainment were limited to 80 percent of outlays. Tax preferences benefiting defense contractors, banks, oil companies, and other industries were narrowed. On top of all these changes, the minimum tax for both individuals and business was retained and strengthened.

Finally, the individual and corporate tax rates were cut drastically. Under the individual income tax, two rates—15 and 28 percent—were substituted for the earlier schedule of 14 rates, which rose to a maximum of 50 percent. However, the benefits of the lowest rates and of the personal exemptions were phased out for higher income taxpayers at a 5 percent rate. As a result, the new individual income tax rate structure has four brackets, with rates of 15, 28, 33, and 28 percent (see Table 7). The general corporate rate was cut from 46 percent to 34 percent. Despite these large rate cuts, the act was expected to be roughly revenue neutral in total over the first five years, but to shift about $25 billion of tax annually from individuals to corporations.

The distributional effect of the 1986 act is distinctly progressive, especially if the increase in corporate tax liabilities is taken into account. I have calculated the change in average effective tax rates of the nation's families on the basis of the distribution of income estimated from the Brookings MERGE file (Table 5). Total federal tax burdens decline in the lower nine deciles and rise in the top decile. In the lower deciles, the tax reductions result from increases in the personal exemptions, standard deduction, and the earned income credit under the individual income tax. The increases at the top reflect the broadened individual income tax base, as well as the increase in corporate tax liability, which is assumed to fall on owners of capital in these calculations. However, as already noted, this increase in progressivity only partially reversed the reductions that had taken place in the 1970s and early 1980s.

**Table 5** Changes in Individual and Corporate Income Tax Liabilities
Under the Tax Reform Act of 1986, by Population Percentile, 1988

| Population Percentile[a] | Percent Change in | |
|---|---|---|
| | Federal Individual and Corporate Income Taxes[b] | Total Federal Taxes |
| 1st Decile | −44 | −16 |
| 2nd Decile | −32 | −11 |
| 3rd Decile | −24 | −10 |
| 4th Decile | −16 | −7 |
| 5th Decile | −12 | −6 |
| 6th Decile | −8 | −4 |
| 7th Decile | −7 | −4 |
| 8th Decile | −6 | −3 |
| 9th Decile | −6 | −4 |
| 10th Decile | +3 | +2 |
| Top 5 Percent | +4 | +3 |
| Top 1 Percent | +5 | +5 |

*Source:* Brookings MERGE file.

[a]The classification is by a comprehensive definition of income, including imputed rent and corporate earnings allocated to stockholders, whether distributed or not.

[b]Assumes the corporate tax is on capital in general.

## The Unfinished Agenda

Despite the progress made in 1986, the federal income tax in the United States falls considerably short of the comprehensive income target.[40] I assume that we shall continue to tax capital gains on a realization, rather than accrual, basis, and that gifts and bequests will be taxed under a separate transfer tax. Nevertheless, a great deal more could be done to broaden the tax base for equity, efficiency, and revenue reasons.

The personal exemptions, standard deductions, and rate bracket limits are adjusted annually for inflation, but the tax base is not. Of the two types of adjustment, adjustment of the tax base would be by far the more important. Perhaps the major reason why the income tax tends to be in disrepute is the discrimination against capital income inherent in a nominal income tax. An inflation adjustment of asset prices should be incorporated in the tax law as part of the computation of real capital gains and losses, real interest income expense, and real inventory and depreciation allowances. The adjustment of interest is admittedly difficult, but the widespread use of computers should ease the administrative and compliance problems.

Restoration of a tax differential between capital gains and ordinary income should be resisted at all costs. Equalization of the tax rates lowers the incentive to convert other income into capital gains, simplifies business and financial decisions, and reduces income tax complexity. Aside from the correction for inflation, the one additional reform needed in the capital gains tax is to include in the tax base unrealized capital gains transferred by gift or at death. Taxing such gains would reduce the lock-in effect of the tax on transfers of assets and eliminate a source of horizontal inequity.

A major neglected problem in most countries is the erosion of the tax base from the exclusion of employee fringe benefits. Trade unions, as well as employers, staunchly defend the continued exclusion of fringe benefit income, but in fact the largest subsidies go to the highest paid employees. Loopholes for union members and other workers are no more defensible than those for the rich. Taxation of fringe benefits would encourage their conversion into cash compensation, thus giving employees more control over the disposition of their income and the choice of the providers of their services. Australia and New Zealand have shown the way to reform in this area by taxing fringe benefits (other than contributions to pension plans) at the corporate tax rate. This method of handling a difficult, but urgent, problem is simple and effective.

Social Security benefits continue to receive favorable treatment, even though the elderly can no longer be regarded as a disadvantaged group. Under current law, the medical insurance subsidies they receive are not subject to tax, and less than half of retirement and disability benefits is taxable to married couples with income above $32,000 ($25,000 if single). The value of the medical insurance subsidies should be subject to tax in full[41] and retirement and disability benefits should be treated like private pensions without any income thresholds, which would mean that roughly 85 percent of the benefits would be currently taxable.

The treatment of owner-occupied housing remains unsatisfactory. I assume that the exclusion of imputed rent from the tax base and the deduction of mortgage interest by most homeowners are sacrosanct, but it is possible to limit the encouragement of borrowing without promoting rearrangements of debt for tax purposes. The solution is to broaden the limitation on deductions of investment interest to include all interest payments. That is, a deduction for all interest payments would be allowed, but limited to the amount of reported investment income. To accommodate the homeowner lobby, the limit could be raised to net investment plus an arbitrary amount, say, $10,000—enough to take care of the vast majority of homeowners. The broader interest limitation would remove the discrimination against borrowing for other purposes and the incentive to substitute home equity loans for other types of borrowing.

Deductions other than for interest are still too generous. The Simons' definition of income includes all sources of income, without any deductions for the uses of that income. For equity reasons, it is appropriate to permit deductions for such unusual expenses as medical payments and casualty losses. I would retain the deduction for state income taxes to moderate interstate tax differentials.[42] However, the property tax is largely a benefit tax and therefore should not be deductible. Nor is it necessary to allow a deduction for the first dollar of charitable contributions on incentive grounds. Little or no charitable giving would be lost[43] and much revenue would be gained or reductions in tax rates would be possible if the federal deduction for property taxes were disallowed and the deduction for charitable contributions were restricted to amounts in excess of two percent of income. In addition, the tax-exemption for interest on newly issued state and local bonds should be removed.

Although income tax compliance is better in the United States than in most other countries, roughly 15 percent of individual income is still unreported, according to IRS estimates.[44] Extension of withholding to interest and dividends would improve compliance. Congress enacted a withholding system for these income items in 1982, but repealed it the following year under pressure from the financial institutions. Since information returns are required for annual interest and dividend payments of $10 or more, the marginal costs of compliance with a withholding system would be small.

One of the major features of the 1986 tax law was to telescope the schedule of tax rates into two acknowledged and two concealed brackets, a bizarre four-bracket rate structure of 15, 28, 33, and 28 percent. The reduction in the number of brackets was a response to the flat tax proposals that were being promoted when the tax reform bill began its journey through Congress, while the unsightly bulge in the rate schedule was motivated by revenue considerations. It is not necessary to return to 14 brackets, but there is room for more rate graduation without the bulge.

In this connection, consideration needs to be given to improving the structure of estate and gift taxes to compensate for their low average rates. These taxes were almost gutted by increases in the exemptions and reductions in the tax rates when income tax rates were cut in 1981. Now that the top income tax rates are even lower, it is time to rely more heavily on the estate and gift taxes.

The reduction in the tax rates led to two additional changes in the 1986 act that I believe were unfortunate. Congress eliminated the deduction for two-earner couples and ended the privilege of averaging income for tax purposes.[45] Both provisions should be restored in the interest of horizontal equity.

Finally, contrary to the prevailing view among public finance experts, Congress clearly believes that a separate, unintegrated corporate tax is essential for effective income taxation. A separate tax prevents individuals from avoiding the income tax by accumulating earnings at the corporate level, although some might question whether corporations should be taxed at a higher rate than the top bracket individual rate. But in its present form, the corporate tax encourages debt financing. It is alleged to be a major cause of the recent upsurge in leveraged buyouts and mergers. The remedy is not to allow a deduction or credit for dividends received at the individual level. Rather, the deduction of interest by corporations should be denied while reducing their tax rate to the neighborhood of 15 percent to maintain the revenues now produced by the corporate tax.[46] The corporate tax would become a low-rate tax on net corporate income before distributions.

## Tax Rates and Progressivity

The reforms I have suggested would greatly increase the income tax base and permit a realignment of the tax rates to achieve the distributional objectives described earlier. At calendar year 1990 levels, the tax base would increase from $2.4 trillion to $2.8 trillion (Table 6). The increase in the base leaves enough room to cut rates in the lowest taxable income brackets and still keep the top tax rates at reasonably modest levels.

In redesigning the rate structure, I suggest scrapping the multiple schedule system which was developed to reduce the tax advantage of married couples relative to single people under income splitting. It is simpler to use one set of rates and to rely on the personal exemptions to take into account differences in ability to pay of families of different size.[47] The restored deduction for two-earner couples (20 percent of the earnings of the spouse with the lower earnings up to $70,000) would help avoid a significant marriage penalty.

The same revenue and progressivity of present law could be generated by a tax schedule ranging from 7 percent on the first $5,000 of taxable income to 26 percent on taxable income in excess of $35,000, without the bulge in tax rates under current law (see Plan I, Table 7).[48] Thus, a wide margin exists for increasing progressivity at the top of the income scale, while keeping rates moderate. To restore the progressivity of the federal tax system to its 1977 level, the range of graduation would have to be expanded and the rate of graduation increased. A starting rate of 4 percent on the first $5,000 of taxable income rising to 48 percent on taxable income above $250,000 would accomplish this objective (see Plan II, Table 7).[49]

**Table 6** Adjusted Gross Income and Taxable Income Under the Tax Reform Act of 1986 and Under a Comprehensive Income Tax

| | **1990 Billions of Dollars** | |
| Item | **Adjusted Gross Income** | **Taxable Income** |
| --- | --- | --- |
| Tax Reform Act of 1986 | 3,545 | 2,407 |
| Plus: | | |
|     Personal Deductions[a] | 0 | 68 |
|     Transfer Payments[b] | 226 | 164 |
|     Fringe Benefits[c] | 187 | 185 |
|     Two-earner Deduction[d] | −82 | −81 |
|     Other[e] | 43 | 42 |
| Equals: Comprehensive Tax[f] | 3,919 | 2,785 |

*Source:* Congressional Budget Office.

[a]Allows flat standard deduction of $4,000; interest deduction limited to investment income plus $10,000; tax deduction limited to income taxes; 10 percent floor on deductions for medical expenses and casualty losses; 2 percent floors on deductions for charitable contributions and miscellaneous expenses; and no standard deduction for the elderly and the blind.

[b]Includes 85 percent of Social Security retirement and disability benefits for all taxpayers, workers' compensation, and veterans' benefits; and 50 percent of the insurance value of hospital insurance benefits.

[c]Includes premiums paid by employers for health and life insurance and other fringe benefits; interest on life insurance policies; and IRAs of persons covered by employer pension plans.

[d]20 percent of earnings of spouses with lower earnings up to a maximum of $70,000.

[e]Includes unrealized capital gains transferred by gift or at death, interest on newly issued state and local securities, and all preference items now subject to the minimum tax.

[f]An increase in the earned income credit under Plan II (see Table 7) does not affect adjusted gross income or taxable income.

**Table 7** Comparison of Tax Rates Under the Tax Reform Act of 1986
and Under Two Comprehensive Income Taxes, 1990

| Tax Reform Act of 1986[a] | | Comprehensive Income Tax[b] | | |
|---|---|---|---|---|
| **Taxable Income** | **Rate (percent)** | **Taxable Income** | **Rate (percent)[c]** | |
| | | | **Plan I** | **Plan II** |
| $0–$32,400 | 15 | $0–$5,000 | 7 | 4 |
| 32,400–78,400 | 28 | 5,000–10,000 | 10 | 8 |
| 78,400–208,560[d] | 33 | 10,000–20,000 | 15 | 14 |
| 208,560 and over | 28 | 20,000–35,000 | 18 | 14 |
| | | 35,000–70,000 | 26 | 23 |
| | | 70,000–100,000 | 26 | 24 |
| | | 100,000–150,000 | 26 | 29 |
| | | 150,000–250,000 | 26 | 33 |
| | | 250,000 and over | 26 | 48 |

[a]For a married couple with two dependents. Separate rate schedules apply to single persons and heads of household.
[b]Applies to all taxpayers, regardless of marital and family status.
[c]Plan I maintains present progressivity of the federal income tax at 1990 levels; Plan II restores progressivity of the federal tax system as a whole to levels prevailing in 1977. Plan II provides a refundable earned income credit of 14 percent (up to $1,000) to all earners and increases the credit by 4 percentage points for each person in the tax unit above one (with a phaseout between $10,000 and $20,000 of adjusted gross income).
[d]Range within which the 13-percentage point reduction in the first bracket is phased out. Top limit of the range increases or decreases by $11,480 for each personal exemption.

Another change to increase progressivity would be to increase the earned-income credit for low-income families. Today, the credit is the same for all families, regardless of the number of children. The credit would be more effective in combating poverty if it increased with family size. For example, the current 14-percent credit could be maintained for families with one child and four percentage points, or roughly $250, could be added for each additional child. With this modification, the earned income credit would increase the likelihood that a family with several children could earn enough to remain outside the welfare system.

Table 8 reports the average effective federal income tax rates by population deciles under the schedule that restores overall progressivity to 1977 levels (Plan II) and under the schedule that matches 1990 distribution with a broadened base (Plan I). The average effective rates in Plan II are lower than those under present law in the bottom nine deciles and higher in the top decile. For the top 1 percent of the family units, the average effective rate rises from 21 percent to 30 percent, which cannot be regarded as punitive.

I recognize that few people would go as far as I would in broadening the tax base. But that does not mean that the objective of greater progressivity must be abandoned. Even if there were no additional base-broadening between now and 1990, the same degree of progressivity that prevailed in 1977 could be achieved with rates ranging from 7 percent at the bottom to 56 percent at the top.

**TABLE 8** Effective Federal Individual Income Tax Rates Under the
Tax Reform Act of 1986 and Under Two Comprehensive Income Taxes, 1990[a]

| | Percent | | |
|---|---|---|---|
| Population Percentile[b] | Tax Reform Act of 1986 | Comprehensive Income Tax[c] | |
| | | Plan I | Plan II |
| 1st Decile[d] | −0.9 | −0.4 | −1.3 |
| 2nd Decile | 0.0 | 0.1 | −0.8 |
| 3rd Decile | 1.9 | 2.0 | 0.7 |
| 4th Decile | 4.5 | 4.6 | 3.3 |
| 5th Decile | 6.2 | 6.2 | 5.0 |
| 6th Decile | 7.4 | 7.4 | 6.1 |
| 7th Decile | 8.4 | 8.5 | 7.0 |
| 8th Decile | 9.4 | 9.5 | 7.8 |
| 9th Decile | 11.1 | 10.9 | 9.1 |
| 10th Decile | 16.5 | 16.5 | 18.9 |
| Top 5 Percent | 18.0 | 18.1 | 22.3 |
| Top 1 Percent | 20.7 | 20.8 | 30.5 |
| All Deciles[e] | 11.1 | 11.1 | 11.1 |

*Source:* Congressional Budget Office.
[a]Assumes corporate income is borne by capital income.
[b]Arrayed by comprehensive income, which includes all transfer payments, the employer share of payroll taxes, and the corporate income tax (allocated to capital income).
[c]For tax rates under the two plans, see Table 7.
[d]Excludes families with zero or negative incomes.
[e]Includes families with zero or negative incomes.

## CONCLUSION

I conclude that there is no good reason for the disenchantment of economists with the income tax. The main rival of the income tax—the consumption expenditure tax—is distinctly inferior on theoretical as well as practical grounds. The endowment or lifetime perspective of the expenditure tax is indefensible in a world of financial, political, and family instability. The transition problems in moving from an income tax to an expenditure tax are extremely difficult. There is also a danger that the substitution of an expenditure tax for the income tax would greatly increase the concentration of wealth. Moreover, the public regards income, not expenditure, as the best index of ability to pay, and it would be unwise to abandon this familiar and widely approved basis of taxation.

The 1986 reforms have greatly improved the federal income tax by broadening the base and lowering rates. But the progressivity of the federal tax system has been declining for the last two decades. As a result, the distribution of before-tax income, which has been growing more unequal in the 1980s, has become even more unequal on an after-tax basis. I have suggested that the goal of tax policy should be to restore the progressivity of the income tax at least to its level in the mid-1970s.

The 1986 tax reform went a long way toward comprehensive income taxation, but much more can be done to enlarge the tax base and to remove the preferences for capital income. Among the more urgent base-broadening reforms are the inclusion in taxable income of capital gains transferred by gift or at death, elimination of the tax exemption for newly issued state-local securities, taxation of employee fringe benefits, treatment of Social Security benefits like private pensions, reduction of the tax subsidy for homeowners, pruning of the personal deductions, and withholding on interest and dividends. To correct the measurement of capital income for inflation, asset prices should be adjusted for changing prices in order to convert nominal to real incomes for tax purposes. The two-earner deduction and income averaging should be restored to reduce the marriage penalty and equalize the treatment of fluctuating and stable incomes.

A comprehensive income tax along these lines would permit further rate reductions throughout the income scale if the degree of progression enacted in 1986 were to be retained. However, the progressivity of the federal tax system has declined since the mid-1970s, even after taking into account the effect of the 1986 act. To restore the degree of progressivity of the mid-1970s, the rate of graduation of the tax rates would need to be increased. I estimate that this can be accomplished with a rate schedule ranging from 4 percent at the bottom to 48 percent at the top of the taxable income scale—a moderate schedule of rates by any standard.

It is clear from this analysis that the revenue potential of the income tax has not been exhausted in this country. Even if the base is not broadened, the income tax can be used to raise considerable additional revenues in order to eliminate the recurring federal deficits. Each percentage-point increase in the individual and corporate income tax rates would bring in about $30 billion in 1994, so that three points would come close to balancing the overall budget in that year. A top individual income tax rate of 31 percent and a corporate rate of 37 percent cannot be regarded as punitive or harmful to economic incentives.

What is inappropriate in my view would be to introduce a value-added tax, as some are suggesting. The value-added tax is regressive and imposes unnecessarily heavy burdens on the lower income classes. With tax rates as low as they are today, more revenues should come from the income tax, the tax paid by those who have the ability to pay. In view of the recent reductions in the progressivity of the federal tax system, it would be unconscionable to enact the distinctly inferior alternative of a value-added tax.

# NOTES

I have benefited from the comments and suggestions on an earlier draft of this paper by Henry J. Aaron, Richard Goode, Jane G. Gravelle, Robert W. Hartman, Donald W. Kiefer, Herbert E. Klarman, Robert D. Reischauer, Clifford M. Winston, and H. Peyton Young, but they should not be held responsible for the views expressed in this paper. I am indebted to Richard Kasten for various simulations. I am also grateful to Stephen J. Kastenberg for research assistance and to Diane A. Shugart, Valerie M. Owens, and Sara C. Hufham for secretarial assistance.

1. Some of the more extreme supply siders argued that large tax cuts pay for themselves (see, for example, Laffer 1981), but I believe it is fair to say that this view has been totally discredited. For a more reasonable supply-side view, see the *Economic Report of the President 1982.*

2. See, for example, Michael J. Boskin (1978), David E. Bradford (1980), Charles L. Ballard, Don Fullerton, John Shoven, and John Whalley (1985), Paul Courant and Edward Gramlich (1982), Martin Feldstein (1978), Robert Hall and Alvin Rabushka (1985), John Kay and Mervyn King (1983), Charles McLure (1987), Mieszkowski (1980), and Lawrence Summers (1981). It is interesting that the recent popularity of the expenditure tax among economists was stimulated by a tax lawyer, William D. Andrews (1974).

3. See Pechman (1988).

4. See Musgrave (1989) for a statement of similar views.

5. Using Pareto distributions based on income tax data to approximate the upper tail of the U.S. distribution, Rudy Fichtenbaum and Hushang Shahidi (1988) calculated that the CPS underestimation of the Gini coefficient rose from 1.7 percent in 1967 to 7.6 percent in 1984.

6. For the method of calculation, see Pechman (1989, ch.1).

7. According to *Statistics of Income,* the shares of adjusted gross income other than capital gains increased from 6.59 percent in 1981 to 7.64 percent in 1986 for the top 1 percent of tax units, from 17.31 to 18.77 percent for the top 5 percent, and from 35.11 to 36.56 percent for the top 15 percent.

8. See, for example, Frank Levy (1988) and Sheldon Danziger et al. (1989).

9. See Pechman and Benjamin Okner (1974) and Pechman (1985).

10. See Alan Auerbach and James Poterba (1987).

11. Since the income tax affects economic behavior, the before-tax distributions reflect the responses of taxpayers, through portfolio shifts, substitution of nontaxable fringe benefits for cash compensation, and other actions, to the level and structure of the tax system. Hence, the after-tax distribution is more representative of the changes in inequality. For a discussion of these issues, see Eugene Steuerle (1985) and Harvey Galper et al. (1988).

12. The income distributions used in the Brookings MERGE file for 1966 were prepared on the basis of incomes *including* transfer payments. After so many years, it is impractical to reclassify the income and tax data for 1966 by income excluding transfer payments.

13. Little empirical work has been done on trends in the progressivity of the transfer system itself. If it has changed, the movement in the last decade may have been toward less progressivity because welfare payments have not kept up with inflation and the coverage of the unemployment compensation system has narrowed.

14. To be precise, equal *absolute* sacrifice leads to progression, equal *proportionate* sacrifice to still more progression, and equal *marginal* sacrifice to leveling of incomes from the top down until the required revenues are obtained. See Richard Musgrave (1959, 99–102).

15. See Musgrave (1959, ch. 5) and Richard Goode (1976, ch. 2). For a skeptical view of the case for the progressive income tax, see Blum and Kalven (1952).

16. See H. P. Young (1990). I omit discussion of the optimal tax literature, which built on the old sacrifice theory, because it does not yet provide a basis for making judgments

about the optimum degree of progression. This literature suggests that a progressive income tax is appropriate when redistribution is an objective of social policy, but the range of tax rates is very wide depending on the assumptions used. See Glen Hubbard and Kenneth Judd (1986), Nicholas Stern (1987, 49–52), Henry Aaron (1989, 10-12), Rosen (1988a, 1988b) and Slemrod (forthcoming).

17. "The case for drastic progression in taxation must be rested on the case against inequality—on the ethical or aesthetic judgment that the prevailing distribution of wealth and income reveals a degree (and/or kind) of inequality which is distinctly evil or unlovely." Simons (1938, 18–19).
18. See Simons (1950).
19. See Break (1957) and Holland (1969).
20. These estimates are based on a comparison with work effort under a system of lump-sum taxes. The estimates would be reduced substantially if the basis of comparison were a proportional income tax. For summaries of recent studies and their implications for policy, see Bosworth (1984, ch. 5) and Gary Burtless and Robert Haveman (1987). The methodology of these studies is explained by Hausman (1987).
21. See Hausman and Poterba (1987).
22. See Burtless (1989).
23. For a review of the various studies, see Evans (1983) and Bosworth (1984, chaps. 3 and 5).
24. President Ronald Reagan was one of those who believed that tax rate cuts would actually increase revenues (see Reagan 1981, 710). The supply-side view is defended in Raboy (1982). For an analysis of this view, see Meyer (1981).
25. For analyses of the relative merits of the income and expenditure taxes, see Kaldor (1955), Musgrave (1976), Pechman (1980), Aaron and Galper (1985), and Bradford (1986).
26. The identity of lifetime incomes and expenditures holds when there are gifts to others and bequests, provided the gifts and bequests are counted as expenditures. Aaron and Galper (1985) defined such a tax as a "lifetime" income tax, arguing that "there is no logical reason why a particular astronomical regularity should be enshrined in the tax law" (pp. 21-22).
27. See Bradford (1980, 106–109), Bradford (1986, 315), and Musgrave (1976, 11–12). Bradford holds this view while Musgrave does not.
28. For an excellent discussion of the lifetime vs. the short-run perspective as a basis for taxation, see Goode (1980).
29. See, for example, Feldstein (1978), Atkinson and Sandmo (1980), Atkinson and Stiglitz (1980), Auerbach and Kotlikoff (1987, ch. 5), Rosen (1988a, 469), and Gravelle (1988 and 1989).
30. Like the equality between a consumption and an income tax in present value terms, this assumes that tax and interest rates remain constant over a lifetime and there are no gifts and bequests. Let $s$ = saving, $w$ = wages, $c$ = consumption, $r$ = the interest rate, and assume that saving in the first period is consumed during the second, then

$$s_1 = w_1 - c_1$$
$$c_2 = w_2 + (1 + r)s_1$$
$$c_1(1 + r) + c_2 = (1 + r)(w_1 - s_1) + w_2 + (1 + r)s_1$$
$$c_1(1 + r) + c_2 = (1 + r)w_1 + w_2.$$

31. See Hall and Rabushka (1985), Bradford (1986, ch. 14), and McLure et al. (1988, ch. 9).
32. For a discussion of these problems and possible solutions, see Aaron and Galper (1985, 78–79, 99–103) and U.S. Department of the Treasury (1977, chaps. 4 and 6).

33. The combined employer-employee payroll tax rose from 6 percent in 1960 to 12.26 percent in 1985 and 14.1 percent in 1985. It is scheduled to rise further in 1990 to 15.3 percent. The maximum taxable earnings level rose from $4,800 in 1960 to $7,800 in 1970, $25,900 in 1980, $39,600 in 1985, and $48,000 in 1989. The maximum taxable earnings levels have been adjusted for inflation since 1984. For details see Pechman (1987, 332).

34. Specifically, as the basis for revision, I use the distribution of federal tax burdens in 1977 when the CBO tax incidence series begins. I do not mean to imply that the federal tax system in the mid-1970s had exactly the correct degree of equalization.

35. See Simons (1938, ch. II).

36. See Stern (1987, 51), Aaron (1989, 10–12), and Slemrod (forthcoming).

37. For an analysis of the structural features of the 1986 tax reform, see Pechman (1987a).

38. A passive activity is a trade or business in which the taxpayer (or spouse) does not materially participate. All rental activities are regarded as passive.

39. However, the act did not change the deductibility of interest on borrowing to finance business investments.

40. For a detailed analysis of a comprehensive income tax base, see Pechman (1977). Estimates of the revenue effects of specific changes in the tax base needed to reach the comprehensive base are given in Congressional Budget Office (1989).

41. The tax would be imposed on the insurance value of hospital and Medicare subsidies rather than on the dollar benefits actually received. See Congressional Budget Office (1989).

42. See Pechman (1987b, 267–269), for illustrations of aggregate tax rates with various combinations of federal and state tax rates.

43. Clotfelter (1989) reports finds that equations estimated on pre-1986 data relating charitable giving to income, the price of giving, and other variables fail utterly to predict the response of charitable giving to the Tax Reform Act of 1986.

44. Kenadjian (1988).

45. For discussions of the function of a two-earner deduction and the need for income averaging, see Pechman (1987a, 102–107 and 127–128).

46. To prevent undue hardship to highly leveraged firms, the denial of the interest deduction might be phased in over a period of years.

47. To avoid the old community property problem (see Pechman 1987b, 102–107), the brackets in the rate schedules for married couples filing separate returns would be one-half the size of the brackets for single people.

48. Exemptions and the standard deduction would remain the same as in 1989, that is, exemptions would be $2,000 per capita and the standard deduction would be $3,100 for single persons, $4,550 for heads of households, and $4,200 for married couples, all adjusted for inflation.

49. Between 1977 and 1990 the weight of the relatively regressive payroll tax in federal revenues increased. Thus, the income tax must be more progressive in 1990 than it was in 1977 to restore overall progressivity to its 1977 level.

# REFERENCES

Aaron, Henry J. "Politics and the Professors Revisited." *American Economic Review 79* (May 1989) Papers and Proceedings (1988): 1–15.

Aaron, Henry J., and Harvey Galper. *Assessing the Income Tax.* Washington, D.C.: Brookings Institution (1985).

Andrews, William D. "A Consumption-Type or Cash Flow Personal Income Tax." *Harvard Law Review 87* (April 1974): 1113–1188.

Atkinson, Anthony B., and Agnar Sandmo. "Welfare Implications of the Taxation of Savings." *Economic Journal 90* (September 1980): 529–549.

Atkinson, Anthony B., and Joseph E. Stiglitz. *Lectures on Public Economics.* New York: McGraw-Hill (1980).

Auerbach, Alan J., and Laurence J. Kotlikoff. *Dynamic Fiscal Policy.* London: Cambridge University Press (1987).

Auerbach, Alan J., and James M. Poterba. "Why Have Corporate Tax Revenues Declined?" *Tax Policy and the Economy, vol. 1,* Lawrence H. Summers, ed., Cambridge, Massachusetts: MIT Press, (1987).

Ballard, Charles L., Don Fullerton, John B. Shoven, and John Whalley. *A General Equilibrium Model for Tax Policy Evaluation.* Chicago: University of Chicago Press (1985).

Blum, Walter J., and Harry Kalven. "The Uneasy Case for Progressive Taxation." *University of Chicago Law Review 19* (Spring 1952): 417–520.

Boskin, Michael J. "Taxation, Saving, and the Rate of Interest." *Journal of Political Economy 86* (April 1978): pt. 2, S3–S27.

Bosworth, Barry P. *Tax Incentives and Economic Growth.* Washington, D.C.: Brookings Institution (1984).

Bradford, David F. "The Case for a Personal Expenditure Tax." *What Should Be Taxed: Income or Expenditure?* Washington, D.C.: Brookings Institution (1980): 75–113.

————. *Untangling the Income Tax,* Cambridge: Harvard University Press (1986).

Break, George F. "Income Taxes and Incentives to Work: An Empirical Study." *American Economic Review 5* (September 1957): 529–549.

Burtless, Gary. "The Supply-Side Legacy of the Reagan Years: Response of Labor Supply," unpublished paper (July 3, 1989).

Burtless, Gary, and Robert Haveman. "Taxes Transfers, and Labor Supply: The Evolving Views of U.S. Economists." *The Relevance of Public Finance for Policy-Making.* Detroit: Wayne State University Press (1987).

Clotfelter, Charles. "The Impact of Tax Reform on Charitable Giving: A 1989 Perspective," paper prepared for a Conference on the Economic Effects of the Tax Reform Act of 1986, Ann Arbor, Michigan (November 10–11, 1989).

Congressional Budget Office. *The Changing Distribution of Federal Taxes: 1975–1990* (October 1987).

————. *The Changing Distribution of Federal Taxes: A Closer Look at 1980* (July 1988).

————. *Reducing the Deficit: Spending and Revenue Options* (February 1989).

Economic Report of the President. Washington, D.C.: U.S. Government Printing Office (February 1982).

Courant, Paul N., and Edward M. Gramlich. "Tax Reform: There Must be a Better Way." National Policy Papers, Washington, D.C.: *National Policy Exchange* (November 1982).

Danziger, Sheldon, Peter Gottschalk, and Eugene Smolensky. "How the Rich Have Fared, 1973–87." *American Economic Review, Papers and Proceedings 1988 79* (May 1989): 310–314

Evans, Owen J. "Tax Policy, the Interest Elasticity of Saving, and Capital Accumulation: Numerical Analysis of Theoretical Models." *American Economic Review 73* (June 1983): 398–410.

Feldstein, Martin. "The Welfare Cost of Capital Income Taxation." *Journal of Political Economy 86* (April 1978): S29–S51.

Fichtenbaum, Rudy, and Hushang Shahidi. "Truncation Bias and the Measurement of Income Inequality. *Journal of Business and Economic Statistics 5* (July 1988): 335–337.

Fisher, Irving. "Income in Theory and Income Taxation in Practice." *Econometrica 5* (January 1937): 1–55.

Galper, Harvey, Robert Lucke, and Eric Toder. "A General Equilibrium Analysis of Tax Reform," in *Uneasy Compromise: Problems of a Hybrid Income-Consumption Tax,* Henry J. Aaron, Harvey Galper, and Joseph A. Pechman, eds., Washington, D.C.: Brookings Institution (1988), 59–114.

Goode, Richard. *The Individual Income Tax,* rev. ed., Washington, D.C.: Brookings Institution (1976).

————. "Long-Term Averaging for Income Tax Purposes," in *The Economics of Taxation*, Washington, D.C.: Brookings Institution (1980), 159–178.

Gravelle, Jane G. "Assessing a Value-Added: Efficiency and Equity." *Tax Notes* (March 7, 1988): 1117–1123.

————. "Income, Consumption, and Wage Taxation in a Life Cycle Model: Separating Efficiency from Redistribution," unpublished paper (June 1989).

Hall, Robert E., and Alvin Rabushka. *The Flat Tax.* Stanford, California: Hoover Institution Press (1985).

Hausman, Jerry A. "Taxes and Labor Supply," in *Handbook of Public Economics,* vol. 1, Alan J. Auerbach and Martin Feldstein, eds., Amsterdam: North-Holland (1987): 213–263.

Hausman, Jerry A., and James M. Poterba. "Household Behavior and the Tax Reform Act of 1986." *Journal of Economic Perspectives 1* (Summer 1987): 101–120.

Holland, Daniel M. "The Effect of Taxation on Effort: Some Results for Business Executives," in *Proceedings of the Sixty-Second Annual Conference on Taxation, 1969,* Columbus OH: National Tax Association (1970), 428-517.

Hubbard, R. Glen, and Kenneth L. Judd. "Liquidity Constraint, Fiscal Policy, and Consumption." *Brookings Papers on Economic Activity 1* (1986): 175-208.

Kaldor, Nicholas. *An Expenditure Tax,* London: Allen & Unwin (1955).

Kay, John A., and Mervyn A. King. *The British Tax System,* 3rd ed., Oxford: Oxford University Press (1983).

Kenadjian, Bardj, Internal Revenue Service. "Gross Tax Gap Trends According to New IRS Estimates, Income Years 1973–1992." *Statistics of Income Bulletin 8* (Summer 1988): 23–33.

Laffer, Arthur B. "Government Exactions and Revenue Deficiencies." *Cato Journal 1* (Spring 1981): 1-21.

Levy, Frank. *Dollars and Dreams: The Changing American Income Distribution.* New York: Norton (1988).

McLure, Charles E., Jr. "Where Tax Reform Went Astray." *Villanova Law Review 31* (1987): 1619–1663.

McLure, Charles E., Jr., John Mutti, Victor Thuroni, and George Zodrow. *The Taxation of Income from Business and Capital in Colombia.* Colombia: Direccion General de Impuestos Nacionales, Ministerio de Haciendia y Credito Publico (1988).

Meade, James, et al. *The Structure and Reform of Direct Taxation.* London: Allen & Unwin (1978).

Meyer, Lawrence H., ed. *The Supply-Side Effects of Economic Policy.* The Hague: Kluwer Nijhoff Publishing (1981).

Mieszkowski, Peter. "The Advisability and Feasibility of an Expenditure Tax System", in *The Economics of Taxation,* Henry J. Aaron and Michael J. Boskin, eds., Brookings Institution (1980): 179-202.

Mill, John Stuart. *Principles of Political Economy,* W. J. Ashley, ed., London: Longmans, Green (1929), Bk 2, ch. 2, sec. 4.

Musgrave, Richard A. *The Theory of Public Finance: A Study in Public Economy.* New York: McGraw-Hill (1959).

———. "ET, OT, and SBT." *Journal of Public Economics 6* (July–August 1976): 3–16.

———. *Strengthening the Progressive Income Tax: The Responsible Answer to America's Budget Problem.* Washington, D.C.: Economic Policy Institute (1989).

Pechman, Joseph A., ed. *Comprehensive Income Taxation.* Washington, D.C.: Brookings Institution (1977).

———, ed. *What Should be Taxed: Income or Expenditure?* Washington, D.C.: Brookings Institution (1980).

———. *Who Paid the Taxes, 1966–85?* Washington, D.C.: Brookings Institution (1985).

———. *Who Paid the Taxes, 1966–85? Revised Tables.* Washington, D.C.: Brookings Institution (1987).

———. "Tax Reform: Theory and Practice." *Journal of Economic Perspectives 1* (Summer 1987a): 11–28.

———. *Federal Tax Policy,* 5th ed., Washington, D.C.: Brookings Institution (1987).

———, ed. *World Tax Reform: A Progress Report.* Washington, D.C.: Brookings Institution (1988).

———. *Tax Reform, The Rich and the Poor.* Washington, D.C.: Brookings Institution (1974).

Pechman, Joseph A., and Benjamin A. Okner. *Who Bears the Tax Burden?* Washington, D.C.: Brookings Institution (1974).

Raboy, David G. *Essays in Supply Side Economics.* Washington, D.C.: Institute for Research in the Economics of Taxation (1982).

Reagan, Ronald. *Public Papers of the Presidents of the United States, 1981,* Washington, D.C.: U.S. Government Printing Office (1982).

Rosen, Harvey S. *Public Finance,* 2nd ed., Homewood, Illinois: Irwin (1988a).

———. "Does Progressive Taxation Survive Optimal Theory?" unpublished paper (1988b).

Simons, Henry C. *Personal Income Taxation: The Definition of Income as a Problem of Fiscal Policy.* Chicago: University of Chicago Press (1938).

———. *Federal Tax Reform.* Chicago: University of Chicago Press (1950).

Slemrod, Joel. "Optimal Taxation and Optimal Tax Systems." *Journal of Economic Perspectives* (forthcoming).

Stern, Nicholas. "The Theory of Taxation and Optimum Income Taxation: An Introduction," in *The Theory of Taxation for Developing Countries,* David Newberry and Nicholas Stern, eds., Washington, D.C.: Oxford University Press for the World Bank (1987), 22–59.

Steuerle, C. Eugene. *Taxes, Loans and Inflation: How the Nation's Wealth Becomes Misallocated.* Washington, D.C.: Brookings Institution (1985).

Summers, Lawrence H. "Capital Taxation and Accumulation in a Life-Cycle Growth Model." *American Economic Review 71* (September 1981): 533–544.

U.S. Department of the Treasury. *Blueprints for Basic Tax Reform.* Washington D.C.: U.S. Government Printing Office (1977).

Young, H. Peyton. "Progressive Taxation and Equal Sacrifice." *American Economic Review 80* (March 1990): 253–266.

**PERSONAL INCOME TAX**
**Topic of Interest:**
*Tax Reform and Behavioral Changes*

## S E L E C T I O N    2 3

Martin Feldstein

# Behavioral Responses to Tax Rates:
# Evidence from the Tax Reform Act of 1986

Although economists are in agreement about the theoretical effects of taxation, a great deal of disagreement exists about what actually happens. Points of controversy concerning the validity of various empirical estimates include which factors or variables are important (and which ones can be omitted), the specification or measurement of the variables, levels of aggregation, and the time period or years contained in the study. Most often, however, it is simply the lack of appropriate data that has stymied economists in their empirical work. But this may have changed—at least with respect to the federal income tax.

In this selection, Martin Feldstein summarizes recent research on the behavioral responses of taxpayers. As Feldstein states, "the Tax Reform Act of 1986 (TRA86) is the most important natural experiment since the start of the income tax." Thus, the data collected before and after these tax changes is particularly significant for its uniqueness as well as for its ability to help us understand the impact of various tax programs. The effects of tax rate changes on labor supply, taxable income, and realized capital gains are analyzed, and compared to previous empirical studies on these issues. On the basis of this work, several implications for future tax policies are proposed.

### Questions to Guide the Reading
1. According to Feldstein, what are the "three quite different reasons" that make the Tax Reform Act of 1986 significant for economic research?

Feldstein, Martin. "Behavioral Responses to Tax Rates: Evidence from the Tax Reform Act of 1986." *American Economic Review* 85 (May 1995): 170-174.

**Martin Feldstein** is Research Associate and President of the National Bureau of Economic Research and Professor of Economics at Harvard University.

2. How does Eissa's study complement the previous research literature on the effects of tax policy on labor supply?
3. Why is it "totally wrong to say that taxes do not affect the labor supply of men"?
4. Theoretically, why would taxable income rise when the marginal income tax rate falls? Why does Feldstein believe this response is more important than changes in labor supply?
5. How does Feldstein support his contention that realized capital gains are quite sensitive to the capital-gains tax rate?
6. What are possible implications of these studies for future tax policy-making?

For those of us who study the effects of taxation, the Tax Reform Act of 1986 (TRA86) is the most important natural experiment since the start of the income tax. Although we are just beginning to examine the evidence, the lessons based on studying TRA86 are likely to have profound effects on academic thinking and on the design of tax policies in the years ahead.

The 1986 tax legislation is so useful as a basis for research for three quite different reasons. First, it involves a wide variety of tax rate changes for different individuals. The marginal tax rate fell by 44 percent for the top income earners and by 100 percent for low income earners but actually rose for nearly a third of all taxpayers (Hausman and Poterba 1987). The tax rate on capital gains rose by as much as 40 percent for some taxpayers while changing very little for others. This variety makes it possible to separate the effects of changes in tax rates from the background forces that affected all taxpayers during the middle years of the 1980s.

Second, the magnitude and character of the tax change was largely unexpected before 1986, making it possible to compare 1985 and earlier years with the years after 1986 (Feldstein 1994; Fullerton 1994). Third, and in some ways most significant, the quality of government data on household behavior in the 1980s is superior to anything that researchers have had in the past. In addition to the Treasury public-use sample of more than 100,000 individual tax returns for each year, there is also a panel-data sample of taxpayers that permits researchers to follow the same individuals before and after the 1986 tax change. Researchers are beginning to study these data sources and also to explore what can be learned from a variety of other sequential cross-section data sets. With this rich array of microeconomic data, it is no longer necessary to try to learn something about the effects of tax changes in the 1980s from a handful of aggregate time-series observations.

By analyzing these data we can hope to develop the information needed to forecast how potential changes in tax rules and tax rates would alter tax revenue and the deadweight loss of the tax system. Sometimes our analytic goals have to be more modest. We cannot always translate behavioral changes into measures of economic efficiency. But even in those cases, we can hope to provide useful information by estimating how much a proposed change in tax rules would increase such economic variables as charitable contributions or private saving or capital-gains realizations per dollar of revenue loss. Of course, in some cases the analysis may point to policy changes that actually raise revenue while also increasing some desired form of economic behavior.

# I. TAX RATES AND LABOR SUPPLY

Although there is still very little statistical analysis of the behavioral changes induced by TRA86, the available evidence points to several important conclusions. I begin with the research on labor supply and then turn to the more general effect of tax rates on taxable income and to the specific effect of tax rates on capital gains.

There is a long and econometrically sophisticated literature on the effects of taxes on labor supply based on cross-section samples that predate the 1986 tax reform[1] (Hausman 1981, 1985; Hausman and Ruud 1984; Pencavel 1986; Mroz 1987; Triest 1990; MaCurdy 1992; Heckman 1993). The general conclusions of these studies are that the working hours and participation rates of men are quite insensitive to net wages and to exogenous income but that working hours and participation rates of married women are substantially more sensitive to both. It is clear however that, even for married women, the literature contains a wide variety of parameter estimates. These estimates appear to be sensitive to the particular parametric specification of the labor-supply function and to the treatment of the unknown wages for women who are out of the labor force, a particularly serious problem since labor-force participation is generally found to be more responsive than the hours worked among the employed group of married women.

Eissa (1995) has used the TRA86 experience to estimate the sensitivity of married women's labor supply to taxes in a way that avoids the problems of earlier studies. She reasoned that the change of a married woman's marginal tax rate between the years immediately before 1986 and the years immediately after 1986 depended on her husband's initial income level. Women with high-income husbands experienced bigger declines in marginal tax rates than women whose husbands had lower incomes. Eissa classified women in the Current Population Survey (CPS) by their husbands' incomes in this way and calculated the changes in labor-force participation rates and the corresponding changes in the marginal net-of-tax shares (i.e., 1 minus the marginal tax rate) for these income groups in pre- and post-1986 CPS samples. Comparing the change in participation rates between the two periods for two different income groups to the corresponding change in marginal tax rates for the two different income groups provides an estimate of the local elasticity of participation with respect to the net-of-tax share. Eissa also applies this differences-in-differences approach to estimating the response of hours among women who work.[2]

This differences-in-differences estimation procedure avoids the problem of the unobserved wage rate in earlier cross-section studies (by assuming only that the proportional change in the wage of women is the same in the different husband-income groups). It also avoids the requirement of cross-section studies to specify a precise functional form for the labor-supply equation.

Eissa's (1995) analysis found a compensated elasticity of the participation rate with respect to the net-of-tax share (or, equivalently, to the net-of-tax wage) of 0.42 at the means of the variables and a corresponding elasticity of hours worked among those who are employed of 0.45. These effects have fully occurred within five years of the change in tax rates. The combined effect of the two elasticities implies an elasticity of total hours worked of about 1.0. Although this is not substantially different from the central tendency in the previous literature, it is an important contribution because the estimation method is more robust, and the parameter estimates are therefore more reliable.

It is important, however, not to confuse changes in participation and in average hours with changes in labor supply. The amount of "labor" that an individual supplies depends also on the intensity of work effort, the nature of the occupation, the assumption of risk and responsibility, the location of work, the amount of travel, the on-the-job- acquisition of skills, and many other dimensions *all of which can be influenced by changes in tax rates.* It is totally wrong to say that taxes do not affect the labor supply of men when what the data show is that their participation rate and their average hours do not appear to vary in the short term. Similarly, although it is possible to observe women's response to tax changes in the form of participation rates and average hours, women will also respond over time by changing the same wide range of labor-supply behavior. Only further imaginative research will show how much more elastic the total long-run labor supply is than the currently measured changes in participation and average hours.

## II. TAX RATES AND TAXABLE INCOME

A decrease in marginal tax rates causes not only an increase in labor supply (broadly defined), but also a shift in the form of compensation (from fringe benefits and other nontaxed income to taxable cash compensation) and a reduction in deductible expenditures as the relative price of ordinary consumption falls relative to the price of such tax-favored consumption as mortgage payments and charitable contributions. Taxable income therefore rises substantially more than aggregate hours.

In Feldstein (1993), I used the Treasury Department's panel of tax returns to estimate the response of taxable incomes to changes in the net-of-tax share. I grouped taxpayers by their 1985 marginal tax rates and compared each taxpayer's adjusted taxable incomes in 1985 and 1988 to the group's change in the marginal net-of-tax share. This differences-in-differences approach avoids the identification problems of traditional regression estimates.

For example, taxpayers in the highest marginal tax rate class in 1985 had an average rise of 42.2 percent in their marginal net-of-tax share between 1985 and 1988. Taxpayers in the next lower group, with marginal tax rates of 42–45 percent in 1985, experienced a 25.6-percent average rise in their net-of-tax share. The corresponding increases in the adjusted taxable income for the two groups (adjusted to exclude capital gains and modified in other ways) were 44.8 percent and 20.3 percent. Comparing these changes in taxable incomes and in the net-of-tax shares implies a taxable income elasticity of 1.48. Other differences-in-differences comparisons for taxpayers with 1985 marginal tax rates of 22 percent and higher implied taxable income elasticities of 1.25 and 1.04.

Gerald Auten and Robert Carroll (1994) of the Treasury Department's Office of Tax Analysis subsequently reestimated the same elasticity using the much larger panel of tax returns for 1985 and 1989 that is available only inside the Treasury. Their sample includes more than 5,000 taxpayers with 1985 marginal tax rates of 50 percent. They report an elasticity of 1.33 with a standard error of 0.15.[3]

In a related study, Daniel Feenberg and Poterba (1993) showed that the share of total adjusted gross income (AGI) received by the top one-half percent of taxpayers rose gradually from 1981 to 1986 and then increased sharply in the next few years. Although some of the post-1986 increase is due to the inclusion of all of capital gains in AGI after 1986 and to the shift in some incomes from ordinary small business corporations to Subchapter-S corporations (which are part of individual AGI), the substantial remainder of the increased AGI no doubt reflects the taxpayers' decisions to take more of their income in taxable form rather than in untaxed benefits.

Although labor supply has been the traditional focus of tax studies of individual behavior, the induced change in taxable income is actually the more important response. It is the uncompensated change in taxable income that determines the change in revenue when tax rates change. And it is the compensated change in taxable income, rather than the more limited change in working hours and wage income, that determines the change in the deadweight loss of the tax system (Feldstein 1995).

## III. TAX RATES AND REALIZED CAPITAL GAINS

Because capital gains are only taxed when they are realized and losses can be offset against gains, the level of net realized capital gains can be expected to be quite sensitive to the capital-gains tax rate. I found such sensitivity in a number of studies done in the late 1970s (e.g., Feldstein and Yitzhaki 1978; Feldstein et al., 1980). That conclusion has been questioned by researchers who argue that the cross-section results were distorted by responses to temporary changes in individual tax rates (see e.g., the recent paper by Leonard Burman and William Randolph [1994] of the Congressional Budget Office). The analysts at the Treasury and the CBO who are responsible for projecting the effects of capital-gains taxes appear to take the view that changes in capital-gains tax rates have very little long-term effect.

The experience since 1986 is therefore very informative. Although there has been no explicit microeconomic research on capital-gains realizations since 1986, we can compare the history of aggregate realizations with the predictions of the Treasury and the CBO. Here are the facts. Realized capital gains surged in 1986 (jumping to 190 percent of the 1985 level) as taxpayers took gains in advance of the already legislated sharp 1987 rise in capital-gains tax rates. The real value of realized capital gains then declined in 1987 and 1988 to $155 billion, 16 percent below the 1985 level. At that point, the Treasury and the CBO, based on their statistical model of realizations, projected that capital gains would rise rapidly over the next several years. The Treasury staff projected that capital gains would reach $256 billion in 1992, while the CBO projected capital gains of $287 billion (Gideon 1990, 216). In fact, capital gains have continued to decline since 1988, falling nearly 40 percent in real terms (to $118 billion in 1992) despite a 34-percent rise in the real level of prices. The actual 1992 level of capital gains was only 41 percent of the level projected by the Congressional Budget Office.

It would appear from these data that the capital-gains realizations are far more sensitive to tax rates than the Treasury and CBO analysts have assumed. Only a careful analysis of the microeconomic data on realizations will determine whether they are consistent with the estimates based on earlier experience.

## IV. SOME IMPLICATIONS

Although evidence based on the 1986 experience is just beginning to accumulate, some clear implications already emerge. First, the substantial sensitivity of married women's labor supply implies that the efficiency of the tax system could be increased significantly by reducing the marginal tax rates of these women relative to their husband's marginal tax rates (Feldstein and Feenberg 1996). More generally, the sensitivity of taxable income to the net-of-tax share implies that lower marginal tax rates would involve much less revenue loss than is traditionally assumed and would bring a much more substantial reduction in the deadweight loss of the tax system (Feldstein 1993, 1995) than is implied by calculations based on labor supply alone. These estimates and the experience with capital gains suggest that the process of projecting taxpayer responses that lies at the heart of revenue estimation and therefore of Congressional tax policy-making would be substantially improved by incorporating the accumulating evidence on how taxpayers have responded to the Tax Reform Act of 1986.

## NOTES

1. Although the demographic characteristics of the women in the different groups do not differ substantially, Nada Eissa (1995) controlled for the effects of these differences by a regression equation within the differences-in-differences framework.
2. Hausman and Poterba (1987) projected the effects of TRA86 based on Hausman's

(1981) parameter estimates. Barry Bosworth and Gary Burtless (1992) discuss the effects of the 1986 legislation, but their evidence is limited to means for data aggregated by income quintiles.

3. These estimates for TRA86 are broadly consistent with the analysis of the 1981 tax reductions by Lawrence Lindsey (1987) and John Navratil (1994).

# REFERENCES

Auten, Gerald and Robert Carroll. "Taxpayer Behavior and the 1986 Tax Reform Act." Mimeo, National Bureau of Economic Research Summer Institute, Cambridge, Massachusetts (July 1994).

Bosworth, Barry, and Gary Burtless. "Effects of Tax Reform on Labor Supply, Investment, and Saving." *Journal of Economic Perspectives* 6(1) (Winter 1992): 3–25.

Burman, Leonard, and William Randolph. "Measuring Permanent Responses to Capital-Gains Tax Changes in Panel Data." *American Economic Review 84*(4) (September 1994): 794–809.

Eissa, Nada. "Taxation and Labor Supply of Married Women: The Tax Reform Act of 1986 as a Natural Experiment." National Bureau of Economic Research (Cambridge, Massachusetts) Working Paper No. 5023 (1995).

Feenberg, Daniel, and James M. Poterba. "Income Inequality and the Incomes of Very High Income Taxpayers," in James M. Poterba, ed., *Tax Policy and the Economy,* vol. 7. Cambridge, Massachusetts: MIT Press (1993), 145–177.

Feldstein, Martin. "The Effect of Marginal Tax Rates on Taxable Income: A Panel Study of the 1986 Tax Reform Act." National Bureau of Economic Research (Cambridge, Massachusetts) Working Paper No. 4496 (October 1993), *Journal of Political Economy* (forthcoming).

————. *American Economic Policy in the 1980's.* Chicago: University of Chicago Press (1994).

————. "Tax Avoidance and the Deadweight Loss of the Income Tax." *National Bureau of Economic Research* (Cambridge, Massachusetts) Working Paper No. 5505 (1995).

Feldstein, Martin, and Daniel Feenberg. "The Taxation of Two Earner Families," in Martin Feldstein and James Poterba, eds., *The Empirical Foundations of Household Taxation.* National Bureau of Economic Research (Cambridge, Massachusetts) Conference Volume (1996, forthcoming).

Feldstein, Martin, Joel Slemrod, and Schlomo Yitzhaki. "The Effects of Taxation on the Selling of Corporate Stock and the Realization of Capital Gains." *Quarterly Journal of Economics 94*(4) (June 1980): 111–191.

Feldstein, Martin, and Schlomo Yitzhaki. "The Effect of the Capital Gains Tax on the Selling and Switching of Common Stock." *Journal of Public Economics 9*(1) (February 1978): 17–36.

Fullerton, Donald. "Inputs to Tax Policymaking: The Supply Side, the Deficit and the Level Playing Field," in Martin Feldstein, ed., *American Economic Policy in the 1980's,* Chicago: University of Chicago Press (1994): 165–208.

Gideon, Kenneth. "Testimony," in *Tax Incentives for Increasing Savings and Investments.* Senate Finance Committee Senate Hearing 101–981, March 1990, Washington, DC: U.S. Government Printing Office (1990), 27–28.

Hausman, Jerry. "Labor Supply," in Henry Aaron and James Pechman, eds., *How Taxes Affect Economic Behavior.* Washington, D.C.: Brookings Institution (1981), 27–83.

———. "Taxes and Labor Supply," in Alan Auerbach and Martin Feldstein, eds., *Handbook of Public Economics,* vol. I. Amsterdam: North-Holland (1985), 213–263.

Hausman, Jerry, and James Poterba. "Household Behavior and the Tax Reform Act of 1986." *Journal of Economic Perspectives 1*(1) (Summer 1987): 101–119.

Hausman, Jerry, and Paul Ruud. "Family Labor Supply with Taxes." *American Economic Review 74*(2) (Papers and Proceedings) (May 1984): 242–248.

Heckman, James. "What Has Been Learned About Labor Supply in the Past Twenty Years?" *American Economic Review 83*(2) (Papers and Proceedings) (May 1993): 116–121.

Lindsey, Lawrence. "Individual Taxpayer Responses to Tax Cuts, 1982–1984: With Implications for the Revenue Maximizing Tax Rate." *Journal of Public Economics 33*(2) (July 1987): 173–206.

MaCurdy, Thomas. "Work Disincentive Effects of Taxes: A Reexamination of Some Evidence." *American Economic Review 82*(2) (Papers and Proceedings) May 1992: 243–249.

Mroz, Thomas. "The Sensitivity of an Empirical Model of Married Women's Hours of Work to Economic and Statistical Assumptions." *Econometrica 55*(4) (July 1987): 765–799.

Navratil, John. "Evidence on Individual Tax Payer Behavior from Panel Tax Return Data." Mimeo, National Bureau of Economic Research, Cambridge, Massachusetts (1994).

Pencavel, John. "Labor Supply of Men: A Survey," in Orley Ashenfelter and Richard Layard, eds., *Handbook of Labor Economics,* vol. I. Amsterdam: North-Holland (1986), 3–102.

Triest, Robert. "The Effect of Income Taxation of Labor Supply in the United States." *Journal of Human Resources 25*(3) (Summer 1990): 491–516.

# S E L E C T I O N   2 4

Joel Slemrod

# Did the Tax Reform Act of 1986 Simplify Tax Matters?

The direct burden of taxation is easy to measure: the total dollar value of all collected tax revenues. But while not as easy to measure, the excess burden (or welfare cost) is just as real, and includes any additional resources expended as a result of taxation. Thus, both efforts on the part of government officials to prevent tax evasion as well as efforts on the part of taxpayers to find "tax shelters" contribute to the excess burden of taxation. Intriguingly, tax simplification is argued to be a more effective means of decreasing both evasion and avoidance efforts—more effective than enforcement measures such as increasing the number and extent of audits. Because the choice not to pay taxes or to spend resources to avoid paying taxes reflects a rational calculation, this decision is based, in part, on the costs of complying with tax laws. Thus, tax simplification should lower compliance costs, making tax evasion less attractive and tax avoidance less possible.

One of the celebrated promises of the Tax Reform Act of 1986 was that it would lower compliance costs by way of a drastically streamlined federal tax system. In this selection, Joel Slemrod examines to what extent this legislation actually simplified the personal income tax. He provides quantitative measures of the costs of complexity and compliance. While the Tax Reform Act of 1986 sharply reduced income tax rates, and eliminated many deductions, exemptions, and exclusions, Slemrod argues that compliance costs have not fallen overall. At best, the Act may have simply prevented compliance costs from increasing to even higher levels.

·····················································································

Slemrod, Joel. "Did the Tax Reform Act of 1986 Simplify Tax Matters?" *Journal of Economic Perspectives* 6 (Winter 1992): 45-57.

**Joel Slemrod** is Professor of Economics, Professor of Business Economics and Public Policy, and Director of the Office of Tax Policy Research at the University of Michigan. He is a past Senior Economist on the President's Council of Economic Advisors.

## Questions to Guide the Reading

1. What are the policy implications of placing simplicity "next to equity and efficiency as important criteria by which to judge a tax system"? What are the total resource costs of collecting taxes?
2. What major simplifications were provided by the 1986 tax reform?
3. How was the Tax Reform Act of 1986 supposed to help in "leveling the playing field"? Are there any indications that greater transactional simplicity was achieved?
4. What indirect measures support the argument that the Act did not decrease the complexity of the tax system?
5. What comprehensive measure of complexity is advocated by Slemrod? What are the flaws of this measure? What conclusions have been drawn from relevant survey evidence?
6. What tradeoffs occurred in attempting to simplify the tax system in 1984–1986? Why is it possible that the Omnibus Budget Reconciliation Act increased tax compliance costs?

Simplification was a major concern when the tax reform debate began in earnest in 1984. The Treasury Department's proposal issued in November of that year was entitled *Tax Reform for Fairness, Simplicity, and Economic Growth*. It proposed a tax system simple enough that two-thirds of all taxpayers could switch to "return-free" filing, in which the IRS could calculate tax liability based on information reports from third parties. President Reagan's tax proposal, released after six months of debate both in public and within the Administration, relegated simplicity to the third and last goal of its title. The tax bill that eventually was signed into law on October 22, 1986, the Tax Reform Act of 1986, was certainly not the elegant simplification that many had hoped for. In fact, it was widely argued that the original goal of simplicity had been left by the wayside in the rush to devise a politically acceptable compromise that would meet the constraints of revenue and distributional neutrality.

This paper attempts to assess whether the Tax Reform Act of 1986 simplified tax matters significantly, or at all. I conclude that, despite a few scattered signs that tax-related financial planning has declined, the compliance cost of the income tax system is probably higher now that it was in the early 1980s. This suggests that the Tax Reform Act achieved little, if any, simplification in the tax system, although it remains possible that the Act dampened what would have been an even greater increase in compliance cost.

Before proceeding, two cautions are in order. First, this paper is concerned only with changes made by the Tax Reform Act of 1986 in individual income taxation. The cost of compliance with business taxation is also large, according to one estimate approximately twice as large as the cost of compliance with individual income taxation (Arthur D. Little 1988) There is widespread agreement, though no hard evidence, that the Tax Reform Act further increased this cost, especially with regard to foreign-source income and pensions. Second, it is unavoidable that any large change in the tax law will increase the cost of compliance for a while as taxpayers learn about and adjust to the new law. For this reason, even a tax change that simplified the tax system in the long run might increase the cost of compliance in the short run. This caveat suggests that evidence from the years immediately following the Tax Reform Act of 1986 might understate its contribution to simplification. It also underlines that stability of the tax system is an important element of simplicity.

## COMPLEXITY AND COMPLIANCE COSTS

It is entirely appropriate that simplicity be placed next to equity and efficiency as important criteria by which to judge a tax system. According to recent estimates, the cost of collecting income tax—including the value of the time spent by taxpayers—is between 5 and 10 percent of tax revenue, of the same order of magnitude as some recent estimates of the standard distortionary costs of taxation (Slemrod and Sorum 1984; Arthur D. Little 1988; Blumenthal and Slemrod 1991). Complexity also has impacts, usually deleterious ones, on the horizontal equity of how the tax burden is shared. When it is understood that the tax system entails not only the structure of rates and bases but also the facts of administration and enforcement, the complexity of the process is an important aspect to consider in the design of tax policy.

Of course, there is generally a tradeoff between simplicity and the other objectives of the tax system. Some of the complexity arises in an attempt to distinguish among taxpayers in equitably assessing the tax burden.

Complexity has several dimensions. The aspect that first comes to mind for most taxpayers is the time and expense involved in completing the tax return, including not only complying with the filing requirement, but also of identifying and documenting the deductions, credits, and reductions in taxable income to which they are entitled. This aspect, often called compliance cost, can be further divided into the cost required to comply with the law and the cost incurred by taxpayers in an effort to reduce taxable income. The effort to reduce taxable income includes both taking full advantage of tax-reducing provisions and arranging one's financial affairs with tax implications in mind. To the tax collection agency, complexity in large part relates to the administrative cost of raising revenue, and in particular relates to the encouragement that some tax provisions provide for the use of complicated schemes to avoid tax payments. Frequent changes in the tax structure add to both of these costs, as taxpayers and tax collectors must learn about and adjust to the new system. The compliance cost, administrative cost, and the costs borne by third parties in the tax collection process (like employers operating the withholding system) sum to the total resource costs of collecting taxes.

# HOW THE TAX REFORM ACT
# OF 1986 AFFECTED SIMPLICITY

The Tax Reform Act of 1986 addressed the problem of complexity directly by eliminating several special provisions and some structural sources of complexity, and addressed it indirectly by reducing marginal tax rates. However, some of the provisions added to the complexity of tax compliance, often in an attempt to reduce the incentive to engage in complex tax-motivated financial transactions.

Before proceeding further, a few words about the importance of the number of tax brackets are in order. The collapsing of 14 tax brackets (15, for single filers) to three, although promoted by the Administration as a key element of simplification, is actually an insignificant change in the complexity of the system. Once taxable income is computed, finding tax liability from the tax tables is a trivial operation and is not significantly simplified by having fewer brackets. This change, though, may improve the perceived simplicity of the system and may, because arguably most taxpayers know their marginal tax rate better after the Tax Reform Act than before it, make for more informed decisions.

In theory, the lowering of marginal tax rates should reduce the resource cost of collecting taxes, because it reduces the incentive of taxpayers to invest in finding ways to cut their taxable income. After all, the return to reducing taxable income by a dollar is exactly the marginal tax rate. Thus, a general reduction in marginal tax rates should cause a substitution away from the use of the taxpayer's own time and expenditure in the tax return filing process. However, empirical research reported in Slemrod (1989a) suggests that in practice there may be only small resource cost savings from moving toward a tax structure with lower marginal tax rates. This empirical conclusion, though, rests on the assumption that taxpayers' sources of income remain unchanged when the rate structure changes. This assumption results in an underestimate of the cost saving from a lower rate structure to the extent that it discourages involvement in relatively high compliance cost activities such as self-employment or real estate investment.

By increasing the standard deduction, eliminating the deduction for personal interest payments and sales taxes, subjecting miscellaneous deductions to a floor, and increasing the floor on deductible medical expenses, the Tax Reform Act of 1986 ensured that the fraction of taxpayers who itemize their deductions would decline, and it reduced the complexity of itemizing for those who remained itemizers. In addition, the increase in the threshold income for filing a return reduced the number of taxpayers who need file at all. However, it is worth noting that the Act did not reduce marginal tax rates for all taxpayers. In this journal, Hausman and Poterba (1987) estimated that, although the majority of taxpayers (58.9 percent) had their marginal rate reduced, only 11.2 percent received reductions of more than 10 percentage points; furthermore, 13.8 percent had the same marginal tax rate and 27.3 percent faced higher marginal tax rates as a result of the Act.

Several provisions of the Tax Reform Act directly reduced record-keeping requirements. In this category I put the repeal of the credit for political contributions, the deduction for adoption expenses, the two-earner deduction, and income averaging, as well as the new limitations on eligibility for Individual Retirement Accounts. In addition, the Tax Reform Act allows income to be adjusted for employee business expenses and other miscellaneous deductions only to the extent that the sum of those items exceeds 2 percent of a taxpayer's adjusted gross income. On the other hand, several provisions of the Act complicated the tax filing process, including limitations on passive losses and the new tracing rules to determine to what extent interest payments are deductible (necessitated by the phased-in elimination of the deductibility of interest on personal loans and the retention of full deductibility of mortgage interest).

The efforts in the Tax Reform Act to reduce the disparities in effective taxation of capital income across real assets and the financial packaging of these assets— "leveling the playing field," as it was often called—should have reduced the "transactional complexity" of the tax system.[1] As Steuerle (1985) and others have stressed, the combination of differentially taxed vehicles for savings and different marginal tax rates on savers creates a wide range of opportunities for those individuals who invest in playing the tax arbitrage game. The Act limited these gains by reducing the tax differentials across assets (largely through eliminating the investment tax credit and capital gains preference), by flattening the distribution of marginal tax rates, and by directly limiting the ability of individuals to play the tax arbitrage game of borrowing, paying fully deductible interest, and then buying lightly taxed assets. Furthermore, the Act limited the extent to which intra-family transfers of income-producing property can be used to reduce tax liability by shifting income from the parent's high marginal tax rate to a child's generally lower tax bracket. By so doing, it reduced the incentive to transfer asset ownership purely for tax reasons.

## INDIRECT MEASURES OF TAX REFORM'S IMPACT ON COMPLEXITY

### Itemized Deductions

Itemizing deductions is an important component of compliance cost. A regression analysis using the data from Slemrod and Sorum (1984) suggests that, holding demographic factors and other tax return characteristics constant, in 1982 itemization added an average of $111 per return to compliance cost, compared to an overall average compliance cost for all taxpayers, including itemizers, of $275. Since 34 percent of taxpayers itemized in 1982, these numbers head to the conclusion that in 1982 about $4 billion, or 13.7 percent of all compliance cost, was due to itemization.

As mentioned above, the Tax Reform Act reduced the incentive to itemize by increasing the standard deduction, by eliminating some deductions (notably sales tax and consumer interest payments) and by disallowing the deductibility of miscellaneous deductions under a floor of 2 percent of adjusted gross income). Table 1 shows that the total number of returns with itemized deductions fell from 40.7 to 31.9 million between 1986 and 1989, and fell as a fraction of total returns from 39.5

**Table 1** Total Returns, Returns with Itemized Deductions, and Returns with Paid Preparer Signature, 1980–1989 (in millions)

|  | Total Returns | Returns with Itemized Deductions | Percent Itemizing | Returns with Paid Preparer Signature | Percent with Paid Preparer Signature |
|---|---|---|---|---|---|
| 1980 | 93.90 | 28.95 | 30.83 | n.a. | n.a. |
| 1981 | 95.40 | 31.75 | 33.09 | 39.53 | 41.44 |
| 1982 | 95.34 | 33.43 | 35.07 | 42.12 | 44.18 |
| 1983 | 96.32 | 35.23 | 36.38 | 43.26 | 44.91 |
| 1984 | 99.44 | 38.20 | 38.42 | 45.22 | 45.48 |
| 1985 | 101.66 | 39.85 | 39.20 | 46.69 | 45.92 |
| 1986 | 103.05 | 40.67 | 39.47 | 48.05 | 46.63 |
| 1987 | 107.00 | 35.51 | 33.19 | 50.99 | 47.66 |
| 1988 | 109.81 | 31.79 | 28.95 | 51.51 | 46.91 |
| 1989 | 112.28 | 31.93 | 28.44 | 52.81 | 47.03 |

Source: Internal Revenue Service, *Statistics of Income,* various years, and *SOI Bulletin,* Spring 1990 and Spring 1991.

percent to 28.4 percent. A rough calculation based on Pitt and Slemrod (1989) suggests that saving 8.8 million taxpayers from having to itemize would result in a resource cost saving of about $0.24 billion per year, in 1982 dollars.[2] These calculations take into account that those taxpayers that cease itemizing when the standard deduction rises incrementally are those with a relatively low level of itemizable deductions and a relatively low compliance cost of itemizing. This is one reason why the average resource cost of these taxpayers that shift our of itemizing is less than the overall average of $111 per return.

## Use of Professional Tax Assistance

Taxpayers retain professional tax assistance for a variety of reasons, including the desire to reduce their tax liability and to minimize their own investment in learning how to comply with the tax law. It is reasonable to suppose that the demand for professional tax assistance is, other things equal, positively correlated to the complexity of the tax system and therefore changes since 1986 in usage of professional assistance would be an indirect measure of how complexity has changed. Table 1 shows that the fraction of total returns with a paid preparer signature did in fact fall in 1988, reversing a decade-long upward trend, but the 1989 fraction crept up slightly. The 1988 and 1989 figures, however, still lie above every other year in the 1980s except for 1987.

However, the reliability of this simple fraction as an index of the impact of the Tax Reform Act on complexity is questionable. The Act limited the deductibility to the taxpayer of hiring professional assistance, by putting tax return preparation in the category of miscellaneous deductions which are deductible only to the extent that they exceed 2 percent of adjusted gross income.[3] Thus, the average net cost to some taxpayers increased. The fact that use of such professionals was approximately constant, even after this increase in price, suggests that complexity of the tax code, if anything, increased.

## Number of Tax Returns Filed

By increasing both the personal exemption and standard deduction, the Tax Reform Act of 1986 increased the minimum income threshold for filing a return. Between 1986 and 1988, the filing threshold for married couples filing jointly rose from $5,830 to $8,900; for single filers it rose from $3,560 to $4,950.[4] This change was expected to take as many as six million taxpayers off the tax rolls completely, and thereby reduce their compliance costs immediately to zero.[5] (After 1988, the filing threshold was indexed for inflation.) Table 1, though, shows no decline after 1986 in the number of returns filed. In fact, the annual rate of increase between 1986 and 1988 was the highest of any two-year period in the 1980s.

There remains somewhat of a puzzle regarding why the anticipated decline in low-income returns filed did not materialize, but two factors are commonly cited. First, many lower-income taxpayers with zero tax liability continued to file to receive the (refundable) earned income tax credit, which was made more generous by the Tax Reform Act. The number of returns which had zero tax before credits and an earned income credit, and thus presumably would not otherwise have been filed, increased from 1.4 million in 1986 to 4.1 million in 1988. This increase could account for part, but not all, of the unexpected increase in total returns filed between those two years. Geiman (1990) argues that a more important factor was the change holding that if a person could be claimed as a dependent on someone else's tax return, they are not entitled to a personal exemption on their own tax return. Although the repeal of this personal exemption was offset somewhat by changes in the rules concerning use of the standard deduction by dependents, the net effect was generally to reduce the filing threshold. Geiman claims that through tax year 1988, this provision added about 4.1 million more dependent taxpayers to the tax roll than would have occurred under prior law. These two factors, plus the fact that many others continued to file in order to claim refunds for withheld taxes—or just out of habit—were apparently strong enough that the predicted decline in the number of returns filed never materialized.[6]

One of the simplification successes of the Tax Reform Act was the sharp decline in the number of returns subject to the alternative minimum tax (AMT), which is itself a very cumbersome calculation. The number of returns subject to AMT filed in tax year 1989 was 101,176, down from 608,907 in 1986. The precipitous drop was largely due to the fact that many taxpayers had been subject to the AMT because they had large long-term capital gains, of which 60 percent was excluded from regular taxable income. The AMT had been designed to recapture some of that exclusion. But the Tax Reform Act subjected long-term capital gains to full taxation. For many taxpayers, this change dropped the potential AMT liability to below the regular income tax liability, and rendered it inapplicable.

## Indirect Measures of Transactional Simplicity

As mentioned earlier, one of the main goals of the Tax Reform Act of 1986 was to reduce the incentive to reduce tax liability by engaging in complex financial activities. For example, eliminating the provision that excluded 60 percent of long-term capital gains realizations from taxation reduced the incentive to repackage capital income (or even labor income) as capital gain. The limitations of passive losses and interest deductions were designed to reduce the gain from tax arbitrage—borrowing with fully deductible interest payments to purchase partially taxed or untaxed assets. The restriction on the gains from intra-family—ladder tax income shifting was designed to reduce the gain from transferring the ownership of assets.

For taxpayers who continued to engage in the affected activities, some of the new provisions undoubtedly increased the cost of compliance. However, to the extent that these provisions discouraged some taxpayers from engaging in complex tax-motivated transactions, the cost of the tax system declined.[7]

Indirect measures of tax-induced financial transactions do suggest a decline in transactional complexity after 1986. The financial planning industry, which had thrived on tax shelters and the high commissions they paid, has apparently fallen upon hard times. In 1986, the International Association of Financial Planners had more than 24,000 members. By the beginning of 1990 its membership was slightly over 17,000. No doubt some of this decline can be attributed to the stock market crash of 1987, which scared many individual investors out of the market. Privately sold limited partnerships, whose attraction was almost entirely tax-related, were a $10.5 billion business in 1985, but in 1990 have declined to $1.4 billion annual flow.[8]

Tax return data up to 1987 cited by Nelson and Petska (1990) suggest that the Act had already begun to induce people to move out of tax shelters.[9] For example, there was a decline in 1987 in the number of partnerships that reported losses and in the size of their losses, while there were increases in the number and profits of partnerships reporting gains. For high-income taxpayers, partnership losses as a percentage of total positive income fell from 11.3 percent in tax year 1985 to 8.5 percent in tax year 1987.

The trends in the financial planning industry generally and limited partnerships specifically are consistent with a decline in transactional complexity, although it is difficult to quantify the resource savings associated with the trends. In the next section, I turn to what evidence exists about the net effects of all of the changes of the Tax Reform Act of 1986 on complexity.

## DIRECT MEASURES OF TAX REFORM'S EFFECT ON COMPLIANCE COST

The indirect measures discussed in the previous section can be helpful in assessing the success of certain features of the Tax Reform Act of 1986, or in providing indicators of its overall success in simplifying the tax system. These measures are not particularly helpful in an overall assessment of whether the Act has simplified tax matters. For this, some comprehensive measure of complexity is required.

In earlier work, I have suggested that the total cost of collection is a useful, though flawed, index of the complexity of a tax system (Slemrod 1984). Among its flaws is that it does not distinguish on the taxpayer side between collection costs which must be expended to comply with the law and those collection costs which are incurred in an effort to reduce one's tax liability, whether through legal or illegal means. On the tax collection agency's side, it does not distinguish between the cost of administering the tax system and the cost of enforcing it—that is, dealing with potential evaders of the tax law. Although these distinctions are important to make in any analytical treatment of simplification, all are costs of operating the tax system and should be considered in a basic assessment of how simply it operates.

In some cases, this index of complexity may conflict with intuition. As an example, consider the case where the record-keeping and calculation requirements of a particular credit are loosened, so that only half as many resources as before are required to calculate and qualify for the credit. Suppose that, as a result, there is a quadrupling of the number of households who apply for and receive the credit (and that any changes needed to make up the lost revenue have no collection cost implications). According to the cost-based index, the tax system has become more complicated. The credit procedure itself has become simpler to understand, but the system as a whole is, by the index of costliness, more complex, since the total number of hours spent on that line item has increased.

Or to choose a more extreme example of the same problem, the U.S. General Accounting Office (1979) estimated that in 1976 over six million taxpayers who should have filed income tax returns did not do so. The GAO found that the average educational level of the nonfilers was below the national norm, and suggested that the reason for nonfiling was often that the process was too complicated to be understood. The compliance cost associated with this group is approximately zero. A change in the tax system which, by making the process easier to comprehend, induces those currently not filing to file would almost certainly add to total privately-borne compliance costs. Thus, although the tax system may have become simpler to understand, it has become more complicated (that is, more costly) to collect the revenue. The cost-based measure of complexity embraces the latter judgment.

Because a large component of compliance cost consists of taxpayers' own time, comprehensive measures are generally based on survey evidence. The work of Sandford et al. (1989) on the United Kingdom is the outstanding example of this research. For the United States, the most notable attempts to measure the cost of collection of the tax system before 1986 are Slemrod and Sorum (1984) and Arthur D. Little (1988). Based on a mail survey of 2,000 Minnesota residents, Slemrod and Sorum estimated that in tax year 1982 the total resource cost of taxpayers' time and monetary expenditure on complying with federal and state individual income taxes amounted to between $17 and $27 billion. This consisted of approximately 2 billion hours of taxpayer's time (or about 20 hours per taxpayer spread over a tax year, or the equivalent of one million tax administrators working 2,000 hours a year).

The Arthur D. Little study was commissioned by the IRS to provide a methodology for the paperwork burden imposed on the public as a result of the federal tax reporting system. The data for the analysis was obtained from two national taxpayer surveys: a diary study of approximately 750 individual taxpayers who were asked to keep track daily of the time spent completing their 1983 tax returns, and a retrospective mail questionnaire of about 6,200 taxpayers.[10] This study estimated the total burden on individuals to be 1,549 million hours, of which 714 million were for recordkeeping, 255 million for learning, 478 million for preparing the return, and 147 million for sending the return. This aggregate figure was broadly consistent with the Slemrod and Sorum results for 1982. The aggregate figures were about 20 percent lower, which could be explained by broader, and arguably more accurate, coverage of low-income taxpayers and the national coverage of the survey (the 1982 Minnesota state tax return was definitely more complex than average).

To assess the impact of tax reform on complexity, the survey methodology of Slemrod and Sorum (1984) was repeated in 1990, for tax year 1989, by Blumenthal and Slemrod (1991). The preliminary results from that survey suggest that there was an increase in compliance cost between 1982 and 1989. The average amount of time spent on tax matters rose from 21.7 hours in 1982 to 27.4 hours in 1989. The average expenditure for professional assistance increased from $42 to $66, in 1989 dollars. Increases in time spent were registered in all components of compliance cost (recordkeeping, research, and time spent with practitioners). A preliminary analysis of the causes of the increase reveals that having rental income is associated with more compliance cost in 1989 compared to 1982, as is having self-employment income. That rental income is now associated with more compliance cost is not surprising, given the complicated rules restricting the extent to which losses from real estate investment can offset other income.[11]

Of course, not all of the increase in compliance cost between 1982 and 1989 can be attributed to the Tax Reform Act. In fact there is indirect evidence of a trend toward higher compliance costs over this period, due to the drift of taxpayers into categories, both demographic and income source, that are associated with higher compliance cost. While between 1982 and 1989 the total number of returns filed increased by 18 percent, the total number of returns with self-employment income rose by 41 percent, those with capital gains increased by 57 percent, and those receiving pension and/or annuity income rose by 93 percent. In the absence of quantitative evidence on this trend, it is conceivable that compliance costs in 1990 would have been, in the absence of the Act, higher than they in fact were. Nevertheless, these preliminary numbers seem to rule out any significant decline in complexity owing to the Tax Reform Act.

## CONCLUSIONS

It's no surprise that the legislation eventually produced by the great tax reform debate of 1984–1986 was not the radical simplification that many had hoped for.

The debate itself brought out clearly the tradeoffs between simplicity and other objectives of the tax system. For example, the Treasury Department rejected a pure flat tax on distributional grounds, while recognizing its potential for simplifying the tax system. On the other hand, the "Treasury I" proposal of November 1984 did contain an innovative scheme for indexing capital income for inflation; this idea was eventually rejected, in large part because of the complexity of administering the system.

Yet the Tax Reform Act of 1986 did deliver on some potentially important simplifications—notably the reduction in itemizers, the flattening of marginal rates, and the more level playing field, which included the abandonment of the exclusion of 60 percent of long-term capital gains. There was a cost, though, to these potential simplifications. To level the playing field, complex restrictions on passive losses were introduced. To raise the revenue required to keep reform revenue-neutral while cutting tax rates, the deductibility of consumer interest was curtailed—necessitating complex rules for tracing borrowing—and the highly complex alternative minimum tax was expanded.

The sparse and preliminary quantitative evidence that is now available suggests that the Tax Reform Act of 1986 did not turn the tide of growing complexity of the tax system. Although there is indirect evidence that tax-induced transactional complexity has declined since 1986, preliminary measures of the overall compliance cost of the individual income tax system show a significant increase in all components of compliance cost.

Nor does the most recent experience with deficit reduction, culminating in the Omnibus Budget Reconciliation Act of 1990, offer much in the way of optimism about future simplification. This bill restored a small preference for capital gains, established a system of phasing out itemized deductions which will add to the opaqueness of the system and, worst of all from the standpoint of simplicity, introduced a new tax on certain luxury consumption goods which not only requires a new administrative machinery but opens a host of avoidance options. This new tax will raise a fairly small amount of revenue from upper-income taxpayers while avoiding the simpler—but less politically acceptable—alternative of rate increases. It is not a hopeful sign that simplicity will cease being the poor stepchild of equity, efficiency, and political deal-making as a tax policy goal.

However, there are other more encouraging developments, especially the simplification efforts of lawyers' and accountants' professional associations.[12] In my view, one critical element that helps to keep simplicity on the political agenda is having quantitative measures of the costs of complexity and compliance. Further research on the successes and failures of the Tax Reform Act of 1986 in reducing tax system complexity will help to sharpen these measures.

## NOTES

An earlier version of this paper was presented at the American Economic Association meetings, December 28–30, 1990 in Washington, D.C. I am grateful to Rebecca

London for invaluable research assistance, and to Don Fullerton, Russell Geiman, and Don Skadden for helpful comments on an earlier draft.

1. See Bradford (1986, ch. 12) for an excellent discussion of which structural features of a tax system contribute to transactional complexity.

2. Pitt and Slemrod (1989) estimate that increasing the standard deduction by $1,000 would reduce the number of itemizers by 6.8 million and save $0.18 billion, and that increasing it by $2,000 would reduce itemizers by 13.4 million and save $0.37 billion. A linear interpolation suggests that dropping 8.8 million itemizers would save $0.24 billion.

3. Some taxpayers undoubtedly shifted their professional assistance expenditures to Schedule C (self-employment income), in which context unrestricted deductibility was retained.

4. Separate and higher filing thresholds apply to taxpayers when at least one taxpayer is blind or over 65.

5. Hausman and Poterba (1987) estimated 6 million; Pechman (1987) estimated 4.8 million.

6. There has also been a shift toward greater reliance on the use of the 1040A and 1040EZ forms. More than half of the growth in returns between tax year 1986 and 1988 were in these simpler forms, although they comprise only about 35 percent of all returns (Geiman 1990).

7. The very complexity of the tax provisions may discourage some taxpayers from the activity. In response to the question, "Have you ever chosen not to undertake some type of business activity (such as buying or selling real estate) because of the hassle or expense of complying with the tax laws?" 15.4 percent of a random sample of tax-payers said yes in 1982 and 29 percent answered yes in 1989 (Blumenthal and Slemrod 1991). This raises the intriguing possibility that making a step in the tax compliance process more complex can, by discouraging participation in the activity, reduce the cost of compliance. This possibility is discussed further in the next section of this paper, and in Slemrod (1984).

8. The figures on limited partnerships in 1990 and the financial planning industry are taken from Waggoner (1990).

9. The principal attraction of these shelters was their ability to generate fully deductible losses in the early years of the investment; whatever gains that materialized in the later years were often in the form of preferentially taxed capital gains. Thus investments which for tax purposes were losses could offer an attractive after-tax return.

10. There was also a third survey of business taxpayers performed in 1984, in which 4,000 partnerships and corporations were sent a mail questionnaire. For business taxpayers the total burden in hours, which includes the equivalent value of professional tax assistance acquired, came to 4,342 million hours for tax year 1983.

11. Based on the national mail survey of over 500 tax practitioners conducted in the summer of 1989, Long (1989) also concludes that the compliance burden increased significantly as a result of the Tax Reform Act of 1986.

12. I have in mind the Invitational Conference on Reduction of Income Tax Complexity, jointly sponsored by the American Institute of Certified Public Accountants Tax Division and the American Bar Association Section of Taxation, held in Washington, D.C. on January 11 and 12, 1990. Both groups have forwarded simplification suggestions to the House Ways and Means Committee.

# REFERENCES

Arthur D. Little. "Development of Methodology for Estimating the Taxpayer Paperwork Burden." Final Report to the Department of the Treasury, Internal Revenue Service, Washington, D.C. (June 1988).

Bittker, Boris. "Tax Reform and Tax Simplification." *University of Miami Law Review 29* (1975): 1–20.

Blumenthal, Marsha, and Joel Slemrod. "The Compliance Costs of the U.S. Individual Income Tax System: A Second Look After Tax Reform," unpublished manuscript, Office of Tax Policy Research, The University of Michigan (1991).

Bradford, David. *Untangling the Income Tax.* A Committee for Economic Development Publication. Cambridge, Massachusetts and London, England: Harvard University Press (1986).

Geiman, Russell. "Selected Impacts of the Tax Reform Act of 1986 on Individual Returns," in *Trend Analyses and Related Statistics–1990 Update,* Internal Revenue Service Publication 1500 (August 1990): 73–82.

Gustafson, Charles, ed. *Federal Income Tax Simplification.* Philadelphia: American Law Institute (1979).

Hausman, Jerry, and James Poterba. "Household Behavior and the Tax Reform Act of 1986." *Journal of Economic Perspectives 1:*1 (Summer 1987): 101–119.

Long, Susan. "The Impact of the Tax Reform Act of 1986 on Compliance Burdens: Preliminary National Survey Results." Paper presented at the IRS Tax Research Conference, Washington, D.C. (November 1989).

Nelson, Susan, and Tom Petska. "Partnerships, Passive Losses, and Tax Reform." *Statistics of Income Bulletin,* Winter 1989–1990. Internal Revenue Service. Washington, D.C.: U.S. Government Printing Office (1990): 31–39.

Pechman, Joseph. "Tax Reform: Theory and Practice." *Journal of Economic Perspectives 1:*1 (Summer 1987): 11–28.

Pitt, Mark, and Joel Slemrod. "The Compliance Cost of Itemized Deductions: Evidence from Individual Tax Returns." *American Economic Review 79:*5 (December 1989): 1224–1232.

Sandford, Cedric, Michael Godwin, and Peter Harwick. "Administrative and Compliance Costs of Taxation." Bath, England: Fiscal Publications (1989).

Slemrod, Joel. "Optimal Tax Simplification: Toward a Framework for Analysis," Proceedings of the 76th Annual Conference of the National Tax Association (1984).

Slemrod, Joel. "The Effect of Tax Simplification on Individuals." In *Economic Consequences of Tax Simplification,* The Federal Reserve Bank of Boston Conference Series No. 26 (1986).

Slemrod, Joel. "The Return to Tax Simplification: An Econometric Analysis." *Public Finance Quarterly 17:*1 (January 1989a): 3–28.

Slemrod, Joel. "Optimal Taxation and Optimal Tax Systems." *Journal of Economic Perspectives 4*:1 (Winter 1990):157–178.

Slemrod, Joel, and Nikki Sorum. "The Compliance Cost of the U.S. Individual Tax System." *National Tax Journal 37*:4 (December 1984): 461–474.

Steuerle, C. Eugene. *Taxes, Loans and Inflation.* Washington, D.C.: Brookings Institution (1985).

Surrey, Stanley. "Complexity and the Internal Revenue Code: The Problem of Management of Tax Detail," *Law and Contemporary Problems 34*:4 (Autumn 1969): 673–710.

U.S. Department of the Treasury. Office of the Secretary, "Tax Reform for Fairness, Simplicity, and Economic Growth." Washington, D.C. (November 1984).

U.S. General Accounting Office. "Who's Not Filing Income Tax Returns." GGD-79-69. Washington, D.C.: U.S. Government Printing Office (1979).

Waggoner, Lyle. *USA Today* (April 18, 1990).

# S E L E C T I O N   2 5

R. Glenn Hubbard

# Corporate Tax Integration: A View from the Treasury Department

"Eliminate double taxation" is an often repeated proposal for tax reform. Dividend income is subject to double taxation: first, corporations pay a corporate income tax on earnings distributed as dividends; and second, shareholders pay a personal income tax on dividends received from the corporations. Also, earnings which are retained and reinvested within the corporation will be taxed as personal income if these earnings result in future capital gains to the stockholders.

Proposals to avoid double taxation on corporation income are known as corporate tax integration plans. Supporters of such plans argue that the corporate tax distorts investment decisions, and therefore, elimination of double taxation through tax integration would increase the overall efficiency of the tax system and the U.S. economy. In this selection, Glenn Hubbard analyzes several methods of integration and assesses the probable effects on corporate decisions and financial markets. Hubbard organizes his discussion around the basic prototypes for corporate tax integration put forth by the U.S. Department of the Treasury. Although recommending the adoption of a specific prototype, the Treasury Report also attempted to clarify the issues that must be addressed in order to ensure a successful transition to any of the proposed corporate tax integration plans.

Hubbard, R. Glenn. "Corporate Tax Integration: A View from the Treasury Department." *Journal of Economic Perspectives 7* (Winter 1993): 115-132. This selection is an abridged version of the original article.

**R. Glenn Hubbard** is Professor of Economics and Finance, Graduate School of Business and Department of Economics at Columbia University. Hubbard also served as Deputy Assistant Secretary for Tax Analysis, U.S. Department of the Treasury.

### Questions to Guide the Reading

1. In what ways might the corporate income tax violate notions of tax equity or fairness?

2. How does the present tax system distort corporate decisions regarding organizational form? Financing methods? Dividend distributions?

3. What four issues does the Treasury Report argue must be addressed by any corporate tax integration plan? What specific problems are caused by open economies?

4. Full integration (also known as the partnership method) would eliminate the corporation income tax. Why does the Treasury recommend against this plan?

5. According to the author, "most integrated tax systems use imputation credit prototypes." How does the imputation credit system eliminate double taxation?

6. What three primary concerns obstruct the implementation of a tax integration plan? Can they be resolved? Explain.

---

Current U.S. income tax law treats corporations and their investors as separate entities. Under this so-called "classical" system of corporate taxation, two levels of tax are levied on earnings from investments in corporate equity. First, income earned by corporations is taxed at the corporate level. Second, when the corporation distributes dividends to shareholders, the income is taxed at the shareholder level as ordinary income. Undistributed earnings, which increase share values, are also double taxed, since they are taxed at capital gains rates when shares are sold.

In contrast, investors who conduct business activity in noncorporate form, such as a sole proprietorship or partnership (or in corporate form through an S corporation), are taxed once on their earnings at their individual tax rate. Corporate earnings distributed as interest to suppliers of debt capital are generally taxed to U.S. taxpayers as ordinary income.[1] However, interest paid is generally deductible by the corporation, and thus not subject to tax at the corporate level.

"Integration" of the corporate and individual income taxes refers to any plan in which corporate income is taxed only once, rather than taxed both when earned and when distributed to shareholders as dividends. Integration has many variants. In January 1992, the U.S. Treasury Department released a study of corporate tax integration, *Integration of the Individual and Corporate Tax Systems* (hereafter "the Treasury Report").[2] The Treasury Report documents the economic distortions caused by the current two-tier tax system and the need to change the way in which the United States taxes corporations and their shareholders, and presents the issues involved with alternative approaches.

Despite their differences, the methods of integration studied in the Treasury Report reflect a common goal: To the extent practicable, fundamental economic considerations, not the tax structure, should guide investment, organizational, and financial decisions. Although the Tax Reform Act of 1986 reduced the effect of taxation on many business decisions, that reform did not directly address distortions in business organizational and financing decisions under current law. Thus, integration can be viewed as the next logical step in tax reform.

## THE NEED FOR INTEGRATION

The current system of corporate taxation raises questions of fairness because it creates differences in the taxation of alternative sources of income from capital. A taxpayer conducting an equity-financed business in corporate form faces a different tax burden than a taxpayer conducting the same business in noncorporate form. A corporation that raises capital in the form of equity faces a different tax burden than a corporation that raises the same amount of capital from debt.[3] A similar disparity exists in the treatment of corporations that finance investment with retained earnings and those that pay dividends and finance investment with new equity. Because of its bias towards debt, the current tax system encourages taxpayers to engage in practices that tend to disguise equity as debt. This effort represents a wasteful use of resources, and imposes significant administrative costs in attempting to distinguish debt from equity. These arguments for integrating the corporate and individual income tax systems have been put forth by economists and legal specialists for more than a generation. Why is the time now right to advance the debate? Let me suggest three reasons.

First, the 1980s witnessed an explosion of corporate borrowing in the United States. Indeed, many observers believe that this activity—and the accompanying financial distress it brought in many sectors of the economy—was influenced significantly by the tax bias against equity finance. While the greater reliance on debt had its origin in many factors (Gertler and Hubbard 1992), the use of debt contracts with virtually no provisions to index repayments to shifts in industry-wide or economy-wide conditions almost surely reflects the tax preference given such debt under current law. Financial decisions, which may leave firms more vulnerable to a downturn in the economy, should be based on fundamental economic considerations, not the tax code. The tax bias against equity finance needs to be addressed.

Second, these distortions have economic costs. Integration of the individual and corporate tax systems would reduce or eliminate these economic distortions. The potential economic gains could be substantial, as discussed below.

Third, aside from these efficiency gains, the various integration prototypes, especially those that also focus on the taxation of interest, provide a mechanism for addressing a problem which has increasingly troubled many governments—the difficulty of taxing income from capital in a global economy. It is desirable to keep the overall tax rate on income from capital as low as possible. However, the ability of some investors to avoid or reduce taxation of capital income, while other investors cannot, is not an adequate surrogate for a uniform lower rate of taxation on all income from capital.

This paper does not attempt to provide a summary of the Treasury Report, but rather places it in the context of economists' arguments for integration, policy judgments for selecting a prototype for integration, and other outstanding issues. This sort of discussion is in the spirit of the Treasury Report, which does not contain specific legislative recommendations, nor present an exhaustive analysis, but was intended to encourage discussion of the different issues and prototypes.

Integration is not a cure-all. Even an integrated tax system is unlikely to attain complete neutrality with respect to the taxation of capital income. In addition, integration focuses on improving the allocation of the nation's capital stock, rather than on reducing the overall tax rate on capital income. However, the Treasury Report and many discussions of corporate tax integration do demonstrate that the current system of corporate taxation merits further fundamental change, and that the potential benefits from integration are substantial.

## THE CORPORATE TAX AND ECONOMIC DISTORTIONS

The classical corporate tax system distorts three economic and financial decisions. Namely, whether to: (1) invest in noncorporate rather than corporate form; (2) finance investments with debt rather than equity; and (3) retain rather than distribute earnings.[4] In addition to the corporate and individual tax considerations, each of these decisions has nontax attributes, as well.

### Organizational Form

Traditional arguments for integrating corporate and individual income taxes emphasize distortions of business organizational form (Harberger, 1962, 1966). By taxing corporate equity income twice, the classical corporate tax system discourages equity-financed investment by corporate organizations. Also, it means that the corporate sector must earn a higher pretax rate of profit to prevent capital from flowing to the noncorporate sector. The tax distorts the allocation of resources by discouraging the use of the corporate form even when incorporation would provide nontax benefits—such as limited liability for the owners, centralized management, free transferability of interests, and continuity. Since Harberger's seminal research, more sophisticated models have been constructed to determine the costs of the economic distortions caused by the corporate income tax (see studies reviewed in the Treasury Report; Shoven and Whalley 1984). For example, Harberger's original model delineated only noncorporate and corporate sectors; some researchers developed models with more sectoral detail.

More recently, models emphasizing shifts in the relative importance of corporate and noncorporate producers within an industry have suggested greater distortions under the corporate tax than suggested by earlier approaches (Gravelle and Kotlikoff 1989). The additional cost arises because corporate and noncorporate producers within an industry possess differential advantages. Corporations may be better able to exploit scale economies, while noncorporate organizations may be better able to encourage entrepreneurial skill. Distorting the choice between these corporate forms thus means diminishing the use of scale economies, as well.

The tax bias against corporate equity investment must be placed in the context of other tax considerations.[5] For example, when the source of corporate equity investment is retained earnings, rather than new share issues, then the funds for investment are taxed at the corporate level and as capital gains to investors. At various times and in certain industries, the combination of the corporate tax rate and the effective tax rate on capital gains has been greater than, equal to, and less than the individual income tax rate on business income. In this way, differences among tax rates may reduce, eliminate, or even reverse the bias against investment by corporations. An additional mitigating factor is the use of debt finance; to the extent that corporations finance investments through debt, the relative tax advantage for noncorporate businesses is reduced.

## Corporate Capital Structure

Corporations have three alternatives for financing new investments: issuing new equity, using retained earnings, or issuing debt. The classical corporate tax system discriminates against equity financing of new corporate investment; because corporate profits are taxed twice, the cost of equity capital generally exceeds the cost of debt capital. Projects funded with new equity or retained earnings therefore require a higher pretax rate of return than projects financed with debt. The lower effective tax rate for debt-financed than for equity-financed corporate investment encourages the use of debt finance by corporations, holding nontax factors constant.[6]

Indeed, if debt issuance involved no nontax considerations, corporate borrowing would be an efficient type of "self help" integration, since interest payments are deductible. Stiglitz (1973), for example, demonstrates that in the absence of nontax benefits and costs of debt finance, the corporate tax does not distort marginal investment decisions (since firms will use debt finance at the margin to take advantage of the deductibility of interest payments). The burden of the corporate tax would be borne by the initial equity. However, since (as I argue below) alternative corporate financing arrangements can have important nontax benefits and costs, the tax system should avoid prejudicing financial decisions.

Leverage may well offer nontax benefits. Those analysts who are most sanguine about high levels of corporate debt and debt-service burdens typically maintain that the "discipline" of debt is desirable because it empowers lenders with an indirect means to monitor the activities of managers (Jensen 1986). Lenders brandishing the threat of pushing a firm into bankruptcy may well have more power to monitor the performance of a firm's managers than fragmented shareholder ownership.

But in practice, increased debt financing may be an ineffective way to improve managerial incentives. It works best when most of the variation is common across business enterprises—as with industry-wide or business cycle fluctuations (Gertler and Hubbard 1990, 1992). Thus, even when there are incentive benefits associated with debt finance, the most efficient financial arrangements will involve both debt and equity, with equity serving as a cushion against economy-wide fluctuations in profitability.

Higher debt levels can increase nontax costs of debt, including costs associated with financial distress. Even when corporations avoid formal bankruptcy proceedings, they can incur costs of entering into covenants that restrict operating flexibility when they cannot meet their interest obligations. The costs can include extra demands on executives' time, supply disruptions, declines in customers' confidence, and significant legal fees. Corporations must therefore evaluate the tax and nontax benefits of additional debt relative to these costs. The Treasury Report concludes that tax-induced distortions in corporations' comparisons of nontax advantages and disadvantages of debt entail significant efficiency costs.

## Corporate Dividend Distributions

The current system of corporate income taxation may also distort a corporation's choice between distributing or retaining earnings and, if amounts are distributed, whether they are paid in the form of a nondividend distribution, such as a share repurchase. Distributing earnings through dividends will be taxed relatively highly versus distributing earnings through capital gains generated by reinvested earnings or share repurchases.

Financial economists have offered two explanations to explain why corporate dividends are paid despite the tax bias against dividend distributions (Treasury Report 1992; Poterba and Summers 1985).[7] The first—known as the "traditional view"—argues that dividends offer nontax benefits to shareholders that offset their apparent tax disadvantage. For example, analogous to the earlier discussion of nontax benefits of debt finance, high dividend payouts may decrease managerial discretion over internal funds. Alternatively, dividends may provide signals to investors about a firm's prospects or relative financial strength, although the need to maintain dividend payments as a signal will constrain the use of retained earnings as a corporation's source of financing for new investments. Under the traditional view, firms set dividend payments so that, for the last dollar of dividends paid, the incremental nontax benefit of dividends equals their incremental tax cost. Thus, the amount of dividends paid out is expected to decrease as the tax burden on dividends relative to capital gains increases. Based on the empirical evidence, this traditional approach is the one taken by the Treasury Report.

The second explanation, or "tax capitalization view," assumes that dividends offer no nontax benefits to shareholders relative to retained earnings.[8] An additional assumption in this view is that corporations have no alternative to dividends (like share repurchases) for distributing funds to shareholders. As a result, investor-level taxes on dividends reduce the value of the firm (as they are capitalized in share value), but would generally affect neither corporate dividend nor investment decisions. Under the assumptions of the tax capitalization view, corporate tax integration would not encourage corporations to increase dividend payouts, but would confer a windfall on holders of existing equity.

The distortions of business organizational and financial decisions under the current classical corporate tax system suggest that corporate tax integration might be desirable. But deciding upon a particular method of integrating the corporate and individual tax systems requires coming to grips with a variety of complex real-world issues.

## ISSUES IN SELECTING AN INTEGRATION PROTOTYPE

It would be far easier to design an integrated tax system if all shareholders were taxed at the same rate, shareholder and corporate tax rates were the same, all corporate income were taxed in the same manner, and the United States were a closed economy. The real world is not so simple, and evaluating alternative prototypes for integrating the corporate and individual tax systems requires a number of policy decisions.

Selecting a prototype for corporate tax integration requires making judgments on four issues, relating to the treatment of corporate-level tax preferences (for example, accelerated appreciation or tax-exempt interest on municipal bonds); corporate income received by tax-exempt investors; corporate income received by foreign shareholders; and foreign taxes paid by U.S. corporations. This section will summarize the Treasury Report recommendations in these four areas; the next section will discuss how various prototypes comport with these recommendations.

1. *The benefit of corporate-level tax preferences should not be extended to shareholders.* Integrating the individual and corporate tax into a single structure raises the question of whether individuals should be able to take direct advantage of corporate tax preferences. Doing so would lead to a large loss in revenue, a loss which presumably would have to be offset by raising other distorting taxes. However, the decision not to do so—in other words, to use corporate tax preferences only in calculating corporate income—does maintain a bias toward the corporate form of organization for those firms whose corporate tax preferences are significant.

2. *Corporate tax integration should not reduce taxes paid on corporate capital income by tax-exempt investors.* The current system taxes corporate-level income without regard to whether shareholders are taxable or tax-exempt. But if the corporate and individual taxes are unified, then does income flowing to tax-exempt investors end up bearing no tax at all? The revenue cost of such a step would be substantial. In principle, for example, one could deal with the problem by imposing a tax on the investment income of tax-exempt investors. Since that tax rate could be set at any level between zero and the statutory corporate

rate, tax-exempt entities could be accorded some degree of preferential treatment. Other integration options discussed below offer alternative approaches to this problem.

3.  *The benefits of integration should not be extended to foreign shareholders by statute, though benefits may be extended by treaty.* Under a classical tax system, corporate tax revenue has generally been collected by the source country, while the country of residence has generally maintained the primary claim on taxing dividends. But if the corporate and individual taxes are to be integrated, these two levels of taxation must become one and the same. If the new, single level of taxation is done at the investor level, for example, then foreign investors would be relieved of paying taxes on their U.S. investment. This raises the concern that U.S. investors could continue to face double taxation in their foreign investments, while foreign investors in the U.S. benefited from an integrated tax code. Using treaties to assure reciprocal treatment of foreign investors has been the approach followed by virtually all of the U.S. major trading partners (except Australia).

4.  *Foreign taxes paid by U.S. corporations should not be treated identically by statute to taxes paid to the U.S. government, though extending the benefits of integration to foreign-source income could be accomplished through bilateral treaty negotiations.*[9] If the United States treated foreign taxes paid as identical to U.S. taxes, foreign earnings abroad taxed at rates higher than the U.S. rate (34 percent) would not be taxed by the United States at the corporate level. Under an integrated corporate tax, presumably foreign corporate earnings taxed abroad would not face U.S. taxes at the individual level, either. Some treaty arrangement for reciprocal treatment makes far more sense than engaging in a battle where each country seeks to tax foreign companies at higher rates.

Any integration prototype must be judged by how it copes with these issues.

## PROTOTYPES FOR CORPORATE INTEGRATION

### Full Integration

One method of integration would treat the corporation as a conduit, taxing all corporate earnings, irrespective of whether they are distributed, once.[10] One way to implement this would be a "shareholder allocation" prototype, in which shareholders would include their share of the corporation's income in their income subject to tax. Tax would be withheld at the corporate level, and shareholders could apply the credits for corporate taxes paid against their income tax liability. [11]

How would shareholder allocation address the policy judgments discussed in the previous section? To be consistent with the Treasury Report's recommendations regarding tax-exempt and foreign shareholders, the credit for corporate taxes paid would count against other tax liabilities, but would not be refundable. In addition, the Treasury's prototype would retain the withholding tax on dividends paid by U.S. corporations to shareholders abroad (currently 30 percent), subject to reductions negotiated by treaty.

In contrast to the Treasury Report's recommendations regarding the treatment of preference income, however, preferences and foreign tax credits would be passed through to shareholders, since they would be included in the calculation of corporate income. Avoiding such passthroughs would be both inconsistent with the spirit of full integration and administratively complex. For this reason and because of the general administrative complexity of the prototype, the Treasury did not recommend its enactment.

## Dividend Relief

Most proposals for integration have focused on eliminating the double taxation of those earnings that are distributed; in short, dividend relief. A number of options are possible. In an "imputation credit" system, tax is collected at the corporate level, but shareholders receive a credit to apply against investor-level taxes. In a "dividend deduction" system, corporations could deduct dividend payments just as they do interest payments in calculating taxable income. Or in a "dividend exclusion" system, shareholders would not be taxed on dividend income.

The imputation credit prototype might work this way: Corporations would determine their income for tax purposes as they do now and would pay a corporate-level tax. Shareholders would include in their income the "grossed-up" amount of the dividend—that is, including both the dividend and the associated tax paid at the corporate level. They could apply toward individual tax payments a credit equal to the amount of corporate tax that would be associated with gross dividends. This system is similar to the taxation of wages and salaries for employees, in which an employee includes gross wages in taxable income and receives a credit equal to the amount of tax withheld.

An imputation credit system can be shaped to conform to a number of different policy judgments. For example, the prototype suggested by the Treasury would make the credit nonrefundable, so that corporate income accruing to tax-exempt and foreign shareholders would still be subject to one level of tax.[12] Alternatively, making credits refundable would extend the benefits of integration to these shareholders. While the Report did not recommend this prototype for dividend relief because of its relative complexity—it would create a new regime for taxing corporate dividend distributions—the fact that most integrated tax systems use imputation credit prototypes suggests that it should continue to be studied.

A dividend deduction system would treat dividends and interest payments symmetrically at the corporate level.[13] From the point of view of the basic policy judgments delineated earlier, a dividend deduction system would violate the Treasury's recommendation that the benefits of integration not be extended to tax-exempt and foreign shareholders. Moreover, a proposal to deduct dividends paid—at least the portion attributable to income on which corporate tax has been paid—would be significantly more expensive than other forms of dividend relief.

Recent dividend deduction proposals include the "Allowance for Corporate Equity" proposal of the Capital Taxes Group of the British Institute for Fiscal Studies (Gammie 1991), which would allow a corporation to deduct in its calculation of taxable income an allowance equal to the product of a specified interest rate times stockholders' equity. This example illustrates an important point: Dividend deduction systems do not have to be tied to dividends actually paid, which is a concern often expressed by high-technology industries with low dividend payouts. Deductions can be based on an imputed cost of equity and the average level of shareholders' equity. The American Law Institute (1989) also proposed a dividend deduction system limited to dividends paid on new equity capital: the deduction would be equal to the product of a specified interest rate and net contributed capital (less extraordinary dividends and nondividend distributions).[14]

The Treasury Report recommended a dividend exclusion prototype for dividend relief as the most straightforward means of implementing the general policy recommendations requiring the least change from current law. Under this prototype, corporations would pay the corporate income tax, computing taxable income in the same way as under current law. However, dividends paid out of fully taxed corporate income would not be taxed again at the investor level.

To address the goals of the previous section, the dividend exclusion program might be arranged in this way: Fully taxed income would be tracked by corporations in an "Excludable Dividend Account" (EDA) based on corporate taxes paid. For example, corporate tax payments of $34 would permit $66 to be contributed to the EDA. That is, since the $34 of tax paid is equivalent to paying the statutory corporate tax rate on $100 of earnings, the corporation would be allowed to add $100 – $34, or $66 to its EDA, from which it could pay excludable dividends to its shareholders. Amounts of dividends distributed which are greater than the EDA balance, like distributions from corporate tax preference income, would be taxable at the individual level.

Under the dividend exclusion prototype, tax-exempt investors would not pay tax either on "excludable" or on "taxable" dividends, but would not be granted a refund of applicable corporate taxes. Essentially, those shareholders bear the same tax burden on corporate equity income as they now bear. Foreign shareholders would also be treated as they are under current law: a withholding tax of 30 percent on dividends paid by U.S. firms to foreign shareholders would remain (with lower rates available by treaty). With respect to foreign-source income earned by U.S. firms, corporations would be permitted to credit foreign taxes paid against U.S. corporate tax (as under current law). However, the EDA would not be increased by U.S. corporate tax liabilities offset by foreign tax credits.

Though not usually considered in traditional analyses of corporate tax integration, the existence of capital-market imperfections affect the choice of an integration prototype. Under the simplest neoclassical model of the firm with perfect capital markets, the decision of whether to grant dividend relief at the firm level or the investor level is determined by whether one believes that corporate income should be taxed once at the corporate tax rate or once at progressive shareholder tax rates, and by administrative considerations. However, transactions costs of issuing securities and costs arising from asymmetric information can make external finance more expensive than internal finance (for example, Greenwald et al. 1984; Fazzari et al. 1988). As a result, it may be inappropriate to allow firms and shareholders to benefit from integration only to the extent that internally generated funds are paid out as dividends.

Because retained (already fully taxed) earnings would bear a greater tax burden than distributed earnings under dividend relief models, corporations would have an incentive to distribute rather than retain earnings. The dividend exclusion prototype could be easily extended to avoid the double taxation of retained earnings. The Report outlines a "dividend reinvestment plan" (DRIP), which would allow a corporation to declare deemed dividends (up to the amount of its EDA balance), treating the dividend as reinvested in the corporation. Hence, shareholders would be treated as if they had received an excludable dividend, and the stock's basis would be increased, avoiding a subsequent capital gains tax on retained earnings.

## More Neutral Treatment of Debt and Equity

Integration prototypes reduce the differences in the tax treatment of debt and equity finance. Differences need not be eliminated, however. For example, the Treasury Report's imputation credit and dividend exclusion prototypes would retain the current level of corporate taxes on equity income received by tax-exempt and foreign investors. As long as interest payments remain deductible, the tax system would still create a bias toward debt investments by such investors. This problem can be addressed at either the investor level or the firm level, as was the case for dividend relief.

An imputation credit system could be extended to equate the treatment of debt and equity by implementing a "bondholder credit" system. Under such a system, corporate interest deductions would be disallowed. Corporate tax paid on earnings used to pay interest or dividends would be passed through to bondholders and shareholders as imputation credits. Bondholders and shareholders would then include in their income, for tax purposes, the sum of the (cash) interest or dividend payments and the imputation credits. Credits could be used to offset tax on interest income. A similar prototype was actually introduced in legislation by Representative Vander Jagt in 1990 (H.R. 4457, 101st Congress, 2nd Session, 1990). To conform to the Treasury's decision regarding the appropriate tax treatment of tax-exempt and foreign shareholders, such shareholders would not be able to claim refunds of imputation credits. Taxable shareholders would be able to use excess credits to reduce their tax on other income, but not to claim refunds.

However, the Treasury Report took a different approach to this problem, and developed in detail a broad extension of the dividend exclusion prototype to interest. Treasury's prototype—the Comprehensive Business Income Tax (CBIT)—would apply to all businesses, noncorporate and corporate, with the exception of very small firms. CBIT would represent fundamental shifts in the taxation of capital income, and the Report presents it as a long-term option.

Under the CBIT prototype, neither deductions for payments to debtholders and nor to equity holders would be permitted, and a tax would be collected at the entity level (at a rate equal to the highest marginal individual tax rate, currently 31 percent).[15] However, both interest and equity distributions generally would be excludable from income by investors.

The Treasury Report does not take a stand on whether capital gains would continue to be taxed under CBIT; it presents CBIT variants with and without taxation of the capital gains. However, if all business income were taxed at the entity level and investors excluded all interest and dividend income, taxing capital gains would create a significant disparity between distributed and retained earnings. An exemption for capital gains (and disallowance of losses) on equity and debt of CBIT entities would be consistent with the general exemption of dividends and interest from the investor-level tax under CBIT.

To conform to the Treasury Report's general recommendations, CBIT would not extend benefits of entity-level preferences to investors. This would be accomplished by establishing Excludable Dividend Accounts, as in the case of the dividend exclusion prototype. That is, payments received by debtholders and equityholders would be excludable up to the amount of the EDA balance, and distributions in excess of that balance would be taxable. With respect to tax-exempt and foreign shareholders, the entity-level tax would be nonrefundable, thereby ensuring that one level of tax is collected. The Treasury Report does, however, recommend that the current 30 percent withholding tax on dividends paid by U.S. corporations to foreign shareholders be repealed. CBIT would allow foreign taxes paid by U.S. firms to be credited against the U.S. entity-level tax, but the income sheltered from tax by such credits would not go into the EDA. However, the calculation of the foreign tax credit limitation would be modified to prevent the use of excess foreign tax credits due to the expanded tax base under CBIT.

CBIT would eliminate tax distortions in organizational form, capital structure, and dividend policy more completely than any of the other prototypes. However, it would also be a substantial departure from current law, and issues surrounding its implementation require significant additional analysis. Two of the key issues include: how CBIT might affect investment by tax-exempt and foreign investors in U.S. private and government debt; and how it might affect the portfolios of banks, insurance companies, and other financial institutions.

## HOW LARGE ARE THE BENEFITS OF INTEGRATION?

The direction of the tax biases under current law is clear. The size of the resulting inefficiency will be determined by how much households and firms respond to these tax considerations. Formal economic analysis is difficult since behavioral responses in one market affect other markets. For example, when the corporate tax drives capital from the corporate sector, rates of return in the noncorporate sector are affected.

These economic interrelationships can be studied using computable general equilibrium models. An advantage of these models is that they are detailed representations of the U.S. economy and its actual (and proposed) tax system. Some warnings apply, however. First, since any given model can create some odd results, the Treasury Report diversifies its presentation with simulation results based on four different models. Second, the computable general equilibrium models offer comparison of steady-state tax regimes—that is, assuming that behavioral adjustments have taken place. This focus on the long run is instructive, since the goal of improving the long-term performance of the economy reason behind integration, but it does ignore transition effects, which can be substantial. Finally, the models incorporate costs of financial distortions in an ad hoc fashion.[16]

To examine the economic effects of switching to an integrated tax system, it is necessary to specify an experiment. For example, if integration were modeled as a cut in the tax rate on corporate capital income, it would be difficult to separate the economic effects of a reduction in capital taxes from the economic effects of integration per se. Accordingly, the Report assumes that other taxes are changed to offset the revenue effects of integration. While many such experiments are possible, the Report focuses on two: the use of offsetting lump-sum and uniform capital income taxes. While lump-sum replacement taxes are sometimes used in studies of efficiency gains from tax reforms, they have the drawback of biasing comparisons of prototypes in favor of prototypes that lose the most revenue (because the lump-sum tax is nondistorting). As a result, the offset of increasing or reducing all tax rates on capital income is more meaningful. Such results indicate economic effects of integration per se, holding constant the total tax rate on capital income.

The economic benefits from corporate tax integration appear to be significant. The gains result from improved allocation of real resources, reductions in the likelihood of firms experiencing financial distress, and the shift toward allowing corporations to make capital structure and dividend decisions based on nontax benefits and costs. Estimated increases in economic well-being from integration are in many cases as large as gains suggested for the reforms in the Tax Reform Act of 1986 (Fullerton et al. 1987; Gravelle 1989).

The Treasury Report offers estimates of the effect of shareholder allocation, imputation credit, dividend exclusion, and CBIT prototypes. Depending on the prototype, model, and financing assumption, this expansion ranges from a 2 percentage-point increase in the share of capital used in the corporate sector to a 8 percentage-point increase. In addition, the integration prototypes generally encourage corporations to use less debt. Estimated debt-to-asset ratios decrease by from 1 percentage point to 7 percentage points, depending on the model, financing assumption, and prototype. The integration prototypes encourage corporations to increase the portion of earnings distributed as dividends. Depending on the model, financing assumption, and prototype, dividend payout ratios rise modestly by between 2 and 6 percentage points.

By shifting resources into the corporate sector, reducing corporate borrowing, and encouraging dividends, the prototypes generate changes in economic well-being. Each prototype improves economic welfare, with improvement ranging from an amount equivalent to 0.07 percent of annual consumption (that is, total consumer spending on goods and services) to an amount equivalent to 0.73 percent of consumption, or a range of from $2.5 to $26 billion per year. In other words, these annual gains might amount to as much as 28 percent of the tax revenue currently generated from corporate capital income. The gains are largest for the CBIT prototype, because it generally eliminates the tax bias against corporate equity issues and dividend distributions. Remember that all of these efficiency gains assume that taxes on capital income would be increased, as necessary, to compensate for any revenue lost as a result of integration.

## OUTSTANDING ISSUES

Integrating the corporate and individual income tax systems would likely increase economic efficiency, even if the switch to an integrated tax system is revenue-neutral, and paid for by higher taxes on capital income. Why, then, is integration not more popular in business and policy-making communities?

One answer lies in the general heading of "transition problems." A well-known adage holds that an old tax is a good tax, but corporate integration would change significantly the taxation of capital income. Investors and firms have made decisions based on the existing classical tax system: to invest in noncorporate or corporate businesses; or in equity rather than debt; or to retain or distribute corporate earnings; or to issue debt or equity. A shift to integration will impose costs and uncertainty.

However, transition problems are not insurmountable; in fact, they are a common feature of most tax reform programs. One common answer is to phase-in new provisions; for example, the Tax Reform Act of 1986 phased in passive loss disallowance rules, the personal interest disallowance rules, and the new investment interest limitations. An alternative transition strategy would be to treat "old" and "new" capital separately. The Treasury Report rejected this strategy on policy grounds, but it would be administratively complex as well. For example, a permanent "grandfather" rule would require maintaining a distinction between old and new assets and equity interests and, for the CBIT prototype, old and new debt as well. Under a phase-in approach, integration would be introduced gradually over a designated period, but no distinction between old and new equity or debt would be made. (The ongoing analysis of corporate taxation by the American Law Institute has suggested a similar approach.) Such phase-ins could be relatively simple for integration through dividend relief.

A second broad concern about integration, beyond the problems of transition, involves issues of integration in an open economy. Three of the four computable general equilibrium models used in the Report's economic analysis treat the United States as a closed economy; the effects of integration might be very different in an open economy. For example, in a closed economy, a successful saving incentive might be expected to lower the cost of capital and increase domestic investment. In contrast, in a small open economy, which takes the real interest rate in the international capital market as given, much of the added saving might flow abroad with very little effect on the domestic capital stock. The Report does offer one open-economy computable general equilibrium model to examine the effects of integration prototypes on foreign investment in the United States, U.S. investment abroad, the components of the balance of payments, and the U.S. domestic capital stock (see also Mutti and Grubert 1985), but more research is needed before reaching firm conclusions. Two issues are particularly unknown and important—the extent to which capital is internationally mobile and the relative mobility of debt and equity capital.

A third group of concerns about integration probably reflects a confusion of different goals in reforming corporate income taxation. A number of economists and policymakers believe that enacting an integration proposal that holds the level of capital income taxation constant is less important than reducing the overall level of taxation of capital income to reduce intertemporal distortions in consumption decisions and raise national saving. In this view, more attention should be paid to introducing broad incentives for saving in the tax code, or to switching from an income tax system to a consumption tax system. As an example of these differing goals, some business interests traditionally supported dividend deduction schemes for companies over dividend relief for shareholders (via imputation credit or dividend exclusion schemes) because making dividends deductible would lower the cost of capital for firms. Such a comparison confuses the effect of a reduction in the level of capital taxation (which may well be laudable) with integration. A similar problem arises in the comparison of the relative desirability of investment incentives (like accelerated depreciation), and integration. Integration is conceptually separate from any particular level of corporate taxation. Rather than debating a level of taxation versus a method, one should rather ask about the relative contributions of these alternatives toward increasing economic efficiency holding the level of capital income taxation constant.

Corporate tax integration could be combined with a goal of reducing the overall level of corporate taxation. For example, the revenue cost of integration could be offset by higher taxes on noncapital income. In addition, some integration prototypes such as dividend exclusion or CBIT would be compatible with a transition from the current income tax to a consumption tax alternative (Bradford 1986). However, a shift from an income tax to a consumption tax would have to address similar difficult transition and open economy issues raised by discussions of integration.

## CONCLUSION

Integrating the corporate and individual income tax systems is not a new topic. I believe it is fair to say that a consensus is emerging from the ongoing studies of integration, both within the Treasury and outside, that integration is desirable.

Further advancing the integration debate requires three steps, all of which will require significant interaction between economists, politicians, and the business community. Additional research is needed on the factors affecting the organizational and financial decisions of firms, particularly including international dimensions, and on the costs of a transition to an integrated tax system. Then, discussion should focus on basic policy judgments, such as those made by the Treasury regarding the treatment of tax-exempt and foreign shareholders. Finally, with a better understanding of the economic benefits of integration and basic policy judgments, individual prototypes can be debated.

## NOTES

I am grateful to Dave Bradford, Lowell Dworin, Gerry Gerardi, Jane Gravelle, Michael Graetz, Jim Nunns, Joseph Stiglitz, and Timothy Taylor for helpful comments and suggestions. Any opinions expressed are my own and not necessarily those of the Treasury Department.

1. Interest income received by foreign lenders from U.S. corporations, however, is not generally subject to U.S. tax.

2. The interested reader should also consult the recently completed study of and proposals for integration in American Law Institute (1992).

3. Differences in the total effective tax rates (that is, incorporating corporate and individual taxes) on income from corporate equity, noncorporate equity, and corporate debt can be substantial. Under plausible assumptions (including an inflation rate of 4 percent, a dividend payout ratio of 57 percent, an average holding period of seven years, and a holding of two-thirds of capital gains until death), Gravelle (1991) estimates that a noncorporate equity income facing a 28 percent tax rate would face a 48 percent total effective tax rate if it were in the form of corporate equity and a 20 percent total effective tax rate on corporate debt. Moreover, accounting for the importance of holdings of tax-exempt institutions creates even larger differences among tax rates on different forms of capital income. See also Gordon and MacKie-Mason (1990) and Gertler and Hubbard (1992) for a discussion of the total effective tax rates on debt and equity income.

4. One might also add the distortion of intertemporal consumption decisions resulting from the overall level of capital income taxation. That problem is not unique to the classical system, however, and I will set it aside here.

5. While the use of an S corporation can provide nontax benefits of the corporate form, while avoiding the problem of double taxation, there are a number of restrictions on their use that limit their applicability. Nonetheless, the use of S corporations has increased significantly.

6. In fact, debt-financed investments can have a negative marginal effective tax rate because the corporation deducts the inflationary component of the nominal interest rate at the corporate rate, which is generally higher than a noncorporate lender's tax rate.

7. It is fair to say that the question of why distributions take the form of dividends (instead of, say, share repurchases) is an open question for research.

8. American Law Institute (1989) assumed the tax capitalization view of the dividend decision. American Law Institute (1992) generally argues the traditional view as a general description.

9. This author hopes that any prototype actually proposed by Treasury will extend the benefits of integration to foreign-source income earned by U.S. corporations with reciprocal treatment by other countries.

10. For a discussion of full integration, see McLure (1979). A full integration prototype has never been enacted, though the Carter Commission recommended such a prototype for Canada in the 1960s (Royal Commission on Taxation 1966) and the U.S. Treasury (1977) analyzed a prototype in its *Blueprints* study. Germany's Tax Reform Commission rejected full integration in 1971, because of administrative complexity (Gourevitch 1977).

11. The basis of shares would rise by the amount of allocated taxable income plus the amount of preference income. Basis would fall by the amount of distributions to shareholders, and distributions greater than basis would be taxed as a gain.

12. The American Law Institute (1992) study proposed an imputation credit prototype in which shareholders would receive a refundable credit for taxes paid at the corporate level, and in which the benefits of certain tax preferences would be passed through to investors.

13. The U.S. Treasury Department (1984) recommended a 50 percent dividends-paid deduction and the President's 1985 tax proposals included a 10 percent deduction, though no dividends-paid deduction was adopted in the Tax Reform Act of 1986.

14. The American Law Institute (1989) proposals would reduce the tax bias against finance from new, but not from existing, equity. This restriction reflected that study's adoption of the tax capitalization view of the dividend decision.

15. The Treasury Report's CBIT prototype would not include U.S. government debt and home mortgage obligations as CBIT debt. Accordingly, interest received on such debt would be taxable, and mortgage interest payments would be deductible, as under current law.

16. Space does not permit a thorough review of the assumptions of and findings generated by the CGE models; see Chapter 13 of the Treasury Report for details.

## REFERENCES

American Law Institute, Federal Income Tax Project. *Reporter's Study Draft, Subchapter C (Supplemental Study).* Philadelphia (1989). (Memo written by Professor William D. Andrews of the Harvard Law School.)

American Law Institute, Federal Income Tax Project. *Reporter's Study Draft, Integration of the Individual and Corporate Income Taxes.* Philadelphia (1992). (Memo written by Professor Alvin C. Warren of Harvard Law School.)

Ault, Hugh, J. "Corporate Integration, Tax Treaties, and the Division of the International Tax Base: Principles and Practices." *New York University Tax Law Review* (forthcoming).

Bradford, David F. *Untangling the Income Tax.* Cambridge: Harvard University Press (1986).

Fazzari, Steven, R. Glenn Hubbard, and Bruce C. Petersen. "Financing Constraints and Corporate Investment." *Brookings Papers on Economic Activity 1* (1988): 141–195.

Fullerton, Don, Yolanda Kodrzycki Henderson, and James Mackie. "Investment Allocation and Growth Under the Tax Reform Act of 1986," in *Compendium of Tax Research, 1987.* Washington, D.C.: U.S. Government Printing Office (1987).

Gammie, Malcolm. "Corporate Tax Harmonization: An 'ACE' Proposal." *IBFD European Taxation 12* (1991).

Gertler, Mark, and R. Glenn Hubbard. "Taxation, Corporate Capital Structure, and Financial Distress," in Lawrence H. Summers, ed., *Tax Policy and the Economy, 4*, Cambridge: MIT Press (1990): 43–72.

————. "Corporate Financial Policy, Taxation, and Macroeconomic Risk," mimeo, Columbia University (August 1992).

Gordon, Roger H., and Jeffrey K. MacKie-Mason. "Effects of the Tax Reform Act of 1986 on Corporate Financial Policy and Organizational Form," in Joel B. Slemrod, ed., *Do Taxes Matter?: The Impact of the Tax Reform Act of 1986*. Cambridge: MIT Press (1990): 91–131.

Gourevitch, Harry G. "Corporate Tax Integration: The European Experience." *Tax Lawyer 31*:1, (Fall 1977): 65–112.

Gravelle, Jane G. "Differential Taxation of Capital Income: Another Look at the 1986 Tax Reform Act." *National Tax Journal 47* (December 1989): 441–463.

Gravelle, Jane G. *Corporate Tax Integration: Issues and Options*. Washington, D.C.: Congressional Research Service (1991).

Gravelle, Jane G., and Lawrence Kotlikoff. "The Incidence and Efficiency Costs of Corporate Taxation When Corporate and Noncorporate Firms Produce the Same Good." *Journal of Political Economy 97*:4 (August 1989): 749–780.

Greenwald, Bruce, Joseph E. Stiglitz, and Andrew Weiss. "Information Imperfections in the Capital Market and Macroeconomic Fluctuations." *American Economic Review 74* (May 1984): 194–199.

Harberger, Arnold C. "The Incidence of the Corporation Income Tax." *Journal of Political Economy 70*:3 (June 1962): 215–240.

Harberger, Arnold C. "Efficiency Effects of Taxes on Income from Capital," in Marian Krzyzaniak, ed., *Effects of the Corporation Income Tax*, Detroit: Wayne State University Press (1966): 107–117.

Jensen, Michael C. "Agency Costs of Free Cash Flow, Corporate Finance, and Takeovers." *American Economic Review 76*:2 (May 1986): 323–329.

McLure, Charles E., Jr. *Must Corporate Income Be Taxed Twice?* Washington. D.C.: The Brookings Institution (1979).

Mutti, John, and Harry Grubert. "The Taxation of Capital Income in an Open Economy: The Importance of Resident-Nonresident Tax Treatment." *Journal of Public Economics 27*:3 (August 1985): 291–309.

Poterba, James M., and Lawrence H. Summers. "The Economic Effects of Dividend Taxes," in Edward Altman and Marti Subrahmanyam, eds., *Recent Advances in Corporate Finance*, Homewood: Richard D. Irwin (1985): 227–284.

Royal Commission on Taxation. *Report of the Royal Canadian Commission on Taxation, 4*, chapter 19. Ottawa: Queen's Printer (1966).

Shoven, John B., and John Whalley. "Applied General Equilibrium Models of Taxation and International Trade: Introduction and Survey." *Journal of Economic Literature 22*:3 (September 1984): 1007–1051.

Stiglitz, Joseph E. "Taxation, Corporate Financial Policy, and the Cost of Capital." *Journal of Public Economics 2* (February 1973): 1–34.

U.S. Department of the Treasury. *Blueprints for Basic Tax Reform.* Washington, D.C.: U.S. Government Printing Office (1977).

U.S. Department of the Treasury. *Tax Reform for Fairness, Simplicity, and Economic Growth: The Treasury Department Report to the President.* Washington, D.C.: U.S. Government Printing Office (1984).

U.S. Department of the Treasury. *Integration of the Individual and Corporate Tax Systems: Taxing Business Income Once.* Washington, D.C.: U.S. Government Printing Office (1992).

The White House. *The President's Proposals to the Congress for Fairness, Growth, and Simplicity.* Washington, D.C.: U.S. Government Printing Office (1985).

# S E L E C T I O N     2 6

Ernest S. Christian

# The Tax Restructuring Phenomenon: Analytical Principles and Political Equation

Recent years have seen a number of proposals in the United States to institute a flat rate (proportional) tax on a comprehensive definition of income. Proponents argue that if tax preferences—exclusions, exemptions, and deductions—are eliminated, a surprisingly low flat rate can raise the same amount of revenue as a tax system which exempts income such as employer contributions for medical insurance, social security benefits, charitable donations, and home-mortgage interest. While generally in agreement with the desirability of broadening the income tax base, opponents defend progressive taxation on equity grounds, believing it to be an appropriate means of reducing the inequality of income in the United States. Replacing a progressive tax system with a flat rate system is asserted to increase tax burdens on low and middle income taxpayers and decrease burdens on high income taxpayers.

In this selection, Ernest Christian compares two actual versions of a flat rate tax system. One version was introduced in U.S. Senate bill S.722 in 1995—the Unlimited Saving Allowance or USA Tax. The other version is simply referred to as the Flat Tax and is consistent with the well-known proposal by economists Robert Hall and Alvin Rabushka, who promise that "Tax forms could fit on postcards" (see Suggested Further Readings). Christian argues that the main goal of both alternatives should be to simplify the tax system and eliminate any tax bias against saving and investment. More specifically, by removing special provisions and graduated rates, flat tax proposals should lower taxpayer compliance costs. In addition, a flat-rate income tax should enhance economic

Christian, Ernest S. "The Tax Restructuring Phenomenon: Analytical Principles and Political Equation." *National Tax Journal* 48 (September 1995): 373-385. This selection is an abridged version of the original article.

**Ernest S. Christian** is Attorney and Chief Counsel for the Center for Strategic Tax Reform, Washington, D.C.

growth and international competitiveness by avoiding some of the disincentives to save and invest, which have been associated with higher marginal income tax rates.

### Questions to Guide the Reading

1. Both the Flat Tax and the USA Tax would replace the traditional corporate income tax. While many provisions are identical, how do the two plans differ in their treatment of direct compensation paid to employees (labor income)?

2. Flat tax proponents have not reached agreement on the treatment of income generated by multinational firms operating within the borders of the United States. How do the Flat Tax and USA Tax differ in their explicit border adjustments?

3. What are the business tax rates proposed by the two plans? What are the implications of these rates for total tax revenues collected from the business sector?

4. Some argue that both the Flat Tax and USA Tax are "modified" flat tax proposals, and that the only "true" flat tax would levy a single, unchanging rate on all types of income at the individual level. While the Flat Tax has a single nominal rate of 20 percent, why is the Flat Tax not, in fact, a single, unchanging tax on wage income? Referring to Table 5, what are the effective rates?

5. The Flat Tax allows no credit for the 7.65 percent FICA tax paid by employees. What does this feature imply about the real marginal rate on wage income (up to $61,500) of a 20 percent flat tax? Referring to Table 6, what does this imply about the real effective tax rates for various levels of income with the payroll tax included?

6. Both the Flat Tax and USA Tax attempt to eliminate any tax bias against saving. How do the Flat Tax and the USA Tax differ in the treatment of individual savings?

7. What would be the aggregate revenue results of the USA Tax and the Flat Tax? What differences would exist between the two taxes in the resulting share of taxes collected from individuals versus businesses? In the resulting shift in the distribution of the tax burden among family income groups?

8. At the individual income tax level, what modifications of the Flat Tax (as presented by the author) might make it more politically workable?

# INTRODUCTION

There is a high likelihood that the federal income tax of today will soon be replaced by a new American tax system.[1] The long reign of federal income tax has had an enormous impact on the daily lives and behavior of 250 million Americans. It is thoroughly embedded in their consciousness. Abandoning it in favor of a new tax system will be a historic event that will have far-reaching consequences for generations to come. As bad and unpopular as the present Internal Revenue Code is, it will not be an easy task to enact a proper replacement. It is not hard to construct a tax system that would be both simpler and better than the present one. It is, however, not so easy to construct a tax system that the American people will accept and that will actually be enacted into law. It is even harder to enact a new American tax system that is based on core principles of enduring merit that will continue to serve the nation as political and economic circumstances change in the future.

The two leading competitors to replace the present income tax are the Flat Tax and the USA Tax.[2] Either would be vastly superior to the present incumbent. Both are highly sophisticated in the sense of minimalism.

*The art of using the fewest and simplest elements to achieve the greatest effect.*

While structurally different, both approaches derive from the same analytical roots. Both share many of the same goals. Both have many of the same consequences, most particularly with respect to simplification and in eliminating the bias against saving and investment. In fact, the USA Tax is a version of the Flat Tax and vice versa. By evaluating the similarities as well as the differences, the purpose here is to put both in perspective and to speculate about how these two seemingly separate paths toward tax restructuring may merge into one (see Figures 1 and 2).

## BUSINESS-LEVEL TAXES: PARTICULAR SIMILARITIES AND DIFFERENCES

Both the USA Tax and the Flat Tax would replace the present corporate income tax with a new form of annual business tax that includes U.S. sales revenues and deducts amounts paid to other businesses. Both would eliminate the present law distinction between incorporated and unincorporated businesses, and both would uniformly apply the business tax to partnerships and proprietorships, as well as to corporations of all types. Neither would allow a deduction for dividends paid and neither would include in income dividends received. Both would disallow the present law deduction for interest paid and both would exclude interest received. Both would abandon the depreciation concept and would, instead, allow capital purchases to be expensed (see Table 1).

Up to this point—except for the tax rate—the Flat Tax and the USA Tax at the business level are identical, but there is more to the story. Businesses also pay

**Figure 1** The Flat Tax

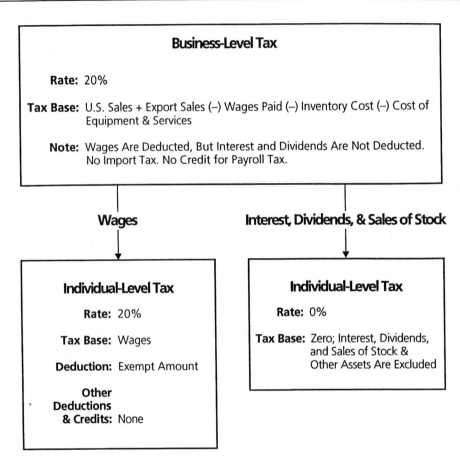

Business-Level Tax

**Rate:** 20%

**Tax Base:** U.S. Sales + Export Sales (–) Wages Paid (–) Inventory Cost (–) Cost of Equipment & Services

**Note:** Wages Are Deducted, But Interest and Dividends Are Not Deducted. No Import Tax. No Credit for Payroll Tax.

**Wages**

**Interest, Dividends, & Sales of Stock**

Individual-Level Tax

**Rate:** 20%

**Tax Base:** Wages

**Deduction:** Exempt Amount

**Other Deductions & Credits:** None

Individual-Level Tax

**Rate:** 0%

**Tax Base:** Zero; Interest, Dividends, and Sales of Stock & Other Assets Are Excluded

compensation to employees, and it is here that big differences between the USA Tax and the Flat Tax start to emerge. The Flat Tax allows a deduction for direct compensation paid to employees. The USA Tax does not. On the other hand, the USA Tax allows a business a tax credit for the FICA payroll tax it pays on employee wages. The Flat Tax does not. Because the USA Tax allows no deduction for either direct or indirect compensation to employees, it is border adjustable for exports and imports. Because the Flat Tax allows a deduction for direct compensation, it is not border adjustable for exports and imports. The USA Tax provides appropriate transitional rules for business capital assets and inventory acquired prior to the effective date of the new tax system. Apparently, the Flat Tax does not, although it could and may do so when fully drafted and introduced in legislative form (see Table 2).

**Figure 2** The USA Tax

---

## Business-Level Tax

**Rate:** 11%

**Tax Base:** Sales Revenues (–) Exports (–) Inventory Cost (–)
Cost of Equipment & Services

**Payroll Tax:** Tax Credit for Employer-Paid Payroll Tax

**Imports:** 11% Tax on Imported Inventory, Equipment & Services

**Note:** No Deduction for Wages Paid, Dividends Paid, or Interest Paid.

**Wages**       **Interest, Dividends, & Sales of Stock**

## Individual-Level Tax

**Rates:** Progressive, Initially 19%, 27%, and 40%, But Soon
Decline to 8%, 19%, and 40%

**Tax Base:** Wages + Interest + Dividends + Sales of Stock and Other
Assets (–) Savings

**Savings Deduction:** A Deduction Is Allowed for Savings, i.e., Stocks, Bonds,
Deposits, etc.

**Withdrawal from Savings:** Principal and Earnings on Principal Are Taxed When
Withdrawn from Savings

**Other Deductions & Credits:** Deduction for Exempt Amount & Deductions for Home
Mortgage Interest, Charitable Contributions & Secondary
Education; Credit for Employee-Paid Payroll Tax & EITC

**Table 1** Initial Similarities and Differences

|  | USA Tax | Flat Tax |
|---|---|---|
| Rate of tax | 11% | 20% |
| Applies to corporate and noncorporate businesses alike | Yes | Yes |
| Territorial tax (U.S. sales only) | Yes | Yes |
| Expenses capital purchases the same as inventory and supplies | Yes | Yes |
| Excludes dividends received, and no deduction for dividends paid | Yes | Yes |
| Excludes interest received, and no deduction for interest paid | Yes | Yes |

**Table 2** Additional Similarities and Differences

|  | USA Tax | Flat Tax |
|---|---|---|
| Deducts direct compensation to employees | No | Yes |
| Deducts indirect compensation to employees | No | No |
| Allows credit for employer FICA tax | Yes | No |
| Taxes export sales | No | Yes |
| Imposes import tax | Yes | No |
| Provides transitional rules | Yes | No |

At an 11 percent business tax rate, the USA Tax is designed to raise about the same aggregate amount of revenue (inclusive of the employer payroll tax) from the business sector as present law. If the 11 percent rate remains constant year-to-year as the amortization deductions for pre-effective date capital and inventory costs decline, the USA Tax will, over time, moderately increase the aggregate amount of taxes collected at the business level—especially if the tax on net imports is attributed entirely to domestic business firms instead of being attributed in part to the foreign-sited capital and labor factors that produced and sold those imports. A business tax rate that gradually declines from roughly 11 percent to roughly 9 percent in the out years would have an entirely revenue-neutral result at the business level over time. Because labor services comprise roughly 80 percent of gross domestic product (GDP), about the same proportion of business tax revenues under the USA Tax comes from the output value of labor. The remainder comes from a combination of net (in excess of cost) returns to capital invested after the effective date, gross returns to old capital in excess of transitional amortization deductions, and from net imports.

At a 20 percent tax rate, the Flat Tax could substantially increase business taxes and the percentage of total tax revenues that is collected from the business sector. Absent transitional adjustments, immediately after enactment of the business tax, revenues will come from gross returns to old capital investment that will decline year-by-year, net (in excess of cost) returns to new capital investment, and output value of labor as measured by indirect compensation.

As is standard in such exercises, the foregoing general projections of revenue results assume the same levels of future capital investment and GDP growth as would be the case if the present income tax continued in effect. Proponents of the Flat Tax and the USA Tax would expect GDP to grow more rapidly after the present income tax is replaced. The USA Tax would, in all cases, continue to collect from the business sector about the same percentage of the total taxes as under present law.

## THE INDIVIDUAL-LEVEL TAXES: PARTICULAR SIMILARITIES AND DIFFERENCES

Both the Flax Tax and the USA Tax would replace the present federal income tax on individuals. Both are designed to eliminate the bias against income that is saved and both are intended to be less complex and less intrusive than the present personal income tax. When viewed in traditional and somewhat superficial terms of income definition, deductions allowed, rates of tax, and credits against tax, the USA Tax and the Flat Tax do, however, present markedly different pictures as shown in Table 3.

The Flat Tax has a single nominal rate for individuals (here illustrated as 20 percent). Under the rigid constraint imposed by the basic structure of the Flat Tax, the individual tax rate must always be exactly equal to the business tax rate. The USA Tax in S.722 has three nominal rates that vary somewhat by filing status as shown in Table 4.

Both the Flat Tax and the USA Tax have family (personal) exemptions and dependent exemptions that effectively modify the nominal rate (rates). In the case of the Flat Tax, these exemptions appear to be as set forth below, although they may be modified when the Flat Tax is fully articulated in legislative bill form.

| | |
|---|---|
| Joint return | $26,200 |
| Single filer | $13,100 |
| Head of household | $17,200 |
| Per dependent | $ 5,300 |

The USA Tax in S.722 has the following exemptions:

| | |
|---|---|
| Joint return | $ 7,400 |
| Single filer | $ 4,400 |
| Married/separate | $ 3,700 |
| Head of household | $ 5,400 |
| Per filer and dependent | $ 2,550 |

As evidenced by the fact that they are substantially larger, the exemptions play a much more significant role under the Flat Tax. Because the flat exemptions decrease as a percentage of income as income rises, they are the way by which the Flat Tax achieves some degree of graduation on an effective rate basis. However, because only wage income is included and taxed on the individual tax return, it is only on wage income that the tax is graduated.

**Table 3**  Basic Similarities and Differences

|  | USA Tax | Flat Tax |
| --- | --- | --- |
| Progressive rates | Yes | No |
| Flate rate | No | Yes |
| Includes wages and salaries in income subject to tax | Yes | Yes |
| Allows credit for employee FICA payroll tax | Yes | No |
| Allows a deduction for income that is saved | Yes | No |
| Allows deductions for the following: | Yes | No |
| Charitable contributions | Yes | No |
| Home mortgage interest |  |  |
| Education expenses |  |  |
| Allows deduction for state income and property taxes | No | No |
| Allows a substantial level of exempt income before tax applies | Yes | Yes, but much larger than under USA Tax |
| Allows personal and dependency exemptions | Yes | Yes |
| Maintains an earned income tax credit (EITC) for the working poor | Yes | No |

**Table 4**  Rates and Brackets by Filing Status

| Taxable Income Above | 1996 | 1997 | 1998 | 1999 | 2000 |
| --- | --- | --- | --- | --- | --- |
| Married/Joint Return |  |  |  |  |  |
| $     0 | 19% | 15% | 13% | 10% | 8% |
| 5,400 | 27% | 26% | 25% | 20% | 19% |
| 24,000 | 40% | 40% | 40% | 40% | 40% |
| Married/Separate Returns |  |  |  |  |  |
| $     0 | 19% | 15% | 13% | 10% | 8% |
| 2,700 | 27% | 26% | 25% | 20% | 19% |
| 12,000 | 40% | 40% | 40% | 40% | 40% |
| Head of Household |  |  |  |  |  |
| $     0 | 19% | 15% | 13% | 10% | 8% |
| 4,750 | 27% | 26% | 25% | 20% | 19% |
| 21,100 | 40% | 40% | 40% | 40% | 40% |
| Single |  |  |  |  |  |
| $     0 | 19% | 15% | 13% | 10% | 8% |
| 3,200 | 27% | 26% | 25% | 20% | 19% |
| 14,400 | 40% | 40% | 40% | 40% | 40% |

Assuming a joint return with no children, various effective rates of tax on wage income are shown in Table 5. (If one or more $5,300 dependent exemptions were also included, the effective rates would also vary among taxpayers with the same wage incomes.)

Thus, despite the nominal flat rate, the Flat Tax is not a proportionate tax insofar as wage income is concerned and, in fact, is significantly graduated in the range of income that includes nearly all wage earners—going from 5 percent at

**Table 5** Illustrative Effective Tax Rates

| Nominal Marginal Rate | Exemption | Wage Income | Effective Rate |
|---|---|---|---|
| 20% | $26,200 | $ 26,200 | 0 |
| 20% | $26,200 | $ 35,000 | 5% |
| 20% | $26,200 | $ 52,400 | 10% |
| 20% | $26,200 | $ 61,500 | 11% |
| 20% | $26,200 | $ 78,600 | 13% |
| 20% | $26,200 | $131,000 | 16% |
| 20% | $26,200 | $262,000 | 18% |
| 20% | $26,200 | $524,000 | 19% |

$35,000 to 18 percent at $262,200. The Flat Tax is *flat* only at the bottom end of the income scale (0 percent up to $26,200 in Table 5) and at the top of the income scale (19 percent, plus a fraction, above $524,000 in Table 5).

Under the theory and construct of the Flat Tax, it is also flat and proportional on nonwage income such as interest, dividends, and gains without regard to amount. The *graduated* Flat Tax on wage income and the *flat* Flat Tax on nonwage income can both be seen in a simple comparison.

> Example 1: *A retired couple whose savings (stock) has earned a pretax dividend of $35,000 would "prepay" a 20 percent tax at the business level and receive an after-tax dividend of $28,000. An unretired couple who earned $35,000 of wages would pay tax at an effective rate of 5 percent and have after-tax income of $33,250 before taking into account the 7.65 percent FICA payroll tax. After payroll taxes, this couple would have take-home pay of $30,753.*

Although primarily related to graduation versus proportionality under the Flat Tax, example 1 also helps to illustrate the "prepayment" concept on the basis of which the Flat Tax excludes nonwage income from the individual tax return. The theory is that after paying and deducting wages to employees, and paying and deducting the cost of its capital equipment, the corporation has taxable income of $35,000 on which it, on behalf of the retired couple, paid a 20 percent or $7,000 tax. Example 1 further illustrates that while the 20 percent nominal rate may be the real rate on dividends and other nonwage income, the real marginal rate under the Flat Tax on each additional dollar of wage income is, in most cases, higher than 20 percent. Because the Flat Tax allows no credit for the 7.65 percent FICA tax paid by employees, the real marginal rate on wage income up to $61,500 is 27.65 percent.

As a consequence, the real effective rates of tax on wage income are also higher than previously illustrated in Table 5 in the case of a joint return. When restated assuming only the basic exemption of $26,200, the results are in Table 6.

Because the USA Tax allows a credit for the 7.65 percent FICA payroll tax, its nominal rates (19, 27, and 40 percent on a joint return in 1996) are inclusive of the payroll tax and are, therefore, the real marginal rates. A useful comparison to the Flat Tax is set forth as follows:

| | Real Marginal Rates | |
|---|---|---|
| Flat Tax (wage income over $61,500) | 20% | |
| Flat Tax (wage income up to $61,500) | 27.65% | |
| USA Tax | 1996 | 2000 |
| | 19% | 8% |
| | 27% | 19% |
| | 40% | 40% |

A somewhat different comparison can also be made between the rate (rates) of tax on wage income under the Flat Tax and the USA Tax. If the FICA payroll tax is ignored (on the ground that it will continue to be paid in all events), the additional rate of the Flat Tax on all wage income is 20 percent. On the other hand, the additional rate of the USA Tax on wage income up to $61,500 is in each case 7.65 percentage points less than the applicable nominal rate. The additional rates (joint return in the case of the USA Tax) illustrated as follows:

| | Additional Rates | |
|---|---|---|
| Flat Tax (all wage income) | 20% | |
| USA Tax | 1996 | 2000 |
| | 11.35% | 0.35% |
| | 19.35% | 11.35% |
| | 32.35% | 32.35% |

Although the foregoing comparison of additional rates may be used to illustrate another way of looking at the payroll tax credit allowed by the USA Tax on wage income, the fact remains that the actual rates on a USA Tax joint return are 19, 27, and 40 percent, and these rates are inclusive of the payroll tax.

These rates, and the comparable rates for individuals in other filing status, apply uniformly to nonwage income (such as dividends and interest) as well as to wage income. Unlike the Flat Tax, which uses the yield-exemption approach to eliminate the tax bias against savings, and where, as a consequence, the individual tax return only includes wage income, the USA Tax individual tax return includes both wage income and nonwage income. At the individual level, both types of income are taxed exactly at the same progressive rates.

**Table 6**  Illustrative Effective Tax Rates with Payroll Tax Included

| Real Marginal Rate | Exemption | Income | Real Effective Rate |
|---|---|---|---|
| 27.65% | $26,200 | $ 26,200 | 7.65% |
| 27.65% | $26,200 | $ 35,000 | 7% |
| 27.65% | $26,200 | $ 52,400 | 14% |
| 27.65% | $26,200 | $ 61,500 | 16% |
| 27.65% | $26,200 | $ 78,600 | 19% |
| 27.65% | $26,200 | $131,000 | 20% |
| 27.65% | $26,200 | $262,000 | 20% |
| 27.65% | $26,200 | $524,000 | 20% |

Because the USA Tax includes and taxes at the individual level earnings on income that has previously been saved and, therefore, become "capital," the USA Tax uses the traditional approach of allowing a deduction for saving, in order not to tax both the income that is saved and the earnings on savings. The Flat Tax allows no deduction for saving because it uses the yield-exemption approach, which excludes earnings on savings.

While the familiar deduction approach under the USA Tax and the less familiar yield-exemption approach both eliminate the tax bias against saving and although the return on savings is, all else equal, the same in both cases, the cash flow results to the saver in the year the saving occurs are not the same. Ignoring the payroll tax, the different current-year cash flow results are easily seen in a simple comparison.

> Example 2: *By working overtime, a two-earner couple earns an additional $1,000 that is taxable at 20 percent under the Flat Tax and that comes within either the 19, 27, or 40 percent tax bracket under the USA Tax. They desire to save $1,000. Under the Flat Tax, which allows no deduction for savings, they must pay an additional $200 of tax. In order to save $1,000, they must cut back their current standard of living by $200. Under the USA Tax, which allows a deduction for saving, they pay no additional tax and can save the full $1,000 without reducing their current standard of living.*

The USA Tax and the Flat Tax have different aggregate revenue results, counting the individual taxes and business taxes together. In total, the USA Tax is revenue-neutral relative to present law and maintains about the same split between individuals and businesses as under present law.

In contrast, the proponents of the Flat Tax apparently intend that it reduce aggregate revenues by about $40 billion in the first year. Some preliminary estimates by the Treasury have suggested substantially higher revenue losses at a 20 percent rate, but those estimates are disputed. In the absence of a fully articulated Flat Tax in legislative bill form and official revenue estimates, the split between individuals and businesses is unclear, but it would appear that over time the business share would increase and the individual share would decrease, relative to present law and relative to the USA Tax.

The USA Tax is neutral with respect to the distribution of the tax burden by expanded family income class. As shown in Table 7, the USA Tax maintains and makes slightly more "progressive" the present law distribution.

No comparable income class distribution table has been put out by the proponents of the Flat Tax, and one needs to be circumspect in making comparisons on this sensitive subject, but it seems to be the case that the Flat Tax would significantly redistribute a percentage of the tax burden from upper income groups to middle and lower middle income groups and, therefore, by traditional standards, be "regressive" even though the Flat Tax is somewhat graduated. For example, and stated somewhat differently, the Treasury has indicated that proposals along the lines of the Flat Tax would amount to a 7 to 17 percent increase in federal taxes for families with incomes under $200,000 and a 26 percent decrease in federal

**Table 7** USA Tax Distributed by Income Class

| Expanded Family Income | Percent Change (Increase or Decrease) in Tax Liability for Class |
|---|---|
| 0–$10,000 | –75% |
| $10,000–$20,000 | –9% |
| $20,000–$30,000 | –14% |
| $30,000–$50,000 | –5% |
| $50,000–$75,000 | 0 |
| $75,000–$100,000 | 0 |
| $100,000–$200,000 | +3% |
| Over $200,000 | +4% |

taxes for families with incomes above $200,000. Quibbles about the precise percentages are not important. These estimates may be somewhat off the mark but they probably do indicate the general direction of the shift in tax burden that occurs under the Flat Tax.

## OVERVIEW: STEPPING BACK FOR ANOTHER LOOK

Against the background of long experience with the present federal income tax, the Flat Tax presents a startling contrast—no deductions instead of many, not even for charity and home ownership. There are no credits, not even child care. The Flat Tax uses a single rate that applies to the rich and poor alike and everyone in between. Only wage earners file personal tax returns. There is not even a line on the tax return for interest and dividends. On the positive side, of course, there is the idea that the tax return filed by most Americans might be only the size of a postcard. Furthermore, relieving the tax bias against saving may be the key to a much more prosperous future for this generation of Americans and the next. That is hard to argue with.

Repealing all deductions and having a flat tax rate might seem fundamental to the Flat Tax and the positive goals it is intended to achieve. From some perspectives, that may be true. Many proponents of the Flat Tax would say so. From other perspectives, there is nothing fundamental about having or not having a few deductions, or about one instead of two or more rates of tax. For example, from the perspective of the highly flexible structure of the USA Tax, the deduction and rate aspects of the Flat Tax are merely policy choices. They are important ones in terms of the consequences to affected persons such as charities and homeowners, but they are choices nevertheless. The flexible structure of the USA Tax can readily accommodate either multiple rates or a single flat rate. In fact, relative to steeply progressive tax rates in the past, the multiple rates in S.722 are actually fairly flat. The USA Tax in S.722 has only three rates and as a practical matter has only two rates of major significance. The top rate kicks in fairly quickly and, as a consequence, the income brackets to which the two lower rates apply are not very wide. In addition, judged by historical standards, the higher of these two principal rates is not all that much greater than the lower (e.g., in 1996, 40 percent compared to 27 percent on a joint return).

Similarly, the flexible structure of the USA Tax could easily accommodate a policy choice to have no personal deductions in the traditional sense. In fact, along with the deduction for personal saving, which is critical, the USA Tax only allows a few basic deductions. The charitable contribution deduction is not the source of any appreciable complexity, and certainly the home mortgage interest deduction is not complex at all. All anyone has to do is transfer one number from the statement furnished by the mortgage lender onto the tax return. In fact, the Flat Tax, itself, will almost certainly retain the home mortgage interest deduction for existing mortgages. Otherwise, many families, especially young couples, would no longer be able to afford the mortgage payments on houses already purchased and contractually committed to prior to the enactment of the Flat Tax. Repealing the home mortgage interest deduction for new families in the future may have some substantial consequences, but a simpler tax return with fewer lines will not be one of them.

Given the fact that the few deductions retained by the USA Tax are not complicated, and given that having one tax rate instead of two or three rates has almost nothing to do with simplification, why then is the Flat Tax so rigid in that regard and why do its proponents focus so heavily on these aspects? There must be some other reason. The same question can be asked about using the yield-exemption approach to eliminate the tax bias against saving, instead of the more familiar and likely more politically palatable deduction approach under the USA Tax. The Flat Tax appears to totally exclude interest, dividends, and gains from tax, and to tax only wage income. That appearance may be hard to dispel and is rife with possibilities for both genuine misunderstanding and political demagoguery. In addition, it can be said, with some degree of truth, that the different current-year cash flow results under the USA Tax make it more attractive to new savers, whereas the yield-exemption approach is most attractive to those people who already have savings.

The answer to these questions is clear. It is the same answer that explains why the Flat Tax does not contain explicit border-tax adjustments for imports and exports, even though many who otherwise favor the Flat Tax idea consider these border adjustments to be an important goal of tax restructuring. All these results and rigidities arise directly from the bifurcated structure of the Flat Tax. As shown by the schematics at the beginning of this paper, both the Flat Tax and the USA Tax are vertically bifurcated, viz., a tax is imposed at the business level when income is produced and a tax is imposed at the individual level when income is received. That Flat Tax, but not the USA Tax, is then also horizontally bifurcated, viz., at the business level only capital income is included and taxed, and, at the individual level, only labor income (wages and salaries) is included and taxed. In contrast under the construct of the USA Tax, both labor income and capital income are included in the tax base at both the business level and the individual level.

The doubly bifurcated structure of the Flat Tax is highly rigid and constrains choices. For example, within that structure a deduction for charitable contributions could only be allowed against wage income, but if such a deduction is going to be allowed, it is anomalous for people with only interest and dividend income not to also get that deduction. Many of them are most likely to be the largest donors. Further, for example, the doubly bifurcated structure virtually mandates a flat rate. If progressive rates were applied, they could only be applied to wage income. However, in order for the average rate in a multiple rate system for wage income to produce the same revenue as a 20 percent flat rate, the top rate on wage income would be higher than 20 percent and higher than the 20 rate on nonwage income that is implicit in the prepayment concept of the Flat Tax where capital income is taxed only at the business level. Similarly, and for the same reasons, the present construction of the Flat Tax generally precludes use of the deduction approach to personal saving. In addition, border tax adjustments at the business level are precluded because the present construction of the Flat Tax requires that wage income be deducted at the business level because it is taxed at the full Flat Tax rate at the individual level.

## ACHIEVING THE MAIN GOALS

The main goal of both the Flat Tax and the USA Tax should be to serve the national interest by actually enacting into law a simplified tax system that eliminates the tax bias against savings and enhances our ability to compete in international markets.

The main debate will be political, focused on whether the main goal will be achieved with or without changing the existing distribution of the tax burden between high-, middle-, and low-income groups as determined by the very inexact process and methodology of distributional analysis. That political debate will alone be enough of a problem without adding additional political barriers that arise out of the basic structure of the Flat Tax itself and without using a basic structure that can achieve the main goal only if the political debate is resolved in a certain way.

In order to isolate the main goals from the political debate about progressivity, and to ensure the enactment of a new American tax system in all events, the proponents of the Flat Tax should express it within the highly flexible framework of the USA Tax where labor income and capital income are taxed at both the business level and the individual level, and where the border tax adjustments can be made. The business-level taxes would be identical. At the individual level, there would be the following two, highly workable versions of the Flat Tax:

1. One with a single rate, no personal deductions (other than the savings deduction), and no payroll tax credit.
2. Another with two additional rates, a few personal deductions for charity, home mortgage interest, education, and so on (plus the savings deduction), and a payroll tax credit.

\* \* \*

# NOTES

1. As of May 1995, nearly all announced presidential candidates plus the Majority Leader of the Senate (also a presidential candidate), the Speaker of the House, the Majority Leader of the House, the Chairman of the Committee on Ways and Means, the Chairman of the Committee on Finance, and an array of other leading members of Congress have either introduced legislation to replace the income tax or have indicated substantial support for the general idea.

2. The Flat Tax is as generally described by Robert E. Hall and Alvin Rabushka and leading congressional proponents as of May 1995 (See Hall and Rabushka [1995]). When fully drafted and introduced in legislative form, the basic structure of the Flat Tax may be modified; either as suggested in this paper or otherwise. The USA Tax is as contained in S.722, with was introduced on April 25, 1995. A prototype for the USA Tax is explained in Christian and Schutzer (1995).

# REFERENCES

Christian, Ernest S., and George J. Schutzer. "USA Tax System—Description and Explanation of the Unlimited Savings Allowance Income Tax System." *Tax Notes 66:* 11 (March 10, 1995): 1482–1575.

Hall, Robert E., and Alvin Rabushka. *The Flat Tax,* 2d ed. Stanford: Hoover Institution Press (1995).

Gilbert E. Metcalf

# Value-Added Taxation: A Tax Whose Time Has Come?

In the United States, fundamental federal tax reform continues to be a prominent subject of political debate. Proposals have included plans to flatten the income tax rate structure, to integrate corporate and individual taxation, to institute effective wealth transfer taxes, and to change the financing of the social security system. However, one of the most radical proposals has been to introduce broad-based consumption taxation—a completely new method of federal taxation for the United States. The prime consumption tax candidate has been the value-added tax (VAT), essentially a multi-stage sales tax collected from firms at each stage of production. (In contrast, a state or local sales tax is a single-stage tax.) Many proponents of value-added or consumption taxation believe the benefits of changing to this new system of taxation will far outweigh the costs of transition.

In this selection, Gilbert Metcalf begins by illustrating the "ABCs" of value-added taxation—the various methods of calculating a VAT. Metcalf then provides a brief summary of the history of the value-added tax around the world. In particular, this tax is a significant source of revenue in many European countries. After dispelling several common misconceptions, the author focuses on the potential impact of a value-added tax on savings and labor supply as well as on the controversy concerning distributional effects. Metcalf continues by addressing particular VAT design issues, including how to mitigate any negative impact on the elderly during transition to a VAT and possible problems related to

..........................................................................................

Metcalf, Gilbert E. "Value-Added Taxation: A Tax Whose Time Has Come?" *Journal of Economic Perspectives 9* (Winter 1995): 121–140.

**Gilbert E. Metcalf** is Assistant Professor of Economics at Tufts University and Faculty Research Fellow, National Bureau of Economic Research.

administration and compliance costs as well as state and local concerns over tax competition with might be considered a federal sales tax.

### Questions to Guide the Reading

1. How does the general cash flow equation for a firm demonstrate that the VAT is effectively a tax on wage income and old capital?
2. The author demonstrates that the total revenue collected by a broad-based uniform VAT would be identical to that collected with a retail sales tax. What differences exist in the design and administration of the two taxes?
3. How did the European turnover tax work, and why was it replaced by a VAT? How does Canada's Goods and Services Tax compare to a typical credit style VAT?
4. According to the author, what are some of the common myths associated with the VAT—and why are they myths?
5. How might a VAT impact the supply of labor? Why do proponents consider blandness to be one of the VAT's main virtues—even referring to the VAT as a "vanilla tax"?
6. How could one argue that a broad-based VAT is not regressive? What are two important caveats to this conclusion?
7. What are some of the transitional concerns with implementing a VAT? Why are political concerns about the impact of a VAT on the elderly likely to be of particular importance?

---

Is the United States ready for a value-added tax (VAT)? Ten years ago, the answer would have been an emphatic "no." Comprehensive consumption taxation has been an unpopular concept among most policymakers, and periodic efforts to transform existing business taxes to a consumption base tax have been failures.[1]

However, in early 1993 several members of the Clinton administration floated the idea of paying for health care reform with a VAT. According to the *Washington Post*, Health and Human Services Secretary Donna Shalala stated "[c]ertainly we're looking at a VAT," while OMB deputy director Alice Rivlin told the National Association of Manufacturers in April 1993 that "a VAT or a general sales tax has a good deal to recommend it." In an interview with *Fortune* (1993), Bill Clinton said, "The question for America becomes . . . whether we should lower either income or payroll taxes and substitute a progressive VAT." While the trial balloon was quickly brought back down, it is remarkable that the idea was even broached. There appears to have been a shift in mind-set toward the tax; it no longer lingers in the world of ideas economists think important and everyone else thinks outlandish.

Someone once quipped that a VAT has never passed in the United States because liberals worry that it would be regressive and conservatives worry that it would become a money machine for the government. However, the joke continues, a VAT will be passed when liberals recognize that it could be a money machine and conservatives recognize that it is regressive. Does this joke accurately describe a VAT? The purpose of this paper is to answer this and other questions that are often asked about value-added taxes and to consider how a VAT might be implemented in the United States. I begin this paper by describing how value-added taxation works and then give a brief description of the evolution of the use of VATs around the world. The remainder of the paper considers the economic impact of a VAT as well as design issues that are likely to arise.

## THE ABCs OF VALUE-ADDED TAXATION

A value-added tax, or VAT , taxes the value added in production through the various stages of production. Value added is simply the difference between the value of the goods (or services) sold and the value of goods (or services) purchased as intermediate inputs. There are several ways to impose such a tax. We could tax gross sales net of intermediate goods purchases at each stage of production. This forms the basis for a "subtraction method" VAT. A second method of imposing a VAT would be to tax gross sales and allow a credit for taxes paid by other firms at previous stages of production on intermediate goods. The "credit method" VAT works in this fashion.

A third method of taxing value added relies on understanding the general cash flow equation for a firm. The following equation notes the sources and uses of cash in a firm:

$$S + K^+ = L + M + K^-$$

The equation notes that cash comes into a firm from two sources: capital inflows ($K^+$ includes both new equity and borrowing) and proceeds from the sale of a good or service ($S$). Cash is used for payments for labor ($L$) and intermediate goods ($M$). In addition, cash is used for dividend and interest payments as well as any retirement of debt and equity ($K^-$). At this elementary level, intermediate goods are simply any goods purchased from another company, including capital goods.[2]

From the "subtraction method" VAT, we know that $S - M$ is one measure of value added. But this implies that rearranging the terms in the cash flow equation will provide an alternate measure. That is, value added ($V$) will equal:

$$V = S - M = L + K^- - K^+$$

In short, value added will also equal payments to labor and net capital outflows, whether they occur as dividend or interest payments, or as equity and debt retirements net of new debt or equity. This approach highlights a distinction between "old" and "new" capital. Old capital—that is, capital already in the firm as debt or equity—is taxed either as it is retired or as income is paid to it. New capital, however, is excluded from the tax base and untaxed. This distinction between old and new capital is important when considering transitional concerns with consumption taxation; I return to this issue below.

Finally, we could impose a tax equivalent to a VAT by imposing a retail sales tax. This equivalence has often led to a VAT being termed a national sales tax. While the economic effects of the two taxes would be the same, the design and administration of the taxes differ. The various methods of VAT taxation are perhaps most easily seen by considering a simple example. Table 1 illustrates the production and sale of an economics textbook. We begin with two primary inputs: the author's manuscript and the paper that will be used in production of the book. For simplicity, ignore any inputs used for producing these two intermediate goods. I have somewhat arbitrarily labeled the payments to the author as a payment to labor. Of the $50 in sales of paper, $35 goes to labor and $15 to the owners of the paper company.

Note that we can compute value added in a number of ways. For the manuscript preparation, value added equals $100. This equals both sales less intermediate purchases, and labor plus returns to capital. Value added for paper manufacture, publishing, and retailing can be similarly computed. The publisher purchases paper and the manuscript (at cost $150) and sells a printed text to a retailer for $250 (value added equals $100). The retailer applies a 100 percent markup (out of which payments to labor and capital come) for a retail cost of $500.[3]

The most common way of administering a VAT is to levy a tax on the total value of sales at each stage of production and allow a credit for any VAT paid on inputs in production. For purposes of claiming the credit, a firm is typically required to show proof (usually an invoice) that the VAT has been paid by its supplier. This

**Table 1**  Textbook Production

| | Manuscript Preparation | Paper | Publisher | Retailer | TOTAL |
|---|---|---|---|---|---|
| Sales | 100 | 50 | 250 | 500 | 900 |
| Labor | 100 | 35 | 50 | 200 | 385 |
| Intermediate Goods | 0 | 0 | 150 | 250 | 400 |
| Return to Capital | 0 | 15 | 50 | 50 | 115 |
| Value Added | 100 | 50 | 100 | 250 | 500 |
| | | | | | |
| *Credit Method VAT* | | | | | |
| Gross VAT Liability (10% of gross sales) | 10 | 5 | 25 | 50 | 90 |
| Credits | 0 | 0 | 15 | 25 | 40 |
| Net VAT Liability | 10 | 5 | 10 | 25 | 50 |
| | | | | | |
| *Subtraction Method VAT* | | | | | |
| VAT Liability (10% of sales less purchase of intermediate goods) | 10 | 5 | 10 | 25 | 50 |

provides a form of self-regulation in VAT enforcement, since firms have an incentive to ensure that the VAT that their supplier claims to have paid has in fact been paid. The middle part of Table 1 illustrates this approach. Total value in manuscript production is $100. A 10 percent VAT would collect $10 at this stage of production. There would be no credit for any VAT paid at previous levels of production as there are no previous stages. Similarly, $5 is paid as paper is sold to the publisher. Total value for the publisher is $250, and the gross VAT liability equals $25. However, with a credit of $15 for the VAT paid on the manuscript and paper used to produce the book, the publisher's VAT payment net of credit would equal $10. Similarly, the retailer has a gross liability of $50 but gets to take as a credit the $25 in VAT paid at previous stages of production. Total VAT paid is $50; that is, 10 percent of the total value added. Applying a 10 percent retail sales tax would raise the same amount of revenue showing the equivalence of a broad-based uniform VAT to a retail sales tax.

The subtraction method VAT is subtly different from the credit method VAT. The next part of Table 1 indicates that the tax base is simply gross sales less purchases of intermediate goods that have already been subject to the VAT. Unlike the credit method, there is no effort made to document the actual payments made by suppliers. Rather, it is assumed that the tax is paid at the same rate at all stages of production. If this is true, then the subtraction VAT and credit VAT are equivalent.

The Congressional Budget Office (1994a) estimates that a comprehensive 5 percent VAT, like the one illustrated in Table 1, would raise nearly $100 billion in its first full year of operation and over $600 billion in its first five years. For comparison, eliminating the deduction for home mortgage interest and taxing employer contributions for health insurance (but allowing an individual tax credit for premiums up to a limit) would raise slightly more than $500 billion over five years. Alternatively, raising individual marginal tax rates by approximately 7 percent (to a 16/30/33/38/42 percent rate structure) would raise less than $200 billion over five years. The large revenue raising capacity of a VAT is a major reason the tax is both alluring and frightening, depending on one's perspective.

However, the United States is unlikely to enact a comprehensive VAT, for a number of reasons. First, the administrative costs of a VAT would likely lead to certain classes of firms being exempted from taxation. Second, distributional concerns would likely lead to a VAT with multiple tax rates. One of those rates is likely to be zero—meaning that certain items on which the poor spend a high proportion of their income might not be taxed at all.

Whether a reduced rate will actually alter the distribution of tax liabilities depends on how it is applied. Consider "zero rating" publishers' sales of textbooks with a credit method VAT. Zero rating means that firms file all paperwork for a VAT and keep all necessary records. However, they apply a zero rate to their gross sales before claiming a credit for VAT paid at previous levels. In our example, the books would be taxed at a zero rate, and the invoice transferred to the retailer would record a zero tax payment. However, the publisher would still be able to claim the credit for VAT paid at previous stages of production and would receive a check from the government for $15, as shown in the first line of Table 2.

**Table 2**  Net VAT Liability with a Modified Tax Base: Credit Method VAT

|  | Manuscript Preparation | Paper | Publisher | Retailer | TOTAL |
|---|---|---|---|---|---|
| Zero Rating Publishers | 10 | 5 | −15 | 50 | 50 |
| Zero Rating Retailing | 10 | 5 | 10 | −25 | 0 |
| Exempting Retailing | 10 | 5 | 10 | 0 | 25 |
| Exempting Publishing | 10 | 5 | 0 | 50 | 65 |

Net VAT liability through the publishing stage would be zero. Moving to the next production stage, the retailer would not be able to take a tax credit for the $25 of taxes previously paid by the publisher. His net VAT liability increases from $25 to $50, and the total VAT liability is unchanged at $50.

On the other hand, if the retailer may zero rate textbook sales, there will be a change in VAT collections (line 2 of the table). The retailer applies a zero rate to gross sales for a gross VAT liability of zero. It then takes a credit of $25 for previous VAT payments and receives a refund of $25 from the tax authorities. Total net VAT liability is zero—textbook sales are untaxed. These are general results. Zero rating intermediate production has no effects on tax collections with a credit method VAT. However, zero rating at the final stage of production will eliminate the tax liability.

Administrative concerns with the record keeping associated with a VAT raise the possibility of exempting certain sectors of the economy from the tax. VAT exemption simply means that some stage of production is not part of the tax system. The exemption releases firms from the responsibility for collecting the VAT or filing any paperwork on sales and purchases. Small businesses are the most likely candidates for exemption.

While exempting small businesses would reduce their paperwork, it could also increase the tax liability on the products they sell. If retailers are exempt, they do not file a tax and incur no VAT liability. However, they also receive no rebate of taxes paid at previous stages of production. Thus, in our example, the net VAT liability if retailers are exempt is $25 (line 3 of Table 2). Note that exemption at the retail level is *not* the same as zero rating. It reduces but does not eliminate the tax liability. However, if the publisher is exempt, the outcome is different (line 4). Now, the publisher incurs no VAT liability but is unable to take a credit for VAT payments made by the author and the paper manufacturer. The retailer is unable to take a credit for those VAT payments either as there is no invoice documenting those payments. The result is that exempting the publisher (and so breaking the chain of payments and invoices) actually *increases* the total VAT liability. This happens because we have double taxed the value added by the author and the paper manufacturer, the second time at the retail stage when gross rather than net value added was taxed.[4]

The examples above employ the European credit method—so called because most of the European countries use this method to administer the tax. Devices like exemptions and zero rating are more complicated if a subtraction-type VAT is employed. A subtraction VAT looks like a corporate income tax, with the important difference that investment is expensed and labor and interest costs are not allowed as deductions. Value added is simply the difference between the value of a firm's sales and its purchases (both capital and intermediate goods). Our example in Table 1 recorded sales on a tax exclusive basis. The cost of intermediate goods for the publisher would actually be $165 if the tax is passed forward. For the subtraction VAT, the publisher would compute the tax exclusive value of its purchases by assuming that a VAT liability was included in the cost of its materials. Thus the firm would net out the tax by dividing the cost of materials by one plus the tax rate. In our example, material costs of $165 would be divided by 1.10 to obtain the tax exclusive cost of $150. The tax base for the publisher would then be $250 – $150, or $100.

The need to net out the VAT paid on materials raises difficulties if the subtraction VAT is implemented with multiple rates. Table 3 illustrates how exemptions and lower rates affect tax collections with a subtraction style VAT.[5] If publishers are exempt from the VAT, the retailer now has a tax inclusive cost of intermediate goods equal to $265. Dividing by one plus the tax rate yields a tax exclusive base of $241 and a tax liability of nearly $26. Total VAT liability has been reduced roughly by 10 percent of the value added in publishing. The rest of Table 3 illustrates exempting retailing and applying lower tax rates. In general, exemptions are less problematic if they occur at the retail level rather than at a price stage of production. While it is possible to track multiple VAT rates through sales, it removes one of the greatest advantages of the subtraction of VAT, the lack of paperwork and record keeping that exists with the credit style VAT.

## A SHORT HISTORY OF THE VALUE-ADDED TAX

Pechman (1987) attributes the modern idea of value-added taxation to a post-World War I German industrial executive.[6] But nothing came of the concept until the Shoup mission to Japan proposed and implemented a short-lived VAT in postwar Japan. France was the first European country to adopt a limited VAT in 1954; the form was a wholesale-level VAT to replace a multistage production tax. With the formation of the European Community (EC), nee the European Economic Community (EEC), and the interest in tax harmonization within Europe, greater attention was paid to the

**Table 3** Net VAT Liability with a Modified Tax Base: Subtraction Method VAT

| | Manuscript Preparation | Paper | Publisher | Retailer | TOTAL |
|---|---|---|---|---|---|
| Exempting Publishers | 10 | 5 | 0 | 25.90 | 40.90 |
| Exempting Retailing | 10 | 5 | 10 | 0 | 25 |
| 5% Rate on Retailing | 10 | 5 | 10 | 12.50 | 37.50 |
| 5% Rate on Publishing | 10 | 5 | 5 | 25.45 | 45.45 |

variety of production taxes that existed in Europe. A common tax used by European countries prior to the introduction of VATs was the turnover tax—basically a tax on sales at each level of production. This leads to "cascading" whereby the taxes get levied on taxes collected at earlier stages of production so that in a production process with sales across a number of firms, the tax rate on value added substantially exceeds the statutory rate. Moreover, cascading creates incentives for vertical integration. As Aaron (1982) notes, the unpopularity of the turnover taxes paved the way for their replacement with VATs. Denmark was the first European country to adopt the VAT (1967), followed in short order by France, Germany, the Netherlands, Luxembourg, Belgium, Ireland, Italy, and the United Kingdom.

The original Treaty of Rome that established the EC in 1957 called (in article 99) for consideration of tax legislation that would harmonize the members' tax codes. Ten years later, two directives were adopted by the Council of Ministers that led to VATs being implemented by member countries. The first directive called for the replacement of the existing system of cumulative (that is, cascading) taxes with a noncumulative VAT, and the second directive laid out ground rules for constructing VATs. Additional directives were adopted that clarified various issues with respect to VAT taxation. Finally, in 1977, the sixth directive on VAT brought together the various previous directives on VAT and established consistent rules for VATs in the EC. Subsequent countries that have joined the EC (Greece, Portugal, and Spain) have introduced a VAT.[7] As the European Community moves toward a single market, harmonization of tax rates is increasingly important (Buckett 1992).

Canada and Japan have also introduced some form of value-added taxation. Japan introduced a subtraction style VAT in 1989. It differs from a standard VAT in allowing firms to take a credit for purchases from exempt businesses despite the fact that no VAT was paid on those purchases. Roughly two-thirds of all businesses in Japan are completely exempt from the VAT, and additional businesses are partially exempt (JCT 1992). This credit has the effect of lowering the tax burden and creating an incentive for Japanese firms to purchase from tax-exempt domestic businesses rather than from importers (who do not receive the credit).

Canada introduced a federal VAT called the Goods and Services Tax in 1991. Unlike a typical credit style VAT, the Goods and Services Tax is levied on the purchaser with vendors responsible for collecting the tax. In this sense, the Goods and Services Tax is a federal sales tax. This tax replaced the Manufacturers' Sales Tax, a tax on manufacturing activity in Canada. The MST was rightly criticized for favoring retail, wholesale, and service industries (among others) over manufacturing and for favoring imports over exports (Whalley and Fretz 1990).

Table 4 provides information on rates and the fraction of GDP or total tax collections deriving from goods and services taxes (VATs, general sales taxes, and excise taxes) for various OECD countries. Rates vary widely, from a low of 3 percent in Japan to a high of 22 percent in Norway. These rates are the "standard" rates—those applied to the majority of purchases. Many countries zero rate or apply a reduced rate to a variety of items. Moreover, exempting certain sectors has the effect of altering (raising or lowering) the tax rate on other commodities.

**Table 4** VATs in Other Countries

| Country | VAT Rate | Goods and Services Taxes As Percentage | |
|---|---|---|---|
| | | of GDP | of Taxes |
| Belgium | 19.5 | 7.2 | 16.0 |
| Canada | 7 | 5.3 | 14.1 |
| Denmark | 15 | 9.9 | 20.6 |
| France | 18.6 | 7.9 | 17.8 |
| Germany | 15 | 6.4 | 16.4 |
| Greece | 18 | 9.9 | 25.9 |
| Italy | 19 | 5.7 | 14.3 |
| Japan | 3 | 1.4 | 4.4 |
| Luxembourg | 15 | 7.2 | 14.9 |
| Netherlands | 18.5 | 7.3 | 15.6 |
| New Zealand | 12.5 | 8.6 | 23.8 |
| Norway | 22 | 8.2 | 17.4 |
| Portugal | 16 | 6.8 | 19.0 |
| Spain | 15 | 5.5 | 15.9 |
| Switzerland | 6.5 | 3.0 | 9.7 |
| Turkey | 12 | 6.5 | 22.2 |
| United Kingdom | 17.5 | 6.7 | 18.5 |

*Source: Price Waterhouse Guide to Doing Business In . . . various countries, and Eurostat (1993). Rates are as of January, 1, 1993. Revenue Figures are for 1991 and are from OECD Revenue Statistics.*

Goods and service taxes in the OECD countries range in importance from 10 percent of GDP in Greece down to 1.4 percent for Japan. Readers may be surprised to see that none of the countries (save Greece) collects more a quarter of their tax revenues from a VAT. In most countries, 15 to 20 percent is more the norm. As a rough rule, VATs replace income taxes (in the sense that most countries that employ a VAT collect a significantly smaller fraction of tax revenues from personal and corporate income taxes). This fact will be relevant in the discussion of administrative costs below. An argument against introducing a VAT in this country is that the administrative costs would be dramatically higher than in the EC because it would be a supplementary tax here rather than a major tax as in Europe. However, the numbers in Table 4 indicate that a VAT in all countries is simply part of the mix of taxes employed and by no means the dominant tax. A 5 percent VAT in the United States combined with state and local sales taxes would mean that goods and services taxes in the United States would comprise roughly 13 percent of tax revenues.

## MISCONCEPTIONS ABOUT A VAT

Introducing a value-added tax in the United States would likely have significant impacts on the economy. Before turning to more substantive impacts, I focus in this section on dispelling a few myths about the impact of a VAT.

One concern typically raised is that a VAT would be inflationary. This view confuses a one-time price increase with a continual increase in prices. Whether prices rise or not depends on whether the tax is passed forward or passed back in the form of lower factor payments. Which happens will depend on the response of the Federal Reserve. An accommodating monetary policy would allow consumer prices to increase by the amount of the tax while a tight policy would force factor payments to fall. Note that in either case, real factor payments would fall. The distributional impact of a VAT would depend on monetary policy, in part because of the existence of unindexed transfers. I return to this point below.

A VAT can be levied on an "origin" or a "destination" basis. A second fallacy about a destination basis VAT is that it will improve the trade balance. A destination VAT would tax consumption based on the location of consumption; exports would be excluded from the tax base while imports would be taxed. An origin VAT, on the other hand, would tax consumption based on the origin of production; exports would be subject to the VAT and imports would be zero rated (or in some other fashion excluded from the tax base). The treatment of exports and imports (border tax adjustments) leads some to argue that destination VATs "favor" exports while origin VATs "discourage" exports. As President Clinton put it when discussing a destination style VAT in a *Fortune* (1993) interview, "The VAT is the only internationally recognized, legal way to favor your exports and to impose a burden on imports. All our competitors do it."

In fact, a VAT that taxes imports and rebates the tax on exports would have no impact at all on the trade balance. Consider the decision of a domestic consumer to purchase an automobile. Introducing a VAT will not alter the relative prices of domestic and imported cars. Both will go up by a percentage amount equal to the VAT rate (assuming the tax is passed forward), in the case of the domestic car because of the imposition of the VAT throughout the production process and in the case of the import because of the border tax adjustment (plus any value added after entry into the United States). Similarly, the relative price of exported goods to foreign goods in other countries will be unaffected by the imposition of the VAT, since exports are not subject to the VAT under the border adjustment.

Of course, a border adjustment is not necessary to maintain neutrality between domestically produced and foreign produced goods, so long as prices or the exchange rate is flexible. This result is well known to trade theorists and can be motivated by thinking about importable and exportable goods separately. Consider a VAT under the origin principle. For exportable goods, the producer price for domestically consumed goods or exported goods is unchanged since the VAT is paid regardless of the destination of the good. But the consumer price of the exported good cannot rise (otherwise foreigners would substitute foreign produced goods for the exported good). The tax is passed back to domestic producers. For importable goods, arbitrage in a competitive market will require that the domestic consumer price of a good equal the foreign price. But the imported good is not subject to the VAT. Thus, the origin style VAT is once again passed back to domestic producers. Relative consumer prices for the importable versus exportable goods are unchanged under the origin principle, and relative domestic producer prices for both goods are also unchanged; that is, both fall by the amount of the tax.[8]

## SAVINGS, LABOR SUPPLY, AND A VAT

A VAT differs from the current income tax system by taxing consumption, whether in the present or in the future, at the same rate. By contrast, the present U.S. income tax hits savers twice: once when they earn the income, and again when they receive interest on their savings. A VAT eliminates the intertemporal consumption distortion that arises from taxing savings, which is one of its great appeals for many economists. By raising the after-tax return to savings, a VAT will also increase the amount of savings, if the savings elasticity with respect to the interest rate is positive. The VATs potential impact on savings appeals to the many economists who feel that savings rates in the United States are too low. Unfortunately, it is not clear that the savings elasticity with respect to the interest rate is very large. For example, Hausman and Poterba (1987) summarize research during the 1980s and conclude that this elasticity is probably close to zero. Whether implementing a VAT would increase savings rates is an open question.

A VAT is equivalent to a tax on wages, which is to say that leisure is untaxed by a VAT. The issue of a VAT's impact on labor supply is often overlooked. As Heckman (1993, 118) notes in a survey of research on labor supply, changes in net wages can have strong effects "at the extensive margin—at the margin of entry and exit—where the elasticities are definitely not zero." On this margin, a VAT could have substantial effects on labor supply. However, Heckman also notes that the direct effect on hours worked of a change in the real wage is probably quite small. As he puts it (p. 118), "A revision is in order for George Stigler's dictum that all elasticities are 1 in absolute value. A dictum closer to the truth would be that elasticities are closer to 0 than 1 for hours-of-work equations...."

Whether a VAT would affect labor supply likely depends on its impact through cross-price elasticities. As an example, assume that housing services and leisure are substitutes (as suggested by Triest 1992). In a world with no existing taxes, implementing a VAT that zero rated housing would affect labor supply through two channels. First, the VAT would drive down the real wage, leading to a reduction in labor supply (to the extent that the uncompensated labor supply elasticity with respect to the wage is positive). Second, zero rating housing would induce a substitution away from leisure toward more housing consumption. Thus the net effect on labor supply would be ambiguous. In fact, with a zero labor supply elasticity, the VAT cum zero rating for housing would increase labor supply.

Whether the effect on labor supply through cross-price elasticities is important is an empirical matter. Perhaps a more important channel through which a VAT could affect labor supply is in the treatment of work-related expenses. If a VAT is applied to work clothing, child care, domestic help, and other work-related expenses, there would be a considerable disincentive for work, especially for secondary earners in a household.

Except for its possible effect on labor supply, a VAT is remarkably free of distortions. This has been one of its main virtues among its proponents. McLure (1987, p. 28) put it this way; "The economic effects of introducing a value-added tax are, for the most part, not very interesting. . . . That the economic effects of the VAT are rather bland—we might call it a vanilla tax—is one of its chief advantages."[9] Of course, this presumes that there will not be exempted or zero-rated sectors. But if other countries provide guidance, goods and services like housing, medical services, banking and insurance, and food are likely to be exempt from VAT or taxed at lower rates.

Housing is particularly interesting since there is a simple solution to the problem of exempting housing from the VAT (as is done in most countries). Exempting existing housing creates a consumption distortion between the purchase of new and existing housing. A better policy would be to subject all housing to the VAT once.[10] For new housing, this would occur at time of construction; for existing housing, it would occur at the first transfer of the property after the tax was passed. In practical terms, an attachment to the deed of a house after that time could certify that the house is now "VAT free." This does raise the knotty transitional problem that we are taxing old capital. Let me return to this problem below. But suffice it to say here that this approach would mean that existing housing is treated the same as other forms of old capital.

## DISTRIBUTIONAL IMPACT OF A VAT

One traditional complaint about a broad-based VAT has been that it would be regressive. Pechman's (1985) work on the U.S. tax system is typically cited on this point. He finds that the system of excise taxes used in the United States is highly regressive.[11] However, there are problems with using the present patchwork of federal, state, and local excise taxes to draw conclusions about a VAT. A broad-based VAT would tax all (or most) goods and services at the same rate. But as Fullerton and Rogers (1993, Table 3-6) point out, excise tax rates in 1984 varied widely among goods from a low of zero (on shelter and financial services) to a high of over 70 percent (on alcohol and tobacco).

Moreover, Pechman's (1985) analysis was based on an annual measure of economic well being. Recent tax incidence research has focused on the lifetime burden of taxation. Shifting from an annual to a lifetime perspective is particularly important for consumption taxation (for example, see Caspersen and Metcalf 1994). The reason is that in an annual framework, the regressivity of a broad-based VAT depends on the extent to which savings rates rise with income. Since the rich consume a lower proportion of their income than the poor, a consumption tax will take a lower share of their income—that is, it appears regressive. Now turn to the lifetime perspective. In the absence of bequests, lifetime income will equal the present discounted stream of consumption. From this view, a proportional broad-based consumption tax would exact the same fraction of lifetime income from everyone, and the tax appears proportional rather than regressive.[12]

There are two especially important caveats to the conclusion that a VAT is not regressive: one involving nontaxed consumption (like leisure), the other involving nontaxed bequests. The labor supply effects of a VAT were discussed earlier. Whether incorporating endogenous labor supply makes a VAT regressive over the lifetime depends on whether lifetime leisure is a luxury good with respect to lifetime income. If the income elasticity of leisure exceeds one, then the taxable consumption to lifetime potential income (income in the absence of any leisure) will fall with income, and the tax will be regressive. However, the income elasticity of leisure is not likely to exceed one.[13] As a result, the fact that leisure is not taxed benefits the poor and middle class more than the rich. In this way, not taxing leisure adds progressivity to a VAT.

It has long been argued that excluding bequests from the base of a broad-based consumption tax makes the tax more regressive (Menchik and David 1982). A similar argument can be made about bequests as was made about leisure. Whether their exclusion from the tax base makes the tax more regressive depends on whether bequests are a luxury good or not.

However, the issue of bequests is complicated by the fact that while they would not be explicitly taxed under a VAT, they may be implicitly taxed— depending on one's view of the bequest motive. One motivation for bequests follows from the bequest giver deriving utility from the gift (Blinder 1974). Presumably, the utility derives from the consumption that the recipient of the bequest obtains from the gift rather than the monetary amount. Since the recipient is subject to the VAT when he or she consumes the bequest, the giver of a bequest has his or her utility reduced by the imposition of a VAT. In other words, the bequest is implicitly taxed.[14]

Moreover, including the bequest in the base of the tax would create a distortion against bequests. A VAT that did not include bequests would apply equally to the consumption of both parents and children, and thus create no distortion. Including bequests under a VAT would mean that they were taxed twice; once as a bequest, and again when consumed by the recipients.

An alternative perspective views bequests as a payment for services elicited from one's children, as in the strategic bequest model of Bernheim, Shleifer, and Summers (1985). To the extent these services provided by children are untaxed personal services (visits, phone calls, favors), a VAT that did not tax bequests in effect allows parents to purchase certain services tax free from their children, and thus could distort behavior.[15] Understanding the motive for bequests is important for determining how the presence of bequests affects the incidence of VAT.

Let me raise two additional distributional issues concerning a VAT. First, political pressure will likely lead to extensive zero or reduced ratings on certain products to increase the progressivity of a VAT. For administrative reasons, a better approach would be to maintain a single rate and give a lump sum payment to poor families to offset a portion of their VAT liability. Alternatively, the earned income tax credit could be increased, thereby targeting the payment toward the working poor. Second, the incidence of the VAT will depend in part on how the

Federal Reserve reacts and how Congress treats unindexed transfer payments like AFDC. If the Federal Reserve accommodates a one-time price increase from imposing a value-added tax, prices will rise, and part of the burden will fall on those whose income is not indexed against inflation, like the very poor. Alternatively, as Browning (1985) has pointed out, if real benefits from transfer programs are kept constant, the burden of the VAT will fall on workers (along with owners of old capital), rather than consumers as a group.

## TRANSITIONAL CONCERNS

One of the most vexing issues with implementing a VAT is the treatment of old capital in the transition. In practice, this translates into a concern about a VAT's impact on the elderly during the transition. As noted earlier, a VAT is effectively a tax on wage income and old capital. Auerbach et al. (1983) point out that the tax on old capital is a lump sum tax that mitigates efficiency losses for the VAT as compared, say, with the wage tax alone. But a capital levy is perceived to be unfair. Moreover, political concerns dictate some consideration for a VAT's impact on the elderly when designing a tax.

One approach would simply be to announce a VAT today to be effective at some date in the future. Delay has been suggested by Graetz (1980), among others. Delaying enactment reduces the loss for current capital owners. This occurs partly because income from capital is not subject to a VAT for some time into the future. This reduces the present value of the capital loss (drop in asset prices); when the VAT is actually implemented there will be no additional capital loss at that time, since it will have been fully anticipated. The loss is also mitigated because capital formation will be reduced during the period leading up to enactment, thereby increasing the return to capital. This is clearly a shortcoming of delay given current efforts to raise saving rates, in part to accommodate the large increases in retirement expected early in the next century.

Perhaps a better approach would be to zero rate or exempt items consumed by the elderly. Besides the obvious administrative problems that result from different taxes on various consumption goods, it is difficult to target such a subsidy precisely to the elderly. A better approach would be to exempt the elderly from sales tax at the retail level. This approach is still imperfect, since many capital owners are not elderly (and vice versa). Also, the possibilities for tax evasion are rife. An even better approach would be to increase the elderly exemption on the income tax to offset the additional consumption taxes that they would have to pay. This would also mitigate some of the political opposition from this potent and large interest group.

## VAT AND THE SIZE OF THE PUBLIC SECTOR

One argument against a VAT is that it increases the size of the public sector. While this point is widely asserted, the available evidence does not offer much support for this claim. Stockfisch (1985) found that the growth in tax collections relative to GDP is not appreciably different between the VAT and non-VAT countries. The ratio of growth rates in both sets of countries was roughly 1.19 on average prior to implementing a VAT; for the period after VATs were enacted, the ratio of growth rates on average was 1.15 in the VAT countries and 1.08 in the non-VAT countries.[16] However, since there is no formal test for differences in these ratios, Stockfisch's (p. 549) conclusion that "the simple prima-facie view that imposition of a value-added tax increases government spending...is not supported" cannot strictly speaking be accepted.

But it is likely that the comparison that Stockfisch (1985) makes is biased toward finding that enacting a VAT increases spending. If countries that enacted a VAT were under pressure to raise revenues for existing programs, one would expect a higher growth rate ratio for the VAT countries relative to the non-VAT ones. Of course, this would be a misleading correlation, since it would follow from fiscal pressures driving needs for new revenue sources rather than new revenues allowing growth in spending. But Stockfisch doesn't find any connection at all. [17]

## ADMINISTRATIVE AND COMPLIANCE COSTS

The General Accounting Office (1993) recently estimated that the total costs of administering a fully implemented broad-based VAT in 1995 would be $1.8 billion per year. In addition, there would be one-time transition costs of about $800 million. Substantial savings can be achieved by exempting small businesses. Exempting firms with annual receipts of less than $25,000 would reduce the number of returns needing to be filed by about one-half while raising the exemption to $100,000 would reduce returns filed by nearly two-thirds. Administrative costs in this latter case would fall by one-third. According to the GAO report, business taxpayers in 1987 under the $25,000 threshold accounted for 0.7 percent of gross receipts. Business taxpayers under a $100,000 threshold accounted for only 2.6 percent of gross receipts. Thus, they project little fall in tax collections from exempting small firms.

As noted above, exempting small firms would affect effective tax rates depending on whether the small firms are at the end of the production chain or in the middle. One possible outcome of exempting these firms would be to discriminate against small intermediate production firms and favor small final producers. The adverse effects of exemption could be eliminated by making registration optional for small firms. Those with significant expenditures on VAT-taxed inputs would be inclined to register to take advantage of the credit in a credit invoice VAT system. Of course, this reduces some of the administrative savings that arose from allowing the exemption in the first place. The figures cited above assume voluntary registration.

A VAT with multiple rates or other complexities would drive up the administrative costs of the tax. GAO (1993) estimates that audit costs would rise between $400 and $700 million and taxpayer services about $140 million with a more complex tax. Transition costs would also increase.

In addition to administrative costs for the government, taxpayers will incur compliance costs as well. Based on the experience in the United Kingdom, the Congressional Budget Office (1992) estimates private compliance costs between $4 and $7 billion in 1988 for a VAT that exempted business with gross receipts less than $25,000.[18] This compares to an estimated compliance cost of $21 to $33 billion (in 1988 dollars) for federal and state income taxes (Slemrod and Sorum 1984).

Offsetting these higher costs are the administration and compliance costs that are avoided by implementing a VAT rather than raising existing tax rates. Higher marginal tax rates for existing taxes are likely to increase tax avoidance and evasion activities thereby requiring increases in monitoring, administration, and compliance costs for existing taxes. Whether a new VAT is preferable from the point of view of administrative and compliance costs to increasing revenues from existing taxes is not clear a priori.

## VAT AND STATE AND LOCAL SALES TAXES

A final concern involves the relationship between a federal VAT and the system of state and local sales taxes already in effect. Many state and local officials are concerned that a federal VAT would encroach on their ability to levy sales taxes. There are two issues here. The first issue is a true administrative issue: how would one design a collection system to levy both federal VAT and state and local sales taxes? Presumably, it is not difficult to program cash registers to track VAT and state or local sales taxable sales separately. Integrating tax collections is probably easier if the tax base is the same across a VAT and sales taxes. State and local sales taxes tend to use the same tax base (the local tax typically piggybacks on the state tax base). If a VAT were implemented, states would probably move to a tax base matching the VAT base. The advantage of this would be the standardization of sales tax bases across states. This would reduce the incentives for shopping across state borders, although such incentives will continue as long as tax rates vary across states.

The second issue is whether a VAT would encroach on state and local sales tax collections. The political economy argument—that a VAT would require states to lower their sales tax rates—is not persuasive. Provincial and federal sales taxes coexist in Canada with no particular problems. Additionally, the economic argument is made that a VAT will cause consumption to fall, thereby reducing the state sales tax base as well as collections. But this would likely be true for *any* tax that was implemented, not just a VAT tax.

## ALTERNATIVES TO A VAT

Much has been written on the different ways that comprehensive consumption taxes can be implemented, and it is not the point of this article to reinvent the wheel. But it is worth commenting on a couple of alternatives to a VAT to clarify the advantages and disadvantages that are particular to a VAT. I will comment on a cash flow income tax and the $X$ tax.

A cash flow tax would eliminate the corporate income tax and modify the personal income tax to allow a deduction for all net additions to saving. Since consumption simply equals income less saving, the cash flow income tax gets at consumption by measuring income adjusted for changes in wealth. In effect, it is equivalent to a broad-based VAT. A simple way to think about this form of consumption tax is to imagine extending tax deductibility for IRAs to all net saving. For this to work, it would be necessary to create registered savings accounts so that net flows can be accurately measured. An obvious compliance problem is the ability to hide existing assets out of which taxpayers could consume without paying tax.

The $X$ tax, due to Bradford (1987), is like a subtraction style VAT combined with a wage tax.[19] Firms pay a flat tax on sales net of the cost of all inputs, including capital purchases and labor. If the deduction for labor costs were not allowed, this would be a subtraction style VAT exactly. At the individual level, there is a progressive tax on wage income (net of an exemption based on family size). The exemption and progressive rate schedule add progressivity to the $X$ tax. If the individual rate were fixed at the business rate and there were no allowance, the $X$ tax would be identical to a subtraction style VAT. However, the $X$ tax allows greater flexibility to adjust progressivity.

The prime advantage of either the cash flow or $X$ tax is that either requires only modest modification of the existing tax system. The $X$ tax in particular is easily implemented. Expensing of investment replaces depreciation schedules, and interest payments no longer are deducted. At the individual level, all employment compensation (including salaries and wages, as well as pension income) would be included in the tax base while all capital income is excluded.

The prime difficulty with either of these taxes is that taken alone, they would probably be difficult to enact. A revenue-neutral shift from an income to a consumption base has little political appeal. Such a shift would require raising marginal tax rates on wage income to offset the exclusion of capital income from taxation. At the same time, there would be a shift away from corporate income taxation as new investment is expensed. The recent debates over the merits of reducing the taxation of capital gains suggest this shift would be controversial at best and unworkable at worst. A VAT, on the other hand, is likely to be perceived as a new tax; it may be more politically feasible to enact a VAT if packaged with a particular program, like financing Medicare for the elderly or paying for a major new program such as some version of health care reform.

## CONCLUSION

Should the United States implement a value-added tax? It is a sobering fact that the on-budget federal deficit is projected to be $276 billion in fiscal year 1997—3.6

percent of GDP (Congressional Budget Office, 1994b). Feldstein (1994) argues that this number may be low by as much as $115 billion. Moreover, health care reform could add an additional $20 billion to the deficit in 1997, according to the Congressional Budget Office.

While spending cuts can reduce the deficit, it is hard to imagine serious progress can be made without some tax increases. In this situation, one may more properly ask not whether the nation should raise taxes, but rather which tax we should raise. In that light, a value-added tax begins to look very attractive.

## NOTES

I am grateful to David Bradford, Carl Shapiro, and Timothy Taylor for their thoughtful comments.

1. A recent effort was the bipartisan "Uniform Business Tax" proposed in 1991 by Reps. Schulze (R) and Guarini (D) (H.R. 3170). In the general explanation accompanying their bill, they state that the UBT resembles a combination of a employer-paid payroll tax and a "fundamentally reformed and simplified business tax system." Nowhere is it described as a consumption tax.

2. Allowing full deduction for purchase of capital is a property of a consumption-type VAT. Alternatively, an income-type VAT would allow a depreciation deduction only. VATs are generally of the consumption type.

3. Depending on the subject matter and the publisher, $500 is either the gross proceeds from textbook sales or the price of a single book, or both. I leave it to the reader to choose the appropriate units.

4. Note the incentive for vertical integration. Exemptions typically occur to reduce administrative burdens on small producers. There is an incentive for production carried out by small exempt firms to be done by a larger taxable firm and thereby avoid breaking the tax chain.

5. Zero rating and exempting a stage of production is equivalent in a subtraction style VAT.

6. For a more comprehensive history of value-added taxation, see Shoup (1990) or U.S. Treasury (1984).

7. Greece was allowed a deferral of the date of introduction of a VAT in the fifteenth VAT directive (1984).

8. Grossman (1980) shows that if there is a traded intermediate good, a VAT is not neutral under the origin principle if the tax is imposed as a general sales tax. For the European style credit invoice VAT to be neutral on an origin basis, one must credit an imputed VAT on an imported intermediate good even though no tax has actually been paid.

9. Of course, optimal tax theory does not imply that uniform commodity taxation is optimal.

10. In effect, this policy would tax the consumption stream of housing services on a tax prepayment basis.

11. Pechman's work, as well as other's work on consumption tax incidence, assumes competitive markets and forward passing of the tax. Recent work by Besley and Rosen (1994) challenges the assumption of competitive markets and finds evidence of overshifting for a number of commodities. Computing the incidence of taxes in the presence of imperfectly competitive markets is an important research topic for public finance economists.

12. The argument that a broad-based consumption tax is proportional over the lifetime applies equally to a broad-based sales tax. This argument is developed further in Metcalf (1994).

13. Defining leisure is a bit problematic (do we include sleep?), but as an approximation, mean leisure is probably at least as large as mean labor supply. If equal, then the income elasticity of leisure equals (in absolute value) the income elasticity of labor supply; if leisure exceeds labor supply, the elasticity is smaller than the elasticity of labor supply.

14. This is not inconsistent with the view that the bequest giver does in fact derive utility from the size of the gift itself (as in the bumper sticker, "He who dies with the most toys wins"). Presumably, utility derives from the size of the gift in real rather than nominal terms. A VAT would reduce the bequest in real terms.

15. It is not clear a priori whether the untaxed services would increase or decrease if a VAT were implemented. Because the services are untaxed there would be a rightward shift of the demand curve for services. From the children's point of view, a VAT is analogous to a wage tax, and the supply curve for services would shift left if the supply elasticity is positive.

16. The ratio of growth rates fell in eight of the twelve VAT countries after a VAT was enacted and also fell in eight of the twelve non-VAT countries. For the VAT countries, the before and after period is relative to when the VAT was enacted, while for the non-VAT countries the two periods are 1964–1971 and 1972–1981, as 1971 was the median year that a VAT was enacted for the VAT countries.

17. Using a different sort of evidence, Feenberg and Rosen (1987) conclude that there is no empirical support for the view that the form of a state's tax structure independently affects the growth of the public sector. They look at differences in state tax structures and find no evidence that variations in the elasticity of state tax revenues with respect to income have any effect on the growth of the public sector.

18. On a positive note, one advantage of a VAT is that the underground economy is brought into the tax system. While income may go unreported, it will be more difficult to evade taxes on consumption of that income.

19. Bradford chose the name so that people would consider the tax on its merits without preconceived notions about income or consumption taxes. See also the discussion of a two-tiered consumption tax in Bradford (1986). A variation on the X tax is the Hall-Rabushka flat tax discussed in Hall and Rabushka (1983).

## REFERENCES

Aaron, Henry Jr. *VAT Experiences of Some European Countries.* Deventer, the Netherlands: Kluwer (1982).

Auerbach, Alan, Laurence Kotlikoff, and Jonathan Skinner. "The Efficiency Gains from Dynamic Tax Reform." *International Economic Review 24* (February 1983): 81 –100.

Bernheim, B Douglas, Andrei Shleifer, and Lawrence Summers. "The Strategic Bequest Motive." *Journal of Political Economy 93* (December 1985): 1045–1076.

Besley, Timothy, and Harvey Rosen. "Sales Taxes and Prices: An Empirical Analysis," mimeo, Department of Economics, Princeton University (1994).

Blinder, Alan. *Toward an Economic Theory of Income Distribution.* Cambridge, Massachusetts: MIT Press (1974).

Bradford, David. *Untangling the Income Tax.* Cambridge, Massachusetts: Harvard University Press (1986).

————. "On the Incidence of Consumption Taxes," in C. Walker and M. Bloomfield, eds., *The Consumption Tax: A Better Alternative?* New York: Ballinger (1987): 243–261.

Browning, Edgar. "Tax Incidence, Indirect Taxes, and Transfers." *National Tax Journal 38* (December 1985): 525–533.

Buckett, Alan. *VAT in the European Community.* London: Butterworths (1992).

Caspersen, Erik, and Gilbert Metcalf. "Is a Value Added Tax Regressive?" *National Tax Journal* (1994): forthcoming.

Feenberg, Daniel, and Harvey Rosen. "Tax Structure and Public Sector Growth." *Journal of Public Economics 32* (March 1987): 185–201.

Feldstein, Martin. "The U.S. Fiscal Problem: Where We Are, How We Got Here And Where We're Going: A Comment." *National Bureau of Economic Research* (May 1994).

*Fortune* Magazine. "Clinton Speaks on the Economy." (August 23, 1993): 58–62.

Fullerton, Don, and Diane Rogers. *Who Bears the Lifetime Tax Burden?* Washington, D.C.: Brookings Institution (1993).

Graetz, Michael. "Expenditure Tax Design," in J. Pechman, ed., *What Should Be Taxed: Income or Expenditures?* Washington D.C.: Brookings Institution (1980): 161–276.

Grossman, Gene. "Border Tax Adjustments: Do They Distort Trade?" *Journal of International Economics 10* (February 1980): 117–128.

Hall, Robert, and Alvin Rabushka. *Low Tax, Simple Tax, Flat Tax.* New York: McGraw-Hill (1983).

Hausman, Jerry, and James Poterba. "Household Behavior and the Tax Reform Act of 1986." *Journal of Economic Perspectives 1* (Summer 1987): 101–120.

Heckman, James. "What Has Been Learned About Labor Supply in the Past Twenty Years?" *American Economic Review 83* (May 1993): 116–121.

Joint Committee on Taxation. *Comparison of the Tax Systems of the United States, Germany, and Japan,* JCS-13-92 (July 20, 1992).

Menchik, Paul, and Martin David. "The Incidence of a Lifetime Consumption Tax." *National Tax Journal 35* (June 1982): 189–203.

Metcalf, Gilbert. "The Lifetime Incidence of State and Local Taxes: Measuring Changes During the 1980's," in J. Slemrod, ed., *Tax Progressivity and Income Inequality,* New York: Cambridge University Press (1994): 59–88.

McLure, Charles. *The Value-Added Tax: Key to Deficit Reduction?* Washington, D.C.: American Enterprise Institute (1987).

Pechman, Joseph. *Who Paid the Taxes, 1966–85?* Washington, D.C.: Brookings Institution (1985).

————. *Federal Tax Policy.* Washington, D.C.: Brookings Institution (1987).

Shoup, Carl. "Choosing Among Types of VATs," in M. Gillis, C. Shoup, and G. Sicat, eds., *Value Added Taxation in Developing Countries,* Washington, D.C.: World Bank (1990): 3–16.

Slemrod, Joel, and Nikki Sorum. "The Compliance Cost of the U.S. Individual Income Tax System." *National Tax Journal 37* (December 1984): 461–474.

Stockfisch, J. "Value-Added Taxes and the Size of Government: Some Evidence." *National Tax Journal 38* (December 1985): 547–552.

Triest, Robert. "The Effect of Income Taxation on Labor Supply When Deductions are Endogenous." *Review of Economics and Statistics 74* (February 1992): 91–99.

U.S. Congressional Budget Office. *Effects of Adopting a Value Added Tax.* Washington, D.C.: U.S. Government Printing Office, 1992.

————. *Reducing the Deficit: Spending and Revenue Options.* Washington D.C.: U.S. Government Printing Office (1994a).

————. *The Economic and Budget Outlook.* Washington, D.C.: U.S. Government Printing Office (1994b).

U.S. Department of the Treasury. *Tax Reform for Fairness, Simplicity, and Economic Growth,* Volume 3. Washington, D.C.: Department of the Treasury (1984).

U.S. General Accounting Office. *Value Added Tax: Administrative Costs Vary with Complexity and Number of Businesses.* Washington, D.C.: General Accounting Office (May 1993).

*Washington Post* (April 15, 1993): A8.

Whalley, John, and Deborah Fretz. *The Economics of the Goods and Services Tax,* Canadian Tax Foundation, Canadian Tax Paper No. 88 (1990).

# S E L E C T I O N   2 8

Henry J. Aaron and Alicia H. Munnell

# Reassessing the Role for Wealth Transfer Taxes

Arguments for and against "tax the rich" are often intensely emotional and deeply divided: Tax the rich—and everyone else's tax burden can be lowered, resulting in a more equitable tax system. Tax the rich—and entrepreneurs will work less and invest less, resulting in a real decline in economic growth. While the debate is often focused on capital gains taxation or the high-bracket income tax rates, an equally controversial issue concerns estate and inheritance taxes on wealth—death duties.

In this selection, Henry Aaron and Alicia Munnell address the question: Are taxes on wealth transfers appropriate in the modern industrial economy of the United States? Using several perspectives, the authors answer "yes." From a life-cycle theoretical perspective, a comprehensive tax on lifetime income should combine an inheritance tax with an earnings tax or a bequest tax with a consumption tax. From an empirical perspective, the richest one percent control over thirty percent of the wealth in the United States. Aaron and Munnell argue effective estate taxes could be used to deconcentrate the wealth distribution, and at the same time, to help disperse any wealth-related economic, social, or political power.

**Questions to Guide the Reading**
1. How is the life-cycle perspective used to support taxation of inheritances or bequests? Why is wealth transfer taxation more difficult to defend under the "dynastic" theory of consumption?

Aaron, Henry J., and Alicia H. Munnell. "Reassessing the Role for Wealth Transfer Taxes." *National Tax Journal 45* (June 1992): 119-143. This selection is an abridged version of the original article.

**Henry J. Aaron** is Program Director of Economic Studies at The Brookings Institution. **Alicia H. Munnell** is Member Nominee to the Council of Economic Advisors.

2. How does life-cycle theory define wealth? How do the authors' three empirical measures of wealth differ? What rationale is given for the use of each one? In particular, why is the first wealth measure considered the "best index of economic power"?

3. Empirical estimates of the role of inheritance in wealth accumulation vary substantially—from 20 to 80 percent of total wealth. How does the use of different definitions of life-cycle wealth and of an intergenerational transfer explain the inconsistent estimates? What estimation approach do the authors advocate (and with what result)?

4. George Cooper (1979) claimed that the U.S. estate tax is a "voluntary tax." Explain. What are the most common mechanisms of avoidance, and how do they work?

5. In what ways might tax avoidance impact the U.S. economy?

6. With reference to ability-to-pay, why do the authors assert that estate and gift taxes in the United States "should be restructured or replaced"? What are the potential advantages and disadvantages of replacing the estate tax with an inheritance tax?

---

ALL developed countries rely extensively on progressive personal income taxes. None derives significant revenue from taxes on the transfer of wealth. In one sense, this situation is not surprising, since taxes on wealth transfers are exceedingly difficult to administer and many view any taxes on wealth as a form of double taxation. In another sense, the situation is surprising, since the life-cycle framework suggests that wealth transfers—by bequest or inheritance—belong in the tax base as much as annual flows of earnings or consumption. Moreover, to the extent that wealth conveys benefits above its ability to support consumption, wealth transfer taxes could prevent undue concentrations of economic, social, or political power.

This article explores the role of wealth transfer taxes in a modern industrial economy.... The conclusion, which is summarized in the final part, consists of five points. First, ownership of wealth in all industrialized countries is highly concentrated. Second, neither the United States nor the other countries we survey do much through their tax systems to reduce that concentration. Third, the life-cycle framework suggests, on equity grounds, that wealth transfers should be taxed. This conclusion would be reinforced if wealth were to provide utility above and beyond the ability to consume or if it were shown that wealth concentrations produced adverse social or political effects. Fourth, the evidence suggests that bequests and inheritances play a significant role in the accumulation and distribution of wealth, so that effective wealth transfer taxes could reduce the concentration of wealth holdings. Fifth, the excess burdens associated with current wealth taxes are very large relative to revenue generated. In short, wealth transfer taxes deserve a serious reassessment.

## THE RATIONALE FOR WEALTH TRANSFER TAXATION

If people can borrow and lend freely at a given interest rate, total lifetime economic resources are equal to either of two sums: the discounted present value of earnings plus inheritances, or the discounted present value of consumption plus bequests.[1] For those who can borrow and lend freely, this life-cycle perspective leads on equity grounds to either of two prescriptions: that personal taxes should be levied on earnings plus inheritances, or that personal taxes should be levied on consumption plus bequests (with suitable averaging to allow for variations in tax rates). Which of these quantities should be subject to tax and the extent to which they should be taxed hinge on a number of other considerations: the efficiency effects of taxing alternative bases, the realism of the assumption of perfect capital markets and the importance of violations of this assumption, and variations in the need for revenues over time.

This line of argument is based on the concept of wealth as potential consumption. If wealth is deemed to provide utility above and beyond financing consumption—for example, as a source of economic power and control—then standard ability-to-pay theory would call for a separate tax on the holding or transmission of wealth apart from any tax on earnings plus inheritances or on consumption plus bequests.[2]

The "dynastic" theory of consumption, espoused by Barro (1974) and others, provides less clear guidelines for wealth transfer taxation.[3] Under this theory, household saving, consumption, and labor supply are determined by the wealth available not to a single generation but to many generations of a family or household. This theory provides no basis for adding inheritances or bequests to earnings or consumption in a personal tax base, but would allow for the taxation of wealth or wealth transfers in some fashion if wealth provides utility apart from its use to finance consumption or if wealth-related social, political, or economic power were deemed appropriate to tax. For constructing a national tax system, we believe that the life-cycle framework is a more useful model than one that assumes virtually infinite time horizons on the part of individuals.[4]

One could ask, however, how the prescriptions of the life-cycle model for wealth transfer taxes fit into a tax system based on comprehensive income as the optimal personal tax base. Including wealth (or its surrogate, capital income) makes sense on equity grounds within a utility-based framework only if one holds that planning horizons are no longer than the taxable period and that capital markets preclude the transfer of resources across taxable periods.[5] In effect, a taxable unit would "inherit" each period a stock of wealth bequeathed from itself in the preceding period. Adopting these (unrealistic) assumptions and applying the logic used above would suggest an annual tax on net worth. The tax on capital income could be seen as an alternative means of achieving that objective, although the implied tax rate on capital income should then exceed that on earnings.[6]

In practice, of course, the effective rate of tax on capital income falls well short of that on labor income in most countries in most situations, because of sheltered pension savings, the failure to fully tax capital gains, and evasion of taxes on interest and dividend income. One particularly glaring loophole, at least in the United States, is the ability of individuals to completely escape tax on appreciated assets by passing them from one generation to another as bequests, since the basis for determining capital gains on inherited property is the fair market value on the date of the decedent's death. As a result of this and other provisions, actual, as opposed to theoretical, income taxes look more like taxes on earnings than comprehensive levies on all sources of income.

The failure of the income tax to reach most capital income and gains means that, in the absence of wealth transfer taxes, an important portion of the tax base suggested by the life-cycle model escapes taxation altogether. While this portion averages roughly 8 percent for the population as a whole, it is significant for the most affluent members of society, since wealth holdings are highly concentrated.[7] In fact, in the United States, proponents of strengthening the estate tax cite failures of the income tax as a major justification (Graetz 1983 and Gutman 1983).

In short, the life-cycle model provides a strong intellectual case on equity grounds for taxing wealth transfers as well as earnings or consumption. This goal is met inequitably and incompletely through attempts to include capital income in the personal income tax base. The comprehensive income tax reaches some income from life-cycle accumulations, which under a life-cycle income tax should be wholly exempt. And it falls at a negligible rate on inherited wealth, which should be taxed more heavily. The analytically correct levy is one on either bequests or inheritances. The justification for such a levy is reinforced by the notion that wealth may well provide utility above and beyond the ability to consume, or the potential that great concentration of wealth holdings can produce adverse social or political outcomes.

## DEFINING AND MEASURING WEALTH

It is one thing to decide that wealth transfers should be taxed; it is another to determine what constitutes wealth. Within the life-cycle theory, wealth is the sum of resources available to people over their lives and is simply the discounted present value of inheritances, earnings, and returns on saving that differ from the rate of discount. This means that the life-cycle definition includes "human capital," as represented by the value of future earnings, as well as physical and financial capital.

If wealth enters the utility function of people because it is a source of power or social standing, independent of the consumption it can finance, a more limited concept is appropriate. In that event, the relevant measure is the stock of financial or real assets under control of the taxable unit. Empirical studies of the distribution of wealth generally have focused on this narrower measure, suggesting a view that wealth conveys power and influence independent of consumption. To put it in the boldest terms, traditional empirical studies on the distribution of wealth suggest that people who earn enormous incomes and have enormous life-cycle wealth, but who save little, are not wealthy, even though they may be regarded as rich.

For the remainder of this article, we shall follow the conventional route of measuring wealth excluding human capital. In reviewing data from the United States, we shall use three definitions of wealth that vary according to the control the household has over particular assets (Table 1). All three definitions include the replacement value of tangible assets, the market value of equities, and the book value of bonds. To these basic ingredients, the narrowest wealth concept, $W_1$, adds the cash surrender value of trusts and pension funds—typically small amounts that a household could realize if it tried to sell its holdings. This narrow measure could be useful for analyzing the behavior of persons with limited capacity to borrow against other assets, or of myopic consumers. It also provides the best index of economic power.

A broader wealth concept, $W_2$, includes the full value of both trusts and pension funds.[8] To the extent that pensions are fully funded, pension assets reflect future pension benefits—a factor that, according to the life-cycle model, would be expected to influence a household's saving and capital accumulation.

If future pension benefits influence household decisions, as implied by the use of $W_2$, then so should the present discounted value of social insurance pension benefits, which are included in the third wealth measure, $W_3$. If households foresee future social insurance entitlements, they should also recognize the taxes that will be necessary to pay for these benefits; hence, $W_3$ includes net rather than gross social security wealth. This comprehensive concept would be appropriate for most life-cycle consumption models.

**Table 1** Definitions of Wealth Concepts

| Concept | Definition |
| --- | --- |
| $W_1$ | $W_1$ is defined as the cash surrender value of total assets less liabilities and is a measure of the wealth currently available to the household or individual. The assets include owner-occupied housing, other real estate, all consumer durables, demand deposits and currency, time and savings deposits, bonds and other financial securities, corporate stock, unincorporated business equity, trust fund equity, the cash surrender value of insurance, and the cash surrender value of pensions. Liabilities include mortgage debt, consumer debt, and other debt. Trusts are measured at their actuarial value, which represents roughly 50 percent of the total reserves of trusts. Pensions are measured at their cash surrender value, which represents a very small percentage, around 5 percent, of their total reserves. All other tangible and financial assets and liabilities are measured at full value. |
| $W_2$ | $W_2$ is a broader measure of wealth than $W_1$, and is defined as $W_1$ plus the full reserves of trust funds and the full reserves of private pension funds less their actuarial values included in $W_1$. |
| $W_3$ | An even broader measure of wealth, $W_3$ equals $W_2$ plus the present discounted value of expected social security benefits. |

All three measures are valuable, since the appropriate definition of wealth for policy deliberations varies with the issue under consideration. Those concerned that an undue concentration of wealth puts too much power in the hands of a few should probably look at the distribution of $W_1$, a measure of assets directly controlled by households. On the other hand, $W_2$ (or even $W_3$) is a superior measure if the issue is the role played by wealth in supporting consumption, because these measures include public and private pensions.

## The Amount and Composition of Wealth in the United States: 1900–1990

The three measures of net worth are shown in Figure 1.[9] These estimates are an updated and slightly modified version of data originally compiled by Wolff (1989).

$W_1$, $W_2$, and $W_3$ are virtually identical in the United States until 1922, at which time $W_2$ begins to exceed $W_1$ because of the emergence of private pensions. By 1990 pensions grew to 14 percent of total assets and 18 percent of net worth. $W_3$ began to diverge from $W_2$ in the late 1930s after the enactment of the social security program. By 1990 the present value of accumulated social security entitlements equalled roughly 40 percent of marketable net worth of households.

The balance sheet data contain hints about shifts in the distribution of wealth ownership. Assets can be divided into "life-cycle wealth" and "capital wealth." Life-cycle wealth includes owner-occupied housing, consumer durables, cash and demand deposits, and pensions, less mortgage and consumer debt—assets and liabilities whose accumulation depends on the age of household members as predicted by the life-cycle model. Capital wealth includes tenant-occupied housing, time deposits, financial securities, corporate stock, trust fund equity, and unincorporated business equity less other liabilities—wealth that appears to be built up primarily to create estates for succeeding generations.[10] These classifications are interesting, crude as they may be, because life-cycle wealth consists of assets that are distributed broadly among both the middle and upper classes, while capital wealth is concentrated among those with the highest incomes. Hence, a significant shift in the share of one or the other compared to the total could signal a major shift in the distribution of asset holdings.

As it turns out, the extent to which a shift appears to have taken place depends critically on the definition of wealth adopted. According to the narrowest wealth concept, $W_1$, the ratio of life-cycle wealth to total wealth increased from 18 percent to 30 percent between 1930 and 1950, and fluctuated around 30 percent after 1950. Life-cycle wealth as a share of the total declined sharply in the 1980s, suggesting an increase in the concentration of wealth holdings. $W_2$ presents a somewhat different picture; the increase in life-cycle wealth as a share of the total continued through 1980 and then leveled off. In other words, the apparent decrease in life-cycle wealth, with its implication of increasing wealth concentration, disappears once the full value of employer-sponsored pensions is included in the calculation. Expanding the wealth concept even further to include the present discounted

**Figure 1**  Real Net Worth Per Capita (1990 Dollars)

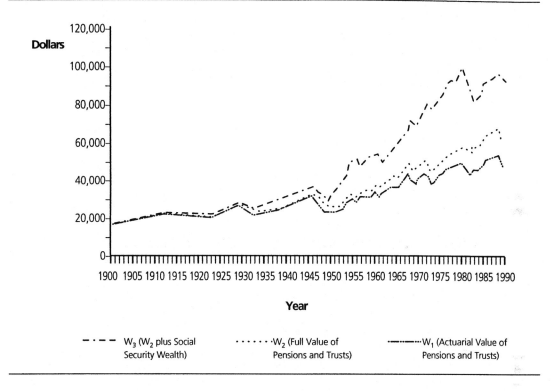

Year

— · — W₃ (W₂ plus Social Security Wealth)  
· · · · · · W₂ (Full Value of Pensions and Trusts)  
———— W₁ (Actuarial Value of Pensions and Trusts)

value of net social security benefits, $W_3$, the ratio of life-cycle to total wealth depicts a steady trend toward deconcentration in household asset holdings.

\* \* \*

## Overall Assessment of U.S. Wealth Distribution Data

Crude manipulations with the national balance sheets, estimates from estate tax data, and solid evidence from cross-section surveys conducted by the Federal Reserve Board all indicate that holdings of wealth in the United States are highly concentrated. Using the narrow definition, the top 1 percent of wealth holders control about 30 percent of net worth. Broader definitions reduce this value, but the holdings of the top of the distribution remain significant.

Although the estate tax data suggest a major deconcentration of wealth in the first half of the century, some researchers have suggested that this apparent trend toward equalization might simply reflect *intra*household equalization in wealth holdings between spouses, rather than reduction in the *inter*household concentration of wealth. More importantly, no trend toward deconcentration is evident in the post-war era. Rather, data on income equality during the 1980s suggested that the concentration of wealth holdings would be likely to increase (U.S. House of Representatives 1991)....

## THE ROLE OF BEQUESTS IN WEALTH ACCUMULATION

According to the traditional life-cycle theory, people choose a consumption path based on the relationship between their personal rate of time preference and the rate of return they can earn on savings. If the former exceeds the latter, people choose to consume more when young than when old, and conversely. When the two rates are equal, people seek unchanging consumption over their lifetimes. Under the assumed hump-shaped earnings profile, people save during their working years and draw down accumulated assets in retirement. Although the life-cycle theory can accommodate a bequest motive, bequests have been accorded slight weight, and Modigliani has argued that they probably account for a small portion of asset holdings. Members of each cohort are assumed to consume most of what they have saved before they die, and to transmit wealth to the next generation only because the exact date of death is uncertain or because annuity markets are imperfect.[11] If this theory accurately characterized wealth accumulation in the United States, it would leave a small role for wealth transfer taxes to affect the distribution of the nation's wealth.

In 1981 Kotlikoff and Summers challenged the conventional wisdom, claiming that intergenerational transfer rather than life-cycle saving explained most wealth accumulation in the United States.[12] They based their conclusion on two calculations—one derived from the flow of bequests and one from cumulating life-cycle saving.[13] Under the former, Kotlikoff and Summers used wealth data from the Federal Reserve's 1962 Survey of Financial Characteristics of Consumers and age-specific mortality rates to estimate annual intergenerational transfers. They transformed the flow of bequests into a stock of wealth by assuming that beneficiaries, on average, receive a constant fraction of their lifetime labor income in bequests and that the average age gap between bequeathers and inheritors is unvarying. These assumptions mean that the relationship between bequests and the stock of inherited wealth depends on the size of the age gap, the rate of growth of the economy, and the real rate of return. Using this approach, Kotlikoff and Summers concluded that inherited wealth accounted for 46 percent of the total wealth.

The direct calculation of life-cycle wealth produced the even more startling result that inherited wealth accounted for nearly 80 percent of the stock,[14] and that life-cycle wealth was only 22 percent of the total. In calculating these figures, Kotlikoff and Summers defined life-cycle wealth as the accumulated difference between the past streams of labor income and past streams of consumption. Procedurally, this meant distributing total labor income and total consumption in each year by age and sex groups (based on cross-section information), calculating the difference between these values for each group, capitalizing and cumulating these values to arrive at life-cycle wealth for each age and sex group, and finally aggregating across groups to arrive at total life-cycle wealth in a given year.

Modigliani (1984 and 1988) countered that the preponderance of evidence, including his own research, places life-cycle—not inherited—wealth at 80 percent of total wealth.[15] He identified two key issues that accounted for most of the difference between his results and those of Kotlikoff and Summers—namely, the definition of life-cycle wealth and the definition of an intergenerational transfer.

Kotlikoff and Summers calculated life-cycle wealth as the difference between the past streams of *labor income* only and consumption; Modigliani argued that it should be the difference between *total income* and consumption. Thus, Modigliani would include as life-cycle saving any income earned on previously received intergenerational transfers. He argued that, by adding income on inheritances to inheritances, Kotlikoff and Summers grossly overstated the role of intergenerational transfers.

With respect to the definition of intergenerational transfers, Kotlikoff and Summers included as bequests payments received by financially dependent individuals after age 18. The largest such transfer in the United States is college tuition. The issue of how to treat college tuitions and other such payments arose because Kotlikoff and Summers used a specific age, rather than the formation of the household, as the point from which to date accumulation. Under their procedure, college students over 18 who have no income but consume tuition provided by their parents are treated implicitly as if they were life-cycle dissavers. This means that the value of college tuitions is subtracted from life-cycle saving and added to inherited wealth.

Our assessment of the controversy at this stage is that the Kotlikoff-Summers treatment of earnings on previously inherited assets is preferable to Modigliani's, but that on balance their treatment of college tuition payments is not. The inclusion of earnings on previous inheritances simply standardizes in present value terms inheritances received at various times in the past. The standard definition of life-cycle income, as noted earlier, is simply the discounted present value of earnings *plus inheritances.*

The issue of whether to treat parental payments for college tuition as bequests or as parental consumption is more difficult. At some point, parental gifts to adult children clearly should be treated as bequests. Cash gifts made by elderly parents to middle-aged offspring are an effective means of avoiding estate taxes, for example. On the other hand, parental support of dependent children normally is treated as parental consumption. A continuum of circumstances exists between these extremes. If one is forced to put tuition payments in one category or the other, they probably should be treated on balance as transfers to dependent children.

Adjusting the estimates to eliminate educational expenditures and making two other technical adjustments suggested by Modigliani[16] bring the Kotlikoff-Summers ratio of bequests to total wealth to 32 percent using the flow-of-bequest approach and to 52 percent using the cumulation of life-cycle saving approach.[17]

These numbers are consistent with the results of a recent detailed study of estate tax returns, which concluded that between 25 and 40 percent of the U.S. capital stock results from intergenerational transfers (Barthold and Ito 1991)....

The most persuasive piece of evidence, from our perspective, is a simple calculation based on data from the 1986 SCF and 1986 estate tax returns. The distribution of wealth from the 1986 SCF combined with total wealth from the 1986 household balance sheets and age-specific death rates indicate that $215 billion was in the hands of decedents in 1986 (Table 2). Through the decedents' instructions, some of this wealth went to spouses, some to charity, and the remainder to members of succeeding generations. Since estate tax returns for 1986 decedents reported 45 percent of net worth being transferred across generations (Johnson 1990), annual intergenerational bequests for the population as a whole were assumed to equal $97 billion (45 percent of $215 billion)....These values imply that inherited wealth in 1986 totaled $3.4 trillion, 30 percent of national net worth. This estimate is a lower limit, as it excludes intergenerational transfers other than by bequest.

Despite the appearance of some consistency among the estimates, the role of bequests in wealth accumulation is clearly controversial and unresolved. Part of the controversy reflects a genuine ambiguity regarding when an expenditure should be regarded as consumption and when as a transfer. Beyond such conceptual issues, current estimates are just not very precise. For the purpose of this article, however, the central finding is that intergenerational wealth transfers are of sufficient size to establish a potential role for wealth transfer taxes to affect the distribution of wealth.

**Table 2** Estimate of Total Net Worth in Hands of Decedents, 1986

| Age Group | Percent of Total Net Worth[a] | Net Worth[b] ($ Billions) | Death Rate[c] | Net Worth in Hands of Decedents[d] ($ Billions) |
|---|---|---|---|---|
| Under 25 | 0.5 | $ 56 | 0.0007 | [e] |
| 25–34 | 6.3 | 709 | 0.0013 | $ 1 |
| 35–44 | 14.3 | 1,604 | 0.0021 | 3 |
| 45–54 | 21.9 | 2,455 | 0.0050 | 12 |
| 55–64 | 24.3 | 2,729 | 0.0126 | 34 |
| 65–74 | 23.1 | 2,598 | 0.0280 | 73 |
| 75+ | 9.6 | 1,079 | 0.0846 | 91 |
| All Groups | 100.0 | 11,229 | | 215 |

[a]The distribution of wealth by age calculated from the "1986 Survey of Consumer Finances," using household net worth excluding pensions by age of household head.
[b]Distribution of wealth by age applied to the total 1986 net worth of the household sector ($W_1$) as calculated for this paper.
[c]Deaths in each age group divided by the total U.S. population in the same age group. Excludes infant deaths.
dNet worth multiplied by the death rate.
[e]Less than $500,000.
*Source:* Federal Reserve Board of Governors, 1986, Survey of Consumer Finances, Machine Readable Data; National Center for Health Statistics, 1989, *Vital Statistics of the United States, 1986*, vol. 2, Mortality, Tables 1–3, 8–3; and authors' calculations.

## WEALTH TRANSFER TAXES

Most developed nations impose some kind of tax on the transfer of wealth by gift or bequest. Without exception, the taxes yield little revenue and the trend in collections has been down, if any trend can be detected. Moreover, the costs of avoidance, at least in the United States, are formidable. This combination of circumstances—low yield and high collection (or noncollection) costs—suggests the need for reform of wealth transfers taxes.

## Wealth Transfer Taxation in Selected Countries

**United States Experience** The United States has built a legally elaborate system for taxing wealth transfers that yields little revenue. The federal government taxes gifts and estate transfers and imposes a separate tax on generation-skipping trusts. In addition, all states but one tax estates, nineteen states tax inheritances, and seven states tax gifts.

At the federal level, Congress experimented with rudimentary inheritance and gift taxes in the late nineteenth century, but enacted an estate tax in 1916 when with the revenue needs of World War I. An estate tax was chosen over the inheritance tax because it was viewed as easier to administer and was thought to produce more revenue. Net estates in excess of $50,000 were subject to a progressive levy that ranged from 1 percent to 10 percent. Wealthy individuals promptly discovered that they could avoid the estate tax by giving away their property before death. To close this loophole, Congress enacted the gift tax in 1924.

After remaining relatively untouched for its first 60 years of existence, except for changes in rates and exemptions and adjustments in the treatment of married couples, the wealth transfer tax system was overhauled substantially in 1976. The three most important changes were: (1) unifying the gift and estate taxes into one system that applies a single progressive rate schedule to combined lifetime and death transfers, (2) introducing a comprehensive levy on generation-skipping transfers, and (3) expanding the marital deduction. These positive developments, from the perspective of tax reformers, were offset by a more than three-fold increase in the general exemption in 1981.

**Experience in Selected Countries** In contrast to the United States, most industrialized countries tax wealth transfers under an inheritance rather than an estate tax. Typically, small transfers are exempt. Transfers among close relations, especially spouses, are taxed at lower rates than transfers to others in France, Sweden, and Germany. The tax schedules are progressive in every country, with nominal rates rising to levels as high as 70 percent.

Despite the high marginal rates, the yields are meager. No developed industrial country derives significant revenues from wealth transfer taxes. This should not be surprising, however, given that the wealth of decedents in any one year is not a large percentage of GDP (5 percent in 1986 in the United States). Wealth transfer taxes yield between 0.2 and 0.3 percent of gross domestic product in France, the United Kingdom, and the United States, even less in Germany, Japan, and Sweden, and virtually nothing in Canada, which repealed national wealth transfer taxes in 1972 (Table 3).[18]

This pattern of high nominal rates that few actually pay raises the question of how taxpayers escape these taxes. If the mechanisms are inexpensive, the result may only be disrespect for the taxing authority. If the mechanisms are costly, then the ratio of excess burdens to revenues generated may be quite large, a circumstance that heightens the need for reform.

## Tax Avoidance in the United States

One U.S. expert writing on the wealth transfer tax system in the United States entitled his 1979 book for The Brookings Institution *A Voluntary Tax?* The author concluded:

> *In sum, because estate tax avoidance is such a successful and yet wasteful process, one suspects that the present estate and gift tax serves no purpose other than to give reassurance to the millions of unwealthy that entrenched wealth is being attacked. The attack is, however, more cosmetic than real and the economy is paying the price in fettered capital and distorted property ownership for this cosmetology (Cooper 1979, p. 82).*

More recent statements in the popular estate planning literature echo the same theme:

> *With proper planning, practically no family, even the quite wealthy, need pay wealth transfer taxes (Auster 1987, p. 116).*

> *Fortunately, the federal tax code contains an assortment of opportunities for you to protect your estate from the government's grasp (Anrig 1985, p. 60).*

**Table 3** Estate/Inheritance and Gift Tax as a Percent of Gross Domestic Product

| Year | Germany | France | Sweden | Canada | Japan | United Kingdom | United States |
|------|---------|--------|--------|--------|-------|----------------|---------------|
| 1965 | .07 | .20 | .14 | .39 | .13 | .80 | .49 |
| 1970 | .08 | .25 | .14 | .31 | .19 | .73 | .46 |
| 1975 | .05 | .27 | .11 | .09 | .21 | .29 | .38 |
| 1980 | .07 | .23 | .10 | .02 | .19 | .20 | .31 |
| 1985 | .08 | .27 | .13 | .01 | .34 | .24 | .22 |
| 1986 | .10 | .30 | .12 | a | .42 | .25 | .23 |
| 1987 | .11 | .34 | .11 | a | .52 | .25 | .24 |
| 1988 | .11 | .38 | .09 | a | .50 | .23 | .23 |
| 1989 | .09 | .38 | .10 | a | .52 | .23 | .24 |

[a]Less than 0.01 percent.
*Source:* Organisation for Economic Cooperation and Development, 1991, *Revenue Estimates of OECD Member Countries: 1965–1990* (Paris, France: OECD).

*As long as you are not caught by surprise, almost everyone can pass along their estate to heirs without losing anything to the IRS [Internal Revenue Service] (Anrig 1985, p. 66).*

Estate tax statistics confirm these sentiments (Table 4). Of the $123 billion of wealth slated to be transferred across generations in 1986,[19] only $36 billion showed up on estate tax returns. Total federal taxes paid amounted to only $6 billion. Thus, despite high, progressive rates, the effective rate of tax on transferred wealth was about 5 percent.[20] Informed observers think that decedents could have avoided even this modest toll if they had taken the time to do so.

## Mechanisms of Avoidance

Even with the generous exemption, the steeply progressive rates of the U.S. estate and gift tax could reduce the concentration of wealth if avoidance were not so prevalent. Wealthy people avoid estate taxes by employing an array of estate planning techniques that fall into three major categories: freezing the estate, creating tax-exempt wealth, and disposing of wealth already accumulated. Placing a low value on wealth already accumulated may be the primary method of tax avoidance.

"Freezing" the size of the wealthy person's current estate and diverting future growth to the intended heirs is much easier, in estate planning terms, than disposing of substantial wealth after it has accumulated. The most straightforward option is simply to give away large portions of the estate as gifts as early as possible. The problem is that gift taxes can become burdensome and the original owner loses control over the property. To avoid these difficulties, estate planners have developed several procedures that allow the donor to retain control over the property, reduce or avoid the need to pay immediate gift tax on the transfer, or transfer more property than is apparent.

"Preferred stock recapitalization" used to be an ideal solution, but it has been reined in recently by new restrictions. The way it used to work is as follows: an owner of a closely held business who wanted to transfer future growth in the business to an heir would cancel the company's outstanding common stock and issue in its place a combination of preferred stock, which would receive most of the company's current net profits and perhaps effective voting control over the company, and common stock, which would be entitled to the fruits of future growth but would receive little current income and enjoy little control. The owner would receive the preferred stock, and heirs would get the common stock. The terms and conditions on the preferred would be set in such a way as to minimize the value of the common stock. This procedure would allow the owner to transfer all future growth to the heirs, without excessive gift tax and without sacrificing control.[21]

The Omnibus Budget Reconciliation Act of 1987 placed severe limits on the use of estate freezing. Most importantly, it required that the value of the transferred stock and its subsequent appreciation be included in the transferor's estate. The rules, however, changed again in 1990, so that the transferor now pays gift tax on the value of the common stock at the time of the transfer, but subsequent appreci-

**Table 4** Federal Estate Tax Returns Filed, Selected Years 1925–1988[a]
Dollar Amounts in Millions

| | Gross Returns | | Taxable Returns | | | | Net Estate | Estate Tax as a Percent of | |
|---|---|---|---|---|---|---|---|---|---|
| Year | Number | Percent of all Decedents | Number | Percent of all Decedents | Gross Estate | Taxable Estate | Net Estate Tax Revenues | Gross Estate | Taxable Estate |
| 1925 | 14,013 | 1.1 | 10,642 | 0.8 | $ 2,958 | $ 1,621 | $ 86 | 2.9 | 5.3 |
| 1930 | 8,798 | 0.6 | 7,028 | 0.5 | 4,109 | 2,377 | 39 | 0.9 | 1.6 |
| 1935 | 11,110 | 0.8 | 8,655 | 0.6 | 2,435 | 1,317 | 154 | 6.3 | 11.7 |
| 1940 | 15,435 | 1.1 | 12,907 | 0.9 | 2,633 | 1,479 | 250 | 9.5 | 16.9 |
| 1945 | 15,898 | 1.1 | 13,869 | 1.0 | 3,437 | 1,900 | 531 | 15.4 | 27.9 |
| 1950 | 25,858 | 1.8 | 17,411 | 1.2 | 4,918 | 1,917 | 484 | 9.8 | 25.2 |
| 1955 | 36,595 | 2.4 | 25,143 | 1.6 | 7,467 | 2,991 | 778 | 10.4 | 26.0 |
| 1961 | 64,538 | 3.8 | 45,439 | 2.7 | 14,622 | 6,014 | 1,619 | 11.1 | 26.9 |
| 1963 | 78,393 | 4.3 | 55,207 | 3.0 | 17,007 | 7,071 | 1,841 | 10.8 | 26.0 |
| 1966 | 97,339 | 5.2 | 67,404 | 3.6 | 21,936 | 9,160 | 2,414 | 11.0 | 26.4 |
| 1970 | 133,944 | 7.0 | 93,424 | 4.9 | 29,671 | 11,662 | 3,000 | 10.1 | 25.7 |
| 1977 | 200,747 | 10.6 | 139,115 | 7.3 | 48,202 | 20,904 | 4,979 | 10.3 | 23.8 |
| 1983[b] | 63,251 | 3.1 | 35,148 | 1.7 | 50,390 | 26,483 | 5,170 | 10.3 | 19.5 |
| 1986 | 42,125 | 2.0 | 23,731 | 1.1 | 59,805 | 31,635 | 6,383 | 10.7 | 20.2 |
| 1987 | 45,113 | 2.1 | 21,335 | 1.0 | 66,564 | 35,914 | 6,358 | 9.6 | 17.7 |
| 1988 | 43,683 | 2.0 | 18,948 | .9 | 70,625 | 37,250 | 6,299 | 8.9 | 16.9 |
| 1989 | 45,695 | 2.1 | 20,695 | 1.0 | 77,997 | 42,161 | 7,466 | 9.6 | 17.7 |
| 1990 | 50,367 | 2.3 | 23,104 | 1.1 | 87,117 | 48,566 | 8,999 | 10.3 | 18.5 |

[a]These data are not entirely comparable with those discussed in the text because these figures represent returns filed in a given year, while the data discussed in the text represent data for those who died in 1986. Unfortunately, a consistent series of data on estates by year of death rather than filing year is not available.

[b]1983 figures are for returns with gross estates in excess of $300,000. However, the majority of returns filed in 1983 were for 1982 decedents. Consequently, to the extent that gross estates between $225,000 and $300,000 had net taxable estates greater than $225,000, these 1983 figures understate actual amounts.

Source: U.S. Congress, Joint Committee on Taxation, 1981, *Background and Description of Bills (S. 395, S. 404, S. 574, and S. 858) Relating to Estate and Gift Taxes,* Washington, D.C.: Government Printing Office, April 30, Table 4; U.S. Bureau of the Census, 1987, *Statistical Abstract of the United States, 1988,* 108th ed., Washington, D.C.: Government Printing Office, Table 112; National Center for Health Statistics, 1989, *Vital Statistics of the United States, 1986,* vol. 2, Mortality, part A; DHHS Pub. No. (PHS) 88-1101, Washington, D.C.: Government Printing Office, Table 1-1; Mary F. Bentz, 1984, "Estate Tax Returns, 1983," *Statistics of Income Bulletin,* Table 1; Barry Johnson, 1990, "Estate Tax Returns, 1986–1988," *Statistics of Income Bulletin,* Tables 1, 1B, and 1C; U.S. Department of the Treasury, Internal Revenue Service, 1992, "Estate Tax Statistics for 1989 and 1990," *Statistics of Income Bulletin,* Tables 1 and 2.

ation once again goes untaxed under the estate levy. Although the current provisions are significantly more lenient than those resulting from the 1987 reforms, the transferor can no longer set the value of the common stock at zero. Additionally, the preferred stock retained by the parent must earn market rates of return.

Estate "freezing" is but one approach to estate planning and applies particularly to wealthy business owners, entrepreneurs, investors, and others whose activities generate capital growth. While this group accounts for the majority of wealthy individuals, high-salaried executives constitute another significant segment. The major estate planning opportunity for these persons is to take advantage of possibilities for creating tax-exempt wealth.

The most important item in this category is life insurance. Corporations commonly provide their high-paid executives with large amounts of employer-funded group term insurance. Such policies frequently exceed $1 million, yet proceeds easily are excluded from the executive's estate. All that is required is to transfer ownership either directly to the prospective heirs or to a trust on their behalf.[22]

Disposing of accumulated wealth is the most difficult estate planning task. "A dollar in the hand is worse than two in the bush from an estate planning perspective" (Cooper 1979, 38). Nevertheless, numerous options are available to reduce or to eliminate transfer tax liabilities. For example, a couple with numerous beneficiaries and foresight can easily give away several million dollars tax free under the current exemption of $20,000 per year per recipient; and, of course, gifts also transfer future appreciation without tax.

While planned giving is ideal for those with foresight, the private annuity can save the estates of those who realize suddenly and belatedly that death is nigh and the estate tax collector not far behind. Under this arrangement, a parent could transfer all property to the children in return for an annuity. As long as the annuity fairly reflects the value of the property and actuarial probabilities—but not necessarily the specific illnesses facing the potential decedent—the transaction is not subject to gift tax or estate tax, even if the parent dies the day after the transfer takes place.[23]

Placing a low estimate on the value of the estate is perhaps the most popular way to avoid taxes. This technique is particularly useful in the case of closely held corporations where a low value can sometimes be assigned to the outstanding stock. Stock values are usually calculated in two steps. The first consists of the valuation of the company based on the book value of underlying assets, current and projected earnings and dividends, values of similar publicly-traded companies, and other objective factors. Expert appraisers usually prepare such estimates according to conventional rules and methods.

At the second stage, a series of special factors are considered that can cause fair market value to diverge from the step-1 estimates. For example, the estimated value of a large block of stock may be reduced because of the possibility that abrupt sale would depress the market price. Alternatively, the value of a small block of stock may be reduced because it does not confer voting control. The value of a relatively unknown company may be discounted because the lack of reputation would depress the value of its stock on the open market.

Several options also exist for real estate. Alternative valuation procedures for real estate used in farming or closely held businesses can lower values significantly below what the market would bring. The conservation easement is sometimes an attractive option for suppressing property values for tax purposes. The primary example of this is the creation of open-space easements that are donated to charitable conservation organizations. If the easement is created during life, the wealthy individual gets the benefit of a current charitable income tax deduction as well as the reduction in value of the property for gift and estate tax purposes.[24] Valuation is a delicate art that can reduce dramatically the value of an estate and whose skillful practice is compensated generously by satisfied clients.

The wealthy can always reduce their estate by donating an undivided or split interest in property to charity. Split interest gifts can take the form either of a charitable "remainder trust," which involves a life interest to an individual and the remainder to charity, or a charitable "lead trust," which provides income to a charity for a term of years followed by a remainder to an individual.[25]

## Overall Assessment of Wealth Transfer Taxes

Subjecting wealth transfer taxes to the conventional tools of economic analysis is particularly difficult. Estate and gift taxes cause taxpayers to structure financial transactions in ways that reduce tax liability. To some degree such tax avoidance affects real economic behavior, such as the nature of investment or property use. For the most part, however, tax avoidance consists of hiring skilled legal talent to arrange property rights in appropriate ways.

The economic cost of arranging such avoidance is not trivial. The American Bar Association reports that over 16,000 lawyers, roughly 5 percent of its total membership, cite trust, probate, and estate law as their area of concentration. Accountants engage in estate planning as well, and are trying eagerly to increase their share of the estate planning market. To the compensation of these professionals must be added the efforts of those who are trying to avoid the taxes. In total, the compliance costs of the transfer tax system must amount to a sizable fraction of the total yield of $6 billion.

If wealth transfer taxes are indeed "voluntary taxes," as Cooper alleged, they are hardly related to ability-to-pay in the usual sense. Rather, they are penalties imposed on those who neglect to plan ahead or who retain unskilled estate planners. These are not the customary indices of economic capacity. In short, the estate and gift taxes in the United States have failed to achieve their intended purposes. They raise little revenue. They impose large excess burdens. They are unfair. And they should be restructured or replaced.

Two broad options are available within the framework of the life-cycle identity; the choice is between taxing earnings plus inheritances or consumption plus bequests. This framework might seem inappropriate, because most countries claim to apply comprehensive income taxes. In fact, none does. Capital income is incompletely and in some cases negatively, taxed.[26] As a result, the actual personal income tax bases in most countries more nearly resemble labor income taxes. These are linked to a combination of *ad rem* consumption taxes on value added, sales, and various individual commodities.

Starting from a consumption tax norm would lead one to try to perfect the taxation of estates and gifts. A variety of restrictions could be added to limit avoidance of estate and gift taxes. For example, the U.S. Treasury has put forward new regulations concerning estate freezing that are intended to narrow opportunities for tax avoidance. Even if additional such amendments could expand significantly the bequest tax base, which they probably cannot, the estate tax is the wrong levy to link to what is essentially a tax on labor income.

The life-cycle framework suggests that an earnings tax, which personal income taxes in most countries approximate, be paired with an inheritance tax. A comprehensive tax on accessions through inheritance or gift would permit countries to tax lifetime income in full. Moreover, most experts agree that a wealth transfer tax system with graduated rates based on the circumstances of the inheritor is more equitable than one based on the wealth of the decedent, since most assume that the recipient ultimately bears the burden of the tax regardless (Surrey et al. 1987). Furthermore, an inheritance tax should encourage the dispersion of large estates, since the tax would be much greater for a single inheritor than if the estate were divided among several beneficiaries.[27]

An inheritance or accessions tax has several potential drawbacks, three minor, but two more serious. First, the administrative burden of enforcing such a tax would most likely increase, simply because it would involve collecting from several inheritors rather than one estate. This issue is more complex under an accessions tax, since the tax would be based on the amount received from all donors. This difficulty could be mitigated somewhat by deducting the duty at the source, rather than from the individual. The second minor problem is that yields may decrease if the estate is split among several beneficiaries, but this decrease could be offset by raising rates or lowering exemptions. Third, a shift from an estate to an inheritance tax would require a significant transition period to allow people to adjust to the new rules. The final problems are more serious. Tax avoidance through the use of trusts is more complicated under an inheritance tax than under an estate tax.[28] Additionally, the valuation problems that plague the estate tax would still arise under an inheritance tax.

Although the inheritance tax has several technical problems, most could be mitigated by structuring the system carefully. Moreover, the theoretical appeal of an inheritance tax given our reliance on labor income taxes—namely its inherent fairness compared to the estate tax and its greater ability to break up large estates—argues for giving serious consideration to exploring the adoption of such a levy.

## CONCLUSION

Wealth transfer taxation persists, but just barely, in developed industrial countries. Administrative problems partly explain its light use. In the United States, resources spent on avoiding wealth transfer taxes are of the same general magnitude as the yield, suggesting that the ratio of excess burden to revenue of wealth transfer taxes is among the highest of all taxes.

Whatever the administrative problems, a good intellectual case exists for increased reliance on wealth transfer taxes. Within the life-cycle framework a tax on wealth transfers—bequests or inheritances—is essential to the definition of lifetime income. Outside the normal utility-based framework employed by economists, an additional basis for taxing both wealth and wealth transfers exists if wealth independently confers economic, social, or political power. To the extent that such economic power produces utility, it can be incorporated within the traditional framework of welfare economics and ability to pay. To the extent that large and durable concentrations of economic power are regarded as antithetical to economic and social mobility, taxes can be used to hinder the transfer of such advantages across generations.

Evidence from the United States suggests that wealth remains highly concentrated, although less so than it was early in the twentieth century. Other countries have displayed similar trends. In the United States, increasing inequality in the distribution of income over the 1980s suggested that wealth concentration might follow the same trend. Recent evidence has borne this out.

The unsatisfactory current state of wealth transfer taxes, the trends in income and wealth distributions, and the need for wealth transfer taxes for the proper definition of income add up to a strong case for reform of this tax.

## NOTES

This paper was originally prepared as the Joseph A. Pechman Memorial Lecture for the 47th Congress of the International Institute of Public Finance. The opinions expressed in this paper do not necessarily reflect the views of the trustees, officers, or staff of The Brookings Institution, or the official position of the Federal Reserve Bank of Boston or the Federal Reserve System. The authors would like to thank Leah Cook and Karan Singh for their extensive support in preparing this paper, and two anonymous referees of this journal.

1. Gifts received should be regarded as inheritances. Gifts given should be regarded as bequests. See Atkinson and Stiglitz (1980).
2. Economists seldom include power or control in the utility functions they use in analysis. Psychologists, sociologists, and many others would find its omission a bit peculiar. We suggest that the explicit inclusion of wealth in the utility function and an exploration of the implications for tax policy of doing so, although rather trivial in one sense, might be instructive.
3. Musgrave (1985) notes that in a model with an infinite number of periods, any wealth transfer tax would violate equity considerations, and a pure income or consumption tax eventually would tax all resources. This paper assumes, however, that the life-cycle framework with a finite horizon is the more appropriate model.
4. Interestingly, the life-cycle theory may provide a superior description of the behavior of most families. while the dynastic theory may provide a better description of the accumulation and transmission of most wealth. The explanation for this anomaly is that most people inherit and bequeath very little. but a few households accumulate large estates, hold them. and pass them on to their heirs. For an empirical and theoretical critique of the infinite-horizon theory of household behavior, see Bernheim (1987).
5. It makes sense on efficiency grounds if the efficiency gains from a lower tax on earnings more than offset the efficiency losses from the disturbance of intertemporal consumption neutrality caused by taxing capital income. More generally, the optimal tax literature has shown that uniform tax rates on different consumption goods (where differences include the timing as well as the type of consumption) minimize utility loss only under rather strong assumptions.

6. Under the life-cycle theory, the tax rate on the stock of capital inherited at the start of life is the same as that on labor income. Application of this principle annually would imply a tax rate on the stock of capital equal to that on labor income. The tax rate implied for capital income, $t_k$, would be $t_l/r$, where $t_l$ is the tax rate on labor income and $r$ is the ratio of capital income to capital value. Typically, $t_k$ would exceed 100 percent.

7. In 1986, assets in the hands of decedents amounted to $215 billion (see Table 2). Total earnings in that year amounted to $2,483 billion ($2,095 billion of wages and salaries, $199 billion of other labor income, and assume two-thirds of $282 billion of proprietors' income). Hence, wealth transfers amounted to 8 percent of the recommended earnings-plus-inheritance tax base.

8. Even though trusts are a small portion of total wealth, their treatment is one of the most complicated aspects of the various definitions. In the case of trusts over which individuals have complete control, their cash surrender value of $W_1$ and their full market value of $W_2$ are identical. Where the beneficiary and owner are different, however, as in the case of second or third party trusts, the trust has no cash surrender value to the beneficiary; the beneficiary cannot liquidate the trust, since the beneficiary does not control the assets. In this case, $W_1$ includes the actuarial value of the trust, which is the full value of trust assets discounted over the expected lifetime of the second and/or third parties. $W_2$, on the other hand, includes the full market value of trust assets.

9. Few data on the size and distribution of wealth were available in the United States before the 1980s, when the Federal Reserve Board began publishing national balance sheets with both tangible and financial assets. Earlier information consisted largely of pioneering research by Goldsmith on national aggregates since 1900 (Goldsmith 1962). A 1962 survey by the Federal Reserve Board provided the first glimpse of the distribution of wealth among households, but the Fed did not undertake another comprehensive survey until 1983. Follow-up surveys in 1986 and 1989 and a detailed set of longitudinal surveys by the Census Bureau beginning in 1983 have provided policymakers with access to fairly good information about the magnitude and composition of national wealth and who owns it. See the original paper for a full discussion of sources and methods used in compiling all of the data in this section, and for detailed tables.

10. This categorization was suggested by Wolff (1981).

11. An early study by Tobin (1967) provided some empirical support for the notion that life-cycle saving could explain most of the capital stock.

12. Kotlikoff and Summers acknowledged that their methodological approach was similar to that of Darby (1979) and Brittain (1978). Darby used cross-section data on wealth, earnings, and consumption to divide current wealth into that portion that would be consumed and that portion that would be transferred to succeeding generations. He inferred longitudinal age-consumption and age-earnings profiles from the cross-section data and concluded that no more than 29 percent of U.S. private net worth was used for life-cycle consumption. Brittain also concluded that inheritance played a major role in wealth accumulation and inequality.

13. To bolster the case that life-cycle saving plays a minor role in wealth accumulation, Kotlikoff (1988) cited several other developments that he believed cast doubt on the life-cycle theory itself. These included the slow rate of asset decumulation among the elderly, the apparent lack of demand for annuities, and the steady saving rate despite the substantial extension of the retirement period. These items must be interpreted

cautiously, however. First, asset decumulation appears much more rapid if one also includes the drawing down of pension and social security wealth. Second, private and public retirement systems provide most of retirement income as annuities and may well satisfy retirees' demand for this form of financial arrangement. Finally, the introduction of the social security program probably satisfied the need for additional saving to finance the extended period of retirement. Social security, however, traditionally has been financed, more or less, on a pay-as-you-go basis, and therefore would not raise the saving rate.

14. A referee informed us that Kotlikoff recently has revised this figure downward to 55 percent, after accounting for the effect of inheritances on labor supply and earnings.

15. Other evidence cited by Modigliani (1988) included survey results, where participants reported that they had received only a small share of their total wealth from gifts and inheritances (Morgan et al. 1962, Projector and Weiss 1964, and Barlow et al. 1966), evidence based on probate statistics (David and Menchik 1982, Menchik and David 1983), a direct estimate of life-cycle wealth (Ando and Kennickell 1985), and an estimate from the United Kingdom (Royal Commission on the Distribution of Income and Wealth 1977).

16. The largest of these adjustments deals with the treatment of durable goods and affects the cumulation of life-cycle saving estimate. Originally, Kotlikoff-Summers (1981) included expenditures on durable goods in consumption, as the National Income and Product Accounts do. Modigliani (1984) countered that this treatment is incorrect; durables should be treated like other investments and included in life-cycle saving. Using Kotlikoff-Summers data, he included depreciation of durables in consumption and net purchases of durables in saving. This correction was not entirely consistent, since it added durables to life-cycle wealth but not to total wealth. Kotlikoff-Summers responded (1986) with an alternative correction that omitted the accumulation of durables from both life-cycle wealth and total wealth. This procedure is troublesome for two reasons: it completely ignores a piece of wealth, and the excluded item exhibits a strong life-cycle pattern of accumulation. It seems that the appropriate correction has now been made by Modigliani (1988), who, includes the accumulation of durables in both life-cycle wealth and total wealth. This correction reduces the initial Kotlikoff-Summers share of bequests in total wealth by 14 percentage points.

The other adjustment affects the flow-of-bequest estimate by altering the assumption of timing of bequests. Kotlikoff-Summers assume that, on average, bequests occur 10 years before death, at age 65. Modigliani instead assumes that bequests occur at the time of death, which reduces the ratio of bequest wealth to total wealth by roughly 5 percentage points.

17. If these same adjustments were applied to Kotlikoff's revised estimate under the cumulation of life-cycle saving approach, they would reduce the new estimate from 55 percent to 27 percent.

18. Four of the seven countries shown in Table 3 also impose net wealth taxes—Germany, France, Sweden, and Canada. In each case, the yield of the net wealth taxes exceeds that of the corresponding wealth transfer taxes.

19. This $123 billion of transferred wealth differs from the $97 billion reported at the end of the section entitled "The Role of Bequests in Wealth Accumulation" because it represents the pretax value of estates, whereas the $97 billion is a posttax figure.

20. This figure excludes state and local estate and inheritance tax paid. Including these taxes brings the effective tax rate up to 6 percent.

21. The only negatives to a preferred stock recapitalization are that the corporation becomes loaded with a heavy preferred dividend requirement and the owner becomes the recipient of additional ordinary income that has already been taxed at the corporate level. The latter problem is reduced to the extent that payment of profits is shifted to payments of interest, which are deductible at the corporate level in the United States.

22. In view of the unlimited marital deduction, the most common procedure is to assign ownership to the children with the spouse having access to both interest and principal during his or her lifetime. Moreover, this approach is as effective for whole life as it is for term insurance. Since the amount of insurance is unlimited by law and can be offered by any corporation, the possibilities for tax avoidance through life insurance are staggering. The data, however, show that this possibility is not being exploited fully.

23. The annuitant might have the bad luck to survive and live to full life expectancy. In this case, he or she will receive all the payments, be forced to pay income tax on the payments plus capital gains on appreciation on the transferred assets, and will end up with assets equal to the property transferred in the first place.

24. For example, an owner of a large rustic fishing lodge, who wants to preserve the rustic conditions, can give to a charitable institution an easement barring any development of most of the surrounding land. This will preserve the property as a natural sanctuary and not alter the owner's use, while drastically reducing the value of the property for tax purposes.

25. For example, under a charitable remainder trust, a 60-year-old person might transfer $1 million of appreciated securities to an annuity trust for his alma mater, retaining an annuity of $80,000 (8 percent) for life. The IRS, using a 10 percent discount rate, values a life annuity for a 60-year-old at $592,928. An immediate income tax deduction is allowed for the remainder of $1 million less $592,928, or $407,072. When the person dies, the value of the trust is included in his estate but is offset immediately by a charitable deduction for the same amount.

26. Capital income is taxed negatively when payments are deductible at higher average rates than apply to receipts. This outcome is widespread in the case of interest expense and interest income, since fully taxable interest typically is deducted by fully taxable payers and received by partially or fully exempt recipients.

27. The wealth-dispersing feature of the tax could be limited if the estate is bequeathed only to the immediate family, since close relations are taxed at lower rates under the inheritance tax. This drawback could be alleviated through careful design of the system, however.

28. The use of trusts basically presents two difficulties. Under an inheritance tax, the distribution of trust property, not the contribution or creation of the trust, is the taxable event. Since trusts can be structured to indefinitely postpone the distribution of the property, this can result in virtually unlimited tax deferral. This difficulty can be addressed by including a provision on property left in trust that would operate largely as a mechanism for prepayment of inheritance taxes on the ultimate distribution of this property. The second problem arises because most accessions tax proposals involve graduated rates that vary with the beneficiary's relationship to the decedent. This creates a difficulty in the case of remainderman trusts. Consider, for example, a woman who sets up property in a trust that will pay income to her sister for life with the remainder passing to her sister's son. The question becomes whether the son should be treated as if he inherited the property from his mother or from his aunt. Hence, one needs to decide whether the final inheritors should be taxed as if they received property from the original testator or the previous trustee.

# REFERENCES

Aaron, Henry J., and Harvey Galper. *Assessing Tax Reform.* Washington, D.C.: The Brookings Institution (1985).

Ando, Albert, and Arthur Kennickell. "How Much (or Little) Life Cycle Is There in Micro Data? Cases of U.S. and Japan." Paper presented at Instituto Bancario San Paolo di Torino Conference to Honor Franco Modigliani, at Martha's Vineyard, Massachusetts, (September 19–21, 1985).

Anrig, Greg, Jr. "How to Avoid Estate Taxes." *Money 14* (December 1985): 60–66.

Atkinson, Anthony B., and Joseph E. Stiglitz. *Lectures on Public Economics,* New York: McGrawHill Book Company, Inc. (1980).

Auster, Rolf. "Estate Planning Strategies After 1986." *Taxes 65* (February 1987): 116–123.

Barlow, Robin, H. E. Brazer, and J. N. Morgan. *Economic Behavior of the Affluent.* Washington, D.C.: The Brookings Institution (1966).

Barro, Robert J. "Are Government Bonds Net Wealth?" Journal of Political Economy 82:6 (November/December 1974): 1095–1117.

Barthold, Thomas A., and Takatoshi Ito. "Bequest Taxes and Accumulation of Household Wealth. U.S.-Japan Comparison." NBER Working Paper 3692. Cambridge, Massachusetts: National Bureau of Economic Research (1991).

Bentz, Mary F. "Estate Tax Returns, 1983." *Statistics of Income Bulletin 4*:2 (Fall 1984): 1–12.

Bernheim, B. Douglas. "Ricardian Equivalence: An Evaluation of Theory and Evidence," in Stanley Fischer, ed., *NBER Macroeconomics Annual 1987,* Cambridge, Massachusetts: The MIT Press (1987): 263–303.

Brittain, John A. *Inheritance and the Inequality of Material Wealth.* Washington, D.C.: The Brookings Institution (1978).

Cooper, George. *A Voluntary Tax? New Perspectives on Sophisticated Tax Avoidance.* Washington, D.C.: The Brookings Institution (1979).

Darby, Michael R. *Effects of Social Security on Income and the Capital Stock.* Washington, D.C.: American Enterprise Institute (1979).

David, Martin A., and Paul Menchik. "Distribution of Estates and Its Relationships to Intergenerational Transfers," in U.S. Department of the Treasury, Internal Revenue Service, Statistics of Income Division, *Statistics of Income and Related Administrative Record Research: 1982* (October 1982): 103–108.

Federal Reserve Board of Governors. Survey of Financial Characteristics of Consumers, Machine Readable Data (1962).

———. "Balance Sheets for the U.S. Economy" (April 1981).

———. Survey of Consumer Finances, Machine Readable Data (1983 and 1986).

————. "Balance Sheets for the U.S. Economy, 1945–1990." C.9 Release (April 1991).

Goldsmith, Raymond W. *The National Wealth of the United States in the Postwar Period.* National Bureau of Economic Research. Princeton, New Jersey: Princeton University Press (1962).

Graetz, Michael J. "To Praise the Estate Tax, Not to Bury It." *Yale Law Journal 93:*2 (1983).

Gutman, Harry L. "Reforming Federal Wealth Transfer Taxes After ERTA." *Virginia Law Review 69:*7 (October 1983): 1183–1272.

Johnson, Barry W. "Estate Tax Returns, 1986–1988." *Statistics of Income Bulletin 9:*4 (Spring 1990): 27–61.

Kotlikoff, Laurence J. "Intergenerational Transfers and Savings." *Journal of Economic Perspectives 2:*2 (Spring 1988): 41–58.

Kotlikoff, Laurence J., and Lawrence H. Summers. "The Role of Intergenerational Transfers in Aggregate Capital Accumulation." *Journal of Political Economy 89:*4 (August 1981): 706–732.

————. "The Contribution of Intergenerational Transfers to Total Wealth: A Reply." NBER Working Paper 1827. Cambridge, Massachusetts: National Bureau of Economic Research (1986).

Menchik, Paul, and Martin David. "Income Distribution, Lifetime Saving and Bequests." *The American Economic Review 73:*4 (September 1983): 672–690.

Modigliani, Franco. "Measuring the Contribution of Intergenerational Transfers to Total Wealth: Conceptual Issues and Empirical Findings." Paper presented at a seminar on Modeling the Accumulation and Distribution of Personal Wealth, in Paris France (September 1984).

————. "The Role of Intergenerational Transfers and Life-Cycle Saving in the Accumulation of Wealth." *Journal of Economic Perspectives 2:*2 (Spring 1988): 15–40.

Morgan, J. N., M. H. David, W. J. Cohen, and H. E. Brazer. *Income and Welfare in the United States.* New York: McGraw-Hill Book Company, Inc. (1962).

Munnell, Alicia H., with C. Nicole Ernsberger. "Wealth Transfer Taxation: The Relative Role for Estate and Income Taxes." *New England Economic Review* (November/December 1988): 3–28.

Musgrave, Richard A. "Death and Taxes," in Horst Hanusch, Karl W. Roskamp, and Jack Wiseman, eds., *Public Sector and Political Economy Today,* Stuttgart: Gustav Fischer Verlag (1985): 149–155.

Musgrave, Richard A., and Peggy B. Musgrave. *Public Finance in Theory and Practice,* 4th ed., New York: McGraw-Hill Book Company (1984).

Organisation for Economic Cooperation and Development. *Revenue Estimates of OECD Member Countries: 1965–1990.* Paris, France: OECD (1991).

Pechman, Joseph A., *Federal Tax Policy,* 5th ed. Washington, D.C.: The Brookings Institution (1987a).

————. "Inheritance Taxes," in John Eatwell, Murray Millgate, and Peter Newman, eds., *The New Palgrave: A Dictionary of Economics,* vol. 2, New York: The Stockton Press (1987b): 855–857.

Projector, Dorothy, and Gertude S. Weiss. *Survey of Financial Characteristics of Consumers.* Washington, D.C.: Board of Governors of the Federal Reserve System (1964).

Royal Commission on the Distribution of Income and Wealth. *Report No. 5, Third Report on the Standing Reference.* London, England: Her Majesty's Stationery Office (1977).

Surrey, Stanley S., Paul R. McDaniel, and Harry L. Gutman. *Federal Wealth Transfer Taxes: Cases and Materials,* 2nd ed., University Casebook Series, Mineola, New York: Foundation Press Inc. (1987).

Tobin, James. "Life Cycle Saving and Balanced Growth," in William Fellner et al., eds., *Ten Economic Studies in the Tradition of Irving Fisher,* New York: John Wiley and Sons, Inc. (1967): 231–256.

U.S. Department of the Treasury, Internal Revenue Service. "Estate Tax Statistics for 1989 and 1990." *Statistics of Income Bulletin 11:3* (Winter 1992): 63–70.

U.S. House of Representatives, Committee on Ways and Means. *Overview of Entitlement Programs, 1991 Green Book.* Washington, D.C.: Government Printing Office (1991).

Wolff, Edward N. "The Accumulation of Household Wealth Over the Life-Cycle: A Microdata Analysis." *Review of Income and Wealth,* Series 27, no. 1 (March 1981): 75–96.

————. "Trends in Aggregate Household Wealth in the U.S., 1900–1983." *Review of Income and Wealth,* Series 35 no. 1 (March 1989): 1–29.

Wolff, Edward N., and Marcia Marley. "Long-Term Trends in U.S. Wealth Inequality: Methodological Issues and Results," in R. E. Lipsey and H. Tice, eds., *The Measurement of Saving, Investment, and Wealth, Studies in Income and Wealth,* vol. 52, Chicago: University of Chicago Press (1989): 765–844.

## S E L E C T I O N     2 9

Charles T. Clotfelter and Philip J. Cook

# On the Economics of State Lotteries— Updated

The popularity of state lotteries in the United States has grown rapidly in recent years. In 1980, only fourteen states operated lotteries, and in 1985, seventeen states. However, today the number is well over thirty. Only North Dakota has failed to pass a lottery referendum in the past three decades. Public demand for lottery games is high, even though the odds of winning are extraordinarily low compared to private gambling ventures. State governments make money from lotteries in the same way any business makes profits—more is collected in sales (revenues) than is paid out in prizes and expenses (costs). Thus, although moral, tax-equity, and other concerns are often raised over state-sponsored gambling, state governments seem unable to resist the attractiveness of this "voluntary tax" on lottery winnings. Certainly, when budget crunches are the rule rather than the exception, the choice to finance government activities through a voter-supported lottery rather than an increase in sales or state-income taxes does not seem hard to understand.

In this selection, Charles Clotfelter and Philip Cook first summarize the historical experience of government-sponsored lotteries. The authors then focus on the demand for lottery products by the public. Clotfelter and Cook also examine elements of the supply of lotteries, explaining why multi-state lottery consortiums like "LottoAmerica" have formed. Because state lotteries seem to be guided by a single objective—to raise money for state treasuries—it is also not surprising that most states have made private lotteries illegal. As a government enterprise, the lottery agency can thus enjoy a near-monopoly position,

Clotfelter, Charles T., and Philip J. Cook. "On the Economics of State Lotteries." *Journal of Economic Perspectives 4* (Fall 1990): 105-119. This selection is an abridged version of the original article.

**Charles T. Clotfelter** and **Philip J. Cook** are both Professors of Public Policy Studies and Economics at Duke University. Professor Cook kindly updated the data in this reading for inclusion in this anthology.

competing essentially only with other state lotteries and earning monopoly-like economic profits.

### Questions to Guide the Reading

1. In general, how does the payout rate for lotteries compare to those for private forms of gambling? What is the evidence for "increasing returns to scale in the provision of lottery products"?
2. What changes have occurred in the lottery "product line" since the early 1970s?
3. Why may otherwise risk-averse individuals purchase lottery tickets with unfavorable odds?
4. How have marketing strategists attempted to make playing the lottery appealing to more segments of the population?
5. What socioeconomic characteristics are good predictors of who plays the lottery?
6. What evidence suggests that lottery products are not substitutes for each other?
7. Although taxes and lotteries both contribute to state treasuries, how do lottery sales differ from other types of "tax" collection?

State lotteries can be evaluated from either of two perspectives familiar to economists: as a consumer commodity or as a source of public revenue. As a commodity, the lottery is notable for its broad market penetration and rapid growth. Sixty percent of the adults in lottery states play at least once in a year. The annual growth in real per capita sales in lottery states has averaged over 9 percent, rising in 1994 dollars from $26 in 1975 to $140 in 1994. Lotteries account for a rather modest fraction of revenue in states that run them (less than 3 percent in most states),[1] but they are nonetheless one of the most visible state government activities. Lottery sales exceed those of all other products sold directly by state governments to the public and are larger than all but three major activities of state government: education, public welfare, and highways (Clotfelter and Cook 1989, Table 2.5).

Moreover, lotteries are a qualitatively new activity for state governments, in that they are a business operated, in effect, for profit. State liquor stores are perhaps the closest analog, but they were created to encourage temperate drinking practices and do not engage in the sales promotion and marketing activities that are characteristic of the lotteries.

Lotteries enjoy an honored place in American history as a device for raising funds for public purposes. Funding for such institutions as the Jamestown settlement, Harvard College, and the Continental Army, as well as hundreds of bridges, fire houses, and schools came from lotteries. But after the notorious Louisiana lottery of the post-Civil War era,[2] lotteries were prohibited by every state in this century until 1963, when New Hampshire adopted one. Thus, modern lotteries are a restoration of a device for exploiting the widespread interest in gambling at long odds for the sake of funding worthy activities. Since 1963, thirty-two states and the District of Columbia have created lotteries, and it is a good bet that other states will follow in the next few years.

This article examines several aspects of the economics of state lotteries, focusing primarily on the demand for lottery products. We begin by giving a descriptive overview. The succeeding sections examine the motivations for playing lottery games and evidence on the determinants of lottery demand. The final section considers the welfare economics of the apparent objective of lotteries—to maximize profits for the state.

## AN OVERVIEW OF STATE LOTTERY OPERATIONS

Table 1 provides summary information on the thirty-seven American state lotteries (including the District of Columbia) during 1994. Included in this table are the year the lottery began operation, total and per capita sales, and the distribution of revenues. Table 1 displays an interestingly high variation between states in sales per capita. For example, Massachusetts' per capita "profits" (net revenues) are double those of neighboring Connecticut and triple those of New Hampshire and Vermont, despite the fact that they all have well-established lotteries. These interstate differences suggest that tastes for lottery gambling differ widely across population groups.

The last three columns of Table 1 show how each state distributes its lottery revenues. On average, only 57 percent of all lottery revenues are returned in the form of prizes, a ratio that is much lower than that offered by other forms of commercial gambling such as bingo (75 percent), horseracing (79 percent), or casino gambling (96 percent) (*International Gambling and Wagering Business*, [August 1, 1995]: p. 1940). In 1994 the payout rate for lotteries ranged from a low of 47 percent in New York to a high of 68 percent in Massachusetts.[3] Operating expenses, which include the roughly 5 percent of sales paid as commissions to retail sales agents, average 11 percent of gross revenues. There is some evidence of increasing returns to scale. For example, the eleven biggest states with 1994 sales exceeding $1 billion had median costs of 10 percent while the twelve smallest, with sales less than $250 million, had median costs of 16 percent.[4]

The "profit" or net revenue remaining after prizes and operating expenses are deducted goes to the state treasury. These transfers can be thought of as implicit taxes levied on the purchase of lottery tickets. Expressed in a form comparable to excise tax rates these implicit taxes are extraordinarily high: the average profit rate of 32 percent (of gross revenues) is equivalent to an excise tax rate of 47 percent (of expenditures net of this tax).[5]

The product line offered by state lotteries today bears little resemblance to the games available in the early 1970s. As late as 1973, the only significant lottery

**Table 1** U.S. Lottery Sales and Distribution of Revenues

| State | Year Began | 1994 Sales (millions) | 1994 Sales per capita | Payout Prizes | Operation Costs | Net Revenue |
|---|---|---|---|---|---|---|
| Arizona | 1981 | $ 249 | $ 61 | 49% | 16% | 35% |
| California | 1985 | 1,931 | 61 | 50% | 16% | 34% |
| Colorado | 1983 | 287 | 79 | 59% | 15% | 26% |
| Connecticut | 1972 | 552 | 169 | 56% | 10% | 34% |
| Delaware | 1975 | 101 | 143 | 52% | 14% | 34% |
| District of Columbia | 1982 | 210 | 368 | 51% | 16% | 33% |
| Florida | 1988 | 2,208 | 158 | 52% | 10% | 38% |
| Georgia | 1994 | 1,127 | 160 | 51% | 16% | 33% |
| Idaho | 1989 | 72 | 64 | 57% | 21% | 22% |
| Illinois | 1974 | 1,529 | 130 | 56% | 8% | 36% |
| Indiana | 1989 | 575 | 100 | 58% | 13% | 29% |
| Iowa | 1985 | 207 | 73 | 57% | 15% | 28% |
| Kansas | 1988 | 152 | 60 | 52% | 16% | 32% |
| Kentucky | 1989 | 480 | 125 | 59% | 15% | 26% |
| Louisiana | 1991 | 350 | 143 | 50% | 14% | 36% |
| Maine | 1974 | 145 | 117 | 55% | 14% | 31% |
| Maryland | 1973 | 984 | 197 | 52% | 9% | 39% |
| Massachusetts | 1972 | 2,443 | 404 | 68% | 7% | 25% |
| Michigan | 1972 | 1,343 | 141 | 52% | 10% | 38% |
| Minnesota | 1990 | 331 | 72 | 58% | 24% | 18% |
| Missouri | 1986 | 351 | 67 | 54% | 15% | 31% |
| Montana | 1988 | 37 | 43 | 49% | 27% | 24% |
| Nebraska | 1994 | 53 | 33 | 51% | 21% | 28% |
| New Hampshire | 1964 | 120 | 106 | 48% | 20% | 32% |
| New Jersey | 1970 | 1,431 | 181 | 51% | 7% | 42% |
| New York | 1967 | 2,369 | 130 | 47% | 10% | 43% |
| Ohio | 1974 | 1,920 | 173 | 58% | 10% | 32% |
| Oregon* | 1985 | 2,499 | 810 | 85% | 7% | 8% |
| Pennsylvania | 1972 | 1,566 | 130 | 50% | 9% | 41% |
| Rhode Island* | 1974 | 196 | 197 | 56% | 15% | 29% |
| South Dakota* | 1988 | 478 | 663 | 63% | 23% | 14% |
| Texas | 1992 | 2,758 | 150 | 55% | 11% | 34% |
| Vermont | 1978 | 53 | 91 | 55% | 13% | 32% |
| Virginia | 1988 | 875 | 134 | 53% | 12% | 35% |
| Washington* | 1982 | 315 | 59 | 53% | 16% | 31% |
| West Virginia | 1986 | 185 | 102 | 64% | 13% | 23% |
| Wisconsin | 1988 | 496 | 98 | 55% | 12% | 33% |
| United States | | $30,978 | $140 | 57% | 11% | 32% |

*The state operates video lottery terminals, which offer a higher payout rate than other lottery games.
Sources: Gaming and Wagering Business 11 (February 15, 1990, 30); (May 15, 1990, 47); North American Gaming Report 1995, Supplement to International Gaming & Wagering Business (July 1, 1995). State populations for 1994 are from the Statistical Abstract; unpublished information obtained from state lottery agencies.

product was a sweepstakes game conducted in much the same way as colonial lotteries; it was essentially a raffle in which bettors bought tickets and waited days or weeks to see if their ticket was drawn. Today this old-fashioned game is virtually extinct, having been replaced by games with quicker payoffs, bigger prizes, and greater intrinsic "play value." The lotteries' first major innovation was the instant game ticket, offering players a chance to discover immediately if they had won a prize. The second new lottery product was a daily numbers game, a computerized imitation of the illegal game that has long been popular in many cities. Designed to appeal largely to this preexisting market, this game (like its illegal counterpart) lets players choose their own numbers, thus providing an opportunity to become actively involved in the gambling process.

The on-line computer network that supports the numbers game also made it possible to offer a third major lottery product in the early 1980s: lotto. This game features long odds and huge jackpots that build from one drawing to the next if there are no winners. One typical format is a 6/44 game, in which players select six out of 44 numbers, with a probability of 1 in 7.1 million of picking all six numbers correctly. With jackpots (typically stated as the undiscounted sum of 20 annual payments) reaching as high as $100 million, lotto has garnered enormous public interest. As shown in Table 1, most lottery states now offer all three of these games—instant, numbers, and lotto—and there is every indication that the states will continue to develop new products in the quest for increased sales. Oregon introduced sports betting in 1989, and a number of states are considering video game slot machines.[6]

## WHY PEOPLE PLAY

Setting aside its game-playing aspect for a moment, a lottery ticket is a sort of risky financial asset, offering a prospect of prizes in return for an investment of 50 cents or a dollar. Since the expected value of the prizes is typically only half the ticket price, the question naturally arises as to why so many adults consider this investment worthwhile. It is true that well-informed players who schedule their bets carefully can improve on the standard 50 percent payout rate. When a lotto jackpot grows sufficiently large through rollovers accumulating from a series of drawings in which no one wins, it may even be possible to place a favorable bet, that is, one with an expected return greater than the cost of the ticket (Thaler and Ziemba 1988; Chernoff 1981). But such occasions are rare indeed, and it is safe to say that normally this asset has no place in the portfolio of a prudent investor. Nonetheless, it has very broad appeal.

For some, playing the lottery is an amusing pastime, one that offers the modest pleasures of discovering whether an instant ticket is a winner or discussing lotto strategy with workmates. When players in California were asked whether they played the lottery more for fun or the money, the respondents were about evenly divided. However, of those with incomes below $30,000, 25 percent more respondents cited money than fun, while the reverse was true at upper incomes (*Los Angeles Times* Poll 1986). In addition to promoting the idea that it is fun to play, lotteries encourage people to think of playing as a public-spirited activity, with the proceeds going to support education or other public services, and that thought may indeed strengthen some citizens' motivation to play.[7] But surely, the hope of private gain is what sells the bulk of lottery tickets.

The challenge to the analyst is understanding why the risky prospects offered by lottery games appeal to people who exhibit some aversion to risk in other circumstances. As a simple example of risk aversion, it has been shown that most people, when given a choice between a 50 percent chance of receiving $1,000 and a sure thing of $400, prefer the latter (Kahneman and Tversky 1979) The propensity to gamble at unfavorable odds was the subject of the classic article by Milton Friedman and L. J. Savage (1948). They suggested that people may perceive a disproportionate benefit to a prize that is large enough to elevate their social standing, and may be willing to pay a premium for that sort of chance.

The Friedman-Savage explanation for why otherwise risk-averse people may buy unfavorable chances at large prizes is intuitively appealing. Among other things, it helps explain why lottery games with a relatively modest top prize appeal primarily to low-income players (for whom $500 may be enough to buy a quantum improvement in standard of living, at least temporarily), whereas games with comparatively large jackpots attract more middle-class players (Clotfelter and Cook 1987, 538).

A quite different line of explanation for why rational people would accept unfair bets at long odds is offered by the cognitive psychology literature. In the usual lotto format, the odds against hitting the jackpot are several million to one. Such probabilities are well beyond the realm of experience gained from playing the game, and as a result players cannot be expected to have much intuition about their chances. For example, someone who spends $20 per week on a 6/49 lotto game for his or her adult lifetime would have less than 1 in 200 chance of winning the jackpot. Faced with such a remote chance, people tend to assess the prospect on the basis of rough heuristics like what Tversky and Kahneman (1974) called "availability," defined as the ease with which instances of the event can be brought to mind. In the case of lotteries, the ability to visualize such instances is aided by the steady stream of winners, who are announced each week with considerable fanfare, and by the advertising of lottery agencies.

We documented how lottery advertising emphasizes the chance of winning big with a sample of over 151 television and radio ads from thirteen of the largest state lotteries. These ads included very little objective information on the probability of winning. Only 12 percent of our sample ads provided any information about the odds of winning, and none of them stated the probability of winning one of the large prizes. On the other hand the dollar amount of prizes were mentioned in fully half the ads, and in most cases the reference was to the largest prize.

These ads accentuated the possibility of winning. Out of the fifty-two television ads in the sample that portrayed a lottery player, two-thirds showed at least one person winning a prize. Some ads debunked pessimists who claimed it was unlikely to win big, or offered themes like: "Somebody's going to win. Why not you?" Such messages, implicit or explicit, help make the dream of wealth credible. By aiding "availability," such ads may tend to produce an exaggerated sense of the likelihood of winning. A gamble which is objectively unfair may thus be perceived as attractive by people who normally are averse to risk.

Tversky and Kahneman's explanation may appeal to economists because it preserves a view of the lottery player as an objective, albeit poorly informed, assessor of the risky prospect offered by a game. However, a more fundamental departure from the economist's expected utility framework may be necessary to explain the existence of an apparently profitable business of providing advice to players on how to choose their numbers. Although every possible play in numbers or lotto has the same chance of winning, many players are willing to pay for advice in the form of "dream books," consultations with astrologers, tabloids offering numerology columns, and computer software that facilitates the analysis of patterns in recent drawings of winning numbers. There is a common tendency to deny the operation of chance even in situations that are entirely chance-determined: an "illusion of control," to use psychologist Ellen Langer's term. She has demonstrated in several gambling experiments that this illusion is heightened if subjects are asked to make choices, even if their efforts have no effect on the probability of winning (Langer 1975, 1978). Thus the success of the lottery may in part reflect the widespread illusion that choosing winning numbers is partly a matter of skill.

## WHO PLAYS THE LOTTERY?

Most adults who live in lottery states have played the lottery at least once, but a small percentage of lottery customers are so active as to account for the bulk of all sales. In any given week about one-third of all adults play; over the course of a year participation broadens to encompass 60 percent of the adult public.[8] Among those who do play, the most active 10 percent of players account for 50 percent of the total amount wagered, while the top 20 percent wager about 65 percent of the total.

Interestingly, the degree of concentration among players (as indicated by these percentages) does not depend on the time interval under consideration.[9] This pattern of concentration of sales is typical of consumer products. One rule of thumb in marketing, the "law of the heavy half," holds that the top 20 percent of consumers of any commodity account for about 80 percent of total purchases.[10] Unless heavy players are appreciably less responsive to advertising than occasional players, this concentration implies that the "typical" (median) consumer is of little relevance in marketing the lottery, since it is the atypical, relatively heavy player who accounts for most of the sales. It appears that the primary instrument for converting moderate or inactive players into active players is product innovation, rather than advertising.

Socioeconomic patterns of lottery expenditures have received considerable attention from social scientists as well as lottery marketing directors. We obtained information on the characteristics of players from a number of sources, including several household surveys. Whether measured by participation rate, average expenditure, or the prevalence of heavy players, certain consistent generalizations emerged from our analysis of these sources. Men play somewhat more than women. Adults play more in their middle years than when young (18 to 25) or old (65 and over). Catholics play more than Protestants, approximately half again as much. And lottery play is systematically related to social class, although perhaps not always as strongly as the conventional wisdom would suggest in this regard.

The pattern is clear with respect to one indicator of social class: lottery play falls with formal education. For example, a survey in California found that the proportion of adults who participated during one week in July 1986 ranged from 49 percent for those with less than a high school education to 30 percent for those with a college degree. With respect to occupation, in the California survey lottery play was most common among laborers (including both skilled and unskilled) at 46 percent, and least among advanced professionals (25 percent). Retired people and students played least of all. With respect to race, survey evidence suggests that Hispanics in the west and blacks in the east play more than non-Hispanic whites.

Remarkably, the same sources of data do not demonstrate any consistent relationship between lottery play and household income over the broad middle range; the average expenditure in dollars for households making $10,000 is about the same as for those making $60,000. One implication of this pattern of demand is that the tax implicit in lottery finance is regressive, in the sense that as a percentage of income, tax payments decline as income increases.

It is interesting to note that even when all these socioeconomic factors are taken into account, there remain certain individuals who simply display a strong propensity toward gambling that is strongly predictive of lottery play. The most complete survey of gambling participation ever conducted in the United States was the National Study of Gambling, a national survey conducted in 1975 involving 1,735 respondents (Commission on the Review of the National Policy Toward Gambling 1976). Questions were asked concerning participation in all forms of commercial gambling, both legal and illegal. For the respondents from lottery states, lottery participation was twice as high among gamblers as among those who did not participate in other commercial gambling (74 percent as opposed to 36 percent), and that association remained strong in a multivariate analysis.

However, the majority of lottery players were not otherwise involved in commercial gambling, and would not have been in the absence of the lottery. For example, a person with the socioeconomic characteristics associated with a 27 percent likelihood of participating in some form of commercial gambling if living in a non-lottery state had a participation probability of 52 percent in a lottery state. In sum, the lottery has an especially strong appeal to established gamblers, but it also recruits many people who would not otherwise become involved in commercial gambling.

## THE EFFECT OF CHANGING PRICES AND PAYOFFS

An appropriate definition of price is not obvious in the case of lottery products because there is no single best definition of quantity. One reasonable definition of the quantity unit is "one dollar's worth of expected prize value." Price would then be the cost of buying that unit, or the reciprocal of the payout rate. Consider, for example, the straight three-digit numbers game, in which the probability of winning is 1 in 1,000. Most states pay off at a rate of 500 to 1, for an average pay-out rate of 50 percent and a price, by this definition, of $2.00. In Massachusetts, which is unique in paying 700 to 1 on a straight three-digit bet in its numbers game, the price would be $1.43. Although quantities of different lottery games cannot be added together—one "unit" of the numbers game cannot be added to one "unit" of lotto to get a meaningful total—total expenditures may be.

It would be surprising indeed if a reduction in price (an increase in the payout rate) did not increase expenditures somewhat. One common pattern of lottery play is for players to "reinvest" small prizes in additional tickets (Clotfelter and Cook 1989, 111), which virtually ensures an expenditure increase from a hike in the payout rate, even if players' evaluation of the game does not change.[11] If it is true that total expenditures are stimulated by an increase in the payout rate, then by definition the demand for lottery products is elastic. But knowing that would not be sufficient for a lottery designer who requires assurance that an increase in the payout rate will increase the lottery's profitability, a result that would require under current payout rates a price elasticity greater than 2 in absolute value.[12]

This issue cannot be resolved with available data, simply because payout rates over time and across states are too uniform to create the necessary contrast. For example, as of 1986 numbers games in all states except for Massachusetts offered a payout rate of 50 percent. Lotto exhibits slightly more interstate variation in pay-out rates, but it also differs across states in format and the size of the betting pool, which may also influence sales and make specifying a demand equation difficult. Our regression analyses suggested that sales were quite sensitive to price, but the coefficient estimate was not very stable with respect to alternative specifications for cross-section data on states.[13]

Much more clear-cut is the evidence that lotto sales are responsive to rollovers in the jackpot. Under typical lotto rules, if a drawing fails to produce a winner the money in that jackpot is "rolled over" to the subsequent drawing. If several con-secutive drawings produce no winners, the jackpot continues to accumulate and the expected value of a bet grows accordingly.[14] This form of price reduction stim-ulates sales.[15] We estimate an equation using data on 170 consecutive drawings in the Massachusetts lotto game, covering the period from July 18, 1984 to March 1, 1986. For each thousand dollars of "rollover" added to the jackpot, we estimated an increase of sales of $418, with a standard error of $19.[16] The stimulus to betting is insufficient in this case to make it worthwhile for the state to augment the jack-pot "artificially," in the absence of a rollover.

There is also intriguing evidence on the cross-price elasticity of demand for closely related lottery products. Although each number in the numbers game has the same probability of winning, some players choosing the numbers do not view them as perfect substitutes. They see some numbers as "luckier" than others; 777 and 333 are perennial favorites. In most states, there is a fixed payout (500 to 1), so that every number has the same price. But a few states calculate payoffs on a pari-mutuel basis, so that popular numbers have a lower payout and higher price than unpopular numbers. A comparison of patterns of play in two states suggests that players are responsive to differences in price for specific numbers. In Maryland, where numbers have equal payout rates, players concentrate their bets on popular numbers. Players in the pari-mutuel state of New Jersey, on the other hand, tend to spread their bets out, placing fewer bets on the most popular numbers and more on the least popular numbers.

## ARE LOTTERY PRODUCTS SUBSTITUTES FOR EACH OTHER OR OTHER GAMES?

Most lotteries added lotto to their existing product line during the 1980s, and in the majority of states it soon became the sales leader. It is natural to suppose that lotto sales would to some extent come at the expense of reducing the sales of the numbers and instant games.[17] But surprisingly, the evidence indicates that the sales of existing game have not been hurt by the introduction of lotto. We compared the average growth rates in sales for numbers and instant games during the two-year periods before and after the introduction of lotto for a sample of thirteen states. In only four states did the growth rate decrease, as would be expected if lotto were a substitute for the other games. The growth rate of the other games *increased* in the other nine states.

Another type of evidence supports this conclusion, too. Lotto sales tend to vary widely from drawing to drawing, depending on the size of the jackpot (as determined by the rollovers from previous drawings). If lotto were a substitute for other games, then the run-up in lotto sales when there is a large jackpot would depress sales of other games. An analysis of Massachusetts numbers sales data for 85 consecutive weeks was conducted to test for this possibility; it revealed that the size of the lotto jackpot, which had an enormous effect on lotto sales, had *no* discernible effect on sales of the numbers game. The additional betting on lotto was "new" money.

It would be of great interest to know whether this result extends to illegal gambling, and especially the illegal numbers games of which the state numbers games are a direct imitation. Not surprisingly, there is no reliable evidence on the illegal game's profitability or sales, although it has clearly survived the introduction of the legal game. Whatever their effect on the illegal numbers game, we do know that the state lotteries have greatly broadened participation in commercial gambling, legal and illegal included.

## THE PECULIAR ECONOMIES OF SCALE OF LOTTO

For the game of lotto, bigger is better. Small states appear to be unable to mount a lotto game that attracts much public interest because the jackpots are inevitably small compared to the multimillion-dollar bonanzas generated in California and New York. As a result, multistate lottery consortiums have formed to offer a lotto game that, by combining the populations of several small states, rivals the games of the largest states. The first such consortium was the Tri-State (Maine, New Hampshire, and Vermont). The second was LottoAmerica, initiated in 1988, with the District of Columbia and five widely scattered states with a combined population of about 12 million.

Lotto is a game with peculiar economies of scale. It is a pari-mutuel game, with the jackpot set equal to a percentage of the amount bet (typically about 25 percent). If a drawing has no jackpot winner, the money in that jackpot rolls over into the jackpot for the next drawing. When several players win, the jackpot is divided among them. The reason that the population base is important to lotto sales, but not sales of other lottery games, hinges on the role of the jackpot in attracting lotto action. An example may help explain how this works.

Suppose state A has an adult population of 10 million and state B has only 100,000. Given equally attractive games, we assume that lotto purchases in both states will average $1 per capita at each drawing. In state A the initial jackpot is then worth $2.5 million, compared with only $25,000 in state B. If both states set the probability of winning at 1 in 100,000 with the average price per winner the same in both states, then state A will have an average of 100 winners while state B will have one winner. Given these rules, the games in the two states do not appear to differ much. However, state A has the option of reducing the probability of winning to, say, 1 in 10 million, in which case each state has only one winner on the average.

Under these rules, state A offers one hundred times the jackpot of state B and only 1 percent of state B's probability of winning. For reasons discussed above, most players prefer state A's game to state B's. The prize in state A is the stuff that dreams are made of, and in case anyone is not paying attention, the lottery agency will focus its advertising on the magnitude of this jackpot. Yet the offsetting large difference in probabilities between the two states has little influence on potential players. As long as most drawings produce a winner, the prospect of winning will be credible in both states.

## THE GOVERNMENT'S BUSINESS

As they are presently constituted, state lotteries are guided by one objective: to raise as much revenue as possible for state treasuries. This objective is sometimes stated explicitly in state law and often in the annual reports of lottery agencies and in state government studies.[18] It is also evident in the lotteries' high price (implied by the 50 percent average payout rate) and the vigorous style of marketing. By focusing on net revenue, the lotteries are behaving as if the public are shareholders in this state enterprise, and hence that the "bottom line" is a valid guide to the public interest.[19]

However, the normative perspective guiding this revenue maximization objective is incomplete. It ignores the fact that the lottery is a commodity as well as a revenue source. This fact opens the door to a consideration of alternative objectives for government. If the commodity were seen as a more or less harmless form of entertainment, reducing the markup over cost would be welfare-enhancing. Alternatively, the government might believe that lottery games are harmful, perhaps creating negative externalities for nonplayers. After all, gambling has long been viewed as a vice that justifies public concern and government regulation. In that case, high prices would be justified as a means for discouraging consumption, either on efficiency grounds, to reflect negative externalities, or on sumptuary grounds, to signal society's disapproval.

However, two aspects of existing lotteries make it very clear that revenue maximization, and not a desire to curtail consumption, motivate the high price of lotteries. First, the percentage of lottery sales going to the state treasury exceeds the comparable tax rates on alcoholic beverages and on cigarettes, both of which are more harmful commodities by any metric. Although we lack the necessary knowledge about parameters of demand to apply formulas of optimal taxation, it seems very likely that the implicit tax rate on lottery purchases is too high relative to taxes on other commodities.[20] The high price/low payout strategy may serve the public well in their role as "stockholders," but it shortchanges the majority of the public in their dual role as consumers.

The other reason the sumptuary pricing argument fails to explain lottery prices becomes obvious when one examines the second important characteristic of supply—the active marketing of the product. The agencies seek to recruit new players by improving distribution networks and offering coupons and tie-in sales to encourage novices to try playing. To increase sales to regular players they have increased the frequency of drawings, offered some bets on a subscription basis, and (in one state) packaged instant game tickets together in groups of five. Advertising, publicity, and product innovations boost sales by recruiting new players and increasing the activity of existing players. In short, the lottery agencies are clearly *not* interested in discouraging sales of their products. The low payout rate is motivated by revenue rather than sumptuary concerns.

A lottery could be operated in other ways. A state could license one or more private firms to take the place of its lottery agency. This would allow the state to distance itself from the promotion of gambling, but it would also lessen the state's control over operations, which to date has been effective in keeping the games free of corruption. Furthermore, the lottery agencies could increase payout rates to levels typical of other forms of commercial gambling, increasing consumer surplus at the expense of state revenue collections. Another option would be to require lottery agencies to disclose more information on the probability distribution of prizes, and to be more candid in characterizing the value of jackpots paid out in the form of annuities. Restrictions on advertising, of the sort currently in effect in Virginia and Wisconsin, could be adopted in other states.[21] However, states appear to have little enthusiasm for making any major changes in what has become a popular and profitable formula for raising revenue.

# NOTES

The authors are grateful to the National Bureau of Economic Research and Duke University for research support and to Henry Aaron and the editors of *Journal of Economic Perspectives* for helpful comments.

1. See Table I of Szakmary and Szakmary (1995). They report the ratio of net lottery revenue to general state revenue for each lottery state in 1992. This ratio exceeded 3 percent in Maryland, Ohio, and Florida. The average over all thirty-three states was 1.5 percent.

2. From 1878 until 1894, the Louisiana Lottery Company offered the only legal game in the country. Most of its sales were to residents of other states, where lotteries were outlawed. In response to increasing demands for federal intervention, Congress enacted a series of restrictions on the use of the mails to conduct lotteries, and finally in 1895 barred all lottery activity in interstate commerce. The Lottery Company earned its reputation of corruption by routinely bribing Louisiana legislators to continue its monopoly charter in the state.

3. Oregon has a payout rate of 85 percent, but this rate is not comparable to most of the other states. Much of Oregon's revenues comes from video lottery terminals, which offer a much higher payout rate than other lottery games.

4. The ten states in between have a median cost of 13.5 percent. In making these calculations we exclude the four states that make heavy use of video lottery terminals.

5. These figures refer to implicit tax rates and do not relate to the administrative costs of lottery finance. Some have suggested that lotteries are an especially inefficient form of taxation since it "costs," say, 11 cents to raise 32 cents, which is much higher than the ratio of administrative costs per dollar of revenue raised for most taxes. This comparison is flawed because the 11 cents per dollar of operating costs for lotteries pays for the provision of a product, not just the collection of revenue. The lottery is not simply a tax.

6. South Dakota has such devices in place as lottery outlets. Its video lottery terminals offer an electronic version of poker and several other games. West Virginia lottery has recently introduced video keno at racetracks.

7. A marketing strategist for one of the largest lottery suppliers, Scientific Games, Inc., argued that the Colorado Lottery's decision to earmark revenues for parks and recreation made it possible to sell tickets to many citizens who would otherwise not have played. See "Scientific Games Lures Lifestyles," *American Demographics 8* (October 1986): 26–27.

8. Personal communication from Irving Piliavin, estimated from a national telephone survey conducted by the University of Wisconsin Letters & Science Survey Center between June and August, 1989 ($n = 733$). Results from this survey also show that 20 percent of adults living in states without a lottery played at least once in the preceding year, yielding an overall national participation rate of 47.5 percent.

9. The figures cited are based on *Los Angeles Times* Poll 104, March 1986. Measures of concentration are virtually identical for three surveys that asked respondents to report lottery expenditures for some period preceding the interview: a one-week period (Maryland, 1984), a two-month period (California, 1985), and a twelve-month period (all lottery states combined, 1974). For a discussion of these surveys, see Clotfelter and Cook (1989).

10. This is also referred to as Pareto's law of the "80/20 rule." See Buell (1986, 8–10).

11. This behavior could be understood as an effort by players to limit their net expenditures on lottery products, staying within a self-imposed budget that allocated a certain amount to lottery play each week.

12. Let $C(Q)$ represent operating costs as a function of quantity units, where one quantity unit is defined as one dollar in expected value of prizes. The lottery agency's net profits are given by $N = PQ - Q - C(Q)$, where $P$ is the price charged for a quantity unit. The first-order condition for profit maximization can be written

$$-E_{PQ} = P(1 - C')/[P(1 - C') - 1].$$

If marginal operating costs are 6 percent of sales and the payout rate is 50 percent, we have $P = 2$ and $C' = 0.12$, implying that the price elasticity of demand at maximum profit is $-2.3$. For an increase in the payout rate to increase profits, $E_{PQ}$ must exceed 2.3 in absolute value.

13. Log-linear equations were estimated for per capita numbers and lotto sales, where independent variables were population, income, percent black, percent urban, and payout rate. The estimated elasticities of sales with respect to the payout rate (with $t$-statistics in parentheses) were 3.05 (0.7) for numbers and 2.55 (2.3) for lotto. The equations were estimated with 15 and 16 observations, respectively. For the complete equations, see Clotfelter and Cook (1989, Table A.4).

14. If players play randomly, it can be shown that the expected value of a lotto bet increases monotonically with the total amount bet, assuming there is no rollover in the jackpot. The expected value of a lotto bet for a given number of bettors is of course increased if a rollover is added to the pot. Thus the addition of a rollover to the jackpot increases the jackpot both directly, by increasing the available prize money, and indirectly, by attracting more action which also increases the amount of available prize money.

15. The prospect offered by a lotto bet when the jackpot has been augmented by rollovers is qualitatively different from when there are no rollovers; the probability of winning remains the same, but the probability distribution for the amount won (which depends on the number of other winners, since the jackpot is divided among them) is transformed by the increase in the number of players. Thus, strictly speaking, the difference between a lotto drawing with and without rollovers present is not just a difference in "price," as we have defined that term. But the qualitative difference in the two products is slight enough that we believe our regression results can sustain the interpretation offered above.

16. We extended the analysis to take account of the fact that the rollover generates more action and hence a still larger jackpot than the rollover itself would produce. In this "rational expectations" formulation, each $1,000 of increase in predicted jackpot size increases play by $333 (S.E. = $15) (Cook and Clotfelter 1989).

17. This intuition follows from the presumption that players will view lotto as a substitute for other lottery games. Alternatively, a transactions cost argument suggests one basis for complementarity. The introduction of lotto broadens participation in the lottery, and some of these new bettors may not limit themselves to lotto tickets when they make a lottery purchase.

18. Of course, this objective is constrained in various ways. In some states the enabling legislation specifies revenue as the primary objective subject to preservation of "the dignity of the state" (Arizona), "the general welfare of the people" (Michigan), or "the public good" (West Virginia). Every state bans sales to minors, and two states have placed limits on the content of advertising.

19. This bottom line ignores the fact that lottery expenditures affect other sources of tax revenues. Clotfelter and Cook (1989, Chap 11, App.) offer a general equilibrium model suggesting that the lottery reduces other tax collections by a few percentage points. More important is the question of how lottery promotion affects the public's propensity to work, save, invest, and otherwise engage in productive economic activity. If the image of easy wealth undermines productive activity, the effect on public revenues over the long run could be considerable.

20. The optimal excise tax rate on a commodity depends on its price elasticity, whether it produces externalities, and the distribution of its consumption over income. Ignoring externalities and distribution, the efficient assignment of excise tax rates require minimization of deadweight loss by taxing those items with elastic demand less heavily than those with inelastic demand. If it is indeed true that the price elasticity of demand for lottery tickets exceeds one in absolute value, as argued above, then lottery taxation generates proportionately greater deadweight loss than taxation of items with inelastic demand. One natural comparison is between the implicit tax rates on lottery products to excise tax rates on alcohol and tobacco. The implicit lottery tax rate in the U.S. exceeds the others, yet on the basis of externality and distributional considerations, and perhaps price elasticity as well, lotteries should probably be taxed less rather than more heavily relative to those elasticity as well, lotteries should probably be taxed less rather than more heavily relative to those commodities. For a discussion of this point, see Clotfelter and Cook (1987).

21. For a discussion of alternative models of lottery operations, see Clotfelter and Cook (1990).

# REFERENCES

Buell, Victor P., ed. *Handbook of Modern Marketing* 2nd ed. New York: McGraw-Hill (1986).

Chernoff, Herman. "How to Beat the Massachusetts Numbers Game: An Application of Some Basic Ideas in Probability and Statistics." *Mathematical Intelligencer 3* (1981): 166–172.

Clotfelter, Charles T., and Philip J. Cook. "Implicit Taxation in Lottery Finance." *National Tax Journal 40* (December 1987): 533–546.

————. *Selling Hope: State Lotteries in America.* National Bureau of Economic Research Monograph. Cambridge: Harvard University Press (1989).

————. "Redefining 'Success' in the State Lottery Business." *Journal of Policy Analysis and Management 9* (Winter 1990): 99–104.

Commission on the Review of the National Policy toward Gambling. *Gambling in America.* Washington, D.C.: Government Printing Office (1976).

Cook, Philip J., and Charles T. Clotfelter. "The Economics of Lotto." Duke University (1989).

Friedman, M., and L. J. Savage. "The Utility Analysis of Choices Involving Risk." *Journal of Political Economy 56* (August 1948): 279–304.

Kahneman, Daniel, and Amos Tversky. "Prospect Theory: An Analysis of Decision Under Risk." *Econometrica 47* (March 1979): 263–291.

Langer, Ellen J. "The Illusion of Control." *Journal of Personality and Social Psychology 32* (1975): 311–328.

———. "The Psychology of Chance." *Journal for the Theory of Social Behavior 7* (1978): 185–207.

*Los Angeles Times*. Poll 104 (March 1986).

Szakmary, Andrew C., and Carol Matheny Szakmary. "State Lotteries as a Source of Revenue: A Reexamination." *Southern Economics Journal 61* (1995): 1176–1177.

Thaler, Richard H., and William T. Ziemba. "Anomalies: Pari-mutuel Betting Markets: Racetracks and Lotteries." *Journal of Economic Perspectives 2* (Spring 1988): 161–174.

Tversky, Amos, and Daniel Kahneman. "Judgment Under Uncertainty: Heuristics and Biases." *Science 185* (1974): 1124–1131.

![SELECTION 30]

Alan J. Auerbach, Jagadeesh Gokhale, and Laurence J. Kotlikoff

# Generational Accounting: A Meaningful Way to Evaluate Fiscal Policy

The U.S. federal government has operated in deficit since 1970. Not surprisingly, the increasingly higher levels of national debt (sum total of all budget deficits) have not escaped attention. Voters are concerned about the impact of government deficits on their standard of living—both today and in the future. Heated debates continue in Washington over the federal budget. Beneath the public rhetoric are fundamental economic questions such as what impact current deficits have on future generations, whether government borrowing reduces capital formation, and whether debt-financing is equivalent to taxation. But essential to answering these and related questions is: How should the deficit be measured? No consensus exists among economists or politicians—even the Congressional Budget Office (CBO) reports three different measures, a "standardized employment" deficit, an "on budget" deficit, as well as an "official" deficit.

In this selection, Alan Auerbach, Jagadeesh Gokhale, and Laurence Kotlikoff introduce and demonstrate generational accounting, a novel, comprehensive approach to public-budget measurement. Generational accounting provides a systematic way to address the question of the burden of the national debt on today's and future generations. Based on a given set of fiscal policies, this technique attempts to value the different amounts current and future generations pay in taxes, net of transfers, to

..........................................................................

Auerbach, Alan J., Jagadeesh Gokhale, and Laurence J. Kotlikoff. "Generational Accounting: A Meaningful Way to Evaluate Fiscal Policy." *Journal of Economic Perspectives* 8 (Winter 1994): 73-94. This selection is an abridged version of the original article.

**Alan J. Auerbach** is Professor of Economics and Law, and Robert D. Burch Professor of Tax Policy and Public Finance at the University of California at Berkeley. **Jagadeesh Gokhale** is Economic Advisor at the Federal Reserve Bank of Cleveland. **Laurence J. Kotlikoff** is Professor of Economics at Boston University and Research Associate at the National Bureau of Economic Research.

the government. This amount is termed the "generational account" or "lifetime net payment." Since the measurement is calculated over a lifetime, generational burdens of alternative government fiscal policies can be compared. The authors find that the lifetime net payments of each generation have risen steadily during this century. And specifically, if U.S. fiscal policy remains unchanged, future generations will pay a much higher share of their incomes to the government than today's generations—possibly 71 percent of their projected lifetime earnings. Auerbach and his colleagues also illustrate how this new budget tool can be applied to analyze changes in particular public policies such as Social Security payroll taxes.*

## Questions to Guide the Reading
1. How does the choice of labeling government receipts and expenditures influence the value of a particular deficit measure?
2. Why are current deficit measures inadequate tools to use in evaluating alternative fiscal policies? In general, how do generational accounts differ from current deficit measures?
3. How does the government's intertemporal budget constraint reflect the zero sum nature of fiscal policy? What is the implication of a reduction in a generation's "account"?
4. Why are the net payments (in Tables 1 and 2) negative for older individuals? Why do differences exist between male and female generational accounts?
5. Why might generational accounting be superior to deficit accounting? Specifically, what policy implications might be missed if deficit accounting were relied upon to evaluate alternative tax reforms?
6. What changes in public policy could correct the current intergenerational imbalance, in order to bring about "generational equity"? How might lifetime net tax rates contribute to a policy debate concerning the fiscal burden of future generations?

How large should the federal budget deficit be? Any economist or policymaker seeking to answer this question is immediately confronted with a range of questions about how to measure the deficit. Should the deficit be measured including or excluding Social Security's cashflow surpluses? Should it include all or part of the recent savings and loan bailout? Should it be adjusted for growth, inflation,

*Editors' note: Generational accounting, however, is not without its critics. A good summary of the concerns about this method can be found in Robert Haveman's companion article (see Suggested Further Readings). The response to Haveman by Auerbach, Gokhale, and Kotlikoff is found at the end of the unabridged version of their original article.

and the state of the economy? Should the deficit be measured net of government investment? Should the deficit include changes in the unfunded liabilities of Medicare, Social Security, and the civil service and the military retirement systems? The answers one gives to these and the plethora of similar questions make all the difference in the world to the measured size of the deficit.

For want of agreement on the "correct" way to measure the deficit, the Congressional Budget Office now routinely offers the public a menu of deficits from which to choose. Take fiscal year 1992. For that year, the CBO reported that the "official" deficit, as measured for Congressional budget purposes, was $290 billion (CBO 1993, Table 2-1). But it also reported that the "on-budget" deficit, which excludes the large surplus of the social security system and the small deficit of the postal service, was $340 billion. The CBO also offered a "standardized employment" deficit, which was only $201 billion, as well as a $292 billion deficit that excluded the net payments received to help finance Operation Desert Storm as well as those made to bolster the nation's deposit insurance system. These alternative deficit measures differ not only in their magnitudes (the difference between the largest and smallest equals 2.3 percent of GDP), but also in their time-trends. For example, the difference between the standardized employment deficit and the official deficit is projected to narrow considerably by fiscal year 1998, while the difference between the official and on-budget deficits is projected to grow considerably, as the annual surpluses of the social security system rise.

Which deficit is the right one, and to which deficit trend should we pay attention? No consensus exists among economists, and for good reason. Economic theory suggests that the deficit is not a well-defined economic concept, but rather an arbitrary number whose value depends on how the government chooses to label its receipts and payments (Kotlikoff 1986, 1992, 1993; Auerbach and Kotlikoff 1987).

To understand the arbitrary nature of any particular deficit measure, consider how the U.S. government might characterize $1.00 that it "borrows" from a citizen this year, through the sale of a one-year Treasury bill, and the $1.03 of "principal plus interest" that it gives the citizen next year, through the payment of principal plus interest on the T-bill. One way to relabel these transactions is to say that the government is "taxing" the citizen $1.00 this year and making a "transfer payment" of $1.03 to the citizen next year. Another way is for the government to say that it is, this year, "borrowing" $5.00 from the citizen as well as "transferring" $4.00 to the citizen and that next year it is " repaying principal plus interest" of $5.15 to the citizen as well as levying a " tax" on the citizen of $4.12.

There are countless ways of labeling the government's extraction of $1.00 from this citizen this year and its giving the citizen $1.03 next year. The reported deficit can be wildly different, although the citizen is in exactly the same economic position. This ambiguity applies to every dollar the government takes in, whether labeled " taxes" or "borrowing," and every dollar the government distributes, whether described as "transfer payments" or "repayment of principal plus interest."[1] In short, it is *impossible* to measure the debt and the change in the debt—the deficit—in a way which carries a useful underlying economic meaning.

Even were there agreement about which deficit measure were "correct," such a measure would still be of limited use in understanding fiscal policy for two reasons. First, fiscal policy is dynamic and cannot be described by a short-term measure that entirely ignores the likely course of future policy. Second, a single deficit measure cannot identify the intergenerational distribution of the burden of government finance at any given time. Without dealing with these issues it is impossible to evaluate the impact of fiscal policy on the aggregate economy or identify how the burden of fiscal policy is distributed across individuals—supposedly the major questions the deficit is supposed to help us address.

To make an assessment of generational fiscal burdens that is independent of the words the government uses to label its receipts and payments, we have developed "generational accounting" (Auerbach, Gokhale, and Kotlikoff 1991). Generational accounts indicate, in present value, what the typical member of each generation can expect to pay, now and in the future, in net taxes (taxes paid net of transfer payments received). Generational accounting indicates not only what existing generations will pay, but also what future generations must pay, given current policy and the government's intertemporal budget constraint. This constraint requires that those government bills not paid by current generations must ultimately be paid by future generations.

This paper first describes the method of generational accounting, and provides some limited analysis of its sensitivity to economic assumptions. It offers some representative applications of this new tool to proposed Social Security and budget policies. . . .

## UNDERSTANDING GENERATIONAL ACCOUNTS

The government's intertemporal budget constraint at each date requires that the subsequent net tax payments of current and future generations be sufficient, in present value, to cover the present value of future government consumption, as well as pay off the government's initial net indebtedness (net of initial government assets). Failure to satisfy this constraint means that the government will default on its liabilities, in essence satisfying the constraint through a tax on its creditors. A common, but incorrect, interpretation of this constraint is that it implies that the national debt will be paid off. In fact, the only requirement is that the debt be serviced through payments by existing and future generations. The way in which generational accounts—the present value of the remaining lifetime net tax payments of current generations as well as the entire lifetime net tax payments of future generations—enter into the government's intertemporal budget constraint can be expressed by a simple equation.[2]

| present value of remaining net tax payments of existing generations | + | present value of net tax payments of future generations | = | present value of all future government consumption | − | government net wealth |
|---|---|---|---|---|---|---|

This equation indicated the zero sum nature of fiscal policy, when it is properly viewed from an intergenerational perspective. Holding the present value of government consumption fixed, a reduction in the present value of net taxes extracted from current generations (a decline in the first term in the equation) necessitates an increase in the present value of net tax payments of future generations. The equation also demonstrates that we cannot determine the fiscal burden being imposed on future generations without knowing the future path of government purchases and the generational accounts of those currently alive, which depend on the net taxes to be paid by these generations. Hence, it is impossible to assess the stance of generational policy without making assumptions about the paths of these future variables.

A set of generational accounts is simply a set of values, one for each existing and future generation, with the property that their combined present value adds up to the present value of government consumption less initial government wealth.[3] The same principles can be extended to distinguish male and female cohorts within each generation, which we have done in our work to date, and to distinguish among other demographic characteristics as well as lifetime income levels. Don Fullerton and Diane Lim Rogers (1993) have recently made some progress toward such intragenerational accounting.

Since generational accounts reflect only net taxes paid to the government (taxes less transfers received), they do not impute to particular generations the value of the government purchases of goods and services made to provide them with education, highways, national defense, and other services.[4] Therefore, they do not show the full net benefit or burden that any generation receives from government policy as a whole, although they can show a generation's net benefit or burden from a particular policy change that affects only taxes and transfers.

Note that any reduction in a generation's "account" expands its remaining lifetime budget constraint, thereby permitting it to engage in more consumption.[5] This, then, is the channel by which redistributing across generations can lower national saving. Policies that lower the accounts of current generations (necessitating increases in the accounts of future current generations) will stimulate current consumption.[6] Armed with cohort-specific propensities to consume, one can estimate how changes in fiscal policy will alter each generation's and, thus, aggregate consumption by multiplying the generation's propensity to consume by the change in its generational account, as shown in Auerbach, Gokhale, and Kotlikoff (1992b).

## CONSTRUCTING GENERATIONAL ACCOUNTS

The methodology and data sources used in calculating generational accounts are discussed in detail in Auerbach et al. (1991) and OMB (1993). We summarize that discussion here.

The basic approach to calculating generational accounts proceeds as follows. Based on projections of current tax and transfer plans, we calculate generational accounts for the current generation, the first term in the left-hand side of the equation in the text. This requires projections of the population by age and sex, and projections of average taxes and transfers for each generation in each year in which at least some member of the generation will be alive. For population, we use the Social Security Trustees' 1992 intermediate (alternative II) projections of population by age and sex through 2066 and extend these projections beyond 2066 using the fertility, mortality, and immigration probabilities projected to prevail in 2066.

Our projections of average future taxes and transfers by age and sex are based on current and projected values of National Income and Product Accounts (NIPA) totals of all federal, state, and local taxes and transfers. These projections incorporate the Social Security Trustee's long-term forecasts of social security total contributions and benefit payments, the Health Care Financing Administration's long-term forecasts of spending on Medicare and Medicaid, and OMB's long-term forecasts of federal taxes and transfer payments other than those of Social Security, Medicare, and Medicaid. Beyond the period in which these government long-term forecasts are available, we assume that particular tax and transfer aggregates grow to keep pace with demographics and productivity growth. The current and projected future NIPA tax and transfer totals are distributed to generations, as defined by age and sex, based on corresponding distributions in cross-section survey data. These surveys include the Survey of Income and Program Participation, the Survey of Consumer Expenditures, and the Current Population Survey.

The second task is to calculate the present value of future government consumption. Federal purchases of goods and services through 2004 are taken from OMB's 1992 Mid-Session Review extended beyond 1997 and updated for the actual fiscal year 1992 results. State and local purchases through 2004 are kept at the same ratio to GDP as in 1991. Federal, state, and local purchases after 2004 were divided between those made on behalf of specific age groups, the young, middle-aged, and elderly (such as educational expenditures), and those that are more nearly pure public goods (such as defense and public safety). Purchases per person in each of the three age groups, and purchases of public goods per capita, increase at the assumed rate of productivity growth.[7]

For making present value calculations in each of these cases, we need to decide on an appropriate discount rate. Future government receipts and expenditures are risky, which suggest that they be discounted by a rate higher than the real rate of interest on government securities. On the other hand, government receipts and expenditures appear to be less volatile than the real return on capital, which suggests that they be discounted by a lower rate than that. The baseline calculations assume a 6 percent real discount rate, which is roughly halfway between the real historical returns on government bonds and private sector capital.

For the second term on the right-hand side, we need an estimate of the initial stock of government net wealth. Our measure of government wealth should, in principle, equal all government assets less liabilities. In practice, we include only government net financial wealth.[8] Our estimate of government net debt (the negative of government net wealth) for 1992 is formed by adding together annual National Income Account deficits (federal, state, and local) from 1900 through 1991.

With the present value of net taxes of current generations, the present value of government spending, and an estimate of government wealth in place, we can then calculate the total collective net tax payment required of future generations, expressed as a present value. Given this total, we determine the average lifetime net tax payment of each member of each future generation under the assumption that the average lifetime net tax payment of successive generations rises at the economy's rate of productivity growth.[9]

Perhaps the easiest way to evaluate the burden faced by the typical future generation is to compare it to the lifetime net tax payments of current newborns. The generational accounts of both newborns and future generations take into account net tax payments over these generations' entire lifetimes; the only difference is the growth adjustment just mentioned. Of course, one could make many alternate assumptions about the tax payments of future generations. But while considering alternatives is a useful purpose of generational accounting, it makes sense to begin by calculating the intergenerational imbalance of present fiscal policy.

## BASELINE GENERATIONAL ACCOUNTS

Tables 1 and 2 present generational accounts as of 1991 (reprinted from OMB 1993, Tables F-1 and F-2) for every fifth generation of males and females alive in that year. The calculations assume a real discount rate of 6 percent and a real productivity growth rate of 0.75 percent per year, and that no policy changes will affect the fiscal burdens of generations currently alive.

The first column of each table, labeled "net payment," is the difference between the present value of taxes that a member of each generation will pay, on average, over his or her remaining life and the present value of the transfers he or she will receive. The second column shows the average present values of the different federal, state, and local taxes; this includes labor income taxes, capital income taxes, payroll taxes, and excise taxes. The final column gives the values of the corresponding transfers, which includes Social Security, disability, health, and welfare transfers. As an example, take the case of 30-year-old males. On average, the 1991 cohort of 30-year-old males will pay $205,500 to the government over the course of their remaining lives. This figure reflects the difference between the $258,500 present value of payments to the government and the $53,000 present value of transfers. The largest source of payments (in present value) is payroll taxes ($89,800), followed by income taxes ($80,400), excise taxes (which include state sales taxes and total $48,500) and capital income taxes ($39,900). For this same cohort, health-related transfers (including Medicare) are the single largest transfer category, followed by social security and welfare programs (such as AFDC).

The present value of the future taxes to be paid by the young and middle-aged generations exceeds the present value of the future transfers they will receive. The

**Table 1**  The Composition of Male Generational Accounts
(present values in thousands of dollars)

| Generation's Age in 1991 | Net Payments | Tax Payments | Transfer Receipts |
|---|---|---|---|
| 0 | 78.9 | 99.3 | 20.4 |
| 5 | 99.7 | 133.2 | 33.5 |
| 10 | 125.0 | 155.3 | 30.3 |
| 15 | 157.2 | 195.0 | 37.8 |
| 20 | 187.1 | 229.6 | 42.5 |
| 25 | 204.0 | 251.9 | 47.9 |
| 30 | 205.5 | 258.5 | 53.0 |
| 35 | 198.8 | 259.1 | 60.3 |
| 40 | 180.1 | 250.0 | 69.9 |
| 45 | 145.1 | 227.2 | 82.1 |
| 50 | 97.2 | 193.8 | 96.6 |
| 55 | 38.9 | 153.1 | 114.2 |
| 60 | −23.0 | 112.1 | 135.1 |
| 65 | −74.0 | 76.8 | 150.8 |
| 70 | −80.7 | 56.3 | 137.0 |
| 75 | −75.5 | 41.5 | 117.0 |
| 80 | −61.1 | 30.2 | 91.3 |
| 85 | −47.2 | 23.2 | 70.4 |
| 90 | −3.5 | 8.8 | 12.3 |
| | | | |
| Future Generations | 166.5 | | |
| Percentage difference | 111.1 | | |

present value of net payments peaks at age 30 for males and age 25 for females. These amounts are large because these generations are approaching their peak tax-paying years, but still relatively far from the reduced net payments that occur during retirement (when income subject to tax falls and transfer payments increase). For newborn males and females, on the other hand, the present value of the net payment is much smaller, $78,900 and $39,500 respectively, because they will not pay much in taxes for a number of years.

The differences in male and female generational accounts reflect differences in labor force participation, family structure, and mortality. For example, older women are projected to receive a greater present value of health-related transfers because they will live longer, on average.

As a group, older generations, both male and female, will receive more Social Security, Medicare, and other future benefits than they will pay in future taxes. However, one must remember that the figures in these tables show the *remaining* lifetime net payments of particular generations, and do not include the taxes a generation paid or the transfers it received in the past. Males who are now 65, for example, paid considerable taxes when they were younger, and these past taxes are not included in the remaining lifetime net payments shown in their generational accounts. Therefore, the remaining lifetime net payment by one existing

**Table 2** The Composition of Female Generational Accounts
(present values in thousands of dollars)

| Generation's Age in 1991 | Net Payments | Tax Payments | Transfer Receipts |
|---|---|---|---|
| 0 | 39.5 | 62.6 | 23.1 |
| 5 | 48.7 | 77.4 | 28.7 |
| 10 | 59.4 | 94.6 | 35.2 |
| 15 | 72.4 | 115.7 | 43.3 |
| 20 | 84.0 | 133.3 | 49.3 |
| 25 | 86.4 | 139.8 | 53.4 |
| 30 | 81.1 | 138.5 | 57.4 |
| 35 | 71.9 | 136.0 | 64.1 |
| 40 | 55.3 | 129.2 | 73.9 |
| 45 | 29.5 | 117.2 | 87.7 |
| 50 | −2.2 | 101.3 | 103.5 |
| 55 | −39.5 | 84.2 | 123.7 |
| 60 | −80.8 | 66.8 | 147.6 |
| 65 | −112.5 | 51.3 | 163.8 |
| 70 | −110.6 | 40.4 | 151.0 |
| 75 | −100.6 | 30.3 | 130.9 |
| 80 | −83.3 | 21.2 | 104.5 |
| 85 | −65.6 | 13.7 | 79.3 |
| 90 | −9.8 | 2.0 | 11.8 |
| Future Generations | 83.4 | | |

generation cannot be directly compared with that of another. Such a comparison requires a different methodology, and will be discussed in a later section.

These calculations can also show the amount future generations of males and females will have to pay to balance the government's budget constraint, assuming that subsequent generations pay this same amount except for an adjustment for growth. These amounts come out to $166,500 for men and $83,400 for women, which represents an increase of 111.1 percent over the burden faced by current newborns, who have been assumed to face current tax and transfer rules. This imbalance is striking in its magnitude. Of course, making more optimistic assumptions about discount rates and productivity can reduce the size of this gap. But even assuming a discount rate of just 3 percent and a productivity growth rate of 1.25 percent, future generations will still have to pay 65 percent more than current newborns (OMB 1993, Table F-3). Thus, the evidence for significant generational imbalance in U.S. fiscal policy is quite robust.

## APPLICATIONS OF GENERATIONAL ACCOUNTING

The superiority of generational accounting over deficit accounting is immediately clear when one compares the effects of particular policies on deficits and generational accounts. Policies that change the pattern of generational burdens need not affect the deficit, while other policies may change the deficit without affecting the pattern of generational burdens. Our purpose here is to show the advantages of generational accounting in examining fiscal and intergenerational consequences of alternate policies; to use generational accounting as a reminder of the necessity of specifying the future consequences of current policy changes; and to see how generational accounting can be used to design policies that can achieve an equitable intergenerational distribution of the burden of paying for the government's bills.

## Three Hypothetical Policies

To begin, consider three hypothetical policies which shift the fiscal burden, at least to some extent, to young and future generations. The first policy is a five-year, 20 percent reduction in the average federal income tax rate, with the tax rate increased above its initial value after five years to maintain a constant debt-to-GNP ratio. The second policy is an immediate and permanent 20 percent increase in Social Security benefits, financed on a pay-as-you-go basis by increases in payroll taxes. The third policy involves an equal revenue switch in tax structure—a permanent 30 percent cut in payroll taxes financed by increased sales taxes.

Notice that only the first policy of cutting taxes now and raising them in the future affects the budget deficit. The other two policies are "revenue-neutral" in the standard budgetary sense. Thus, if an analyst is using the budget deficit as the measure of intergenerational tax burdens and fiscal policy, the first policy would be seen as a stimulus and something that imposes additional burdens on future generations, while the second and third policies would appear to have no impact at all.

A generational accounting approach offers a much more informative analysis. Given the assumptions used earlier, the temporary 20 percent income tax cut benefits all generations over age 25 while burdening those younger. The greatest benefit accrues to those currently about age 55, while the greatest burden lands on those currently age 15–20. Although the second policy of a pay-as-you-go increase in Social Security benefits has no effect on the deficit, as typically measured, it has more pronounced generational implications: old men and old and middle-aged women gain substantially from this policy; young and future generations, especially men, lose. The third policy of switching from payroll to sales and excise taxes also leaves the deficit unchanged over time, but results in young and middle-aged men *gaining* at the expense of older male and all female generations. This pattern of redistribution arises because the ratio of male to female payroll tax payments is much higher than their ratio of indirect tax payments. Hence, compared to females, payroll tax reduction benefits males, especially younger ones, relatively more than increases in sales and excise taxes hurts them.

Without a correct assessment of such generational effects, it is also impossible to evaluate the macroeconomic effects of these policies. Consider again the 20 percent increase in Social Security benefits that leaves the deficit unchanged because payroll taxes are increased simultaneously. Given evidence that the marginal propensity to consume out of remaining lifetime resources rises with age (Auerbach et al. 1992a), this policy will raise the consumption of the elderly by a larger amount than it reduces the consumption of the young and middle-aged.[10] However, if the deficit is used as a measure of economic stimulus, the analyst would mistakenly conclude that this policy has no impact on aggregate consumption demand.

Along with failing as a guide to changes in consumption, the deficit also fails to help us understand how fiscal policies affect national saving, and through this channel, changes in capital-labor ratios and factor prices (wages and real interest rates). As discussed in Auerbach and Kotlikoff (1987), understanding changes in factor prices is important for assessing fully the intergenerational incidence of fiscal policy. Hence, knowing how generational accounts change in response to policy is essential to understanding not only the direct generational welfare effects of government policy, but also the indirect effects associated with factor price changes.

## The Moynihan Proposal

One lesson of generational accounting is that any short-term policy changes also require a long-term policy adjustment. Take, for example, Senator Daniel Patrick Moynihan's proposal to cut payroll taxes in the short term by 30 percent, and thus to avoid building up a surplus in the Social Security trust fund.[11] Generational accounting emphasizes that any such proposal for tax cuts must ultimately be paid for, and it forces the analyst to state how the government's intertemporal budget constraint would be satisfied.

Consider three ways of paying for Moynihan's proposal. The first alternative is that specified in the Senator's proposal, namely raising payroll taxes after 2020 to levels above those that would otherwise have prevailed. The second is cutting Social Security benefits after 2020. The third is making up the shortfall in payroll tax revenue by immediately raising income tax rates. A generational accounting analysis shows that cutting Social Security taxes until the year 2020 and increasing them thereafter benefits all except the very young and future generations of both sexes. Cutting benefits, rather than increasing taxes, after 2020 produces the same pattern of gains and losses. However, in this second approach, the gains of middle-aged generations are not as large as under the first policy: these generations pay no payroll taxes when old under the first policy and, hence, escape the future hikes in payroll tax rates under that policy. However, they do suffer reduced benefits under the second policy. Under the second policy, because the gains of working generations are not as large as under the first policy, the losses of future generations are also lower. The third option—a switch from payroll to income taxation—produces large losses for older generations while providing moderate gains for young and future generations. Unlike payroll taxation, income taxation contains an element of capital income taxation which falls relatively more heavily on older generations—the major asset-owners in the economy.

## Generational Accounting as a Guide to Generational Equity

Generational equity is an ethical concern, and our choice of any particular norm for purposes of illustration is not meant to impose this norm as our preferred ethical judgment. Rather, we simply choose a norm we think is of general interest: namely, that generations born in the future should not pay a higher share of their lifetime incomes to the government than today's newborns. In the U.S. context, satisfying this norm—equalizing the lifetime net tax rate of today's and tomorrow's children—requires the elimination of the current fiscal policy's 111 percent imbalance in growth-adjusted generational accounts.

There are many possible ways of making this adjustment, of course. One method would be to raise, immediately and permanently, all taxes at all levels of government by 11.7 percent. The second way is to reduce, immediately and permanently, all transfer payments made by all levels of government by 24.9 percent. Both policies would lead to an equalization, on a growth-adjusted basis, of the generational accounts of current newborns and future generations. But the two policies are significantly different in other respects.

Increasing all taxes by 11.7 percent will impose especially heavy sacrifices on young and working-aged generations. In contrast, a policy of reducing all transfer payments by 24.9 percent will place heavy burdens on older generations. In fact, older females suffer relatively more from reductions in transfer payments because of their relatively lower mortality and because they earn Social Security and health benefits based on their spouses' greater earnings in the past. In either approach, however, current adult generations would have to make a considerable sacrifice to keep their children and/or future generations from bearing much higher burdens than they themselves must bear. According to our preliminary calculations, such sacrifices are about three times as large as those called for by President Clinton's first budget, enacted in August 1993—and Clinton's budget passed by only a single vote in both the House and the Senate. The political prospects for far greater sacrifices do not appear great.

## RETROSPECTIVE CALCULATIONS: LIFETIME TAX RATES

The analysis so far has considered only the present value of future taxes and transfers. This sort of prospective analysis can compare a generation's account before and after a policy change, and it can compare the lifetime fiscal burdens of the newly born and future generations, because their entire lifetimes are in the future. However, it cannot directly compare the generational accounts of one existing generation with that of another—say the generation born in 1940 with the generation born in 1960—because prospective analysis does not take into account the taxes and transfer payments all living generations have paid and received in the past.

Making comparisons of the lifetime net tax treatment of existing generations requires retrospective calculations that combine past taxes and transfers with the remaining generational accounts for these generations. Tables 3 (aggregate) and 4 (for males and females separately) show the results of such "lifetime" generational accounts for different generations born since 1900, expressed in terms of lifetime net tax rates, defined as the generation's account at birth divided by the present value, also evaluated at birth, of its lifetime labor income.[12] As described in OMB (1993), the lifetime net tax rates in the table are calculated using historical data on estimates of actual taxes paid and transfers received by age and sex in the years 1900 through 1992, along with the projections for 1993 and subsequent years of taxes paid and transfers received by age and sex that are used to form the generational accounts presented above.

Looking first at Table 3, we observe that generations born in 1900 bore, on average, a lifetime net tax rate of about 22 percent. This rate has edged up gradually, but steadily, for generations born in subsequent years. Under baseline policy, today's newborn generations will bear lifetime net tax rates of just under 34 percent. But, as we already have learned, baseline policy is clearly unsustainable, leaving an enormous fiscal burden to be paid by future generations—equal to 71 percent of their projected lifetime labor income!

As Table 4 indicates, the lifetime net tax rate for males in the base case exhibits a strong upward trend. The rate for females started much higher than for males (35 percent versus 18 percent), but then declined until 1950. Since 1950, the net tax rate has been about the same for males and females. This pattern is attributable to the increasing labor force participation of women and the fact that many taxes paid by the household (such as sales taxes) are attributed according to consumption rather than income. The lower female earnings thus contribute to a higher female tax rate, especially on those born during the early decades of this century.

Tables 3 and 4 also show the gross tax and transfer rates, whose difference equals the net tax rate. This breakdown reveals the expansion of government

**Table 3** Lifetime Tax Rates (average for males and females)

| Year | Net Tax Rate | Tax Rate | Transfer Rate |
|------|------|------|------|
| 1900 | 21.5 | 24.8 | 3.3 |
| 1910 | 24.7 | 29.8 | 5.2 |
| 1920 | 26.3 | 32.5 | 6.2 |
| 1930 | 28.1 | 35.3 | 7.2 |
| 1940 | 29.3 | 37.3 | 8.0 |
| 1950 | 30.6 | 39.9 | 9.3 |
| 1960 | 32.1 | 42.3 | 10.2 |
| 1970 | 33.2 | 44.5 | 11.3 |
| 1980 | 33.8 | 45.5 | 11.7 |
| 1990 | 33.6 | 45.7 | 12.2 |
| 1991 | 33.5 | 45.8 | 12.2 |
| Future Generations | 71.1 | | |

Topic of Interest: Generational Accounts

**Table 4** Lifetime Tax Rates

| Year | Males | | | Females | | |
|------|----------|-----|----------|----------|-----|----------|
| | **Net Tax Rate** | **Tax Rate** | **Transfer Rate** | **Net Tax Rate** | **Tax Rate** | **Transfer Rate** |
| 1900 | 17.8 | 19.6 | 1.8 | 35.3 | 43.9 | 8.7 |
| 1910 | 21.8 | 24.6 | 2.8 | 35.7 | 49.6 | 13.9 |
| 1920 | 24.2 | 27.7 | 3.5 | 34.0 | 50.4 | 16.5 |
| 1930 | 26.4 | 30.5 | 4.1 | 34.4 | 52.8 | 18.5 |
| 1940 | 28.2 | 33.0 | 4.8 | 32.7 | 50.6 | 17.9 |
| 1950 | 30.6 | 36.8 | 6.2 | 30.6 | 46.9 | 16.3 |
| 1960 | 32.3 | 39.6 | 7.2 | 31.5 | 47.9 | 16.4 |
| 1970 | 33.6 | 41.7 | 8.1 | 32.5 | 50.3 | 17.8 |
| 1980 | 34.1 | 42.4 | 8.3 | 33.1 | 51.6 | 18.5 |
| 1990 | 33.9 | 42.7 | 8.7 | 32.9 | 52.0 | 19.1 |
| 1991 | 33.9 | 42.7 | 8.8 | 32.8 | 52.0 | 19.2 |
| Future Generations | 71.5 | – | – | 69.3 | | |

transfer payments during the past century. It also shows that the similarity between males and females in lifetime net tax rates masks very different gross tax and transfer rates. Each rate is much higher for females, which reflects females' lower lifetime earnings (which lowers the denominators of the tax and transfer rates) and greater longevity (which increases females' lifetime transfer payments).

\* \* \*

## CONCLUSION

Generational accounting represents a new and comprehensive method of long-term fiscal planning. Unlike the budget deficit, generational accounting is not an arbitrary accounting construct. Rather it is a prescription, based on economic theory, for how to assess the generational burden and macroeconomic effects of fiscal policy. While improvements in the methodology remain to be made, generational accounting is now routinely being used by the U.S. government. It is also being used or developed by the governments of several other countries, including Japan, Italy, and Norway.

Generational accounting describes not only the burdens that fiscal policy places on different generations, but also the changes in policy needed to alter the distribution of such burdens. In the case of U.S. fiscal policy, achieving the goal of stabilizing lifetime tax rates of future generations of Americans will require a much more significant sacrifice by current generations than politicians seem to realize. As long as our politicians rely on deficit accounting, they are likely not to recognize the extremely serious consequences of their delay in addressing the current generational imbalance in U.S. fiscal. policy.

# NOTES

This paper draws from our other work, including Auerbach, Gokhale, and Kotlikoff (1991, 1992a, 1992b), Auerbach et al. (1993), Kotlikoff (1992), and from Office of Management and Budget (1993). We thank Robert Kilpatrick, Bruce Baker, Barry Anderson, and other economists at OMB for their collaboration. We are very grateful to Mr. Lawrence Benenson for funding research on generational accounting. Auerbach also acknowledges the support of the National Science Foundation (grant #SES9022707), and the Edward Netter Research Fund.

1. This statement may be true even in the context of liquidity constraints once one takes into account the endogenous determination of the liquidity constraints. Hayashi (1987) and Kotlikoff (1993) discuss this point.

2. For those more comfortable seeing such relationships expressed in algebraic form:

$$\sum_{s=0}^{D} N_{t,t-s} + \sum_{s=1}^{\infty} N_{t,t+s} = \sum_{s=t}^{\infty} G_s(1+r)^{t-s} - W_t^g$$

The term $N_{t,k}$ stands for the account of the generation born in year $k$. The index $s$ in the first summation runs from age 0 to age $D$, the maximum length of life. Hence, the first element of this summation is $N_{t,t}$, which is the present value of net payments of the generation born in year $t$; the last term is $N_{t,t-D}$, the present value of remaining net payments of the oldest generation alive in year $t$, namely those born in year $t - D$. The second summation starts with the term $N_{t,t+1}$ the present value in year $t$ of the payments of the generation born in year $t + 1$. The values of government consumption in year $s$, given by $G_s$, are discounted by the pretax real interest rate, $r$. The remaining term on the right-hand side, $W_t^g$ denotes the government's net wealth in year $t$.

3. A set of generational accounts is simply a set of values $N_{t,k}$, defined by:

$$N_{t,k} = \sum_{s = \max(t,\, k)}^{k+D} T_{s,k} P_{s,k} (1+r)^{t-s}$$

In this expression, $T_{s,k}$ stands for the projected average net tax payment to the government made in year $s$ by a member of the generation born in year $k$. The term $P_{s,k}$ stands for the number of surviving members of the cohort in year $s$ who were born in year $k$. For generations who are born prior to year $t$, the summation begins in year $t$. For generations who are born in year $k$, where $k > t$, the summation begins in year $k$. Regardless of the generation's year of birth, the discounting is always back to year $t$.

4. Imputations appear feasible for certain types of government purchases, such as for primary school education, and they could be included in future improvements of generational accounts.

5. The lifetime budget constraint of each generation specifies that the present value of its consumption must equal its current net wealth, plus the present value of its human wealth, plus the present value of its net private intergenerational transfers, less the present value of its net payments to the government, its generational account (its $N_{t,t}$). For

the generation born in year $k$ the year $t$ remaining lifetime budget constraint is given by:

$$\sum_{s=t}^{k+D} [C_{s,k} + I_{s,k}] P_{s,k}(1 + r)^{t-s} = W_{t,k} + \sum_{s=t}^{k+D} E_{s,k} P_{s,k}(1 + r)^{t-s} - N_{t,k}$$

In this equation, the terms $C_{s,k}$, $I_{s,k}$, and $E_{s,k}$ stand, respectively, for the average values in years of consumption, private net intergenerational transfers, and labor earnings of the generation born in year $k$. The term $W_{p,k}^{t}$ stands for the year $t$ net wealth of the generation born in year $k$.

6. This assumes that current generations do not offset such government intergenerational redistribution through changes in private intergenerational transfers. As Altonji, Hayashi, and Kotlikoff (1992) show, there is no evidence in U.S. data to support the intergenerational altruism needed for such a result.

7. To date we have not attempted to measure the value of existing government capital, such as highways, nor have we added the imputed rent on this measure of government consumption spending. However, the omission of such adjustments has little impact on our assessment of the imbalance in the net taxation of current and future generations. If we value the capital at the present value of its imputed rent, these two adjustments to the right-hand side of the equation in the text would cancel. For example, our exclusion of Yellowstone National Park from initial government assets is offset by our exclusion of the park's implicit rent from future government purchases.

8. As just mentioned in the previous footnote, this omission is not as serious as it may at first appear.

9. In our calculations, "generation" refers to sex-specific birth cohorts.

10. Note that by the zero-sum nature of intergenerational redistribution, the increase in resources to the current elderly exceeds the reduction in resources to the current young and middle-aged with the difference equal to the reduction in resources of future generations. Hence, even if the elderly had the same (rather than a larger) propensity to consume as the young and middle-aged, there would be an increase in aggregate consumption.

11. Statement of Senator Daniel Patrick Moynihan on the Social Security Tax Cut Act of 1991, released January 14, 1991.

12. Since lifetime taxes, transfers, and income have trended upward and have fluctuated to some extent, it is more appropriate to compare the relative fiscal burden on different generations in terms of lifetime net tax rates rather than in terms of absolute amounts.

## REFERENCES

Altonji, Joseph, Fumio Hayashi, and Laurence J. Kotlikoff. "Is the Extended Family Altruistically Linked? Direct Tests Using Microdata." *American Economic Review 82*:5 (December 1992): 1177–1198.

Auerbach, Alan J., and Laurence J. Kotlikoff. *Dynamic Fiscal Policy.* Cambridge: Cambridge University Press (1987).

Auerbach, Alan J., Jagadeesh Gokhale, and Laurence J. Kotlikoff. "Generational Accounts: A Meaningful Alternative to Deficit Accounting," in D. Bradford, ed., *Tax Policy and the Economy,* vol. 5, Cambridge: MIT Press (1991): 55–110.

————. "Generational Accounting: A New Approach to Understanding the Effects of Fiscal Policy on Saving." *Scandinavian Journal of Economics* 94:2 (June 1992a): 303–318.

————. "Social Security and Medicaid Policy from the Perspective of Generational Accounting," in J. Poterba, ed., *Tax Policy and the Economy* vol. 6. Cambridge: MIT Press (June 1992b): 129–145.

Auerbach, Alan J., Jagadeesh Gokhale, Laurence J. Kotlikoff, and Erling Steigum, Jr. "Generational Accounting in Norway: Is Norway Overconsuming Its Petroleum Wealth?" mimeo, Boston University (1993).

Congressional Budget Office. *The Economic and Budget Outlook: Fiscal Years 1994–1998* (January 1993).

Fullerton, Don, and Diane Lim Rogers. *Who Bears the Lifetime Tax Burden?* Washington, D.C.: Brookings Institution (1993).

Hayashi, Fumio. "Tests for Liquidity Constraints: A Critical Survey and Some New Observations," in Truman F. Bewley ed., *Advances in Econometrics, Fifth World Congress,* vol. 2, Cambridge: Cambridge University Press (1987).

Kotlikoff, Laurence J. "Deficit Delusion." *The Public Interest 84* (Summer 1986): 53–65.

————. *Generational Accounting—Knowing Who Pays, and When, for What We Spend.* New York: Free Press (1992).

————. "From Deficit Delusion to the Fiscal Balance Rule—Looking for a Sensible Way to Measure Fiscal Policy." *Journal of Economics,* Supplement 7 (1993): 17–41.

Office of Management and Budget. *Budget Baselines, Historical Data, and Alternatives for the Future* (January 1993): Appendix, ch. F.

# S E L E C T I O N   3 1

Wallace E. Oates

# An Economic Approach to Federalism

The United States is said to have a federal form of government because it is composed of a central government, state governments, and local governments. Fiscal federalism refers to the partition of taxation and expenditure functions among the various levels of government. A multilevel governing system creates some interesting and important questions. How do decisions made at one level impact governments at other levels? What are the benefits and costs of a system in which households and businesses can choose among subnational governments with alternative tax and expenditure policies? What are the potential organizational benefits of fiscal federalism—or more simply, is some bureaucracy useful?

Taken from his classic book *Fiscal Federalism,* the focus of this selection by Wallace Oates is on the question: which functions of government can best be performed at each level? Oates compares centralized, decentralized, and federal forms of government. Some believe that local governments perform the economic functions of the public sector most efficiently, while others assert that state or national governments have the advantage. In reality, Oates argues, it is more likely that each level of government has a comparative advantage in performing certain governmental functions.

### Questions to Guide the Reading
1. According to Oates, why is a centralized government better suited to addressing the problem of economic stabilization?
2. What limits the effectiveness of local poverty or income redistribution programs?
3. What types of goods and services would tend to be underproduced by local governments? Why?

..........
Oates, Wallace E. "An Economic Approach to Federalism," in *Fiscal Federalism,* New York: Harcourt Brace Jovanovich, Inc. (1972), 3-20. This selection is an abridged version of the original article.

**Wallace E. Oates** is Professor of Economics at University of Maryland and Fellow at Resources for the Future.

4. What are possible economic advantages of decentralization to local citizens?
5. How does Oates's economic definition of federalism differ from the meaning given to "federalism" by political scientists?

---

*The federal system was created with the intention of combining the different advantages which result from the magnitude and the littleness of nations.*

— Alexis de Tocqueville, *Democracy in America*

The functions of the public sector are to ensure an efficient use of resources, to establish an equitable distribution of income, and to maintain the economy at high levels of employment with reasonable price stability. The concern in this chapter is the organization of the public sector that will best allow the government to perform these tasks. In short, the question is, What form of government promises the greatest success in resolving the allocation, distribution, and stabilization problems? To get at this issue, it is useful to consider at a conceptual level two polar or nearly polar forms of government. At one end of the spectrum is complete centralization: a unitary form of government. In this case, the central government, in the absence of other levels of government, assumes full responsibility for the three economic functions of the public sector. As we move in the opposite direction on this spectrum of governmental forms, we approach total decentralization of government. For my purposes, it is useful to stop a bit short of total decentralization, which would presumably represent a state of anarchy. Rather, let us consider as our opposite extreme a highly decentralized system in which the central government is almost completely devoid of economic responsibility. In this instance, a system of small local governments performs virtually all the economic tasks of the public sector. In both cases, however, the society under consideration is understood to be a nation with a single currency and with an absence of restrictions on the movements of goods and services within the system. The sole difference in the two cases is the extent of decentralization of the public sector.

While these cases, especially the latter, are admittedly highly unrealistic (and this in a way is the point), it is instructive to consider briefly the relative economic advantages of the two alternatives. From such an examination, a powerful economic case for federalism emerges.

## THE ECONOMIC CASE FOR CENTRALIZED GOVERNMENT

An examination of the stabilization problem suggests that a centralized, or unitary, form of government would possess a far greater capability to maintain high levels of employment with stable prices than would a public sector characterized by extreme decentralization. At the outset, it is obvious that there must exist a central agency to control the size of the money supply. If, in contrast, each level of government was able to create and destroy money, there would exist an irresistible incentive to rapid monetary expansion. By simply using a printing press, any local government could create paper with which to purchase real goods and services from neighboring communities. It would clearly be in the interest of each municipality to finance its expenditures by creating money rather than by burdening its own constituents with taxation. The likely outcome would be rampant price inflation; for this reason, some form of centralized monetary control is imperative.

Without access to monetary policy, local governments would have to rely on fiscal policy—that is, expenditure and revenue programs—to stabilize their respective economies. The scope, however, for an efficacious fiscal policy is severely limited. First, small local economies are, in general, highly open economies, as their constituents typically purchase a large portion of the goods and services they consume from other localities. This implies that the leakages from a marginal dollar of private spending are likely to be quite large. As a result, in a simple Keynesian system, the expenditure multiplier (that is, the reciprocal of the sum of the marginal propensity to save and the marginal propensity to import out of income) will tend to be quite small. Much of the expansionary impact of a local tax cut, for example, will be dissipated, since only a relatively small proportion of the new income generated will be spent on locally produced goods and services.

* * *

Second, the use of Keynesian deficit-finance policies to stimulate the local economy carries with it a cost to local residents, a cost that is largely absent for such policies at the national level. The cost stems from the nature of local government debt. Within a national economy, there normally exists a high degree of mobility of financial capital; debt issued in one community is generally held to a large extent by residents of other communities. This means, as Alvin Hansen and Harvey Perloff have pointed out, that the use of debt finance by a local government will tend to saddle the community with an external debt.[1] In later years, repayment of principal and interest will necessitate a transfer of real income from the residents of the community to outsiders. In contrast, since the international mobility of capital is normally far less than that which exists within a nation, interest-bearing debt issued by the central government will take the form primarily of an internal debt. The central government is thus in a position to stimulate the economy without burdening society with the prospect of future income transfers to outsiders.

The logic therefore suggests that, as regards the stabilization problem, a unitary form of government is distinctly superior to a government organization exhibiting an extreme degree of decentralization. A central government is in a position to make good use both of monetary and of fiscal policy in maintaining the economy at high levels of output without excessive inflation. Local governments, in contrast, are seriously constrained in their capacity to regulate the aggregate level of economic activity in their jurisdictions. Moreover, it should be stressed that, among a highly interdependent group of local economies, movements in levels of business activity tend to parallel one another. Contractions or booms in some areas are rapidly communicated to neighboring areas through a contracted or increased demand for exports. This means that cyclical movements in aggregate economic activity are largely national in scope and as such can best be treated by countercyclical policies operating on a nationwide scale.

As in the case of the stabilization problem, the resolution of the distribution problem is a difficult matter in a system characterized by a high degree of decentralization of the public sector. Suppose that the members of society desire a more egalitarian distribution of income than that which emerges from the unfettered operation of the market system. Assume, moreover, that the socially desired distribution of income is one in which the disposable income of each individual or family depends only on the unit's level of income before any redistributive taxes and transfers. The idea here is simply that the desired distribution of income requires the transfer of certain amounts of income from the wealthy to the poor, and the tax paid, or, alternatively, the subsidy received, by a particular individual depends solely on his level of income. In this case, the program required to achieve society's desired pattern of income distribution is clearly a negative income tax. The existing distribution of income can be translated into the desired one by adopting a certain tax-subsidy schedule by which higher-income units pay taxes that are distributed in the prescribed pattern to lower-income units.

The difficulty is that within the highly decentralized fiscal system, local governments working independently to achieve differing redistributional objectives are likely to run into real trouble. Consider, for example, a community that adopts a strong negative income-tax program designed to achieve a significantly more equalitarian distribution of income than exists in the rest of the nation. Such a program, in view of the relatively high degree of individual mobility that characterizes a national economy, would create strong incentives for the wealthy to move out to neighboring municipalities and for the poor to migrate into the community. A more nearly equal distribution of income might well result, but it would be caused largely by an outflow of the rich and an influx of the poor, with a consequent fall in the level of per-capita income in the community under consideration.

The curious part is that this could happen even if all the members of the community, including the wealthy, genuinely desired to eliminate poverty through an explicitly redistributive policy. Every individual might stand willing to vote for a negative income tax program, and yet, if any one person perceived an avenue through which he could avoid his own contribution to the program, it might well be in his interest to do so. The point is that the contribution of any single person or family to the general elimination of poverty in a society is likely to be negligible. There is, therefore, a real incentive for so-called free-rider behavior by which an individual would leave to others the burden of financing redistributive programs. For this reason, the migration of relatively wealthy individuals from a locality that adopts an aggressive redistributive program may be perfectly consistent with a general commitment on the part of that society to a policy aimed at reducing or eliminating poverty.

The scope for redistributive programs is thus limited to some extent by the potential mobility of residents, which tends to be greater the smaller the jurisdiction under consideration. This suggests that, since mobility across national boundaries is generally much less than that within a nation, a policy of income redistribution has a much greater promise of success if carried out on the national level. A unitary form of government is therefore likely to be far more effective in achieving the redistributional objectives of the society than is a governmental organization at the opposite end of the spectrum.

Turning last to the allocation problem, one finds again that, for a certain class of goods and services, a highly centralized government is likely to be far more successful in providing appropriate levels of output than is a system of local governments. It is the responsibility of the public sector as a whole either to institute incentives for private production or, alternatively, to provide directly appropriate levels of output of those goods and services not forthcoming in efficient quantities through the operation of free markets. Some of these goods and services may be of such a character that they confer, or could confer, significant benefits on everyone in the nation. Consider, for example, a pure public good whose benefits extend to the individuals in all communities. The production of $X$ units of the commodity in one community implies that $X$ units are consumed by the residents of all municipalities. A rough approximation to such a commodity might be a missile system established by one community that is bound by an alliance to other communities to regard an attack on one as an attack on all. Under these circumstances, a missile system in any single community would serve as a deterrent to a potential aggressor against any of the others, for the enemy would have to expect missile retaliation should he invade any of the localities. In this case, then, a missile system in one community serves as a substitute for a similar system in a neighboring jurisdiction.

For such a public good, is a system of decentralized decision-making likely to result in the efficient level of output of the commodity? Will the individual communities, each seeking to maximize the welfare of its own constituents, end up providing a missile system such that the cost of a marginal missile is equal to the sum of the values placed on that missile by the residents of all the communities? The answer, as Mancur Olson and Richard Zeckhauser has shown, is generally no.[2] The reason is that each community in determining whether it will or will not produce an additional unit of the good (that is, another missile emplacement) considers only the benefits its own residents will receive from the marginal unit. As a result, the full social value of an additional unit of the good is not taken into consideration. As Olson and Zeckhauser explain it, a subefficient output results *because each ally gets only a fraction of the benefits of any collective good that is provided, but each pays the full cost of any additional amounts of the collective good. This means that individual members of an alliance or international organization have an incentive to stop providing the collective good long before the Pareto optimal [that is, economically efficient] output for the group has been provided. This is particularly true of the smaller members who get smaller shares of the total benefits accruing from the good, and who find that they have little or no incentive to provide additional amounts of the collective good once the larger members have provided the amounts they want for themselves, with the result that the burdens are shared in a disproportionate way.[3]*

The one special case in which an efficient output may be attained is where the various communities have an agreement to share the cost of an additional unit of the good in the same proportion as they share the benefits. In this case, all communities would be willing to support the production of an additional missile site if the value of the marginal missile exceeded its cost. However, in general, one would expect such public goods to be underproduced in a system of decentralized decision-making. In contrast, under a unitary form of government, assuming that public decision-makers seek to maximize the welfare of the entire citizenry, the value of a marginal unit of the public good to members of all the communities would presumably be taken into account. One would therefore expect a central government to provide a better approximation to the efficient level of output of those public goods that benefit the members of all communities than would a system of decentralized decision-making.

The preceding discussion suggests that a unitary form of government has several important advantages over its counterpart at the opposite end of the spectrum. In a system comprising only local governments, the public sector would be seriously handicapped in its capacity to meet its economic responsibilities. Local governments, I have argued, would find it extremely difficult to stabilize their respective economies, to realize the most equitable distribution of income, and to provide efficient levels of output of those public goods that confer benefits on the members of all or several communities. A central government, in contrast, is much more capable of performing these tasks satisfactorily. Nonetheless, a system of local governments does possess attractive economic attributes to which we turn next.

## THE ECONOMIC CASE FOR DECENTRALIZED GOVERNMENT

A basic shortcoming of a unitary form of government is its probable insensitivity to varying preferences among the residents of the different communities. If all public goods are supplied by a central government, one should expect a tendency toward uniformity in public programs across all communities. The problem here is that the level of consumption of a public good almost always involves compromise. Some individuals may prefer an expanded and high-quality program of public services, while others may want less public output and the accompanying reduced level of taxes. For truly national public goods (that is, those goods all individuals consume in identical quantities regardless of their community of residence), such compromise is inevitable. However, for other public goods whose benefits are limited to a specific subset of the population (for example, the members of a single community), there is at least a partial solution in greater decentralization of the public sector.

Consider, for example, a public good whose consumption is limited to the residents of the community in which it is provided. If provided by the central government, the most likely outcome would be similar levels of consumption of the good in all communities. However, such uniform levels of consumption may not be efficient, because they do not take into consideration possible variations in the tastes of residents of differing communities. If, in contrast, each community had its own local government, one might expect variations in the level of provision of this public good across the different localities, variations that would, to some extent at least, reflect the differences in tastes of the constituencies of the communities. The point here is that economic efficiency is attained by providing the mix of output that best reflects the preferences of the individuals who make up society, and if all individuals are compelled to consume the same level of output of a good when variations in individual consumption—or, in this case, variations in consumption among different subsets of the population—are possible, an inefficient allocation of resources is the likely result. A decentralized form of government therefore offers the promise of increasing economic efficiency by providing a range of outputs of certain public goods that corresponds more closely to the differing tastes of groups of consumers.

The possibilities for welfare gains through decentralization are further enhanced by the phenomenon of consumer mobility. As Charles Tiebout has argued, in a system of local government, a consumer can to some extent select as his place of residence a community that provides a fiscal package well suited to his preferences.[4] One can envision a system of local governments where, for example, each community provides a different level of consumption of a local public good and in which the consumer by "voting on foot" selects the community that provides the level of public output that best satisfies his tastes. Through this mechanism, one can get a sort of market solution to the problem of producing efficient levels of output of some public goods. A decentralized form of government thus possesses the advantage of allowing various levels of output of certain public goods, by means of which resources can be employed more efficiently in satisfying the preferences of consumers.

Decentralization may, moreover, result in greater experimentation and innovation in the production of public goods. With a large number of independent producers of a good, one might expect a variety of approaches (for example, varying techniques of instruction in local public schools) that, in the long run, promises greater technical progress in modes of providing these goods and services. Closely connected to this point are the competitive pressures that result from an enlarged number of producers; such pressures will tend to compel the adoption of the most efficient techniques of production. If, for example, public officials in one community have discovered a particularly effective way of providing a certain service, the governments of neighboring jurisdictions will, in all probability, be compelled to adopt similar techniques of production in order to avoid serious criticism from local residents. In contrast, if a single central government provides all public goods with no competitors, one might well expect the forces inducing innovation and efficiency to be less strong. A system of local government may thus promote both static and dynamic efficiency in the provision of public goods and services.

Finally, there is some reason to believe that decentralization may lead to more efficient levels of public output, because expenditure decisions are tied more closely to real resource costs. If a community is required to finance its own public program through local taxation, residents are more likely to weigh the benefits of the program against its actual costs. In the United States, for instance, proposals to improve local school systems are frequently submitted to the local electorate along with a proposed increase in property tax rates to fund the program. In contrast, if funds for local public projects come wholly from a central government, residents of a given community have an incentive to expand levels of local public services as far as possible, since they may bear only a negligible part of the costs of the program. To discourage this tendency, the central government could adopt other fiscal measures; it could, for example, require a community to bear the cost of many of its own programs by varying tax rates among communities or, where possible, by employing user charges. Often, however, this is not an easy matter; the federal government in the United States, for example, is prohibited by the Constitution from levying direct taxes with rates that vary on a geographical basis.

In summary, a decentralized public sector possesses several economically desirable characteristics. First, it provides a means by which the levels of consumption of some public goods can be tailored to the preferences of subsets of the society. In this way, economic efficiency is enhanced by providing an allocation of resources that is more responsive to the tastes of consumers. Second, by promoting increased innovation over time and by providing competitive pressures to induce local governments to adopt the most efficient techniques of production, decentralization may increase both static and dynamic efficiency in the production of public goods. Third, a system of local government may provide an institutional setting that promotes better public decision-making by compelling a more explicit recognition of the costs of public programs.

## THE OPTIMAL FORM OF GOVERNMENT: A FEDERAL SYSTEM

The preceding discussion suggests that both a unitary form of government and one characterized by extreme decentralization possess distinct advantages and serious shortcomings in performing the three fundamental economic tasks of the public sector. A central government can best resolve the stabilization and distribution problems, but in the absence of what I have called local governments, serious welfare losses from uniformity in the consumption of public goods and technical waste in their production are quite likely. What is clearly desirable is a form of government that combines the advantages of these two polar forms and avoids the most serious shortcomings of each; a federal organization of government meets this need.

Federalism represents, in one sense, a compromise between unitary government and extreme decentralization. In a federal system there exist both a central government and subcentral government units, each making decisions concerning the provision of certain public services in its respective geographical jurisdiction. From an economic standpoint, the obvious attraction of the federal form of government is that it combines the strengths of unitary government with those of decentralization. Each level of government, rather than attempting to perform all the functions of the public sector, does what it can do best. The central government presumably accepts primary responsibility for stabilizing the economy, for achieving the most equitable distribution of income, and for providing certain public goods that influence significantly the welfare of all members of society. Complementing these operations, subcentral governments can supply those public goods and services that are of primary interest only to the residents of their respective jurisdiction. In this way, a federal form of government offers the best promise of a successful resolution of the problems that constitute the economic *raison d'etre* of the public sector. It is in this sense that federalism may, in economic terms, be described as the optimal form of government.

\* \* \*

The argument presented thus far suggests that a federal structure of the public sector has, at least in economic terms, compelling advantages over alternative forms. If this is true, one would expect to find the federal structure the typical form of government. And yet, political scientist Daniel Elazar's list of federal countries numbers only sixteen nations.[5] Even this list would be considered by some to be overly inclusive; Kenneth C. Wheare, writing in the 1940s, was willing to grant federal status to only four nations. This suggests that the economic meaning of federalism differs in some fundamental way from its meaning to most political scientists, which is in fact the case. Therefore, in order to place the analysis in a clearer perspective, it will prove useful to examine more closely what an economist means by a federal system.

## THE ECONOMIC MEANING OF FEDERALISM

In his pioneering study of federalism, which has provided the basis for much of the later work on federal political institutions, Kenneth C. Wheare defined federalism as ". . . the method of dividing powers so that the general and regional governments are each, within a sphere, co-ordinate and independent."[6] From this definition and from his observations of actual governments (largely that of the United States), Wheare was able to set forth a number of characteristics that a political system must possess in order to qualify as federal; these were primarily constitutional provisions that protected the autonomy of different levels of government. I think it is fair to say that this largely legalistic approach, though not employed in nearly so restrictive a fashion as by Wheare, has characterized much of the later work in political science on this subject.

Such an approach makes a good deal of sense for a political study of federalism. Since a political scientist is interested in the division and use of power, there is real reason to exclude from the federal category a system in which, for example, the power of subcentral governments is exercised solely at the convenience of the central government. A system in which a central government merely delegates certain decision-making functions to regional or local governments will typically have a quite different power structure from one in which the scope of responsibility and independence of each level of government is carefully defined and protected by a written constitution. Related to this, Poul Meyer, among others, has been careful to distinguish between "decentralization," which represents a genuine possession of independent decision-making power by decentralized units, and "deconcentration," which implies only a delegation of administrative control to lower levels in the administrative hierarchy.[7] On the basis of such distinctions, political scientists have naturally been willing to recognize as federal countries only the limited number of nations in which, to a significant extent at least, different levels of government each possess an explicitly independent scope of responsibility and authority.

The problem of federalism is, however, quite different for an economist. In particular, the economist's central concerns are the allocation of resources and the distribution of income within an economic system. The structure of government is, for this reason, of interest to him only to the extent that it carries with it implications for patterns of resource use and income distribution. From this perspective, decentralization of the public sector is of importance primarily because it provides a mechanism through which the levels of provision of certain public goods and services can be fashioned according to the preferences of geographical subsets of the population. Therefore, I suggest the following *economic* definition of federalism:

> Federal Government: *A public sector with both centralized and decentralized levels of decision-making in which choices made at each level concerning the provision of public services are determined largely by the demands for these services of the residents of (and perhaps others who carry on activities in) the respective jurisdiction.*

One element of this definition requires special comment. In contrast to the conception of federalism in political science, it makes little difference to the economist whether or not decision-making at a particular level of government is based on delegated or constitutionally guaranteed authority. What matters is simply that decisions regarding levels of provision of specified public services for a particular jurisdiction (be they made by appointed or elected officials, or directly by the people themselves through some form of voting mechanism) reflect to a substantial extent the interests of the constituency of that jurisdiction.

This is not to say, however, that constitutional provisions are wholly irrelevant to the economics of federalism. On the contrary, constitutional constraints may make it quite difficult or costly in some instances for central government agencies to interfere with local government decisions. To this extent, a formally federal constitutional structure may typically result in a process of public decision-making in which local interests have a relatively major impact on choices affecting primarily the welfare of local residents. Legalistic factors may thus have a real influence on decision-making procedures. However, it is to be emphasized that it is the extent to which the decisions themselves reflect local interests that matters for the economist, and constitutional structure assumes importance only to the degree that it affects the responsiveness of the provision of local services to local preferences.

This is obviously a far broader view of federalism than that typically employed in political science. In fact, the most useful way for an economist to approach this issue is to treat federalism not in absolute but in relative terms.[8] As suggested earlier, we can envision a spectrum of structures of the public sector along which the difference is essentially one of degree rather than kind. At one end of the spectrum is a unitary form of government with all decisions made by the central authority, and at the opposite pole is a state of anarchy. Aside from the two polar points themselves, the other positions on the spectrum represent federal organizations of the public sector moving from a greater to a lesser degree of centralization of decision-making.

This would imply, however, that *in economic terms* most if not all systems are federal. Aside from an absolute degree of centralization of decision-making—which in practice is almost impossible to imagine—the public sectors of all countries would be federal, with distinctions being made in terms of differing degrees of centralization. I think this is the most useful way to see the issue; and it explains the ease with which I was able to reach the conclusion that, from an economic perspective, a federal system is the optimal form of organization of the public sector.

Of course, the problem is that within this framework such a conclusion is a vacuous one. If all public sectors are more or less federal in structure, it is obviously tautological to say that federalism is the optimal form of government. The real issue becomes the determination of the appropriate degree of decentralization for a particular government sector. Where along this centralization spectrum should a particular public sector be?

To answer this question requires matching public functions, including the provision of each public service, with appropriate levels of decision-making. This, as I see it, is the central theoretical problem of the subject of fiscal federalism: the determination of the optimal structure of the public sector in terms of the assignment of decision-making responsibility for specified functions to representatives of the interests of the proper geographical subsets of society. This suggests, moreover, that the arguments developed in this chapter, although they may have led initially to a conclusion without great substance, do take us some way into the analysis of the real problem; they indicate, in rough terms at least, a general outline for the appropriate division of fiscal functions between the central and decentralized levels of government. A more careful examination of this issue reveals, however, that the selection of the proper level of government to provide a particular public good or service is not an easy problem; there are typically a number of variables that figure in this decision, and in most instances, some form of trade-off between welfare gains and losses is involved.

## NOTES

1. *State and Local Finance in the National Economy,* New York: W. W. Norton (1944): 194–200. For an alternative view of the relative burden of internal and external debt on later generations, see James Buchanan, *The Principles of Public Debt: A Defense and Restatement,* Homewood, Illinois: Richard D. Irwin (1958).
2. "An Economic Theory of Alliances." *Review of Economics and Statistics 48* (August 1966): 266–275.
3. Ibid., 278.
4. "A Pure Theory of Local Expenditures." *Journal of Political Economy 64* (October, 1956): 416–424.
5. "Federalism," in David L. Sills, ed., *International Encyclopedia of the Social Sciences,* vol. 5, New York: Macmillan (1968): 365.
6. Wheare, *Federal Government,* p. 10.
7. *Administrative Organization,* Copenhagen: Nyt Nordisk Forlag Arnold Busck (1957), 56–61.
8. This is the approach suggested by Livingston, "A Note on the Nature of Federalism."

## S E L E C T I O N    3 2

Charles M. Tiebout

# A Pure Theory of Local Expenditures

Charles Tiebout presents his classic model of a household which choos-es to live in a locality with the mix of government-provided goods and services (and taxes) most closely matching its preferences. As Oates argued in the previous reading, fiscal federalism offers people the unique opportunity to choose their local governments. Thus, with many local governments present in an area, "consumer-voters" who do not like the government where they live can "vote with their feet" by mov-ing to another jurisdiction.

Such mobility establishes a pattern of public sector demands result-ing in a wide variety of output and taxes from different governments. State or local governments compete for voters by providing services in exchange for taxes. Government officials often complain that such com-petition can lead to inefficiently low levels of public services, if subna-tional governments compete only by holding taxes low. However, just as competition among firms benefits shoppers who consider both price and quality when buying private goods, Tiebout argues that intergovern-mental competition should benefit citizens by leading to the availability of more preferred mixes of locally-provided public services and taxes.

### Questions to Guide the Reading

1. Tiebout focuses on goods which can be optimally provided by local governments—goods which many modern public finance economists refer to as "local public goods." How do these "public" goods differ from the type of public good modeled by Samuelson and Musgrave?
2. Tiebout's model assumes that "an optimal community size" exists. What are some of the factors which may determine optimal size?

.............
Charles M. Tiebout. "A Pure Theory of Local Expenditures." *Journal of Political Economy 64* (February 1956): 416-424. Reprinted by permission of the author and The University of Chicago. This selection is an abridged version of the original article.

**Charles M. Tiebout,** former Professor of Economics at the University of Washington, passed away in 1968.

3. Tiebout compares the results of his model with one which could yield the severe outcome of "making each person his own municipal government." How does Tiebout's model "fall short" of providing each individual with a one-person community—precisely tailored to match each person's preferences?
4. How does voting with one's feet provide the "local public-goods counterpart to the private market's shopping trip"?
5. What might be some policy implications of interjurisdictional externalities—what Tiebout refers to as external economies and diseconomies?
6. What are possible policy implications of Tiebout's analysis? Under what circumstances would municipal integration be most likely to occur?

---

One of the most important recent developments in the area of "applied economic theory" has been the work of Musgrave and Samuelson in public finance theory.[1] The two writers agree on what is probably the major point under investigation, namely, that no "market type" solution exists to determine the level of expenditures on public goods. Seemingly, we are faced with the problem of having a rather large portion of our national income allocated in a "non-optimal" way when compared with the private sector.

This discussion will show that the Musgrave-Samuelson analysis, which is valid for federal expenditures, need not apply to local expenditures. The plan of the discussion is first to restate the assumptions made by Musgrave and Samuelson and the central problems with which they deal. After looking at a key difference between the federal versus local cases, I shall present a simple model. This model yields a solution for the level of expenditures for local public goods which reflects the preferences of the population more adequately than they can be reflected at the national level. The assumptions of the model will then be relaxed to see what implications are involved. Finally, policy considerations will be discussed.

## THE THEORETICAL ISSUE

Samuelson has defined public goods as "*collective consumption goods* $(X_n + 1, ..., X_n + n)$ which all enjoy in common in the sense that each individual's consumption of such a good leads to no subtraction from any other individual's consumption of that good, so that $X_n + j = X_i^i + j$ simultaneously for each and every $i$th individual and each collective good."[2] While definitions are a matter of choice, it is worth noting that "consumption" has a much broader meaning here than in the usual sense of the term. Not only does it imply that the act of consumption by one person does not diminish the opportunities for consumption by another but it also allows this consumption to be in another form. For example, while the residents of a new government housing project are made better off, benefits also accrue to other residents of the community in the form of the external economies of slum clearance. Thus many goods that appear to lack the attributes of public goods may properly be considered public if consumption is defined to include these external economies.

A definition alternative to Samuelson's might be simply that a public good is one which should be produced, but for which there is no feasible method of charging the consumers. This is less elegant, but has the advantage that it allows for the objections of Enke and Margolis.[3] This definition, unfortunately, does not remove any of the problems faced by Musgrave and Samuelson.

The core problem with which both Musgrave and Samuelson deal concerns the mechanism by which consumer-voters register their preferences for public goods. The consumer is, in a sense, surrounded by a government whose objective it is to ascertain his wants for public goods and tax him accordingly. To use Alchian's term, the government's revenue-expenditure pattern for goods and services is expected to "adapt to" consumers' preferences.[4] Both Musgrave and Samuelson have shown that, in the vertically additive nature of voluntary demand curves, this problem has only a conceptual solution. If all consumer-voters could somehow be forced to reveal their true preferences for public goods, then the amount of such goods to be produced and the appropriate benefits tax could be determined. As things now stand, there is no mechanism to force the consumer-voter to state his true preferences; in fact, the "rational" consumer will understate his preferences and hope to enjoy the goods while avoiding the tax.

The current method of solving this problem operates, unsatisfactorily, through the political mechanism. The expenditure wants of a "typical voter" are somehow pictured. This objective on the expenditure side is then combined with an ability-to-pay principle on the revenue side, giving us our current budget. Yet in terms of a satisfactory theory of public finance, it would be desirable (i) to force the voter to reveal his preferences; (ii) to be able to satisfy them in the same sense that a private goods market does; and (iii) to tax him accordingly. The question arises whether there is any set of social institutions by which this goal can be approximated.

## LOCAL EXPENDITURES

Musgrave and Samuelson implicitly assume that expenditures are handled at the central government level. However, the provision of such governmental services as police and fire protection, education, hospitals, and courts does not necessarily involve federal activity. Many of these goods are provided by local governments. It is worthwhile to look briefly at the magnitude of these expenditures.

Historically, local expenditures have exceeded those of the federal government. The thirties were the first peacetime years in which federal expenditures began to pull away from local expenditures. Even during the fiscal year 1954, federal expenditures on *goods and services exclusive of defense* amounted only to some 15 billions of dollars, while local expenditures during this same period amounted to some 17 billions of dollars. There is no need to quibble over which comparisons are relevant. The important point is that the often-neglected local expenditures are significant and, when viewed in terms of expenditures on goods and services only, take on even more significance. Hence an important question arises whether at this level of government any mechanism operates to insure that expenditures on these public goods approximate the proper level.

Consider for a moment the case of the city resident about to move to the suburbs. What variables will influence his choice of a municipality? If he has children, a high level of expenditures on schools may be important. Another person may prefer a community with a municipal golf course. The availability and quality of such facilities and services as beaches, parks, police protection, roads, and parking facilities will enter into the decision-making process. Of course, non-economic variables will also be considered, but this is of no concern at this point.

The consumer-voter may be viewed as picking that community which best satisfies his preference pattern for public goods. This is a major difference between central and local provision of public goods. At the central level the preferences of the consumer-voter are given, and the government tries to adjust to the pattern of these preferences, whereas at the local level various governments have their revenue and expenditure patterns more or less set. Given these revenue and expenditure patterns, the consumer-voter moves to that community whose local government best satisfies his set of preferences. The greater the number of communities and the greater the variance among them, the closer the consumer will come to fully realizing his preference position.

## A LOCAL GOVERNMENT MODEL

The implications of the preceding argument may be shown by postulating an extreme model. Here the following assumptions are made:

1.  Consumer-voters are fully mobile and will move to that community where their preference patterns, which are set, are best satisfied.
2.  Consumer-voters are assumed to have full knowledge of differences among revenue and expenditure patterns and to react to these differences.
3.  There are a large number of communities in which the consumer-voters may choose to live.
4.  Restrictions due to employment opportunities are not considered. It may be assumed that all persons are living on dividend income.
5.  The public services supplied exhibit no external economies or diseconomies between communities.

Assumptions 6 and 7 to follow are less familiar and require brief explanations:

6. For every pattern of community services set by, say, a city manager who follows the preferences of the older residents of the community, there is an optimal community size. This optimum is defined in terms of the number of residents for which this bundle of services can be produced at the lowest average cost. This, of course, is closely analogous to the low point of a firm's average cost curve. Such a cost function implies that some factor or resource is fixed. If this were not so, there would be no logical reason to limit community size, given the preference patterns. In the same sense that the average cost curve has a minimum for one firm but can be reproduced by another there is seemingly no reason why a duplicate community cannot exist. The assumption that some factor is fixed explains why it is not possible for the community in question to double its size by growth. The factor may be the limited land area of a suburban community, combined with a set of zoning laws against apartment buildings. It may be the local beach, whose capacity is limited. Anything of this nature will provide a restraint.

In order to see how this restraint works, let us consider the beach problem. Suppose the preference patterns of the community are such that the optimum size population is 13,000. Within this set of preferences there is a certain demand per family for beach space. This demand is such that at 13,000 population a 500-yard beach is required. If the actual length of the beach is, say, 600 yards, then it is not possible to realize this preference pattern with twice the optimum population, since there would be too little beach space by 400 yards.

The assumption of a fixed factor is necessary, as will be shown later, in order to get a determinate number of communities. It also has the advantage of introducing a realistic restraint into the model.

7. The last assumption is that communities below the optimum size seek to attract new residents to lower average costs. Those above optimum size do just the opposite. Those at an optimum try to keep their populations constant.

This assumption needs to be amplified. Clearly, communities below the optimum size, through chambers of commerce or other agencies, seek to attract new residents. This is best exemplified by the housing developments in some suburban areas, such as Park Forest in the Chicago area and Levittown in the New York area, which need to reach an optimum size. The same is true of communities that try to attract manufacturing industries by setting up certain facilities and getting an optimum number of firms to move into the industrially zoned area.

The case of the city that is too large and tries to get rid of residents is more difficult to imagine. No alderman in his right political mind would ever admit that the city is too big. Nevertheless, economic forces are at work to push people out of it. Every resident who moves to the suburbs to find better schools, more parks, and so forth, is reacting, in part, against the pattern the city has to offer.

The case of the community which is at the optimum size and tries to remain so is not hard to visualize. Again proper zoning laws, implicit agreements among realtors, and the like are sufficient to keep the population stable.

Except when this system is in equilibrium, there will be a subset of consumer-voters who are discontented with the patterns of their community. Another set will be satisfied. Given the assumption about mobility and the other assumptions listed previously, movement will take place out of the communities of greater than optimal size into the communities of less than optimal size. The consumer-voter moves to the community that satisfies his preference pattern.

The act of moving or failing to move is crucial. Moving or failing to move replaces the usual market test of willingness to buy a good and reveals the consumer-voter's demand for public goods. Thus each locality has a revenue and expenditure pattern that reflects the desires of its residents. The next step is to see what this implies for the allocation of public goods at the local level.

Each city manager now has a certain demand for $n$ local public goods. In supplying these goods, he and $m - 1$ other city managers may be considered as going to a national market and bidding for the appropriate units of service of each kind: so many units of police for the $i$th community; twice that number for the $j$th community; and so on. The demand on the public goods market for each of the $n$ commodities will be the sum of the demands of the $m$ communities. In the limit, as shown in a less realistic model to be developed later, this total demand will approximate the demand that represents the true preferences of the consumer-voters—that is, the demand they would reveal, if they were forced, somehow, to state their true preferences. In this model there is no attempt on the part of local governments to "adapt to" the preferences of consumer-voters. Instead, those local governments that attract the optimum number of residents may be viewed as being "adopted by" the economic system.[5]

## A COMPARISON MODEL

It is interesting to contrast the results of the preceding model with those of an even more severe model in order to see how these results differ from the normal market result. It is convenient to look at this severe model by developing its private-market counterpart. First assume that there are no public goods, only private ones. The preferences for these goods can be expressed as one of $n$ patterns. Let a law be passed that all persons living in any one of the communities shall spend their money in the particular pattern described for that community by law. Given our earlier assumptions 1 through 5, it follows that, if the consumers move to the community whose law happens to fit their preference pattern, they will be at their optimum. The $n$ communities, in turn, will then send their buyers to market to purchase the goods for the consumer-voters in their community. Since this is simply a lumping together of all similar tastes for the purpose of making joint purchases, the allocation of resources will be the same as it would be if normal market forces operated. This conceptual experiment is the equivalent of substituting the city manager for the broker or middleman.

Now turn the argument around and consider only public goods. Assume with Musgrave that the costs of additional services are constant.[6] Further, assume that a doubling of the population means doubling the amount of services required. Let the number of communities be infinite and let each announce a different pattern of expenditures on public goods. Define an empty community as one that fails to satisfy anybody's preference pattern. Given these assumptions, including the earlier assumptions 1 through 5, the consumer-voters will move to that community which *exactly* satisfies their preferences. This must be true, since a one-person community is allowed. The sum of the demands of the $n$ communities reflects the demand for local public services. In this model the demand is exactly the same as it would be if it were determined by normal market forces.

However, this severe model does not make much sense. The number of communities is indeterminate. There is no reason why the number of communities will not be equal to the population, since each voter can find the one that exactly fits his preferences. Unless some sociological variable is introduced, this may reduce the solution of the problem of allocating public goods to the trite one of making each person his own municipal government. Hence this model is not even a first approximation of reality. It is presented to show the assumptions needed in a model of local government expenditures, which yields the same optimal allocation that a private market would.

## THE LOCAL GOVERNMENT MODEL REEXAMINED

The first model, described by the first five assumptions together with assumptions 6 and 7, falls short of this optimum. An example will serve to show why this is the case.

Let us return to the community with the 500-yard beach. By assumption, its optimum population was set at 13,000, given its preference patterns. Suppose that some people in addition to the optimal 13,000 would choose this community if it were available. Since they cannot move into this area, they must accept the next best substitute. If a perfect substitute is found, no problem exists. If one is not found, then the failure to reach the optimal preference position and the substitution of a lower position becomes a matter of degree. In so far as there are a number of communities with similar revenue and expenditure patterns, the solution will approximate the ideal "market" solution.

Two related points need to be mentioned to show the allocative results of this model: (1) changes in the costs of one of the public services will cause changes in the quantity produced; (2) the costs of moving from community to community should be recognized. Both points can be illustrated in one example.

Suppose lifeguards throughout the country organize and succeed in raising their wages. Total taxes in communities with beaches will rise. Now residents who are largely indifferent to beaches will be forced to make a decision. Is the saving of this added tax worth the cost of moving to a community with little or no beach? Obviously, this decision depends on many factors, among which the availability of and proximity to a suitable substitute community is important. If enough people leave communities with beaches and move to communities without beaches, the total amount of lifeguard services used will fall. These models then, unlike their private-market counterpart, have mobility as a cost of registering demand. The higher this cost, *ceteris paribus*, the less optimal the allocation of resources.

This distinction should not be blown out of proportion. Actually, the cost of registering demand comes through the introduction of space into the economy. Yet space affects the allocation not only of resources supplied by local governments but of those supplied by the private market as well. Every time available resources or production techniques change, a new location becomes optimal for the firm. Indeed, the very concept of the shopping trip shows that the consumer does pay a cost to register his demand for private goods. In fact, Koopmans has stated that the nature of the assignment problem is such that in a space economy with transport costs there is *no* general equilibrium solution as set by market forces.[7]

Thus the problems stated by this model are not unique; they have their counterpart in the private market. We are maximizing within the framework of the resources available. If production functions show constant returns to scale with generally diminishing factor returns, and if indifference curves are regularly convex, an optimal solution is possible. On the production side it is assumed that communities are forced to keep production costs at a minimum either through the efficiency of city managers or through competition from other communities. Given this, on the demand side we may note with Samuelson that "each individual, in seeking as a competitive buyer to get to the highest level of indifference subject to given prices and *tax*, would be led as if by an Invisible Hand to the grand solution of the social maximum position."[8] Just as the consumer may be visualized as walking to a private market place to buy his goods, the prices of which are set, we place him in the position of walking to a community where the prices (taxes) of community services are set. Both trips take the consumer to market. There is no way in which the consumer can avoid revealing his preferences in a spatial economy. Spatial mobility provides the local public-goods counterpart to the private market's shopping trip.

## EXTERNAL ECONOMIES AND MOBILITY

Relaxing assumption 5 has some interesting implications. There are obvious external economies and diseconomies between communities. My community is better off if its neighbor sprays trees to prevent Dutch elm disease. On the other hand, my community is worse off if the neighboring community has inadequate law enforcement.

In cases in which the external economies and diseconomies are of sufficient importance, some form of integration may be indicated.[9] Not all aspects of law enforcement are adequately handled at the local level. The function of the sheriff, state police, and the FBI—as contrasted with the local police—may be cited as resulting from a need for integration. In real life the diseconomies are minimized in so far as communities reflecting the same socioeconomic preferences are contiguous. Suburban agglomerations such as Westchester, the North Shore, and the Main Line are, in part, evidence of these external economies and diseconomies.

Assumptions 1 and 2 should be checked against reality. Consumer-voters do not have perfect knowledge and set preferences, nor are they perfectly mobile. The question is how do people actually react in choosing a community. There has been very little empirical study of the motivations of people in choosing a community. Such studies as have been undertaken seem to indicate a surprising awareness of differing revenue and expenditure patterns. The general disdain with which proposals to integrate municipalities are met seems to reflect, in part, the fear that local revenue-expenditure patterns will be lost as communities are merged into a metropolitan area.

## POLICY IMPLICATIONS

The preceding analysis has policy implications for municipal integration, provision for mobility, and set local revenue and expenditure patterns. These implications are worth brief consideration.

On the usual economic welfare grounds, municipal integration is justified only if more of any service is forthcoming at the same total cost and without reduction of any other service. A general reduction of costs along with a reduction in one or more of the services provided cannot be justified on economic grounds unless the social welfare function is known. For example, those who argue for a metropolitan police force instead of local police cannot prove their case on purely economic grounds. If one of the communities were to receive less police protection after integration than it received before, integration could be objected to as a violation of consumers' choice.

Policies that promote residential mobility and increase the knowledge of the consumer-voter will improve the allocation of government expenditures in the same sense that mobility among jobs and knowledge relevant to the location of industry and labor improve the allocation of private resources.

Finally, we may raise the normative question whether local governments *should*, to the extent possible, have a fixed revenue-expenditure pattern. In a large, dynamic metropolis this may be impossible. Perhaps it could more appropriately be considered by rural and suburban communities.

## CONCLUSION

It is useful in closing to restate the problem as Samuelson sees it:

> However, no decentralized pricing system can serve to determine optimally these levels of collective consumption. *Other kinds of "voting" or "signaling" would have to be tried.... Of course utopian voting and signaling schemes can be imagined.... The failure of market catallactics in no way denies the following truth: given sufficient knowledge the optimal decisions can always be found by scanning over all the attainable states of the world and selecting the*

*one which according to the postulated ethical welfare function is best. The solution "exists"; the problem is how to "find" it.*[10]

It is the contention of this article that, for a substantial portion of collective or public goods, this problem *does have* a conceptual solution. If consumer-voters are fully mobile, the appropriate local governments, whose revenue-expenditure patterns are set, are adopted by the consumer-voters. While the solution may not be perfect because of institutional rigidities, this does not invalidate its importance. The solution, like a general equilibrium solution for a private spatial economy, is the best that can be obtained given preferences and resource endowments.

Those who are tempted to compare this model with the competitive private model may be disappointed. Those who compare the reality described by this model with the reality of the competitive model—given the degree of monopoly, friction, and so forth—*may* find that local government represents a sector where the allocation of public goods (as a reflection of the preferences of the population) need not take a back seat to the private sector.

## NOTES

I am grateful for the comments of my colleagues Karl de Schweinitz, Robert Eisner, and Robert Strotz, and those of Martin Bailey, of the University of Chicago.

1. Richard A. Musgrave, "The Voluntary Exchange Theory of Public Economy, *Quarterly Journal of Economics LII* (February 1939): 213–217; "A Multiple Theory of the Budget," paper read at the Econometric Society annual meeting (December 1955); and his forthcoming book, *The Theory of Public Economy;* Paul A. Samuelson, "The Pure Theory of Public Expenditures," *Review of Economics and Statistics XXXVI:* 4 (November 1954): 387–389; and "Diagrammatic Exposition of a Pure Theory of Public Expenditures," ibid., XXXVII: 4 (November 1955): 350–356.
2. "The Pure Theory...," op. cit., p. 387.
3. They argue that, for most of the goods supplied by governments, increased use by some consumer-voters leaves less available for other consumer-voters. Crowded highways and schools, as contrasted with national defense, may be cited as examples (see Stephen Enke, "More on the Misuse of Mathematics in Economics: A Rejoinder," *Review of Economics and Statistics XXXVII* [May 1955]: 131–133; and Julius Margolis, "A Comment on the Pure Theory of Public Expenditure," Review of Economics and Statistics XXXVII [November 1955]: 247–249).
4. Armen A. Alchian. "Uncertainty, Evolution and Economic Theory." *Journal of Political Economy, LVIII* (June 1950): 211–221.
5. See Alchian, op. cit.
6. Musgrave, "Voluntary Exchange...," op. Cit.
7. Tjalling Koopmans, "Mathematical Groundwork of Economic Optimization Theories," paper read at the annual meeting of the Econometric Society (December 1954).
8. "The Pure Theory...," op. cit., 388. (Italics mine.)
9. I am grateful to Stanley Long and Donald Markwalder for suggesting this point.
10. "The Pure Theory...," op. cit., 388–389.

# SUGGESTED FURTHER READINGS

········································································································

## BY TOPIC AREA

### General Introduction to Public Finance and Government

Aaron, Henry J., and Charles L. Schultze (eds.). *Setting Domestic Priorities: What Can Government Do?* Washington, D.C.: The Brookings Institution, 1992.

Auerbach, Alan J. "Public Finance in Theory and Practice." (Symposium on Economics in the Policy Process.) *National Tax Journal 46* (December 1993): 519–526.

Auerbach, Alan J., and Martin Feldstein (eds.). *Handbook of Public Economics, Volumes I & II.* Amsterdam: North-Holland, 1985.

Buchanan, James M. *Economics: Between Predictive Science and Moral Philosophy,* complied and with preface by Robert D. Tollison and Viktor J. Vanberg. College Station, Texas: Texas A&M University Press, 1987.

———. "The Potential and the Limits of Socially Organised Humankind." *Interdisciplinary Science Reviews 16* (1991): 168–174.

———. *Public Finance in Democratic Process: Fiscal Institutions and Individual Choice.* Chapel Hill: University of North Carolina Press, 1967.

———. "Richard Musgrave, Public Finance, and Public Choice." *Public Choice* (June 1989): 289–291.

Dreze, Jacques H. "Forty Years of Public Economics: A Personal Perspective." *Journal of Economic Perspectives 9* (Spring 1995): 111–130.

Feldstein, Martin (ed.). *American Economic Policy in the 1980s.* Chicago: University of Chicago Press, 1994.

Friedman, Milton. *Capitalism and Freedom.* Chicago: University of Chicago Press, 1962.

Hammond, Peter J. "Theoretical Progress in Public Economics: A Provocative Assessment." *Oxford Economic Papers 42* (1990): 6–33.

Hare, Paul G. (ed.). *Surveys in Public Sector Economics.* Oxford, United Kingdom: Basil Blackwell, 1988.

Haveman, Robert H., and Julius Margolis (eds.). *Public Expenditure and Policy Analysis* (3rd edition). Dallas: Houghton Mifflin, 1983.

Heller, Walter W. "What Is Right with Economics." *American Economic Review 65* (March 1975): 1–26.

Laffont, Jean-Jacques. *Fundamentals of Public Economics.* Cambridge, Massachusetts: The MIT Press, 1988.

Menchik, Paul L. "The Distribution of Federal Expenditures." *National Tax Journal 44* (September 1991): 269–276.

Musgrave, Richard A. *Public Finance in a Democratic Society: Collected Papers Volumes I & II.* New York: New York University Press, 1986.

———. *The Theory of Public Finance: A Study in Public Economy.* New York: McGraw-Hill, 1959.

Musgrave, Richard A., and Alan T. Peacock (eds.). *Classics in the Theory of Public Finance.* London: Macmillan and Company Limited, 1964.

Quigley, John M., and Eugene Smolensky (eds.). *Modern Public Finance.* Cambridge, Massachusetts: Harvard University Press, 1994.

Starrett, David A. *Foundations of Public Economics.* Cambridge: Cambridge University Press, 1988.

## Public Finance Analysis

Aaron, Henry J., Thomas E. Mann, and Timothy Taylor (eds.). *Values and Public Policy.* Washington, D.C.: The Brookings Institution, 1994.

Arrow, Kenneth J. "Social Responsibility and Economic Efficiency." *Public Policy 21* (Summer 1973): 303–317.

———. "Values and Collective Decision Making," in *Philosophy, Politics, and Society,* edited by P. Luslett and W. Runcman (215–232). New York: Barnes Noble, 1967.

Atkinson, A. B. (ed.). *Modern Public Finance, 2 Volumes.* Brookfield, Vermont: Edward Elgar Publishing, 1991.

Barr, Nicholas. "Economic Theory and the Welfare State: A Survey and Interpretation." *Journal of Economic Literature 30* (June 1992): 741–803.

Bator, Francis. "The Anatomy of Market Failure." *Quarterly Journal of Economics* (August 1958): 351–379.

———. "The Simple Analytics of Welfare Maximization." *American Economic Review* (March 1957): 22–59.

Boadway, Robin W., and Neil Bruce. *Welfare Economics.* Oxford, United Kingdom: Basil Blackwell, 1989.

Cairncross, Alec. "Economics in Theory and Practice." *American Economic Review 75* (May 1985): 1–14.

Chelimsky, Eleanor. "On the Social Science Contribution to Governmental Decision-Making." *Science 254* (October 11, 1991): 226–231.

Feldman, Allan M. *Welfare Economics and Social Choice Theory.* Boston: Kluwer Nijhoff Publishing, 1980.

Friedman, Milton. *Essays in Positive Economics.* Chicago: University of Chicago Press, 1953.

Hanusch, Horst (ed.). *Public Finance and the Quest for Efficiency.* Detroit: Wayne State University Press, 1984.

Johansson, Per-Olov. *An Introduction to Modern Welfare Economics.* Cambridge: Cambridge University Press, 1991.

Le Grand, Julian. "Equity versus Efficiency: The Elusive Trade-Off." *Ethics 100* (April 1990): 554–568.

Mayer, Thomas. "Friedman's Methodology of Positive Economics: A Soft Reading." *Economic Inquiry 31* (April 1993): 213–223.

Mishan, E. J. *What Political Economy Is All About: An Exposition and Critique.* Cambridge: Cambridge University Press, 1982.

O'Connell, John F. *Welfare Economic Theory.* Boston, Massachusetts: Auburn House Publishing, 1982.

Schultz, Charles L. "The Role of Responsibilities of the Economist in Government." *American Economic Review 72* (May 1982): 62–66.

Schultz, George. "Reflections on Political Economy." *Challenge 17* (March/April 1974): 6–11.

Stigler, George F. *The Citizen and the State.* Chicago: University of Chicago Press, 1975.

"Symposium: Economists as Policy Advocates." *Journal of Economic Perspectives 6* (Summer 1992): 59–78.

Tresch, Richard W. *Public Finance: A Normative Theory.* Plano, Texas: Business Publications, 1981.

Zajac, Edward E. *The Political Economy of Fairness.* Cambridge, Massachusetts: The MIT Press, 1995.

# Externalities

Arnott, Richard, and Kenneth Small. "The Economics of Traffic Congestion." *American Scientist 82* (September–October 1994): 446–455.

Arrow, Kenneth, Bert Bolin, Robert Costanza, Partha Dasgupta, Carl Folke, C. S. Holling, Bengt-Owe Jansson, Simon Levin, Karl-Goran Maler, Charles Perrings, and David Pimentel. "Economic Growth, Carrying Capacity, and the Environment." *Science 268* (April 28, 1995): 520–521.

Atkinson, Scott, and Thomas H. Tietenberg. "Market Failure in Incentive-Based Regulation: The Case of Emissions Trading." *Journal of Environmental Economics and Management 21* (1991): 17–31.

Barthhold, Thomas A. "Issues in the Design of Environmental Excise Taxes." *Journal of Economic Perspectives 8* (Winter 1994): 133–151.

Baumol, William J. "On Taxation and the Control of Externalities." *American Economic Review 62* (June 1972): 307–322

Baumol, William J., and Wallace E. Oates. *Economics, Environmental Policy, and the Quality of Life,* 2nd edition. New York: Harcourt Brace Jovanovich, 1982.

Blinder, Alan S. "Cleaning Up the Environment: Sometimes Cheaper Is Better," in *Hard Heads, Soft Hearts: Tough-Minded Economics for a Just Society* (ch. 5, 138–159). Reading, Massachusetts: Addison-Wesley, 1987.

Bloom, David E. "International Public Opinion on the Environment." *Science 269* (July 21, 1995): 354–358.

Breslow, Marc. "Taxing Trash." *Dollars and Sense* (May/June 1994): 26–29, 42.

Cnossen, Sijbren, and Herman Volebergh. "Toward a Global Excise on Carbon." *National Tax Journal 45* (March 1992): 23–36.

Cook, Philip J., and Michael J. Moore. "This Tax's for You: The Case for Higher Beer Taxes." *National Tax Journal 47* (September 1994): 559–573.

Cordes, Joseph J., Eric M. Nicholson, and Frank J. Sammartino. "Raising Revenue by Taxing Activities with Social Costs." *National Tax Journal 43* (September 1990): 343–356.

Cornes, Richard, and Todd Sandler. *The Theory of Externalities, Public Goods, and Club Goods.* Cambridge: Cambridge University Press, 1986.

Crandall, Robert W. "Corporate Average Fuel Economy Standards." *Journal of Economic Perspectives 6* (Spring 1992): 171–180.

Dahlman, Carl J. "The Problem of Externality." *Journal of Law and Economics* (April 1979): 141–162.

Dasgupta, Partha S. "Population, Poverty and the Local Environment." *Scientific American 272* (February 1995): 40–45.

Delong, James V. "Of Mountains and Molehills: The Municipal Solid Waste Crisis." *The Brookings Review* (Spring 1994): 34–39.

Demsetz, Harold. "Towards a Theory of Property Rights." *American Economic Review 57* (May 1967): 347–359.

Dorfman, Robert, and Nancy S. Dorfman (eds.). *Economics of the Environment: Selected Readings,* 3rd edition. New York: WW Norton, 1993.

Dwyer, John P. "California's Tradable Emissions Policy and Greenhouse Gas Control." *Journal of Energy Engineering 118* (August 1992): 59–76.

Eskeland, Gunnar S., and Emmanuel Jimenez. "Curbing Pollution in Developing Countries." *Finance & Development 26* (March 1991): 15–18.

Farrell, Joseph. "Information and the Coase Theorem." *Journal of Economic Perspectives 1* (Fall 1987): 113–129.

Foster, Vivien, and Robert W. Hahn. "Designing More Efficient Markets: Lessons from Los Angeles Smog Control." *Journal of Law and Economics 38* (April 1995): 19–48.

Goldstein, Avram, and Harold Kalant. "Drug Policy: Striking the Right Balance." *Science 249* (September 28, 1990): 1513–1521.

Goulder, Lawrence H. "Carbon Tax Design and the U.S. Industry Performance," in *Tax Policy and the Economy Volume 6*, edited by James M. Poterba (59–104). Cambridge, Massachusetts: The MIT Press, 1992.

Grossman, Michael, Jody L. Sindelar, John Mullahy, and Richard Anderson. "The Economic Case Against Higher Alcohol Taxes: Response." *Journal of Economic Perspectives 9* (Winter 1995): 210–212.

Hahn, Robert W., and Robert N. Stavins. "Economic Incentives for Environmental Protection: Integrating Theory and Practice." *American Economic Review 82* (May 1992): 464–468.

Hall, Jane V., Arthur M. Winer, Michael T. Kleinman, Frederick W. Lurmann, Victor Brajer, and Steven D. Colome. "Valuing the Health Benefits of Clean Air." *Science 255* (February 14, 1992): 812–817.

Hayes, Dennis. "Harnessing Market Forces to Protect the Earth." *Issues in Science and Technology 7* (Winter 1990): 46–51.

Heien, Dale. "The Economic Case Against Higher Alcohol Taxes." *Journal of Economic Perspectives 9* (Winter 1995): 207–209.

Helm, Dieter (ed.). *Economic Policy Towards the Environment.* Oxford, United Kingdom: Blackwell, 1991.

Hemenway, David. "Nervous Nellies and Dangerous Dans." *Journal of Policy Analysis and Management 12* (1993): 359–363.

Hoeller, Peter, and Jonathan Coppel. "Carbon Taxes and Current Energy Policies in OECD Countries." *OECD Economic Studies* (Winter 1992): 167–193.

Hoffman, Elizabeth, and Matthew L. Spitzer. "Experimental Tests of the Coase Theorem with Large Bargaining Groups." *Journal of Legal Studies 15* (January 1986): 149–171.

Inhaber, Herbert. "Of LULUs, NIMBYs, and NIMTOOs." *The Public Interest 107* (Spring 1992): 52–64.

Johnson, David B. "Meade, Bees, and Externalities." *Journal of Law and Economics* (April 1973): 35–52.

Katz, Michael L., and Carl Shapiro. "Systems Competition and Network Effects." *Journal of Economic Perspectives 8* (Spring 1994): 93–115.

Lee, Dwight R. "Environmental Economics and the Social Cost of Smoking." *Contemporary Policy Issues 9* (January 1991): 83–92.

Levenson, Leo, and Deborah Gordon. "DRIVE+: Promoting Cleaner and More Fuel Efficient Motor Vehicles through a Self-Financing System of State Sales Tax Incentives." *Journal of Policy Analysis and Management 9* (Summer 1990): 409–415.

Meade, J. E. "External Economics and Diseconomies in a Competitive Situation." *Economic Journal* (March 1952): 54–67.

Mishan, Edward J. "The Relationship between Joint Products, Collective Goods, and External Effects." *Journal of Political Economy* (May/June 1969): 329–348.

Montgomery, Claire A., Gardner M Brown, Jr., and Darius M. Adams. "The Marginal Cost of Species Preservation: The Northern Spotted Owl." *Journal of Environmental Economics and Management 26* (March 1994): 111–128.

Moore, Basil J. "Fuel Efficiency Standards and the Motor Vehicle Explosion." *Challenge 33* (May–June 1990): 56–59.

Moore, Stephen. "So Much for 'Scarce Resources.'" *The Public Interest 106* (Winter 1992): 97–107.

Nakamura, Leonard I. "Information Externalities: Why Lending May Sometimes Need a Jump Start." *Business Review of the Federal Reserve Bank of Philadelphia* (January–February 1993): 3–14.

Nivola, Pietro S. "Deja Vu All Over Again: Revisiting the Politics of Gasoline Taxation." *The Brookings Review* (Winter 1990/1991): 29–35.

———. "Gridlocked or Gaining Ground? U.S. Regulatory Reform in the Energy Sector." *The Brookings Review* (Summer 1993): 36–41.

Nivola, Pietro S., and Robert W. Crandall. "The Extra Mile: Rethinking Energy Policy for Automotive Transportation." *The Brookings Review* (Winter 1995): 31–33.

Pogue, Thomas F., and Larry G. Sgontz. "Taxing to Control Social Costs: The Case of Alcohol." *American Economic Review 79* (March 1989): 235–243.

Portney, Paul R. "Economics and the Clean Air Act." *Journal of Economic Perspectives 4* (Fall 1990): 173–181.

Rahn, Robert W. "Economic Prescriptions for Environmental Problems: How the Patient Followed the Doctor's Orders." *Journal of Economic Perspectives 3* (Spring 1989): 95–114.

Repetto, Robert. "Environmental Productivity and Why It Is So Important." *Challenge 33* (September/October 1990): 33–38.

Repetto, Robert, Roger C. Dower, and Robert Gramlich. "Pollution and Energy Taxes: Their Environmental and Economic Benefits." Challenge 36 (July–August 1993): 9–14.

Rousso, Ada S., and Shvetank P. Shah. "Packaging Taxes and Recycling Incentives: The German Green Dot Program." *National Tax Journal 47* (September 1994): 689–702.

Ruff, Larry. "The Economic Common Sense of Pollution." *The Public Interest 19* (Spring 1970): 69–85.

Sawicki, David S. "The Tragedy of the Common: A First Case Assignment for Students of Policy Analysis." *Journal of Policy Analysis and Management 10* (Winter 1991): 150–163.

Segerson, Kathleen, and Thomas H. Tietenberg. "The Structure of Penalties in Environmental Enforcement: An Economic Analysis." *Journal of Environmental Economics and Management 23* (September 1992): 179–200.

Small, Kenneth A. "Urban Traffic Congestion: A New Approach to the Gordian Knot." *The Brookings Review* (Spring 1993): 6–11.

Starr, Roger. "Recycling: Myths and Realities." *The Public Interest 119* (Spring 1995): 28–41.

———. "Waste Disposal: A Miracle of Immaculate Consumption?" *The Public Interest 105* (Fall 1991): 17–29.

Stavins, Robert N. "Harnessing the Marketplace." *EPA Journal 18* (May/June 1992): 21–25.

Stavins, Robert N., and Bradley W. Whitehead. "Dealing with Pollution: Market–Based Incentives for Environmental Protection." *Environment 34* (September 1992): 7–43.

Stigler, George J. "Law or Economics?" *Journal of Law and Economics 35* (October 1992): 455–468.

Summers, Lawrence. "The Case for Corrective Taxation." *National Tax Journal 44* (September 1991): 289–292.

Tietenberg, Thomas H. *Environmental Economics and Policy.* New York: HarperCollins, 1994.

———. "Transferable Discharge Permits and the Control of Stationary Source Air Pollution: A Survey and Synthesis." *Land Economics 56* (November 1980): 391–416.

———. "Using Economic Incentives to Maintain Our Environment." *Challenge 33* (March–April 1990): 42–46.

Tomkins, J. M., and J. Twomey. "International Pollution Control: A Review of Marketable Permits." *Journal of Environmental Management 41* (May 1994): 39–47.

Tucker, William. "Marketing Pollution." *Harper's 262* (May 1981): 31–38.

Turvey, Ralph. "On Divergences between Social Cost and Private Cost." *Economica* (August 1963): 309–313.

Veljanovski, C. G. "The Coase Theorems and the Economic Theory of Markets and Law." *Kyklos* (1982, Fasc.1): 53–74.

Viscusi, W. Kip. "Cigarette Taxation and the Social Consequences of Smoking," in *Tax Policy and the Economy 9,* edited by James M. Poterba (pp. 51–102). Cambridge, Massachusetts: The MIT Press, 1995.

Zerbe, Richard O., Jr. "The Problem of Social Cost in Retrospect." *Research in Law and Economics* (1980): 83–102.

Zilberman, David, Andrew Schmitz, Gary Casterline, Erik Lichtenberg, and Jerome B. Siebert. "The Economics of Pesticide Use and Regulation." *Science 253* (August 2, 1991): 518–522.

## Public Goods

Arrow, Kenneth J. "Information and Economic Behavior," lecture presented to the Federation of Swedish Industries, Stockholm (1973), reprinted in *Volume 4 of Collected Papers of Kenneth J. Arrow: The Economics of Information,* 136–152. Cambridge: The Belknap Press of Harvard University Press, 1984.

Bardhan, Pranab. "Symposium on Management of Local Commons." *Journal of Economic Perspectives 7* (Fall 1993): 87–92.

Barrett, Scott. "The Problem of Global Environmental Protection." *Oxford Review of Economic Policy 6* (1990): 68–79.

Beckerman, Wilfred, and Jesse Malkin. "How Much Does Global Warming Matter?" *The Public Interest 114* (Winter 1994): 3–16.

Berkes, F., D. Feeny, B. J. McCay, and J. M. Acheson. "The Benefits of the Commons." *Nature 340* (13 July 1989): 91–93.

Buchanan, James M. *The Demand and Supply of Public Goods.* Chicago: Rand McNally, 1968.

———. "An Economic Theory of Clubs." *Economica* (February 1965): 1–14.

Clarke, Edward H. *Demand Revelation and the Provision of Public Goods.* Cambridge, Massachusetts: Ballinger, 1980.

Coase, Ronald H. "The Lighthouse in Economics." *Journal of Law and Economics 17* (October 1974): 357–76.

Cohen, Joel E. "Population Growth and Earth's Human Carrying Capacity." *Science 269* (July 21, 1995): 341–346.

Cowen, Tyler. "Law as a Public Good: Economics of Anarchy." *Economics and Philosophy 8* (October 1992): 249–267.

———. *Public Goods and Market Failures.* New Brunswick, New Jersey: Transaction, 1992.

Diamond, Peter A., and Jerry A. Hausman. "Contingent Valuation: Is Some Number Better than No Number?" *Journal of Economic Perspectives 8* (Fall 1994): 45–64.

Dornbusch, Rudiger, and James M. Poterba (eds.). *Global Warming: Economic Policy Responses.* Cambridge, Massachusetts: The MIT Press, 1991.

Hanemann, W. Michael. "Valuing the Environment through Contingent Valuation." *Journal of Economic Perspectives 8* (Fall 1994): 19–43.

Hanusch, Horst (ed.). *Public Finance and the Quest for Efficiency.* Detroit: Wayne State University Press, 1984.

Head, John G. *Public Goods and Public Welfare*. Durham, North Carolina: Duke University Press, 1974.

Holtermann, S. E. "Externalities and Public Goods." *Economica* (February 1972): 78–87.

Kindleberger, Charles P. "International Public Goods without International Government." *American Economic Review 76* (March 1986): 1–13.

Klein, Daniel B. "The Voluntary Provision of Public Goods? The Turnpike Companies of Early America." *Economic Inquiry 28* (October 1990): 788–812.

Lovell, Michael C. "Sponsoring Public Goods: The Case of CAI on the PC." *Journal of Economic Education 22* (Winter 1991): 39–53.

Marwell, Gerald, and Ruth E. Ames. "Economists Free Ride, Does Anyone Else? Experiments on the Provision of Public Goods, IV." *Journal of Public Economics 24* (June 1981): 295–310.

Miller, David. "Public Goods without the State." *Critical Review 7* (1993): 505–523.

Nordhaus, William D. *Managing the Global Commons: The Economics of Climate Change*. Cambridge, Massachusetts: The MIT Press, 1994.

———. "An Optimal Transition Path for Controlling Greenhouse Gases." *Science 258* (November 20, 1992): 1315–1319.

Pommerehne, Werner, Lars P. Feld, and Albert Hart. "Voluntary Provision of a Public Good: Results from a Real World Experiment." *Kyklos 47* (Fasc. 4, 1994): 505–518.

Portney, Paul R. "The Contingent Valuation Debate: Why Economists Should Care." *Journal of Economic Perspectives 8* (Fall 1994): 3–17.

Poterba, James M. "Global Warming Policy: A Public Finance Perspective." *Journal of Economic Perspectives 7* (Fall 1993): 47–63.

Samuelson, Paul A. "Diagrammatic Exposition of a Theory of Public Expenditures." *Review of Economics and Statistics* (November 1955): 360–366.

Sandler, Todd. "After the Cold War, Secure the Global Commons." *Challenge 35* (July–August 1992): 16–23.

———. *Collective Action: Theory and Applications*. Ann Arbor, Michigan: University of Michigan Press, 1992.

Schelling, Thomas C. "Some Economics of Global Warming." *American Economic Review 82* (March 1992).

Schmidtz, David. "Market Failure." *Critical Review 7* (1993): 525–537.

———. *The Limits on Government: An Essay on the Public Goods Argument*. Boulder, Colorado: Westview, 1991.

Schnytzer, Adi. "An Economic Model of Regime Change: Freedom as a Public Good." *Public Choice 79* (1994): 325–339.

Seabright, Paul. "Managing Local Commons: Theoretical Issues in Incentive Design." *Journal of Economic Perspectives 7* (Fall 1993): 113–134.

Stonebraker, Robert J. "Optimal Church Size: The Bigger The Better?" *Journal for the Scientific Study of Religion 32* (1993): 231–241.

Swallow, B. M., and M. Woudyalew. "Evaluating the Willingness to Contribute to a Local Public Good: Application of Contingent Valuation to Tsetse Control in Ethiopia." *Ecological Economics 11* (1994): 153–161.

Tideman, Nicolaus T. "Ethical Foundations of the Demand Revealing Process." *Public Choice* (Spring 1977, Supplement): 71–77.

Tideman, T. Nicolaus, and Tullock, Gordon. "A New and Superior Process for Making Social Choices." *Journal of Political Economy 84* (December 1976): 1145–1159.

Varian, Hal. "Markets for Public Goods?" *Critical Review 7* (1993): 539–557.

## Optimal Government Intervention

Arnott, Richard. "Time for Revisionism on Rent Control?" *Journal of Economic Perspectives 9* (Winter 1995): 99–120.

Backhaus, Jurgen G. "Assessing the Performance of Public Enterprises: A Public–Choice Approach." *European Journal of Law and Economics 1* (December 1994): 275–287.

Baumol, William J., and David F. Bradford. "Optimal Departures from Marginal Pricing." *American Economic Review 60* (June 1970): 265–283.

Bennett, James T., and Thomas J. DiLorenzo. *Underground Government: The Off–Budget Public Sector.* Washington, D.C.: Cato Institute, 1984.

Bennett, James T., and Manuel H. Johnson. "Tax Reductions without Sacrifice: Private-Sector Production of Public Services." *Public Finance Quarterly* (October 1980): 363–396.

Bhattacharyya, Arunava, Elliot Parker, and Kambiz Raffiee. "An Examination of the Effect of Ownership on the Relative Efficiency of Public and Private Water Utilities." *Land Economics 70* (May 1994): 197–209.

Boarman, Patrick M. "Antitrust Laws in a Global Market." *Challenge 36* (January–February 1993): 30–36.

Borcherding, Thomas E. "The Causes of Government Expenditure Growth: A Survey of the U.S. Evidence." *Journal of Public Economics 28* (1985): 359–382.

Borcherding, Thomas E., Werner W. Pommerehne, and Friedrich Schneider. "Comparing the Efficiency of Private and Public Production: The Evidence from Five Countries." *Journal of Economics* (1982): 127–156.

Bridge, Gary. "Citizen Choice in Public Services: Voucher Systems," in *Alternatives for Delivery of Public Services: Toward Improved Performance*, edited by E. S. Savas (51–109). Boulder, Colorado: Westview Press, 1977.

Browning, Edgar K. "Subsidies Financed with Distorting Taxes." *National Tax Journal 46* (June 1993): 121–134.

Buchanan, James M. *Fiscal Theory and Political Economy: Selected Essays.* Chapel Hill: University of North Carolina Press, 1960.

Congressional Budget Office. *Controlling the Risks of Government-Sponsored Enterprises.* Washington, D.C.: U.S. Government Printing Office, April 1991.

Dowd, Kevin. "Is Banking a Natural Monopoly?" *Kyklos 45* (Fasc. 3, 1992): 379–392.

Ellwood, John W., and Eric M. Patashnik. "In Praise of Pork." *The Public Interest* (Winter 1993): 19–33.

Foster, C. D. *Privatization, Public Ownership and the Regulation of Natural Monopoly.* Oxford, United Kingdom: Blackwell Publishers, 1992.

Friedman, Milton. *Capitalism and Freedom.* Chicago: University of Chicago Press, 1962.

Gramlich, Edward M., and Daniel L. Rubinfeld. "Voting on Public Spending: Differences between Public Employees, Transfer Receipts, and Private Workers." *Journal of Policy Analysis and Management 1* (1982): 516–533.

Hollas, Daniel R., and Stanley R. Stansell. "The Economic Efficiency of Public vs. Private Gas Distribution Utilities." *Annals of Public and Co–operative Economy 65* (1994): 281–300.

Joulfaian, David, and Michael L. Marlow. "The Relationship Between On–Budget and Off–Budget Government." *Economics Letters 35* (1991): 307–310.

Korszyk, Sophie M. "Private Finance for Public Works: The U.S. Experience." *Annals of Public and Cooperative Economics 63* (1992): 103–118.

Lawson, Colin. "The Theory of State-Owned Enterprises in Market Economies." *Journal of Economic Surveys 8* (September 1994): 283–309.

Lloyd, Robert E. "Government–Induced Market Failure: A Note on the Origins of FHA Mortgage Insurance." *Critical Review 8* (Winter 1994): 61–71.

Lowry, Edward D. "Justification for Regulation: The Case for Natural Monopoly." *Public Utilities Fortnightly* (November 8, 1973): 17–22.

Meltzer, Allan H., and Scott F. Richard. "A Rational Theory of the Size of Government." *Journal of Political Economy 89* (October 1981): 914–927.

Moe, Ronald C., and Thomas Stanton. "Government-Sponsored Enterprises as Federal Instrumentalities: Reconciling Private Management with Public Accountability." *Public Administration Review* (July/August 1989): 321–329.

Munnell, Alicia H. "Infrastructure Investment and Economic Growth." *Journal of Economic Perspectives 6* (Fall 1992): 189–198.

Musolf, Lloyd. "Government-Sponsored Enterprises and Congress." *Public Administration Review 51* (March/April 1991): 131–137.

Naysnerski, Wendy, and Tom Tietenberg. "Private Enforcement of Federal Environmental Law." *Land Economics 68* (February 1992): 28–48.

Peltzman, Sam. "The Growth of Government." *Journal of Law and Economics 23* (October 1980): 209–288.

Pilgrim, Tim A. "Newspapers as Natural Monopolies: Some Historical Considerations." *Journalism History 18* (1992): 3–10.

Plott, Charles R., Alexandre Borges Sugiyama, and Gilad Elbaz. "Economies of Scale, Natural Monopoly, and Imperfect Competition in an Experimental Market." *Southern Economic Journal 61* (October 1994): 261–287.

Roberts, Russell D. "Government Subsidies to Private Spending on Public Goods." *Public Choice 74* (September 1992): 133–152.

Sanders, Heywood T. "What Infrastructure Crisis?" *The Public Interest* (Winter 1993): 3–18.

Seidman, Harold. "Government Sponsored Enterprises: One View." *Public Budgeting & Finance 9* (Autumn 1989): 76–80.

Stanton, Thomas H. "Government Sponsored Enterprises: Another View." *Public Budgeting & Finance 9* (Autumn 1989): 81–86.

———. *A State of Risk: Will Government–Sponsored Enterprises Be the Next Financial Crisis?* New York: HarperCollins, 1991.

Steiner, Peter O. "The Public Sector and the Public Interest," in *Public Expenditure and Policy Analysis,* edited by Robert H. Haveman and Julius Margolis (3–41). Boston: Houghton Mifflin Company, 1983.

Summers, Lawrence. "Some Simple Economics of Mandated Benefits (What Can Economics Contribute to Social Policy?)." *American Economic Review 79* (May 1989): 177–183.

Tatom, John A. "Public Capital and Private Sector Performance." *Review of the Federal Reserve Bank of St. Louis 73* (May/June 1991): 3–15.

Train, Kenneth E. *Optimal Regulation: The Economic Theory of Natural Monopoly.* Cambridge, Massachusetts: The MIT Press, 1991.

Tullock, Gordon. *Private Wants, Public Means.* New York: Basic Books, 1970.

U.S. Department of Treasury. *Report of the Secretary of the Treasury on Government Sponsored Enterprises.* Washington, D.C.: U.S. Government Printing Office, May 1990.

Weicher, John C. "The New Structure of the Housing Finance System." *Federal Reserve Bank of St. Louis Review 76* (July/August 1994): 47–66.

Weisskopf, Thomas E. "Challenges to Market Socialism: A Response to the Critics." *Dissent* (Spring 1992): 250–261.

Winston, Clifford. "Economic Deregulation: Days of Reckoning for Microeconomists." *Journal of Economic Literature 31* (September 1993): 1263–1289.

———. "Efficient Transportation Infrastructure Policy." *Journal of Economic Perspectives 5* (Winter 1991): 113–127.

Wolf, Charles, Jr. "A Theory of Non-Market Failures." *The Public Interest 55* (Spring 1979): 114–133.

Woodward, G. Thomas. "Government Sponsored Enterprises: Another View." *Public Budgeting & Finance 9* (Autumn 1989): 87–93.

Wray, Randall L. "Book Reviews—A State of Risk: Will Government-Sponsored Enterprises Be the Next Financial Crisis? by Thomas H. Stanton." *Journal of Economic Issues 26* (March 1992): 275–285.

Zajac, Edward E. "Basic Ramsey Prices in the Regulated Sector," in *Fairness or Efficiency: An Introduction to Public Utility Pricing* (21–32). Cambridge, Massachusetts: Ballinger Publishing, 1978.

## Public Choice

Abbott, Alden F., and Gordon L. Brady. "Welfare Gains from Innovation-Induced Rent Seeking." *Cato Journal 11* (Spring/Summer 1991): 89–97.

Allen, Stuart D., Joseph M. Sulock, and William A. Sabo. "The Political Business Cycle: How Significant?" *Public Finance Quarterly 14* (January 1986): 107–112.

Arrow, Kenneth J. *Social Choice and Individual Values,* 2nd edition. New York: Wiley, 1963.

Bennett, James T., and William P. Orzechowski. "The Voting Behavior of Bureaucrats: Some Empirical Evidence." *Public Choice 41* (1983): 271–283.

Black, Duncan. *The Theory of Committees and Elections.* Cambridge, United Kingdom: Cambridge University Press, 1958.

Blair, Douglas H., and Pollak, Robert A. "Rational Collective Choice." *Scientific American 249* (August 1983): 88–95.

Bonner, John. *Introduction to the Theory of Social Choice.* Baltimore, Maryland: Johns Hopkins University Press, 1986.

Bowen, Richard L., James E. T. Moncur, and Richard L. Pollock. "Rent Seeking, Wealth Transfers and Water Rights: The Hawaii Case." *Natural Resources Journal 31* (1991): 429–448.

Bowles, Samuel, Herbert Gintis, and Bo Gustafsson (eds.). *Markets and Democracy: Participation, Accountability and Efficiency.* Cambridge, United Kingdom: Cambridge University Press, 1993.

Brunner, Karl, and Meckling, William H. "The Perception of Man and the Conception of Government." *Journal of Money, Credit, and Banking 9* (February 1977): 70–85.

Buchanan, James M., and Tullock, Gordon. *The Calculus of Consent.* Ann Arbor: University of Michigan Press, 1962.

Carter, John R., and David Schap. "Line-Item Veto: Where Is Thy Sting?" *Journal of Economic Perspectives 4* (Spring 1990): 103–118.

Congleton, Roger D. "Evaluating Rent Seeking Losses: Do the Welfare Gains of Lobbyists Count?" *Public Choice 56* (1988): 181–184.

Coughlin, Peter J. "Majority Rule and Election Models." *Journal of Economic Surveys 3* (1990): 157–188.

Cowen, Tyler, Amihai Glazer, and Henry McMillan. "Rent Seeking Can Promote the Provision of Public Goods." *Economics and Politics 6* (July 1994): 131–145.

Doel, Hans van den, and Ben van Velthoven. *Democracy and Welfare Economics,* 2nd edition. Cambridge: Cambridge University Press, 1993.

Downs, Anthony. *An Economic Theory of Democracy.* New York: Harper & Row, 1957.

Ekelund, Robert, Jr. "An Economic Model of the Medieval Church: Usury as a Form of Rent Seeking." *Journal of Law, Economics, and Organization 5* (Fall 1989): 307–331.

Feenstra, Robert C. "How Costly Is Protectionism?" *Journal of Economic Perspectives 6* (Summer 1992): 159–178.

Feldman, Allan. "Manipulating Voting Procedures." *Economic Inquiry 27* (July 1979): 452–474.

Glazer, Amihai. "On the Incentives to Establish and Play Political Rent-Seeking Games." *Public Choice 75* (1993): 139–148.

Green, Jerry, and Jean–Jacques Laffont. *Individual Incentives in Public Decision-Making.* Amsterdam: North Holland, 1979.

Hardin, Russell. *Collective Action.* Baltimore, Maryland: Johns Hopkins University Press, 1982.

Hazlett, Thomas W., and Robert J. Michaels. "The Cost of Rent-Seeking: Evidence from Cellular Telephone License Lotteries." *Southern Economic Journal 59* (January 1993): 425–435.

Joulfaian, David, and Michael L. Marlow. "Incentives and Political Contributions." *Public Choice 69* (1991): 351–355.

Kalt, Joseph, and Mark Zupan. "Capture and Ideology in the Economic Theory of Politics." *American Economic Review 74* (June 1984): 279–300.

Kelman, Steven. "'Public Choice' and Public Spirit." *The Public Interest 87* (Spring 1987): 80–94.

Littlechild, S. C. and Jack Wiseman. "The Political Economy of Restriction of Choice." *Public Choice 51* (1986): 161–171.

MacKay, Alfred F. *Arrow's Theorem: The Paradox of Social Choice.* New Haven, Connecticut: Yale University Press, 1980.

MacKay, Robert, and Carolyn Weaver. "Agenda Control by Budget Maximizers in a Multi-Bureau Setting." *Public Choice 37* (1981): 447–472.

McNutt, Patrick A. "Rent-Seeking and X-Inefficiency." *Public Choice 75* (1993): 371–378.

Medema, Steven C. "Another Look at the Problem of Rent-Seeking." *Journal of Economic Issues 25* (December 1991): 1049–1065.

Migue, Jean–Luc, and Richard Marceau. "Pollution Taxes, Subsidies, and Rent Seeking." *Canadian Journal of Economics 26* (May 1993): 355–365.

Mueller, Dennis C. *Public Choice II.* Cambridge, United Kingdom: Cambridge University Press, 1989.

Niskanen, William A., Jr. *Bureaucracy and Representative Government.* Chicago: Aldine-Atherton, 1971.

Paul, Chris, and Al Wilhite. "Illegal Markets and the Social Cost of Rent-Seeking." *Public Choice 79* (1994): 105–115.

Peltzman, Sam. "An Economic Interpretation of the History of Congressional Voting in the Twentieth Century." *American Economic Review 75* (September 1985): 656–675.

Riker, William H. "Arrows Theorem and Some Examples of the Paradox of Voting," in *Mathematical Applications in Political Science* edited by John M. Claunch (41–60). Dallas: Arnold Foundation, 1965.

Rivlin, Alice M. "Economics and the Political Process." *American Economic Review 77* (March 1987): 1–10.

Rowley, Charles K., Robert D. Tollison, and Gordon Tullock (eds.). *The Political Economy of Rent-Seeking.* Boston: Kluwer Academic Publishers, 1988.

Saari, Donald G. *Geometry of Voting.* Berlin: Springer-Verlag, 1994.

Schnytzer, Adi. "Changes in the Budgetary Allocations and International Comparisons of the Social Cost of Rent-Seeking: A Critical Note." *Public Choice 79* (1994): 357–362.

Schultze, Charles L. "Excerpts from a Political Handbook for Economic Policy Advisors" (317–324), in *Money, Macroeconomics, and Economic Policy: Essays in Honor of James Tobin,* William C. Brainard, William D. Nordhaus, and Harold W. Watts (eds.). Cambridge, Massachusetts: The MIT Press, 1991.

Scully, Gerald W., and Daniel J. Slottje. "Ranking Economic Liberty across Countries." *Public Choice 69* (1991): 121–152.

Steen, Lynn A. "Election Mathematics: Do All Those Numbers Mean What They Say?" Reprinted in *Scientific American 243* (October 1980): 16–26B.

Stevens, Joe B. *The Economics of Collective Choice.* Boulder, Colorado: Westview Press, 1993.

Stewart, Ian. "Election Fever in Blockvotia." *Scientific American* (July 1995): 88–89.

Sulock, Joseph M. "The Free Rider and Voting Paradox 'Games'." *Journal of Economic Education 21* (Winter 1990): 65–69.

"Symposium: Economics of Voting." *Journal of Economic Perspectives 9* (Winter 1995): 3–98.

Thorbecke, Willem. "Rent Seeking and the Cost of Protectionism." *Journal of Economic Perspectives 7* (Spring 1993): 213–215.

Tullock, Gordon. *Autocracy.* Dordrecht, The Netherlands: Martinus Nijhoff Publishers, 1987.

———. "Rents, Ignorance, and Ideology," in *The Economics of Special Privilege and Rent Seeking* (ch. 2, 11–27). Boston: Kluwer Academic Publishers, 1989.

———. "The Welfare Costs of Monopolies, Tariffs, and Theft." *Western Economic Journal 5* (Fall 1967): 224–232.

Wilson, James Q. *Bureaucracy: What Government Agencies Do and Why They Do It.* New York: Basic Books, 1989.

## Cost–Benefit Analysis

Adams, John. "The Emperor's Old Clothes: The Curious Comeback of Cost–Benefit Analysis." *Environmental Values 2* (1993): 247–260.

Anderson, Lee G. and Russell F. Settle. *Benefit-Cost Analysis: A Practical Guide.* Lexington, Kentucky: D. C. Heath, 1977.

Arrow, Kenneth J. "Criteria for Social Investment." *Water Resources Research 1* (1965): 1–8.

Boardman, Anthony, Aidan Vining, and W. G. Waters. "Costs and Benefits through Bureaucratic Lenses: Example of a Highway Project." *Journal of Policy Analysis and Management 12* (1993): 532–555.

DiIulio, John J., Jr., and Anne Morrison Piehl. "Does Prison Pay: The Stormy National Debate over the Cost-Effectiveness of Imprisonment." *The Brookings Review* (Fall 1991): 28–35.

Gelles, Gregory M. "Costs and Benefits of HIV-1 Antibody Testing of Donated Blood." *Journal of Policy Analysis and Management 12* (1993): 512–531.

Gillespie, Stephen. "Are Economic Statistics Overproduced?" *Public Choice 67* (December 1990): 227–242.

Gilroy, John Martin. "The Ethical Poverty of Cost-Benefit Methods: Autonomy, Efficiency and Public Policy Choice." *Policy Sciences 25* (1992): 83–102

Gomez–Ibanez, Jose A. "Rescission of the Passive Restraints Standard: Costs and Benefits," in *Cases in Microeconomics* by Jose A. Gomez–Ibanez and Jospeh P. Kalt (95–106). Englewood Cliffs, New Jersey: Prentice-Hall, 1990.

Gramlich, Edward M. *A Guide to Benefit-Cost Analysis,* 2nd edition. Englewood Cliffs, New Jersey: Prentice Hall, 1990.

Greenberg, David H. "Conceptual Issues in Cost/Benefit Analysis of Welfare-To-Work Programs." *Contemporary Policy Issues 10* (October 1992): 51–64.

Hocking, Martin B. "Paper Versus Polystyrene: A Complex Choice." *Science 251* (February 1, 1991): 504–505.

Joskow, Paul L., and Donald B. Marron. "What Does Utility-Subsidized Energy Efficiency Really Cost?" *Science 260* (April 16, 1993): 281, 370.

Krupnick, Alan J., and Paul R. Portney. "Controlling Urban Air Pollution: A Benefit-Cost Assessment." *Science 252* (April 26, 1991): 522–528.

Larovere, E. L., L. F. L. Legey, and J. D. G. Miguez. "Alternative Energy Strategies for Abatement of Carbon Emissions in Brazil—A Cost–Benefit Analysis." *Energy Policy 22* (1994): 914–924.

Levy, David T., and Ted R. Miller. "A Cost-Benefit Analysis of Enforcement Efforts to Reduce Serving Intoxicated Patrons." *Journal of Studies on Alcohol 56* (March 1995): 240–247.

Meeks, Thomas J. "The Economic Efficiency and Equity of Abortion." *Economics and Philosophy 6* (April 1990): 95–138.

Mishan, Edward J. *Cost-Benefit Analysis.* New York: Praeger, 1976.

Nelson, Julianne. "Persuasion and Economic Efficiency: The Cost-Benefit Analysis of Banning Abortion." *Economics and Philosophy 9* (October 1993): 229–252.

Pack, Janet Rothemberg. "You Ride, I'll Pay." *The Brookings Review* (Summer 1992): 48–51.

Pearce, David W. *Economic Values and the Natural World.* Cambridge, Massachusetts: The MIT Press, 1993.

Pimentel, David, C. Harvey, P. Resodudarmo, K. Sinclair, D. Kurz, M. McNair, S. Crist, L. Shpritz, L. Fitton, R. Saffouri and R. Blair. "Environmental and Economic Costs of Soil Erosion and Conservation Benefits." *Science 267* (February 24, 1995): 1117– 1123.

Stevens, T. H., R. Glass, T. More, and J. Echeverria. "Wildlife Recovery: Is Benefit-Cost Analysis Appropriate?" *Journal of Environmental Management 33* (1991): 327–334.

Trumbell, William N. "Who Has Standing in Cost-Benefit Analysis?" *Journal of Policy Analysis and Management 9* (1990): 201–218.

Williams, Alan. "Cost-Benefit Analysis: Bastard Science? And/Or Insidious Poison in the Body Politick?" in *Public Expenditure and Policy Analysis* (3rd edition) edited by Robert H. Haveman and Julius Margolis (535–560). Dallas: Houghton Mifflin, 1983.

Wisniewski, Stanley C. "Analyzing the Contracting-Out of Government Services: Relevant Cost-Benefit Considerations." *Public Budgeting and Finance 11* (Summer 1991): 95–107.

# Distribution of Income

Aaron, Henry J., Thomas E. Mann, and Timothy Taylor (eds.). *Values and Public Policy.* Washington D.C.: The Brookings Institution, 1994.

Ackerman, Bruce A. *Social Justice in the Liberal State.* New Haven: Yale University Press, 1980.

Arrow, Kenneth J. "Some Ordinalist-Utilitarian Notes on Rawls's Theory of Justice." *Journal of Philosophy 70* (1973): 245–263.

Barthold, Thomas A. "How Should We Measure Distribution?" *National Tax Journal 46* (September 1993): 291–299.

Baynes, Kenneth. *The Normative Grounds of Social Criticism: Kant, Rawls, and Habermas.* Albany, New York: State University of New York Press, 1992.

Blinder, Alan S. "The Level and Distribution of Economic Well Being," in *The American Economy in Transition,* edited by Martin Feldstein (415–479). Chicago: University of Chicago Press, 1980.

Bond, Doug, and Jong-Chul Park. "An Empirical Test of Rawls's Theory of Justice: A Second Approach, in Korea and the United States." *Simulation & Gaming 22* (December 1991): 443–462.

Bound, J., and G. Johnson. "Changes in the Structure of Wages in 1980s." *American Economic Review 82* (June 1992): 371–392.

Burtless, Gary. "The Contribution of Employment and Hours Changes to Family Income Inequality." *The American Economic Review 83* (May 1993): 131–135.

Cutler, David M., and Lawrence F. Katz. "Untouched by the Rising Tide: Why the 1980s Economic Expansion Left the Poor Behind." *The Brookings Review* (Winter 1992): 41–45.

Danziger, Sheldon, and Peter Gottschalk (eds.). *Uneven Tides: Rising Inequality in America.* New York: Russell Sage Foundation, 1993.

Foley, Duncan K. "State Expenditure from a Marxist Perspective." *Journal of Public Economics 9* (1978): 221–238.

Gaertner, Wulf. "Distributive Justice: Theoretical Foundations and Empirical Findings." *European Economic Review 38* (1994): 711–720.

Inhaber, Herbert, and Sidney Carroll. *How Rich Is Too Rich? Income and Wealth in America.* New York: Praeger, 1992.

Kosters, Marvin H. "The Rise in Income Inequality: What it Means for a Society Like Ours." *The American Enterprise* (November–December 1992): 29–37.

Krugman, Paul. "The Income Distribution Disparity." *Challenge 33* (July–August 1990): 4–6.

Kukathas, Chandran, and Philip Pettit. *Rawls: A Theory of Justice and Its Critics.* Stanford: Stanford University Press, 1990.

Miller, David. "Distributive Justice: What the People Think?" *Ethics 102* (April 1992): 555–593.

Mueller, Dennis C. "Achieving the Just Policy." *American Economic Review 64* (May 1974): 147–152.

Nussbaum, Martha, and Amartya Sen (eds.). *The Quality of Life.* Oxford: Clarendon Press, 1993.

Okun, Arthur. *Equality and Efficiency: The Big Trade-Off.* Washington, D.C.: Brookings Institution, 1975.

Phillips, Kevin. *The Politics of Rich and Poor: Wealth and the American Electorate in the Reagan Aftermath.* New York: Random House, 1990.

Rawls, John. "Concepts of Distributional Equity: Some Reasons for the Maximin Criterion." *American Economic Review 64* (May 1974): 141–146.

Ricoeur, Paul. "On John Rawls' A Theory of Justice: Is a Pure Procedural Theory of Justice Possible?" *International Social Science Journal 42* (1992): 553–564.

Rose, Stephen J. "Declining Family Incomes in the 1980s: New Evidence from Longitudinal Data." *Challenge 36* (November–December 1993): 29–36.

Schokkaert, Erik, and Bart Capeau. "Interindividual Differences in Opinions about Distributive Justice." *Kyklos 44* (Fall 1991): 325–345.

Sen, Amartya. *Choice, Welfare, and Measurement.* Cambridge, Massachusetts: The MIT Press, 1982.

———. *Inequality Reexamined.* Cambridge Massachusetts: Harvard University Press, 1992.

———. *On Economic Inequality.* New York: WW Norton, 1973.

Sen, Amartya and Bernard Williams (eds.). *Utilitarianism and Beyond.* Cambridge, United Kingdom: Cambridge University Press, 1982.

Thurow, Lester C. "A Surge in Inequality." *Scientific American* (May 1987): 30–37.

Tietenberg, Thomas H. "The Poverty Connection to Environmental Policy." *Challenge 33* (September/October 1990): 26–32.

Tullock, Gordon. *Welfare for the Well-to-Do.* Dallas: Fisher Institute, 1983.

Waldrop, Judith. "Choose the Income That's Right for You." *American Demographics 14* (December 1992): 9–10.

## Poverty Programs

Asher, Martin A., Robert H. Defina, and Kishor Thanawala. "The Misery Index: Only Part of the Story." *Challenge 36* (March–April 1993): 58–62.

Atkinson, A. B. "The Welfare State and Economic Performance." *National Tax Journal 48* (June 1995): 171–198.

Bell, Carolyn Shaw. "What Is Poverty?" *American Journal of Economics and Sociology 54* (April 1995): 161–162.

Blank, Rebecca M. "Proposals for Time-Limited Welfare." *Journal of Economic Perspectives 8* (Fall 1994): 183–193.

Browning, Edgar K. "Effects of the Earned Income Tax Credit on Income and Welfare." *National Tax Journal 48* (March 1995): 23–43.

————. "The Marginal Cost of Redistribution." *Public Finance Quarterly 21* (January 1993): 3–32.

Burtless, Gary. "The Economist's Lament: Public Assistance in America." *Journal of Economic Perspectives 4* (Winter 1990): 57–78.

————. "Employment Prospects of Welfare Recipients," in *The Work Alternative: Welfare Reform and the Realities of the Job Market,* edited by Demetra Smith Nightingale and Robert H. Haveman (ch. 4, 71–106). Washington, D.C.: The Urban Institute Press, 1995.

————. "Inequality in America: Where Do We Stand?" *The Brookings Review* (Summer 1987).

————. "Paychecks or Welfare Checks: Can AFDC Recipients Support Themselves?" *The Brookings Review* (Fall 1994): 34–37.

————. "When Work Doesn't Work: Employment Programs for Welfare Recipients." *The Brookings Review* (Spring 1992): 27–29.

Colburn, Christopher B. "A Public Choice Explanation for the Decline in Real Income Transfers." *Public Finance Quarterly 18* (January 1990): 123–134.

Currie, Janet. "Welfare and the Well-Being of Children: The Relative Effectiveness of Cash and In-Kind Transfers," in *Tax Policy and the Economy, Volume 8,* edited by James M. Poterba (1–43). Cambridge, Massachusetts: The MIT Press, 1994.

Currie, Janet, and Duncan Thomas. "Does Head Start Make a Difference?" *American Economic Review 85* (June 1995): 341–363.

Cutler, David, and Lawrence F. Katz. "Raising Inequality? Changes in the Distribution of Income and Consumption in the 1980s." *American Economic Review 82* (May 1992): 546–551.

Danziger, Sheldon. "Relearning Lessons of the War on Poverty." *Challenge 34* (September–October 1991): 53–54.

Delorme, Charles D., Jr., David R. Kamerschen, and David C. Redman. "The First U.S. Food Stamp Program: An Example of Rent Seeking and Avoiding." *American Journal of Economics and Sociology 51* (October 1992): 421–434.

Dickert, Stacy, Scott Houser, and John Karl Scholz. "The Earned Income Tax Credit and Transfer Programs: A Study of Labor Market and Program Participation," in *Tax Policy and the Economy 9,* edited by James M. Poterba (1–50). Cambridge, Massachusetts: The MIT Press, 1995.

Ellwood, David T., and Summers, Lawrence H. "Is Welfare Really the Problem?" *The Public Interest* (Spring 1986): 57–78.

Friedman, Milton. "The Case for the Negative Income Tax," in *Republican Papers,* edited by Melvin R. Laird (202–220). New York: Praeger, 1968.

Fuchs, Victor R., and Diane M. Reklis. "America's Children: Economic Perspectives and Policy Options." *Science 255* (3 January 1992): 41–46.

Gardner, Bruce L. "Changing Economic Perspectives on the Farm Problem." *Journal of Economic Literature 30* (March 1992): 62–101.

Gist, John R. "Entitlement Spending: Myths and Realities." *Tax Notes* (December 20, 1993): 1515–1519.

Gramlich, Edward M. "Economists' View of the Welfare System." *The American Economic Review 79* (May 1989): 191–196.

Gueron, Judith M. "Work and Welfare: Lessons on Employment Programs." *Journal of Economic Perspectives 4* (Winter 1990): 79–98.

Hancock, K. E. "Can Pay? Won't Pay? Or Economic Principles of Affordability." *Urban Studies 30* (February 1993): 127–145.

Haveman, Robert. "When Problems Outrun Policy." *Challenge 36* (May–June 1993): 28–35.

———. "Who Are the Nation's Truly Poor? Problems and Pitfalls in (Re)Defining and Measuring Poverty." *The Brookings Review* (Winter 1993): 24–27.

Haveman, Robert, and John Karl Scholz. "Transfers, Taxes, and Welfare Reform." *National Tax Journal 47* (June 1994): 417–434.

Holtzblatt, Janet, Janet McCubbin, and Robert Gillette. "Promoting Work through the EITC." *National Tax Journal 47* (September 1994): 591–607.

Jenkins, Vlad. "The Urban League and the Youth Subminimum Wage," in *Cases in Microeconomics,* edited by Jose A. Gomez–Ibanez and Joseph P. Kalt (152–173). Englewood Cliffs, New Jersey: Prentice Hall, 1990.

Kosters, Marvin H. "The Earned Income Tax Credit and the Working Poor." *The American Enterprise* (May–June 1993): 65–72.

LaLonde, Robert J. "The Promise of Public Sector–Sponsored Training Programs." *Journal of Economic Perspectives 9* (Spring 1995): 149–168.

Levitan, Sara, and Frank Gallo. "Wanted: Federal Public Service Program." *Challenge 34* (May–June 1991): 32–40.

Mazur, Jay. "The Minimum Wage Revisited." *Challenge 38* (July–August 1995): 23–28.

Mead, Lawrence M. "The New Politics of the New Poverty." *The Public Interest* (Spring 1991): 3–20.

Melnick, R. Shep. "Interpreting Entitlements: The Politics of Statutory Construction." *The Brookings Review* (Winter 1994): 40–45.

Mincy, Ronald B., Isabel V. Sawhill, and Douglas A. Wolf. "The Underclass: Definition and Measurement." *Science 248* (27 April 1990): 450–453.

Moffit, Robert. "An Economic Model of Welfare Stigma." *American Economic Review 73* (December 1983): 1023–1035.

———. "Incentive Effects of the U.S. Welfare System: A Review." *Journal of Economic Literature 30* (March 1992): 1–61.

Nerlove, Marc, Assaf Razin, and Efraim Sadka. "Children: A Capital Good or a Base for Income Redistribution Policies." *Public Finance–Finances Publique 48* (1993): 78–84.

Nightingale, Demetra Smith, and Robert H. Haveman (eds.). *The Work Alternative: Welfare Reform and the Realities of the Job Market.* Washington, D.C.: The Urban Institute Press, 1995.

Ohls, James C., and Harold Beebout. *The Food Stamp Program: Design Tradeoffs, Policy, and Impacts.* Washington, D.C.: The Urban Institute Press, 1993.

Phelps, Edmund S. "Raising the Employment and Pay of the Working Poor: Low-Wage Employment Subsidies versus the Welfare State." *American Economic Review 84* (May 1994): 54–70.

———. "Low-Wage Employment Subsidies versus Welfare State." *American Economic Review 84* (May 1994): 54–58.

Press, S. James, and Judith M. Tanur. "The Confluence of Sociology, Statistics, and Public Policy in the Quality Control of the Food Stamps, AFDC, and Medicaid Family Assistance Programs." *Evaluation Review 15* (June 1991): 315–332.

Pressman, Steven. "The $1000 Question: A Tax Credit to End Child Poverty?" *Challenge 35* (January–February 1992): 49–52.

Sawhill, Isabel V. "Poverty in the U.S.: Why Is It So Persistent?" *Journal of Economic Literature 26* (September 1988): 1073–1119.

Smeeding, Timothy M. "Why the U.S. Antipoverty System Doesn't Work Very Well." *Challenge 35* (January–February 1992): 30–35.

Smeeding, Thomas M., and Barbara Boyd Torrey. "Poor Children in Rich Countries." *Science* (November 11, 1988): 873–878.

Standing, Guy. "The Road to Workfare: Alternative to Welfare or Threat to Occupation?" *International Labour Review 129* (1990): 677–691.

Steuerle, C. Eugene. "Tax Credits and Family Values." *The Responsive Community 5* (Summer 1995): 44–49.

———. "Tax Credits for Low-Income Workers with Children." *Journal of Economic Perspectives 4* (Summer 1990): 201–212.

Tullock, Gordon. *Economics of Income Redistribution.* Boston: Kluwer–Nijhoff Publishing, 1983.

Wagner, Richard E. *To Promote the General Welfare: Market Processes vs. Political Transfers.* San Francisco: Pacific Research Institute for Public Policy, 1989.

## Public Education

Brown, Frank. "Privatization of Public Education: Theories and Concepts." *Education and Urban Society 27* (February 1995): 114–126.

Brown, Frank, and Richard C. Hunter. "Introduction: Privatization of Public School Services." *Education and Urban Society 27* (February 1995): 107–113.

Chubb, John E., and Terry M. Moe. "America's Public Schools: Choice Is a Panacea." *Brookings Review* (Summer 1990): 4–12.

Couch, Jim F., William F. Shughart, II, and Al L. Williams. "Private School Enrollment and Public School Performance." *Public Choice 76* (1993): 301–312.

Edlin, Aaron S. "Is College Financial Aid Equitable and Efficient?" *Journal of Economic Perspectives 7* (Spring 1993): 143–158.

Feldstein, Martin. "College Scholarship Rules and Private Saving." *American Economic Review 85* (June 1995): 552–566.

Friedman, Milton. "The Role of Government in Education," in *Capitalism and Freedom* (ch. VI, 85–107). Chicago: University of Chicago Press, 1962.

Glenn, Charles L. "Controlled Choice in Massachusetts Public Schools." *The Public Interest* (Spring 1991): 88–105.

Hauptman, Arthur M. "Navigating the Maze of New College Financing Options." *Brookings Review* (Summer 1990): 32–38.

Kane, Thomas J., and Cecilia Elena Rouse. "Labor-Market Returns to Two- and Four-Year College." *American Economic Review 85* (June 1995): 600–614.

Kohl, Herbert. "In Defense of Public Education." *Dissent* (Spring 1993): 227–232.

McPherson, Michael S., and Morton Owen Schapiro. *Keeping College Affordable: Government Educational Opportunity.* Washington, D.C.: Brookings Institution, 1991.

———. "Paying for College: Rethinking the Role of the States and the Federal Government." *Brookings Review* (Summer 1991): 14–19.

Monk, David H. "Productivity Issues in Education Finance: The Connection Between Research and Policy." *1993 Proceedings of the Eighty-Sixth Annual Conference on Taxation.* Columbus, Ohio: National Tax Association, 1994.

Reschovsky, Andrew. "Fiscal Equalization and School Finance." *National Tax Journal 47* (June 1994): 185–197.

Salop, Steven C., and Lawrence J. White. "Antitrust Goes to College." *Journal of Economic Perspectives 5* (Summer 1991): 193–202.

Sander, William. "Expenditures and Student Achievement in Illinois: New Evidence." *Journal of Public Economics 52* (1993): 403–416.

Stiglitz, Joseph E. "The Demand for Education in Public and Private School Systems." *Journal of Public Economics* (November 1974): 349–385.

Zimmerman, Dennis, and Barbara Miles. "Substituting Direct Government Lending for Guaranteed Student Loans: How Budget Rules Distorted Economic Decisionmaking." *National Tax Journal 47* (December 1994): 773–787.

# Social Insurance

Aaron, Henry J. "Social Security: The Labrea Tar Pits of Public Policy." *National Tax Journal 43* (September 1990): 363–369.

Aaron, Henry J., Barry P. Bosworth, and Gary Burtless. *Can America Afford to Grow Old? Paying For Social Security.* Washington, D.C.: The Brookings Institution, 1989.

Arrau, Patricio, and Klaus Schmidt–Hebbel. "Pension Systems and Reforms: Country Experiences and Research Issues." *Revista de Analisis Economico 9* (June 1994): 3–20.

Atkinson, Anthony B., and John Micklewright. "Unemployment Compensation and Labor Market Transitions: A Critical Review." *Journal of Economic Literature 29* (December 1991): 1679–1727.

Axinn, June, and Mark J. Stern. "Social Security Policy Reconsidered." *Challenge 33* (July–August 1990): 22–27.

Burtless, Gary. "The Tattered Safety Net: Jobless Pay in the United States." *Brookings Review* (Spring 1991): 38–41.

Carlson, Keith M. "The Future of Social Security: An Update." *Review of the Federal Reserve Bank of St. Louis 73* (January/February 1991): 33–49.

Deere, Donald R. "Unemployment Insurance and Employment." *Journal of Labor Economics 9* (October 1991): 307–324.

Diamond, Peter. "Privatization of Social Security: Lessons from Chile." *Revista de Analisis Economico 9* (June 1994): 21–33.

Diamond, Peter and Salvador Valdes-Prieto. "Social Security Reforms," in *The Chilean Economy: Policy Lessons and Challenges,* edited by Barry P. Bosworth, Rudiger Dornbusch, and Raul Laban (ch. 6, 257–320). Washington, D.C.: The Brookings Institution, 1994.

Dilnot, Andrew, and Steven Webb. "A Practical Framework for the Analysis of Social Security Reform." *Fiscal Studies 12* (November 1991): 33–55.

Feldstein, Martin S. "Unemployment Insurance: Time for Reform." *Harvard Business Review* (March–April 1975): 51–61.

Feldstein, Martin, and Andrew Samwick. "Social Security Rules and Marginal Tax Rates." *National Tax Journal 45* (March 1992): 1–22.

Gillion, Colin. "Social Security and Protection in the Developing World." *Monthly Labor Review 117* (September 1994): 24–31.

Hansen, W. Lee, and James F. Byers (eds.). *Unemployment Insurance: The Second Half-Century.* Madison, Wisconsin: University of Wisconsin Press, 1990.

Hurd, Michael D. "Research on the Elderly: Economic Status, Retirement, and Consumption and Saving." *Journal of Economic Literature 28* (June 1990): 565–637.

Iyer, Subramanian N. "Pension Reform in Developing Countries." *International Labour Review 132* (1993): 187–207.

McLaughlin, Eithne. "Work and Welfare Benefits: Social Security, Employment and Unemployment in the 1990s." *Journal of Social Policy 20* (October 1991): 485–508.

Meyer, Bruce C. "Lessons from the U.S. Unemployment Insurance Experiments." *Journal of Economic Literature 33* (March 1995): 91–131.

———. "Unemployment Insurance and Unemployment Spells." *Econometrica 58* (July 1990): 757–789.

Meyer, Charles W., and Nancy Wolff. *Social Security and Individual Equity: Evolving Standards of Equity and Adequacy.* Westport, Connecticut: Greenwood Press, 1993.

Nelissen, Jan H. M. "Lifetime Income Redistribution by Social Security." *Journal of Population Economics 8* (1995): 89–105.

Noguchi, Yukio. "Aging of Population, Social Security, and Tax Reform," in *The Political Economy of Tax Reform,* edited by Takatoshi Ito and Anne O. Krueger (211–230). Chicago: University of Chicago Press, 1992.

Parrott, Alec L. "Social Security: Does the Wartime Dream Have to Become a Peacetime Nightmare?" *International Labour Review 131* (1992): 367–386.

Pattison, David, and David E. Harrington. "Proposals to Modify the Taxation of Social Security Benefits: Options and Distributional Effects." *Social Security Bulletin 56* (Summer 1993): 3–21.

Rejda, George E. *Social Insurance and Economic Security,* 4th edition. Englewood Cliffs, New Jersey: Prentice Hall, 1991.

Rivlin, Alice M. "Four Reasons Not to Cut Social Security Taxes." *The Brookings Review* (Spring 1990): 3–8.

Schmid, Gunther, Bernd Reissert, and Gert Bruche. *Unemployment Insurance and Active Labor Market Policy: An International Comparison of Financing Systems.* Detroit: Wayne State University Press, 1992.

Steuerle, C. Eugene, and Jon M. Bakija. "How Social Security Redistributes Income." *Tax Notes* (March 28, 1994): 1763–1175.

———. *Retooling Social Security for the 21st Century: Right and Wrong Approaches to Reform.* Washington, D.C.: Urban Institute Press, 1994.

Thompson, Lawrence H. "The Social Security Reform Debate." *Journal of Economic Literature* (December 1983): 1425–1467.

Tobin, James. "The Future of Social Security: One Economist's Assessment," in Theodore R. Marmor and Jerry L. Marshaw, eds., *Social Security in Contemporary American Politics,* Princeton, New Jersey: Princeton University Press, 1988.

Vijlbrief, J. A. "Equity and Efficiency in Unemployment Insurance." *De Economist 141* (1993): 214–237.

von Maydell, Bernd. "Perspectives on the Future of Social Security." *International Labour Review 133* (1994): 501–510.

Vroman, Wayne. "Why the Decline in Unemployment Insurance Claims?" *Challenge 34* (September–October 1991): 55–58.

Weaver, Carolyn L. (ed.). *Social Security's Looming Surpluses: Prospects and Implications.* Washington, D.C.: The American Enterprise Institute for Public Policy Research, 1990.

# Health Care

Aaron, Henry J. "Issues Every Plan to Reform Health Care Financing Must Confront." *Journal of Economic Perspectives 8* (Summer 1994): 31–43.

———. *Serious and Unstable Condition: Financing America's Health Care.* Washington, D.C.: Brookings Institution, 1992.

———. "Tax Issues in Health Care Reform." *National Tax Journal 47* (June 1994): 407–416.

Aaron, Henry J., and William B. Schwartz. "Rationing Health Care: The Choice Before Us." *Science 247* (1990): 418–422.

American Medical Association. *Health Access in America: The AMA Proposal to Improve Access to Affordable, Quality Health Care.* Chicago: American Medical Association, 1990.

Arrow, Kenneth. "Uncertainty and the Welfare Economics of Medical Care." *American Economic Review 53* (December 1963): 941–973.

Azevedo, D. (1992): "No Kidding—There's a State Where Doctors like Medicaid." *Health Economics 69* (1992): 126–35.

Barer, M. L., W. P. Welch, L. Antioch. "Canadian/U.S. Health Care: Some Reflections on the HIAA's Analysis." *Health Affairs 10* (Fall 1991): 229–236.

Bruner, Sally T., Daniel R. Waldo, and David R. McKusick. "National Health Expenditures Projections through 2030." *Health Care Financing Review 14* (Fall 1992).

Burman, Leonard E., and Jack Rodgers. "Tax Preferences and Employment-Based Health Insurance." *National Tax Journal 45* (September 1992): 331–346

Congressional Budget Office. *Projections of National Health Expenditures.* Washington, D.C.: U.S. Government Printing Office, October 1992.

Cutler, David M. "Public Finance Issues in Health Reform." *1994 Proceedings of the Eighty-Seventh Annual Conference on Taxation.* Columbus, Ohio: National Tax Association, 1995.

Daniels, Norman. "Equity of Access to Health care: Some Conceptual and Ethical Issues." *Milbank Memorial Fund Quarterly 60* (1982): 51–81.

De Lew, Nancy, George Greenberg, and Kraig Kinchen. "A Layman's Guide to the U.S. Health Care System." *Health Care Financing Review 14* (1992): 151–169.

Ellis, Randall P., and Thomas G. McGuire. "Supply-Side and Demand-Side Cost Sharing in Health Care." *Journal of Economic Perspectives 7* (Fall 1993): 135–151.

Feldstein, Martin, and Jonathan Gruber. "A Major Risk Approach to Health Insurance Reform," in *Tax Policy and the Economy 9,* edited by James M. Poterba (103–130). Cambridge, Massachusetts: The MIT Press, 1995.

Feldstein, Paul J. *Health Care Economics.* Albany New York: Delmar, 1992.

Fuchs, Victor R. "Best Health Care System in the World?" *Journal of American Medical Association 268* (1992): 916–917.

————. "Health System Reform: A Different Approach." *Journal of American Medical Association 272* (August 17, 1994): 560–563.

Gold, Marxha, Karyen Chu, Suzanne Felt, Mary Harrington, and Timothy Lake. "Effects of Selected Cost-Containment Efforts: 1971–1993." *Health Care Financing Review 14* (1993): 183–213.

Hurst, Jeremy W. "Reform of Health Care in Germany." *Health Care Financing Review 12* (1991): 73–86.

Iglemart, John. "Perspectives of an Errant Economist: A Conversation with Tom Schelling." *Health Affairs 9* (Summer 1990): 109–121.

Ikegami, Naoki. "The Economics of Health Care in Japan." *Science 258* (October 23, 1992): 614–618.

Marmor, Theodore R. "Canada's Health Care System: A Model for the United States?" *Current History* (December 1991): 422–423.

McPherson, K. "International Differences in Medical Care Practice." *Health Care Financing Review 10* (1989): 9–19.

Neuschler, E. *Canadian Health Care: The Implications of Public Insurance.* Washington, D.C.: Health Insurance Association of America, 1990.

Newhouse, Joseph. "Medical Care Costs: How Much Economic Loss." *Journal of Economic Perspectives 6* (Summer 1992): 3–22.

Newhouse, Joseph, and the Insurance Experiment Group. *Free for All: Lessons from the RAND Health Insurance Experiment.* Cambridge, Massachusetts: Harvard University Press, 1993.

Pauly, Mark V. "The Economics of Moral Hazard: Comment." *American Economic Review 58* (June 1968): 531–537.

———. "Taxation, Health Insurance, and Market Failure in the Medical Economy." *Journal of Economic Literature 24* (June 1986): 629–675.

Peet, John. "Survey: Health Care." *The Economist* (July 6, 1991): Special Section 1–18.

Phelps, Charles E. "Diffusion of Information in Medical Care." *Journal of Economic Perspectives 6* (Summer 1992): 23–42.

———. *Health Economics.* New York: HarperCollins, 1992.

Phelps, Charles E., and S. T. Parente. "Priority Setting for Medical Technology and Medical Practice Assessment." *Medical Care 28* (1990): 703–723.

Raffel, Marshall W., and Norma K. Raffel. *The U.S. Health System: Origins and Functions,* 4th edition. Albany, New York: Delmar Publishers, 1994.

Reinhardt, Uwe. "Resource Allocation in Health Care: The Allocation of Lifestyles to Providers." *The Milbank Quarterly 65* (1987): 153–176.

Rice, Dorothy P. "Ethics and Equity in U.S. Health Care: The Data." *International Journal of Health Services 21* (1991): 637–651.

Rice, Mitchell F., and Mylon Winn. "Black Health Care and the American Health System: A Political Perspective," in *Health Politics and Policy,* 2nd edition, Theodore Litman and Leonard S. Robins (eds.), Albany, New York: Delmar, 1993.

Rothschild, M. and J. Stiglitz. "Equilibrium in Competitive Insurance Markets: An Essay on the Economics of Imperfect Information." *Quarterly Journal of Economics 90* (1976): 629–649.

Schieber, George J., Jean-Pierre Poullier, and Leslie M. Greenwald. "U.S. Health Expenditure Performance: An International Comparison and Update." *Health Care Financing Review 13* (1992): 1–87.

Stevens, Carl. "Health Care Cost Containment: Some Implications of Global Budgets." *Science 259* (January 1, 1993): 16–17, 105.

"Symposium: Health Care Reform." *Journal of Economic Perspectives 6* (Summer 1992): 3–58.

Torrens, Paul R., and Stephen J. Williams. "Understanding the Present, Planning for the Future: Dynamics of Health Care in the United States in the 1990s," in *Introduction to Health Services,* 4th edition, edited by Paul R. Torrents and Stephen J. Williams. Albany, New York: Delmar, 1993.

Weisbrod, Burton A. "The Health Care Quadrilemma: An Essay on Technological Change, Insurance, Quality of Care, and Cost Containment." *Journal of Economic Literature 29* (June 1991): 523–552.

# Taxation

Akbari, Ather H. "The Public Finance Impact of Immigrant Population on Host Nations: Some Canadian Evidence." *Social Science Quarterly 72* (June 1991): 334–346.

Altig, David, and Charles T. Carlstrom. "The Efficiency and Welfare Effects of Tax Reform: Are Fewer Tax Brackets Better than More?" *Economic Review of the Federal Reserve Bank of Cleveland 30* (1994): 30–42.

Atkinson, A. B. "Optimal Taxation and the Direct versus Indirect Tax Controversy." *Canadian Journal of Economics* (November 1977): 590–606.

Atkinson, Anthony B., and Joseph E. Stiglitz. *Lectures on Public Economics.* London: McGraw–Hill Book Company (UK) Limited, 1980.

Ballard, Charles L., and Don Fullerton. "Distortionary Taxes and the Provision of Public Goods." *Journal of Economic Perspectives 6* (Summer 1992): 117–131.

Ballentine, J. Gregory. "The Structure of the Tax System versus the Level of Taxation." *Journal of Economic Perspectives 6* (Winter 1992): 59–68.

Bator, Francis M. "Why We Must Raise Taxes." *Challenge 33* (March–April 1990): 50–51.

Becsi, Zsolt. "The Long (and Short) on Taxation and Expenditure Policies." *Economic Review of the Federal Reserve Bank of Dallas* (July 1993): 51–64.

Boskin, Michael J. "On Some Recent Econometric Research in Public Finance." *American Economic Review 66* (May 1976): 102–109.

Bosworth, Barry, and Gary Burtless. "Effects of Tax Reform on Labor Supply, Investment, and Saving." *Journal of Economic Perspectives 6* (Winter 1992): 3–25.

Bradford, David F., and Rosen, Harvey S. "The Optimal Taxation of Commodities and Income." *American Economic Review 66* (May 1976): 94–101.

Browning, Edgar K. "On the Marginal Welfare Cost of Taxation." *American Economic Review 77* (March 1987): 11–23.

Buchanan, James M. "The Political Efficiency of General Taxation." *National Tax Journal 46* (December 1993): 401–410.

Burtless, Gary T., and Haveman, Robert H. "Taxes and Transfers: How Much Economic Loss?" *Challenge 30* (March–April 1987): 45–51.

Davie, Bruce F. "Tax Expenditures in the Federal Excise System." *National Tax Journal 47* (March 1994): 39–62.

de Vanssay, Xavier, and Zane A. Spindler. "Is Tax Reform in the Public Interest? A Rent-Seeking Perspective." *Public Finance Quarterly 22* (January 1994): 3–21.

Devaragar, S., D. Fullerton, and R. Musgrave. "Estimating the Distribution of Tax Burdens: A Comparison of Alternative Approaches." *Journal of Public Economics* (April 1980): 155–182.

Feenberg, Daniel R., and James M. Poterba. "Income Inequality and the Incomes of Very High-Income Taxpayers: Evidence from Tax Returns." *Tax Policy and the Economy 7,* edited by James M. Poterba (145–177). Cambridge, Massachusetts: The MIT Press, 1993.

Feldstein, Martin. "On the Theory of Tax Reform." *Journal of Public Economics 6* (1976): 77–104.

Feldstein, Martin. "The Effect of Marginal Tax Rates on Taxable Income: A Panel Study of the 1986 Tax Reform." *Journal of Political Economy 103* (June 1995): 551–572.

———, ed. *The Effects of Taxation on Capital Accumulation.* Chicago: University of Chicago Press, 1987.

Fullerton, Don, and Diane Lim Rogers. *Who Bears the Lifetime Tax Burden?* Washington, D.C.: The Brookings Institution, 1993.

Gravelle, Jane G. "Equity Effects of the Tax Reform Act of 1986." *Journal of Economic Perspectives 6* (Winter 1992): 27–44.

Goode, Richard. "'Economics in the Policy Process': A Comment." *National Tax Journal 47* (June 1994): 403–405.

———. "Tax Advice to Developing Countries: An Historical Survey." *World Development 21* (1993):37–53.

Harberger, Arnold C. *Taxation and Welfare.* Boston: Little, Brown and Company, 1974.

Haveman, Robert M. "Optimal Taxation and Public Policy," in *Modern Public Finance,* edited by John M. Quigley and Eugene Smolensky (ch. 9, 247–256). Cambridge, Massachusetts: Harvard University Press, 1994.

Holcombe, Randall G., and Jeffrey A. Mills. "Is Revenue-Neutral Tax Reform Revenue Neutral?" *Public Finance Quarterly 22* (January 1994): 65–85.

Hubbard, R. Glenn. "On the Use of 'Distribution Tables' in the Tax Policy Process." *National Tax Journal 46* (December 1993): 527–537.

Hulten, Charles R., and Robert M. Schwab. "A Haig-Simons-Tiebout Comprehensive Income Tax." *National Tax Journal 43* (March 1991): 67–78.

Ishi, Hiromitsu. "The Conflict between Efficiency and Equity of Tax Administration." *Hitotsubashi Journal of Economics 33* (December 1992): 129–147.

Ito, Takatoshi, and Anne O. Krueger (eds.). *The Political Economy of Tax Reform.* Chicago: The University of Chicago Press, 1992.

Jorgenson, Dale W., and Kun-Young Yun. "The Excess Burden of Taxation in the United States." *Journal of Accounting, Auditing, and Finance 6* (Fall 1991): 487–508.

Khalilzadeh–Shirazi, Javad, and Anwar Shah. "Tax Reform in Developing Countries." *Finance & Development* (June 1991): 44–47.

Krauss, Melvin B., and Harry J. Johnson. "The Theory of Tax Incidence: A Diagrammatic Analysis." *Economica* (November 1972): 357–382.

Lile, Stephen E. "Family Tax Burdens: How Do the States Compare?" *Spectrum: The Journal of the State Government 65* (Fall 1992): 6–15.

Musgrave, Richard A. "Horizontal Equity, Once More." *National Tax Journal 43* (June 1990): 113–122.

———. "Short of Euphoria." *Journal of Economic Perspectives 1* (Summer 1987): 59–71.

———. "Social Contract, Taxation and the Standing of Deadweight Loss." *Journal of Public Economics 49* (1992): 369–381.

Musgrave, Richard A., Ching–huei Chang, and John Riew (eds.). *Taxation and Economic Development Among Pacific Asian Countries.* Boulder, Colorado: Westview Press, 1994.

Payne, James L. *Costly Returns: The Burdens of the US Tax System.* San Francisco: ICS Press, 1993.

———. "The End of Taxation?" *The Public Interest* (Summer 1993): 110–118.

Pechman, Joseph A. "Tax Reform: Theory and Practice." *Journal of Economic Perspectives 1* (Summer 1987): 11–28.

Poterba, James M. "Empirical Public Finance—Taxation and Housing: Old Questions, New Answers." *The American Economic Review 82* (May 1992): 237–242.

———. "Is the Gasoline Tax Regressive?" in *Tax Policy and the Economy, Volume 5,* edited by David Bradford (144–164). Cambridge, Massachusetts: The MIT Press, 1991.

———. "Lifetime Incidence and the Distributional Burden of Excise Taxes." *The American Economic Review 79* (May 1989): 325–336.

Quiggin, John. "Taxation When Borrowing Is Costly." *The Economic Record 69* (December 1993): 416–427.

Ramsey, Frank P. "A Contribution of the Theory of Taxation." *The Economic Journal 37* (March 1927): 47–61.

Razin, Assaf, and Joel Slemrod (eds.). *Taxation in the Global Economy.* Chicago: The University of Chicago Press, 1990.

Rivlin, Alice M. "The Continuing Search for a Popular Tax." *American Economic Review 79* (May 1989): 113–117.

Rosen, Harvey S. "Income Tax Progressivity: A Century–Old Debate." *Business Review of Federal Reserve Bank of Philadelphia* (January–February 1990): 3–12.

Sandford, Cedric (ed.). *Key Issues in Tax Reform.* Perrymead, United Kingdom: Fiscal Publications, 1993.

Sgontz, Larry G. "An Excise Tax that Reduces Price." *National Tax Journal 45* (March 1992): 115–117.

———. "Optimal Taxation: The Mix of Alcohol and Other Taxes." *Public Finance Quarterly 21* (1993): 260–275.

Slemrod, Joel. "Do Taxes Matter? Lessons from the 1980s." *American Economic Review 82* (May 1992): 250–256.

————. "Income Creation or Income Shifting? Behavioral Responses to the Tax Reform Act of 1986." *The American Economic Review 85* (May 1995): 175–180.

————. "Optimal Taxation and Optimal Tax Systems." *Journal of Economic Perspectives 4* (Winter 1990): 157–178.

————. "Professional Opinions about Tax Policy: 1994 and 1934." *National Tax Journal 48* (March 1995): 121–147.

————. "Taxation and Inequality: A Time-Exposure Perspective," in *Tax Policy and the Economy, Volume 6,* edited by James M. Poterba (105–127). Cambridge, Massachusetts: The MIT Press, 1992.

————, ed. *Do Taxes Matter? The Impact of the Tax Reform Act of 1986.* Cambridge, Massachusetts: The MIT Press, 1990.

Steinmo, Sven. "The End of Redistribution? International Pressures and Domestic Tax Policies." *Challenge 37* (November–December 1994): 9–17.

Steinmo, Sven. "The Truth about Taxes." *Challenge 38* (January–February 1995): 57–58.

Stella, Peter. "Tax Farming: A Radical Solution for Developing Country Tax Problems?" *IMF Staff Papers 40* (March 1993): 217–225.

Steuerle, C. Eugene. *The Tax Decade: How Taxes Came to Dominate the Public Agenda.* Washington, D.C.: Urban Institute Press, 1992.

Stuart, Charles. "Welfare Costs Per Dollar of Additional Tax Revenue in the United States." *American Economic Review 77* (June 1987): 352–362

Thurow, Lester C. "The Economics of Public Finance." *National Tax Journal* (June 1975): 185–194.

U.S. Department of the Treasury. *Restructuring the U.S. Tax System for the 21st Century: An Option for Fundamental Reform.* Washington, D.C.: U.S. Government Printing Office, December 1992.

Vickrey, William. "Federal Policy for the 1990s: An Updated Agenda for Progressive Taxation." *The American Economic Review 82* (May 1992): 257–262.

Wallace, Sally, Michael Wasylenko, and David Weiner. "The Distributional Implications of the 1986 Tax Reform." *National Tax Journal 44* (June 1991): 181–198.

Zodrow, George R. "Grandfather Rules and the Theory of Optimal Tax Reform." *Journal of Public Economics 49* (1992): 163–190.

# Personal Income Tax

Aaron, Henry J. "The Capital Gains Tax Cut: Economic Panacea or Just Plain Snakeoil?" *The Brookings Review* (Summer 1992): 30–33.

Abramowicz, Kenneth F. "Taxation of Scholarship Income." *Tax Notes* (November 8, 1993): 717–725.

Alm, James. "Marriage and the Marriage Tax." *1992 Proceedings of the Eighty-Fifth Annual Conference on Taxation.* Columbus, Ohio: National Tax Association, 1993.

Alm, James, Michael McKee, and William Beck. "Amazing Grace: Tax Amnesties and Compliance." *National Tax Journal 43* (March 1990): 23–37.

Auerbach, Alan J. "On the Design and Reform of Capital-Gains Taxation." *The American Economic Review 82* (May 1992): 263–267.

Auten, Gerald E., and Joseph J. Cordes. "Cutting Capital Gains Taxes." *Journal of Economic Perspectives 5* (Winter 1991): 181–192.

Bakija, Jon, and Eugene Steuerle. "Individual Income Taxation Since 1948." *National Tax Journal 44* (December 1991): 451–475.

Blumenthal, Marsha, and Joel Slemrod. "The Compliance Cost of the U.S. Individual Income Tax System: A Second Look after Tax Reform." *National Tax Journal 45* (June 1992): 185–202.

Bordignon, Massimo. "A Fairness Approach to Income Tax Evasion." *Journal of Public Economics 52* (1993): 345–362.

Bovenberg, A. Lans. "Tax Policy and National Saving in the United States: A Survey." *National Tax Journal 42* (June 1989): 123–138.

Bradford, David F. *Untangling the Income Tax.* Cambridge, Massachusetts: Harvard University Press, 1986.

Browning, Edgar K., and Jacquelene M. Browning. "Why Not a True Flat Rate Tax?" *The Cato Journal 5* (Fall 1985): 629–650.

Buchanan, James M., and Yong J. Yoon. "Rational Majoritarian Taxation of the Rich: With Increasing Returns and Capital Accumulation." *Southern Economic Journal 61* (April 1995): 923–935.

Carroll, John S. "How Taxpayers Think about Their Taxes: Frames and Values," in *Why People Pay Taxes: Tax Compliance and Enforcement,* edited by Joel Slemrod (43–63). Ann Arbor: University of Michigan Press, 1992.

Cordes, Joseph J., Arjo Klamer, and Thomas C. Leonard. "Academic Rhetoric in the Policy Arena: The Case of Capital Gains Taxation." *Eastern Economic Journal 19* (Fall 1993): 459–479.

Dubin, Jeffrey J. A., Michael J. Graetz, and Louis L. Wilde. "The Effect of Audit Rates on the Federal Income Tax, 1977–1986." *National Tax Journal 43* (December 1990): 395–409.

Feenberg, Daniel R., and Harvey S. Rosen. "Recent Developments in the Marriage Tax." *National Tax Journal 48* (March 1995): 91–101.

Feenberg, Daniel, and Lawrence Summers. "Who Benefits from Capital Gains Tax Reductions?" in *Tax Policy and the Economy,* Volume 4, edited by Lawrence H. Summers (1–24). Cambridge, Massachusetts: The MIT Press, 1990.

Ferleger, Louis, and Jay R. Mandle. "Americans' Hostility to Taxes." *Challenge 34* (July–August 1991): 53–55.

––––––. "Irrelevant Measures of Americans' Hostility to Taxes." *Challenge 34* (September–October 1991): 48–50.

Goode, Richard. "The Economic Definition of Income," in *Comprehensive Income Taxation,* edited by Joseph A. Pechman (1–30). Washington, D.C.: The Brookings Institution, 1977.

Graville, Jane. "Do Individual Retirement Accounts Increase Personal Saving?" *Journal of Economic Perspectives 5* (Spring 1991): 133–148.

Hall, Robert E., and Alvin Rabushka. *The Flat Tax.* Stanford, California: Hoover Institution Press, 1995.

––––––. "Tax Forms Could Fit on Postcards." *Consumer's Research Magazine 78* (April 1995): 23–28.

Kinsey, Karyl A., Harold G. Grasmick, and Kent W. Smith. "Framing Justice: Taxpayer Evaluations of Personal Tax Burdens." *Law and Society Review 25* (November 1991): 845–873.

Kotlikoff, Laurence J. "Taxation and Savings—A Neoclassical Perspective." *Journal of Economic Literature* (December 1984): 1576–1624.

Minarik, Joseph J. "Capital Gains Taxation, Growth, and Fairness." *Contemporary Policy Issues 10* (July 1992): 16–25.

Owens, Jeffrey, and Mark Robson. "Taxation and Household Saving." *The OECD Observer 191* (December 1994–January 1995): 27–30.

Pechman, Joseph A., and Gary V. Engelhardt. "The Income Treatment of the Family: An International Perspective." *National Tax Journal 43* (March 1): 1–23.

Pollack, Gerald A. "Should Capital Gains Be Indexed?" *Challenge 34* (July–August 1991): 56–60.

Ram, Rati. "Share of Individual Income Tax in Government Revenue: An Intertemporal Multicountry Study." *Public Finance—Finances Publiques 48* (1993): 97–109.

Reckers, Philip M. J., Debra L. Sanders, and Stephen J. Roark. "The Influences of Ethical Attitudes on Taxpayer Compliance." *National Tax Journal 47* (December 1994): 825–836.

Shapiro, Matthew D., and Joel Slemrod. "Consumer Response to the Timing of Income: A Change in Tax Withholding." *American Economic Review 85* (March 1995): 274–283.

Sheppard, Lee A. "'Something Borrowed': The Tax Treatment of Marla's Tiara." *Tax Notes* (December 27, 1993): 1541–1543.

Slemrod, Joel (ed.). *Why People Pay Taxes: Tax Compliance and Enforcement.* Ann Arbor: The University of Michigan Press, 1992.

# Corporation Income Tax

Abrutyn, Stephanie, and Robert W. Turner. "Taxes and Firms' Dividend Policies: Survey Results." *National Tax Journal 43* (Nbr. 4): 491–497.

Anderson, Patricia M., and Bruce D. Meyer. "The Unemployment Insurance Payroll Tax and Interindustry and Interfirm Subsidies." *Tax Policy and the Economy 7,* edited by James M. Poterba (111–144). Cambridge, Massachusetts: The MIT Press, 1993.

Blumenthal, Marsha. "The Compliance Costs of the U.S. Corporate Income Tax for Large Corporations." *1993 Proceedings of the Eighty-Sixth Annual Conference on Taxation.* Columbus, Ohio: National Tax Association, 1994.

Cummins, Jason G., Kevin A. Hassett, and R. Glenn Hubbard. "Have Tax Reforms Affected Investment?" in *Tax Policy and the Economy 9,* edited by James M. Poterba (131–150). Cambridge, Massachusetts: The MIT Press, 1995.

Daly, Michael, and Joann Weiner. "Corporate Tax Harmonization and Competition in Federal Countries: Some Lessons for the European Community." *National Tax Journal 46* (December 1993): 441–461.

Feldstein, Martin. "Tax Policy and International Capital Flows." *Weltwirtschaftliches Archiv 130* (1994): 675–697.

Fiekowsky, Seymour. "Tax Incentives as Viewed by Economists and Lawyers." *National Tax Journal 44* (September 1991): 325–340.

Gerardi, Geraldine, Michael J. Graetz, and Harvey S. Rosen. "Corporate Integration Puzzles." *National Tax Journal 43* (September 1990): 307–315.

Goulder, Lawrence H., and Philippe Thalmann. "Approaches to Efficient Capital Taxation." *Journal of Public Economics 50* (February 1993): 169–196.

Gravelle, Jane G. *The Economic Effects of Taxing Capital Income.* Cambridge, Massachusetts: The MIT Press, 1994.

––––––. "The Corporate Income Tax: Economic Issues and Policy Options." *National Tax Journal 48* (June 1995): 267–277.

––––––. "What Can Private Investment Incentives Accomplish? The Case of the Investment Tax Credit." *National Tax Journal 46* (September 1993): 275–290.

Jorgenson, Dale W. "Tax Reform and the Cost of Capital: An International Comparison." *Tax Notes International* (April 19, 1993): 981–1008.

Kale, Jayant R., and Thomas H. Noe. "Taxes, Financial Distress, and Corporate Capital Structure." *Quarterly Review of Economics and Finance 32* (Spring 1992): 71–83.

Meyer, Laurence H., Joel L. Prakken, and Chris P. Varares. "Designing an Effective Investment Tax Credit." *Journal of Economic Perspectives 7* (Spring 1993): 189–196.

"Open Letter: Fixing the U.S. Economy." *Challenge 35* (March–April 1992): 64–65.

Poterba, James M. "Why Didn't the Tax Reform Act 1986 Raise Corporate Taxes?" in *Tax Policy and the Economy,* Volume 6, edited by James M. Poterba (43–58). Cambridge, Massachusetts: The MIT Press, 1992.

Rollinson, Barbara L. "Guidelines for Taxing International Capital Flows: An Economic Perspective." *National Tax Journal 46* (September 1993): 309–315.

Scholes, Myron S., and Mark A. Wolfson. "The Role of Tax Rules in the Recent Restructuring of U.S. Corporations," in *Tax Policy and the Economy*, Volume 5, edited by David Bradford (1–24). Cambridge, Massachusetts: The MIT Press, 1991.

Sheppard, Lee A. "The Investment Tax Credit: New Age Intervention and Old Politics." *Tax Notes* (March 22, 1993): 1575–1579.

Sinn, Hans–Werner. "Taxation and the Cost of Capital: The 'Old' View, the 'New' View, and Another View," in *Tax Policy and the Economy*, Volume 5, edited by David Bradford (25–54). Cambridge, Massachusetts: The MIT Press, 1991.

Sorensen, Peter Birch. "Changing Views of the Corporate Income Tax." *National Tax Journal 48* (June 1995): 279–294.

# Other Taxes

Aaron, Henry J., Harvey Galper, and Joseph A. Pechman (eds.). *Uneasy Compromise: Problems of a Hybrid Income-Consumption Tax*. Washington, D.C.: The Brookings Institution, 1988.

Blankart, Charles B. "Income Taxation, Consumption Taxation, Intergenerational Transfers, and Government Behavior." *Public Finance—Finances Publiques 48* (1993): 7–15.

Bowman, John H., George E. Hoffer, and Michael D, Pratt. "Current Patterns and Trends in State and Local Intangibles Taxation." *National Tax Journal 43* (December 1990): 439–450.

Carroll, Sidney L. "Taxing Wealth: An Accessions Tax Proposal for the U.S." *Journal of Post Keynesian Economics 12* (Fall 1989): 49–69.

Congressional Budget Office. *Effects of Adopting a Value-Added Tax*. Washington, D.C.: U.S. Government Printing Office, February 1992.

Due, John F. "Some Unresolved Issues in Design and Implementation of Value-Added Taxes." *National Tax Journal 43* (December 1990): 383–394.

Duncombe, William. "Economic Change and the Evolving State Tax Structure: The Case of the Sales Tax." *National Tax Journal 45* (September 1992): 299–313.

Felix, David. "Financial Globalization and the Tobin Tax." *Challenge 38* (May–June 1995): 56–59.

Fox, William F. (ed.). *Sales Taxation: Critical Issues in Policy and Administration*. Westport: Praeger, 1992.

Friedman, David A., and Joel Waldfogel. "The Administrative and Compliance Cost of Manual Highway Toll Collection: Evidence from Massachusetts and New Jersey." *National Tax Journal 48* (June 1995): 217–228.

Gale, William G., and John Karl Scholz. "Intergenerational Transfers and the Accumulation of Wealth." *Journal of Economic Perspectives 8* (Fall 1994): 145–160.

Gravelle, Jane, and Dennis Zimmerman. "Cigarette Taxes to Fund Health Care Reform." *National Tax Journal 47* (September 1994): 575–590.

Hafer, R. W., and Trebing, Michael E. "The Value-Added Tax: A Review of the Issues." *Federal Reserve Bank of St. Louis Review 62* (January 1980): 3–10.

Harmelink, Philip J., and Janet Furman Speyrer. "An Evaluation of Alternative Methods of Taxing Social Security Benefits." *Journal of Post Keynesian Economics 15* (Fall 1992): 3–30.

McLure, Charles E. Jr. "Economic, Administrative, and Political Factors in Choosing a General Consumption Tax." *National Tax Journal 46* (September 1993): 345–358.

———. "International Aspects of Tax Policy for the 21st Century." *The American Journal of Tax Policy 8* (1990): 167–185.

————. "Substituting Consumption-Based Direct Taxation for Income Taxes as the International Norm." *National Tax Journal 45* (June 1992): 145–154.

Metcalf, Gilbert E. "Life Cycle Versus Annual Perspectives on the Incidence of a Value Added Tax," in *Tax Policy and the Economy,* Volume 8, edited by James M. Poterba (45–64). Cambridge, Massachusetts: The MIT Press, 1994.

Mieszkowski, Peter M. "The Property Tax: An Excise Tax or a Profits Tax?" *Journal of Public Economics* (April 1972): 73–96.

Musgrave, Peggy B. "Substituting Consumption-Based Direct Taxation for Income Taxes as the International Norm: A Comment." *National Tax Journal 45* (June 1992): 179–184.

Pomp, Richard D., and Oliver Oldman. "A Normative Inquiry into the Base of a Retail Sale Tax: Casual Sales, Used Goods, and Trade Ins." *National Tax Journal 43* (December 1990): 427–437.

Price, Charles E., and Thomas M. Porcano. "The Value-Added Tax: Is It a Reasonable Alternative to Raise Federal Revenue?" *Journal of Accountancy* (October 1992): 44–48.

Purohit, Mahesh C. "Adoption of a Value Added Tax in India: Problems and Prospects." *Economic and Political Weekly 28* (March 6, 1993): 393–404.

Reinstein, Alan, Gerald H. Lander, and William H. Henson. "Michigan's Value-Added Tax Experience: A Model for Federal Enactment." *Taxes—The Tax Magazine 68* (August 1990): 588–594.

Rousslang, Donald J., and Pieter Van Leeuwen. "Using a VAT to Reduce the Federal Deficit: The Consequences for U.S. Trade." *Applied Economics 22* (1990): 179–186.

Sabelhaus, John. "What is the Distributional Burden of Taxing Consumption?" *National Tax Journal 46* (September 1993): 331–344.

Sarkar, Shounak, and George R. Zodrow. "Transitional Issues in Moving to a Direct Consumption Tax." *National Tax Journal 46* (September 1993): 359–376.

Seidman, Laurence S. "Is a Consumption Tax Equivalent to a Wage Tax?" *Public Finance Quarterly 18* (1990): 65–76.

Siegfried, John J., and Paul A. Smith. "The Distributional Effects of a Sales Tax on Services." *National Tax Journal 44* (March 1991): 41–53.

Smith, Peter. "Lessons from the British Poll Tax Disaster." *National Tax Journal 44* (December 1991): 421–436.

Snell, Ronald K. "Our Outmoded Tax Systems." *State Legislatures 20* (August 1994): 16–21.

Temple, Judy A., and James D. Rodgers. "Recent Trends in Local Government Reliance on Sales and Income Taxes." *1994 Proceedings of the Eighty-Seventh Annual Conference on Taxation.* Columbus, Ohio: National Tax Association, 1995.

Trebby, James. "An Analysis of the Value-Added Tax as an Alternative Source of Federal Revenue." *Akron Business and Economic Review 21* (Winter 1990): 6–18.

Viscusi, W. Kip. "Promoting Smokers' Welfare with Responsible Taxation." *National Tax Journal 47* (September 1994): 547–558.

Wassmer, Robert W. "Property Taxation, Property Base, and Property Value: An Empirical Test of the 'New View.'" *National Tax Journal 46* (June 1993): 135–158.

Weidenbaum, Murray. "A New Kind of Tax: Adopting a Consumption Tax." *Current* (May 1993): 17–21.

Wong, Lung–Fai, Joel Michael, and Doug Wilson. "The Distributive Effect of Expanding the Sales Tax." *Public Finance Quarterly 18* (1990): 465–479.

# Government Deficits and Debt

Abel, Andrew. "Can the Government Roll Over Its Debt Forever?" *Business Review of the Federal Reserve Bank of Philadelphia* (November–December 1992): 3–18.

Auerbach, Alan J. "Taxes and Spending in the Age of Deficits: A View from Washington and Academe." *National Tax Journal 45* (September 1992): 238–241.

Auerbach, Alan, Jagadeesh Gokhale, and Laurence J. Kotlikoff. "Generational Accounts and Lifetime Tax Rates: 1990–1991." *Economic Review of the Federal Reserve Bank of Cleveland 1* (1993): 2–13.

————. "Social Security and Medicare Policy from the Perspective of Generational Accounting," in *Tax Policy and the Economy,* Volume 6, edited by James M. Poterba (129–145). Cambridge, Massachusetts: The MIT Press, 1992.

Alesina, Alberto, and Roberto Perotti. "The Political Economy of Budget Deficits." *IMF Staff Papers 42* (March 1995): 1–31.

Bahl, Roy, and William Duncombe. "State and Local Debt Burdens in the 1980s: A Study in Contrast." *Public Administration Review 53* (January–February 1993): 31–40.

Barro, Robert J. "The Ricardian Model of Budget Deficits," in *Debt and the Twin Deficits Debate* edited by James M. Rock (133–148). Mountain View, California: Mayfield Publishing, 1991.

Bernstein, Peter L., and Robert L. Heilbroner. "The Relationship Between Budget Deficits and the Savings/Investment Imbalance in the United States: Facts, Fancies, and Prescriptions," in *Debt and the Twin Deficits Debate,* edited by James M. Rock (109–131). Mountain View, California: Mayfield Publishing Company, 1991.

Blejer, Mario I., and Adrienne Cheasty. "The Measurement of Fiscal Deficits: Analytical and Methodological Issues." *Journal of Economic Literature 29* (December 1991): 1644–1678.

Blinder, Alan S. "Is the National Debt Really—I Mean, Really—a Burden?" in *Debt and the Twin Deficits Debate,* edited by James M. Rock (173–187). Mountain View, California: Mayfield Publishing Company, 1991.

Bohn, Henning. "Budget Deficits and Government Accounting." *Carnegie-Rochester Conference Series on Public Policy 37* (December 1992): 1–84.

Carter, John R., and David Schap. "Line-Item Veto: Where Is Thy Sting?" *Journal of Economic Perspectives 4* (Spring 1990): 103–118.

Collender, Stanley. *The Guide to the Federal Budget, Fiscal 1993.* Washington, D.C.: Urban Institute Press, 1992.

Congressional Budget Office. *Reducing the Deficit: Spending and Revenue Options.* Washington, D.C.: U.S. Government Printing Office, February 1993.

Croushore, Dean. "How Big Is Your Share of Government Debt?" *Business Review of the Federal Reserve Bank of Philadelphia* (November–December 1990): 3–12.

Duggan, James E. "Social Security and the Public Debt." *Public Finance—Finances Publiques 46* (1991): 382–404.

Eisner, Robert. "Debunking the Conventional Wisdom in Economic Policy." *Challenge 33* (May–June 1990): 4–11.

————. "Deficits, Saving & Economic Policy." *American Economist 38* (Fall 1994): 3–11.

————. "Deficits and Us and Our Grandchildren," in *Debt and the Twin Deficits Debate,* edited by James M. Rock (81–107). Mountain View, California: Mayfield Publishing Company, 1991.

————. "Deficits: Which, How Much, and So What?" *The American Economic Review 82* (May 1992): 295–298.

————. "National Saving and Budget Deficits." *Review of Economics and Statistics 76* (February 1994): 181–186.

Eisner, Robert, and Paul J. Pieper. "A New View of the Federal Debt and Budget Deficits." *American Economic Review 74* (March 1984): 11–29.

Etzioni, Amitai. "Deficit Reductions in a Populist Age: How to Sell Shared Sacrifice." *Challenge 36* (March–April 1993): 22–25.

Fardmanesh, Mohsen. "Economic Growth and Alternative Deficit-Reducing Tax Increases and Expenditure Cuts: A Cross–Sectional Study." *Public Choice 69* (1991): 223–231.

Fieleke, Norman S. "The United States in Debt." *New England Economic Review* (September–October 1990): 34–54.

Friedman, Benjamin M. "Learning from the Reagan Deficits." *The American Economic Review 82* (May 1992): 299–304.

———. "New Directions in the Relation Between Public and Private Debt." *Science* (April 1987): 397–403.

Gale, William G., and Robert E. Litan. "Saving Our Way Out of the Deficit Dilemma." *The Brookings Review* (Fall 1994): 6–11.

Galston, William, and Amitai Etzioni. "Communitarian Economics: How to Cut the Deficit and Put America Back to Work." *Challenge 35* (November–December 1992): 53–55.

Galbraith, James K., and William Darity, Jr. "A Guide to the Deficit." *Challenge 38* (July–August 1995): 5–12.

Garner, Alan. "The Social Security Surplus: A Solution to The Federal Budget Deficit?" *Economic Review of the Federal Reserve Bank of Kansas City* (May 1989): 25–39.

Gramlich, Edward M. "U.S. Budget Deficits: Views, Burdens, and New Developments," in *Debt and the Twin Deficits Debate,* edited by James M. Rock (173–187). Mountain View, California: Mayfield Publishing Company, 1991.

Gramlich, Edward, Richard Kasten, and Frank Sammartino. "Deficit Reduction and Income Redistribution." *The American Economic Review 79* (May 1989): 315–319.

Haveman, Robert. "Should Generational Accounts Replace Public Budgets and Deficits?" *Journal of Economic Perspectives 8* (Winter 94): 95–111.

Hewitt, Paul S. "Owe, Susannah: How Much the National Debt Will Make You Cry." *Policy Review* (Winter 1994): 46–48.

Holcombe, Randall G., Jackson, John D., and Zardkoohi, Asghar. "The National Debt Controversy." *Kyklos 34* (1981): 186–202.

Ippolito, Dennis S. "The Budget Process and Budget Policy: Resolving the Mismatch." *Public Administration Review 53* (January–February 1993): 9–12.

Joines, Douglas H. "How Large a Federal Budget Deficit Can We Sustain?" *Contemporary Policy Issues 9* (July 1991): 1–11.

Kesselman, Jonathan R. "Innovation in Public Debt Management to Reduce the Federal Deficit." *Canadian Public Policy—Analyse de Politiques 18* (1992): 327–352.

Kotlikoff, Laurence. *Generational Accounting: Knowing Who Pays, and When, For What We Spend.* New York: The Free Press, 1992.

Kowalcky, Linda K., and Lance T. LeLoup. "Congress and the Politics of Statutory Debt Limitation." *Public Administration Review 53* (January–February 1993): 14–26.

Lee, Dwight R., and Richard K. Vedder. "Friedman Tax Cuts vs. Buchanan Deficit Reduction as the Best Way of Constraining Government." *Economic Inquiry 30* (October 1992): 722–732.

Mann, Thomas E., and Charles L. Schultze. "Getting Rid of the Budget Deficit: Why We Should and How We Can." *The Brookings Review* (Winter 1988/89): 2–17.

McIntyre, Robert S. "Tax Inequality Caused Our Ballooning Budget Deficit." *Challenge 34* (November–December 1991): 24–33.

Niskanen, William A. "The Case for a New Fiscal Constitution." *Journal of Economic Perspectives 6* (Spring 1992): 13–24.

"Open Letter: Economists Oppose Balanced Budget Amendment to the U.S. Constitution." *Challenge 35* (May–June 1992): 59–60.

Penner, Rudolph G. (ed.). *The Great Fiscal Experiment.* Washington, D.C.: The Urban Institute Press, 1991.

Rabin, Jack. "Public Debt: A Symposium." *Public Administration Review 53* (January/February 1993): 8.

Reischauer, Robert D. "Taxes and Spending Under Gramm-Rudman-Hollings." *National Tax Journal 43* (September 1990): 223–232.

Rock, James M. (ed.). *Debt and the Twin Deficits Debate.* Mountain View, California: Mayfield Publishing Company, 1991.

Sabelhaus, John. "Deficits and Other Intergenerational Transfers: Restoring the Missing Link." *Challenge 37* (January–February 1994): 45–50.

Schultze, Charles L. "Is There a Bias toward Excess in U.S. Government Budgets or Deficits?" *Journal of Economic Perspectives 6* (Spring 1992): 25–43.

———. "Of Wolves, Termites, and Pussycats: Or, Why We Should Worry About the Budget Deficit." *The Brookings Review* (Summer 1989): 26–33.

Seater, John J. "Ricardian Equivalence." *Journal of Economic Literature 31* (March 1993): 142–190.

Sill, D. Keith. "Managing the Public Debt." *Business Review of the Federal Bank of Philadelphia* (July–August 1994): 3–14.

"Symposium: Budget Deficit." *Journal of Economic Perspectives 3* (Spring 1989): 17–94.

Tobin, James. "Thinking Straight About Fiscal Stimulus and Deficit Reduction." *Challenge 36* (March–April 1993): 15–18.

Vickrey, William. "Meaningfully Defining Deficits and Debt." *The American Economic Review 82* (May 1992): 305–310.

# Fiscal Federalism

Alm, James, Michael McKee, and Mark Skidmore. "Fiscal Pressure, Tax Competition, and the Introduction of State Lotteries." *National Tax Journal 46* (December 1993): 463–476.

Atlas, Cary M., Thomas W. Gilligan, Robert J. Hedershott, and Mark A. Zupan. "Slicing the Federal Government Net Spending Pie: Who Wins, Who Loses, and Why." *American Economic Review 85* (June 1995): 624–629.

Bartik, Timothy. *Who Benefits from State and Local Economic Development Policies?* Kalamazoo, Michigan: Upjohn, 1991.

Bird, Richard M. "Threading the Fiscal Labyrinth: Some Issues in Fiscal Decentralization." *National Tax Journal 46* (June 1993): 207–227.

Brauer, Jurgen, and John Tepper Marlin. "Converting Resources from Military to Non-Military Uses." *Journal of Economic Perspectives 6* (Fall 1992): 145–164.

Break, George F. *Financing Government in a Federal System.* Washington, D.C.: The Brookings Institution, 1980.

Brennan, Geoffrey, and James Buchanan. *The Power to Tax: Analytical Foundations of a Fiscal Constitution.* Cambridge, United Kingdom: Cambridge University Press, 1980.

Brinner, Roger E., and Charles T. Clotfelter. "An Economic Appraisal of State Lotteries." *National Tax Journal 28* (December 1975): 395–404.

Brown, Charles C., and Wallace E. Oates. "Assistance to the Poor in a Federal System." *Journal of Public Economics 32* (April 1987): 307–330.

Buchanan, James M. "Federalism and Fiscal Equity." *American Economic Review 40* (September 1950): 583–599.

Bucks, Dan R., and Michael Mazerov. "The State Solution to the Federal Government's International Transfer Pricing Problem." *National Tax Journal 46* (September 1993): 385–392.

Case, Anne C., and Harvey S. Rosen. "Budget Spillovers and Fiscal Policy Interdependence: Evidence from the States." *Journal of Public Economics 52* (October 1993): 285–307.

Coffman, Richard B. "Tax Abatements and Rent–Seeking." *Urban Studies 30* (1993): 593–598.

Clotfelter, Charles T., and Philip J. Cook. "Implicit Taxation in Lottery Finance." *National Tax Journal 40* (December 1987): 533–546.

————. "Redefining 'Success' in the State Lottery Business." *Journal of Policy Analysis and Management 9* (Winter 1990): 99–104.

Courant, Paul N., and Edward M. Gramlich. "The Impact of the TRA on State and Local Fiscal Behavior," in *Do Taxes Matter? The Impact of the Tax Reform Act of 1986,* edited by Joel Slemrod. Cambridge, Massachusetts: The MIT Press, 1990.

Courant, Paul N., and Daniel L. Rubenfeld. "Tax Reform: Implications for the State-Local Public Sector." *Journal of Economic Perspectives 1* (Summer 1987): 87–100.

Gramlich, Edward M. "The Economics of Fiscal Federalism and Its Reform," in *The Changing Face of Fiscal Federalism,* edited by Thomas R. Swartz and John E. Peck (152–174). London: Sharpe, 1990.

————. "Federalism and Federal Deficit Reduction." *National Tax Journal 38* (September 1987): 299–313.

————. "A Policymaker's Guide to Fiscal Decentralization." *National Tax Journal 46* (June 1993): 229–235.

Grewal, Bhajan S., Geoffrey Brennan, and Russell L. Mathews. *The Economics of Federalism.* Canberra: Australia National University Press, 1980.

Heil, James. "Searching for Leviathan Revisited." *Public Finance Quarterly 19* (July 1991): 334–346.

Kenyon, Daphne A., and John Kincaid (eds.). *Competition Among States and Local Governments: Efficiency and Equity in American Federalism.* Washington, D.C.: Urban Institute Press, 1991.

Marlow, Michael L. "Intergovernmental Competition, Voice and Exit Options and the Design of Fiscal Structure." *Constitutional Political Economy 3* (1992): 73–88.

McLure, Charles E., Jr. *Fiscal Federalism and the Taxation of Natural Resources.* Lexington, Massachusetts: D. C. Heath, 1983.

————. "Tax Competition: Is What's Good for the Private Goose Also Good for the Public Gander?" *National Tax Journal 39* (September 1986): 222–232.

Michelman, Hans H., and Panayotis Soldatos (eds.). *Federalism and International Relations.* Oxford: Clarendon, 1990.

Micksell, John L. "State Lottery Sales and Economic Activity." *National Tax Journal 47* (March 1994): 165–171.

Mieszkowski, Peter, and George R. Zodrow. "Taxation and the Tiebout Model: The Differential Effects of Head Taxes, Taxes on Land Rents, and Property Taxes." *Journal of Economic Literature 27* (September 1989): 1198–1146.

Mills, Edwin S. (ed.). *Handbook of Urban Economics.* Amsterdam: North Holland, 1987.

Musgrave, Richard A. "Who Should Tax, Where, and What?" in *Tax Assignment in Federal Countries,* edited by Charles E. McLure, Jr. Canberra: Australian National University Press, 1983.

Neenan, William B. "Suburban-Central City Exploitation Thesis: One City's Tale." *National Tax Journal 32* (June 1979): 117–139.

Oates, Wallace E. "Federalism and Government Finance," in *Modern Public Finance,* edited by John M. Quigley and Eugene Smolensky (ch. 5, 126–151). Cambridge, Massachusetts: Harvard University Press, 1994.

————. "Fiscal Decentralization and Economic Development." *National Tax Journal 46* (June 1993): 237–243.

————, ed. *The Political Economy of Fiscal Federalism.* Lexington, Massachusetts: Lexington Books, 1977.

Quigley, John M., and Eugene Smolensky. "Conflicts Among Levels of Government in a Federal System." *Public Finance—Finances Publiques 47 Suppl.* (1993): 202–215.

Rivlin, Alice M. "A New Vision of American Federalism." *Public Administration Review 52* (July/August 1992): 315–321.

———. *Reviving the American Dream: The Economy, the States & the Federal Government.* Washington, D.C.: The Brookings Institution, 1992.

Rosen, Harvey S. (ed.). *Studies in State and Local Public Finance.* Chicago: University of Chicago Press, 1986.

Schwab, Robert M., and Wallace E. Oates. "Community Composition and the Provision of Local Public Goods: A Normative Analysis." *Journal of Public Economics 44* (1991): 217–237.

Szakmary, Andrew C., and Carol Matheny Szakmary. "State Lotteries as a Source of Revenue: A Re–Examination." *Southern Economic Journal 61* (April 1995): 1167–1181.

Wallis, John J. "The Political Economy of New Deal Fiscal Federalism." *Economic Inquiry 24* (July 1991): 510–524.

Yinger, John, and Helen F. Ladd. "The Determinants of State Assistance to Central Cities." *National Tax Journal 42* (December 1989): 413–428.

Zodrow, George R. *Local Provision of Public Services: The Tiebout Model after Twenty–five Years.* New York: Academic Press, 1983.